THE LIFE OF
JESUS

Lives of Jesus Series

LEANDER E. KECK, *General Editor*

THE LIFE OF JESUS

by

FRIEDRICH SCHLEIERMACHER

Edited and with an Introduction by
JACK C. VERHEYDEN

Translated by
S. MACLEAN GILMOUR

FORTRESS PRESS
Philadelphia

This book is a translation of *Das Leben Jesu. Vorlesungen an der Universität zu Berlin im Jahr 1832*, edited by K. A. Rütenik (Berlin: Georg Reimer, 1864).

Copyright © 1975 by Fortress Press

Library of Congress Catalog Card Number 72-87056

ISBN 0-8006-1272-8

3467C73   Printed In U.S.A.   1-1073

FOREWORD TO THE SERIES

In a time when a premium is placed on experimentation for the future and when theological work itself values "new theology," the reasons for reissuing theological works from the past are not self-evident. Above all, there is broad consensus that the "Lives of Jesus" produced by our forebears failed both as sound history and as viable theology. Why, then, make these works available once more?

First of all, this series does not represent an effort to turn the clock back, to declare these books to be the norm to which we should conform, either in method or in content. Neither critical research nor constructive theology can be repristinated. Nevertheless, root problems in the historical-critical study of Jesus and of theological reflection are perennial. Moreover, advances are generally made by a critical dialogue with the inherited tradition, whether in the historical reconstruction of the life of Jesus or in theology as a whole. Such a dialogue cannot occur, however, if the tradition is allowed to fade into the mists or is available to students only in handbooks which perpetuate the judgments and cliches of the intervening generation. But a major obstacle is the fact that certain pivotal works have never been available to the present generation, for they were either long out of print or not translated at all. A central aim, then, in republishing certain "Lives of Jesus" is to encourage a fresh discovery of and a lively debate with this tradition so that our own work may be richer and more precise.

Titles were selected which have proven to be significant for ongoing issues in Gospel study and in the theological enterprise as a whole. H.S. Reimarus inaugurated the truly critical investigation of Jesus and so was an obvious choice. His *On the Intention of Jesus* was reissued by the American Theological Library Association in 1962, but has not really entered the discussion despite the fact that questions he raised have been opened again, especially by S. G. F. Brandon's *Jesus and the Zealots*. Our edition, moreover, includes also his previously untranslated discussion of the resurrection and part of D. F. Strauss's evaluation of Reimarus. That Strauss's *Life of Jesus* must be included was clear from the start. Our edition, using George Eliot's translation, will take account of Strauss's shifting views as well. Schleiermacher's *Life of Jesus* is here translated, partly because it is significant for the study of Schleiermacher himself and partly because he is the wellspring of repeated concern for the inner life of Jesus. One of the most influential expressions of this motif came from Wilhelm Herrmann's *The Communion of the Christian with God*, which, while technically not a life of Jesus, emphasizes more than any other work the religious significance of Jesus' inner life. In fresh form, this emphasis has been rejuvenated in the current work of Ernst Fuchs and Gerhard Ebeling who concentrate on Jesus' own faith. Herrmann, then, is a bridge between Schleiermacher and the present. In such a series, it was also deemed important to translate Strauss's critique of Schleiermacher, *The Christ of Faith and the Jesus of History*, for here important critical issues were exposed. Probably no book was more significant for twentieth-century study of Jesus than Johannes Weiss's *Jesus' Proclamation of the Kingdom of God*, for together with Albert Schweitzer, Weiss turned the entire course of Jesus-research and undermined the foundations of the prevailing Protestant theology. From the American scene, Shailer Mathews's *Jesus on Social Institutions* was included. There can be no substantive dialogue with our own theological tradition which ignores his work, together with that of Shirley Jackson Case. Case's *Jesus: A New Biography* was originally planned for inclusion, but its availability in two other editions has made that unnecessary. Finally, A. Loisy's *The Gospel and the Church* has been added in order to acquaint both Protestants and Catholics with an important alternative to the liberal Protestant view of the relation between Jesus and the church. Doubtless other works could have been included with justification; however, these will suffice to enliven the theological scene if read perceptively.

In each case, an editor was invited to provide an introductory essay and annotations to the text in order to assist the reader in seeing the book in perspective. The bibliography will aid further research, though in no case was there an attempt to be comprehensive. The aim is not to produce critical editions in a technical sense (which would require a massive apparatus), but a useable series of texts with guidance at essential points. Within these aims the several editors enjoyed considerable latitude in developing their contributions. The series will achieve its aim if it facilitates a rediscovery of an exciting and controversial history and so makes our own work more fruitful.

The present volume makes Schleiermacher's lectures on the life of Jesus available in English for the first time. The translation was prepared by the late S. MacLean Gilmour of Andover Newton Theological School. For a brief explanation of the present Table of Contents see. pp. lix-lx of the editor's Introduction.

The editor of the present edition is Jack C. Verheyden, Professor of Theology at the School of Theology at Claremont and chairman of the Department of Religion at the Claremont Graduate School. After receiving his B.A. from Rice University, Professor Verheyden earned the B.D. and Ph.D. (1967) at Harvard. His steady concern for the problem of history and theology is evidenced by his dissertation, "Christology and Historical Knowing: A Study based on Friedrich Schleiermacher and the New Quest of the Historical Jesus," and by the fact that he is working on a major study of Schleiermacher's Christology. Furthermore he expects to publish shortly his Rockwell Lectures at Rice University, under the title "The Historical Course of the Knowing of God."

Leander E. Keck

CONTENTS

Foreword to the Series by Leander E. Keck   v

Introduction by Jack C. Verheyden   xi

Select Bibliography   lxi

THE TEXT OF THE LIFE OF JESUS

Introduction   3
  A. The Concept of a Biography   3
  B. Theological Aspects of Writing a Life of Christ   8
  C. The Problem of the Sources   36
  D. The Three Periods of the Life of Christ   43

FIRST PERIOD:
The Life of Christ before His Public Appearance   45
  A. The Birth of Christ and Attendant Issues   45
  B. The Problem of the Two Natures of Christ   81
  C. Christ's God-Consciousness and Its Development   87
  D. The Spontaneous Emergence of His Mission   123
  E. The Transition to a Constant Public Activity   135
    1. Christ's Baptism   135
    2. Christ's Temptation   144

SECOND PERIOD:
The Public Life of Christ until His Arrest   156
  A. External and Internal Aspects of His Activity   156
  B. The External Aspect of Christ's Activity   164
    1. The Locality and Christ's Disposition of Time   164
    2. Miracle-working Activity   190

C. The Internal Aspect of Christ's Activity 229
    1. His Self-communication in the Form of
      Teaching 229
        a. His Teaching Concerning His Person 245
        b. His Teaching Concerning His Vocation 286
    2. His Activity in Founding a Community 338
D. The Developing Catastrophe 362

THIRD PERIOD:
From the Arrest to the Ascension 392
A. The Passion Story 392
    1. Arrest and Trials 396
    2. The Problem of the Reality of Christ's Death 415
    3. Circumstances Accompanying Christ's Death 420
B. The Story of Christ's Resurrection until His
    Ascension 431
    1. The Resurrection Accounts 434
    2. The Nature and Purpose of Christ's Second
      Life 460
    3. Christ's Final Departure and Its Unimportance
      for Faith 469

INTRODUCTION

by Jack C. Verheyden

Friedrich Schleiermacher was the first person to lecture publically on the topic of the life of Jesus.[1] Books had appeared on this subject prior to his time, but the history of Jesus as a distinct part of academic studies apparently commenced with Schleiermacher's lectures in 1819, a series which he repeated four times during the subsequent twelve years. Therefore, even though Schleiermacher himself never published a book on the life of Jesus, he had great influence in stimulating a recognition of the theological and historical importance of this subject both through his lectures and through his epochal publications in systematic theology.

It is doubtful whether any other thinker has combined so many of the various strands of the problematic as has Schleiermacher. His fame as the "father of modern Protestant theology" deservedly rests on his ability as a systematic theologian, as chiefly exemplified in his magnum opus, *The Christian Faith;* and the questions and interests of doctrine have loomed large in the discussion about the history of the life of Jesus. Yet there have been few major systematic theologians of the modern world who have also operated with distinction as New Testament critical historians. Schleiermacher contributed significantly in this respect, both in regard to the Gospels and in regard to other parts of the New Testament as well. Alongside this versatility, however, he also possessed a substantial philosophical mind. Indeed, Schleiermacher is the only man since the Enlightenment who, while pursuing the vocation of Christian preacher and theologian, at the same

---

1. Karl Hase, *Die Geschichte Jesu* (Leipzig, 1876), p. 1; Albert Schweitzer, *The Quest of the Historical Jesus,* trans. W. Montgomery, 1906 (New York: Macmillan, 1961), p. 62; Emanuel Hirsch, *Geschichte der neueren evangelischen Theologie* (Gütersloh, 1960), 5:34.

time gains a separate chapter devoted to his thought in some of the most noted histories of philosophy.[2] Included in his philosophical explorations was sustained reflection upon the character of historical interpretation and the nature of language. These philosophical matters concerning the object of historical knowledge and the manner in which such knowledge takes place constitute an important strand in the fabric of an attempt to write a history of the life of Jesus.

The question of writing a history of Jesus and what this task means theologically has shifted over the generations, and one should not assume that our inquiries and interests in the subject are the same as those of a century or two ago. For many today, having lived entirely within the intellectual times when approaching matters historically is a self-evident practice, it may be hard to grasp that even in the eighteenth century this approach was not shared in large proportion by educated people, particularly in theology. Whereas today it is usual amidst theological discussion for the charge to arise concerning a christological position "that it is unhistorical," in the eighteenth century it was generally considered a theological weakness if a thinker allowed critical questions of general historiography to intrude into his discussion. A theology that did so usually earned itself the designation of "rationalist" or "liberal" — these not being congratulatory phrases in the eyes of most. And, as a matter of fact, the great majority of writers of lives of Jesus in the eighteenth and nineteenth centuries were departing at significant points in their theological perspectives from the orthodox traditions of Christianity, and this was not confined to the formal tradition concerning the inspired text of Scripture. As a result, certain common interests run through this literature.

This commonality can be briefly noted by recalling the broader lines of christological doctrine. First, in regard to the person of Jesus Christ, orthodox doctrine has referred to him as uniting in himself two natures which form a person perfect

2. Frederick Copleston, *A History of Philosophy* (London: Burns and Oates, 1965), vol. 7; Friedrich Ueberweg, *Grundriss der Geschichte der Philosophie* (Berlin, 1923), vol. 4. There is an English translation of an earlier edition of Ueberweg, *History of Philosophy*, trans. G. S. Morris (New York: Scribner, 1903).

both in deity and in humanity. The humanity of his person was without sin. Jesus Christ, therefore, is consubstantial with God and consubstantial with man. These categories for interpreting the person of Jesus Christ were forged in the day when Greek metaphysical terms provided a common scientific language. The ongoing change of history has largely eroded this common scientific language as to just what is meant by consubstantiality. This is true not only for the divine nature of Christ, which has been the one usually questioned because of the difficulty of comprehending how a man could still be human if a divine nature resided in him; it is also true for the consubstantiality of his human nature. The sociology of knowledge and the awareness of the relativities of history raise the question of what a "human nature" is. What is this "nature" or "substance" relationship which a man centuries later has to the figure of Jesus?

Second, there is a common setting for the quest of the historical Jesus in regard to orthodox doctrine concerning the work of Christ. Particularly in Protestant orthodoxy, although not only there, the weight of the interpretation of the work of Christ rested upon his satisfying the offended honor and justice of God by enduring the punishment rightfully deserved by the rest of the human race. This punishment is bestowed through Christ's suffering death. Indeed, he suffered precisely enough to allow God to be merciful. Political and ethical changes in the modern world concerning the representation of one person by another made this statement increasingly artificial and unconvincing to large numbers of people in Christendom. In fact, many abhorred this doctrine as implying an unworthy conception of God. Another way of relating the Christian man to Jesus Christ became necessary.

Third, there arose as a concomitant of modern science great tensions in the Christian church over the miracles of the Bible, at first in regard to the Old Testament, but eventually also with respect to the Gospels. These tensions revolved around the problem of the relation of nature, as a realm of lawful processes analyzable by scientific control and experiment, to the biblical reports of occurrences which violated such lawfulness. Was the effectiveness of Jesus constituted by such miraculous occurrences, or did it reside in something possessing more continuity with the world of modern science? This also was an impetus toward historical questioning about the life of Jesus.

One way of bringing all of these features together is by noting the difference between the message of Jesus and the preaching of the primitive church. The propensity for speaking of Jesus as having a divine nature, as rendering a propitiatory atonement, and as miraculously walking on the water was not present in the teaching of Jesus itself but arose only in the course of the church's transformation of Jesus' own message. Consequently, these writers on the life of Jesus found a separation between Jesus as he really was and views which would foster the establishment of the orthodox doctrines of traditional Christology which increasingly were found wanting by thinkers of the Enlightenment and the nineteenth century. The teaching of Jesus himself, then, became the all-controlling category to replace the role assigned him in the church's doctrines of atonement.

The literature on the historical Jesus during this era, therefore, manifested a definite ambivalence. On the one hand, it reflected a positive interest in attesting that the new situation of the scientific handling of critical data did not abrogate the stature of the One who is the subject of the church's christological statements. On the other hand, it displayed an interest in showing that critical handling of historical evidence did establish that this figure could not be what the doctrines of the church hold him to be. And to complicate the picture, this ambivalence of interest cannot be simply divided among the different figures who participated in the historical investigation. On the contrary, both concerns are likely to be found in the same man, though in varying degrees. A writer on the life of Jesus could be convinced of the positive stature of Jesus and that Jesus himself had a message for men that had been obscured by the church. Therefore, such a writer as J. R. Seeley in England with his *Ecce Homo* was interested in a reform of the life and doctrine of the church by means of the historical Jesus, even though he may have agreed also with those holding that a critical handling of historical evidence indicated that Jesus could not be what the doctrines of the church held him to be.[3] And one guided by the latter interest, such as Ernest Renan, might very well agree that Jesus was a figure of considerable stature, even though the particular writer had no interest whatsoever, except negatively, in the church.[4] It has become common today to find disdainful comments about these authors because they allowed their own religious questions and convictions so to shape their histories, even though the commenters themselves share so many of the same objections to the tradition from which these writers were departing and are quick to avail themselves of the importance of "the critical point of view" in intellectual matters.

The decade of the 1860's was a busy one in the nineteenth-century life of Jesus research. Renan's book appeared in 1863 and *Ecce Homo* in 1866, while Theodor Keim's superior work was first published in 1867.[5] In 1863 Heinrich Holtzmann's disentangling of the synoptic Gospels pointed the way for the great strides made in critical research at this time. But 1864 was the banner year for activity. Karl Weizsäcker gave firm support for the priority of Mark and strengthened the case for the second source present in the Synoptics.[6] Timothée Colani took apocalyptic eschatology seriously enough in the Gospels to dedicate a full monograph to denying its applicability, even when this meant excising parts of the text as deriving from Jesus.[7] But the most famous book of all and the one with the widest audience was Daniel Schenkel's *Das Charakterbild Jesu,* a work which was also accused of attempting to reform conservative ecclesiastical politics by means of a "liberal" Jesus. Concurrently, the older David Friedrich Strauss came with his second book on Jesus, a more popular version which he entitled, *A New Life of Jesus for the German People.* It was in this same year that

3. J. R. Seeley, *Ecce Homo* (London, 1866).
4. Ernest Renan, *The Life of Jesus,* trans. W. Carleton (New York, 1863).
5. Theodor Keim, *Die Geschichte Jesu von Nazara* (Zurich, 1867), vol. 1.
6. Karl Weizsäcker, *Untersuchungen über die evangelische Geschichte, ihre Quellen und den Gang ihrer Entwicklung* (Gotha, 1864).
7. Timothée Colani, *Jesus-Christ et les croyances messianiques de son temps* (Strassburg, 1864). Besides these books, Albert Schweitzer lists twenty-four other publications on the life of Jesus question in 1864, eighteen of them in Germany, examining the work of Renan; cf. *Quest of the Historical Jesus.* pp. 188-91.

Schleiermacher's lectures on the life of Jesus were published, thirty years after his death, a time during which the critical discussion had changed considerably. The editor, K. A. Rütenik, in his Preface gives the impression of being in such a hurry to get the volume to the public, even at the price of not being able to avail himself of a superior manuscript which arrived too late, that he intended a supplementary volume to follow shortly.[8] After three decades one wonders why he has to move so precipitately — unless the publisher wanted to join the burgeoning life of Jesus market of that 1864 season!

SCHLEIERMACHER'S CAREER

The versatility attested in Schleiermacher's theological, historical, and philosophical achievements is reflected in his life. Acquaintance with his biography easily brings one to the point of marveling that he had time to engage in so many diverse endeavors. The sixty-five years of his life, spanning the closing third of the eighteenth century and the opening third of the nineteenth century in Germany, took place in the arena of far-reaching historical movements and events in both political and intellectual life. It was the time of the closing years of the Enlightenment and of Pietism, the emerging of German Romanticism, the French Revolution with its ensuing Napoleonic invasions, the formation of the German nation, the union of Lutheran and Reformed Church communions, vigorous intellectual activity by the Prussian Academy of the Sciences and the surge of philosophical creativity in idealism, decisive advances in historiography, including the blooming of systematic research into the life of Jesus. In one manner or another, Schleiermacher's career is caught up in a relation to all of these, even as he pursued continuously his last forty years the vocation of a Christian preacher.

Born in 1768, Schleiermacher came from a family filled with clergy on both his paternal and maternal sides. His father was a Reformed (or Calvinistic Protestant) chaplain to the Prussian army who in his travels had become exposed to the pietism of the Moravian Brethren and resolved that his children would be educated in the context of their religious

8. There is no evidence that such a supplement was published.

vitality. Therefore, Friedrich attended the Moravian schools, including seminary, until he finally became dissatisfied with certain aspects of its religious teaching and the separation from cultural life that marked these institutions; thus he repaired to a university to study the philosophy of Immanuel Kant and the history of philosophical thought in general. He then accompanied an uncle to a parish charge, assisting him in the duties of the pastorate, and this experience eventually led Schleiermacher to ordination in the Reformed church in 1790. In 1796 he came to Berlin as chaplain to a hospital for the poor, and, at the same time, became deeply involved in the high tide of Romanticism present amidst cultural circles in the city.

It was such an audience which Schleiermacher had in mind when in 1799 he published his first and most famous book: *On Religion: Speeches to Its Cultured Despisers.* The book appeared anonymously, but its author was soon discovered and it made Schleiermacher "overnight" a famous man in Germany. The *Speeches* had a wide impact well beyond those specifically interested in religion, and later opponents and critics of Schleiermacher as diverse as the conservative Lutheran ecclesiastic Klaus Harms and the philosopher Hegel, were significantly influenced by its message.[9] Schleiermacher's basic thrust was to oppose all attempts to understand religion in terms of metaphysical systems and the usual canons of morality. He held instead that the real nature of the religious, however embodied, lies in the realm of intuition and feeling, through which one is attuned to the infinite which resists all externalizing. Art and music are important to understanding religion because of their appreciation of individuality and affection. Further, the Enlightenment's quest for a universal, natural religion is a chimera; religion is irreducibly social in

9. For the influence of *On Religion* — hereinafter referred to as the *Speeches* — on Hegel, see Richard Kroner, *Von Kant bis Hegel* (Tübingen: J.C.B. Mohr, 1924), 2:53-67, esp. 53, 56, and 63; also Wilhelm Dilthey, *Die Jugendgeschichte Hegels, Gesammelte Schriften* (Berlin and Leipzig, 1921), 4:149; cf. Richard Brandt, *The Philosophy of Schleiermacher* (New York: Harper, 1941), p. 141. On the relation of Schleiermacher's 1803 *Outline of a Critique of Previous Ethical Theory* to Hegel's 1807 *Phenomenology of Spirit*, see Rudolf Haym, *Die Romantische Schule* (Berlin, 1870; 5th ed. 1928), pp. 926-28.

character and the concreteness of the historical faiths is the source of their vitality.

Drawing even more heavily on Romantic terminology Schleiermacher followed in 1800 with a more personally oriented analysis of individuality, entitled *Soliloquies.* He soon left Berlin for another preaching position as a result of an unhappy experience in love, but returned to the city a few years later following the Napoleonic invasions of Germany. Henceforth, his life was spent pursuing the dual occupations of Reformed preacher to Berlin's Trinity Church, and holding the first chair in theology at the University of Berlin, an institution which he had helped found. There had been some academic experience for him previously at Halle before Napoleon closed the university in 1806. Schleiermacher's own household possessions had been confiscated by the conquering armies and he was reduced to a fare of the most meager rations.

Despite the fact that his formal academic exposure was comparatively small when the new university opened in 1810, Schleiermacher had gained a reputation not only through the *Speeches* and *Soliloquies,* but also through more formal publications on religious, philosophical, and historical subjects including an *Outline of a Critique of Previous Ethical Theory.* One major task that had been begun was the translation of the dialogues of Plato into the German language for the first time. Schleiermacher was involved in this work for over thirty years, his death in 1834 preventing him from completing the entire corpus. However, his translations are still used today.

Schleiermacher did not confine himself to theological matters in his teaching at the University of Berlin but lectured extensively on philosophical subjects as well. The more than thirty volumes that comprise his collected works include separate volumes on ethics and the philosophy of culture, psychology, theory of education, history of philosophy, aesthetics, political theory, hermeneutics, and dialectic. The latter two have brought him the most philosophical recognition, the one on dialectic treating the principles involved in the relation of the social nature of thinking to the givenness of being.

Schleiermacher published a remarkable piece of theological analysis in 1811 entitled *Brief Outline on the Study of Theology* which specified the divisions inherent in Christian theology and the principles which unify these divisions into a coherent whole. In subsequent years he elaborated the contents of many of these divisions by lecturing not only on philosophical theology and dogmatics — lectures which finally assumed published form in *The Christian Faith* in 1821-22 and 1830-31 — but also on subjects later published posthumously, including a comprehensive account of Christian ethics, as well as practical theology, church history, introduction to the New Testament, and the life of Jesus. Additionally, he published separate treatises on the doctrine of election, the doctrine of the Trinity, the three Pastoral Epistles, the evidence from Papias concerning the Gospels of Matthew and Mark, and two long open letters concerning the issues in Christian doctrine he was considering while preparing the second edition of his systematic theology. Schleiermacher was still engaged in creative intellectual activity alongside his preaching and lecturing when he succumbed to pneumonia on February 12, 1834, at sixty-five years of age.

The material in the present volume comes from his lectures on the life of Jesus, mainly following the presentation in 1832. In editing the material, Rütenik distinguished two types of materials: Schleiermacher's handwritten outlines, from which he lectured, and the recorded notes of five of his students. Schleiermacher's manuscript is printed first, as the lecture heading, under which Rütenik gathered the student notes which correlate to that part of the manuscript. The distinction between Schleiermacher's own outlines and the student notes is a very important one, particularly when one keeps in mind David Friedrich Strauss's comment that taking notes under Schleiermacher was like attempting to photograph — with equipment *circa* 1860 — a dancer in full motion![10]

10. David Friedrich Strauss, *Der Christus des Glaubens und der Jesus der Geschichte* (Berlin, 1865), p. 8.

The nature of the materials which constitute these lectures makes it all the more important that we take account of what Schleiermacher published on questions relating to the life of Jesus from other contexts, including his christological thought in general. The text of the New Testament is not the sole source that Schleiermacher thinks pertinent for a life of Jesus.

Three Interpreters of Christmas

An interesting fact about the career of Schleiermacher's lectures on the life of Jesus is that they have been so involved with David Friedrich Strauss. Albert Schweitzer often emphasizes the relation of Strauss to Schleiermacher and indicates that it was Strauss's reading of lecture notes from Schleiermacher's course that spurred his own life of Jesus into publication.[11] When Schleiermacher's volume of lectures finally appeared in 1864, the same year as Strauss's *A New Life of Jesus,* Strauss wrote a critique on the published lectures, *Der Christus des Glaubens und der Jesus der Geschichte.*[12] He had already taken Schleiermacher to task over christological matters in his first life of Jesus; Schleiermacher is the main foe in the concluding section of the book when Strauss reflects upon the dogmatic import of his own critical examination.[13]

This is all the more noteworthy because Strauss, both critically and constructively, echoes some opinions briefly expressed by a literary figure created by Schleiermacher. In 1835, the year after Schleiermacher's death, Strauss applied the category of myth to the text of the Gospels in such a manner that his book, *The Life of Jesus Critically Examined,* marked a far-reaching shift in the discussion of New Testament criticism. The actual history of Jesus appeared to fade into obscurity in comparison with the robust transformation of the

11. *Quest of the Historical Jesus,* p. 71; cf. Hase, *Geschichte Jesu,* pp. 124-25.
12. Strauss's critique is to be included in the Lives of Jesus series in a volume to be translated and edited by Leander E. Keck. So the relation continues. Strauss's book is the only full-length study of Schleiermacher's lectures on the life of Jesus, which have received a notable lack of attention in the past century. There is a penetrating brief discussion in Richard R. Niebuhr, *Schleiermacher on Christ and Religion* (New York: Scribner, 1964), pp. 220-28.
13. On the other hand, Strauss could be quite appreciative of Schleiermacher when Christology was not the subject. Cf. "Schleiermacher und Daub, in ihrer Bedeutung für die Theologie unserer Zeit," *Charakteristiken und Kritiken* (Leipzig, 1844).

actual events of Jesus' life by the imagination of the primitive church. This same point had been made by Schleiermacher's literary figure, who has the name of Leonhardt, in a little book first published by Schleiermacher in 1806, and then again twenty years later in a slightly revised version under the title, *Christmas Eve Celebration: A Dialogue.* This work represents one of the earliest attempts to deal, even though in miniature, with the relation of Christian convictions about Jesus Christ to the results of "radical" New Testament historical criticism. While it does not directly treat the specifics of the history of Jesus, the *Christmas Eve* does evidence the theological framework that Schleiermacher brings to bear in the context of historical questioning, and for that reason is an exceptionally illuminating introduction to his christological thought, including the lectures on the life of Jesus.

Schleiermacher produced the book on Christmas while under the initial momentum of his first Plato translations and the dialogical theory of truth which he found in the master of the Academy.[14] The *Christmas Eve* dialogue, then, is an attempt to depict the life of Christian people celebrating the festival of Christmas through mood, personal life experiences, music, and the occasion of the spoken word. Schleiermacher's view of Plato's dialogical intent is that truth emerges out of the whole complex of the living interchange among living personalities, and not out of any one of these personalities taken separately. This tenet is important in understanding the discourses of three men which come at the close of the book when they attempt to give a reflective interpretation of the meaning and importance of the Christmas festival.

The first figure to speak is the man named Leonhardt, who holds that the life of Christianity virtually creates itself out of its festive occasions. Scriptural narratives and formal doctrines are too remote from common, uneducated folk to have a decisive impact upon religious life. "Suppose we leave out the Roman church, where the Scriptures are seldom if ever put into their hands, but stick to our own (Protestant) people; it is manifest how little inclined even they are to read the

14. Cf. *Great Thinkers on Plato,* ed. Barry Gross, (New York: Putnam, 1968), pp. 64-92.

Bible or prepared even to understand it in proper perspective."[15] Belief in the miraculous attests to this fact. Belief in miracles arises from the moving impressions which festivals make in the present, this being illustrated in the case of miracles attributed to the saints by the Roman Catholic church. It is the holy days set up to honor the saints which give rise to belief in the saints' miraculous activities. Festivals, therefore, instigate belief, and the Christian church reflects such a process in regard to Jesus Christ, and also Mary as the Blessed Virgin.

The consequence for Christianity which Leonhardt finds in this spontaneous creativity of the imagination is that the personal activity of Jesus on earth is not particularly relevant. A scrutiny of the history of Jesus uncovers such contradictory diversity that the historical mind, on the whole, is left in precarious confusion; and what one is able to affirm regarding Jesus indicates that he was much more like John the Baptist than would be gathered from the apostolic testimony. This indicates, Leonhardt thinks, that what is crucial about Jesus for Christianity is his death and resurrection—not as events tied to a particular temporal moment of the past, but rather as a mythical display of a spiritual power which was present no differently in the first century than it is now.

Leonhardt, in isolation, cannot be taken as representing Schleiermacher's position, as is evidenced by the fact that one of the women in the dialogue convivially refers to Leonhardt as "an unbelieving rascal." What is so interesting about Leonhardt is his proto-representation of certain major points later found in David Friedrich Strauss's *Life of Jesus Critically Examined.* Albert Schweitzer stated that the Strauss book rendered obsolete previous approaches to the subject. "For the questions raised by the latter's (Strauss's) life of Jesus, published in 1835, Schleiermacher had no answer, and for the wounds which it made, no healing."[16]

This may well be true but, with an eye toward Leonhardt, not because Schleiermacher was unacquainted with the pos-

15. *Christmas Eve,* trans. T. N. Tice (Richmond: John Knox, 1967), p. 71.
16. *Quest of the Historical Jesus,* p. 62. The fourth edition of Strauss's book (translated by George Eliot) is included in this Lives of Jesus series in a volume edited by Peter C. Hodgson.

sibilities which Strauss pursued. The two succeeding speakers in the Christmas dialogue, in replying to the issues raised by Leonhardt, also provide keys to those aspects of Schleiermacher's thought which influence his account of the life of Jesus, including those which differentiate him theologically from Strauss.

The next man to speak on the meaning of Christmas, and thereby the Christian church's relation to Jesus Christ, is named Ernst. While Ernst says he is not so skeptical about some of these historical questions as is Leonhardt, he approaches the entire matter from a different angle. What interests Ernst is the new life in which Christians participate, a new life which is experienced in a mood and disposition so well symbolized by the Christmas festival. The mood is that of joy and the disposition one of giving to others; these characterize the nature of Christian life, a life which is communal in its very fabric. This Christian spirit is also enduring as opposed to an experience which belongs to the transitory moment. The efficacy of Christian redemption provides stability and continuity to what otherwise would be only a series of temporal changes. Of course, the Christian knows of the contrasts of the temporal as distinct from the eternal, and of that which appears phenomenally at hand as distinct from what is "really real" or being. The Christian is subject to particular delights and sorrows of the moment just as others are; Christian joy, however, overcomes these contrasts and antitheses, not by removing them, but rather by bestowing a more embracing harmony which transcends the antitheses. This joy provides a new context, universal in scope, which transforms the contrasts into a new experienced shape and unity.

The key point which Ernst makes is that *for one who participates in such Christian life* it cannot have been arbitrarily contrived, nor can it have been spontaneously produced out of itself; rather this communal result requires an inner foundation, a common ground which is the source of the heightened existence shared by Christian people. The very nature of the experience of those who constitute the Christian community is that they begin with the separation of natural and spiritual aspects of living, and that they attain the integrated harmony

— so far as they do — which brings joy not out of their own power but from a ground beyond themselves. Precisely for this reason the Christian community must use the language of grace and redemption; this redemption does not come as the report of a forensic decision but through the bestowal of historic influence as this is made concrete in personal relationships. Consequently, the inner ground of the experienced life must lie in a person who possessed this new life in its highest perfection and has imparted it to others from the resources of his own person.[17]

This necessity of a historic redeemer for those participating in the Christian community provides a different perspective on the critical questions from that of Leonhardt. Ernst says that in the context of the new life even the slightest historical traces of the origins of this community in a redeemer are sufficient to convince the Christian that ". . . it is actually Christ to whose powers of attraction this new world owes its formation."[18] Ernst does not say that the Christian community can do without critical history entirely; in that case his emphasis on the necessity of personal concreteness would be in danger of becoming Promethean. Rather, in face of Leonhardt's observation that Jesus is more like John the Baptist than the apostolic testimony, Ernst's point is that Leonhardt is looking at the wrong kind of history. The continuity between Jesus and the primitive church resides in the new life which he has imparted to it.

The final man to speak in the *Christmas Eve* discussion is Eduard,[19] who picks up this same point regarding history and says that Leonhardt has sought out the substance of the matter being considered only in respect to external historical truth. Eduard says he prefers the guidance of the more mystical writer among the evangelists, that is, John, who shows only subordinate interest in particular events and whose real

17. See the outstanding article by Durwood Foster on the parallel of proofs for God to the relation of the church to Jesus Christ, *Christian History and Interpretation,* ed. W. R. Farmer, C. Moule, R. R. Niebuhr (London: Cambridge, 1967), pp. 57-77.
18. *Christmas Eve,* p. 80.
19. There are other speakers after Eduard but not on the subject discussed here. For an analysis of the *Christmas Eve* as a whole, see Richard R. Niebuhr, *Schleiermacher on Christ and Religion* (New York: Scribner, 1964), chap. 1.

concern is with the spiritual meaning. There is a definite overlap between Eduard's position and that of Ernst, illustrated here by both attending to something other than external history; nevertheless, Eduard consistently wants to unfold another dimension of Christianity and the nature of Jesus Christ. Eduard can agree with everything that Ernst has said but his interest is quite different, and this difference in orientation between Ernst and Eduard is an important aid in understanding Schleiermacher's theology.

Ernst's concern is what might be termed "anthropological" or, as we often loosely say today, "existential." He attempts in principle to stay close to the experience of the Christian community and what he finds required is the ground of its new life in an individual person. Ernst apparently has little need to speak directly of God in his comments on Christianity, but Eduard wants to consider the same experienced new life "... from the perspective of the divine" or out of the divine principle.[20] Christian joy and this individual redeemer require explanation: how can an individual person possess this highest perfection of existence so as to bestow it on others, and what constitutes the situation of man so that something historically communicated from one in the past can have such telling significance?

Eduard begins with the Johannine prologue, the Word that was with God and its becoming flesh; but he leaves behind this biblical beginning for a discourse couched in ontological terms. Man is the earth as it becomes conscious of itself. Flesh is limited and sensible nature, while the Word is thinking and coming to know. Man-in-himself, that is, man in his essence, that which constitutes him or makes him human, is life's coming to know itself in its eternal being amid the ever-changing flow of becoming. But when men fail to understand themselves in this essential manner, falling into a state of pure becoming, they thereby bring a disunity of their nature from what they truly are. As a result, they are lost and given over to confusion.

Redemption arises for men when they come to love all becoming, including themselves, in the eternal, willing to be

20. *Christmas Eve,* p. 82.

nothing other "than a thought of eternal being!"[21] The basis for this redemption transpires when men recognize that being has united itself to temporal process, and that this union is not something fortuitous but is an eternal relation exhibited in one who is the Son of man without qualification. Jesus Christ is man-in-himself even as an individual, and as such makes known the union of being and becoming. He is the point from which humanity-in-itself may be formed in each person. Thus Eduard says:

Until he [Christ] enters history, all else is presage: all human life is related to his life, and only through this relation does it partake of goodness and divinity. And now that he has come, in him we celebrate not only ourselves but all who are yet to come as well as all who have been before us, for they only were something insofar as he was in them and they in him.[22]

This common ontological participation which is recognized in the fellowship of the church is expressed in Christianity as love.

Just as Leonhardt taken singly is not equatable with Schleiermacher, so Eduard does not directly sound like Schleiermacher because of the overtly ontological language that he utilizes to bring out "the divine perspective." Similarly, Ernst's tone is much warmer, or more sentimental — depending on the reader's taste — than anything to be found in Schleiermacher's formal and academic theological works. But all three of these interpreters of Christmas embody points which reveal themselves in Schleiermacher's theological thinking as a whole and the lectures on the life of Jesus in particular. Their statements can thus alert interpreters of Schleiermacher to the fact that his theology will emerge only dialectically out of the interchange of various approaches and emphases. Further, the three orientations are fruitful keys to the various moments which find their way into Schleiermacher's Christology. We will explore his thinking further by allowing Leonhardt to represent historical theology and criticism, Ernst to represent the elucidation of the religious consciousness and

21. Ibid.
22. Ibid., p. 84.

its Christian pattern, and Eduard to stand for "man-in-himself" as this finds reformulated expression.

Historical Theology and Criticism

Schleiermacher did not look upon the probing of external, critical history only as a skeptical activity to be combatted by experience and the interests of faith, however much Ernst and Eduard represent Schleiermacher's conviction that the reality of religious life cannot be simply collapsed into the results of such probing. Actually, Schleiermacher in his *Brief Outline of the Study of Theology* formulated an organization of Christian theology which places historical knowledge of the Bible and church history in a most prominent place in the theological curriculum; indeed, it is doubtful whether any work of Protestant theology is comparable to it in the rationale it offers for the importance of a historically informed ministry.[23]

The general view of the interrelating of the branches of theological study that Schleiermacher executes in the *Brief Outline* sharply highlights the dialectical character of Christian theology as a reciprocal interchange of philosophical theology with historical theology. Philosophical theology deals with the nature of religion and religious communions as these are necessary in the development of the human spirit in order to formulate the essence of Christianity. Historical theology, on the other hand, treats the actual past of the community which provides the distinctive shape and content of Christianity's modification of human self-consciousness. There is a historical givenness about Christianity which cannot be expunged and makes theology in Schleiermacher's words "a positive science" arising out of "a determinative mode of faith."[24] This is put succinctly in the introduction to *The Christian Faith* where it is specified that the essence or unity of a religion, including Christianity, must be arrived at by this dialectical procedure:

> Every particular formation of communal religiousness possesses a unity which is partly external in continuously deriving

23. *Brief Outline of the Study of Theology*, trans. T. N. Tice (Richmond: John Knox, 1966); § 26-28 are particularly sharp expressions of this view.
24. Ibid. , § 1 and § 2.

from a definite historical beginning and partly internal as a
distinctive modification of everything which is found in a struc-
tured mode of faith of the same type and stage; and it is from
both of these taken together that the distinctive essence of each
individual formation of communal religiousness is to be
discerned.[25]

Heinrich Scholz, in his introduction to the critical edition
of the *Brief Outline* in 1910, emphasizes the importance of
Schleiermacher's holding to the historical given in defining
the essence of Christianity during his time. The struggle which
Schleiermacher waged for the historical given of external history of a particular time and place was felt as a kind of sin
against the holy spirit of idealistic knowledge, so powerful
was the metaphysics of the human spirit in his day.[26] But
Scholz goes on to say that Schleiermacher's importance in
this respect has become dated, although the energy and
courage with which he conducted the victorious battle should
not be forgotten. Rather, Scholz continues, the situation has
now become reversed and it is empiricism which has come
more and more to the position of tyranny. Therefore, it is the
onesidedness of a positivistic historicism which has to be
combatted, so that it is the other side of the dialectic, the one
that holds that: "Insofar as one tries to make do with a merely empirical method of interpreting Christianity, he cannot
achieve a genuine knowledge of it . . ." which needs to be
heard.[27] A merely empirical method can provide no criterion
for distinguishing what is enduring in that which is changing.

Undoubtedly in Scholz's day in 1910 there was good
reason for maintaining such to be the case. However, his
assumption that Schleiermacher's protest against pure ontology as being no longer relevant for coming to what is essential in Christianity has itself become dated. Actually, the
same issues concerning how these two, the philosophical and
the empirical, should be related still pervade the theological
scene.

25. *The Christian Faith*, trans. H. R. Mackintosh and J. S. Stewart
(Edinburgh: T. & T. Clark, 1928), § 10; hereinafter cited as *CF*.
26. *Kurze Darstellung des theologischen Studiums* (Hildesheim, G. Olms,
1961), pp. xxxii-iii.
27. *Brief Outline*, § 21.

Schleiermacher's concern for the historical given was not confined to the events of Scripture, but included the whole course of the Christian church; nevertheless, the distinctive character of Christianity is most clearly manifested in what he termed exegetical theology, that dealing with the New Testament. These writings present "the normative documents which concern the action and effect of Christ both on and with his disciples, and also those which concern the common action and effect of his disciples toward the establishment of Christianity."[28] This means that part of the historical given that is essential to Christianity in exegetical theology is a consideration of the history of Jesus; it should not be forgotten, however, that for Schleiermacher this occurs in the context of the historical probing of the sweep of church history as a whole.

The focus of Schleiermacher's own activity in historical theology was located in exegetical theology. In 1807 he published a work on 1 Timothy which argued that Paul was not the author of this letter, a new observation at the time. His reputation as a critic was immeasurably increased in 1817 with his book, *A Critical Essay on the Gospel of Luke*. This was the first of Schleiermacher's works to receive full translation into English, this being performed in 1825 by Connop Thirlwall, who actually promulgated the piece anonymously lest public identification with it endanger his ecclesiastical standing. The book was considered by many to have made an "epoch in the history of English theology" because of the freedom of inquiry it displayed in judging the New Testament text.[29] One historian of the nineteenth century notes that in England "the name of Schleiermacher became a kind of bogey word" because of his shredding of the Gospel narratives.[30]

A prominent issue in New Testament criticism in Schleiermacher's day was whether the interrelation of the synoptic Gospels resulted from literary dependence, or whether it derived from the existence of a common source which each of

28. Ibid. , § 105; cf. § 108.
29. J. Estlin Carpenter, *The Bible in the Nineteenth Century* (London, 1903), p. 16.
30. Stephen Neill, *The Interpretation of the New Testament, 1861-1961* (New York: Oxford, 1966), p. 9.

them had modified independently. One New Testament critic of the day whom Schleiermacher respected, a man by the name of Gieseler, argued that this common source was the oral tradition.[31] Schleiermacher himself agreed with Gieseler and others who held basically to the latter view but he did not agree with Gieseler that the common source was only oral tradition, nor did he agree with those that held to another "Urgospel" on which Matthew, Mark, and Luke were commonly based. Rather, Schleiermacher thought that before the present Gospels were formed the oral tradition had come to be written down in various pieces, some of which were available to a particular canonical author and others of which were not.[32] This means that the sources which a Gospel writer possessed were in the form of detached incidents and separate discourses resting upon earlier oral tradition. Certain aggregates, such as the parables, had been carried forward from different times and placed together in blocks.[33]

Schleiermacher draws one important conclusion from this judgment of the nature of the Gospel sources: "It is undeniable that we cannot achieve a connected presentation of the life of Jesus.[34]" The materials that are available do not offer the means for this to be done. In recent theological literature, one often reads that the nineteenth-century researchers of Jesus' history attempted to present a chronological, cause-and-effect, unfolding development of his life. This generalization, accurate or not, certainly does not apply to Schleiermacher.

Since Schleiermacher held that the Synoptics were basically aggregates of individual incidents which had been collected at various times and places, he was interested in the influence of the collectors and writers upon the material. He said that if one compares the Gospels with one another, it is evident that the writers deviate from each other less on the words of Jesus than on other matters. That is, the modification of the material is much greater in the setting and context than in the words of Jesus themselves; and even in the words them-

31. *A Critical Essay on the Gospel of Luke,* trans. Connop Thirlwall (London, 1825), translator's Introduction.
32. Ibid., pp. 1-13.
33. *Hermeneutik und Kritik, Sämmtliche Werke* (Berlin: G. Reimer, 1838), I, 7: 111.
34. See the text of *The Life of Jesus,* p. 43; hereinafter cited as *LJ.*

selves, there is less deviation in regard to that which forms the real point of the narrative. This indicates that the discourses of Jesus that we have are abridgments in which the chief lines have been given prominence and retained.[35] Usually the briefer the sentence the more precisely the Gospel texts agree. Therefore, Schleiermacher's *Critical Essay on Luke* attempted to shift the focus of the synoptic discussion to the examination of each one of the three books, " . . . observing how and according to what rule or from what point of view the several incidents are bound together." Through a grasp of the basic tendency or purpose of the Gospel author much could be learned about the origin of the book and its relation to its sources.[36]

Schleiermacher was, for his day, a radical critic in fragmenting the Synoptics, in emphasizing the flux of the oral tradition upon which they had drawn, and in removing several of their pericopes as having no foundation in the actual events of Jesus' life; but the whole matter was sharply different in respect to the Gospel of John. Schleiermacher denied that the Gospel of Matthew derived from the disciple of that name, nor did he think it tenable that the Gospel of Mark was written under the influence of Peter.[37] But he held that the author of the Fourth Gospel was none other than John, the son of Zebedee. It would be difficult to exaggerate the confidence which Schleiermacher displays throughout his theological writings in the reliability of the Johannine text; only the last chapter of that Gospel has come from a later hand.[38]

It was standard in the early nineteenth century to treat the four Gospels as about equally reliable sources for a life of Jesus.[39] In 1820 Karl Bretschneider published a book, *Probabilia*, which attempted to establish that the Gospel of John was late in origin, probably deriving from the area of Egypt; thus the Johannine question was one which Schleiermacher

35. *Hermeneutik,* p. 111.
36. *Critical Essay on Luke,* p. 17.
37. *Einleitung in das Neue Testament* (Berlin, 1845),I, 3:247-48.
38. Ibid. , p. 343.
39. Karl Hase is representative of this approach, *Das Leben Jesu* (Leipzig, 1829), pp. 1 ff.

specifically had to address in his exegetical courses.[40] In a way, Schleiermacher agreed with Bretschneider's point that the critic must choose between the Synoptics and John, but Schleiermacher chose the latter rather than the former.

The fact that Schleiermacher considered the author of the Fourth Gospel to be a disciple of Jesus did not change the strictures he brought against the possibility of writing a continuous life history of Jesus, even for the time of the public ministry. John's Gospel has a continuous narrative, but its concern is so specialized as to preclude a typical biographical presentation.[41] According to Schleiermacher, the writer of John's Gospel highlights what is fundamentally present throughout Jesus' career; thus he tends to subordinate the external relationships of particular situations in order to emphasize the relation of any individual incident to the whole of John's purpose: "The author wishes to make understandable the disaster in the destiny of Christ together with the authentic nature of his activity, while — regarding the matter from John's own standpoint — the two conflicted with one another."[42]

Another fundamental point which results from the scrutiny of the kind of materials available is that these sources deal with Jesus mainly in his public activity. Schleiermacher thought this of great hermeneutical importance. "The stringency (of the interest of the Gospel writers) has excluded everything which did not belong to the public life of Jesus."[43]

Schleiermacher had a proclivity for schematic arrangement and he does not hesitate to bring it into play in the history of Jesus; undoubtedly, it would have been highlighted even more if we had this work from his own hand. He makes a distinction in the public activity of Jesus between the external and the internal or inner aspects of Jesus' life. To the external aspect belongs the locality where he lived and certain circumstances of his life, including the way he arranged his time.

40. *Einleitung*, pp. 315-16, 332-33.
41. "John is ruled by a definite point of view throughout, but it is not a connected life description, for many of the moments necessary for a biography are entirely lacking in his Gospel." *Hermeneutik*, pp. 223-24. Similar judgments are found in *LJ*, p. 43.
42. *LJ*, p. 159.
43. *Hermeneutik*, p. 171.

"To the inner side belong teaching and the foundation of a community."[44] This quote should be carefully noted in light of later theological discussion of the so-called inner life of Jesus. In the lectures on the life of Jesus Schleiermacher uses "inner" to refer to Jesus' message and the establishing of a community among his disciples as found in his public activity. "Inner" does not refer to some hidden sanctum of Jesus' personality. When examining the words of a man from another time, one should be aware that the use of a word at a later period can come to connote something quite different from what the word meant earlier.

For example, one of the most quoted passages of twentieth-century theology is that taken from Rudolf Bultmann's *Jesus and the Word:* "I do indeed think that we can now know almost nothing concerning the life and personality of Jesus, since the early Christian sources show no interest in either, are moreover fragmentary and often legendary; and other sources about Jesus do not exist."[45] Bultmann goes on to say: "Little as we know of his life and personality, we know enough of his message to make for ourselves a consistent picture."[46] Approaching significant historical figures in a manner which attends to what purpose such persons, including Jesus, had in mind is the appropriate goal: ". . . the work from *their* standpoint is the end they really sought, and it is in connection with their purpose that they are the proper objects of investigation."[47] Therefore, Bultmann concludes, what has been written since the late eighteenth century on the life of Jesus, "his personality and the development of his inner life, is fantastic and romantic."[48]

Comparing Bultmann's statement with the preceding discussion concerning Schleiermacher, it can be seen that when Bultmann speaks about what Jesus purposed in his teaching the reference is to nothing other than that which Schleiermacher speaks of as the "inner" side of the life of Jesus in

---

44. *LJ,* p. 156.
45. Rudolf Bultmann, *Jesus and the Word* (New York: Scribner, 1934), p. 8.
46. Ibid. , p. 12.
47. Ibid. , pp. 9-10.
48. Ibid. , p. 8.

this context of historical theology. Yet Bultmann contrasts this purpose with something very different — an interest in personality and inner life, whereas Schleiermacher contrasts his "inner" side of Jesus with something still more external such as locality and the physical setting of personal circumstances. Undoubtedly, there are both historical and theological differences between Schleiermacher and Bultmann, but they will not be grasped by simply contrasting a Schleiermacherian orientation on the inward with a Bultmannian rejection of the same. In fact, theologically the very reverse of this contrast may have more truth.

In this same vein, Schleiermacher's theory of hermeneutics, which deals with the principles of interpretation, deploys the understanding of what a historical figure purposed under the rubric terms "the psychological interpretation."[49] The reader will find an application of this part of Schleiermacher's hermeneutics in the opening lectures where he discusses the impact of the "directing" man upon his common life.[50] The aim of the psychological interpretation is to understand a man as freely acting through his resolution or act of will having received objectification in the common language.[51] Bultmann, on the other hand, specifies the psychological as a mode of relating to history which precisely excludes freedom; consequently, he wishes to present an alternative of relating to a historical figure through existential personal encounter.[52] The same word, therefore, is used with almost opposite meanings.

What, then, according to Schleiermacher, is this inner aspect manifested in Jesus' teaching and founding of a community? His answer to this question is the nearness of the kingdom of God.[53] Schleiermacher thinks that everything follows from the root of the nearness of the kingdom because it is in Jesus' person that the kingdom's nearness is manifested and it is his work to communicate the power to enter the kingdom. For this reason, Schleiermacher holds that the disjunction between the message *of* Jesus and the message *about*

49. *Hermeneutik*, p. 147.
50. See below, p. 8, n. 1.
51. *Hermeneutik*, p. 154.
52. *Jesus and the Word*, pp. 5-6.
53. *LJ*, p. 245.

Jesus is a false one. In the latter nineteenth century and afterward this separation became even more prominent, but Schleiermacher states that on historical grounds alone it is incorrect. This is true of the Synoptics as well as the Gospel of John. Consequently, there is no teaching about the kingdom which is not also teaching about Jesus himself.[54]

Due to this prominence of the kingdom of God in the teaching of Jesus, his directing activity transforms the Old Testament conceptions of the Jewish people and the various common ideas which entered Israel during intertestamental times. Jesus' message of the kingdom always included a polemical thrust in reference to the Old Testament's use of this idea and the expected Messiah because the prophetic promises were essentially theocratic. This is a point which often recurs in these lectures. The ideas of the Old Testament find their organizing unity in terms of theocracy and it is this theocratic particularism which the message and work of Jesus dissolves.

The end of theocratic particularism provides the rubric in terms of which Schleiermacher understands the imminent eschatological pronouncements of Jesus. Jesus' appearance brings the nearness of the kingdom, and a spiritualization of the idea is entailed. Every prophet's sense of mission includes a predictive dimension, and accompanying Jesus' preaching of the universalization of the kingdom and his own conviction of being sent is the consequent prediction of the fall of Israel's theocratic institutions.[55] Jesus foretells the national catastrophe of Israel, a catastrophe which is impending in the near future. His challenge to the people of Israel to repent and enter the community which it is his vocation to found is pressing because "the generation of those alive at the time would not have died out before that catastrophe occurred."[56] In this manner of interpreting imminent eschatology, Schleiermacher can combine his emphasis on Jesus' spiritualization of the king-

54. Ibid. ,p. 243(S). When the reference is to Schleiermacher's own manuscripts I have appended symbol (S) to differentiate the Schleiermacher material from that in his students' notebooks.
55. Ibid. ,p. 276(S); *CF* § 103, 3.
56. *LJ,* p. 359.

dom with the most concrete and political aspects of the coming judgment for those in power.

The intentional aspect of Jesus' public activity, the nearness of the kingdom of God, Schleiermacher calls a self-communication. His confidence in John leads him historically in this direction because of Jesus' speaking in that Gospel of the Father's having granted the Son to have life in himself (5:26), and of his being the bread of life (6:35), as well as texts such as "My peace I give to you" (14: 27) and "Abide in me and I in you" (15: 4). The real work of Jesus lies in his self-communication to those around him through teaching and gathering men to himself. But since Jesus understands the kingdom to be near with his appearance, his self-communication is always in closest connection with his teaching about God.[57]
Therefore, as Jesus is sent from God, God is depicted as being in search of men who in a spiritual manner will recognize his power and worship him. Again, Jesus spoke of God as his Father, and the Father of his disciples, but not of men in general. It is just through Jesus that God's fatherly relationships are manifested and extended.[58] Since Jesus invites and encourages sinful men to enter the community which he founds through his self-communication, he speaks of God as love. Along with separating the religious from the political found in Old Testament theocracy, he says that God is Spirit. In that Jesus knows that he can do nothing of himself, he speaks of God as ruler.[59] This relational context of Jesus' message points up the fact that Schleiermacher does not see Jesus' self-communication as being distinct from and opposed to his proclamation of the ways of God. His self-communication is itself the nearness of the kingdom.

The emphasis on the public activity of Jesus being a self-communication leads to a characteristically Schleiermacherian twist in relating the life of Jesus to the nature of the sources. As we have noted, Schleiermacher emphasizes that the kind of materials which we possess do not provide the basis for a comprehensively connected presentation of Jesus' life and

57. Ibid. , p. 276(S).
58. Ibid.
59. Ibid. , p. 276(S), pp. 278-79, p. 265.

public ministry. But the very fact that the sources are of this kind, that is, that they are so fragmented and ignore so pervasively a great portion of Jesus' life, is consonant with their subject matter.[60] Precisely this isolated and disjoined external character of the synoptic Gospels is itself peculiarly biographical or life descriptive in respect to their subject, Jesus. Since the activity of Jesus was to communicate the nearness of the kingdom in his own person, an arranged pattern of his activity in regard to the external conditions of his life was irrelevant. A rationally conceived plan of operation and its continuous linear development was inappropriate to the work of self-communication. The kingdom evoked a spontaneity which was not compatible with a set scheme. "Christ required no plan for his influential activity was the pure communication of himself."[61] Thus, there is a congruence between the kind of sources we have and that which defines the vocation of Jesus.

Schleiermacher's emphasis here in the context of exegetical theology on self-communication connects with other features of his theological thought. His doctrinal position on the nature of the person and work of Jesus Christ is consonant with these judgments about the lack of planned procedure and self-communication. They thus provide the transition to his view of the religious self-consciousness.

New Life as the Power of Jesus' God-Consciousness

Ernst's orientation to the experience of joy and the new life in the Christian community, which we have observed in the *Christmas Eve* discussion, points to the dialectical partner of historical theology in Schleiermacher's thought, a subdivision of which we have been examining in his exegetical writings above. Historical theology is always incomplete and requires as its mutually influential partner, philosophical theology, grounded as this latter discipline is in the philosophy of human culture, what Schleiermacher called ethics, and the investigation of religious communions by the philosophy of religion. Without the elucidation which these disciplines bring

60. Ibid. , p. 126.
61. Ibid. , p. 123 (S).

to historical theology, Christian thought would be unable to state what consequences this material from the past has for men in the present. It would be left only with the language of the Bible and the church's earlier expressions. Unless this language relates to a dimension indigenous to the nature of man, it will founder in arbitrariness. Similarly: "Unless religious communities are to be regarded as mere aberrations, it must be possible to show that the existence of such associations is a necessary element for the development of the human spirit."[62] Therefore, the Christian community's experience of joy and new life in the present requires articulation in terms of the religious self-consciousness.

Schleiermacher's account of the inherent religious dimension in the human spirit is most systematically presented in the introduction to *The Christian Faith.* Its focus is the immediate self-consciousness of the unity of personal life and the general condition of finitude. Thus, he says, "If we speak of an original revelation of God to man or in man, the meaning will always be just this, that along with the absolute dependence which characterizes not only man, but all finite existence, there is given to man also the immediate self-consciousness of it, which becomes a consciousness of God."[63] God, as the power unifying all things, can never be immediately grasped by thought; he is "too close" for thinking to embrace. God can only be conceived by reflection upon something more accessible; and this more direct apprehension is the awareness a person has of his own identity and the unity of his self-consciousness. The latter also cannot be grasped conceptionally, but the self's relation to itself can be felt.[64] The quality of this feeling is of such a kind that it brings men to thinking and speaking of God.

Schleiermacher intends by his description of immediate self-consciousness to contrast religiousness with other levels and aspects of consciousness. On the one hand, since it is

---

62. *Brief Outline,* § 22. Paul Tillich's ultimate concern, Bultmann's use of existentialist analysis, and H. R. Niebuhr's faith in a center of value are contemporary approaches in this vein.
63. *Der Christliche Glaube,* ed. Martin Redeker (Berlin: de Gruyter, 1960), § 4, 4. I will cite the German edition when I consider the English translation imprecise.
64. *CF,* § 3, 2.

self-consciousness he is unfolding, he does not mean the unconscious or what we might term "stream of consciousness." These are both too passive and unfocused. On the other hand, he also wants to distinguish *immediate* self-consciousness from ideas of the reasoning mind, even if these ideas are of one's own person. Such thinking is more at the control of the intellect than the "immediate existence-relationship" which religious feeling attests.[65]

This feeling ramifies throughout man's self-consciousness in a variety of ways. In order to clarify these ways, Schleiermacher carries out a dissection of immediate self-consciousness by isolating its ingredients, thereby presenting what we might term a structural or phenomenological account. One element is this felt unity, and this contrasts with that which makes up the sensible element of the self-consciousness in human life, that is, the material of which the feeling is the unity. Schleiermacher does not confine the sensible to matter for it also includes social and moral dimensions. This sensible self-consciousness manifests a reciprocity of "the two most fundamental movements of life, the living receptivity and the free self-activity; for these together in their reciprocal relations, are that by which life is constituted."[66] Each of these mutually complement the other in self-consciousness and mediate the physical feelings of pleasure and pain to the self.

In some relationships either activity or receptivity may diminish to an imperceptible minimum and the other become maximal, and also conversely; but both will always be present in every occasion. In his receptivity a man is conscious of his dependence upon that which modifies him; in his self-activity he is conscious of his freedom to modify that which is over against him. Together they make up the reciprocity between the subject and the corresponding other. What is it that binds this reciprocity together in each unique person? What is the hinge by which the two swing over into one another? This again is the question of the unity of the self. We assume that it is the same self that is freely active and receptively depend-

---

65. *Sendschreiben über seine Glaubenslehre, an* Dr. *Lücke, Sämmtliche Werke* (Berlin: G. Reimer, 1836), I, 2: 586.
66. *Der Christliche Glaube,* § 122, 1.

ent upon that world which surrounds him. What leads a person to assume that it is the same self? This is to come back again to the self's presence to itself, this time providing some means to describe the quality of the feeling. The feeling itself is not the free self-activity or the living receptivity; it is the unity of the two.[67] As the unity of the two, it embraces them both and is known or felt in an embracing contrast to them because it is unqualified by any reciprocity as they are so qualified. Or, as Schleiermacher says in the *Speeches:* "This is the peculiar sphere (of your life) which I would assign to religion — the whole of it and nothing more."[68]

Schleiermacher considered it obvious that this unqualified feeling could not be one of freedom, for this would mean that a man would be totally constituting himself and his world by his self-activity. Therefore, it is an unqualified dependence, the awareness of which is the unity of the self in its free activity and living receptivity. Further, the world cannot be the source of this feeling because over against the world we are conscious of being partially free. This freedom excludes pantheism.[69]

The particular manner in which the feeling of unqualified dependence unites with the sensible self-consciousness Schleiermacher calls an affection. Further: "It goes without saying that the feeling of unqualified dependence, when it unites with a sensibly defined self-consciousness and becomes an affection, must vary also in its strength."[70] The stronger or more intense and stable this relation of the sensible self-consciousness to the feeling of unqualified dependence proves to be, the more religious is the man.[71] That is, he will be more religious in that his awareness of unqualified dependence will contribute more to every moment of his self-consciousness in his reciprocity with the world.

A complicating factor in Schleiermacher's analysis is that while the religious self-consciousness is not to be identified with the intellectual work of the reflective or objective self-

67. *CF,* § 3, 3.
68. *Speeches,* trans. John Oman (New York: Harper, 1958), p. 45.
69. *CF,* § 4, 4.
70. *Der Christliche Glaube,* § 5, 5.
71. *CF,* § 5, 3.

consciousness, it still cannot exist in complete independence from it. The entire development of mental powers causes partial effects for the religious self-consciousness. While the latter may partly proceed on its own way, some forms of religious self-consciousness are nevertheless so incompatible with the scientific and artistic mind that they perish in face of it. This is the case with fetishism and polytheism. That is, a general consciousness of finitude can emerge so that the feeling of unqualified dependence is clearly distinguished from the sensible self-consciousness, thereby removing fetishistic and polytheistic confusion, but the resulting religious affection of the sensible self-consciousness is without strength. The feeling of unqualified dependence plays virtually no role in dominating the sensible self-consciousness even though it is not confused with it. This points to the possible importance of redemption, the need of which is, of course, not confined to a cultured "monotheistic" self-consciousness which does not inform its sensible life by the feeling of unqualified dependence.[72] Schleiermacher says that in its extremest form this condition is one of Godlessness or God-forgetfulness. In the *Speeches*, he says that Christianity presupposes a widely extended Godlessness.[73] The same thing is being maintained when he holds that Christianity is a religion of redemption. Man is in the condition in which he is impotent to bring the elements of his self-consciousness into the dynamic relation by which the feeling of unqualified dependence will dominate the moments of his life.

In this situation the immediate self-consciousness of men exists in a state of misery. Confusion, disorder, apathy, and sorrow reign in them because the unity of their selfhood is fallen into enslavement by its subordination to the sensible self-consciousness. They are unable "to take command of themselves" and are caught in the flow of what Ernst referred to as unrelieved becoming.[74] The result for each of them is that self-consciousness narrows in upon itself rather than inclusively expanding in a direction of universal fellow humanity. Re-

72. Ibid. , § 11, 2.
73. *Speeches*, p. 242.
74. *CF*, § 62, 2.

demption, therefore, means the succor that enables man to live so that the consciousness of unqualified dependence will come to a position of control over the other elements of self-consciousness.

Such redemption, which might be present peripherally in other monotheistic religions, is the central point of Christianity. So Schleiermacher introduces his discussion of grace in Christian doctrine with the words, ''The more distinctly conscious we become that the misery involved in our natural state cannot be removed either by the recognition that sin is inevitable, or by the assumption that it is decreasing of itself, the higher becomes the value we place upon redemption.''[75] This central thrust of Christianity immediately involves another — that is, the locus where this succor is found. There is no way of describing the source of redemption on the basis of a consideration of the elements of immediate self-consciousness. Philosophy of religion cannot establish any particular happening as redemptive. The analysis of the role of religiousness indigenous to the human spirit reaches its limits here and must look to historical theology, just as we saw conversely that historical theology needed philosophical theology in order to elucidate its meaning for the present. The actual locus of the source of this succor is contingent and rests upon an occasion which is historically given. Christianity attests that this ''givenness'' is found in Jesus of Nazareth.

There is another feature of the religious consciousness included in this locus indicated by the figure of Jesus of Nazareth. This one is a differentiation based upon the dynamic relating of the elements of self-consciousness as they refer to the free self-activity and dependent receptivity of man in reference to his social and natural setting. If, say, in a monotheistic self-consciousness the religious determination is of such a kind that the self's receptive moments are taken as the occasion for the moral exercise of free self-activity, then the religion is a teleological one.[76] Its religious affections are goal oriented. Judaism and Christianity are the two monotheistic religions which display this feature. ''In the realm of

75. Ibid., § 86.
76. Ibid., § 9, 1.

Christianity the God-consciousness is always related to the totality of active states in the idea of a kingdom of God.[77] On the other hand, a reverse subordination could take place when the dominance of the sensible self-consciousness by the feeling of unqualified dependence is exercised so that the religious affections are referred to the subject's receptivity, thereby transferring the mark of the religious consciousness from the moral to the passive. Schleiermacher designates the latter as aesthetic religion.

Schleiermacher sums up the Christian God-consciousness in the statement that "Christianity is a monotheistic faith, belonging to the teleological type of religion, and is essentially distinguished from other such faiths by the fact that in it everything is related to the redemption accomplished by Jesus of Nazareth."[78] Jesus provides the redeeming power to shape the elements of self-consciousness in such a way that one's unqualified dependence comes to a control of a moral nature with the kind of telos that Jesus defines, that is, with a universal goal and not a national theocratic one. When the religious self-consciousness receives this power and direction it participates in the joy and manifests the love consonant with this shape. The joy results from the conquest of the old impotence and misery. The love proceeds from the free self-activity being exercised in a moral manner unimpeded by hindering particularism. Together they constitute the new life.

Out of the reciprocal dialectic of the Christian tradition with the conceptual clarification of philosophical theology Schleiermacher can now state the content of Christian doctrine and bring out the import of Jesus' work. His self-communication thereby "assumes the faithful into the power of his God-consciousness, and this is his redemptive activity."[79] The inner side of the public activity of Jesus in teaching and founding a community through his conviction of the nearness of the kingdom of God is the means by which he has communicated to the disciples the power of his God-consciousness.[80] He has set himself forth in word and deed, displaying

77. Ibid., § 9, 2.
78. Ibid., § 11.
79. Ibid., § 100.
80. Ibid., § 101, 4.

publically his dependence upon God and his ordering of that dependence. In the words of Schleiermacher's hermeneutical theory, Jesus objectifies himself into his common language.[81] "The whole work of the Redeemer himself was conditioned by the communicability of his self-consciousness by means of speech."[82] He lays hold of men when his moving presentation leads them to abjure their previous condition and consent to appropriate his activity as a gift. Unbelief is always connected with the lack of self-knowledge which Jesus himself indicated as the limit to his activity.[83]

When Ernst appeals to the new life as the real continuity between Jesus and the apostolic testimony in face of Leonhardt's contrasting opposition of the two in the *Christmas Eve* dialogue, we have a position which Schleiermacher carries through systematically in *The Christian Faith*. His analysis of immediate self-consciousness elucidating this new life formally parallels the general interests and results of the new quest of the historical Jesus in recent theology. The issue involved in the new quest concerns the kind of continuity that exists between Jesus and the New Testament kerygma. Drawing upon existentialist analysis, the new quest locates the continuity in the understanding of existence as this receives various expression in Jesus on the one hand, and in the kerygma on the other.[84] Time and openness to the future replace unqualified dependence but the formal similarities are evident. For instance, in speaking of the parables, Ernst Fuchs says, "They are concerned with the decision for Jesus' understanding of time."[85] Jesus' own understanding of existential past and future are displayed in his message. "Thus the central theme of the sayings of Jesus is the decision which they require. But this requirement is simply the echo of Jesus' own decision."[86]

81. *Hermeneutik*, p. 13.
82. *CF*, § 15, 2.
83. Ibid., § 14, 1.
84. James M. Robinson, *A New Quest of the Historical Jesus* (Naperville, Ill. : Allenson, 1959), pp. 120, 122.
85. Ernst Fuchs, *Hermeneutik* (Bad Canstatt: Müllerschön, 1958), p. 224.
86. Ernst Fuchs, *Zur Frage nach dem historischen Jesus* (Tübingen: J. C. B. Mohr, 1960), p. 157. Eng. trans. *Studies of the Historical Jesus* (London: SCM, 1964), p. 23; see also pp. 104-166 on "Jesus' Understanding of Time." Cf. also James M. Robinson, *Kerygma und historischer Jesus* (Zurich, 1960), p. 141: "If the disciples have understood the decision which constitutes Jesus' existence, then their acceptance of his decision

This formal parallel between Schleiermacher and the new quest, however, leads in somewhat different directions. Schleiermacher proceeds from the actuality of new life in the Christian community, while the new quest analyzes the individual's possibility of decision, and this contrast points to differing orientations on history and Christology. There is some commonality here between Schleiermacher and the American theologian John Knox who similarly wishes to approach Jesus Christ as the inaugurating basis of the Christian life that the church mediates in the present.[87] In Knox's thought, however, the category of ''event'' is central and so encompassing that from Schleiermacher's perspective it threatens to obscure the concrete individuality of Jesus' God-consciousness.[88] It is this emphasis on that which is uniquely Jesus' own self-understanding and the shared participation in it that brings the new quest close to Schleiermacher. However, rather than beginning with the effect of God's redeeming — or creation-completing — impact in the social, historical life of man, the new quest finds a certain possibility enshrined in the New Testament material for which one may or may not decide.

Schleiermacher's beginning with actual transformation and its process means that while he dissects the elements of self-consciousness to elaborate the person-forming work of Jesus, the consequences of this work are very outward. So we find him saying, ''Since the appearance of Christianity is in itself a turning point in the world history, other phenomena approach it in importance only insofar as they resemble it in this respect.''[89] This is both consistent with the ''Ernst'' factor in Schleiermacher's theology and, also, points beyond it to a farther standpoint.

means that they have made his existence their own." Cf. Gerhard Ebeling, *Theology and Proclamation* (Philadelphia: Fortress Press, 1966), pp. 88-89, 124-30; *Word and Faith* (Philadelphia: Fortress Press, 1963), pp. 234-35; *The Nature of Faith* (Philadelphia: Fortress Press, 1961), chap. 4.
87. John Knox, *On the Meaning of Christ* (New York: Harper, 1947); reprinted in *Jesus: Lord and Christ* (1958), p. 203.
88. John Knox, *The Church and the Reality of Christ* (New York: Harper & Row, 1962).
89. *Brief Outline*, § 165.

The Incarnation of Archetypal Humanity

On the basis of the new life communicated by the central figure of the Gospels of the New Testament, the Christian community is related both outwardly and inwardly to Jesus of Nazareth — outwardly as the determinate historical beginning from which the community continually derives, inwardly because it is the power of Jesus' unqualified dependence which is present as the new life. In this sense Jesus is the exemplar of Christian life and fulfills his vocation by communicating vitality and direction to the Christian church. For the Christian, what Jesus imparts is decisive, and therefore the Christian cannot look for that which he is able to receive to be surpassed. The God-consciousness displayed there and participated in by the community is inclusive and universal; consequently the community's task is ever to continue to become according to the pattern it has received. This new shape and personal strength is one which defines the religious self-consciousness and thus is determinate for how Christians experience their unqualified dependence. No limits, then, are placed upon its efficacy and capacity to influence in any future time and place. But, if this is the case — if the new life has such unbounded application — something else must be said about the individual person who is the exemplary and public source of that Christian self-consciousness.

Philosophical theology not only draws on analyses of the human spirit but is also the repository of the concept of "revelation." Revelation signifies the originality of the historical given which lies at the foundation of a religious communion;[90] that is, the religious self-consciousness found in a religious community cannot be explained for the adherents of that communion "by the condition of the circle in which it appears and operates; for if it could, it would not be a starting point, but would itself be the product of a spiritual process."[91] This reflects a valid insight, Schleiermacher believes, not only for a religious communion, but for any entity which manifests something distinctive of its own. For instance, there is an

90. Ibid. , § 45; *CF,* § 10.
91. *CF,* § 13, 1.

analogy to the concept of revelation anytime an individual who is outstandingly endowed becomes the starting point of a new influence. The more prominent founders of the religions possessed such an endowment, which became the historical given that serves to provide the distinctive and original character of their particular communion. But the same is true of figures in other historical bodies. When this concept of revelation or newness is understood from its Christian standpoint, it manifests both continuity and discontinuity with its more generalized use: "But if this is to be applied in the same sense to Christ, it must first of all be said that, in comparison with him, everything which could otherwise be regarded as revelation again loses this character. For everything else is limited to particular times and places."[92] For the Christian, therefore, the originality or newness of the historical given, which provides the basis for the distinctive essence of his religion, is the occurrence which is the turning point of all history. The phrase made famous by Paul Tillich, "the center of history," similar to one used by Schleiermacher himself, catches part of the meaning here, for the influence of what appears in Christ pertains to the entire human race in its constitution and destiny.

The God-consciousness made public by Jesus is the focal point of the historical life of man; and this is not something any individual can simply accomplish himself out of the resources of his own free capacity. A man can influence his fellows through that which is uniquely his, but he cannot posit himself as the turning point of the ages. This could happen only if he in his individuality was at the same time the expression of an influence and direction present in all times and places. In this way, the one who is the exemplar and fountain of Christian self-consciousness for the community not only defines *their* unqualified dependence but the dependence of all men as the finite creatures they are.

Schleiermacher exposits this thrust in several ways in his dogmatics. He speaks of Jesus Christ as the second Adam who completes the creation of human nature.[93] Again, he says

92. Ibid.; cf. *CF*, §94, 2.
93. *CF*, § 89.

that Jesus Christ is like all men in his humanity, but is distinguished from all others by the continuous power of his God-consciousness, and this was "a veritable existence of God in him."[94] Or, the point can be put in terms of God's electing decree which has arranged the whole of things in light of what occurs in Christ.[95] In all of these cases, the "Eduard" side of Schleiermacher's thought, overlapping as it does with "Ernst," takes the individual person who is the source of this new life and explains what Jesus accomplishes in a universal perspective, thereby making Jesus not just another individual man.

The most pointed rubric which Schleiermacher uses to state this universal perspective is the concept indicated by the German word *Urbild* or archetype. The leading proposition dealing with the person of Jesus Christ in *The Christian Faith* says, "If the self-activity of the new common life is original in the Redeemer and proceeds from him alone, then as a historical individual he must have been at the same time archetypal, that is, the archetype must have become completely historical in him, and each historical moment of this individual must have borne within it the archetypal."[96]

The most famous use of *Urbild* in philosophical and theological literature in Germany immediately preceding Schleiermacher's own appropriation of the word is undoubtedly that of Immanuel Kant in his *Religion Within the Limits of Reason Alone*.[97] Kant uses *Urbild* to refer to the noumenal idea of a man well-pleasing to God, and he interprets the Gospel of John's Logos passages by the ideal of duty.[98] The archetype of a "man well-pleasing to God" is God's only begotten Son. This means that "man may then hope to become acceptable to God (and so be saved) through a practical faith in this Son of God (so far as he is represented as having taken upon himself man's nature) . . . he would be unswervingly loyal to the

94. Ibid. , § 94.
95. Ibid. , § 120, 3.
96. *Der Christliche Glaube*, § 90.
97. Immanuel Kant, *Die Religion innerhalb der Grenzen der blossen Vernunft* (1793). Eng. trans. T. M. Greene and H. Hudson, *Religion Within the Limits of Reason Alone* (New York: Harper, 1960).
98. Ibid. , pp. 61-62; Eng. trans. pp. 54-55.

archetype [*Urbild*] of humanity and, by faithful imitation, remain true to his exemplar."[99]

This passage from Kant indicates the prevalent usage of *Urbild* in Germany at the turn of the nineteenth century. The *Urbild* is the archetype of humanity. Herder uses *Urbilder* as equivalent to the Forms in the writings of Plato.[100] *Urbild* could also be employed as the eternal Logos and as the original being of man.[101] Finally, *Urbild* appears as the universal idea or *Idee*.[102]

Kant holds that such an ideal or archetype resides in man's morally-legislative reason as a part of the consciousness of duty. Accordingly, Kant says, "We need, therefore, no empirical example to make the idea of a person morally well-pleasing to God our archetype; this idea as an archetype is already present in our reason."[103] No example in outer experience can be adequate to this archetype of reason, "and the presence of this archetype in the human soul is in itself sufficiently incomprehensible without our adding to its supernatural origin the assumption that it is hypostasized in a particular individual."[104]

Many thinkers of the early nineteenth century did not interpret *Urbild* precisely in the manner of Kant's ideal of duty, but Kant was not alone in denying that this ideal can be hypostasized in a particular individual.[105] Schleiermacher's contention that the archetype became completely historical in Jesus Christ is directly counter to that front. Jesus is not archetypal in any form of human life except that of his God-consciousness. Art, science, and other forms of human activity are not included in this archetype, for these forms of activity do not refer to the unity of self-consciousness which defines the distinctive nature of humanity.[106]

99. Ibid.
100. Jacob Grimm and Wilhelm Grimm. eds., *Deutsches Wörterbuch*, 16 vols. (Leipzig: Hirzel, 1854-1954), XI, 3:2386-87.
101. Ibid.
102. Ibid.
103. *Religion Within the Limits of Reason Alone*, p. 56.
104. Ibid. , p. 57.
105. Friedrich Schelling, *Vorlesungen über die Methode des akademischen Studiums*, ed. O. Braun (Leipzig, 1907); J. G. Fichte, *Die Anweisung zum seligen Leben*, ed. F. Medicus (Hamburg, 1954); Ferdinand Christian Baur, *Die Christliche Gnosis* (Tübingen, 1835).
106. *CF*, § 93, 2.

Although Schleiermacher insisted upon the historical actuality of the archetype of humanity in Jesus Christ, he was not unmindful of the difficulties which this raises for systematic thought:

> But even if it is certain that the source of God-consciousness in such an ever-increasing common life can only be the archetype, it is not by that means easier to understand just how the archetypal is able to come to perception and experience in an individual human being. Surely in general we are able to do nothing other than keep the two apart, and whether considering works of art or forms of nature, we regard each individual only as a complement of the rest and as requiring completion by them.[107]

In the insistence that the archetype became completely historical in Jesus Christ Schleiermacher presents an ontological interpretation of the person of Jesus Christ. It is the humanity of Jesus which defines the relation of God to the whole of the human race. In the order of being, therefore, Jesus Christ is the embodiment of the eternal form of humanity. He is the one through whom God knows the world.

Schleiermacher devotes one division of his lectures on the life of Jesus to a consideration of the questions concerning how Jesus Christ can have an archetypal humanity. He names this division of the lectures "The Life of Christ before His Public Appearance." When one first comes across this heading there is the expectation that one is about to enter a search into those hidden decades of Jesus' life before the baptism. While Schleiermacher touches on such historical matters, they are tangential to the real interest which he pursues in this division of the lectures. Rather, Schleiermacher here deals with that which is "before" Jesus' public appearance not only, or even primarily, chronologically in respect to the baptism, but "vertically," as it were, in the ground and transcendent basis of Jesus' self-consciousness. He propounds here a doctrinal statement on the constitution of the person of Jesus Christ.

Schleiermacher is concerned with the recesses of Jesus' self-consciousness because he thinks the foundational presence of God to Jesus in a unique manner is required for his arche-

107. *Der Christliche Glaube*, § 93, 3.

1

typal nature. Consequently, the life of Jesus "before" his public appearance is the life Jesus receives from God as the basis of Jesus' being able to impart a life that will be efficacious in all times and places. This account is not a historical judgment but a systematic construction of what is required, even though Schleiermacher draws upon such texts as Luke 2:40 "and the child grew and became strong, filled with wisdom" in order to expound the doctrinal points he wishes to develop. While this section on "The Life of Christ before His Public Appearance" stands as the focus of this ideal construction of Jesus' archetypal humanity, Schleiermacher does not confine such discussion to that section alone by any means. Rather, as he explores Jesus' teaching and founding of a community, the designated internal side of the public activity, Schleiermacher also engages in analysis to show that such public activity is the expression that archetypal humanity would take in an individual life. Consequently, Schleiermacher's historical judgments about the public activity of Jesus and his systematic construction of Jesus' archetypal God-consciousness enabling his public work to have such efficacy for the Christian community become tightly intertwined. The result is that despite the fact that Schleiermacher was very concerned as a theologian to distinguish exegetical theology from dogmatic theology in the *Brief Outline,* and to differentiate what could be said of Jesus as if he were any other man from what could be said of him as a subject of faith in the opening lectures of the *Life of Jesus,* the actual execution of the material in these lectures does not evidence this concern.

From the late nineteenth century to the present such relating of history and faith has loomed large in the mind of the theological reader, and in the *Christmas Eve* Schleiermacher shows he was aware of it, but this is not the question that usually engages him in the discussion of the Gospel pericopes in the present volume. Instead of carrying through his lectures from the standpoint of what can be said about Jesus on the basis of critical history as distinct from what might be affirmed as the interpretation of faith — as many today might do — Schleiermacher here turns his efforts to the question of what is humanly conceivable for one who is so uniquely constituted as the archetype become completely historical. Since Jesus is the exemplary source of new life in the Christian community for any future time and place, he is not just another individual but is the embodiment of the divine principle, of God's knowledge and goal of the human race as a whole. But then the question arises: how can Jesus be the incarnation of archetypal humanity resulting from God's unique influence without the conditions and limits of human life being dissolved? This is the problem which Schleiermacher deals with time and again in these lectures. His answers invariably move dialectically between two points, termed by him the docetic and ebionite. If the limitations of human consciousness and the conditions of growth are removed, then docetism is the result. Or conversely, if Jesus is no different in any decisive way from other men, then he has nothing to give and we fall into ebionism.[108] The Christian position must move between these boundaries, so Schleiermacher wants to show that the uniqueness of Jesus does not mean the elimination of what is *logically* conceivable within the limits of humanity. And conversely, if the New Testament indicates something which threatens the distinctive dignity and capacities of Jesus Christ, Schleiermacher attempts to demonstrate that such a text is not really inimical to the unique person of Christ as one moved by the divine influence.

The danger of this tight intertwining of historical judgments and dialectical systematic construction is that he will fall into the trap of deciding specific historical questions on the basis of what his dialectical resolution between docetism and ebionism requires. Schleiermacher does not escape this danger, and it was the defect of this procedure along with his Johannine reliance, that Strauss and Schweitzer found so objectionable. Strauss, however, construed the artificiality of these judgments as an inevitable result of Schleiermacher's

108. "If Christ is to be the Redeemer, i.e., the real origin of constant living unhindered evocation of the God-consciousness, so that the participation of all others in it is mediated through him alone, it is, on the one hand, necessary that he should enjoy an exclusive and peculiar superiority over all others, and, on the other hand, there must also be an essential likeness between him and all men, because otherwise what he has to impart could not be the same as what they need." Ibid. , § 22, 2.

holding that the archetype became completely historical in an individual person. Strauss and the Tübingen school of German theology in general thought such an affirmation an anachronism; however, with much more circumspection and a much less Johannine cast, Karl Barth and Paul Tillich in their differing ways make ontological statements about the humanity of Jesus Christ which echo Eduard's "man-in-himself" and the becoming completely historical of archetypal humanity.[109]

There is more than one issue here in evaluating Schleiermacher. There is his systematic construction in the midst of historical matters and, then, there is his unswerving reliance upon the Gospel of John. The resulting account of Jesus has led some interpreters to state that Schleiermacher did not really have a historical mind.[110] I find this observation understandable but finally incorrect. Not only does his work on 1 Timothy and the Gospel of Luke as well as other New Testament and classical subjects testify to his ability in the historical field, but his readiness to emphasize the conditions of human individuality as applying to Jesus was in advance of most writers during the opening decades of the nineteenth century. Furthermore, as has already been observed (p. xxxi) authorship of the Gospel of John by a disciple was assumed by almost everyone in New Testament scholarship in those years.[111] Is the conclusion, then, to be drawn that none of these

109. See Karl Barth, *Church Dogmatics*, ed. G. W. Bromiley and T. F. Torrance (Edinburgh: T. & T. Clark, 1936-)III, 2:130-31; "He (Jesus) alone is the archetypal man whom all threatened and enslaved creatures must follow ... the Head of a whole body," p. 144. Paul Tillich, *Systematic Theology* (Chicago: University of Chicago Press, 1957), 2:98: "If theology ignores the fact to which the name of Jesus of Nazareth points, it ignores the basic Christian assertion that Essential God-Manhood has appeared within existence and subjected itself to the conditions of existence without being conquered by them. If there were no personal life in which existential estrangement had been overcome, the New Being would have remained a quest and an expectation and would not be a reality in time and space. Only if the existence is conquered in *one* point — a personal life, representing existence as a whole — is it conquered in principle, which means 'in beginning and in power.' This is the reason that Christian theology must insist on the actual fact to which the name Jesus of Nazareth refers."
110. E. g., Schweitzer, *Quest of the Historical Jesus*, p. 62. For a discussion of Schleiermacher's orientation to history, see Hermann Mulert, *Schleiermachers geschichtsphilosophische Ansichten in ihrer Bedeutung für seine Theologie* (Giessen, 1907); also R. R. Niebuhr, *Schleiermacher on Christ and Religion*, chap. 2.
111. It should be remembered that as late as the opening decade of the twentieth century the leading New Testament scholars in England such as

early nineteenth-century writers had really historical minds in the critical sense, even though it was just those years which marked the emergence of great strides in historiography? Such a conclusion would itself be a very "unhistorical" manner of dealing with the past. The acceptance of the Gospel of John as deriving from a disciple cannot convict Schleiermacher and his contemporaries of not having historical minds. This would be analogous to holding that Albert Schweitzer did not have a historical mind because he did not know the results of form criticism.

Therefore, let us examine the other factor, the systematic construction in the midst of historical matters. Schleiermacher certainly attempts something here that contrasts with the twentieth-century characteristic of keeping critical history and doctrine sharply sundered. Such a disjunction is denied by Schleiermacher's attempt to resolve dialectically how Jesus can be uniquely moved by God and at the same time possess a life conceivable within the limits of humanity. That is a valid question for Christian theology even though it is one so largely ignored today — unless one is to say that a Christian historian should present Jesus *etsi Deus non daretur.* Of course, it could be a valid task for a historian to write a history of Jesus "as if God were not there;" but it is also legitimate for one convinced of a distinctive divine initiative in Jesus Christ to attempt to portray these particular human matters as they actually were, that is, in the context of God's influence. Such an endeavor is what Schleiermacher pursues in these lectures on the life of Jesus, and that in itself does not make his mind unhistorical. If he simply blundered into this dialectical treatment of history unaware of what he was doing the matter might be judged differently. But in his introduction Schleiermacher goes to considerable pains to make clear his theological standpoint, even as he wishes to search for histori-

B. F. Westcott, J. B. Lightfoot, and William Sanday also held that the Fourth Gospel was written by a disciple of Jesus; see W. F. Howard, *The Fourth Gospel in Recent Criticism and Interpretation* (London: Epworth, 1931). Karl Bretschneider, who challenged this point in 1820, apparently changed his mind after the ensuing discussion; see Werner Kümmel, *The New Testament: The History of the Investigation of its Problems,* trans. S. MacLean Gilmour and Howard C. Kee (Nashville: Abingdon, 1972), pp. 84 ff. and 420, n. 113.

cal truth whatever the consequences; this theological stand-point also sharpens his cognizance of views which preclude the results in advance in a negative way.

Nevertheless, when both of these factors, the reliance upon the Gospel of John and the dialectical construction, are taken together an unquestionable artificiality often results. It stems, though, not from Schleiermacher's lack of a critical historical mind, however dated his historical judgments now may be, but from something in his basic outlook and view in the present as well as toward the past. This outlook is much too smoothly developmental; it does not allow sharp breaks, revolutionary reversals, and crises waged in fear and trembling. It also excludes new sin arising in the Christian life. Once the Christian self-consciousness has received the power to right itself and, through combat, has brought the consciousness of God to control over the other elements of self-consciousness, an enduring state has been achieved. "Sin in the new man is no longer active, but it is only the aftereffect or descendant of the old man."[112] It is only the remnant of an earlier time. This view of sin is much too retrospective to take account of the devious agility of the human spirit or the continuous struggle necessary if its frailty is to be borne. The implication of this for the matter at hand is that if struggle and conflict against sin in the Christian life results only from the period before conversion, then it follows that a man who is the archetype become completely historical would not be involved in struggle and conflict in his consciousness of God at all. And so it is in Schleiermacher's doctrine of the humanity of Jesus Christ. This also means that there will be no dramatic changes in Jesus' life, for example, after his baptism.

There is about the Jesus of the Fourth Gospel something all too compatible with this aspect of Schleiermacher's view. For instance, the synoptic pericopes about Jesus in the garden of Gethsemane portray trial and apprehension at the coming conflict in being obedient to the will of God. But his sorrow unto death, the petition that the cup of suffering may not be his, the sweat at the prospect that lay before him, these are

112. *CF,* § 109, § 2.

uncongenial to Schleiermacher's mind. A distinction between such weakness and a condition of sin could not successfully be maintained, he says.[113] It is significant, therefore, that the most reliable Gospel does not report any such occurrence. This passage was produced by the church or is a transformation of a parable. It does not apply to Jesus.

From the standpoint of critical history Schleiermacher may well be right here concerning the origin of this story, but such judgments as this mount to the point where Jesus in these lectures seems elevated above some aspects of the earthiness of human life — as is the case with the Johannine Christ.[114] With all his acuteness in emphasizing individuality, of possessing a keen critical sense, and following a method oriented to the personal self-consciousness of man, Schleiermacher cannot include Jesus in the inner conflict and struggle that inhere in the human scene.[115] Despite his emphasis in this volume on the importance of Old Testament ideas for the development of Jesus, it is no coincidence that Schleiermacher's lecturing on a myriad of subjects in philosophy and theology did not include the Old Testament. The earthy struggle of the religious self-consciousness in the Old Testament was discordant to his view. It is the strong inclination to remove this dimension which, when placed in the framework of his dialectical construction, appears falsely to elevate Schleiermacher's Christ. Basically, this defect of his history of Jesus does not arise from an erroneous formal method or a lack of critical historical capacity, judging the latter by the context and questions of Schleiermacher's own day. It comes, rather, from a certain lack in the substance of his own outlook.

Despite the fact that Schleiermacher so closely followed the Gospel of John, his basic christological point — that Jesus through word and deed communicates his sense of dependence

113. *LJ*, pp. 388 (S), 395.
114. Schleiermacher's strictures against conflict should not be confused with his positive emphasis on Jesus' suffering, both inward and outward.
115. Paul Tillich is correct in differentiating his Christology from Schleiermacher's on the basis of the new being's conquest of the distortions of existence through being subjected to them. However, Tillich's other observation that the new being is an ontological term whereas Schleiermacher's *Urbild* is anthropological is misleading; *Urbild* has an ontological character even though the ontology is not the same as Tillich's. See *Systematic Theology*, 2:150.

upon God and by this means awakens and transforms the personal self-consciousness of his fellow men — is not necessarily bound to the Fourth Gospel. Nor does his insistence that the person of Jesus Christ archetypically embodies God's knowledge and goal of the whole race of man have to be allied with a removal of inner struggle. Many of the principles Schleiermacher advances concerning the relation of Christology and history still have much to contribute to theological discussion, even though these principles have often received negative evaluation by those not evidencing a particularly sound grasp of Schleiermacher's own position. Usually such evaluation has taken place by ignoring the setting of Schleiermacher's *The Christian Faith* within the context of his total theological program stated in the *Brief Outline*. This mistake occurred already in Schleiermacher's own time among members of the Tübingen school.

On the other hand, when it is a question of the actual exegetical results to which Schleiermacher comes in his lectures on the life of Jesus, the matter stands differently. Virtually the whole tide of research in the twentieth century — and even before this in Germany — has moved against his position on the Gospel of John. Furthermore, many of the insights for which Schleiermacher contended in his day have by now been developed to a point where it sometimes appears as if they are uncongenial to Schleiermacher. For instance, in the early nineteenth century Schleiermacher intended to emphasize the individuality of Jesus, and that Jesus was influenced by his contemporary life as were other men. By this emphasis, Schleiermacher wished to give prominence to the concreteness of Jesus' humanity. Now, however, his Jesus of Johannine cast appears rather abstract and lacking in concreteness. Or, Schleiermacher tried to accentuate the plurality and fragmentariness of the synoptic Gospels as various precipitates of the oral tradition, but in terms of contemporary scholarship he appears lacking in this very regard, and as a result, engaged in false harmonizing. Add to such considerations as these the fact that Schleiermacher's *question* concerning the life of Jesus — how he can logically be conceived as completely human and yet uniquely moved by God — is not of primary importance to many of a contemporary mind, and the result is adverse for an appreciation of Schleiermacher's efforts as we have them recorded by his hearers in the following pages.

Albert Schweitzer once said that the greatest lives of Jesus have been written out of hate.[116] The hate could be directed against Christianity, or the church's doctrine, or Jesus himself as anything more than a wise man from Nazareth. If such an attitude is a prerequisite for the heights of attainment in this field, then Schleiermacher is excluded, not chiefly by the filters of the hurrying pens of his students, but because he spent his life attempting to foster Christianity, to reconstruct critically its doctrines in the light of modern knowledge, and to maintain that, " There is no other way of obtaining participation in the Christian communion than through faith in Jesus as the Redeemer."[117]

THE TEXT OF *THE LIFE OF JESUS*[118]

The present volume translates K. A. Rütenik's edition of 1864, which, as already noted, reconstructed Schleiermacher's lectures on the basis of their last presentation in 1832. Rütenik's Preface, omitted here, reveals the problems which he had to solve. A certain Mr. Jonas, who undertook to publish Schleiermacher's literary remains, himself doubted whether the life of Jesus materials were publishable inasmuch as only Schleiermacher's notes, from which he lectured extemporaneously, were available. Moreover, for the final part of the lectures, not even these existed. Furthermore, since Schleiermacher lectured five times on the life of Jesus, he varied his exposition of the notes, sometimes expanding and sometimes compressing his previous presentation. Rütenik's careful differentiation between Schleiermacher's own notes and the text which he reconstructed from student notebooks has been preserved here. Rütenik relied on five notebooks, including that of Professor Alexander Schweizer of Zurich, which recorded the last lectures in 1832. A year after this

116. *Quest of the Historical Jesus*, p. 4.
117. *CF*, § 14.
118. This section has been supplied by the series editor.

intricate task of reconstruction was under way, Rütenik received a sixth notebook, more detailed than the others, which he proceeded to incorporate into the final draft — a task which required three years. Even so, Rütenik regarded this edition as a provisional one, for he indicated that within a year he expected to revise the book on the basis of notebooks, already in his possession, from the four earlier lectures in 1819-20, 1821, 1823, and 1829-30; he asked that readers send him still additional notebooks from which to work. Though Rütenik observed that, given Schleiermacher's rapid delivery, the most complete notes are also the most illegible, he reported that he had one especially legible notebook but did not use it for the present work; apparently he reserved it for the more definitive edition which he planned but never produced. Rütenik did, however, record variant versions in footnotes. The present edition includes virtually all of them. However, frequently the brief variants have been placed in parentheses within the text. Although the Rütenik text itself contains parentheses, possibly supplied by Rütenik, the new parentheses are readily identified. Unfortunately, there is no way of being sure of Rütenik's own contribution to the text. Rütenik's longer variants are indicated by asterisks and daggers.[119] Rütenik also supplied occasional content footnotes; these have usually been retained because they refer to related materials in the collected works of Schleiermacher. The present editor's annotations are numbered consecutively. Normally, quotations from the Greek New Testament have been replaced by the RSV. The translator, S. MacLean Gilmour, fortunately completed his work before his death; during the preparation of the volume, however, minor revisions have been made, including the paragraphing and the division of unwieldy sentences.

The present Table of Contents is intended to help the reader; it replaces the analytical one composed by Rütenik, who struggled unsuccessfully to impose a clear structure on the text. Schleiermacher, it should be noted, had the habit of treating a topic in several sessions. Often he began a new

119. Strauss's suggestions for still other readings have not been noted, since it is deemed unwise to further complicate an already complex text.

major division in the middle of a lecture. Consequently there is no congruence between major divisions of the material and the individual lectures. The outline set down in the Table of Contents of this edition makes no effort to provide detailed guidance to the many topics discussed by Schleiermacher; it simply indicates in a general way the location of the major topics discussed. In providing this modern outline, with clearly subordinated sections, a certain arbitrariness was unavoidable. In order not to compound confusion unnecessarily, the new outline has not been imposed on the Rütenik text. The original headings, somewhat modified, are allowed to remain in the middle of the lectures where Schleiermacher (or Rütenik?) placed them.

This is not an easy book to read. Nonetheless, despite the difficulties involved, the experience is rewarding. The work enriches the Schleiermacher materials available in English and makes a significant contribution to the on-going clarification of the task of understanding Jesus and his significance for the Christian faith.

SELECT BIBLIOGRAPHY

BIBLIOGRAPHY

Tice, Terrance N., *Schleiermacher Bibliography*. Princeton: Princeton Theological Seminary (pamphlet no. 12), 1966.

COLLECTED WORKS AND LETTERS

Schleiermacher, Friedrich, *Sämmtliche Werke*. 31 vols. Berlin: G. Reimer, 1835–64.

_____. *Werke: Auswahl in vier Bänden*. Edited by O. Braun and J. Bauer. Leipzig: Meiner, 1911.

_____. *Aus Schleiermachers Leben in Briefen*. 4 vols. Berlin: G. Reimer, 1858–63.

CRITICAL EDITIONS

Schleiermacher, Friedrich. *Der Christliche Glaube*. Edited by Martin Redeker. 2 vols. Berlin: de Gruyter, 1960.

_____. *Hermeneutik*. Edited by Heinz Kimmerle. Heidelberg: Carl Winter, 1959.

_____. *Kurze Darstellung des theologischen Studiums*. Edited by Heinrich Scholz. Leipzig, 1910; Hildesheim: G. Olms, 1961.

_____. *Reden über die Religion*. Edited by G. C. B. Pünjer. Braunschweig: C. A. Schwetschke & Son, 1879.

_____. *Weihnachtsfeier*. Edited by Hermann Mulert. Philosophische Bibliothek, Vol. 117. Leipzig, 1908.

ENGLISH TRANSLATIONS

Schleiermacher, Friedrich. *Brief Outline on the Study of Theology*. Translated by T. N. Tice. Richmond: John Knox, 1966.

_____. *The Christian Faith*. Translated by H. R. Mackintosh and J. S. Stewart. Edinburgh: T. & T. Clark, 1928; New York: Harper Torchbook, 1963.

_____. *Christmas Eve: Dialogue on the Incarnation*. Translated by T. N. Tice. Richmond: John Knox, 1967.

_____. *A Critical Essay on the Gospel of Luke*. Translated by Connop Thirlwall. London: Taylor, 1825.

_____. *The Life of Schleiermacher as Unfolded in His Autobiography and Letters*. Translated by F. Rowan. London: Smith, Elder, & Co., 1860. A translation of most of vols. 1 and 2 of the German edition.

———. "On the Discrepancy Between the Sabellian and Athanasian Method of Representing the Doctrine of a Trinity in the Godhead." Translated by Moses Stuart. *Biblical Repository and Quarterly Observer* 6 (1835): 1–116.

———. *On Religion: Speeches to Its Cultured Despisers.* Translated by John Oman. London, 1893; New York: Harper Torchbook, 1958; also translated by T. N. Tice. Richmond: John Knox, 1969.

———. *Selected Sermons of Friedrich Schleiermacher.* Translated by Mary F. Wilson. London: Hodder and Stoughton, 1890; New York: Funk & Wagnalls, n.d.

———. *Soliloquies.* Translated by Horace Friess. Chicago: Open Court, 1926.

STUDIES OF SCHLEIERMACHER

Barth, Karl. *From Rousseau to Ritschl.* New York: Harper, 1959.

Dilthey, Wilhelm. *Das Leben Schleiermachers.* Berlin, 1870; Göttingen: Vandenhoeck & Ruprecht, 1970.

Friess, Horace L. "Introduction" and "Appendix" to *Schleiermacher's Soliloquies.* Chicago: Open Court, 1926.

Hirsch, Emmanuel, *Schleiermachers Christusglaube.* Gütersloh: Gerd Mohn, 1968.

McCown. C. C. *The Search for the Real Jesus.* New York: Scribner, 1940. (Discussion of Schleiermacher's critical work in the context of the history of the subject.)

Miller, Marlin. *Der Übergang. Schleiermachers Theologie des Reiches Gottes im Zusammenhang seines Gesamtdenkens.* Gütersloh: Gerd Mohn, 1970.

Munro, Robert. *Schleiermacher: Personal and Speculative.* London: Gardner, 1903.

Niebuhr, Richard R. *Schleiermacher on Christ and Religion.* New York: Scribner, 1964.

Redeker, Martin. *Friedrich Schleiermacher: Life and Thought.* Translated by John Wallhausser. Philadelphia: Fortress, 1973.

Schleiermacher as Contemporary. Edited by R. W. Funk. *Journal for Theology and the Church* 7 (1970).

Seifert, Paul. *Die Theologie des jungen Schleiermacher.* Gütersloh: Gerd Mohn, 1960.

Spiegler, Gerhard. *The Eternal Covenant.* New York: Harper & Row, 1967.

Stephan, Horst. *Die Lehre Schleiermachers von der Erlösung.* Tübingen: J. C. B. Mohr, 1901.

THE TEXT OF
THE LIFE OF JESUS

INTRODUCTION

Lecture 1 (May 14). The concept of biography. The contrast between chronicle and history. The task is so to discover the inner quality of his life development as a unity that results can also be achieved on the presupposition of other coefficients. Even at best, however, there are limits to which this can be done.

Gentlemen. In connection with the subject with which we are to concern ourselves in these lectures there are certain important preliminary matters to be dealt with before we proceed to the study itself. The first will be that we must agree on what we actually mean by biography, for that is what we wish to try to provide for the person of Christ. Since a biography is something historical we must recall a peculiar difference that is to be found in all historical accounts. This difference is usually characterized by the saying that the one account is an *actual history,* while the other is a *chronicle.* Life, namely, is a phenomenon that changes with the passage of time. If we begin, then, with time as a divisible entity, the whole of life therefore consists of a series of separate moments that can be isolated and distinguished from one another with greater or lesser accuracy. If this series of moments is all that is noted of a historical subject and if all we are told is only how the individual subject employed each moment, what its content was for him, what we have is nothing other than a chronicle. By this means we obtain only a series of details that were perceptible in the temporal phenomenon. Now to be sure, that is something indispensable, and no one will deny that it belongs to a biography. Naturally, however, the details must always be presented only selectively, for, since time is infinitely divisible, it will always be necessary to gather up what can be divided if one wishes to represent the whole. But even so the changes are differentiated as quantitative entities, and consequently a selection will be necessary: the insignificant are passed over and the more important are articulated. This selection presupposes a standard of judgment, and such a standard contains the seed of something greater than the mere presentation of perceptible details, because there must be a concept in terms of which one change is regarded as of great or of little importance. Accordingly, even a mere chronicle cannot be composed intelligently if no consideration is given at the same time to something other than the perceptible details. However, the more a historical presentation a chronicle is, the more the other factor retreats into the background. In fact, it could even be something that has its ground only in the free discretion of the author and not in the nature of the subject: the author may wish to consider his subject only from a certain viewpoint, and much then appears significant to him which from another viewpoint would be of no consequence. It follows then from this that, if a historical presentation wishes to be actual history, it cannot restrict itself only to what is externally perceptible. But here we note a twofold difference, namely, that to the *particular* as *separable* there is opposed the *unity* as *indivisible*, and to the *externally perceptible* something *inward,* which is not as such perceptible, but can be grasped only in another way. The greater, then, the difference in the subject itself between its unity as something indivisible and that which in it is isolated and the greater the difference between that which is inward and what is externally perceptible, the greater will be the difference between the one and the other manner and method of presentation. Let us now apply all this to biography. Think of an individual whom you especially observe from such a point of view that he fills out a definite place, but he fills out his place in such a way that you at the same time can think of many others who would have filled out the same place in the same way. When you do this, you think of the inner unity, the continuity of the individual life as something recessive, and he (or, he himself) becomes a subject for you only with respect to his externality. That is the case whenever we place the particular under a general category — something which must be done very cautiously, because an injustice can easily lie in its application; thus nothing here is so noted (or:

4

so conceived) except what is externally perceptible: the occurrence of the particular, in which the general occurrences are mirrored. But what is inward is not an object of consideration, because we imagine that a great number of people share the same qualities as the individual, that is to say, if we ascribe to the latter only a slight degree of individuality (or: of its individuality) we must understand the task as finding the unity by means of which just this individual in all his varied appearances is distinguished from every other individual.*

We can now make a somewhat closer approach to the task of a biography which wishes to be a history. With reference to this side of the twofold difference to which attention has been drawn we are compelled to say — we must become conscious of the inward element, the unity, of the life in such a way that we can assert: Even if the particular (or: the circumstances) had been something other than it actually was, we should nevertheless have been able to relate it to the same unity. But how is this one difference related to the other we have noted, (1) the unity, namely, to the isolated particular, which is multitudinous, and (2) the inward to the outward — the inward, which we can only comprehend in a different way, to the outward, which is actually perceptible? To answer this question we are well advised to maintain a firm grip on the following. The difference between the outward and the inward has a reality only to the extent that we can imagine the same outward in relation to a different inward, and the same inward in relation to a different outward. The former is what is expressed in the familiar saying, *duo faciunt idem, sed non est idem,* that is, there may be moments in two different life series which, viewed from without, are not to be distinguished, but the inward to which the one is related is something quite different from that to which the other is related. The manifestation of an individual moment may be the same, but the life determinant of which that is the manifestation is different. The other is this: What is outward is always a

---

* the more we describe the particular from this point of view, the less the description of the detail fulfills the task, but one must seek the unity by which this particular differs from every other particular

5

product of two factors, for every emergent moment of life goes back to another, that is, the life moment may be regarded as a reaction and consequently presupposes an action: something must have acted on me, and my life expression is a reaction to it. To be sure, we may also view the life moment as an original action, but in its manifestation it is determined by the object on which I act. If we only grasp the outwardly perceptible in the activity of a man, the connection is lost and the external element may be presented in great detail without the narrator knowing anything at all about what is inward. "The individual did this and that"— but the actual life determinant which was the basis of it he does not know. Clearly he has not understood the individual man himself at all and cannot say that he knows anything of him if he knows only this external element, just because he assembled these external pieces together. A man's own characteristic being is always one coefficient of that which is external; but if I cannot distinguish these two and consequently do not seek what is inward in what is external, I have failed utterly to understand the man as an acting agent. Viewed from two different sides, this then is the task: to seek for the unity of the particulars and the inward of the externals. In a certain sense the inward is what itself remains the same because it is the same factor in all different results; consequently it is also the unity in the particulars, and therefore it seems as if we had no reason at all to distinguish these two.

But the matter takes on a different form if we ask, How does this relate to the externals, when at the same time it is supposed to be the inward of the externals, that is, how is it related to the fact that the man in his life development remains the same? The life, indeed, is the same, to the extent that it is the inward in its contrast to the external; but even so we cannot say that it is the unity of the particulars. We say, then, that the man in a certain sense is and remains always the same, but that in another sense he becomes someone else. If we meant by this only how he is an outward phenomenon to us, the matter would not belong in this connection, for then it would be the external that had become something different, but we also mean it in the sense

6

that what is inward in him has become something else. Here — and with this we approach a special difficulty with reference to our subject, the biography of Christ — everything depends on how one conceives the relationship between the particular human life and man in general. If we do not think of time at all, but only think of men as they are related to one another, we then must say that the same human nature is in all and there is not anything in anyone (and by this we can only mean) — there is in no one a kind of activity that would not also be in all, but in every individual all these in their relationship one to another are nevertheless again something different, that is, considered as entities that stand in a different relationship to one another. And on the other hand, every individual in the totality of his being, considered as an entity, stands in a different relation to the total task than others do. To this extent we say of every individual that he always remains the same, because we think that in all his different moments of life there is the same difference from all others, in the one and in the other (or: in the other life moment). But it is something else altogether if we consider the individual man in terms of time, for then we find that not all human activities in the same moment are perceptible in the same way.

If in this connection we compare moments of (in a certain sense) identical content with one another, the explanation we give is that in the one moment a certain activity is more apparent and the others recede more and more without, however, being present to a lesser degree; but in the case of moments of different content the matter is quite different. This different content, however, is only the relation to the different life periods, and in respect to these the man becomes an other. Therefore we say: It is not possible to know what will become of a child, because certain forms and activities are still to develop, and consequently we are still unaware of what relation to the others they will assume and how the others will operate; but in like manner during the later life periods certain forms of activity which formerly were prominent recede in such a way that of various people we must say in the same way: We cannot determine how a given youngster will turn out when he grows older, for we have no grounds for calculating in what relation such forms of activity will gradually recede. In this sense, then, there is a difference here also, for the relation of the unity to the particulars and of the inward to the external is not so identical that we should not have to say that the inward is also changeable, although the unity of life is the same, for the person remains the same.

Accordingly, when we ask: What is the actual task of a biography *which is to correspond wholly to the idea of a description of a life?* We have to reply: *The task is to grasp what is inward in the man with such certainty that it can be said: I can say with a measure of assurance how what is outward with respect to the man would have been if what affected him and also what he affected had been different than was actually the case,* for only then do I have an actual knowledge of what is inward in him, because I can also construe it as the constant factor to different results. But we shall be able to achieve only a certain approximation of this; there is a maximum, and even he who possesses the greatest talent for comprehending an inner distinctiveness will only believe he has worked out a solution of the task within certain limits. There is indeed a maximum, and we can establish this inward unity only within certain limits.

Lecture 2 (May 15). No individual can be torn loose from his time, age, and people. In our special case both seem to be applicable, namely, that Christ should be able to be calculated and that he is rooted in the life of his people. So far as the former is concerned, the prior knowledge of the latter places no limits to our consciousness of freedom or to the dignity of Christ, for only those enlightened by him can calculate him. But the limitation is also disadvantageous. In part his exemplary function ceases if we do not know how Christ would now have acted. In part his dignity suffers if he is to be determined by conformity with the life of his people. The relation of the individual to the common life is a twofold one: he directs, or he follows. Christ is absolutely directing; yet in his receptivity he stands also under the power of his common life, because otherwise he would neither have been able to have developed in human terms nor have acted humanly.[1]

1. The German word *dominirend* has been translated as "directing." One possible literal rendition, the word "dominating," has now gained connotations of psychological coercion which would mislead in understanding Schleiermacher's meaning in this lecture. Not only Julius Caesar and Mohammed, but also Michelangelo and Shakespeare, Florence Nightingale

What I set forth at the end of yesterday's lecture as the actual task of a biography, namely, to comprehend and present what is inward in the man with such a clear awareness that one could think with a certain confidence of the same man under different coefficients, that is, under other operative circumstances and forces, and nonetheless forecast the result of his life under other circumstances that are not given — this is the same task that we always set ourselves for everything that we designate by the expression *insight into human character;* its maximum is a kind of prediction, the claim that one knows in advance how the man will reveal himself under certain given circumstances. However, this task can be conceived as a maximum only within certain limits, namely, it is a vain and fruitless undertaking if one wishes to think of one and the same man among a different people or in a different age: such a procedure is wholly unrewarding, for the individual among another people and in a different age would not have been the same. One often hears such questions raised concerning a man who has had a great influence on history as, for instance, how he would have acted if he had lived at this time or that among another people. However, one cannot think of an individual without at the same time thinking of him in connection with the general conditions that determine his existence, and there can be no talk of this unless one sets as a maximum the attempt to establish what a man determined by such conditions would have brought forth as results; but he cannot be torn loose from the general conditions of his individual existence. This must be clear to everyone who has a concept of the influence of the common life upon the individual. The individual comes into being only in and through the common life, and that is a fixed and unalterable relation, and every individual in his development is at the same time a result of the common life. But if we now wish to apply this immediately to our specific task, namely, the biography of Christ, it appears that both what I have set forth as the maxi-

and Mohandas Gandhi, are examples of such directing men according to Schleiermacher's conception. Cf. Schleiermacher's address, "Über den Begriff des grossen Mannes," *Schleiermachers Werke, Auswahl* (Leipzig, 1910), 1: 520-31.

mum soluuon of the task and what I have declared to be its limitation make this special task impossible. If we keep that maximum in mind, we should be able to state the formula as follows. *There can be a representation of the individual which conforms to the idea, that is, one which conforms to the historical idea,* which is not satisfied with externalities alone, *only to the extent that it is possible in a certain sense to calculate the individual man.* No one will easily quarrel with this if he begins with the fact that human nature is the same in all; therefore, that no form of activity can be conceived in a man which would not essentially be also in every other. Consequently we must say that the difference in individuals can only consist in the different relation of the common forms of activity which constitute human history; there is also a calculus here (for every relationship presupposes the possibility of a calculation), and the more incorrect the calculus, the less is the knowledge of the individual; but the more mistaken therewith the knowledge of what is inward, the falser must be the representation of the life.

To pursue the question of the extent to which this stands in general in contradiction to the consciousness of freedom that is present in us all would lead us at this point too far afield. We are all aware, however, that the clarity with which another comprehends and knows me does no harm to my freedom; we rejoice at the clarity of the one who calculates us correctly and yet remain free. But if we ask ourselves whether the thoroughness of a biography of Christ depends on whether he can be calculated in accordance with those general prescriptions, this seems to us to be wholly in contradiction to the way in which we (I am presupposing faith in Christ) distinguish Christ from all men. On the other hand, however, it is quite apparent that, when we speak of the difference of Christ from all other men, of the specific or peculiar dignity of Christ, if that implies essentially that in his human life, in the manner in which what was inward in him came to expression, he is not subject to the same calculus, we should at the same time take away from the concept of Christ its very practical power. For if we ask upon what it depends that Christ nevertheless is given us as an example, we must say that it would

10

be something utterly powerless and wholly vain if we were not able to conceive of Christ as acting in other cases than those individual phenomena in his history that are actually given us. If in this practical application of the knowledge of Christ we were to be limited to the particular incident out of his life which lies before our eyes, this practical application would be of little or no value to us; consequently what on the one hand appears to stand in contradiction to the dignity of Christ is on the other hand a necessity if we are in practice to comprehend Christ. We could not take him as an example if we were not able to construe his way of acting. Consequently the application of the calculus must have its validity also for the life of Jesus, for otherwise his practical effect on us would be inadequate. Accordingly, in spite of that contradiction, this must have its validity.

Now, with reference to the limitation, the first question to be asked is: If we are not permitted to tear any man loose from the general condition of his individual existence, therefore not from his rootage in the life of his people and not from his age, then this appears again to put an end to that application which we postulate is to be made of the knowledge of Christ, for we are in another age and belong to another culture. If therefore we cannot extract Christ from his historical setting in order to think of him within that of our people and our age, it follows again that the knowledge of him has no practical value, for he ceases to have exemplary character. But we can raise the question from another angle. If we are to think of him under the conditions of a definite age and a definite setting in the life of his people, does not this imply a greater diminution of the specific dignity of Christ? To begin with, I wish to direct myself to this latter question, and to answer it we must take a still closer look at the relation of the individual man in the course of his life development to those general conditions.

In this connection I must necessarily presuppose — and believe that I am able to do so because the whole idea of a kingdom of God in its earthly development would otherwise be something empty and valueless — that we have to think of the life in terms of a continuous progression and by no means

11

in terms of an empty circular course. If we include in this presupposition the relation of the individual to the common life, we shall see then that we must think of this as something twofold: namely, on the one hand in such a way that the individual stands to be sure under the power of the common life to which he belongs; but then also, cn the other hand, that the common life stands under the power of individuals. If the former were not the case the whole axiom that the individual is conditioned by the common life in which his existence is cast would be false, but in such a case we should have to regard everything that falls under the form of historical and natural necessity as an accident. But if the latter were false, there could be no historical progression. We cannot go back to the first beginnings of human affairs, but in the common life there could be no development, not in any direction, if it did not stand under the power of individuals. However, there are men whose development goes beyond their people and their time and whose stages of development later enter into the common life; but if the individual furthers the common life by means of results which formerly were not there but later became common property, then the whole stands under the power of the individual life. Among those who exercise such a directing influence on the common life there can, however, be no one who, while directing in one respect, would not stand in another respect under the power of the common life. This duality, therefore, is something that we must recognize in its universality. Now to be sure, there are everywhere individuals in large numbers of whom it certainly cannot be shown that they have exercised a directing influence on the common life. On the contrary, they stand wholly under the power of the common life. That is natural and understandable and belongs to the idea of man as a species. Otherwise there could be no common life, but the influences of the individuals would paralyze each other and there would be nothing but individuals, each for himself; then we should have to say, Among those to whom we ascribe a directing influence of this sort, none can be imagined who, while he exercises such an influence in one respect, does not stand in another respect under the power of the common life. For just because the difference of individuals rests on the relation of various forms of activity of the individual life, so we think of these only as different in every other, namely, with respect to their specific direction, but also as different with respect to their quantity, and the individual can only exercise a directing influence by virtue of those forms of activity which are dominant in himself, but with reference to the other individuals (or: forms of activity) he stands under the influence of the common life.

Having established this and going back to our special task, we are obliged to say that the matter no longer looks as bad as it did at first glance. It no longer seems to us to be a destruction of the special dignity of Christ when we say that he also stands in such a relation to the common life to which he belongs, if we only recall that his relation to the common life was of the sort that he exercised a directing influence. We can say, further, that we distinguish a setting in the life of a particular people and the age, but these distinctions touch each other, and the directing influence of the individual life is, to be sure, greater if it encounters this contiguity: if the individual exercises an influence which extends beyond his people and his age it is greater than if it disappears again with his age. Consequently, without overlooking the fact that there had to be a definite relation of Christ to his people and age, we can nevertheless think of an influence of his activity which extends *over all peoples and over all ages.* But must we accordingly admit that Christ did not stand in any way under the power of his age and his setting in the life of his people? I have often been attacked on the grounds that in the sections on Christology in my *The Christian Faith,* where if one does not wish to propagate a dead letter one must touch on these points, I have so represented this subject that one is obliged to conclude that his setting in the life of his people and also his age must have exerted an influence on Christ. I have been attacked by well-meaning theologians on the grounds that in such a case the peculiar dignity of Christ would be decreased; but I can only explain that as a misunderstanding. Let me be specific. Even if we wish to think of nothing else than the directing influence, we should yet be obliged to say that he could not have been directing if he had not borne in himself

13

the age and life of his people. Every activity of Christ which we wished to think of as divested of such relationships would have been utterly strange to the folk who surrounded him. But such an activity can only be an object of observation. It can reach no further. In actual life one excludes it from attention until he finds something that is shared with others, for only in connection with this latter can a common activity or a living and conscious continuation of the activity of the other be conceived.

I believe it to be our best procedure to go at this point into some detail. Accordingly, we will say, if Christ's knowledge of God is made the object of consideration and someone wished to assert that it came entirely from his people and his age, then, to be sure, the directing influence of Christ, which we previously assumed, would be done away with. Rather, he could only be what he is in our faith to the extent that he determined such a type of the knowledge of God, which can spread over all that is human and all that exists within space and time and can find recognition everywhere. Therefore, what constitutes his specific dignity is to be sought in the most inward ground of his knowledge of God. But if we are to distinguish the most inward ground and in addition only its closest temporal and spatial appearance, then Christ could express himself in no other way than in the language (or: prevailing language) into which he had been born and in which he was reared and on which his fellowship with other men depended, and we ask: Did this contain the absolute knowledge of God, or the capacity to bring this in detail adequately to consciousness? To this we reply, No! for otherwise Christ would not have been necessary at all, but the knowledge of God would have spread of itself by means of the language; and therefore, so far as language was concerned, in the sentient expression of his knowledge of God, he stood under the power of his setting in the life of his people, whose expression was the language he used, and, to be sure, also of his age; and if he were to exercise an effect in this connection he could do so only by means of the current concepts which he had to employ. Indeed, if we assume that the ground of Christ's absolute knowledge of God, which could become

14

a general type for all men, lay in his specific dignity, are we to think that Christ, beginning as a child to speak in his language, already expressed that absolute knowledge of God in his concepts, in the first act of his consciousness? Whoever wishes to maintain that must do so in direct contradiction to the sacred Scripture itself, for in that case Christ could not have increased in wisdom; and at the same time he destroys what is essential to human existence, and that is docetism, an abolition of the true humanity of Christ. Consequently, if we have to think of Christ in this period of his development, we cannot assume as yet any directing influence on his part, for to do otherwise would amount to assuming that Christ even in swaddling clothes performed a miracle (or add: as the apocryphal gospels report). Therefore there must have been a period during which he stood under the power of the common conditions, and in his instance, as in every other, the directing influence only appeared later, although the reason why it had to appear must be assumed to have been something original, just as we have to assume that extraordinary talents in individual men were something original, although they stand in their first development under the power of the common life (or: the common conditions of life). *If true human development in Christ were not assumed, it would be impossible to assume that his life was truly human.*

Lecture 3 (May 17). If we cannot transfer Christ into other times, what is exemplary cannot then be made apparent. But we can become acquainted with the maxims which arose out of his actual life and put these into practice.

For the carrying out of our task we have as material, to be sure, practically only the reports of his disciples, while we should use also those of his opponents in analogous fashion. In the present state of the Christian church we cannot be satisfied to take our departure only from faith in him, or only from faith in the Gospel accounts as inspired truth. On the contrary, in this dispute our faith can become firm and direct only if we establish the facts quite impartially. Firsthand documents of the way opponents thought of him are virtually nonexistent, but, as we are aware, there were contrary judgments.

The principle we have laid down, namely, that we cannot conceive of any individual apart from his relationship to his age and people raises a difficulty which we should have to resolve in such a way that we could calculate him abstracted from this context; for Christ cannot serve as an example if we cannot conceive of him under the circumstances in which we live. This difficulty, to be sure, does not directly affect our present task, but it does have a bearing on the purpose for which we pursue our task, and consequently we must endeavor to deal with it.

So much we shall undoubtedly have to admit, namely, that it would be meaningless to ask in discussion, How would this or that exceptional individual who belonged to another people and age have acted under present circumstances? That is true also of Christ, although only in a certain sense. Let me be more explicit. If we wished to conceive him under present circumstances in the context of his life and with a certain sentient clarity (by sentient I understand the whole context of the spiritual phenomenon), that would be a wholly vain endeavor. If we wish to construct the most graphic picture possible of his life and include the circumstances under which he really lived, then also all exemplary and archetypal effect that he exercises must also proceed from this picture.*

Otherwise we put our own fantasy in its place and then most surely destroy its exemplary value. However, since what is exemplary proceeds entirely from his disposition and this is articulated in the most varied and most comprehensive maxims, maxims in which the individual aspect of the circumstances disappears, we must then say that we have no need at all of that sentient clarity of his behavior under quite different circumstances, but our task is to apply his disposition under those circumstances to ourselves, without imposing our circumstances upon him.[2]

* A graphic picture is obtained only if we think of him under the circumstances of his own time; the picture so obtained contains what is exemplary and archetypal, etc.

2. In *The Christian Faith* Schleiermacher relates Jesus to the directing man by universalizing the latter's historical structure of receiving from his social life and redirecting its movement. Cf. **Introduction, p. xlvij.** Also, compare the following statements from Schleiermacher's essay on the idea of the great man: "The great man's distinctive impact is limited to that sphere to which nature has assigned him, he has a determinate home, whether it may be spatially limited or through a mental type which one finds underlies his power and outside of which he remains without ef-

The main proposition was this: The inner nature of a man in his whole development would have to be so clear by means of such a biography that we could also determine his behavior under other circumstances, although we think of it within those limits. That would be the case with reference to Christ, for instance, if we wished to raise the question, Assuming that Christ's opponents had not gone to work so offensively, had not brought about such a catastrophe, how would Christ have acted in light of this situation? This would not be to abstract Christ from his relation to his people and his time, but, one might say, the ability to calculate another in this way, even if it does no damage to his freedom, nevertheless places us' to some extent above him — to the extent, namely, that we reconstruct him without having at hand what these reconstructions produce. If we think of ourselves in relation to others of our kind in ordinary life, it will certainly have occurred to everyone that a calm observer who has an exact knowledge of another already has a correct idea of how such a one will act, even while the latter himself is still involved in deliberation; at such a time the observer stands above the actor, but only as an observer, and because the actor is not involved in observation but has an entirely different task to carry out. For assuming that another were to report the case in which the third found himself and the question were asked, Will he begin to reflect or will he take advantage of the moment? we shall then have to know this of him in advance and consequently to have construed the earlier situation of deliberation independently of what we see of him. That is based on the fact that observation subsides for a time in the actor; he who is not [involved] in acting is quite free as observer, and the more exactly he knows the other, the more his construction corresponds to what the other does; but does he stand higher than the other because of that? No! — but *in the instance of Christ we must admit that*

feet. . . . Should one be conceived in whom lies the power to awaken a new life in the whole human race of all zones and times and to befriend the whole in one all-encompassing organization, he would be one that surpasses every human measure, and, at the same time, shatters every human greatness. But this mystery which lives in the faith of millions, ever again renewing and purifying itself, we only mention here in order to omit it from our consideration." "Über den Begriff des grossen Mannes," *Schleiermachers Werke* (Leipzig, 1910), 1: 529 and 528.

during Christ's life no one was in a position to calculate him, that as long as his disciples lived with him they were entirely unable to reach such a point, on the one hand because they were always in quite a different situation, one, namely, in which they wished to appropriate him; but, on the other hand also, because they had not yet achieved such a knowledge of his inner nature that it could have led to such a judgment. Assuming, however, that they had been able to do that and that there had been one among them who could have maintained that he could know in advance how Christ would act in this case or in that, *then this would be only the work of Christ himself,* and by extension we shall be able to apply that to all similar cases. The relationship to Christ which the disciples assumed *was his work; it was the first fruits of his directing influence.* The first result of this had to be that such a picture of Christ gradually took shape within them and by no means set them over him: and if a complete knowledge of his life would enable us fully to calculate him, once we had achieved this goal we should *not stand above him, for it would be his work.**

In this way, then, we have arrived at the initial stages of the story of our whole undertaking, for it is apparent that the whole efficacy of Christ, viewed from its historical side, depends actually on the resolution of this task, namely, that such a picture of Christ with this truth emerges as can only take shape as we bring together all separate, scattered elements. Therefore we must also say that every idea of Christ that has passed over in any fashion, either into a written document, or into the institutions of the Christian community, or into any other form of living tradition, is part of the resolution of our task; we therefore must make it clear to ourselves in this history of ours. There we find from the outset the most radical contradiction, with almost all gradations that can be imagined; on the one hand, a surrender to the directing influence of the personality of Christ from the time of his public appearance — this marks the beginnings of

---

* or add: Therefore in this connection any trace of setting ourselves over him would wholly disappear, even if we could reach this goal. When then are we to take a proper standard of criticism?

faith; on the other hand, the most decided opposition, which, however, is also connected with a picture of him. From the beginning, then, a contradiction entered at the same time into the view of Christ. If we now ask, What was the reason for this opposition? we must certainly say that it could not have lain in an effort to form a true and proper picture of Christ, but it could only have its ground in a preconceived opinion, and from such a judgment no true view can arise. The other, opposite idea can also be viewed skeptically, and then the question to be raised would be, Did faith in Christ arise only as the pure result of his influence and of a purely disinterested openness to all human influence? We are at once offered very different answers to this question as criticism of the original conception. One group asserts, Yes, it was the pure effect of Christ himself. The other declares, This conception was conditioned by the way in which the messianic predictions had been formulated among a large part of the Jewish people and by the effect of the circumstance that the fulfillment of these messianic predictions was believed to be at hand, and, viewed as a longing for a different condition, this could naturally also be a germ of error, such as we know to be something quite general in the human soul, namely, that men set their hopes on objects which nevertheless cannot be fulfilled. The question arises: In the whole treatment of our subject, what attitude are we to take to this criticism? It can take various forms. First of all we could say we are at one in faith in Christ; we can admit that at the beginning, to be sure, the disciples may have held false expectations and that therefore they will have explained much that Christ did in quite a different way and will accordingly often have misunderstood him; but that belongs to a time of which we now have no knowledge, but what we have are only the results of a picture of him corrected by Christ himself, after his disciples had wholly abandoned those false hopes. No doubt you are quickly aware that I could have added: We are not only one in faith in Christ, but also in faith in *Scripture*, and regard it as a work of the divine Spirit, and since we therefore trace back to him everything that in these Scriptures is said of Christ we are agreed that nothing is any longer left in them of the possible earlier errors of the disciples.[3] I have been satisfied with my former statement and have not added what follows because all sorts of other objections can be raised to it, but what I have said can be established purely by means of our faith in Christ.

If we now ask ourselves whether, if we were to take our departure from our faith, we should in this way completely solve our problem, the answer would remain in doubt, for we should then not have solved it in a purely historical manner and, with reference to the results our view could have, we ourselves should be at a most distinct disadvantage. In all such proceedings (or: disciplines) we must not leave the present state of the Christian church* out of consideration, for otherwise we ourselves should wholly abandon all hope of exercising an influence on it, and to such a task all we who devote ourselves to theological studies are called. If then, for example, we were to proceed from the fact that we are at one in faith in Christ and therefore take our departure from this faith, our account would have value only for those who in like manner are at one with us in faith in Christ; but we know for a fact that there are remarkable differences in this faith and that a great part of the church, especially in our Fatherland, consists, I will not say of disbelievers, but of those who hold a certain minimum of faith, for whom the presupposition we should make no longer has any validity.[†] Are we to take such a position that would limit our effectiveness? We should actually be able to justify such a procedure only if we believed that if in this connection we were to make some room for another point of view we ourselves could forfeit the

3. This recorded statement taken baldly is anything but a true indication of Schleiermacher's view of Scripture. The canonical and the apocryphal are not closed matters for Protestantism and it is the continual task of the church to approximate ever more closely to the canonical. "As history shows, the sense for the truly apostolic is a gift of the Spirit that is gradually increasing in the church; hence at an early stage much may, through the mistakes of individuals, have crept into the sacred books which a later age can recognize as uncanonical and definitely prove to be so." *The Christian Faith*, trans. H. R. Mackintosh and J. S. Stewart (Edinburgh: T. & T. Clark, 1928), §130, 4; hereinafter cited as *CF*. Scripture does mediate the total impression or picture of Jesus Christ to the Christian. Cf. *CF*, §105, 1.

* or add: from our theological point of view

† has almost been abandoned; or, for these our treatment would be worthless

certainty and firmness of our faith; but that would mean doing an injustice to faith itself, for just because we as theologians find ourselves adopting a scientific viewpoint we must at every step be fully aware of what we are doing, and nothing must happen unexpectedly in our proceedings. And it also must not happen that we unexpectedly lose our faith. Since, however, our faith is faith in a *fact*, it is consequently also dependent on the fact; but for this very reason we must in the interest of our faith regard it as our most important task to make this fact apparent to others as the spring of faith which it is in ourselves. But if we exclude in advance every other conception, we likewise do without this; accordingly we ask: What is the nature of our task?

We must undertake it as we should any other similar one with respect to a man who is no longer in any way an object of faith for us. If we are to investigate truth, the examination of other points of view is also always necessary; and if anyone in any respect is a mark of contradiction, as Christ was in his life and as he is still presented, we should regard anyone as a fool who wished to achieve a true picture of the man and wanted to restrict himself only to the remarks of his friends and defenders. So then, also here we must set to work. Assuming then, that we had narratives from the life of Jesus which had come down to us from his opponents, we should have to make them the object of our investigation with a completely unprejudiced criticism and should have to attempt to establish all points with which they dealt which would emerge as the result of the criticism which is applied to sayings of an opposite tenor. Only if we proceed in this way in every instance and employ views of opponents after this fashion can we carry out our task as it ought to be performed by theologians, and consequently we must begin by lamenting above all that we have so little material other than that contained in the reports of the disciples of Christ. In this connection something which from any other viewpoint would be unsatisfactory can cause us greater concern, namely, that these reports are so constituted that all doubts that can exist about the person of Christ, so far as he is object of a faith such as the faith of Christians, have also been nourished by these reports from ancient times, and consequently they can take the place of such reports as would have issued from his opponents, for we shall never lack interpretations of these reports which proceed from exactly the same attitude and show how in light of this attitude the facts must then have been understood. Therefore if, since the other kind is so greatly lacking, we go back only to the different way of viewing the reports that we have of Christ, we can reach much the same vantage point as though we had richer and more varied historical material. But if I have now said that we are agreed among ourselves in faith in Christ, that we take our departure from a common presupposition, that is, from a common view of his personality in the whole extent of the word as by its very nature the object of such a faith, I have said, to be sure, something which I can justify only in a certain wider and indefinite sense. Consequently we must raise the question whether, granted that we wish to put ourselves on a purely historical level of consideration, in order to come to an understanding and make certain that all are agreed concerning what has been said, we do not have to reach an agreement about, or make some comments on, the identity and difference of the conception of Christ — whether this must not first to some extent be done.

Lecture 4 (May 21). We must take all opinions into consideration, for otherwise we abandon the theological point of view. If the person of Christ is not to be retained, then Christianity as such must be given up and only what is true for itself about it must remain. The Nazorenes (Ebionites) are not to be confused with our contemporaries. The former accepted the miracles, but the latter make the apostles men without judgment and ascribed pious deception to Christ. However, we do not need to dispute their negation of the supernatural because we have not defined the limits of nature. Only, that Christ knew what he was doing makes him unworthy to be an object of reverence.

If we ask how far in the biography of Christ we should or may take an objective view with respect to the different opinions which from the beginning existed concerning the person of Christ, we must admit that we do not possess actual reports and documents of the original opponents. We have hardly any except those that derive from his disciples. These men

founded the Christian church on his commission, and we belong to the Christian church. To this extent we have already
declared ourselves opposed to those who were opponents of
Christ and by an original decision have to a certain extent
made our own the concept of Christ which prevailed among
his disciples. But this "to a certain extent" is the point at
which the difficulty arises, namely, that with respect to the
concept of the person of Christ we have only reports with
great differences which had already emerged among the first
Christians, and these differences have reappeared from time
to time within the Christian church. In fact, if we wish to
restrict ourselves, for example, only to the present, we find
such different representations of the person of Christ issuing
from the Christian church that among them are those of
which we have to say that if one accepts them he can no
longer remain a Christian.*

What attitude on the ground of historical criticism are we
to take to these different views? What correlation with our
religious conviction is possible if we say that we wish to proceed as though we did not have these at all and wish to obtain
the facts purely from the Gospels, in other words, only to form
a conception of his person by means of reflection on the life
of Christ, and therefore then either abandon our faith or by
this investigation become confirmed all the more in our faith?
I believe that as theologians we are not allowed to hesitate
about which way we are to take. If we say we will take no
account of the ideas of those who out of their reflections on
the life of Christ obtained a result adverse to faith, we should
not act theologically; we should abandon the theological
viewpoint, for it does not permit us to decline an investigation. In this connection we can accept only two things: the
fact was either of such a sort that it reflects just these ideas
in the truest fashion, and then the Christian faith as it has
been expressed over the sucession of the centuries lacks the
foundation, since that rests wholly on the person of Christ; or
we should have to say that special circumstances prevailed
that such a phenomenon as the Christian church came into

* views in whose context the name Christ is almost meaningless

23

being from this, which actually was nothing, and we should have to resign ourselves to the fact that it belongs to the guidance of God with reference to the human race that on such a well-meant error so great a part of human formation has been built. The task then would be to get rid of the error in the quietest (or: mildest) way possible and to return to the truth, that is, to establish the religious community, which is the Christian church, with all the truth that is contained in it, so that the concept of the person of Christ would be something of no consequence and what is right would replace what had been false. If it could be demonstrated that this idea really represents the fact, no other way would be open to us but this. If we wish to maintain the scientific viewpoint, we have no option but to pursue the investigation; if we wish to be theologians, the scientific orientation and the Christian faith must be compatible. But if we out of a dark concern attempted to be able to know the results of investigation in advance, we would deceive ourselves. This is something that we can only reject for it would already be a product of unbelief, so that rather than extinguishing unbelief we would legitimate it and, therefore, be in contradiction to ourselves. Consequently there is no other option. We have to undertake the investigation, and we have to include this concept in our presentation.*

Now let us approach the matter more closely and clarify somewhat the state of affairs. It rests on the fact that *the Christian faith, as it has essentially asserted itself in the Christian church, draws a distinction between Christ and all other men.* Please pay very careful attention to the way I have expressed myself, for we cannot deny that at the beginnings of the Christian church there was a faith that did not include this, but that is something quite other than the way of thinking that is now set over against the faith of the church. Those Christians of the early period who were called Nazorenes or Ebionites drew no such distinction between Christ and all other men and attributed no such meaning to the expressions used of Christ in Holy Scripture as did church doctrine at a

* investigation, i.e., take it into consideration

24

later time. They also assumed that the outer human person of Christ had no different manner of origin than other men. They regarded him in essence as a man like all others. But these were Jews who in their faith had already accepted faith in men to whom God revealed himself in a special way, and this was inherent also in their concept of Christ. Regarding him only as the highest among the prophets, they assumed a supernatural revelation in his person analogous to the manner in which God had revealed himself to the prophets and had spoken to men; they assumed the supernatural but said: Christ is not the only man whom we regard as supernaturally endowed. Since the working of miracles was also contained in the concept of the prophets they had also accepted this. But the way in which men in recent times wish to get rid of the distinction between Christ and all other men does not include that but is related to quite other assertions, namely, that there is no such thing as a special revelation and no such thing as a miracle, and because of this the matter is something quite different. The view of Christ held by the Nazorenes puts no barrier in the way of faith in Jesus as the one sent by God, whom men had to follow in order to find their salvation and with reference to whom all that had taken place earlier was only a preparation. But when the neoteric concept of our day declares, It is not possible that Christ should have become man in any other way than all other men; it is not possible that something other than the relation of human activities and abilities should be in an individual member of the human species which distinguishes that individual in a certain way from all others; it is not possible that something can take place in the sphere of nature which transcends nature, and still less possible that a man in one person can be God and man — when men say this they do not yet permit us to see what is the actual content of this negation and what attitude we can take toward it, but they do let us see how this relates to our reports of Christ, who is at the same time the ground of the Christian church, and to the origin of the Christian faith in general. We cannot deny, nor can those who take that point of view, that our Evangelists narrate deeds of Christ which they wish to represent as miracles and that this was the conviction of these authors. If in opposition to this someone says that these authors are not immediate eyewitnesses, that what we have before us are later accounts, then we have to reply that even in the earliest speeches of the heralds of Christianity we find reference to these deeds and that that was the opinion of the first eyewitnesses; indeed, that this opinion was also shared by the people. Well then? If all this happened in a natural way, in the most usual sense of the word, how then does this first proclamation of Christianity relate itself to it, and how does Christ himself relate himself to it? Accordingly, we say, they allowed themselves to be deceived by the superficial appearance; the matter seemed to them to be miraculous. They were, then, people of very poor judgment, and that would be true not only of the authors of the biographies of Christ but also of all the apostles, and the Christian church rests then on the statements of such people, whom we must regard as people of very poor power of judgment. We could even go on to say that the whole matter is not of much importance, for how a phenomenon occurred lies more or less in a physical sphere. All that matters is whether they have correctly presented the *teaching* of Christ.

This brings us back to the question: How then does Christ himself appear to us under that assumption? Was he aware that people were in error when they regarded this act as a miracle? Did he permit faith in him to be grounded at least in part on this act? Did he leave his disciples and the people in this error and put this error to his own use? If that were the case we should have to say that he committed at least a pious deception. We take it for granted that he had a good intention in doing so. He regarded it as a favorable circumstance because it helped to establish his authority. He might have thought that he would accept it as an act of divine providence and make the best use of it in order thereby to tie men firmly to his teaching and to gain admission for his institutions. *If that were the case we should have grave doubts whether to accept him in any way as an object of reverence.* On the contrary, we should have to say, That, to be sure, must have been an act of divine providence, and if Christ would have been so honorable as to deny it and to tell men, "It is no miracle; it is nothing out of the way;" but then the Christian church would not have come into being, and since men were only to be convinced in this way, he wants to regard it as an act of divine providence.* But can we actually maintain, after we have gained this insight, that this structure of the Christian church is to continue in existence only on the statement of Christ and the authority of Christ? To this everyone will answer, No! The church cannot continue to exist on the authority of Christ, for this no longer exists, but it can only continue to exist on what value lies at the basis of it! But then Christ ceases to stand in a special relationship to the Christian church and to the human race in general: we must cling to the general principles and teachings, but the *person* of Christ can no longer have the same value. Hence it will always turn out that *the Christian faith as such cannot continue to exist* with this concept of Christ. If Christ approved of this faith despite the fact that he knew he was not behaving in such a fashion, we must go back to his own truth (or: to what was true for him) and then there is no alternative to the conclusion that for his time he was a bearer of these principles, of this way of life and these insights, which, however, can no longer stand in need of him.

If we now look at the special way in which this concept asserts its influence and how it is developed in its different presentations, still other circumstances come to our attention. On the one hand the matter is so presented that faith in the special dignity of Christ can only have come into being out of earlier concepts, but in such a way that they actually had no basis at all in truth. When you read, for example in Dr. Paulus's *Life of Jesus*,[4] that the Jews at a late date had formed the idea of an eternal or primordial messianic spirit from certain Old Testament sayings, a messianic spirit who had now appeared in the person of Christ, and that faith in Christ based itself on this, that is nothing else than the product of a false interpretation; and if we say, That is not to be found in those passages, we cannot discover it in them as their actual content — then the faith in Christ would have

---

* it would be an act of divine providence

4. H. E. G. Paulus, *Das Leben Jesu als Grundlage einer reinen Geschichte des Urchristentums*, 2 vols. (Heidelberg, 1828).

been without foundation and would have rested on an error, and we also would have to say, Christ was an instrument of God for a certain time; he made use of him to produce this historical phenomenon; but now that we know of what the dignity of Christ consisted, we must abandon this, and only that remains truth that can be completely separated from it. That is the way the matter stands, those are the natural results, if these conceptions are essentially the correct presentation of the fact.

How do we oppose these negations? Can we deprive them of their force? Can we prove that something really miraculous, something absolutely supernatural, lay back of every one, or at least of several, of these narratives of miraculous deeds of Christ? This question includes something for which we do not have the material to provide an answer, for in order to demonstrate that something is absolutely supernatural one must have a complete knowledge of nature; one must be able to determine the limits of nature. This would take us into an area which in the first place is not ours, and in the second place we know how the human spirit is still involved in the investigation of nature, that there is much that formerly would have been regarded as supernatural but which now is generally recognized as natural, and that we cannot undertake to prove the supernatural quality of anything. This, then, is a *dogmatic* assertion which we cannot include in our investigation and still less use as a point of departure. No one can maintain that the positive assertion of an absolute supernaturalness is involved in the way the miracles of Christ were narrated. That is an idea which at that time could not have been conceived in this definite form. Consequently this cannot be the issue on which all else depends, and if this concept which utterly destroys faith has no other ground than that one cannot admit anything absolutely supernatural without at the same time doing away with the concept of nature, then the whole operation rests on a completely wrong (or: unimportant) basis, and such a misunderstanding seems frequently to be basic. But there is a great difference whether we say that we can leave the matter wholly undecided, or that in the way and fashion in which he acted Christ was aware of himself as one then involved in the sphere of nature* and yet permitted faith in something supernatural: this latter involves a pious deception. But between the two assertions there lies such a gulf that it is not necessary to advance the one or the other.

Lecture 5 (May 22). We must likewise oppose what in the broader sense is the docetic view, which arises out of God and man when the divine properties are not allowed to quiesce and which very frequently appears in the usual presentation. This does no harm to faith, but the concept of a coherent life becomes impossible. For the Christian the Holy Spirit is the same for the individual life as [was] the divine in Christ. In the former instance we recognize the necessity of a purely historical conception and yet know how to combine faith with it, because we regard the Holy Spirit only as the inmost driving power, but understand everything that appears externally in purely human terms. Hence in this instance we must also seek such a union. Taking both precautions into consideration, the solution of the task remains possible to the extent that the nature of the sources permits it.

The result of our consideration to this point will lead to the conclusion that this neoteric view of the person of Christ, which explains the miraculous as a mere deception,† does, to be sure, make it easier to present the life of Christ because that life therefore follows the same line as the lives of all ordinary men. However, for this very reason this view wholly does away with an actual faith in him *and, if it wishes to be consistent, must raise the demand that what is true and divine in Christianity be separated from the person of the founder.* In my judgment we are not to be governed by an interest in Christian piety but may only ask whether we can build the whole importance of Christianity for the history of the world on such a basis, whether, in order to present the matter in its pure naturalness, it lies in the nature of things that the historical development should be built in this way on nothing at all.** If with respect to the denial that there can be anything absolutely supernatural in the world of appear-

---

* was not aware of himself as a power which transcended nature as then known

† which remains the minimum that must be presupposed thereby

** whether anywhere important institutions (institutes) are built in this fashion on nothing at all. So we see its inadequacy and unnaturalness

ance and experience we go on to say that we cannot declare against this, since no one can say that we have fully explored nature,* we must in this connection seek to draw a line which forms the boundary. If on the one hand we admit that such a view of the matter could be taken, that both the higher dignity of Christ and in connection with this the individual expressions of it that fall under the character of miracle could appear as according to nature — not ordinary, everyday nature, but nature in the sense that this whole phenomenon in its totality and in detail is involved in the general connection of things in the same way as everything else — if we have to admit this possibility, we can on the other hand draw the strict limit that, if anyone wishes to maintain that there was a deception in the consciousness of Christ himself with reference to his own higher calling and his special relationship to God and that those acts which in the life of Christ are narrated as miracles were either accidental events whose cause lay wholly outside his will, or tricks which he intentionally performed to deceive by using powers known to himself, but which at the same time could have been known also to others, these are the points which cannot be admitted without Christ ceasing to be an object of reverence, for this is incompatible with any kind of deception.

Now let us take into consideration an earlier, contrary view of the person of Christ, and yet one that still today appears essentially as the same. If the special dignity of Christ which specifically distinguishes him from all men, including in it his special relationship to God, is expressed in such a way as sometimes happens in the orthodox declaration of the church, that he was God and man in one person, this can easily be so represented that it includes a real contradiction: unlimited and limited together in a unity of life, in a continuous temporal phenomenon, can hardly be conceived without contradiction. And if an assertion is made in this form — something that Scripture never does — with the intention of placing the peculiar dignity of Christ beyond all contention,

* do not defend, because nature can never be fully measured (will eternally remain unmeasured for us)

then it is natural that if subsequently one must endeavor to dissolve the appearance of contradiction which forces itself on our attention it is not the divine side (or: nature) which must suffer, but the human, and so the *docetic* view comes into being, only in a wider sense than formerly was the case. The idea that Christ did not have a truly human body, but only one that had the appearance of such, may have its basis in this particular occurrence of it more in the idea of matter in various philosophical systems. But if we are to examine that assertion in detail and ask, How did the divine and how did the human manifest themselves in the individual? two ways out are possible. The one: It is asserted that Christ to be sure was God, but during his earthly life the divine qualities in him quiesced. It does not require much reflection to see that this statement consists of nothing but words and that no thought is left, unless other doctrines are to be asserted which likewise run counter to those that Christianity regards as valid; for with that view one must either assume a being of divine essence in him without any activity, or one must separate the divine essence from the divine qualities — something that Christian theology has never permitted. The other way out is that the human was more the external appearance — assumed arbitrarily in this individual instance — than the actual substance; and that is docetism in the widest sense of the word. One of the two natures must be more or less mere appearance.

However, when we consider the kinds of concepts which prevail even today among Christians, as they are presented in conversations in ordinary life, we find very frequent traces of this hidden docetism;* and the stronger the faith in the divinity, the more the faith in the humanity is transformed into a mere appearance. If now the faith in the redemption or the salvation in Christ rests on the presupposition of the divine in Christ, this view of the matter does no harm to faith; but the task of constructing a real view of the life, of the human existence and work of Christ, is thereby quite impossible. If in its

---

* we very often find this docetism in the ordinary concepts of Christ. Still another version: But when we view the Christian kinds of concepts of the ordinary life, we frequently find traces of this hidden docetism

companionship with the divine the human in the same moment is transformed in its essential naturalness into a mere appearance, then even the connection between the one and the other moment, so far as it is to be humanly grounded, can be transformed into mere appearance. As soon as one wishes to explain, for example, the individual moments in the life of Jesus, the most frequent and the most natural, always under the formula of a being together of the divinity and the humanity in the individual moment of life, one must always either go back to the quiescing of the divine qualities, or one must transform the human into a mere appearance, or one returns to the view that a deception is to be assumed in Christ. Whenever Christ asks a question he is then either not omniscient, and then therefore the divine quality quiesces, or he wishes to give the appearance of the human, regardless of the consciousness of omniscience, and in this instance he is perpetrating a deception.

One example alone instead of all will be sufficient here: we shall therefore have to draw a similar result from this side. Let us assume that it is necessary for the continued living action of Christ in the historical connection that we have a living conception of his life and work and that we try to present this coherently in such a way that we stand as little as possible behind those factors which accompany his human appearance upon earth. If we regard that as a necessary task (and it is evident that everything exemplary in Christ depends exclusively upon it), we cannot agree with a view of his person and of his existence upon earth which transforms the human in him into anything that is a mere appearance. To be sure we discover no instruction in this in the original utterances of the Christian faith in our sacred books, but this first arose as a consequence of the later development of the Christian life, whereby we, to be sure, cannot regret enough that such a division arose between that which is dogmatic in its own right and that which is historical in its own right and that the former very early was developed and became authoritative without any connection with the latter.

The task of setting up a formula which would satisfy both

needs in the same way, which would give such a concept of the person of Christ that one can understand *him as the basis, adequate for all time, of the salvation of men* and on the other hand can *conceive his whole existence in a perfectly human way* — this task is one which dogmatic theology must carry out and in whose carrying out it is still engaged, leaning sometimes more to the one side and sometimes more to the other. Only by different moments of both sorts opposing each other can these oscillations become less and less and the opposing directions approximate more and more to each other.

If then we are therefore compelled to regard this task as still unresolved by anyone in any generally recognized way, we shall have to try here also to draw a boundary line to the docetic [as against rationalism] in order that the interest of our task may remain unimperiled. I should like here to permit myself a dogmatic digression for just a moment in order to bring the subject before our eyes from still another point of view. To be explicit, we have a task to carry out with which matters stand the same in respect to the totality of the Christian church as they do with respect to the person of Christ. If, namely, we proceed from the fact that matters stand similarly with the Holy Spirit as the life principle of the Christian church as with the divinity of Christ,* here then something identical is set forth, only that it does not have to do with an individual but with a great totality, which sometime is to embrace all mankind. The Holy Spirit can also be active only in a divine way, and just as one asked with respect to the person of Christ, so here too one would have to ask, How does it stand with the divine properties of the Holy Spirit with respect to that which we regard as its activity in the Christian church? Here, now, because we find ourselves in the area of an immediate present, it will be much more difficult to take the docetic way out; but if on the other hand one takes the way out which the new naturalistic view of the person of Christ has taken, then the peculiar character of the church as a kingdom of God (or: the divine among men) on earth is

* something that is expressed in the trinity

33

lost, just as is the divine character of Christ.[5] But in this area the tasks are not yet laid out, the disputes are not pursued with such formalistic rigidity, and the whole dogmatic development of this article has remained behind the other. As it will occur now to no one to deny the purely human element in all the historical moments of the Christian church or to explain it as a mere appearance — not even to those who maintain the divinity of the Holy Spirit in the same sense as the divinity of Christ — so it must also be possible with respect to our task to present the divinity of Christ in such a way that the human element in the whole phenomenon of Christ in his whole life remains unimperiled.

If one now asks: How does it stand then actually with our faith in the activity of the Holy Spirit? We must answer: If we consider the actual appearance of the Christian church (leaving aside for the moment the canonical time in which lies the composition of Scripture), if we view its entire subsequent course, it will occur to no one to posit that activity as only a purely inward one. But we must comprehend and represent everything actual which comes to light, even the purely human — and not only as form and existence — as also at the same time having come about through the activity of this inner divine principle. And so we shall be able to follow no other rule than this: *everything that appears in Christ's individuality as a life-moment appears as a deed and an action, and it must be able to be apprehended in its historical connection in a purely human way; but nevertheless, we conceive it as the expression or effect of God which was internal.*

If we make such a view basic we shall be able to do justice to our task in terms of the materials we possess by taking under consideration the life of Jesus as a human life without

---

5. Schleiermacher's contention here that the best direction that we have for understanding the presence of God in Jesus Christ is by means of analogy with the presence of the Holy Spirit in the church anticipates a similar procedure which D. M. Baillie applied to understanding the incarnation in his book, *God Was in Christ* (New York: Scribner, 1948). In Baillie's case, however, the analogy proceeds from the individual's conviction of grace as a paradoxical relation of God and man; for Schleiermacher the analogy refers to the church as a communal body. Baillie was the translator of the "introduction" of the English edition of Schleiermacher's *The Christian Faith*. Schleiermacher takes this issue up again below, p. 87.

thereby endangering the essence of the Christian faith, since we continue to presuppose the divine as the inner guiding principle.

Now the question arises: How far are we able to do justice to our task on the strength of the materials we have at our disposal? If we take the task seriously, namely, that of apprehending a life description in general, it cannot be solved in any individual cases in an absolute way, grasping through the description the life of an individual man known as a unity, as a continuum, as the concrete entity which he in actuality has been. Indeed, we shall have to say that taken with this absolute strictness no one even has his own life description, for to be sure we have the consciousness of the unity and the continuity of our life in us, but not in the form of the stringing together of individual moments, for no man possesses his own life wholly in this fashion; rather, it is grasped in memory just as fragmentary in this manner as the life of another can be described to him.

Quite apart from the fact that no one can go back in memory to the beginning of his life, we must say that not even in any given space of time, not even in a short time that is most frequently distinguished, is there such a continuity of memory, but this has gaps. We have the self-consciousness of the unity of life as the basic presupposition, but no one possesses life in its temporarily isolated sections as a connected whole. And if we could conceive the individual moments as a completely executed chronicle in which there could be a most thoroughgoing connection of the individual elements, yet they would always be presented only as discrete entities, and the inner connection would not in this way be brought to light. To this extent, therefore, the task is to be carried out essentially only within certain limits, and then at the same time we rest content with the fact that there is herewith a very great difference of what is more or less given, not only through the difference of the richness of an individual life, for that makes no essential difference herein, because every life is a unity in itself, but that a very great difference is caused by the way and means by which we master the details of a life. With reference to the writing of history in general it has often been said that history is not possible until after the passage of a certain time, that a historical presentation is precluded during the course of, or immediately after, a definite period. On the other hand one ought to reflect that it must be equally true that the further one is away from it the less a history is possible, because all the more moments have disappeared and the recollections have become increasingly fragmentary. Both statements are true, but only in a different connection, in relation to the two sides which we earlier separated from each other in detail.[6]

Lecture 6 (May 23). In addition to the lack of presentations by opponents, concerning the apocryphal gospels in general. Concerning the ambiguity of our sources and the difficulty of giving a presentation from them.

How can we carry out our task by means of the materials we possess? Our four canonical Gospels always remain our main source to which we have to turn. In addition to them there are, to be sure, other similar, so-called apocryphal gospels, that is, such to which the Christian church has not ascribed the authority that would enable them to be regarded as true reporters. We need pay no further heed to this judgment; it must first be confirmed. For the time being we must, to be sure, include them among the sources we are to investigate.[7]

From actual opponents we have very few presentations of any extent, but almost everywhere only *judgments,* which therefore are not to be reckoned among the *sources;* and we have only very few individual statements which have been handed down to us of actual declarations which relate to the life of Christ. Taking all that together we are very inadequately equipped for a task such as is ours. For the purely historical

6. Schleiermacher most probably refers here to the distinction and dynamics of the contrast of history and chronicle with which he began.
7. Schleiermacher did not think that a Protestant position could assume that the present form of the canon is necessarily the correct representation of normative Christianity because the present canon has come about through a decision of the church. Therefore, material now designated apocryphal could through continual testing be ascertained as properly canonical and vice versa. Cf. *Brief Outline on the Study of Theology,* trans. T. N. Tice (Richmond: John Knox, 1966), §104, §105, and §109, §110.

point of view which we must take it is somewhat disadvantageous that we have at our disposal so little of the way the life of Christ was conceived by his opponents; and from all of this that occurs even in our Gospels only very few such judgments can be obtained which go back to something factual. The apocryphal gospels, to the extent they have survived, have virtually nothing to do with those aspects of the actual life of Christ in which we are mostly interested, that is, with his public ministry, but are concerned on the one hand entirely with his childhood and on the other predominantly with the story of his passion.

So far as the four canonical Gospels are concerned, we run into very serious difficulties here also, *which must actually first be cleared up before we attempt to carry out our task; but they are of the sort that we cannot know how soon these difficulties will be removed, and the more important our task is, the less we may await that clarification, although it alone would make us certain of the use that is to be made of the Gospels.* I cannot by any means enter into this dispute in general, but can only touch on that part of it which has an influence on the way we are to carry out our task. This is the state of affairs: strictly speaking we have to say that *so far as our four canonical Gospels are concerned, we have actually only two different sources.* The Gospel of John is the one, and the other three taken together are the other. What I mean, namely, in this connection and so regarded, there is only *one* real difference in kind. The Gospel of John is, namely, in quite a different sense a continuous narrative; the three others are far more aggregations of individual narratives. When I say that these three form only *one* source, what I mean is that if you take a so-called synopsis, where these three Gospels are split up according to the various sections and are placed parallel to each other according to their elements (I have the de Wette synopsis preferably in mind because it offers the great advantage that, in respect to certain parts where these Gospels differ more greatly, each individual Gospel is made the point of departure), this is the way the matter stands: there are a great number of individual narratives from the life of Jesus which these three have in common with each other and

37

only a few in each Evangelist which he alone has.[8] I take the expression "narrative" here in the widest sense, so that I include among it also individual speeches of Christ to the extent that they are narrated. With those individual narratives which the three Gospels have in common this, to be sure, is the way matters stand. They are not always narrated quite in the same way, and the differences in the way they are narrated, even in terms of length, are so varied that in connection with a few such narratives they do not need to be taken into consideration because of their insignificance; however, in connection with others, on the other hand, doubts have arisen whether they deal with the same event or with another. In each individual instance, then, this quantitative interpretation of these differences is always a judgment which is bound up with other judgments which the interpreter has made in another area. There is, namely, a certain strict theory of the inspiration of our New Testament books, and if one has accepted that he can easily reach the point of saying that where such differences occur in two different narratives of one and the same event which cannot be harmonized but occur in such a way that one necessarily cancels out the other, that one element in the one narrative stands in real contradiction to one element in the other — that can no longer be the same event, because he traces back the narrative entirely to the Holy Spirit as the author and accordingly regards it as a narrative of the identical and infallible source. If therefore we look at these narratives common to the three Gospels, the task is then so to construe the fact from the different narratives that one can understand from it at the same time how the different narratives with the contradiction can have arisen, and when this is achieved one has in fact made one narrative out of three different ones and the three writings are therefore handled as writings which must always be regarded as explained by one another.

8. The parallel placing of texts from Matthew, Mark, and Luke enabling simultaneous inspection and study of material which they share in common and that which is peculiar to any one of them is cited here in reference to the production of Wilhelm M. L. de Wette and Friedrich Lücke, *Synopsis evangeliorum Matthaei, Marci, et Lucae cum parallelis Joannis pericopis* (Berlin, 1818).

If we now consider the narratives which are peculiar to individual writings among these Evangelists we must look for the place where these may be inserted, and then we have the task of demonstrating the place in each Evangelist for that occurrence which he does not narrate and which the other does narrate. Since, however, we consider these Gospels from the point of view that they are more aggregates of individual narratives than continuous presentations, because the connection is not everywhere given, accordingly the question arises at once, According to what rules has each combined the individual narratives? This question must first be answered before one can undertake to ascertain the place for each omitted narrative. If one had reason to suspect that these narratives have not always been placed in the temporal sequence in which they followed one another, then in the quest for their place one cannot assume that the chronological order could be established and the point in time in which each Evangelist would have placed the event, for the other Evangelist would have placed it according to another principle.* But only when we have a definite judgment about it and in accordance with that judgment raise the question, How far can we ascertain the chronology (or: chronological order) of the narrated events? — only thereafter, when this would be the case, would we be able to try to present a temporal sequence in the description of the life of Christ. [9]

Matters to be sure are quite different in the instance of the Gospel of John. It is not related to the others in such a way

* so the event will be able to receive a different place in the different writings

9. This passage is an indication of Schleiermacher's anticipation of what in recent years has come to be known as redaction criticism, the study of the purposes of the Gospel authors and how these purposes have shaped their materials in the construction of the Gospels. Schleiermacher's hermeneutical theory well prepares him for this insight because his psychological interpretation, which complements the grammatical interpretation, is couched to sharpen an interpreter's appreciation for the tendency, purpose, and resolution displayed by an author in his writing; *Hermeneutik und Kritik, Sämmtliche Werke* (Berlin: G. Reimer, 1838). Schleiermacher's *A Critical Essay on the Gospel of Luke* states this type of criticism as a basic principle of the work. Cf. Introduction, p. xxxi. Contemporary discussions of redaction criticism are found in Joachim Rohde, *Rediscovering the Teaching of the Evangelists*, trans. Dorothea Barton (Philadelphia: Westminster, 1968); and Norman Perrin, *What Is Redaction Criticism?* (Philadelphia: Fortress, 1969).

that it could be included in such an operation. If one wished to make a synopsis of all four Gospels after the model of de Wette's synopsis, those narratives which John has made basic would be in an entirely different relation than the others. In the Gospel of John the instances would be rare where anything from the others would be placed over against it;* therefore we have here a source which is distinguished in a very definite way from the others. But because of this the difficulty of our whole task is greatly increased. The Gospel of John has been credited from the beginning to an immediate disciple of Christ whose name it bears. That is such an ancient judgment that we can accept it almost as a testimony. But likewise the Gospel of Matthew has been ascribed to another of the twelve disciples of Christ. The other two Gospels were not credited to such authors. The difficulty presents itself in its whole dimension when we place Matthew and John side by side. Both authors, namely, are said to have been men who accompanied Christ during his public ministry and who belonged to the company that surrounded him daily. How then is the fact to be explained that the one represents an aggregation of individual narratives in which, however, so little appears of what the other narrates, and on the other hand that the other gives to a greater extent a continuous narrative in which so little of the details appears which the other has brought together? If we assume then that nevertheless both were companions of Christ, we must assume either that they had quite different intentions in their narratives or that they had quite a different evaluation of the events in the life of Christ. The state of affairs can be understood on either assumption. If, for example, the one had the intention of narrating everything marvelous in the life of Jesus and the other had some other intention, it would be possible to imagine that this other would have left the marvelous wholly to one side; likewise the state of affairs can be explained if one thinks only of the intention of the writing of the account, but both had a different evaluation of the events. Now the task that faces us is to account for

* In the Gospel of John it would be seldom that parallels from the other Gospels could be found for a narrative, whether of speeches or of acts of Christ

this different evaluation or this different intention. If, however, we consider again the relationship of the separate materials we are in no position properly to construe such a difference: whatever one may set forth as the special intention or limitation of purpose, elements would nevertheless be found in the other Gospels which would compel one to say that they ought also to have been included.

Now still another difficulty. There are only very few places in our Gospels where the time difference between the one and the other event is given. Wherever that then is missing, one has actually no gauge for the intervals of time and consequently also no gauge for the whole, so that we could then maintain that the public ministry of Christ had occupied such and such a space of time. This direct measurement can, to be sure, be replaced with another, if the narrated events are brought into connection with facts whose intervals of time are known by other means. Such a means has been at our disposal from ancient times by reference to the Jewish calendar of festivals, for they were regularly recurring festive acts which were linked to certain periods of time, and if in several individual narratives reference were made to such periods, that could supplement the direct mention of intervals of time. Accordingly the attempt has been made from ancient times to arrange the individual events in the life of Christ according to the Jewish calendar of feasts and to determine the chronology of the life of Christ in accordance with the main Jewish festivals. If, for example, reference were made to several passover feasts or to several feasts of tabernacles, one would be enabled to say that if three different passover festivals occur in the public ministry of Christ the latter must have lasted for at least two years; but here we must say again that the synoptic Gospels leave us in this connection wholly in the dark. Only John makes reference on several occasions to festivals, but without specifying exactly what feast he meant; therefore almost everything in this area is also open to dispute, and the views concerning the length of the public ministry of Christ differ significantly from each other; one's view depends on which of the two sources one makes basic. Those who make the synoptic source basic say the Synoptics mention only one passover festival, the one with which Christ's life came to an end; if his public ministry had lasted longer, the three Gospels must have neglected to say that Christ had previously not gone to the passover feast. The one who follows John says that there were more festivals, but the calculation of probabilities according to John has also yielded different results. This is not something merely external or immaterial. We cannot say that it makes no difference whether Christ's public life lasted one year or two or three years; one cannot say that because we must also appraise every life which has its own special purpose in accordance with the earnestness and the power with which that purpose is pursued. If I am to imagine that the public ministry lasted three years but that nothing more happened in them for this purpose than is reported in this relation, another judgment on Christ's method of procedure is forthcoming; but if his life lasted only one year, the intensity of his action would be something else, (or: an absolute maximum), or there must have been much more left unsaid; but this last can only emerge for us from the facts.

Just as difficult also are statements concerning the *locality* of the life of Christ, and again because the three Evangelists stand on one side and John on the other. In the synoptic Gospels,. namely, Galilee is evidently the main stage of Christ's public ministry; only individual and occasional excursions into other parts of the Jewish country occur, which appear as something accidental and temporary, and there is no mention of Jerusalem prior to Christ's going there to the passover festival, at which time his imprisonment took place. On the other hand, John not only brings Christ frequently to Jerusalem, but also, which is very noteworthy, always specifies a reason which Christ had when he leaves Jerusalem for the surrounding country and goes to Galilee. So there are two different views of the locality of Jesus' ministry: *According to the synoptic Gospels it appears that Christ had his actual base of operations in Galilee, and there more specifically in Capernaum. But in the Gospel of John nothing of that at all is to be noted. On the contrary, the presupposition is basic that Galilee was not his usual domicile.* Naturally many differences arise from this, and so we see that also with reference to space and time — information that is quite indispensable when we are thinking in terms of a historical view — our sources cause us much embarrassment.

Lecture 7 (May 24). How the plan must be restricted in accordance with the extent of the materials. Division into three periods.

The Gospel of John has always given me the impression that in a decisive way it bears the character of a coherent, comprehensive presentation, but not to the extent that what it reproduces would be sufficient for our task, for not only does it entirely disregard Jesus' earlier life but also admittedly has many gaps, and therefore a life of Jesus cannot be reconstructed from it as it actually should be; and yet it constitutes all our material! We must therefore confess that, if we take a good look at it, it is very inadequate for our purpose and that even with respect to what it gives us it makes it very difficult to arrive at a definite result, for it is difficult to analyze it so that one might clarify for himself how what in one narrative came into being seems really to contradict what another narrative asserts. Therefore it is undeniable that we cannot achieve *a connected presentation of the life of Jesus.* We must limit our task in accordance with the material at our disposal. *Consequently the only question remaining is: How far can we unite the reports that we have in order to form an outline by which we wish to proceed?*

What we find in Holy Scripture falls into very different periods, and furthermore one period varies greatly with respect to the completeness or the fragmentary character of the presentation from another period.

Three main periods emerge in the whole historical existence of Christ which we have to keep separate from one another. What concerns us the most, from which his actual picture must be formed, is the period of his public ministry — whose length we cannot determine. If we understand this in terms of the narrower limit of *his free influential activity by means of teaching and acting,* the beginning from which we must take our departure, by reason of the state of our reports, is Christ's *baptism.* With this event the narrative in the Gospels of

Christ's activity begins. I am intentionally expressing myself carefully at this point since it is uncertain whether Christ did not carry out a similar activity before his baptism. His free influential activity ends actually with his *arrest*. What he did after this was only reaction to what happened to him; it was not the activity which the idea of his calling expressed. And so we naturally separate this last part of his public life from the earlier part. The narratives we find in the Gospels of Christ's presence with his disciples after his resurrection are, to be sure, again narratives of Christ's free influential activity, but they have a different character. They no longer have the same public nature, but the very opposite is definitely asserted by his disciples, namely, that Christ restricted himself in his appearances to the circle of his disciples. Therefore we have again two periods: the catastrophe of his earthly life in the *passion story*, and the accounts of the time of his *resurrection until his ascension*.

What happens before Christ's public ministry is the first period, of which, however, we have the fewest coherent accounts. Most are detailed narratives of the first beginnings of his life and of what immediately precedes it. But of what immediately precedes his public ministry we actually know nothing at all. As an intermediate act between his birth and his public appearance there exists only the isolated narrative which concerns his boyhood, when, according to the practice of Jewish education, he was instructed in the law. Therefore we shall present these different periods in accordance with the existing accounts and see how far we can succeed in sketching a picture of Christ from what has been handed down which might as closely as possible approach a coherent account of his life.

So far as the externals of the story are concerned, in particular the chronology, there are also many difficulties. These however belong more in the area of the interpretation of individual passages and do not have significance for our task. Whether Christ was born a few years earlier or a few years later than our estimate, or whether he lived a few years more or a few years less, is of little consequence for our presentation and I shall not dwell on the matter.

FIRST PERIOD

The Life of Christ before His Public Appearance

As we wish to make a beginning with the first period we discover a remarkable ambiguity in our Gospels: two of our Evangelists say nothing at all about the birth and the early life of Jesus but introduce him with his public appearance, and what they tell us of earlier matters does not concern his person but the person of him who by his baptism of Christ came into a relation that falls within our concern. The others, namely, Matthew and Luke communicate reports of the birth and ancestry of Christ. When we summarize these reports we stumble at once against all sorts of difficulties — difficulties which increase in number when we take also into consideration the so-called apocryphal gospels and individual data found in other authors. I believe we must here raise first of all a preliminary question, namely, Whence can these reports of the birth of Christ and what is associated with it have come? We are told in most instances when his disciples, who were his constant companions during his public ministry, became acquainted with him; but we cannot assume from the accounts that one of them had been *a companion of Christ's during his youth.* Indeed, the whole character of the account of the baptism of Christ gives the impression that at that time men began to speak of Christ for the first time in a public way.

Now his disciples were in his daily company during his public life, and he was always surrounded at least by several of them, even at those times when he desisted from his public ministry. Can we then believe that accounts of the childhood of Christ originated *with himself,* that his disciples asked him about his earlier life and that he gave them such reports as those we find included in the Gospels? If one has got the impression from the Gospels as a whole of the kind and manner

45

of Christ's companionship with his disciples, of their mutual relationship, it must appear improbable to everyone that the disciples should have inquired after such matters and just as improbable that he should on his own initiative have communicated such accounts to them. On the contrary, it is probable that he used the time with them for what was related immediately to their calling. Indeed, when we consider these reports themselves, how in a certain respect they go into so much detail, how conversations occur in them, poetic effusions, it becomes very improbable that they should have come in this form from Christ himself.

There is, however, another source. We are definitely told in the Gospel of John that after Christ's death John took Mary to his own home, and so we find her at the beginning of the book of the Acts of the Apostles together with Christ's brothers in intimate fellowship with his disciples. Now the time of Christ's public ministry was past and one could imagine that the desire had arisen in his disciples to know more of his life during the time they had not been with him. Also Mary at that time would have been ready to tell of his earlier life, and so one could suppose that the reports in our Gospels had the mother of Christ as their direct source. On the other hand, however, there is also much against this hypothesis, and viewed from another angle it becomes very improbable. In the first place, the one who stood in the closest relationship to Mary was *John*. If we are to assume that his Gospel is wholly his work (or add: as is highly probable), it cannot be denied that we learn from it that he stood in a special relationship to Christ with respect to the subjective qualities of personality, and consequently it would be this point which would usually be the subject of conversation between him and Mary, but his Gospel, most specifically, has nothing to say of all that preceded the public ministry. Indeed, if we assume that the disciples of Christ had now commenced their task and ask ourselves, What would have the greater interest for them, the details of his birth and the earlier events of his life or the story of his further development and the manner in which preparation was made for his public ministry in this? We conclude that the latter were much more important for them, and the

46

earnestness and thoroughness with which they took up the tasks of their apostolic office make it impossible for us to suppose that they should have been interested — I might say, in such a childish fashion — in the marvelous elements which are inherent in these accounts of Christ's beginnings and that these should have been more important to them than what they were able to learn from Mary of his later life and which was not marvelous. I cannot suppose that this would have been true of them, and since we discover no accounts of this period except those of the childhood, I cannot believe that the latter had their origin in conversations of the disciples with Mary.

But whence can they have come? It must be possible to trace all individual accounts back to eyewitnesses. Otherwise they are no longer accounts. So we ask what sort of persons were there who could have had knowledge of these first beginnings? May we assume that the apostles engaged in research into the marvelous beginnings of Christ's life but did not concern themselves at all about his further development? If so we must say that we find that to be the case in two Gospels, of which that of Luke to be sure does not come from an apostle, but the other, even in its present form, is ascribed to an apostle (for that is the predominant opinion). So we shall no longer be able to say that it is the result of direct research that Matthew has only these reports of the first beginnings of the life of Christ and nothing of anything further. If the Gospel of Matthew in its present form has the apostle Matthew as its author, it cannot be due to him that he has been able to impart information only of the first beginnings of Christ's life, but not of his further development. From this it follows that we must leave Mary entirely out of consideration in this connection, for she clearly could have imparted information also of Christ's further development. *Consequently these reports of the birth of Christ must have originated somewhere else. They cannot have come from such a direct source. From this it follows that the written description as we have it cannot belong to a time in which Mary could have been a source of information.*

Now, after Mary, the brothers of Christ are mentioned.

Since Joseph, Christ's father, is referred to no more during Christ's life, it is probable that he did not live to experience Christ's public appearance. But a definite uncertainty overshadows the brothers of Christ. It is a widely disseminated opinion that they were not children of the marriage of Mary with Joseph but that they were sons of Joseph by a previous marriage. Our Gospels say nothing of this, but the apocryphal gospels introduce Joseph before his marriage with Mary as a widower. That, however, is a tradition concerning whose worth we cannot judge, since it is found in connection with many fabulous narratives. It is bound up with the account, namely, that Mary only joined herself to Joseph further to bring up his children and that for that purpose the widower was required to make a choice of them. [No value can be ascribed to this account.]*However, the brothers of Christ, even if they were younger, could know from direct family accounts what had preceded the birth of Christ and what had accompanied it, and therefore the narratives could have come from them. But if they were of an earlier marriage and were considerably older than Christ, it is possible that they were no longer in the paternal house and that they could give no direct information of Christ's further development.

Furthermore, the two accounts in Matthew and Luke do not completely agree with each other. On the contrary, there are three points which contain apparent contradictions. Consequently the two Gospels cannot have drawn from the same source, for only on the hypothesis of different sources can these apparent contradictions be explained. Furthermore, other persons appear in the accounts themselves who we cannot believe were still alive at the time of the collection of such information. Simeon and Anna, for example, are represented as already very aged at the time when Christ was brought into the temple, and they cannot have lived to the time of his public ministry. The same is true of the Bethlehem shepherds, at least if we have in mind the time our narratives were assembled. But we must remain with our hypothesis within this circle: *different sources must be assumed if we wish to admit*

*[The words in brackets may be Rütenik's comments—LEK.]

the validity of both accounts as information in the same way. To be sure, there is a significant difference between the two in this connection. A part of Luke's narrative is poetical in character. Definitely poetic passages occur in them, similar to the psalms and corresponding to the Hebraic poetry of the time. The hymns of thanksgiving of Zechariah and of Mary are of such a sort. Nothing of the kind is found in Matthew. Did someone compose these hymns of thanksgiving in such a way that they could be accepted as information? That must be regarded as highly improbable in view of the fact that the whole event afterwards withdraws into the background. In addition to this lyrical character Luke's whole presentation has also dramatic characteristics. *Zechariah* is set over against *Elizabeth* and *Joseph* over against *Mary.* Then there are angelic appearances, and in one case and in the other there is a different attitude toward them. Consequently there is something here that has something quite other than a purely historical character. *Although it can still be true that a historical element is basic, the reworking of it is such that we must say: The event can hardly have taken place as narrated. On the contrary, the historical accounts have been worked over in the interest of enhancing their lyrical and dramatic character.* One could say that Matthew's accounts have a more strictly historical character, and if the deviations of Luke's accounts from Matthew's consist mainly of elements that are due to the former's method of presentation they can be credited to this method of presentation.

Lecture 8 (May 25). First period before the public appearance. Relationship between the reports of Matthew and Luke. Opposed with respect to Nazareth and Bethlehem. Each Evangelist presupposes what the other narrates.

First of all we want to clarify the facts and only then seek to acquire the proper point of view for the whole. In our Gospels we have narratives of this period only from *Matthew* and *Luke.* This is what we have in Matthew: Christ is born in Bethlehem, though no special circumstances that determined

Bethlehem are mentioned. Earlier we are told that Mary had been "betrothed to Joseph" before Joseph brought her home, and "before they came together she was found to be with child of the Holy Spirit." Joseph did not wish to expose her to a public scandal — a fact which presupposes that he did not regard himself as responsible for the pregnancy — but wanted to divorce her quietly. In a dream, however, he was informed by an angel that the pregnancy was supernatural and resolved to take Mary to himself. After this happened Christ is born in *Bethlehem*. From all this one can draw no other conclusion than that Joseph and Mary at that time *lived in Bethlehem*. The author of the report can have had no other idea than that. If he had thought of Joseph and Mary as living elsewhere he would have let some word fall in the course of the narrative about why Mary had not borne her son at their place of habitation. That is the case with the account in *Luke*. There it is said that Joseph and Mary had not lived in Bethlehem but that Joseph only went to Bethlehem because of the census requirements. At this point, therefore, the two accounts do not agree. *Luke* declares expressly that the angel was sent to Mary who lived in *Nazareth* and that afterward Joseph went to Bethlehem because of the census requirements. Consequently Joseph and Mary lived in Nazareth and it was only by accident that Christ was born in Bethlehem. It is now reported in *Matthew* that after some time, we do not know exactly when, Joseph was warned that *Herod* was laying a plot against the newly born child and that he fled to Egypt. When he returned from Egypt, however, he did not dare to return to Judea — a fact that presupposes that he had formerly lived in Judea — and now it is reported that he settled in Nazareth and a definite reason for this is given. Herein, therefore, there lies a contradiction which plainly cannot be removed. According to the one account there is the presupposition that Galilee had formerly been the place where Joseph and Mary had lived and that Jesus had been born only accidentally in Bethlehem, while in the other account there is the presupposition that Joseph and Mary had been at home in Bethlehem. These two accounts, therefore, cannot come from *one* source, for their statements contradict each other.

The state of affairs is different with all the rest that the one Evangelist has and the other has not. *Matthew* tells the story of the three wise men, the slaughter of the children, and the flight to Egypt. *Luke* does not give these accounts, but his Gospel does not make it impossible that those events happened which are narrated by the other. He only omitted any reference to them. *Luke* tells the story of the shepherds in Bethlehem, which *Matthew* does not tell, but there is nothing in Matthew's account that contradicts it. *Luke* in addition tells of a relationship that had earlier occurred between Mary the mother of Jesus and Elizabeth the mother of John, that these women were blood relatives and were so close to each other that Mary went for a visit of several months to Elizabeth. *Matthew* tells us nothing of this, but in this span of narrative there is no contradiction. But the question arises whether the way Christ later appears can permit us to assume a blood relationship between Christ and John, if such contacts between both mothers had taken place, and this question must be discussed at a later point.

If we now ask: If both narratives cannot be from *one* source, cannot one be traced back to the other without affectations which would destroy all historical procedure, so we ask: Which report is more probably the correct one? Now that is a very difficult question, and we can attempt an answer only by comparing the character of the accounts with each other or by comparing what is narrated with the later circumstances. With respect to the former, in the Gospel of *Luke,* on the one hand, poetic elements appear which we cannot believe can have been transmitted in this fashion by the narration of an eye- or earwitness. Whoever would have communicated his knowledge of the circumstances that accompanied the birth of Christ in response to a question would scarcely have done so in the same context by means of the words with which Zechariah expressed his premonition of the destiny of John or by means of the words with which Mary expressed her hope with respect to the announcement made to her. On the contrary, such a one would have told us that Zechariah broke out into a psalm of thanksgiving and that Mary gave expression to her expectations in several passages of Scripture. That is a certain indication that the reports have been worked over, that they are no longer in their original state. There is also a certain relationship of persons in Luke's account which suggests an artificial assembling: in the first instance, the angelic appearances to Zechariah and to Mary, who both raise objections to what is said to them. For his objections Zechariah is punished by the temporary loss of speech, but Mary is given information that gives her comfort and that leads to a conviction of the truth of the promise. The circumstances are the same, but different persons get different treatment, and consequently these two pairs, Zechariah and Elizabeth, Joseph and Mary,* form a certain dramatic narrative. That does not mean that the persons and the main event were invented, but only that the original reports have been worked over from a special point of view. We find nothing of the sort in *Matthew.* Leaving the miraculous out of consideration, everything is presented in a purely narrative style.† Therefore we are obliged to conclude that, since in *Luke* the narrative has the appearance of a reworking of material and since Luke did not belong to the company of the apostles, we cannot guarantee that he had access to immediate sources as did the apostles, and since the account in Matthew has purely the style of a narrative we would have to be inclined to say that Matthew's account has a purely historical character and consequently must be preferred to Luke's.

But let us look especially at the one item under dispute and from another point of view ask which is the more probable, the report that Joseph and Mary lived in Nazareth, or the report that they lived in Bethlehem. In this connection we must presuppose what both accounts have in common, *that Christ was born in Bethlehem.* The whole account in our Gospels in its context leads us in very many ways to believe that Christ together with those who surrounded him in Jerusalem were regarded as Galileans. When Christ appeared in public there was no connected report of his life

---

* Zechariah and Mary, Joseph and Elizabeth
† apart from the miraculous, everything is presented in a purely prosaic style and manner

anywhere among those to whom he turned.* When people begin to concern themselves about a man they ask about the external events of his life. That he was *reared* in Nazareth, that his mother and brothers and sisters lived there or had lived there or in the neighborhood — these are facts that emerge from individual narratives. So it is a natural assumption that Christ's parents had lived in Nazareth before his birth.† If we believe that Luke's narrative as we have it has been reworked, then perhaps the designation of Nazareth as Christ's birthplace is to be ascribed to this later reworking. It may have arisen from the natural supposition that, since Nazareth was Mary's usual place of residence, this must also have been the case at an earlier time. But now the fact that Jesus had been born in Bethlehem had to be accounted for by some special device and the taking of the census suggested itself. We may easily suppose that the Lukan concatenation of events was constructed from the known fact on the one hand of the political dwelling place of the family and on the other hand from the fact of Christ's birth that took place in Bethlehem at the same time that a census was taken.** And that leads us back to Matthew's account as the more probable, for we cannot see how it could have been due to conjecture.

But now let us consider Matthew's account in similar fashion. If we assume that it is true that a census was taken at the time that Christ was born in Bethlehem, this could also have been the case if Joseph and Mary had previously lived in Bethlehem. He who did not know this ascribed the fact that Christ was born in Bethlehem to the census, but he who did know it had no cause to mention the census, for it was a secondary matter. But is the fact that Christ was born in Bethlehem otherwise authenticated, so that it would be a point we could presuppose with assurance? If we reflect on the fact that Christ was designated as a son of David by those

* or add: Consequently none among them knew of his childhood. So we must assume that, as he became a historical person, there were those who asked whence he had come.
† From these it is a natural assumption to make that his parents had lived in Nazareth also before his birth and *that Christ was born there*
** and consequently Luke's narrative takes on the appearance of a conjecture

53

who believed in his messianic dignity, we raise the question whether this does not make it likely that they believed he must have been born in Bethlehem because Bethlehem was the ancestral seat of the Davidic family. And there is the still further question: Does the fact that Christ was designated son of David indicate a knowledge that he was *really* a son of David, or is the designation due to *the supposition that the Messiah ought to come from the house of David?* Messianic dignity, descent from David, Bethlehem as the ancestral seat of the Davidic family — if these hang together it seems as if they could have been established even without information as a natural conjecture from faith in the messianic dignity of Christ. To be sure, if there had been definite knowledge that Christ was not descended from the Davidic family then those who identified the two in a literal sense, *Messiah* and *descendant of David,* would not have regarded him as Messiah. That is not to be presupposed, and the way he is publicly greeted as son of David, together with the attitude of his opponents, who made use of every weapon against him, would have been able to provide a reason for accusation if he was not a son of David. Consequently, either nothing *to the contrary* must have been known [or such pretentiousness would have given ground for a complaint against him].[10] The genealogies support this. But it may be asked why these can be employed as reliable, especially since they do not agree with each other? This disagreement has been accounted for in various ways, but into this question we cannot enter. But if it be assumed that both these genealogies, or one of them, are incorrect in detail, nevertheless we must say that these genealogies support a fact, and the assumption of Christ's Davidic descent is supported by them. But could it not be objected that the conclusion that Christ must have been born in Bethlehem could have been drawn from the fact of his Davidic descent just as the account that Joseph and Mary had previously lived in Nazareth could have been derived from the fact that they lived there at a later time?

In order to answer the question of where the Messiah must

10. This bracketed editorial addition is specifically identified by Rütenik as being his own.

have been born let us look at the use of the prophetic passage from Micah: "And you, O Bethlehem, in the land of Judah, are by no means least among the rulers of Judah; for from you shall come a ruler who will govern my people Israel." If we look at the passage in its entirety we must say that it does not assert anything more than that the Messiah will be a descendant of David: Bethlehem is mentioned only as the ancestral seat of David, and his descendants might be born anywhere, and any one of them could be called a "Bethlehemite" after the place whence the family originated, even if the individual in question had not been born there. Since we find in Matthew a very strong tendency to trace back to prophetic passages individual details that are not important so far as their content is concerned — that is, circumstances that are not important to the main account — and a tendency to demonstrate agreement in this respect, the former can easily be due to the latter. We cannot regard this tendency as something personal to Matthew but as a widespread characteristic of that time, and as soon as Jesus was regarded as the Messiah, this idea could easily arise if information about his birthplace was lacking: "He must have been born in Bethlehem because he is a son of David." We see that, on the basis of quite another principle, the details as related by Matthew can likewise be regarded as having arisen only out of probable suppositions, and the decided advantage that the one account seemed to have over the other becomes questionable again.

For our faith it is in itself of no consequence whether Christ was born in Bethlehem or in Nazareth (or add: or elsewhere), whether his parents lived in the one place or the other, whether one of the two accounts is literally correct or neither of them. For the authenticity of the Gospel story it is not, to be sure, a matter of no consequence, but there is a great difference whether we have accounts of Christ's birth that are of such doubtful character in the Gospel of *John,* where there is a connected narrative, or in the *synoptic Gospels,* which are only aggregations of separate narratives, for in the former case a concern for the character of the *individual* narrative carries over to *the whole.* In Gospels which are

55

only aggregations of individual accounts that is not the case. On the contrary, in these instances we can say that *a report of the birth of Christ has no essential place in the Gospel narrative, for otherwise it would not be missing from John and Mark.* If no authentic reports of the birth of Christ were extant, *but only those that rest originally on facts but have been expanded by suppositions or additions, then no prejudicial light falls upon these Gospels if they have included narratives which they had at their disposal. The only question is whether we are able with any appropriate degree of certainty to obtain from them the facts that certainly lay back of them.*

Lecture 9 (May 28). Concerning the supernatural conception. Gradation in positive presentation through doubtful assertions and silence to indifference to contrary statements. Faith has no interest in this because the indwelling of the divine can depend not on the lack of human conception but only on the absence of the sinful.[11] So there is no more need of admitting intrigue on Zechariah's part than the seduction of Mary by Chacus. or her adultery with Panthera.

The question concerning *Christ's supernatural birth* is an important one.

A significant gradation is apparent in the New Testament books. There are passages where the Evangelists themselves are not the narrators but where other speakers are introduced who declare that *Joseph was Jesus' father* and where *the Evangelists do not contradict the statement* and appear [as it were] *indifferent* to it. Two Gospels make no mention of Christ's conception and birth, and this silence concerning the assertion of his supernatural origin is associated with a silent overlooking of the contrary assertion. In *Luke's narra-*

11. Schleiermacher's discussion of the virgin birth in *The Christian Faith* maintains that it is an assumption superfluous to Christian doctrine: "The general idea of a supernatural conception remains, therefore, essential and necessary, if the specific preeminence of the Redeemer is to remain undiminished. But the more precise definition of this supernatural conception as one in which there was no male activity has no connection of any kind with the essential elements in the peculiar dignity of the Redeemer." *The Christian Faith,* §97, 2.

tive the assertion of Christ's supernatural origin is not set forth with such exclusive clarity that, if there were no other information about it, one could not explain it otherwise. Let me be specific. The angel's promise *that the power of the Most High would overshadow her* follows, to be sure, in the first instance on Mary's statement that she had no husband, but this latter statement cannot be taken so literally that one could relate the promise *only to it,* since she was betrothed to Joseph and knew of a man from whom she could bring a child into the world. Consequently this promise of the power of the Most High is related more to the fact that the son which would be born would be the Messiah than to any assertion that he would begin life without Mary having been impregnated by a man. In Matthew *this assertion is made most unequivocally* and here is *based on the mistrust of Joseph.* This demonstrates that Joseph was aware that he was not the cause of the origin of this life and that he was restrained from severing his relationship with Mary by the assurance given in a *dream,* an assurance that carried with it the further assurance that no other man was responsible for it. But *Luke* knows nothing of this mistrust on Joseph's part, just as *Matthew* knows nothing of a promise to Mary that preceded the conception of Christ.

If we consider both these facts together, they do not appear to agree with each other: the difference is not such that the statement of the one Evangelist could be related to the *statement* of the other as a mere *omission* on the part of the *one.* If Mary had received such a promise it would have been contrary to the nature of the relationship for her not to have told Joseph of it, and then Joseph's mistrust could not be reconciled with it, since in the other narrative he is represented as receptive to such phenomena and to the truth they bring to light. Accordingly, the two narratives fall short of agreement. They also rest on incompatible presuppositions. On the whole, however, considering the New Testament books in their entirety together, the assertion of the supernatural conception of Christ appears *dissimilarly assessed.* Meanwhile, if we return to the account in which it is presented most forthrightly, that is, to *Matthew's account,* we have not in so doing *returned to any necessity of such an origin so far as it relates to Christ's peculiar dignity and destiny,* but *"in order that the promise might be fulfilled."* There is no presupposition that the Son of God would have to enter into life only in a supernatural way. This, to be sure, has frequently become part of Christian doctrine, and we must always take such a state of affairs into consideration, although it cannot be for us the determining factor. The necessity of belief in the presupposition that Christ was begotten without the cooperation of a man cannot be demonstrated because the purpose associated with it is not thereby achieved. Let me be specific. The necessity of a supernatural birth was connected with the theory of hereditary sin: If the Redeemer was to be free from any share in sin, *and this, I agree, is something essential to the concept of redemption,* he must also have had no share in hereditary sin. *That is a proposition I am ready to admit.* But if I ask, What kind of concept of hereditary sin can be basic in order to justify the assertion: Because Christ was begotten *without the cooperation of a. man,* therefore he was free of hereditary sin! no such concept can be imagined for, if one understands by it a transference of subjection to sin by the *physical* influence of one creature in the begetting of another, that is only half a step, for there is still the influence of Mary to be considered. Two supplementary assertions have been advanced to try to deal with this, although neither has been adopted by the church: firstly, that Mary had no physical influence in Christ's origins — that Christ brought his body from heaven and that Mary was only the channel through which he passed; secondly, that Mary herself was also begotten in a supernatural way. Now, if the former assertion is supernatural and *docetic,* for Christ would not have been truly man if he had brought his body from heaven, and must be rejected, the latter is equally unsatisfactory. In the second instance, sinlessness would have to be carried back to our first parents and in the end be reckoned from Eve.*

That cannot be done, and *no concept of hereditary sin can*

---

* For even Mary stood under the influence of her mother, and consequently the only doctrine of sinless descent that would be of any help would have to be one that traced such sinless descent back to Eve

be in agreement with the idea of redemption through Christ which makes the indispensable demand that, in order to be free from sin, also the first beginning of life must have been free of every physical influence. Consequently we say: *The indwelling of the divine in him cannot rest only on the proposition, viewed in and for itself, that Christ was begotten without the cooperation of a man, but rather on a positive, divine act. Therefore the divine act must also have availed to make Christ free from all connection with hereditary sin, regardless of the physical influence which must have played its part if his life was to be truly a human one.* We can therefore discuss this question *without having to fear a disadvantage for the Christian faith,* even if we have to say that it cannot be maintained that the narrative of the supernatural conception of Christ is a wholly historically founded statement.

If we now relate this purely to the interpretation and consider both Evangelists as independent of each other, then the passage in *Luke* permits another interpretation. It remains possible that Christ was conceived with the cooperation of Joseph, but that *his becoming Son of God* is expressed by the statement that Mary would be overshadowed by the power of the Most High. The narrative in Matthew is nothing else than the account of a *dream,* and then it must follow that it must be demonstrated in another way that *the dream was divinely communicated.* But such a demonstration does not form part of the narrative, and therefore the matter remains uncertain.

Essentially the interest of faith in this matter can only be twofold: on the one hand, interest in the truth of the scriptural passage, in particular with reference to the doctrine of Scripture; on the other hand, with reference to the doctrine of Christ, the interest of faith is only *that nothing sinful entered into the origin of the life of Christ.* When, then, in order to undergird that negative statement with positive content, it has been said that if it is established that Christ was not conceived by the cooperation of *Joseph,* then *another human agent* must have been involved, *it is preferable that this be rejected.* We do find such a statement, and because this is one of the few instances in which we have statements made by opponents recorded by ancient writers we cannot overlook it. *Origen* quotes the statement by *Celsus,* which the latter ascribes to Jewish accounts, which declares that Mary conceived Jesus by sexual intercourse with a soldier, whose name he gives as Panthera, and for this reason she was rejected by her husband and consequently fled with the child to Egypt. Celsus claims to have heard of this from Jews. Some doubts are aroused in my mind by the fact that a specific name is introduced. The naming of the soldier is intended to give the account the appearance of resting on something factual. We also find this name occuring in ecclesiastical narratives. Otherwise it sounds rather strange, but it occurs in book 4 of the writings of John of Damascus, where he speaks of the two genealogies, that of Matthew and that of Luke, and from them derives the genealogy of Mary. In the latter Mary's father is called Joiachim, Joiachim's father is called Bar Panthera, and the latter's father, who would therefore have been Mary's great-grandfather, was called Panthera. Now, it is impossible to conceive of any relation between these two accounts, namely, that Mary had a great-grandfather called Panthera and that she had a seducer called Panthera, except the connection that Jesus was a descendant of Panthera, and so the name was derived from this source.

Recently a couple of hypotheses have been proposed.[12] They would hardly be worthy of comment if it were not noteworthy that anything of the sort could appear that would maintain that it presents a Christian truth and undertakes to provide a rectification of the former assumption in a Christian sense. The former of these hypotheses rests on a passage in Josephus, but not one that has even the remotest connection with the whole story of Christ. In book 17 of the *Antiquities* Josephus tells of a Pharisaic conspiracy in which Bagoas, a eunuch of Herod the Great, and a certain Carus, a favorite of Herod, had been involved and whom Herod had executed, along with others. From the not even precisely demonstrable coincidence that the execution of these con-

12. The first theory which Schleiermacher is discussing is that of Karl H. Venturini, the anonymous author of *Natürliche Geschichte des grossen Propheten von Nazareth* (Copenhagen, 1800-1802). His identity was still unknown at this time.

spirators and the slaughter of the children at Bethlehem took place at the same time the unnamed author of the book concludes that both events are connected, that the plot had in mind the establishment of the Messiah, and that Carus was compelled[13] to seduce Mary and to beget a Messiah of the Davidic line.* All this is a building without any foundation. The other hypothesis is the assertion that Joseph was the natural father of Christ, a fact to which in and for itself (or add: from a moral point of view) no objection can be taken if Joseph and Mary were betrothed, for, since the betrothal in the Jewish sense was regarded as the most important fact, the ceremonies of marriage were only secondary, just as they are now in the Catholic church, because the betrothal validates the marriage. But the important fact is that Zechariah had thought up the project of setting forth the Messiah, that he had persuaded Joseph to cooperate in the venture, and that as a result Christ had been conceived in order to bring forth a Messiah and to assure his appearance.[14] All this was the result of Zechariah's intrigue, for he believed that it was high time that the Messiah should appear and he wished to make his son the Messiah's forerunner. In all this something from the Gospel of Luke is made fundamental that is actually least historical and in addition is distorted by embellishment. Zechariah would have to have fabricated the appearance of the angel to him as well as his dumbness in order to wait and see whether he would actually obtain a son. To my mind this whole connection between Jesus and John the Baptist through a relationship of their mothers is something that can be accepted only as fiction in view of the way John speaks of Jesus as one with whom he was unacquainted. And if

13. Here Rutenik printed nonsense: Carus was "executed." His conjectured emendation has been substituted. [LEK]
* or add: Jesus, son of Carus and the Virgin Mary, was said to be the Messiah set forth by the conspirators, and Carus must have impregnated Mary
14. This second hypothetical construction belongs to Karl von Langsdorf, a former mathematician at the University of Heidelberg of some note, who after his seventieth year turned to theological subjects and published a book containing the theory mentioned here. His idea is that Zechariah tricked Joseph and Mary into the illusion that their son would be the Messiah and that they have passed this to Jesus. *Wohlgeprüfte Darstellung des Lebens Jesu* (Mannheim, 1831).

Luke's narrative suggests that it is a later reworking of facts, we may be permitted to believe that this also did not belong to the original deposit of fact, and on it the whole fictitious account is constructed that claims to be history. And this is said to be a simple presentation of the life of Jesus, which gives one right at the beginning a definite prejudice against the whole.

In Matthew we find immediately after that an account which is peculiar to that Gospel, an account of a recognition of Christ as Messiah soon after his birth, as Messiah in the form of the newborn King of the Jews, and of two events to which that recognition gave rise, namely, the murder of the Bethlehemite children on the one hand, and the flight of Mary with Joseph to Egypt on the other.

Lecture 10 (May 29). In Matthew the incident of the visit of *the wise men* follows, and in Luke that of *the presentation in the temple.* Both events in general are not mutually exclusive, but to the extent that Matthew narrates the journey to Nazareth as something new and Luke regards it as a return home the two events are incompatible. It is also clear that Luke includes all events that took place in Bethlehem within the period of the purification. Consequently it is difficult to believe that either of these narratives could have been recounted by Mary. *Celsus* also tells of the flight to Egypt, and if this is derived from Matthew, then his story of Joseph's expulsion of Mary must have been pure fiction invented for this purpose. This is a probable assumption. But the story of a flight to Egypt must have been more generally known. It cannot have been invented because of Hosea's prophecy, any more than the story of the murder of the children at Bethlehem can have been suggested by the other passage. But the flight to Egypt can have been based on what happened at the presentation in the temple. However, the fact that no one remembered anything of these things at the time of Christ's public appearance indicates that knowledge of all these things on the part of the public was entirely forgotten. It is difficult to understand the figures of the three wise men. If they were wholly non-Jewish they had no occasion to relate the sign they had seen to a Jewish king. If they were proselytes they would have gone with their question not to Herod but to the scribes. It is even more difficult to explain why Joseph did not flee to them rather than to Egypt.

If we consider these Gospel accounts, it appears impossible that *both* could have their direct source in stories that Mary recounted. But if we ask: Cannot one of these accounts have been derived from this source, which we would have to regard as authentic? The answer to this question is also no! If we take Matthew, the relation of the narrative to the prophecy in Hosea (11: 1) is so exact that we have to say that this connection must have been part of the tradition he received. But we find the tendency to make such connections so remarkably dominant in this Gospel that we cannot avoid the conclusion that the author is responsible for them, and we are compelled to say that that addition was the work of the Evangelist. This conclusion is unavoidable.

But let us consider the matter from another angle. Our canonical Gospels owe the exclusive preference they have won in the church above all to the fact that it has been assumed that even those that do not derive from apostles had apostolic sources at their disposal or had received apostolic confirmation. On this assumption it would be possible that, in addition to a narrative of the beginnings of the life of Jesus that is derived from Mary, another could have been preserved in such a way that it would be incorporated into the canonical Gospels along with that from Mary. That, however, has never appealed to me as very probable. If one reflects on how the first Christian community came into being, one must place a high estimate on the apostolic authority. We are speaking at this point only of the origin of the birth narratives. If such accounts of the birth and early childhood of Christ which came from Mary had been current in this circle, they would have been generally familiar, and others that differed significantly from them would not have arisen at all, but would have remained apocryphal. If we take further into consideration that a very powerful formative principle (or: artistic arrangement) prevails in the account in *Luke* and in that of *Matthew*, the connection* with Old Testament sayings, there is here an indication that each is governed by a different kind of concept.

Now, we find in these first beginnings of the life of Jesus, likewise as a part of *Matthew*, the narrative of *the three magi*

* an inclination to Old Testament prophecies

and others that are associated with it, *the murder of the children at Bethlehem* and *the flight to Egypt.* In *Luke,* on the other hand, there is nothing of all this, but there is the story of *the presentation of Christ in the temple* and the announcement of his messianic dignity which is a consequence of it. So, viewed in general, these narratives are so related to one another that it seems possible to insert the one into the other, apart from the fact that it always remains difficult to arrange them in terms of time. In the account in *Matthew* there is here an element that in tendency is miraculous (a definite purpose lies back of this), namely, the sign that those men had in terms of which they looked for the newborn King of the Jews. Of their personality much too little that is specific is told us — whence they had come and who they actually were — so that here also this indefiniteness makes it improbable that this story in this form could have been narrated by Mary. But it is also improbable that, if it had definitely come from her, it could have lost this definiteness in the course of transmission. Such a loss can take place in connection with an aggregation of circumstances, but in the case of quite isolated assertions it is improbable. If, for example, Mary had named a definite area from which the magi had come, it is improbable that this definiteness should have been suppressed in the course of transmission. With respect to the whole connection of the account how the wise men ask in Jerusalem for the newborn King of the Jews and for this purpose turn to King Herod, how Herod then gives them the information and in return stipulates that they provide him with more exact details, how they are warned in Bethlehem that this could lead to the child's destruction and consequently do not return to Jerusalem, how Herod thereupon orders the murder of the Bethlehemite children — with respect to all this we must here note that we have a historian of this period in Josephus by whom, to be sure, the fact that men from the East came to Jerusalem could have been overlooked as something quite insignificant, but who could hardly have neglected to record such a fact as *the slaughter of all children* in a not unimportant center so near to Jerusalem. In light of the character of Herod the atrocity is by no means improbable in itself, for Herod did not hesitate to perpetrate atrocities of this sort, but one thing in this connection is difficult to explain, namely, that Herod was at that time already advanced in years, and if a Messiah had been announced to him who would appear in public in the near future, self-preservation would have impelled him to do everything in his power to circumvent such a threat; but, since he hears of a Messiah who is shortly to be born, it is improbable that he should have taken any notice of a Messiah whose activity he could no longer live to experience.

Now, as soon as a certain improbability is evident in an account one naturally asks whence it probably could have come. This narrative has a very definite content, namely, a recognition of Christ as Messiah, and in fact outside the bounds of his actual fatherland. I do not say that the recognition was by pagans, for if the wise men had not been in touch with Jews they would not have been able to relate the sign in such a fashion to a king of the Jews, and the circumstances point strongly to the conclusion that they stood in some relation to Jews, even if in the widest sense as proselytes. If we assume that as such they had so interpreted the sign and had connected the newborn king of the Jews with the messianic idea, it is difficult to believe that they were so ignorant with respect to Jewish affairs that they should have turned to Herod and not have purposefully avoided any contact with Herod in the course of their journey. So far as the content of the story in its relation to the messianic idea is concerned, this account is quite parallel to that in *Luke:* the recognition of Jesus as Messiah in the course of the *presentation* in the temple has the same tendency. At the beginning of his life the messianic promises are said to have been fulfilled in him and the messianic hopes fixed upon him, just as in Matthew's story attention is directed in this respect to his person. But because the account in *Luke* moves within the natural circle of Jewish life and theocratic faith and contains within it no other element than what is wholly compatible with that time and its circumstances, it has a much greater degree of naturalness than the account in *Matthew.* But if we assume that the later events in Matthew, the Bethlehemite slaughter of children and the flight to Egypt, are assertions of fact, these would not necessarily have followed from the story of the visit of the magi and also do not follow from the tendency to recognize Christ. Consequently the probability is great that these are facts, for the connection with an Old Testament passage in the instance of the murder of the children in Bethlehem in Matthew is such that one could have complete faith in the messianic prophecies, but it would not have been possible that an event in the life of Jesus should have taken place to which this passage about the weeping of Rachel for her children would have had to be related as a prophecy. The event is therefore not to be accounted for by the Old Testament passage, but we must assume that it is based on a *fact*.

You see how skeptically I go to work. If we cannot recognize any original authentic source and it is improbable that the narrative as it stands has come from immediate eyewitnesses, then we are obliged, because we are engaged in a piece of historical research, to place no weight on the difference between canonical and apocryphal writings. On the contrary, we must presuppose as possible that these narratives have an apocryphal character because they are based on such a definite tendency. Therefore it seems to me to be necessary to handle them in such a way. But we cannot enter into these narratives at any greater length.

If we reflect on the facts that *Matthew* narrates and if we assume that these strangers were directed to Bethlehem by Herod, then all that follows is very probable. It required only common knowledge of Herod to make it natural that Joseph and Mary should do everything to dissuade the strangers from returning to Jerusalem, and because of concern for the jealousy of Herod they did not regard themselves as safe, and consequently it needed nothing supernatural to make probable a removal from the jurisdiction of Herod. And so the flight to Egypt was motivated by this fact. In what *Celsus* has to say this is also assumed as a fact, but it is connected with the declaration that Mary was expelled by Joseph. Furthermore, from this the miracles are derived, which consequently are brought into connection with knowledge Christ could

66

have obtained in Egypt — something, to be sure, that presupposes a much longer stay in Egypt than that set forth in Matthew. Now, *Celsus* had no occasion to invent anything of that sort, for he was able to know that there was knowledge of miracles also among the Jews. So it seems to emerge from this that such a fact was known, for *Celsus* cannot have derived it from Matthew. He would have regarded Matthew's account as an alteration if he had known it in its present form. The narrative in *Luke* ignores this fact entirely, and one cannot believe that the author of the narrative, the actual original source of the account in Luke, could have known those circumstances and yet have kept quiet about them, since he could have disposed of them in a few words. Therefore we must admit that the fact was not known in such a general way, and this makes it all the more probable that it does not derive from Mary but from a remoter source, and accordingly began to circulate at a later time. *Luke* does not have to motivate the return of Joseph and Mary to Nazareth because for them it was only a return home. *Matthew,* on the other hand, for whom Bethlehem was their dwelling place from the beginning, has to motivate their assumption of residence in Nazareth and therefore associates it with this return from Egypt.

With this we draw the discussion for the time being to a close and say: That is what our Gospels have to tell us of the beginnings of the life of Jesus, and we have reached a certain plateau. Joseph and Mary are now perfectly united one with the other and live in Nazareth, where Christ is reared. If we take the content of these narratives together and reflect on the two Gospels that contain absolutely nothing of this, we must draw one or the other of the following conclusions. Either narratives from this childhood period of Christ's life, of the events directly associated with his birth, were not in circulation at the time John wrote his Gospel, or at least John regarded them as a not indispensable part of a historical account of Christ, and we can only explain that by a circumstance which, to be sure, becomes very apparent if we think of the total content of the Gospels. Let me be specific. Everything marvelous from the first beginnings of the life of Christ that is here recounted must have been completely forgotten at the time of Christ's public appearance and have remained so from then on, for if these stories had continued to be recalled in any circle the subject of them would have remained in men's memory. If we reflect on how they all end in designating a definite subject as the expected and promised Messiah, we are compelled to conclude that the knowledge of these circumstances would then have been attached to the liveliness of the messianic hope, and whoever shared this hope and at the same time had heard those stories would have connected the two, and these accounts would have been attached everywhere to the messianic hope. To be sure, a long time had passed, and all those to whom the account of these events could have come directly had largely disappeared from the scene when Christ made his public appearance. But if the total impression of the Gospels is that the messianic hope was very widespread and that there was a belief that its fulfillment was near, it follows that a narrative such as this, which designates a specific subject, would have been transmitted along with the living hope, and even if Christ had withdrawn into the shadow, later, at the time of his public appearance, the question must have arisen whether he were the same as the one who at that time had been designated as Messiah. But there is no trace of any such identification at the time of Christ's public appearance. Consequently the birth stories must have been restricted to a very narrow circle and must later accidentally have come again to light, and these events had nothing to do with the appearance of Christ or the origin of faith in him.

Lecture 11 (May 30). In terms of tendency, one should expect that *the wise men,* because they assert the recognition of the Messiah outside Judea, were remembered in Hellenistic circles, whereas the story of *the presentation in the temple* was preserved in Jewish circles, but we do not know how this could result in the fact that the one account came to be recorded in one Gospel and the other in another. Viewed in and for itself, the account of the presentation in comparison to that of the visit of the wise men has the greater inner credibility. It rests wholly on the messianic hope, and it is necessary only to assume a *bath kōl* [a divine revelation]. On the basis of Luke's presupposition it is also natural that Mary personally carried out the custom. (On the other hand, on the basis of the same presupposition, this is not probable in the case of the magi.) The flight to Egypt has more support from external evidence but does require the visit of the wise men. On the contrary, it could have resulted from the *presentation,* for the fear could have arisen that Herod could have learned something of the temple scene.

All that is miraculous in these accounts, taken literally, must have disturbed the natural relation of the parents to Christ. Yet the account of the journey to Jerusalem reflects the very opposite of this. Consequently the impression of the divine must not have been so overwhelming in them that their attitude to him became analogous to that portrayed in the apocryphal gospels. Occasionally a few reports from them.

If we compare this second series of narratives that refer to the childhood of Christ once more, we cannot avoid the conclusion that they likewise cannot be harmonized in such a way that the one could be incorporated into the other. At the beginning I said that the difficulty of arranging all the narratives, each regarded as based on histroy, in a temporal sequence would be disregarded as a matter of secondary importance. However, there is a connection between the temporal sequence and the content of the events themselves, and that we can no longer view as a secondary matter. Take the appearance of the three foreigners in Bethlehem after they had come from Jerusalem and the presentation of Christ in the temple as Luke records it. One of these must be earlier and the other later. If the presentation in the temple is the earlier, then the narrative of the three wise men cannot be incorporated into Luke, for in this Gospel the return to Nazareth follows upon this presentation in the temple. According to Luke, there is no reason why Joseph and Mary should have returned again from Jerusalem to Bethlehem. This fiction has sometimes been advanced, but the way the existence of Joseph and Mary in Bethlehem appears, seems not to agree with the assumption that a useful stay could have developed, and Luke's silence would count strongly against any belief that the narrative comes from any firsthand source. On the other hand, if the appearance of the foreigners in Bethlehem were the earlier, and because of the apprehension that arose the three were advised not to return to Jerusalem and not to give any information to Herod, it is impossible to believe that the child should later have been brought to Jerusalem and practically delivered into the hands· of Herod. It was not an obligatory demand of the law that every mother should go with her child to Jerusalem. On the contrary, if the presentation of the first-born were associated with a sacrifice, the priests could offer that at any place, no matter how remote. If we note in addition that in Luke the journey to Nazareth is narrated definitely as a return to the original dwelling place and in Matthew the flight to Egypt is especially motivated by concern for the child, we see that the presuppositions are so different that everything cannot be harmonized.

Now, from the way this story of the flight to Egypt appears in the apocryphal gospels and in the statements of opponents, it seems very probable that something was known in some form of a stay of Jesus and Mary in Egypt. On the other hand, Luke's account of the presentation of Christ in the temple has such a character of truth and definiteness that in this respect it is very different indeed from the story of the three foreigners. The latter are not named, and their place of origin is only very vaguely intimated. The motive of their appearance is very unsatisfactorily developed, and of the whole account one gets only a very indistinct impression. On the other hand, the story of *Simeon* and *Anna* rests on the natural presupposition of the lively, widespread, and shortly to be realized messianic hope. Consequently it rests on a solid foundation, and the whole event gives the impression of perfect naturalness. If Joseph and Mary had come from such a distance to Bethlehem and if they were about to return to Nazareth, it was natural, after the rites of purification were over, that Mary would be personally present at the presentation of Christ in the course of the journey. It is not necessary to assume something supernatural, astonishing, or unusual to account for Simeon's utterance, but only that some sign *(bath kōl = divine revelation)* had come to him so that he could relate such messianic expectation to the child. Consequently the fact has a general claim to be traced to a genuine origin.*

* or add: In the whole narrative there is not a word that would be out of harmony with an authentic origin of this account.

All the facts when taken together make it probable that something was known of a flight to Egypt. *However, I do not know how to incorporate this story into Luke's account.* The one who assembled these events knew nothing of a flight to Egypt. On the other hand, the flight to Egypt can easily have been motivated by the story of the presentation in the temple, if we leave the narrative of the three magi out of consideration. If the account of the presentation would necessarily become known to many people and if it was true that at that time the child was designated as Messiah, the thought could have arisen that without any doubt the event would become known to Herod, and this could have motivated the departure to Egypt. On the other hand, it appears remarkable that, if the three wise men had come, Joseph and Mary had gone to Egypt and not rather (or: more rapidly whence) whence these three had come, if these had not come from too great a distance.* *So we cannot avoid the conclusion that these two narrative sequences came from two different circles and are connected with each other in the Gospels in such a way that both these contexts cannot at the same time be correct.*

The narrative of the three magi is most open to a certain element of suspicion. In the apocryphal gospels the flight to Egypt appears wholly without any definite connection with the story of the three wise men, and we find in this latter account a definite tendency to assert that Jesus was recognized as Messiah from the beginning outside the actual national Jewish area. Consequently, we get the very strong impression that the narrative could only have arisen as *an expression of this idea incorporated into the account of the beginnings of the life of Christ.* Then, to be sure, this narrative must have come from the less strictly Jewish part of the Christian church. But Matthew's Gospel has a Jewish character throughout, and it is difficult to explain how it came about that the narrative was included in this Gospel. We should have expected it to have been located in the Gospel of Luke. However, since we know so little of how the individual narratives were brought together, we must leave the pro-

* and not to the homeland of the magi, where they would have found the heartiest reception

blem unsolved. But I believe I am able to maintain that *all that has been attempted to bring these two series of narratives into complete agreement is so artificial that it cannot withstand historical criticism.*

If we now at the same time wish to compare the glut of apocryphal gospels, among which the *Gospel of the Infancy* and the *Protevangelium of James* are the most important, we find in them at the start presuppositions from our two Gospels. However, by no means all that these latter offer is used in them, to say nothing of a very notable tendency that is inherent in these productions to harmonize one account with another, so that one might almost believe that the basis of these productions could already have been laid at the time when these narratives were not yet assembled as they are in our present Gospels. On the other hand, we find in them a remarkable tendency to heap up the miraculous and also to multiply analogous events. The *Protevangelium of James* declares, clearly in the style of Luke, that Mary was also conceived in a supernatural fashion, much as Christ was conceived. However, the relationship between Christ and John, which is asserted in Luke, is not mentioned, although Zechariah appears as High Priest and reference is made to Simeon. The persons are the same but the relationships of one to another are different. Joseph receives Mary, whom her parents had dedicated to temple service, from the hands of the High Priest. He obtains her as a widower, not as one betrothed to the woman, in order to educate her further and to preserve her for the service of the Lord. All this is very frivolous. The persecutions of Christ are extended also to *John,* and Elizabeth also flees with John until a mountain opens up and receives them. Everything is so narrated as miraculous that it supports the view that the basis of the narrative is older and that of the Scriptures more recent. Christ is born in a cave and is only laid in a crib for fear of Herod. The story could not have been altered in this fashion if our canonical Gospels had already existed as such. The cave continued at a later time to be identified, and this tradition must therefore have continued to exist in this narrative form. In the *Protevangelium of James* the cave is also the place to which the wise men come, and the star comes to a halt over the cave. If we now consider the *Gospel of the Infancy,* we find that in it the flight to Egypt is preceded by a whole series of miracles which are associated not only with Christ himself, but also with everything that surrounds him, for instance, his swaddling clothes. In this gospel Christ demands of Joseph that he send him to school, and there it is discovered that he already knows everything. In all this the miraculous merges in the docetic. No place is made for the development of the child in the course of education, although that is quite expressly asserted in the canonical Gospels, where we are told that Christ increased in spiritual development in accordance with his advance in years. Although it must be admitted that ancient sources lie at the basis of these productions, which could no longer have arisen at a later time, when our Gospels had achieved canonical authority, nevertheless these productions are very improbable, and actually no real heed need be paid to them.

Both Gospels in narratives that differ from one another ultimately arrive at the same point, namely, that Joseph and Mary took up residence with the child at Nazareth. But we find a great gap, which is only filled by reference to the natural but excellent development of the child, until we come to the only story which Luke narrates of Christ's boyhood. Now the question arises: How can we fill out this gap, if we pay attention to the narratives to this point? They cannot be harmonized if we stop with what we must regard as an individual account. So we are driven to conclude that the conviction that Jesus was the Messiah had already emerged in some specially contrived marvelous fashion at the time of, before, and after his birth, for that is the actual result that becomes clear from all these narratives. If we now ask what was the consequence of this for the further development of Christ, that, to be sure, is something that is very difficult to conceive in any definite way. To be sure, it is something that is analogous to the quite natural way that parents early get a fixed opinion of the excellent destiny of their children, but we cannot say in accordance with experience that that is a good (or: adequate; or: certain) means of producing the right educational activity. For everything which disturbs, by inhibition or overstatement, the unprejudiced attention to what comes forth unexpectedly cannot work advantageously. Now, if both parents had a firm conviction of a divine presence in him, its generality — even though only of a national definition — would extend far beyond the circle on which they could direct their activity; therefore one can scarcely believe, if we think in broad terms of what they could do for the child, that a consistent behavior in education could have emerged from it. In a certain respect that is what the apocryphal gospels narrate. They were led by this, naturally enough, to the constant expectation that something marvelous could develop at any' moment and to regard everything that had to happen for ordinary children as superfluous, just as, on the other hand, they, would have felt themselves very distressed and would have had to follow an obligation which exceeded their powers to fit the child for such a calling as they assigned to him.

The narrative in Luke about Christ's boyhood is of quite a different sort. It exhibits a completely natural treatment of the child by Joseph and Mary. The regulation that was introduced and that was generally adhered to was observed with respect to him. Once upon a time pious Israelites were accustomed, if they could, to go to Jerusalem at least to one of the principal festivals. At that time boys of ten years and up were instructed in the law, and if they understood the sense of it they were eligible to be taken along on the journey to the festival. Both these factors play a part in this story. If Joseph and Mary had been overwhelmed by that miracle and had been led by it in the course of Christ's education, it would be natural that they would always have taken Christ with them because they would always have regarded him as fit to take part in this national religious celebration. Everything takes place so naturally that no one could connect anything with it that rests on a miraculous presupposition. If Mary reproaches Jesus for having made her anxious, then, in the first place, this anxiety does not harmonize with the presupposition of the miraculous, and, in the second place, it also does not harmonize with such a relation of the mother to him that she should have reproached him for anything at all. Consequently this narrative does not indicate that the events earlier narrated had made such an impression on Joseph and Mary that anything of the natural relationship of the parents to the child had been altered. On the contrary, everything follows its natural course. Therefore, whatever may have been the actual basis in fact of those narratives, it must not have been of the sort that with any probability a disturbance of the natural relationship had to result from it.

Lecture 12 (June 1). The miraculous can therefore only have confirmed them in the messianic faith in Jesus, in which, however, there lay as basic only the idea of the identity of prophet and king and not of an innate sharing in the divine, but only of one that would later appear. This then could not disturb the natural relationship. But in what Christ says one cannot mistake the special relation to God which he wishes to' express, which he also later always expressed in such fashion, and if he also extended it to his disciples, that happened unmistakably only by derivation. So the question arises, What kind of consciousness lay at the basis of this utterance, and how can we conceive its human development?

It does not follow that absolutely nothing miraculous accompanied the birth of Christ, but only that it was not of a certain sort. Indeed, it follows that even the idea of the dignity and destiny of Jesus that they formed as a result of all these happenings and promises was not of a kind to alter their relationship to him in any respect. To put the matter in different words: they could not have been clearly convinced that anything was already in the child which would wholly change their relationship to him. Now, we must admit that the messianic idea that was by far the most widespread, the only one they could relate to him, was not of this sort. They could be convinced that the Messiah had been born in this child, but that was a destiny that lay at a distance. To determine the difference between this child and all other men they had no other measure than that which national history offered them of those who were represented as God's specially chosen and blessed. If the prophetic type on the one hand and the kingly on the other were the point to which everything could be traced, then the prophetic dignity was only thought of as resting upon a special sharing in the divine which only became manifest at a certain time, not as an innate difference. Likewise an individual of whom outstanding gifts and powers were presupposed could be destined by God to become king, but not such who could not arise out of a natural development and only presuppose richly endowed human nature. Now, insofar as everything miraculous in those narratives goes back always to the messianic idea, this idea was such as could not alter the relationship of the parents to the children.

What was earlier said in general, namely, that the child grew in age and understanding and in favor with God and man, is likewise only the expression of a favorable and excellent natural development. However, when we view this narrative in the light of how Jesus reveals himself in it, we find something very different. In order to harmonize what I want to say now with the way I have handled this individual narrative to this point, John must now add something. Let me be more specific. Luke's narrative in my judgment gives every indication of being authentic. There is nothing in it to arouse the suspicion that it is told in this way because of a tendency to love. It is the naive expression of a scene which in itself under the circumstances is highly probable. Consequently I see in it no reason to doubt that this account could have come from Mary. It bears witness to a certain bent in Jesus, and that can clearly have been the real reason why it was told, as an occasion on which this decisive bent in him became evident for the first time. Because of this great naturalness we can entertain no doubt of the authenticity of this story, and we view it in quite a different light than the earlier narratives, in which in part a definite tendency is apparent and in part a definite form, all of which points to something artificial and contrived. Christ's behavior as this story records it is also quite natural. Christ is in an environment, in the temple courts, where the individual scribes had their schools, and there he listens to what they have to say. The apocryphal books portray Christ as engaged in teaching, and the creative artists have represented him as such, but that is quite contrary to the story as it appears in our Gospel. Luke represents him as asking questions and giving answers, and that is the manner in which the youthful listeners to the teaching scribes were accustomed to behave. That he remained there for some time after Mary and Joseph had already departed is not something that need be stressed, for festival journeys to and from Jerusalem from a great distance were naturally always undertaken in company with others, but on the other hand it was impossible for all who came from one and the same neighborhood to travel together. Consequently Jesus could believe that he would always find acquaintances among pilgrims on the highway to Galilee, and so he yielded to his interest in listening to those lectures on the law.* Likewise no stress is to be placed on the fact that Joseph and Mary departed on their journey without having ascertained that Jesus was accompanying them. It is clear that, if he knew when and with whom they traveled, they could assume that he would follow with acquaintances. When that did not happen and they looked for him and found him in the temple, he assured them that they could believe that he had remained behind for no other interest than this.

Now comes the question: "How is it that you sought me? Did you not know that I must be in my Father's house?" Here one can raise the question whether those are the words of Jesus on that occasion, or whether Mary had not recalled his *ipsissima verba* but only their sense and had later expressed it as he himself at a later time was accustomed to express himself — that he called God his Father. It is striking in this utterance that thereby a special relationship between God and himself is to be expressed and that he has not spoken as though everyone else could likewise also call God his Father. On the contrary, even where Christ has extended the usage to his disciples, it gives evidence of having derived from him. So the question arises: Did Christ really make use of this expression at that time, or is it an expression which Mary employed, but one taken over from the later way and fashion in which Christ expressed himself? In the latter case there would be nothing of special interest in our story, but in the

* his interest in those lectures assumed priority

77

former case it is a fact that even at this age there was such a consciousness in Jesus, and we should have to ask how that could have taken form in him in the course of his life's development. It is not possible to reject out of hand the latter view of the matter, namely, that the utterance does not consist of the actual words of Christ. One cannot maintain the form of the story as we have it with complete certainty. However, something speaks very strongly for the other opinion, and this has such an influence on our way of thinking that we cannot possibly neglect it a priori. If we reflect on the individual narratives in our Gospels in general, and in particular on those in the Synoptics, such a reflection is the result of an unbiased comparison, but there is also something that first becomes evident to everyone: In all such narratives where any sayings of Christ appear in such a way as to form the actual point of the narrative, the divergent narratives differ from one another to a greater extent and are less in agreement with respect to all other points than with reference to the words of Christ that they communicate, and the shorter the sentence, the more exactly they agree. This fact leads us clearly to the conclusion that Mary must have found the way her son expressed himself about the whole affair most emphatic, and just as she divined in him this higher destiny, so every saying that had any connection with it must have been so remarkable to her that she must have remembered the words of the boy and have told them to others.

Now let us ask, In what sense did Christ actually mean this statement? That, to be sure, is a question that one can answer in many different ways. It often happened in his sayings that he calls himself the Son of God, and this practice later passed over into the speech of his disciples. If we now reflect on how in the period of his public life he justified calling himself the Son of God in passages where he refers to the fact that the expression was also used by others — in fact, by those to whom the word of God was disclosed — we conclude that it must therefore have been able to be used much more by those through whom the word of God was declared to others, so that we can say that his use of it remained wholly analogous to Old Testament usage. If one were now to point out that this expression was also likewise already current as a special synonym for the Messiah, one could say that the whole of Christ's word can be derived from the fact that Jesus already was conscious that the messianic prophecies were to be fulfilled in his person — that he already regarded himself as the promised Messiah. But it is something quite other if we consider this whole question, to which this story contributes only a detail and without which the question would remain the same, from the point of view, not of symbolic church doctrine, but of the generally prevailing faith. As soon as we say that in Christ there was a sharing in the divine which distinguished him from all other men (a rather indefinite expression which is open to various interpretations) and confirm the principle that the development of the human life of Christ must be capable of being viewed in a wholly human way, the question arises: How did it come about that this element of the divine that this faith expresses was in his own self-consciousness and how did it develop and gradually take definite form in his self-consciousness? This question, to be sure, is a difficult one, but it is the general form of the whole way of looking at the life of Jesus that it takes if this presupposition is the point of departure. If we wish for a moment to look at the matter from the opposite point of view and say that this whole assumption of such a Christ, to a certain extent distinguished from all other men innately by a divine communication, was only a product of reverence for Christ, then one could truthfully regard him only as any other man who in this special area was especially characterized by a strong and living consciousness of God. In this case Christ in his self-consciousness could not have had anything that would set him apart from all men. Consequently he could also not have expressed such a special relationship between God and himself as the truth of his self-consciousness, except to the extent that at the same time he likewise exhorted all others to regard their relationship to God in similar fashion. But that is not the form taken by the sayings in his speeches. There it is always *my* Father that is the prevailing form of address, and when Christ extends this expression to his disciples it is always only in the form of a sharing. What is actually typical remains *my* Father and *your* Father, at least wherever the former expression is original. In my judgment one must accept both facts, namely, that Christ so expressed himself and that such a consciousness was in him, without at the same time ascribing a deception to him, which we could not regard as something unconscious. If he had only known himself as he is represented from this point of view, he could have spoken nothing in this way other than to give others another conception of himself than he himself had. *I believe therefore that these two positions are inseparable: a completely naturalistic view of Christ, and that he has permitted a deception* in order to arouse a higher opinion of him than he really had of himself. If one wishes to maintain the one proposition and to dismiss the other out of hand, then one must declare all accounts of Christ that we have to be so uncertain that we cannot use them to form a definite picture of him. The original narrators would have introduced their views everywhere into the speeches of Christ, and then it is impossible to pursue a historical study of the subject. In every account, even in one which is intended to do nothing except present a narrative, the judgment of the narrator always is present, for it is his interpretation. But if we assume that nothing of the speeches of Christ has been handed down without having been tampered with by imposing on it the too high and wrong opinion of his person that arose contrary to his will, then naturally nothing is left,* but this is improbable in the highest degree. If we assume that Christ did not wish to deceive his disciples, we cannot also believe that they could have formed a view of him against his will, a view dissimilar to his own. On the contrary, he would always have corrected them, and then it would not have been possible for a false view to have found a place in the narratives that were handed down. Viewed in its entirety as it lies before us, we can certainly conclude from the evidence that Christ was conscious of a special, peculiar relationship to God, and as soon as we assume that as a fact in his human consciousness we must

---

* or add: but to abandon all historical research concerning Christ, and we can find no calculus for his life

also ask how he arrived at this consciousness, for if this had been in him in an original way from the very beginning of his life, we find ourselves involved at once in the middle of a docetism. Then all identity of human development is lost, because we must assume such a potency of self-consciousness as fixed wherever everything in the child wavers between unconsciousness and the first weak expressions of consciousness. We must therefore clarify for ourselves the origin in time of that consciousness.

Lecture 13 (June 4). Therefore the actual reason for the discord in our theology is the practical necessity of conceiving Christ in purely human terms and the interest of faith in associating the divine with him. In view of the creedal twofold nature it is impossible to bring them together. All artificial expedients fall short of their objective: the quiescing of the divine properties (the identity of essence and properties is lost), a double will, by which the same is intended (the divine will cannot will in temporal terms). From the practical viewpoint the impossibility occurs if Christ is to be completely conceived in the light of our imperfect circumstances, but the noble is not conceived by the ignoble, and consequently does not cease to be doctrine and example. Since every critical (or: uncritical?) theory necessarily becomes docetic, everything always comes back to the question, How can the divine be thought of in human terms in a human setting? However, we have not only the task of thinking this with respect to Christ, but [also] because of the Holy Spirit of doing the same with respect to ourselves, whether it be in personal or in common terms. Here, however, it has always been presupposed that the purely human existence and concept of existence are not therefore abandoned. The closer, then, we adhere to this analogy, the sooner we can achieve the solution.

We stopped at a point which is one of the most difficult. On the one hand one must conceive of something in Christ that specifically distinguishes him from other men, and on the other hand hold fast to the view of really human conditions of life. One cannot say that these two tasks would be carried out in mutual agreement in the course of the usual method of treatment, and one cannot hide the fact from himself that a sufficient reason exists for the division in contemporary theology, a division that has become the more apparent, the more these two tasks have been brought clearly into view. In connection with the customary creedal formulas by which the superhuman, the divine, is ascribed to Christ, a concept of really human conditions of life on his part cannot be retained. The truth of the matter is that those who hold fast to the dogma in this way do not bother about the other, but it can easily be shown that they fall into a docetism which holds that Christ in his true life is no true man, and all artificial aids that have been employed do not achieve what they were intended to achieve. On the other hand it is clear that those who take their departure from the attempt to represent the life of Christ completely as a genuinely human life usually end up by conceiving Christ in such a way that no intelligible reason remains for making him in any way such an object of faith, a central point of the world (or: of mankind), and that is the division that characterizes contemporary theology.

If we begin with the dogmatic point in its usual understanding of a twofold nature in the person of Christ and keep only in mind the disputes that raged in the earlier church, the difficulty of enlarging this doctrine into a clearly intelligible concept becomes already apparent, as well as the fact that the attempt has been unsuccessful. If we say that there is in Christ as a person a divine and a human nature, then from each of these two points results must issue that cancel each other out. The human nature manifests itself everywhere as a definite, limited consciousness, but the divine nature excludes all that is limited.[15] But therewith what is definite, as far as it exists in the man, is terminated. If I am now to think of the consciousness of Christ as a human consciousness, I think of it in every moment as fulfilled in a definite way, *but only in such a way that an infinite variety of consciousness is still possible outside fulfillment, and so one moment is included in the consciousness whereas another moment is not; but the divine nature must be omniscient and exclude such a distinction of the one moment in which one knows something and of the other that does not know it.* Consequently the artificial aid (or: way out) has been devised which asserts that the di-

---

15. Schleiermacher offerred a pointed critique and rejection of the word "nature" as the rubric in terms of which God and man are to be brought together in Jesus Christ. See *CF*, § 96, 1-3

vine properties quiesced during the course of Christ's human life. But it became apparent that men in making use of this expedient are at the same time doing something wrong. What is regarded as the most essential in the knowledge of God ceases to be. It is thereby asserted that there is no relationship in God between essence and properties such as exists in finite things (or: in human nature), but both are the same. If one takes his departure from this and says that in Christ the divine properties are to quiesce, then the divine essence in him also quiesces, and the concept becomes an empty one. Other difficulties that have had to be encountered in a different fashion give rise to the same conclusion. It has been said, for example, that understanding and will belong to a spiritual nature (I do not wish to comment on the correctness of this distinction). Now the same thing is said of God. Men speak of the divine will and understanding. If there is a twofold nature of Christ, then a divine understanding and a divine will are in him, and by reason of his human nature a human understanding and a human will are in him. Now you will recall that with respect to the one point, the will, there arose a well-known controversy within the Christian church. One group declared that the unity of the person rests basically on the unity of the will. Accordingly, if there is to be a unity of person in Christ, he also must possess *only one* will. The other group maintained that with respect to the unity of the person it is not a question of the unity of the will so far as ability and power are concerned, but of the unity of the will in that it always wills only one thing. If several things are willed the unity of the sequence is destroyed. Therefore Christ can have two wills, but with both he wills only one and the same thing. However, how can a human will will the same thing as the divine will and yet remain a human will, and vice versa?* All these expedients are inadequate.

Let us look at the matter from the other side. Those who predominantly take their departure from the other point of view are accustomed to say: If Christ is to have such a relationship to us that we regard him as the absolute teacher and the absolute model, then he must be capable of being con-

* one excludes the other

ceived wholly in human terms. If his thoughts were not truly human (or: divine) we would not grasp them. They would exceed our power of comprehension. If they were truly human but were not his own, then he would always have been engaged in deceiving men and what was actually his own would be superfluous, for it would not contribute to our development. And on the other hand, if we regard him as an absolute model we must think of his action also as actually (or: wholly) human, for otherwise I cannot follow him. In this connection therefore the same situation emerges: If Christ because of his divine properties must have acted quite differently in order to be a model for men, then the divine properties had to quiesce. But then this being amounts to nothing and is superfluous, for he would accomplish the same without it. Since the theologians from the other side must maintain that Christ in just this sense is the perfect teacher and the perfect model, we now inquire what they do if he is to be understood wholly in human terms, with the divine in him, whether it quiesces or not, if no advantage accrues to us in our real relationship to Christ. So the whole theory reduces itself to one essential thing, namely, that this divine had to be in Christ in order to satisfy the divine righteousness, and that is the way and manner that, driven into a corner by the human demand, the theory which presupposes something divine in Christ centers on the doctrine of the representative reconciliation and the satisfaction of the divine righteousness achieved by the sufferings of Christ. This, however, is something quite worthless, for if it is asserted that the divine nature is *apathes* [incapable of suffering], the divine nature as a whole is bereft of meaning. On the other hand, it is not to be denied that the more strictly one undertakes to demonstrate that Christ must be perfectly comprehensible to us — otherwise he cannot be anything of that upon which his influence on the eternal being and life depends — the more easily one reaches the point of denying that specific dignity in its entirety.

But if I am to say what seems to me to be the easier — to be able to ascribe such a specific dignity to Christ from this point of view or, proceeding from that creedal formula of a twofold nature in Christ, to be able to reach a human view of his life — I prefer to undertake the former task rather than the latter. If one believes that the former task results in the abrogation of everything that specifically distinguishes Christ, this belief rests on the fact that in undertaking to demonstrate that he is wholly conceivable one takes his departure at the same time from the imperfect state of our understanding, and this cannot possibly be regarded as an essential demand. The more incomplete the spiritual state of men, the less they are able (or: even?) to comprehend the perfect. If, for instance, we are concerned with how men of a low level of disposition explain to themselves what is noble in human action, we see that they do not comprehend the motives that lie outside their own range of thought. If, however, we were to undertake to show how all men of a higher range of disposition are to be understood by the others, we should abandon the task altogether. On the contrary, *men must gradually be led to become acquainted with the motives of others.* If they were also to comprehend the noble at the very moment it is given them, the task would be impossible. If we wish to apply the same reasoning to human nature, viewed in its development, we must say that, since it is apparent from time to time that individual phenomena lie in any respect far beyond the usual standard (or: standpoint) and that an enlargement of the concept of human nature (or: knowledge) takes place, this is applicable in any conceivable connection (or: area). We must recall, for example, that what is now usually performed in the area of the lordship of man over nature is something that could not have been conceived a number of centuries ago and which at that time lay wholly outside the idea of human nature. If one had said that a man could raise himself into the air, that would have been regarded as a fable (a phantom, Icarus). The same is true in every other area, and therefore we must not demand that every human phenomenon at any given point should be comprehensible, for that would have to cancel out all progress and we would not present human nature as involved in a progressive development. Consequently there is no possibility (or add: open to us?) of pursuing both tasks at the same time. The answer to the problem as it lies before us in symbolic form cannot be found in this way.

But the longer we reflect on it, the more we shall come to see that this rests on a way and manner of philosophizing which cannot any longer be retained. If we ask, for example, with what right these two concepts, the concept of the divine and the concept of nature, are combined, everyone will have to reply, if he reflects carefully on the matter, that the task is actually impossible. The expression "divine nature" has its due and highly appropriate place in every polytheistic system, for it is implicit in such a system that the same one humanly (or: divinely) manifests itself in a variety of forms. However, since we can no longer accept this polytheistic idea, it is impossible for us to accept it in this instance. In another connection this implies a definiteness of being that excludes all else, but also in this connection no one can actually speak of a divine nature, and this is a combination that is wholly inadequate for a scientific presentation. It is probably possible to make use of it if one has been persuaded that it is intended in a figurative way, but in a theory it cannot be employed. The concept of the one, however, seems to involve a difficulty that cannot be removed. If we say that the interest of faith is the governing spirit in the Christian church, as it is until now and also, if that impossibility is not to establish itself, hopefully will remain so, then the interest of faith is always to place something divine in Christ, something that exceeds the human. Anything that could be different, however, would in any case put an end to the human element. For instance, every Arian theory, carried to its logical conclusion, would necessarily be docetic. It would be impossible to assume anything truly human in Christ. As soon as one distinguishes what is higher in Christ from the divine and regards it as something created, it is a *nature,* and then the problem emerges in the truly definite sense that there are two natures in one person, and it is completely insoluble. One of the two must have been appearance. If we maintain the former proposition, we must face the question: Can we possibly conceive of the divine in the human? That is the point about which in the final analysis the matter revolves. If that were wholly inconceivable, we would reach the point at which that interest of faith would have to be abandoned, for what would be positively unthinkable could also possess no reality for us. It could exert no conscious influence except by self-deception,* and then there would be no other choice than to go over to the other side (or: than to become rationalists).

In connection with that interest of faith,† however, we are also expected to reflect on the divine in mankind in general, not only in Christ, for the concept of the Holy Spirit is nothing else than that. The divine becomes located in human beings, among whom we ourselves are included.** We are also to have this element of the divine in our self-consciousness. We shall therefore have to admit that to do justice to the interest of faith with reference to Christ by a theory that does not at the same time do justice to the interest of faith in this respect would be a fragmentation of the Christian doctrine that could be of no help to us (or: would be entirely unsatisfactory). Both ideas, then, must be mutually compatible. And if we ask whether the idea can ever have existed that to assume the activity of the Holy Spirit as something truly divine in the compass of Christianity would in any way put an end to or limit the connection and the truth of what is human, the answer is that no such assertion has ever been made and that virtually no dispute about that has ever arisen. And if I ask someone, Well then, since you assume the activity in yourself of the Holy Spirit, explain what the divine nature in you effects and what the human nature? it necessarily follows that the same questions arise. Consequently it has always been tacitly admitted that it is possible for both the divine and the human to exist in an individual Christian, and the question resolves itself into the problem of accounting for the same conjunction in the instance of the person of Christ and in so doing to postulate nothing that has no bearing on the interest of faith.

Lecture 14 (June 5). If we wished to leave the boyhood story entirely out of consideration, we would later run into similar utterances of Christ concerning himself. We cannot assume that he only

* except as long as the self-deception persists
† or add: in its entire range
** whether as individuals or in the totality of life

reached that conclusion with reference to himself because he had always been told that he was the Messiah and because a special relationship to God had generally been associated with this figure. *He would have ignored the thought had it not been confirmed by an inner experience. Consequently, if we have to assume that something in his consciousness corresponded to these utterances, we must then ask since when and how this developed,[16]and we reach then also the same point. In the first place, then, we think of Jesus in terms of the maximum of the vitality of the consciousness.

This general discussion[†] is only a digression that can help us to see how far we can approach a solution of our problem without in any way reaching a decision concerning the dogmatic articulation of what we as Christians, together with the whole of historical Christianity, see in the person of Christ. Only we must transfer this insight from the general state to the detail of life. We had arrived at such a point in our historical consideration, and now the question arises: How can we view this? To be sure, when Jesus says, "'I must be in my Father's temple," we have to ask whether that was an expression that others also would have used and which can be explained in terms of the pious consciousness of the nation and the time, or was it a peculiar one? Only if we decide on the latter alternative do we have to look for what here is to be presupposed as the actual content of this expression and how Christ reached the point of possessing a consciousness of this sort. Concerning the former alternative there can be no doubt, for we find that later Christ was charged with blasphemy for calling God his Father in this sense. Consequently

---

* Furthermore, this was not really the case. There is no support for Dr. Paulus's view. One who would restore the power of David did not require such a relationship to God, but received his divine communications from without in prophetic fashion or, as the prophets, from within.
16. Compare the statement of A. J. B. Higgins in *Jesus and the Son of Man* (Philadelphia: Fortress, 1964), p. 18: "The Son of God Christology arose not from Jesus' use of the titles Son of God or the Son as a self-designation, but from his consciousness of a unique filial relationship to God as Father." See also p. 196. The question of the development of this relationship is not pursued by Higgins, nor by the vast majority of scholars. It is commonly regarded as an unknowable aspect of Jesus, and as something not necessary to know.
† See the previous lecture.

this expression was something alien to the characteristic type of the piety of his people and his time, and his use of it was called blasphemy because he had no right to employ it. Now the further question arises: Was this later charge made against him in such a sense that basic to it was the idea that if Jesus were really Christ he had the right to assert such a relationship to God, but if he were not Christ the use of such an expression by him would be blasphemy? For many these two alternatives were identical expressions: Christ, the Messiah who is to come, and Son of God. But in this connection it remains true that the one to whom the expression Son of God was applied was also to be credited with a special relationship to God. If we wish to assume that Jesus had learned from his parents that because of the promise given to them he was the Messiah, and because he had assumed that from the beginning he had applied it to himself from his way of thinking, then Jesus must have called himself the Son of God because of an idea current among a section of the people that a special relationship existed between the Messiah and God, and he designated himself in this way for no other reason than that he accepted the idea from his parents that he was the Messiah. This view involves the fewest difficulties, and if we were to accept it there would be nothing left to say about the matter. But I believe that this view of the matter is inadequate if we are to reflect on the life of Christ and on the ruling idea of his time in the relationship to his people that it presents.

Consider on the other hand the fact that the Messiah is also called the son of David and that Christ, because he was regarded as the Messiah, was everywhere designated and accepted as the son of David.* We must admit that it was not generally known as a *historical* item that Mary or Joseph was descended from David. Otherwise the action of his opponents against him would have had to take another direction. Either they would have had to deny the fact or attack it, and of that we have no trace. On the contrary, there is no discussion of his Davidic descent. Least of all can there be any reference to

* even in districts where nothing could have been known of his physical descent

a Davidic descent in those passages in which Christ is designated as a Galilean by virtue of his environment. The idea of his Davidic descent was certainly not a widespread one. The fact that the Messiah was called the son of David clearly implies only that reference was made to the prophetic passages, which for most people were the basis of the messianic hope of the restoration of the Davidic kingdom. It would be an arbitrary, baseless assumption if those who designated the Messiah in this way had had anything but a political idea of the Messiah. If this idea was so widespread, it presupposes no special relationship between God and the Messiah, and much of what is said in many places, especially by Dr. Paulus of Heidelberg, about the universality of the idea of a messianic spirit who would be a higher, heavenly being, is unsatisfactorily documented, without having a truly historical basis. Therefore the more widely distributed the latter idea, the less distributed the former: the more current the messianic expectation of the restoration of the Davidic kingdom and an external might of the Jewish kingdom, the less current the idea of the Messiah who in that inner way had a special relationship to God. If we ask: What then was the nature of the messianic hope of those of whom it first was said that they had related the messianic hopes to the person of Christ? The answer is that in all those utterances the idea that was by far the most common was that of the Messiah as the restorer of the Davidic kingdom, and that the expectation of a political Messiah was the first to be related to the person of Jesus. If the poetic passages in Luke belong only to those productions which give the strong impression of being in a certain sense artistic and if we assume that it is probable that they are to be regarded as genuine utterances of the speakers in question, then it is impossible to demonstrate from them that those who first took a close interest in Jesus had understood the matter in this way. But if definite evidence had existed that these speakers from the beginning had understood the matter otherwise, then it would not have been possible for these productions to have originated at that time. Therefore, to say the least, we have no grounds for maintaining that what Mary and Joseph could have said to Jesus concerning the way he had been designated to them as the Messiah could have been responsible in him for the idea of a special relationship between him and God. This view has no basis in the historical situation as a whole. On the contrary, it can be admitted only as a hypothesis, but one that has the less support the less it can be demonstrated that the idea of such a close relationship with God was inherent in the messianic expectation of the people, and, in light of the physiognomy of the events as they lie before us, we are compelled to draw precisely the contrary conclusion. Consequently this expression on the part of Christ must have had its basis in Christ's own consciousness. We cannot derive it from that authority by reason of which it was assumed that he was the Messiah and from the prevailing thought of the time.

But if we now approach the matter from another direction and ask: What if we bring together Christ's analogous utterances from a later time ... ?* We are driven to conclude that it is highly improbable that such an idea should have taken fixed form and have persisted in Christ only as a result of such a conjunction as: Thou art the Messiah, and between thee and God there must be a special relationship! At the same time we should also have to say that that presupposes that intimation of this relationship must have been given in some fashion. Let it be granted that we presuppose in Christ the belief that he who is Messiah stands also in a special relationship to God and that he believed he was the Messiah because he had been told what had earlier been said of him. In this case he would have had to pay attention to the way in which he would proclaim this special relationship to God, and we should have to conclude that he reflected in this connection and regarded it as a task. *However, if there had been nothing in his inner consciousness to substantiate this idea of such an inner relationship, it could not possibly have survived.* If one awaits confirmation of a hypothesis and such confirmation is not forthcoming, the hypothesis is abandoned. It would then have been necessary for him further to conclude: ''The belief that thou art the Messiah is one that thou

* The question in our sources is incomplete.

91

wilt temporarily retain, but it must be a false belief, for thou findest no support for it in thyself." Consequently such an idea cannot be retained in the way we find that it is retained by Christ.

The fact that this idea was firmly fixed in Christ is documented in large part, to be sure, in the Gospel of John, but not exclusively there. It appears also in the other accounts. In fact, it lies back also of the views that came to be firmly held by his disciples. One might say that this question is of such extreme difficulty that one should avoid it as long as possible in the course of investigation and that it appears inopportune to undertake it in connection with this isolated narrative from Jesus' boyhood, since this narrative stands so much by itself that it would be arbitrary to put any stress on it. However, it has such a high degree of authenticity that I am compelled to conclude that it came into being for a special reason. But if we were to delay the investigation we should nevertheless later have to ask: From what time was this consciousness in Christ? And we should have to return to the fact that in this period of the life of Christ this consciousness existed. Now I wish to hold fast to the canon that has been established and to apply it. If we have sufficient reason to regard it as a part of the self-consciousness of Christ that he was conscious of such a peculiar relationship to God and if we cannot accept the notion that such a consciousness only came into being at a later time, was introduced by his disciples and was a consequence of the interpretation of faith — if we do not wish to adopt this expedient, we must endeavor to understand the origin of this consciousness in as human a way as possible, and in so doing we must retain the analogy of what, because of the same faith, we also say of those who believe in Christ, of the Christian church and its individual members. I repeat what I have already said: *If Christ had only received this idea in such an individual way, as it were from without, he would only have been able to retain it if in his self-consciousness he had found a confirmation of it.* We can take our departure from this and ask what for him could have been a confirmation of such an idea? Then we must say that by the same means by which the idea as one that came into being from without would have been confirmed, it could also have developed from within. If it did not develop from without, it must have developed from within.

If we here establish experience in the first instance on a common level, we find among men in general a very great difference with respect to the human consciousness of a relationship to God. I am not referring to such a specific relationship as we seek to discover in the consciousness of Christ. There is, however, a common element in human consciousness. That is to say, just as much of what is essential in human consciousness develops only gradually in each individual and just as there are times when what is essential has not yet become apparent, we are not disturbed if there are people, whether as individuals or as groups, in whom this consciousness has not yet made an appearance. If we reflect on the natural human conditions, we must regard it as a common element. The concepts of God can be very different, but the consciousness of a relationship to the object of these different concepts is essentially the same.* But in one person we find this as an absolute minimum and in another as a maximum. The actually perfect maximum is this: whenever this consciousness of a relationship to God is an element of every consciousness, whenever it is associated with every natural consciousness which reaches a certain clarity and completeness. On the other hand, if an individual always requires an external impulse in order to develop this consciousness within himself, or if he struggles against the development of this consciousness, this is the minimum. But in this minimum we recognize the fact that the direction thereto must always be inherent in it and that this direction must be a wholly universal one. We now ask ourselves where, then, looking at the matter purely from the human point of view, must we place Christ with reference to this minimum and maximum, if at this period in his life a consciousness of a specifically peculiar relationship to God had developed in him? That clearly presupposes that with reference to this element of the consciousness he must have stood in general on the side of the maximum. As soon as we enter into the va-

* in a certain connection?

rious points of the national development it becomes apparent that, viewing him quite purely (or: simply) as an ordinary child, faith in God had to develop in him in connection with this general thread of communication, and as soon as he reached the stage when instruction in the law began, that became an element which in consequence of the law was applied to his actions and the actions of those who surrounded him, and in this at his age certainly the variety of this relationship will have developed. In the case of many (boys) it will have been a meagre one, but for others it will have become a significant element in their life at an early stage, and if we place Christ at the maximum it is conceivable that the relationship to God can at this time have been a very lively one in him, so that it had entered into all significant elements of life. But that does not make any specific reason (or: difference) apparent for expressing his relationship to God in a way that others did not employ.

Lecture 15 (June 6). If in addition we take the fact into consideration that in Christian faith Jesus' development is believed to have been sinless — which does not mean that there was no human element in Jesus, for we never reckon sin as belonging to the essence of man, but which necessarily follows from a presupposed original divine indwelling — then in comparison to others Christ must have become conscious of his condition as a specific one, but that consciousness was not yet a consciousness of the divine in him. If we wish to ascribe to him such a self-consciousness as the creedal conception usually requires, a consciousness of a singular, pretemporal preexistence of the divine in him, then we must wholly do away with the human element. The exegetical basis of this assumption is very weak. If we hold fast to our canon, namely, the analogy of the indwelling of the Holy Spirit in us, then we find this only in what is most inward, in the principle of the pure volition of the divine will, consequently back of the actual consciousness, for every individual decision always involves human imperfection. Now Christ became aware of this in himself as a living being of God in him. The relationship of Father and Son is comprehensible as a consequence of the comparison of son (full-grown) and servant, the entire divine will, but also as a consciousness that gradually developed until it assumed definite form (greater works manifest it), namely, the entire will with respect to men. So he was able to say, I am the Son of God. According to the creedal conception he would have had to say, I have the Son of God in me.

From this it follows* that a narrative in Luke's Gospel has given rise to our questions, but that question ranges much further afield. This utterance only provides the beginning to a great variety of sayings by Christ, all of which we have to regard as an articulation of the same consciousness. The question actually is this: How can we conceive this under the form of a human consciousness and how can we reconstruct its development in a certain way? The basis for this, to be sure, is the argument with which I ended my lecture yesterday, namely, that in Christ we must presuppose a maximum of sensitivity to the activity of the consciousness of God that had been imparted to him. We took our departure from the fact that we find this everywhere as a constituent of the human consciousness in an individual being, but to a very different degree. It can be reduced to a minimum and it can appear to a maximum extent. But this implies neither something specific in Christ that distinguishes him from all others, nor the relationship of Father and Son.

Let us now abandon this approach in order to pursue the question in a different way. We wish to understand our task from the standpoint of the creedal formulas, and so now wish to say that what Christ wishes in this connection to express in all sayings of this sort is that he was conscious of himself at the same time as the second person in the Godhead. That, to be sure, is what is actually meant in the creedal formulas. Now the question is whether we can think of this as a human consciousness, one compatible with all other human consciousness, and whether in any way we can reconstruct its temporal development, for only then is it a clear concept for us. In that creedal conception the trinitarian relationship is regarded as one immanent in the highest being and at the same time as something eternal, but this eternal is at the same time always regarded as something pretemporal. Consequently everyone who wishes to reflect

* See the conclusion of the preceding lecture.

on the matter with any clarity will have no other alternative than to conclude that in Christ this consciousness existed in the form of the consciousness of a preexistence of the divine in him before all temporal experience. To be sure, individual sayings of Christ have been interpreted in this way, but there is probably nothing easier than to demonstrate that these interpretations are very arbitrary and that, for example, Christ's saying that before the foundation of the world he had possessed a glory that his Father had given him is also open to a different interpretation. We cannot resolve such points of dispute in interpretation, but it probably is necessary to keep them in mind whenever anything in our area of concern rests upon a disputed interpretation, for then it cannot be regarded as resting on a firm foundation. If we now ask whether that can be combined with the total condition of a human consciousness without denying the existence of such a human consciousness and whether we can think of it in terms of the progress and development of our human consciousness, I can only answer both questions in the negative. The consciousness of such a preexistence of the divine in Christ in combination with a human consciousness *cannot be conceived without again putting an end to the unity and personality, and that is the very thing that the creedal formulas never wish to do.* A definite consciousness of the divine in Christ cannot be conceived except as an operative one. However, as soon as we set out to place these two parallel to one another within the unity of a personality, a constantly operative human consciousness and a constantly operative divine consciousness, we clearly put an end to the unity of the personality.

But if we hold fast to the canon that we have established from the connection of the Christian doctrine of faith, namely, that the Christian faith also assumes an element of the divine in Christianity in general, without by so doing in any way denying the completeness of the human consciousness with reference either to the individual being or the total life of the church, then this canon compels us to reject all those formulas out of hand. If the activity of the Holy Spirit is assumed in Christianity, that is not to be conceived as the positive consciousness of a preexistence of this divine element that dwells in us. If we now say we shall be sure of conceiving the divine in the consciousness of Christ only to the extent that we hold fast to this analogy, then we can establish this as a truth, without at the same time accepting the other, namely, the positive consciousness of the divine as something that preexisted. And if we can do this with respect to ourselves, we must also be able to do it with respect to Christ. If we ask: On what does the possibility depend that in Christianity we can regard the divine Spirit as a being dwelling within it, without in the slightest degree putting an end to the relationship to what is human? We can scarcely give any other answer than this: *In this connection the divine is not conceived in the form of a real, discrete consciousness, but only as something that lies at the basis of the total consciousness.* We shall be able to make this clear in perfect agreement with the generally accepted Christian doctrine. If we ask: How does the activity of the divine Spirit express itself in the Christian church? Our answer must be: In the willing and carrying out of the divine will, for everything in this connection is traced back to the divine Spirit. However, if we trace this back in (or: to) the actual consciousness, then every actual human consciousness as one that fills the moment in question is purely a human one. In fact, as soon as we endeavor to attach the activity of the divine Spirit to this form of really moral action we have to say that as soon as we think of the actual definite decision, we think of a human consciousness. We always think of something imperfect in connection with it. Despite all that, we trace this back to the divine Spirit, but what we trace back to it is what lies back of every definite consciousness, namely, the willing of the divine will. If we think of this as the perfectly pure principle, from which, however, all our decisions, in and by themselves imperfect, arise, then this is the only relationship which we can establish between the divine Spirit as at work in the human consciousness and the human connection of what belongs to actual being and doing. If with reference to this we ask: But where, to the extent that it lies back of all different imperfect human decisions, is this divine principle located?

we raise a question that has not yet been perfectly answered in the church's doctrine.

There is uncertainty whether we are to ascribe the divine Spirit its place in the individual as such or in the entire community as such. But the divinity that we ascribe to Christ and in so doing distinguish him from all other men has its seat as object of this divinity only in his personality. In this instance no such uncertainty arises. That is what constitutes the difference, but we can nevertheless retain the analogy. It has its seat in Christ as it does in us,* as we ascribe the divine Spirit its place in the individual and in the entire community, namely, *as the principle and the source of the individual consciousness, but under the form of the actually (actual) individual consciousness. Now, to be sure, we shall have to assert that there is more to the difference than that. It is an essential part of our concept of Christ that what appears as human in him cannot be related to this divine principle in the same way as what appears human in Christianity and in individual Christians is related to the divine principle, namely, as something imperfect to what is perfect, as something adulterated to what is pure. In other words, what appears in Christ as human is as such something definite and therefore also something limited, but in this essentially human form that it possesses it is to be explained, nevertheless, purely by reference to the divine in him.* In this way it will be possible for us to trace this back to the general form of the development as it is represented in the Gospel, when it is said with reference to Christ that as a child he increased in wisdom and in favor with God and man. The latter expression can only refer to what is purely human, that is to say, on the one hand as something developing, a growing object of favor, but (or: on the other hand) this growth can only be conceived purely under this form as something developing from within.

If in this connection we consider the human development, so far as in general we regard the consciousness of God in the Christian church, the activity of the divine Spirit, as basic to it, we recognize the sinful element as a constant one, and

* whether in the individual or in the entire community, as the principle of the temporal consciousness

98

therefore say that the strength of the consciousness of God or the activity of the divine Spirit can only develop in conflict with what has already become the ascendancy of the sensual. We cannot admit that such was the case with Christ if we wish to avoid the view by which he necessarily has to cease being a special object of faith. Consequently we can think of no other form of development than that from complete innocence to an ever more perfect consciousness. I believe that these expressions in their relation to each other cannot contain anything equivocal. The way I have placed innocence over against consciousness involves the belief that innocence is a condition devoid of consciousness. It is a comparative concept, the comparison of an undeveloped consciousness with one that is developed. Innocence is not only opposed to sin, but also to virtue and to merit. It is therefore the state of an undeveloped consciousness, but one in which nothing that differs from the moral demand is involved. As soon as we find such a state in a man who is in the process of development that, if a moral consciousness is given him, he falls into sin, we no longer call him innocent, but only if he is still in such a state that from this state the moral consciousness can develop without sin, and that is the form under which alone we have to place the development of Christ. However, it is conditioned by the fact that the divine that dwells in him personally is not to be equated with what we understand by the expression of the divine Spirit. But this last we also do not assume in anyone as something original, but only as something imparted. If therefore we think only of the difference with (or: on) which we established the faith in the existence and activity of the divine Spirit in the Christian church, the difference between the individual being and Christ, in such a way that after the same fashion the divine as an indwelling principle in him was original, just as in the individual it is something imparted, then that difference in the form of the development follows of itself. Likewise we can only arrive at a clear conception of the spiritual principle as developing into human consciousness in all directions with (or: on) this indwelling of the divine in Christ, without a state of sin intervening, without a difference between the understanding or the insight and what becomes the act, that is the will; so in this way he also must have reached the consciousness of a specific difference between himself and all other men, and he was able to relate this then only to the divine in him. To put the matter in other words, the way by which this consciousness of the divine in him as the principle of all his human existence became a clear consciousness was based on the consciousness of his innocence and sinlessness. It developed in connection with this as the consciousness of a specific difference between himself and all other men. *To be sure, the fact that the divine spirit was in him from the very beginning must be presupposed in all this, and on this presupposition in general rests the view of Christ which makes him the object of faith. Nevertheless, there is nothing in this that stands in contradiction to the essence of a purely human development and personality. It has never been assumed in Christian faith that sin constitutes the essence of man, and on the other hand it has always been assumed in Christian faith that a union with God is possible in terms of man's essence. As soon as we assume that these two things were in Christ from the very beginning, we have assumed in him the specific difference, without having put an end to the essence of man as the concept represents it.*

Now we ask, How did Christ come to articulate this consciousness, as it could have developed in him at the time when he was able to have the consciousness of the antithesis between sin and innocence, in terms of his relationship to God, and thereby to express it by means of these titles of Father and Son? At this point I will undertake only to recall another expression that Christ employed, namely, that he describes this relationship only in terms of its activity in such a way that he says that *the Father is in him*. If we take this literally we are compelled to say that he calls himself the Son insofar as the Father is in him, but not insofar as something divine, which is called Son, dwells in him as a man. If this were not the case he would have falsified rather than have exhausted his concept by this expression, for otherwise he would have had to say: *The Son is in me*. Then it would not have been possible in this way to express the relationship between this Son in him and the Father in conformity with church doctrine, for according to the creeds the Father and the Son are not in each other. Otherwise there would be nothing to the doctrine of the trinity. In another scriptural saying Christ is compared to Moses (Heb. 3: 5-6)* and, while Moses is represented as a faithful servant, Christ is declared to be the Son who is active in the paternal house. Here we see the difference in the knowledge of the total relationship of the divine will. The servant as such is always outside this relationship, but the Son (the Greek word as a rule always designates the full-grown son who has come of age)† is *he who is within this relationship of the Father's will.* Now we can transfer this directly to Christ's saying. That is the type, the actual meaning of this relationship. Christ was always conscious of being within the relationship of the divine will, where this relationship as consciousness must be thought of as something always gradually developing: And so Christ represents himself as always looking to the will of the Father, that is as taking the whole will into himself, and at the same time he says that the Father will show him still greater works. This means in the form of development, as a purely human form. This, then, is the general type to which, as often as we have to return to the divine in Christ, we can again and again clarify for ourselves the coexistence of that divine and a purely human life and being, by means of which we also include both the concept of the Christian church and the self-consciousness of Christians (of this?), without in the slightest being required to disturb the relationship and the truth of the human element. We cannot be more explicit concerning the sequence of the development of Christ's self-consciousness because we have nothing factual about it. On the contrary, we possess only this single point in the whole series, which otherwise stands blank. Consequently, assuming the authen-

---

* See Schleiermacher's festival sermon on the passage.[17]
17. The sermon to which Rütenik refers is found in *Sämmtliche Werke* (Berlin: G. Reimer, 1843), II, 2:299-300, under the title, "The Difference between the Nature of the New and the Old Covenants as Represented in their Founding."
† The Greek word is *huios,* son who has reached his majority, not *teknon.*

ticity of this report, we have to say that already at that time the specific consciousness had developed in Christ.

Lecture 16 (June 7). The possessing of this in himself is to be traced back to the analogy of the omnipresence, since here the discourse concerns a most inward influence. Therefore the consciousness of a divine indwelling can have developed in a purely human way, presupposing a power imparted to him from the beginning adequate to make the consciousness of God continuously, purely, and absolutely effective (that is, so that all moments come to be through it), and such a power is only to be regarded as something divine. We are quite in the dark as to what contributed to the development of this after the twelfth year. Our next interest has to do with how it came about that Jesus, who had been a student of the law, became a teacher. The most natural way would be that of training in a school conducted by Pharisaic or Sadducean scribes. (There are no grounds for speaking in this connection of a school conducted by Essenes, and the fiction that such a school existed is baseless.) Only he must have passed through such a school in such a way that he was unaffected by its errors, for error cannot arise without sin on the way from ignorance through indecision to the truth.[18]

We can believe, to be sure, that a self-consciousness by which he distinguished himself from all other men can have developed in Christ in a wholly natural way if we presuppose an innate power which was a pure representation of the divine, that is to say, which gave him everywhere the direction to the consciousness of God, so that, as long as the intelligent capacity developed, it became more and more for him a continuum and, as far as this necessarily became consciousness of the divine will, had as a moral power an absolute adequacy. However, if we now wished to ask whether what we find in the sayings of Christ is the adequate expression of that, we could justify the one saying as such, namely,

18. The question of errorlessness which Schleiermacher refers to here and at several further points in the lectures concerns the area of Jesus' proper vocation — his God-consciousness and its communication to other men. Errorlessness does not refer to other spheres such as scientific cosmology and art. In the latter Jesus must be a man of his own time and subject to the interpretations of his age. However, matters that pertain to Jesus' unique vocation such as messianic references and the kingdom of God concern him precisely as a man of his time and in these Schleiermacher insists Jesus must be without error. This view is also shared by Karl Hase, *Das Leben Jesu* (Leipzig, 1829), p. 50.

that he places himself in the relationship of the Son, in that definite sense, to God as his Father. But if we consider in addition the other saying, namely, that he says of himself that the Father is in him, or that the Father can be seen in him, so that whoever sees him also sees the Father, it appears that this kind of identification has not yet been justified by the discussion to this point. But if we now ask ourselves what such sayings actually mean, and if we approach the question only from our common conception of God (in the Christian doctrine of God), then we must say that as a matter of fact, apart from that, God is omnipresent and therefore also, properly understood, to be seen in all. Therefore in this saying Christ has said nothing of himself that could not also actually be said in a general sense. However, the fact remains that Christ uttered this saying of himself in a special sense. Only it is necessary for us to rise above the analogy provided by the relation of these sayings to the divine omnipresence. If we ask: How is the highest being anywhere at all, therefore in another? we must pay attention to the fact that already in the earliest period of the Christian church this is expressed in such a way that God is said to be more inward than anything else, but also outside all else, and consequently it is possible to look only at one side of the matter. If at the same time we take our departure from the fact that the divine properties, because they are not distinguished from the divine being, therefore also cannot be distinguished from one another, we must say that the divine omnipresence can be nothing else than another expression for the divine omnipotence. At least, this is the case when one speaks of God in reference to a particular place and God is present only as the almighty one, that is to say, that everything proceeds from him as the original agent.

And if we should now ask: In what sense therefore was Christ able to say of himself, in accordance with this analogy but in a special sense, that the Father was in him? our answer is that it was only insofar as *he was conscious himself of what in him was plainly operative.* Now, that was an eminent sense, and the truth of it is that *he was aware that to do everything only under the form of the divine will and to see*

103

everything only in relation to God was what was operative in him. Consequently God was really what was operative in him, and all individual facts proceed from this. If we now wished (but that lies quite apart from the path we are following, and I can only give the result) to examine our church's creedal formulas, after attempting impartially to remove what is without substance, what would remain after that purging process as the actually true content would be the same thing. Inherent to this result is that this self-consciousness in Christ developed wholly *under the form of the human self-consciousness,* and likewise *gradually became something constant, just as the human self-consciousness in general becomes something constant,* but that he then thought of himself preponderantly under this form of agreement with God as the one who alone was operative in him. If we now return to our story and ask how this expresses itself as act in that narrative, we see that it was quite in accordance with the conditions of the life of that time under which Jesus lived. He informed himself as precisely as possible about what was imbedded in the history and leadership of his people as divine fact, and from the account, therefore, we also get quite a clear picture of the state of human consciousness corresponding to his years and his development. To be sure, however, for our purpose we must very strongly regret that we possess only this single narrative from the whole period of Christ's development until, as a man, he appears on the public stage. If therefore we ask what contributed to the development of the human spiritual powers of Christ, we have to admit that we have absolutely no information bearing on that question and can only resort to analogies. Furthermore, we find it impossible to demonstrate any connection between the conditions under which Christ is presented to us in his childhood and the way he later appeared in public. In the Jewish national development of the day there were two completely different stages of existence. Christ appears in his childhood in the house of Joseph and Mary, and, since Joseph bears the title of *tektōn* [carpenter], he was therefore one who followed several trades. Christ appears later as a teacher. That is quite a different stage, and with reference to the way and manner that he passed from the one to the other we have absolutely no information. What I have said is not to be understood as implying that among Jewish folk there was an order of castes. The only caste was the priestly caste, but the functions of the teacher were not associated with this. On the contrary, if a priest were at the same time a teacher, that was largely something accidental. But the scribes formed the distinguished part of the nation, naturally, because they represented its historical relationship, for informed in the law and informed in history were one and the same, and for this very reason the scribes enjoyed the highest esteem.

We can form a comparatively clear picture of the way and manner that an individual became a scribe. Every Jewish boy received instruction in the law. He had to become acquainted with what he had to observe, and he had to learn the significance of the sacred customs and the sacred festivals and the dignity of holy persons. This could lead to a study of antiquity, but in accordance with its extension this was valued only in terms of the need not to transgress the law out of ignorance and that the national spirit might be implanted so far as possible in every one. There were schools of scribes, and in these a complete knowledge of the legal requirements was furnished, as well as the interpretation of the law, and this was the way by which a man later could appear on his own as a teacher. To this training belonged also, in all probability, the study of the language in which the sacred books had originally been written, for this language at the time was no longer the one in use. However, the scribes of that time were divided into two different sects, the Pharisaic and the Sadducean. I deliberately mention only two. Usually the Essenes are mentioned in addition to those two. This has the support of Josephus's record (or: report) but it is unmistakably apparent from his narrative that the Essenes did not form a sect of the sort represented by the others. They played no part in the public life of the time, but withdrew from it. They formed a separated fellowship and as such were to be found only in scattered areas and made virtually no appearances in public life. They lived in a certain sense only for their separated society. I can probably assume that the conjecture is familiar that Christ had a special relationship to the Essenes and that our question is to be answered by saying that Christ was educated among them, that he took over his special principles from them, and that the way he realized the messianic idea in himself was due to his contact with them. That, however, is a wholly arbitrary construction, for which there is not a single bit of historical documentation. There is no evidence that there were Essenes in Galilee. Their main center, on the contrary, was on the opposite side, on the eastern and southeastern side of Judeà, whither we are least frequently led by our Gospels as an area where Christ at one time or another had ever been active. Furthermore, there is no trace in his public life of any connection during this period with the Essenes, and it is a fiction to assert that the disciples were only in a certain sense the exoteric side of Christ and that he had another secret connection, namely, with the Essenes, which constituted his esoteric side. All that is pure fiction, for which there is not a shred of historical evidence.[19] Therefore, if we ask: How did Christ develop from the point that we find him in the narrative in Luke of his boyhood to the point that he was able to appear as a teacher? we conclude that the hypothesis that he reached that latter point by way of a connection with the Essenes is not only fiction, but is also absolutely improbable, for we have no evidence that public teachers issued from the Essene sect.

We restrict our attention, then, to the two sects which alone come under consideration, and ask: Did Christ obtain the knowledge of the law that was necessary if he were to be able to appear as a public teacher, as well as the familiarity with Scripture and its interpretation, in such a rabbinical school, and if so, did he obtain such skills in a Pharisaic or

19. The idea that Jesus had a secret relation with the Essenes had been advanced by Karl Friedrich Bahrdt in *Briefe über die Bibel im Volkston* (1782) and *Ausführung des Plans und Zwecks Jesu* (1792) and by Karl H. Venturini in *Natürliche Geschichte des grossen Propheten von Nazareth* (Copenhagen, 1800-1802). In Bahrdt's version Jesus was a tool for the group throughout his life, including their staging his miracles and death in order to disabuse the populace of their false messianic hopes. Cf. Albert Schweitzer, *The Quest of the Historical Jesus*, trans. W. Montgomery (New York: Macmillan, 1961), pp. 38-39.

a Sadducean school? No objections can be raised to such an assumption, and I cannot see how it would be out of accord with the dignity of Christ if he were to have learned something for his future calling, and if he were to have been engaged in a process of development in the course of attendance at the national institutes (or: educational establishments). But these public institutes were of two sorts,* and everyone who in this way wanted to become a scribe had to be either a Pharisee or a Sadducee. This is not to say that in these sects there were not several gradations and differences or that it was impossible for individuals to free themselves from involvement in one or the other, but outwardly everyone was affected by this involvement. In this public ministry Christ clearly appears as an opponent of the Pharisees, but not in any way as one associated with the Sadducees. On the contrary, so far as the content of his teaching is concerned, he appears as an opponent of the Sadducees, and therefore, with respect to what was peculiar to them, as one who stood opposed to them, just as in another connection he stood in opposition to the Pharisees.

In any case, then, if he had studied in a Pharisaic or in a Sadducean school, he must have freed himself entirely from its peculiar sectarian character. But we would not be able to think of this emancipation *as a destruction of something that had previously existed*. Rather, from the beginning he must have kept himself free from these biases and, while accepting what was important, *he must have wholly rejected* what was the peculiar view or judgment of these parties. This statement seems to presuppose something that requires still further discussion. If I say: We cannot think of Jesus as having stood for a period in the Pharisaic or Sadducean party and then later as having torn himself loose from it, this statement seems to rest on the assumption that he could not have held a view that he later had to abandon as false. Consequently, not only was his moral development progress without struggle, but also his intellectual development was *progress without error*. At any rate, I am convinced that the one belief

* were organized only by Pharisees and Sadducees

107

cannot consistently be maintained without the other and that both are equally related to the peculiar nature by which Christ becomes an object of faith. In this connection the expression of my conviction has involved me in trouble. On the one hand it is said that this asserts far too much of Christ, while on the other hand I have been blamed for asserting much too little. However, so far as the question belongs to a purely historical conception of Christ, I cannot ignore it, and the parallels between the two views, that of *a moral development without struggle, that is, without the commission of sin,* and that of *an intellectual progression without error,* I regard as so illuminating that they do not require any prior justification. However, the connection between the two is something quite different. Sin in general has often been attributed to error, but, on the other hand, it cannot be denied that error is also to be traced back to sin and that we cannot conceive of error apart from sin.

Let me be more specific. If we consider the relationship of the human spirit to truth we must say: We would be involved in wholly vain endeavors and in a misunderstanding of our whole inner being, indeed, we would actually be dreaming at those moments when we believed we were seeing most clearly, *if we wished to deny that the truth is the natural state of man,* that is, that man's spiritual powers are directed toward the truth, and accordingly that even in their natural activity the truth must be the result of it. Every error is a contradiction of this proposition, and if the proposition is to be true, then at the same time it must be possible along with it to understand how at the same time these contradictions are also true, for otherwise we would have to deny the error. If, in light of this direction of men toward the truth and the nature of men for truth, we undertake, nevertheless, to understand error, we must keep the intermediate states clearly in mind, and therefore we ask: Presupposing that general proposition, in what state does the man exist before, at a certain point, he has the truth? There are only two possible observations to be made. In the first place, he exists in a state of ignorance, that is to say, what is later to become truth for him is not yet a task for him and does not exist for him. It is something of which he has taken no notice. However, if he has already passed this point and it has become a task for him, but if we are to think of him with that concern for the truth as having not yet arrived at the truth, then he must still be engaged in search for the truth. He must still exist in a state of indecision. If we are faced with a task in the area of knowledge and of truth, an area of ignorance disappears. As long as we were unfamiliar with the phenomena which we designate in their essence and general behavior as electricity, a complete ignorance prevailed. When they were observed a task emerged, but it was still a long way from the recognition of the task to a full understanding of the nature of the phenomena. This is the state of indecision, that is to say, of continued preoccupation with the subject without assuming any certainty with reference to it. *Error does not lie on this road from the formulation of the task to the point of decision and insight.* So the question remains: How does error originate? And our answer must be: As the result of sin; as the consequence of a moral deficiency.

Lecture 17 (June 8). The same conclusion does not apply to ideas which are taken over without personal conviction from the general belief of the day and which consequently lie outside the domain of his vocation. Let us take this for granted here. From the accusations of his opponents that Christ had not become familiar with Scripture and from the fact that emerges from such accusations that neither of the two parties charged him with desertion, we conclude that he had not attended any rabbinical school, but that, after having completed the customary course of instruction given to every lad of the day, he had perfected his knowledge of Scripture by his own efforts. That he was familiar with the sacred writings in the original is not subject to doubt, but whether he also knew them in the Alexandrine version is something that cannot be demonstrated, although it is hard to believe that he cannot have known the Greek language. There are no grounds for believing that he acquired Egyptian wisdom, and the supposition of an exclusive preference for *Daniel* is baseless. It is hard to imagine such a preference if Christ made use of the Hebrew original, and there is no trace of such a preference in specific quotations that Christ made from Scripture.

If we assume natural progress in all activity that bears on knowledge, we cannot actually say, presupposing this predetermination of the human spiritual capacity for truth, that in this progress error emerges in the natural course of events. On the contrary, the path of progress is from ignorance, that is to say, from nothing at all, by way of indecision, when something has emerged as a task, to certainty, which then must also be the truth and not error. Assuming that in a specific case, having proceeded from ignorance, we were to arrive, after a task had emerged for us, at an error, without passing through the state of indecision — that is to say, assuming that in such a way we were to reach a certainty which is the opposite of truth — then either we should have to abandon that presupposition, or we should have to conclude that something else than the original bent toward knowledge, from which all this is to proceed, must have been at work. The same thing happens if, having passed through the state of indecision, we later arrive at error rather than at the truth, for the same case occurs as in the former instance, namely, that from ignorance we end up in error. On the basis of our presupposition, however, the result of such a process ought to be the truth. When something opposed to this happens, there must be another reason for it.

How, then, does error originate? If we answer the question empirically, from experience, the answer always involves something immoral. If we think in the first instance, for example, of error in the moral realm, then it is delusion,* which arises from immoral inclination, that brings forth error, for example, whenever we erroneously consider something permissible which cannot be regarded as such. We find the same thing everywhere. This generally recognized fact forms the perfect transition to all else. There is another interest that puts an end to the process, for error emerges only when the desire for knowing is terminated before the truth is reached. This termination of indecision cannot issue from the striving for truth, but this earlier termination is the consequence of an intrusion of another interest. Therefore error often emerges from an excessive hastiness that is due to indolence, and also often from a weariness in the course of investigation,

* corruption of the intelligence

or it may happen that an interest in the result intrudes, and an interest in an untrue result must have an impure motive. Therefore it is impossible to think of error except as combined with sin.

So then, if the person of Jesus is to be, as it is, the object of faith, we must think of his spiritual development from the moral side as without sin and as a transition from innocence to pure morality. It follows from this that we must also think of his intellectual development as the pure transition from ignorance to certainty, without passing through the state of error. I have said that one cannot conclude from what I have argued above that he could not have adopted generally accepted ideas that were erroneous, but ideas that lay entirely outside the area where the discovery of the truth belongs to his vocation, for our argument does not presuppose any final certainty on Christ's own part concerning them. This is an undeniable (Christological*) fact of doctrine, for otherwise we should end up in docetism. Let me give an example. At that time it was not yet known that the earth revolves about the sun and that day and night are the consequence of the movement of the earth about its axis. Whenever we now say that the sun rises, we know that we are referring by that expression only to something that seems to happen, and whenever we are asked whether it is true that the sun rises into the sky, our answer is no. In Christ's day, however, the case was utterly different and the expression at that time signified a truth, that is to say, it expressed what was a generally accepted belief.† Let us now ask what Christ had in mind when he spoke of the rising of the sun. If we wish to say that at that time Christ alone knew that this phenomenon had nothing to do with the movement of the sun, then by that very statement we should do away with the whole true humanity of Christ, for then he would have had in himself all human insight of future times, since what is true of one thing is true of all. In that case he would have possessed an actual omniscience in the form of a human consciousness, something that could not

* The meaning=important for Christology, etc.
† what corresponded fully (purely) to the opinion of the day.

have come into being in a human way. Here and there it is debated whether it is necessary for the whole Christian theory of redemption and the Christian faith in the dignity of Christ to assume Christ's sinlessness and freedom from error. Whenever anyone does not accept this doctrine and maintains that it cannot be stretched to this extent, a horrible cry arises, as if I had said something of Christ that no man could justify. However, no alternative concept is possible. Imagine someone who had the suspicion that we had not yet made much progress in our knowledge of the celestial bodies. If some such person were to have come to Christ and to have asked him: "Do you really know that the sun moves?" Then Christ is said to have answered: "That depends on other factors. However, since the people do not know that, I use the language to which they are accustomed." In such a case Christ would have condescended to accept the error of men, and that idea is quite inconceivable. But my opinion is that Christ would have said: "That has not been the subject of my investigation. That is an acceptance of expressions whose subject in turn is ideas that do not belong in the actual context of life, but which are always employed only for the sake of other ideas." In no way can it be detrimental to the dignity of Christ if I say that he made use of the expressions as he found them current at the time. However, to assume such a certainty in him that he would have wished to defend the truth of such expressions would mean that he was involved in error,* and, according to my presentation, that is something we cannot assume. The same thing can be said of similar ideas.

Presupposing this in general and turning to our specific question I should say: In and for itself I do not consider it impossible, that is, incompatible with our presupposition of Christ, that he could have acquired his knowledge of Scripture and the law by attendance at a Pharisaic or Sadducean school. I should only insist that in doing so he did not accept the one-sided point of view and errors that he heard, but, in the course of his own process of thought, would have raised

* would mean ascribing error to him

a protest against them. I could imagine that this was the course of events. However, we have to admit that there is scriptural evidence against this conclusion, for the scribes themselves alienate the people from faith in Christ by saying that he had not learned Scripture, that is to say, that he had not followed the path that led through the school.* We have no cause to believe that they would have said that had they known the statement was false. It was not a point that they necessarily had to make, since it would have proved an indiscreet claim if someone else were to have appeared and said: "You lied; I know better." Even if he had attended the school in Galilee,† the fact remains that there was a very close connection between all chief centers of education. Consequently we are compelled to conclude that Christ did not attend any such school. Furthermore, according to his discourses Christ appears very definitely as anti-Pharisaic, and we are also told that this from time to time was the occasion of bitterness on the part of the Pharisees. Nevertheless, there is no suggestion that they charged him on this account with being a renegade. The same thing can be said of Jesus' relations with the Sadducees. Therefore it is very probable that Christ never was a student in these schools, but only took the Jewish stages of training that all Jewish youth was obliged to take. Since these last-mentioned stages were associated with the synagogues and provision was made for them everywhere, it was not necessary for him to have been for any time in Jerusalem. Consequently Christ in this respect was self-taught. He acquired his knowledge of Scripture by his own efforts. This does not necessarily mean that during his early years he never asked anyone for advice, that he never solicited another's opinion, that he never sought help from others in solving difficulties. In the course of a natural development of the human consciousness such a dependence on others is unavoidable and does not involve error, but only the state of indecision. How he did this and how far he made the insight of others his own; whether he mastered the Old Testament writings; whether he made himself familiar with the scribal

* Sadducees and Pharisees recognized each other's schools.
† or add: where the main center, Tiberias, had connections with Jerusalem

113

traditions that at that time existed not only in oral but also in written form, and whether he acquired an inclusive or a limited knowledge of them — all these are questions to which available evidence affords no answer. I am convinced that there can be no doubt that he read the Old Testament writings in their original tongue. The study of Hebrew was pursued at the elementary levels of school instruction, and it was possible later to enrich one's knowledge of the language by making use of ordinary linguistic gifts.

Another important question is whether he was also familiar with the Alexandrine translation of the Old Testament books, and in general, whether he had any knowledge of Greek. That is also a question one cannot directly answer from the actual evidence. I am convinced, however, on the grounds of probability, that the question has to be answered in the affirmative. In Galilee, where we have to locate his first period of instruction and where at a later time we find him at least periodically resident and engaged in travel, and in like manner in the Decapolis and in Perea, there were many people who were Greek-speaking. Consequently it can scarcely be imagined that Christ should have been unfamiliar with Greek. In Jerusalem it is well-known that there were synagogues of Hellenistic Greeks who associated with one another because they were unfamiliar with the Semitic dialect employed elsewhere. In such synagogues the Alexandrine translation was certainly used for the public reading of the Old Testament books. I have no intention, of course, of arguing that Christ frequented such synagogues while in Jerusalem. It is very probable, however, that he found it necessary in the course of his life to become familiar with this Old Testament translation, even though there is no evidence in the Gospels that, speaking in Greek, he quoted passages from the Greek translation. However, if we have to assume that he cannot have been wholly unfamiliar with Greek, that he was able to understand and employ that language in ordinary life, it becomes easy to believe that, since he had ready access to it, he could also have known the Alexandrine translation, even though no occasion arose in the course of his immediate activity as a teacher to make use of it. That Christ extended his knowledge beyond the area of his calling is something about which we can say nothing at all.

I should like now to shed a bit more light on two matters that have been raised hypothetically. In the first place, the hypothesis has been advanced that Christ during his stay in Egypt acquired knowledge of nature that had been unknown in Palestine, and this hypothesis has been used to explain his miracles. He was able to produce effects which had to be regarded as miracles in places where this knowledge was not current. I say nothing of what damage this hypothesis does to the moral character of Christ. I only remark that the whole of Christ's stay in Egypt belongs to those problematical accounts which cannot be traced back to any specific authority. But it belongs to the great defects of that method that many conclusions have been drawn from this account and have been represented as natural results. From the narrative as we have it no reason emerges for extending this stay beyond the first years of Christ's life, during which he was quite incapable of assembling such knowledge. On the other hand, also, it is doubtlessly improbable to the highest degree that, even if Christ had remained in Egypt until his boyhood years, he would have acquired knowledge that would not have been current in Palestine. It would be extremely remarkable and improbable if one were to imagine that this journey to Egypt was something unheard of in Palestine. There was always a close connection between Egyptian and Palestinian Jews, and the knowledge which Christ would have assembled would also have been at the disposal of others, and Christ could not have kept this knowledge to himself. Furthermore, it cannot be demonstrated that at that time in Egypt there was a body of knowledge that was derived from the mysteries of the ancient Egyptian caste of priests but that remained the peculiar possession of this caste. Therefore the hypothesis I have been discussing is wholly without value.

Another hypothesis, one that has a greater measure of probability, is that Christ directed his studies in Scripture principally and with special partiality to the writings of *Daniel* and that from these writings in the main he borrowed his messianic idea and his messianic self-consciousness. If one were to believe that Christ had made habitual use of the Alexandrine translation and had drawn his knowledge of Scripture from this version, the hypothesis would be more acceptable, for in the Alexandrine translation *Daniel* stands in the sequence of the ancient prophets. In the Hebrew codex, however, it never stood in the sequence in which it is found in the Septuagint, but only among the third class of writings, where it possessed only a small degree of authority. Such an habitual use of the Alexandrine version on Christ's part is inherently improbable, and if one were to look at the quotations from Scripture that Christ employed one would have to say that he had *Isaiah* much more in mind than *Daniel* and that what could be derived from the latter are ideas which Christ presents as already widely accepted by ordinary folk rather than as his own. He took them from the deposit of generally accepted ideas and employed them in this way, and that requires no hypothesis of a special study of and a special preference for *Daniel*.[20]

Lecture 18 (June 14). Dr. Paulus's hypothesis of a messianic heavenly spirit is wholly untenable. Even the Jewish commentators interpret Daniel 7:12–14 as referring to the Messiah but not to a heavenly spirit. Also the Jews in many instances could not have asked the sort of questions they did if this idea had been a popular one. The hypothesis that Jesus thought of himself as Adam Cadmon (Ben David) is equally unacceptable. I find just as little reason to believe with Paulus that Jesus attended Essene schools, for we do not know that these would have admitted strangers without affiliation. The fact that Christ was called upon to speak at synagogue services supports the belief that he was recognized as a teacher and therefore as one authorized and educated for

20. The question of the possible influence of Daniel upon Jesus emerged as a major thrust of New Testament research at the close of the nineteenth century due to the Son of man passage in Dan. 7: 13-14 and its correlation with intertestamental apocalyptic literature such as the book of Enoch. Johannes Weiss in *Jesus' Proclamation of the Kingdom of God* (Philadelphia: Fortress, 1971), p. 116 (included in the Lives of Jesus series and edited by Richard H. Hiers and D. Larrimore Holland) and Gustaf Dalman, *The Words of Jesus*, trans. D. M. Kay (Edinburgh, 1902), pp. 23-35 both saw this literature as of major importance for Jesus, as did later Rudolf Otto in *The Kingdom of God and the Son of Man* (London: Lutterworth, 1938). The entire issue is still one of the most controverted topics of New Testament research. Cf. Frederick H. Borsch, *The Son of Man in Myth and History* (Philadelphia: Westminster, 1967).

that task. Even after his twelfth year he would have visited the schools on the occasion of festivals and could well have obtained authorization without having attached himself to any specific school of instruction. The story of his rejection at Nazareth makes it clear that he had not spent the whole period of his education, to the time of his baptism, in Nazareth. This conclusion follows, whether there were one incident of rejection or two and whether we adopt Luke's version or Matthew's, for even a year later the residents of Nazareth would have had to mention his own earlier life in their midst and not only that of his brothers and sisters. He may have spent some time in Tiberias and similar places. How *the idea of his influential activity* took form in him raises a much more difficult question. In the first place, any hypothesis of a change in an original plan, that he had first aimed at worldly power, is to be rejected. We must also reject, in the second place, any hypothesis *even of a plan*,[21] for it is not consonant with Christ to be involved always in deliberation, choice of methods, etc., and such a state of indecision on Christ's part is inconceivable.

I want to spend another moment with the question of how Christ as a man obtained the knowledge that he as a teacher had to put to use. It is possible, as we have said, to think of him as having obtained this without attendance at the established rabbinical schools, although there is nothing inherently against the hypothesis that he did receive training there, provided that he appropriated only the philological and historical knowledge they imparted and rejected the onesided and erroneous views that, because of their sectarian character, were actually held in the Pharisaic and Sadducean institutes. However, the former alternative seems to me to be the more probable, for the fact is that Christ was not regarded by the experts in the law themselves as belonging to their circle. In his *Life of Jesus* Dr. Paulus considers it most probable that Christ attended an Essene school, although he guards himself against saying that Jesus was a pupil and agent of the Essenes. Rather, he maintains that Christ may have studied at such a school without having become dependent in the least on the Essenes as a sect or a closed society. This hypothesis seems to me to be improbable in the highest degree. I am convinced that everything we know of the Essenes makes it impossible for us to believe that they

21. See the Editor's Introduction, p. xxxvii.

could have operated under any other form than that of a closed society. [22]

Another fact stands opposed to Dr. Paulus's views, namely, that there is no reason to attribute to Christ in this development of his knowledge any special preference for the Book of *Daniel*. In contradiction to this, Dr. Paulus believes that Christ derived his messianic consciousness in the first instance from this book. As I have already said, it is inherently improbable that Christ should have formed such a preference, for the Book of Daniel was not counted among the actual prophetic writings, but stood in the third division of the canon. The situation would have been quite different had Christ been an Alexandrian, for in the Septuagint Daniel stands among the prophets. The whole hypothesis is based, on the one hand, on the fact that Christ calls himself a Son of man, and, on the other hand, that he speaks of the return of the Son of man on the clouds for judgment. These sayings refer to the material in Daniel 7. On the basis of this passage Dr. Paulus develops his whole hypothesis that in the age of the Maccabees the messianic idea underwent a complete transformation. Originally the Messiah was thought of as a ruler who would be descended from David. Judas Maccabaeus, however, was descended from the line of priests and took over the leadership of the nation. Consequently he was compelled to abandon the belief that the Messiah must be descended from David, and so the idea of a heavenly Messiah arose, the idea of one who would come in the form of a Son of man. However, at the time of Christ it was widely held that the Messiah would be a son of David. If Dr. Paulus is right, the whole idea of the Davidic descent of the Messiah must have lost its validity. But there is not a shred of evidence in the New Testament that the idea was prevalent of a heavenly spirit who would come as Son of man and fulfill

22. The disagreement with Paulus here is not particularly clear cut, for Paulus also insists that Jesus could not have been dependent upon the Essenes as a party forming a secret order, only that there were schools apart from the secret order itself. This judgment that Jesus could never have been part of a secret group was common in the third decade of the nineteenth century. H.E.G. Paulus, *Das Leben Jesu als Grundlage einer reinen Geschichte des Urchristentums,* 2 vols. (Heidelberg, 1828), 1:123; cf. Karl Hase, *Das Leben Jesu* (Leipzig, 1829), p. 51.

what had been associated with the idea of the Messiah. To be sure, in the rabbinical commentary on Daniel 7 the passage in question is interpreted as referring to the Messiah, but not to the Messiah as a higher being. This latter interpretation has been arbitrarily imposed on the passage. In my judgment another idea should be regarded as one that at that time was rather widespread but that had not arisen in the circle of the scribes. The scribes had no other conception of the Messiah than that of one who would be a descendant of David. This is evident from the story of the Magi, which, however much or however little truth it may contain, must have corresponded to the prevailing opinion. *Lazarus Ben David,* a Jewish scholar who died here not long ago, traced the principles of Christianity back to the Cabala. The third return of Adam Cadmon was then to be the coming of the Messiah. This cabalistic idea was certainly not so widespread at the time of Christ that even the scribes would have adopted it. (Enoch, Elijah, the Messiah: the three manifestations of Adam Cadmon.) Therefore I cannot accept it. It is also clear from the New Testament itself that it was not part of the beliefs of the rabbinical schools.

Still another fact is to be noted. Christ is frequently addressed as *rabbi* and is regarded as a teacher, and the use of that title for him was never disputed. He even taught in the *synagogues,* and consequently with a certain degree of publicity. But the synagogues were associated with the rabbinical schools. Therefore, if Jesus had not been regarded in any way as one entitled to teach, he would not have been able to appear in the synagogues. Now, we know from rabbinical sources that those who were recognized as teachers were ordained to the office, that the Sanhedrin administered this ordination, and that those who received such an ordination wore clothing that was an indication of their status. A person was invited to speak at a synagogue service because he was recognized as one entitled to fulfill that duty. Our sources do not say that no one received this ordination who could not prove beyond doubt that he had been in a school, nor can we ascertain from them whether those also could receive the ordination who could prove by actual demonstration that they were not lacking in knowledge of Scripture and the law. The last-mentioned possibility is very probable. Consequently Christ also could have had this authorization, even if he had not graduated from any school. In this way we can explain the fact that he taught not only as a free agent but also in the synagogue.

There is still another question. Where, then, did Jesus live during the period between that last Gospel narrative of his twelfth year and his public appearance? If he had attended Essene schools (as Dr. Paulus maintains), these were located only on the southern or southeastern side of Judea proper, on the Dead Sea. Our Gospels never say that Jesus spent any time in this area during the course of his public ministry. They must deliberately have avoided any mention of it, and this throws a strange light on the hypothesis, for it was natural that Christ would have revisited an area where he had previously been. If, on the other hand, we assume that Christ, without attending a school, had educated himself by making use of the aids at his disposal, that is, by being always present at the time of the great festivals and listening to the teaching of the scribes, as well as employing the aids that were embodied in the Scriptures, then the most natural conclusion is that he remained in Nazareth among his own family. But this conclusion is also quite improbable. In our Gospels we have reports of one or of two visits to Nazareth. (Exegetes disagree as to whether the narratives are different accounts of one visit or accounts of two separate visits.) The Gospel of *Luke* places the story of Christ's appearance at Nazareth at the beginning of his public ministry, and after his visit there we are told that he went to Capernaum. The other main narrative is the one that is found in *Matthew*. There, however, the story is not told until chapter 13. According to Matthew's version, then, the visit could not have been made at the beginning of Christ's public appearance. Nevertheless, it can be that both narratives tell of one and the same event. We are quite unconcerned in this connection with the issue of the debate. What interests us is the way in which the residents of Nazareth express themselves as they observe Christ's public appearance. Is he not the son of Joseph and Mary, and are not his brothers and sisters with them? They would not have been able to speak in this fashion if Christ had lived in Nazareth until shortly before his baptism, and it is a matter of complete indifference whether he appeared in Nazareth shortly after his baptism, as Luke tells it, or at the end of the first year of his public ministry, as Matthew tells it. In either case the people would have had to say: "Until recently he still lived among us and we noticed nothing special about him." In actuality, however, they speak only of members of his family as having lived among them, not of Christ. The story, as it is told, rests upon quite another presupposition and is quite unfavorable to the hypothesis that Christ had lived in Nazareth during this whole period. All this makes it highly probable that he had chosen another place of residence in order that he might put himself into the position in this way of following his vocation of public teaching. If he remained in Galilee he could have gone to Tiberias, the main center of Jewish scribes, for Tiberias lay only a short distance from Nazareth. That he was trained in such a way *as a pupil of some individual teacher,* as Paul was of Gamaliel, *seems to me to be improbable, for this would have led to a relationship of filial regard, into which I cannot believe that Christ can have entered.* These schools were always open to the public to a certain but limited extent, and I can think of Jesus as having attended them in this way.*

We come now, however, to more difficult questions. I can believe that this self-consciousness which Christ expresses when he calls himself a Son of God can have developed in him in the form of the human consciousness. But it is something quite different when we ask: How did the idea of a definite kind and manner of activity develop in him, and why did he not begin this activity at an earlier time? The latter question can be answered rather easily if we assume that Christ in this respect followed the prevailing custom. According to this, no one could appear publicly as a teacher before

---

* The schools had a kind of public character. No one was refused admittance, and so Jesus can have visited them.

his thirtieth year. If Christ had wished to ignore this custom, since he could regard himself as Lord over it as over the Sabbath, he would not have been able to attain his goal. He would not have been recognized as a teacher; his mission would have amounted to nothing for that period. But how the picture of his whole activity took form in him is a very difficult question. I must now confess that the whole expression of *a plan* that Christ had made for himself is something that does not commend itself to me. The idea of a plan suggests to me much too little that is direct and far too much that is constructed in a limited way, and I should not like to think of the matter in this way. Let me make one thing clear at the very beginning. I cannot possibly believe that for a time he shared the common vi .w that the Messiah would have to exercise an external civil power and that he only later changed his opinion. That would be such a fundamental error that, if I were to ascribe it to Christ, he would have to cease to be an object of reverence for me. If at any time he had not known what he wanted to do, then something must have been the cause of that indecision, and I cannot think of such a cause without associating it with sin or corruption. But it is just as difficult for me to think of the development of Christ in terms of the formulation of such a definite plan for his activity because, as we think of it, we always return to the contrast between goal and means, and this contrast bears the marks of moral imperfection so clearly that I should not like to entangle Christ in it. Furthermore, if such a plan comes into being by a process of deliberation and reflection, whether one course or the other is the better, I should not like to ascribe such a process to Christ, for it implies an inner uncertainty. This would place him on the same level as other men and he would not remain an object of reverence. However, there is not a trace of this anywhere. Not even in the most pragmatic narrative in John's Gospel is there anything said of action on Christ's part in accordance with a plan. But now we face the task of understanding how the way was inwardly prepared in Christ for what could not be put into effect as long as he had not attained the legitimate, canonical age.

Lecture 19 (June 15). Christ required no plan, for his influential activity was the pure communication of himself. If he thought of his life as diffused among the masses, the idea of the kingdom of God necessarily arose out of his self-consciousness and his perception of sin. This communication was effected by means of living contact with people, in which we find him engaged as early as the occasion recorded in our narrative. The ability for this increased in a purely human way by practice, and in like manner the basis for this ability was knowledge of men. We would involve ourselves again in a positive error were we to think that the result of his teaching had either exceeded or fallen short of his expectation. He conceived of it in the course of the total historical development in terms of a maximum, but in individual instances as a minimum.

If it does not seem appropriate to me, no matter how the idea is phrased, to speak of a *plan* that Jesus made for his public activity and to ask when and how he came to feel himself ready for his task and by what sort of circumstances he was affected, what shall we put in its place? Before I answer this question I must give a somewhat fuller explanation of my dislike of that way of representing the life of Christ. In all that is subsumed under this concept we always perceive an essential imperfection, and we wish to view the matter only in one or the other area of human activity. So then, let us think of a creative artist. We see a piece of his art and we wish to ask: How did this come into being? Indeed, the fact that it is a work of art means that it did not come into being by haphazard, thoughtless activity. However, if we wish to imagine that the artist has a plan and that such a plan provides you with an explanation of a painting, that the artist wished to represent this idea or that and that this or that was his motive, then in this way only an imperfect work of art can be adequately accounted for. In this case the work of art is a picture, and the picture is said to have originated in an idea. It is said to represent a specific idea. So, between the two there always exists an element of irrationality. The picture is to be viewed as a picture painted for the explicit purpose of representing an idea and so, having originated in this way,* it cannot have an absolute perfection as a picture. Let

* namely, of deliberation

us explain the matter in a different way. Such an artist is only one who is engaged predominantly in the activity of seeing (or: viewing). However, this activity of outer apprehension is not everything. On the contrary, in connection with it there is also an inner activity. Pictures take form within the artist, and the fact that he is such a person[†] is the very thing that makes him an artist. *To have seen the outer shape of something* is the same as *to form an inner picture of it.* The more you think that he, while engaged in his task, has to construct something that was not in the original inner image, the more you think of an imperfection in it, and so everything that requires corrective remedies involves imperfection. However, if the picture represents in its outer form what existed in the inner image, it is perfect.

Now, we could say that all that belongs to a different category and has no application to the question we are considering. However, if we reflect on how, in the widest sense of the word, our actions take place, we shall immediately have to make a large classification and say: There is a kind of action that takes place as the result of ideas and that issues from ideas, but there are also other actions which, just as the painting of the inner image on canvas, become (are) an externalization of something inward. To be sure, we rarely think of this as a series of connected actions, but only as one that is predominantly momentary. However, you will be able to form a picture of it for yourself that is very similar to it. For example, think of two people engaged in conversation with one another. The one says something that seems false to the other. The other, then, has in himself an inner truth concerning this subject, and this is the reason he rejects the statement. We can imagine, on the one hand, that he goes away without saying anything about the matter. On the other hand, we can also imagine that he attempts to correct the other. In this case, however, there is nothing that demands a plan on his part. On the contrary, he allows his inner truth to appear in order that the other may be able to appropriate

[†] or add: by means of this receptivity and spontaneity, viewing and creating

124

it. This action is grounded on nothing else than this inner urge to communicate, and the communication is called forth by the contrast that develops. Think of this on a larger scale. Think of one who wishes to let all his truth appear as much as possible, namely, in a complex of ideas that appears as a work of art, whether it be a scientific one or one of another sort, but who has no other reason for doing so than the inner truth that he allows to appear. The more this complex is related to what is within, as the work of the artist is related to his original inner image, the more perfect it is.

If we then return to the question we have to answer from the vantage point of our historical task — the question, namely, of how a self-consciousness developed in the Redeemer, if there is good reason for our faith in him, in the form of a purely human consciousness — there is only one answer that in the first instance we can give to it. Presupposing the wholly extraordinary power, and in connection with that the contrast that had necessarily to arise from it, nothing ever happened in him that stood in contradiction to this direction of the consciousness of God. In this way we can form a picture for ourselves of the self-consciousness of the Redeemer in the form of a purely human consciousness. Now the question is: Did he find it necessary in the interest of his activity to form any plan, or is it not the most natural thing for us to think of him in light of this specific self-consciousness as involved in such an urge to communicate that his whole activity follows of itself? If we now think of him in this consciousness of the contrast between the complete adequacy of all his spiritual movements to the continuity of the consciousness of God in him and the sin that he constantly observed in the world around him, it lies in the nature of the matter that along with it and at the same time the idea of a kingdom of God in contrast to this purely human being (world) must have come into being by means of that self-consciousness. If he thought of his nature in terms of being wherever he saw anything sinful, he had naturally to think at the same time of this harmony.* Now, we cannot conceive of this as the inner

* or add: harmony of his own ·power and the need of others

truth of a human soul if this at the same time had not been an impulse to transform the world into the kingdom of God by the communication of himself. The consciousness of the power that dwelt in him and the consciousness of the need of the world about him combined to become for him an impulse to constant self-communication. So I am freed from the need of thinking of a plan that Christ made for himself. He desired nothing else than this transformation of the world into the kingdom of God, and to effect it could employ no other means than pure self-communication. So the task does not require that we think of his activity as something that issued from a definite plan. It was something that was the result of an original inner impulse which depends on the consciousness of a divine life. Consequently, it was the desire of a divine life to impart itself.

Now, to be sure, if we also think of the artist on this level, if we think of his work of art as arising out of this inner image, which is a definite externalization of his virtuosity in one area, then we shall have to admit that in the process a great difference of *skill* is apparent when we view works of art that originated under precisely the same circumstances. But this is quite another matter. Let us return to the discussion of the influential activity of Christ. If Christ had proceeded here with a very inferior order of skill, we should have to think that in his activity, which we now describe as the desire to impart himself, a number of elements would have appeared, with the consequence that his self-communication would have been without any result, although he had either desired a definite result, or had presupposed and assumed it. That would be a lack of *skill,* but not something that would make it possible for us to introduce the concept of a definite plan into the idea of his activity in general. In such a case we should obviously have to assume something that we cannot assume, because it is a positive error. If we therefore hold fast in this connection to the conviction that the concept of Christ that represents him as an object of faith does not permit us to think of him as involved in a positive error, because such an error is based on sin, we cannot imagine any such lack of skill on the part of the Redeemer. However, we have the task of understanding as far as possible how he reached this point under the form of a human consciousness and a human activity.

If we ask: What, then, is the skill that in this connection has to be presupposed if I am to think of one engaged in self-impartation, to whom the result in its entirety and in detail always corresponds to what he had in mind, to whom, therefore, the result never falls short of or exceeds his expectations? then our answer must be: Such skill involves nothing other than *knowledge of men*, for it is a question of *whether or not a person correctly understands what will be effected in another by a self-communication*. As Christ appears to us in the course of his whole activity, he must have thought of the result of that activity on the one hand as. an absolute maximum, and on the other hand as an absolute minimum. It was his belief that through him the divine purpose of bringing about the salvation of men would be realized. Consequently, he thought of the result as an absolute maximum. In other words, whatever in the human world could come into being as the greatest approximation to his own state would only come into being as a result of his activity. However, he thought in this instance of the lasting activity of his power in this sphere. But what form did his expectation take so far as the immediate present was concerned? Viewed as a whole, only as a minimum.* Now, however, we must say that even the judgment of his disciples concerning him was that in this respect a complete knowledge of men dwelt in him, that he had a correct estimate of men even in individual instances, and that is all the skill that he required in his activity. How was it possible for that skill to develop in him in a purely human way? There is no other true basis for the knowledge of men than *pure love* and *pure self-consciousness*. Pure love is the desire to enter into men, and, if we assume pure self-consciousness as it was in the Redeemer, it is *index sui et falsi* and was what gave indication of the opposite in others. Whenever we form an incorrect picture of a man, the reason for doing so will turn out to be something connected

* in detail, rather as a minimum; see above.

with sin. Consequently, nothing more was involved in it than the use of life as it developed, but in such a way that it put into effect his whole peculiar power. However, there is no other form of human development of power than practice, and we shall be quite free to construe the whole period in the life of Jesus at the same time as a period of practice, though not as intentional practice, but as practice that issued of itself from his inner impulse and that made use for that purpose of all external events of life as they developed. If he were to obtain this practice, however, we must think of him as in living contact with people, and we find an indication of that as early as the story in Luke of Christ's boyhood. There he appears in one of the halls of the temple in Jerusalem, not merely as a listener, but at the same time as one who asks questions and offers answers, and we must think of that as typical of his entire life. He was always involved in a development that was directed toward the impartation of his self-consciousness.

If we ask: Should we regard it as a serious lack that we have no further definite information concerning this whole preparatory period in the life of Christ? my reply would be: I believe we shall be able to comfort ourselves easily with the thought that the general type of Christ's later development has been given us in Luke's story. We can understand that development in light of the information we have.* If we knew in what locality he lived during this period and with what particular people he came into contact, with whom he entered into a special relationship, then this would only be an enrichment of our historically empirical knowledge of his life, but for our knowledge of his inner development our ignorance of such matters is no real loss. What produces an effect on us is only *his influential activity.* If we knew more than we do, that, to be sure, would be something of interest to the historical scholar as such. However, if we view the matter from the theological standpoint, to the extent that this is directed wholly to the effect upon the church, this loss is not to be taken into account. The only thing that is of any interest

* or add: what comes later being added to it

to us is that we should like to be able to trace back the activity of Christ so far as possible to its first beginnings. To be sure, we also have indications that bear on this, but they go back in part only to those periods during which we cannot assume an actual personal and independent activity on the part of Christ. Such indications are found in what preceded Christ's own development as the relation of the Old Testament prophecies and promises to his person. It would be interesting to ask: With respect to his activity in his *immediate environment,* how may Christ have behaved in the course of his development? But this also is a question that we shall be able to answer in terms of the principles of the analogy, and we do not greatly miss the detail that is lacking. This wholly human view of the life of Christ requires that we think of him as the object of instruction, for otherwise he would not have been a genuine child, and we should become involved in psychological docetism. Even in the period of his instruction as a child, an individual never behaves as a purely passive person, but always as one who himself is active, and as the children are educated, the parents share at the same time in the educational process. This reciprocal effect is a common experience, and, to the degree that Christ developed according to this type, his effect on his environment must already have been in a certain sense a dominant one. That is to say, it must have been much stronger than is the case in ordinary life. In exercising this influence, however, his relationship to people would not have ceased to be a genuine relationship. The narrative in Luke of Christ's boyhood provides us with the basic factors which enable us to reconstruct the whole preparatory period in the life of Christ.

Lecture 20 (June 18). However, if his activity is comprehensible in this fashion as the desire to impart his divine life, how are we to explain the fact that he applied the messianic prophecies to himself — prophecies that did not include any such content? He did not deceive himself. He did not imagine that the prophecies referred to himself as he was. But he also did not deceive others. He need not have anticipated such a dialectically elaborated distinction as is expressed by the Pauline phrases *Israel kata sarka* ["Israel according to the flesh"] and *kata pneuma* ["according to the spirit"]. The idea that conveys his own understanding of his mission is that (such as Simeon held) of a theocracy that includes but extends far beyond the Jewish people. This is what he wanted, and he could consider himself the dominant starting point. All else he regarded only as the raiment in which this idea was wrapped. And so here also we can think of a gradual transition from the complete appropriation of all appearances of this ancient hope to the confident proclamation that the time was fulfilled, without assuming that he had first passed through a period of hesitant vacillation or that he had received a special revelation concerning the matter. This point of view is in sharp contrast to the ordinary one, which represents *his teaching mission as having begun with his baptism,* a viewpoint, to be sure, that has New Testament passages to support it. I grant that it would be possible to distinguish between Christ's communication of himself by means of teaching and the twofold function that really marked his office, namely, that of teaching the people and of gathering his disciples. But even the latter does not actually begin with the baptism. According to Matthew, Christ began to preach after John the Baptist had been arrested. According to John, he already had disciples when he was invited to Cana, a fact that must have been true before the baptism. To lay a heavy stress on the baptism leads either to gnostic conclusions, that the Logos ["Word"] became identified with Jesus on that occasion, or to rationalistic views, that he was made aware of his vocation for the first time on the occasion of his baptism.

There is one question that we cannot avoid: How did Christ come to relate the messianic idea to himself?* To be sure, there are not many sayings of Christ which assert this relationship, but even if we did not have these, few as they are, but were only to reflect on the way Christ allows himself to be identified with the Messiah by his disciples, the problem would remain the same. Now, it cannot be denied that in Christ's time the messianic idea was predominantly understood as the popular hope that was associated with the descendants of David. In other words, it was generally understood as a renewal of the Jewish theocracy. In my judgment, this idea was never and in no way in the thought of Christ, and there are only a few wholly empty intercalations which enable several recent writers to represent the case as, though Christ had accepted that notion to begin with and had later, as it were, changed his plan. I have already given my reasons

* to relate his self-consciousness to the messianic idea and to identify himself with the Messiah

in general for refusing to believe that Christ made use of a plan. However, the idea that served as a vehicle of Christ's own understanding of his mission is that of the theocracy. If it was an essential part of Christ's self-consciousness that in every respect he was governed by the consciousness of God, it follows that he himself, in his personality, was the representation of a theocracy that was determined entirely by the consciousness of the divine will. He endeavored to transmit his life to men, that is, to make them people who would be governed solely by the will of God, and to found a rule of the divine will on the basis of his own person. But he never imagined that this at the same time would be an external rule. On the contrary, everything in his life was a denial of that (that he himself denied it), as is apparent from his last words to Pilate.

Now we may ask: Can his relation of those prophecies to himself be justified in such a way that it involves neither self-deception nor an attempt in any way to deceive others? If he had believed that he himself was actually the subject of those prophecies, there are those who would say that that is what the prophecies meant from the beginning and that the whole idea of a political theocracy was only a misunderstanding. That would be the simplest interpretation, but I do not believe it is the correct one. If we put ourselves back into the period of Jewish history, we are wholly unable to separate the personalities that were active at that time from the type of historical life among the people,* and therefore we shall be unable to believe that those men could have wished to express their expectations in terms of a future rule of the divine will,†which, however, would not immediately result in any particular outer form of life. The actual principle of political theocracy was monotheism. Although monotheism among most of the Jewish people was always based on an underlying polytheistic presupposition, as is apparent from the frequent comparison of Jehovah with other gods, nevertheless it is impossible to deny the principle I have stated. It is certain, then,

* from the total life of the time
† a spiritual rule of the divine will that would not assume any particular outer form

that among the most pious men of the people at all times the expectation of an increase of the influence of the Jewish people in the history of the world was always at the same time an enlargement of the influence of the rule of God among men. Consequently we find the Jewish element in the New Testament (Luke's narrative of Simeon), but at the same time the Messiah is spoken of as a light that was to enlighten the Gentiles, as a prophet by whom the living knowledge of God was to be conveyed also to other peoples. Was it a deception that induced Christ to consider this religious element as the actual truth of the Old Testament prophecies and the political element only as the form in which this truth could be appropriated into their consciousness by the people of the time? As soon as we go back to the true inner reason for all that is appropriated in human life, we must accept this maxim as that in which the pure striving after truth* and, at the same time, love, express themselves as one and the same, for this is apparent from the fact that one regards what is true and good in the acts of men as that by which men are motivated, and all else only as accidental and transitory. Christ, therefore, was unable to act in any other way than this. He did not act as though he still kept something to himself. *The restored glory of the chosen people of God as the means which God employs to spread the knewledge of God among all men, and for this purpose an instrument of God that is unique in its nature: this is what Christ regarded as the actually essential content of the messianic predictions.*†

If we proceed a bit farther in Christian history and consider the idea held by the apostle Paul, we discover that in it the individual elements are much more distinctly presented. That, however, represents a dialectic advance of the Christian idea and was an advance that we do not need to assume had been anticipated by Christ, although the view of the messianic prophecies was wholly identical. The way in which Paul distinguishes "Israel according to the spirit" and "Israel according to the flesh" is the contrast by which the one is wholly

---

* the pure interest in the truth
† or add: He did not think: The prophecies had a political development in mind, but I fulfill them spiritually.

separated from the other. We cannot assume that Christ necessarily thought of it in as distinct a form as this, but the result was the same. The whole remained a unity to him in such a way that he saw only the most essential thing in it, and in this immediacy of consciousness is to be found the reason why he could relate the messianic prophecies in this fashion to himself and regard himself as the one of whom the prophets had written. That more is involved that affects the individual method of interpretation we may readily grant, but it is something that in this connection is not immediately relevant, since it concerns the detail and here we are interested only in the idea in and for itself. But it is apparent from what we maintain that we cannot concede that there was any positive error in Christ. However, the fact that he was able to appropriate ideas concerning which he had no professional competence to form a conviction can be explained by the way in which he entered into the Jewish maxims of interpretation, because the detail for him was only an example of the idea, and his actual task was to hold fast to this idea and to make it vital in the consciousness of men. So we shall always be able to say: To the extent that his special self-consciousness developed in him, to that extent there developed also the conviction that he was the goal of the entire institution of Judaism, and therefore also the one to whom all these presentiments and sayings point which were to identify the fulfillment of this divine decree with the Jewish people. We shall be able to say, then, that his consciousness of himself as the Son of God and his consciousness of himself as the object of the Old Testament promises must be regarded as one and the same thing. We are to think of his conviction that he was the object of the messianic prophecies neither as an idea that took form in him after much vacillation, nor as the result of a special divine revelation, but only as identical with his peculiar self-consciousness, but in this instance in relation to Jewish history and nationality.

From all that has been said it follows that we can only think of the development of the self-consciousness that was peculiar to Christ and of its communication as a gradual transition of the one to the other. And if we take the messianic element also into consideration, we must relate both to the fact that this clarification for himself of the development of the messianic prophecies with reference to himself belonged to his development, and the expression of himself in this connection had therefore to become his proclamation of the kingdom of God. In this way it becomes superfluous to ask when Christ actually began to teach or to appear in public and at what point his activity began and the period of his preparation ended, and we shall be in no position to answer such questions. It was inevitable that the increasing development of his self-consciousness had also to issue in the communication of himself, and it is impossible to mark the end of one process and the beginning of the other. Opposed to this view, however, is the generally accepted belief, which, we must admit, can cite some New Testament passages in its support, that the actual activity of Christ begins with his baptism. His disciples thought of it in this way. Recall the speech that Peter made between the time of Christ's ascension and pentecost, according to which an apostle was to be chosen from among those who had accompanied Christ from the time of his baptism to that of his ascension.

To be sure, there is another special point here that we have to keep in mind. The activity of Christ, as soon as it assumed definite form as such, had two different aspects, and the combination of these two marks the actual beginning of his public ministry. On the one hand there was a rather indefinite influential activity in general, and on the other hand, at the same time, the gathering of a special circle around himself which he then formed into his organism. If someone now says, Whenever we speak of his influential activity, we do not mean his activity in general, but this definite form of it, we shall try to see how far this suggestion carries us. If we examine our various Gospels we get quite disparate results. *Matthew,* for instance, does not say that Christ began to preach the kingdom of God from the time of his baptism. On the contrary, he follows his account of the baptism with that of the temptation. Then he says that John the Baptist was arrested and that only then Christ began to preach. *John* takes us into the environment of the Baptist and makes the Baptist tell his disciples that he sees Jesus again after he had baptized him, but in all this there is nothing said of a preceding activity on the part of Jesus. But if we proceed a bit further in John and read his story that a few days later Jesus returned to Galilee, because there was a marriage at Cana to which he and also his disciples had been invited, we are compelled to ask: How could John say that, if we are not to believe that it was only for the sake of brevity that he said: Christ was invited together with his disciples, instead of: Christ was invited and took his disciples with him? In this case the relationship between Christ and his disciples must have already been established, and there are bits of evidence that Christ had achieved a certain reputation before he allowed himself to be baptized by John. If we return to the fact that Christ was recognized as a public teacher, we must admit that such recognition preceded his baptism, and consequently we can think of an habitual teaching on Christ's part, though not to the same degree. That is to say, we can think of a public appearance in the synagogue, and if he made any lengthy stay anywhere in Galilee between the Sea of Galilee and the coast and appeared there in public, it was always to be presupposed that he had a few people with him who were his students, for such a relationship was in accord with a public appearance in synagogues. This explains the invitation extended to Christ to bring along any disciples whom he happened to have with him. This disposes of any impression that the public appearance of Christ had any association with his baptism. However, Christ's baptism demands some closer consideration.

Concerning the Baptism

How did Christ come to accept baptism from John and what happened at the time of this baptism to give the impression that it marked the actual beginning of Christ's ministry and his divine inauguration? This is a very difficult question. Very frequently, when the importance of this baptism of Christ is stressed, something is in mind comparable to the most ancient heresy, namely, that the divine united with Christ for the first time at his baptism, a view that naturally destroys the whole unity of Christ's life and his whole humanity. There is also a strong tendency in the same direction whenever Christ's baptism is regarded as his necessary inauguration, or whenever, on the other hand, Christ is represented in modern terms as having been previously involved in a measure of uncertainty concerning himself and as having become assured of his divine appointment only at the time of his baptism. His baptism served him as an omen of the truth of his vocation!

Lecture 21 (June 19). The baptism. Objections to a theory of an earlier relationship between Jesus and the Baptist. The account in the Gospel of John must be considered basic. Everything in the other Gospels can be shown to have been derived from it. John's account relates everything marvelous that happened at the baptism to the Baptist. John the Baptist is to be understood according to the analogy of Simeon, only with the commission. Christ could have allowed himself to be baptized only if there were no offer of the forgiveness of sins in connection with the baptism. John the Baptist desired merely that the Jews acknowledge that forgiveness was necessary if they were to share in the mission of the Messiah. Consequently Christ allowed himself to be baptized in part as a symbolic aspect of his proclamation and in part as a recognition of the Baptist and of the relation of the Baptist's mission to his own.[23]

Our first task is to ascertain whether an earlier personal relationship had existed between Jesus and John. The Gospel accounts in this respect are in sharp disagreement. In the Gospel of *John* there is a narrative of the Baptist himself in which *he says that he had not known Jesus*. A recent account of the life of Jesus explains this statement after this fashion: John had not recognized Jesus the moment the latter came

---

23. Schleiermacher's view of the significance of the baptism in *The Christian Faith* is that: "...the explanation which Jesus himself gives of this circumstance forbids the supposition that by this baptism he became something which he had not been before, or that he received an authority or a consecration which was not already his. The former supposition is incompatible with belief in the originality of the divine in his person; and for the latter there is no external authority of any kind in the rite instituted by John. The only value, therefore, which we can attribute to this transaction is that it helps us to understand his public appearance historically: he marked his more open transition from seclusion to public life by an act of confession which inevitably evoked a more definite opinion about him, to which he was able to attach his teaching." §103, 2.

for baptism. However, unless one wishes to deny John all credibility, one cannot say that he had already been acquainted with Christ. The other passage is in the Gospel of Luke. But where in the Gospel of Luke? In that first story that precedes the account of Christ's birth — in the story where the angel informs Mary of the pregnancy of Elizabeth, her relative. This gives rise to the claim: Mary and Elizabeth were related. If they exchanged congratulations and hymns of praise as they thought of the two children that were to be born, it is impossible that they then could have broken off all communication with each other, and it follows that Jesus and John must have come into contact. But these Lukan narratives are the very ones that by a definite parallelism show very clearly definite traces of a degree of artificial revision. If the two accounts are to be brought into harmony, refuge must be taken in artifices. Either the relationship between the two families must have been broken off deliberately, or John the Baptist or John the Evangelist — one or the other — must have covered something up or have falsified the account. In the final analysis, however subtly and ingeniously the pious fraud may be represented, the results are always ingenious hypotheses that remain unconvincing.

Now, we ask, granted that the two accounts in John and Luke cannot be harmonized, which is the more authoritative? There can be no hesitation about which we are to choose. Wherever Luke's narrative may have come from, the evidence that it was assembled and revised for an aesthetic purpose is incontrovertible. It is difficult, however, to distinguish what in this complex of narratives must be regarded as fact and what belongs to the work of the reviser. Consequently my own judgment is that this narrative cannot gainsay the specific statement by the Baptist that he had not known Jesus previously. If you assume that there is truth in the (Luke) narrative, but that in some way John and Jesus had been separated and had never met again, the fact remains that John would have known from his mother that the son of a relative of hers had been designated before his birth as Messiah. Therefore I cannot understand why he would not have added: ''I knew that he was the Messiah, but I didn't know him personally." If anyone prefers to accept such an interpretation in order to assure the complete historicity of Luke's narrative, I shall raise no objections, but, for my part, I cannot persuade myself that it is historical. If we refuse to ascribe any concealment or distortion of fact to the Baptist and insist on the plain meaning of what he said, we are compelled to conclude that there had been no personal relationship between John and Jesus.

What happened at Christ's baptism itself? It is difficult, in fact, in my judgment it is impossible, to harmonize the various accounts. One would have to assume, to say the least, that here and there some misunderstood facts have been introduced into one story that are in contradiction to the others.* In Matthew 3:13 we find a passage in which an earlier acquaintance of John and Jesus is presupposed. Mark epitomizes this narrative in 1:9 ff., but even Mark's story introduces a change into the account. In Mark the voice from heaven addresses Christ, but in Matthew it speaks of Jesus in the third person. According to Matthew, the voice was not directed to Jesus and was therefore intended less for him than for John. In the account in *Matthew,* furthermore, it is doubtful to whom the verb "he saw" refers. It can be interpreted as referring to Jesus, but it can also refer to John, who is the main subject of the sentence. Since the voice in the account in Mark addresses Jesus, we conclude that in this version the voice of the spirit is also intended for him.† In Luke the matter is presented similarly in 3:21 ff. Here we have the same address to Jesus, and so we have two accounts that support each other. Jesus is represented as the one who sees the descent of the dove, and the whole event is related to him, but, in comparison to Mark, strengthened by the phrase *en soi eudokēsa* ["with thee I am well pleased"] instead of the *en hō* ["in whom"] found in Mark [*textus receptus*]. In Matthew it is doubtful whether *hōsei peristeran* ["like a dove"] refers to the form assumed by the Spirit or to the Spirit's movement,

---

* in one or the other of the narratives something must have been introduced that is not compatible with the others

† or add: From this it follows that the baptism was a significant event for Jesus.

138

which may be described as like that of a dove as it flies down. According to the Evangelist *John,* John the Baptist says, *"I myself did not know him,"** and in so doing he contradicts the account in Matthew, where the Baptist at first refuses to baptize Christ. If we are to listen to the Baptist himself as the one who took part in the event, then the account in Matthew, according to which John already knew Jesus *before the baptism,* cannot be correct: "I saw the Spirit descend like a dove from heaven, and, behold, a voice spoke from heaven, 'This is . . . .' "

Here the account of John the Baptist is similar to that of *Simeon* in an earlier Lukan narrative and is not to be regarded as an original revelation. In relation to the messianic expectation that he held, we find that in this case a sign was given him by which he was to recognize the Messiah. At the same time, however, that is bound up with his commission to baptize. In other words, as he exercised his vocation it was granted him that he should recognize the Messiah, a reward, as it were, for exercising his calling. Since that is what John the Baptist himself says, the narrative is related to him.[†] John, however, restricts his reference to this visible sign. There is nothing in his words in John 1:31-34 to confirm Luke's statement about the bodily form. Consequently, either the other narratives are based on other sources, or they have embellished the account in John. Now, there can be no other original source than a narrative that comes from John or a narrative that comes from Christ. Of the latter, however, that coming from Christ, not the slightest trace can be found. Furthermore, a narrative that comes from Christ would be wholly superfluous, for it was to Christ's first disciples that John recounted the incident. Other sources are also impossible to conceive, or the hypothesis, for that matter, that John himself could have given a more detailed account on some other occasion. Since the recognition of the Messiah was the decisive moment in the baptism and the reason why John referred his disciples to Christ, it is impossible to believe that

---

* or add: I saw the Spirit descend as a dove from heaven, and it remained on him.
† or add: In John's account everything is related only to the Baptist.

139

the Baptist omitted reference to such an important element as the physical descent of the dove! It is easy to see how all these elaborations were derived from the original narrative, but in comparison to it they carry no weight. *Everything miraculous that happened at Christ's baptism happened only for John.* In connection with Matthew's account we cannot take refuge in the hypothesis that before the baptism John said to Christ, "It is not my place to baptize you, but yours to baptize me," but after he had recognized the sign he was able to say, "I need to be baptized by you, etc. " We do not need to say that this latter statement is false, but only that it is set in the wrong context. No one can possibly take objection to the fact that something is incorrectly placed in our Gospels, for that is something of which we have any number of examples in other accounts. The New Testament narratives are to be treated like all others, and the correct conclusion is to be drawn from the differences by means of pure historical research. Consequently the whole incident takes on another appearance. The conclusion we reach is not that at the baptism anything miraculous happened for Christ's sake, that at the baptism he learned for the first time that he was the "beloved Son of God", but that everything miraculous happened only for John's sake.

Christ's motive in permitting himself to be baptized by John, regardless of the fact that the act had no special relationship to him, is to be found in Jesus' words, "Thus it is fitting for us to fulfill all righteousness." In other words, he regarded the acceptance of John's baptism as a moment in his life that would have significance for the nation. In what connection did he do that? If we take our departure from the fact that John baptized "for the forgiveness of sins", we are not to understand that in the sense that John thought that forgiveness of sins would be the result of his baptism. If that had been the general opinion, Jesus would not have been able to permit himself to be baptized by John. But that was not what John believed. On the contrary, from the account of typical Johannine practice, the fact emerges that, in view of the imminent appearance of the Messiah, John wished only to awaken the consciousness that members of the Jewish people, if they were to have a part in the Messiah's proclamation, would first have to purge their sins, that in their sins they could not take part in Christ's mission. John wished to counteract the conviction of the Jews of his day that they already had a part in the future messianic kingdom because of the merit that accrued from observance of the law. John's baptism was nothing other than a symbolic act with reference to the position of the Jewish people as such, by which everyone who submitted to it acknowledged that he must abandon the way of sin if he wished to have a part in the messianic kingdom. So there was nothing to prevent Jesus from accepting baptism. But what was his reason for doing so? By accepting baptism Jesus acknowledged that he held the same view of the messianic kingdom that John proclaimed and adopted thereby as his own what as a consequence was to be regarded as a witness to the proclamation of John, but which at the moment was the symbolic beginning of his own proclamation. If he had not done this, John's proclamation could have remained questionable and he would not have given the Baptist the recognition that he was obliged to give of the connection of John's mission with his own. Therefore he said: *By accepting baptism I am obliged to acknowledge you in your mission as my forerunner.*

Lecture 22 (June 20). The marvelous as related only to John and as not involving Christ is actually no concern of ours. The promise given to John can also be explained on the assumption that by it he was directed to observe the one who would eventually appear, and so he may have been wrong in believing that it was fulfilled by that appearance, whose connection with the saying of God rested only on his own interpretation of it. [Accordingly perhaps also the later question, leaving its wholly spiritual interpretation out of consideration, that is involved in the words "he who baptizes with the Holy Spirit."] What is marvelous can be explained by the opening of heaven and the light of the apocryphal gospels as a light phenomenon. The reference to the dove can be understood as a gentle indication either of form or of movement, and the statement that it would remain can only be interpreted as a gradual disappearance on Christ.

The idea that the baptism was an inauguration has obtained much support from the fact that the story of the baptism is followed by that of the temptation. The temptation story cannot be harmonized with the account in John's Gospel, unless we assume that these forty days were located between Christ's baptism and the message to John and that Jesus returned after the temptation to the area in which John was carrying on his work — an assumption that runs counter to the narrative as we have it in Luke's Gospel. Since only Christ can have told the story, the variation in order in the different accounts is difficult to explain. (Elsewhere in our Gospels sayings of Christ exhibit the fewest differences.) We should have to assume that Christ had given separate accounts of the different temptations. However, even the separate temptation narratives are not to be viewed as historical accounts. The changing of stones into bread, if it were necessary, would not have been a sin. The casting of himself down from a pinnacle of the temple could have had no attraction for Christ.

Taking everything into consideration, then, we have to say that Christ's acceptance of baptism was not something that in any respect he did for his own sake. On the contrary, in the course of his life it was only a transition point in a ministry that had already begun but which had not yet assumed its full form. It was such a transition point to the extent that it was an acknowledgment of that theory that was set forth symbolically in the Baptist's institution, namely, of a "kingdom of heaven", of an *'ŏlam ha-ba'* ["age to come"], which could rest only on the basis of a moral transformation and whose new life could not be said to be conditioned by the earlier excellence of the Jewish people. If we consider the baptism of Christ as a public act, it was performed only for John's sake, an acknowledgment (or: recognition) which Christ gave him, and both aspects cannot be separated from each other. To be sure, Jesus could have confirmed John's teaching without permitting himself to be baptized by him, but in so doing he would not have established the historical connection as the nature of the matter demanded. He would have separated John's ministry from his own, whereas by its very nature it had an immediate relationship to his own.

Consequently *the marvelous element* in the narrative of Christ's baptism does not interest us, and we are not obliged in this investigation to form a definite concept of it, since it had to do with John rather than with Jesus and because it only happened in relation to Jesus and his surroundings, but did not proceed from him or come about as a result of his own actions. Furthermore, the accounts differ widely from one another and are difficult to harmonize. The narratives in the other Gospels can easily be accounted for as embellishments of the narrative in the Gospel of John, which is the actual source. The matter is quite different with respect to the apocryphal gospels. These have an element in their versions which is lacking in the canonical Gospels, namely, an extraordinary light, analogous to that which appeared at the time of the apostle Paul's conversion. There is still another point to be taken into consideration. If we compare what John the Baptist declares in his account to have been a divine promise to him and what he says he saw at Jesus' baptism, a certain incongruence between the two becomes apparent. He says that He who sent him to baptize had said to him, "He on whom you see the Spirit descend and remain, this is he who baptizes with the Holy Spirit." We see that this latter was the form in which the idea of Christ was set forth in this discussion between God and the Baptist, and that is a completely spiritual concept. Then John saw the Holy Spirit descend as a dove on Christ and remain on him, and the Baptist acknowledges that he is the Son of God. How is the verb "to remain" to be understood in the one and in the other passage? From the conclusion we see that John regarded the phenomenon as the fulfillment of that divine utterance, but if the descent was something visible, the remaining must also have been something visible, and how are we to understand that? No one can possibly think of the remaining in this connection other than as a brief sojourn — certainly not as a continuous one. In the promise, however, this is not at all what is expressed, for there nothing visible is meant. What we read there is only "the Spirit descended", without any reference to the "dove." Accordingly we can say, We could just as easily understand the promise in a different way, namely, as something that could only be perceived as the result of continued observation, without anything visible being involved,* and on the other hand it would be only the *praesens* that marks the beginning, for the remaining could

* without the sojourn of the Spirit in him constantly remaining

143

only be perceived by viewing his work. If the "remaining" is something temporary, then the promise is incomplete, and also the account, for we do not learn where what John saw descending on Christ remained. If in addition we take the narrative of the apocryphal gospels into consideration and also, according to our Gospels, regard the opening of heaven as preceding the descent, both can easily be combined into one account and it would appear that what John saw was a light phenomenon which came out of a rift in the clouds, and "like a dove" is easily understood as an indication of the form of enclosure or movement.

The usual view — the view that the baptism of Christ was an important and significant event for him himself, an inauguration, as it were, of his public ministry and therefore the opening point of his public life — receives support from the fact that our first three Evangelists attach the story of the *temptation* directly to that of the baptism. Therefore we can do no other than take this temptation story into consideration in connection with that of the baptism and with it bring our account of the transition from the period of Christ's preparation to that of his continuous influential activity to a close, in order then to begin the second main part of his life. In this connection it is worthy of note that the first three Gospels contain the account, whereas in John it is not only entirely missing, but also the very possibility of inserting it does not exist. In the other Gospels this story covers a period of forty days, and it is scarcely possible to find a place in the Gospel of John for such a period after the baptism. This is the way things stand in the Gospel of John: An embassy from Jerusalem comes to the Baptist that inquires concerning his claims, and in his answer he refers to the one who was to come after him and says that that one is already here. On the following day John saw Jesus approaching him and then told his disciples that he it was of whom he had spoken the day before. Then, on the day after that (v. 35), John stood again with two of his disciples and saw Jesus as he walked and said, "Behold, the Lamb of God!" Then two of his disciples went to Jesus, and after Christ's first conversation with them we read at the beginning of chapter 2: On the third day there was a marriage at *Cana,* where the mother of Jesus was also, etc. Therefore no period of forty days can possibly be inserted into the events as they are narrated. The only possibility is that the period of forty days might be located between Christ's baptism and the coming of the embassy to John. If this were the case, Jesus must have returned after the temptation to the area where John had been baptizing, and from there he must have gone to the marriage at Cana, but of such things the other Gospels have nothing to say. Matthew, to be sure, leaves a very large gap at this point. He makes the temptation follow directly upon the baptism. However, he employs "then" as the connecting link, an adverb which in this Gospel is something very indefinite, and after the temptation had come to an end he says only that when Jesus had heard that John had been arrested he withdrew into Galilee. It is possible to think of many things as having happened in between. The story of the temptation in *Mark* is so brief that it emphasizes virtually only the marvelous and magical elements in the event. *Luke,* after mentioning Christ's age, attaches *the genealogy* to the story of the baptism and then says that Jesus, full of the Holy Spirit, returned from the Jordan, was led by the Spirit in the wilderness, and was tempted forty days by the devil. Here we have a definite *contradiction of John,* for there remains no possibility of inserting the period of forty days into John's account if Jesus went from the wilderness to Galilee. According to Luke's account, Jesus could not have gone back to the area in which John at that time was baptizing. The account in *Matthew* raises still other questions, for it speaks at this time already of *the arrest* of John, whereas the Evangelist John represents John the Baptist as baptizing in the area in which Jesus was already permitting his disciples to baptize. Therefore we must *completely ignore* Matthew's chronology of this period and hold fast all the more to that in John.

We have two accounts of the temptation, that in *Matthew* and that in *Luke.* Mark gives only a few external marvelous circumstances that were associated with it. As is well known, both accounts record three temptations of the devil, three attempts to mislead Christ, but these temptations are not recorded in both accounts in the same order. In *Matthew* the first temptation records that the devil proposed to Christ that, because he was hungry, he should transform stones into bread. The second temptation is the suggestion that Christ throw himself down from a pinnacle of the temple. The third is that the devil took him to a very high mountain and showed him all the kingdoms of the world and offered them to him, etc., and only then did Christ order the devil to leave him. Since the very high mountain is not named, we cannot identify the locality exactly. In *Luke* the first temptation is the same as that in Matthew, but no mention is made of the temptations as lasting *for a period of forty days*. On the contrary, we are told that Christ, after he had eaten nothing for forty days, was hungry, and then the first temptation is recorded. In *Matthew* we are not told that Christ *was tempted* for forty days, but that he *had fasted* for that length of time, and then the first temptation began. In *Luke* the temptation that is *the third* in *Matthew* follows upon the first, and *last of all* Satan conducts Christ for the first time to Jerusalem. It is worthy of note in this connection that already in the second temptation Luke makes Christ utter a rejection of Satan, and then Satan tempts him a third time and Christ *actually follows him to Jerusalem*. Even here the accounts in the Gospels are already in disagreement with each other. *Taken individually* the temptations are similarly recorded, but not *in their sequence*. They differ also in their whole view of the event, for in Matthew Christ fasts for forty days, but no one knows *why, and what actually happened during that time*. In Luke Christ is tempted for forty days, but this state of being tempted is referred to only in general. Nothing in detail is mentioned. The detail is introduced only in what follows.

What conclusion are we to draw from this disagreement? If we are to take the accounts as they are represented, as records of an event that took place immediately after Christ's baptism, at a time when nothing is yet said of any disciples of Christ and when Christ alone is represented as having been led by the Spirit into the wilderness, the question that arises first is: Whence do these narratives derive? They can only have come from Christ, for no one was with him. Therefore,

146

unless they are fabrications, they must derive from him. It is a truth that we often find confirmed in these first Gospels that always the fewest deviations occur in what are presented *as sayings of Christ.* So one ought to think that these accounts would probably agree more exactly and thus support the conclusion reached elsewhere. As it is, however, the two narratives cannot be based on the same original account. One Evangelist must therefore have understood what Christ said on the whole quite differently from the other, for the one understood the event as a forty-day temptation, while the other thought of the first temptation as having been preceded by a forty-day fast. In addition to this there is the difference in arrangement of the temptations and in their sequence. So it is natural to ask how it is possible that a narrative that comes from Christ, that he himself told his disciples, could have been composed in such different ways. The first suggestion that comes to mind is that the temptation story as we have it is made up not of *one* account but of *several.* If Christ had spoken of the individual temptations separately rather than as a connected whole, the variations in the final form of the story in Matthew and in Luke would be readily explained. The item of a forty-day fast would belong only to the first temptation, which presupposes that Christ was hungry. If therefore we think only of the two accounts by themselves, the difference between them is reduced to the fact that one speaks of Jesus as "being tempted" for forty days in the wilderness, while the other speaks of him as "fasting" for forty days. If there were originally separate accounts of several temptations, we can understand how they came to be combined in different ways.

Assuming it as probable that the temptation story records a *fact,* the further question arises: What actually was its result? The usual view of the matter is that the temptation of Christ was as it were the *second part* of his inauguration: he had to resist Satan's temptation and by this means as it were overcome him, so that he might bring him under his power, and Christ's driving out of devils is explained from this point of view. The devils had to obey him. But the narrative in the Gospel of *Luke* does not permit such a view and is distinguished in this respect from that in the Gospel of *Matthew*, on which alone the view depends. The conclusion of Matthew's story is different from that in Luke, namely, "until an opportune time," that is, until another occasion, so that there are no grounds for asserting that Satan was overcome as a result of Christ's withstanding of the temptation. Now the question arises: Can we regard these temptations as an actual battle that Christ fought and which gave him victory over Satan? If we reflect on the fact that Jesus was beset with a hunger that threatened his very life and that at that point Satan proposed to him that he change stones into loaves of bread, and then go on to ask: In light of all this, would it have been a *sin* if he had done that? our answer is that no one could *maintain* that. *It was his duty to do what he could to nourish himself in a situation dangerous to his life.* In the second place, Christ would not have waited for Satan to give him advice. In similar fashion it is incredible that Satan should have proposed to Christ that he throw himself down from a pinnacle of the temple. The act would be so valueless spiritually that the sight of it would no doubt have produced amazement but not admiration. The act would have been wholly unworthy of Christ, and one cannot see that he could have hesitated a moment whether to do it or not. The story of this temptation presupposes that Christ had no moral power. It also assumes that Satan did not have much intelligence, for he would not have obtained his goal by this temptation, and the people would have asked: *Cui bono?*

Lecture 23 (June 21). Equally without attraction was the offer by Satan of an earthly lordship, for Christ's nature had no inclination in that direction. But also, taken as a whole, the temptation story is inconceivable. Does Christ know Satan or not? Does he walk visibly with him in the sight of men, or is the event magical? The story is also devoid of all purpose. Consequently other explanations. Vision, dream, or historical expression of an inward experience. The last-mentioned would put Christ on a very subordinate level. The same would be true if we were to accept the hypothesis of a dream, for if Christ had not recognized himself again in it, he would not have related it in such a way that a narrative could have been made out of it. The hypothesis of a vision supernaturally mediated suffers from an absolute lack of purpose. The only other explanation is that the story is a parable. The teachings were valuable for the disciples in the fulfillment of their calling. There are only two difficulties with which we still have to contend: the difference in arrangement and the misinterpretation. The former can be most easily explained as follows: When the parable was first treated as a story, Matthew kept the inner development in mind but, on account of the two journeys with the devil, had to neglect the outer development. Luke tried to make the outer representation of the event more credible, but did an injustice to the inner development. The misinterpretation itself was not original but is the work of a later hand. It was the result of the same way of thinking as that which has preserved it for so long.

Even if we regard Jesus wholly and purely from the human point of view and reflect on the disposition and the individual traits of character that he exhibited in his life, we discover in them no tendency in the direction of a worldly lordship, no trace of any inclination to such an activity, and in the circumstances there exists absolutely no possibility that he could have prepared himself in any way for such a role. To be sure, there are traces enough among the Jewish people of that time, quite unrelated to messianic expectations, of sedition and of a desire to secure independence, but these were wild and imprudent agitations, without any intelligible plan and without any possibility of success. We cannot possibly think of Jesus as involved in such impracticable plots, for his whole disposition was opposed to them. So then, what sort of a temptation could it have been if Satan had offered him all the kingdoms of the world on condition that he should worship him? Such a proposition could have had no attraction for him. It would have had no appeal for him as a temptation!

If we consider the story in and for itself, we see that *in general* it contains absolutely nothing that makes it credible. We are told that the Spirit led Jesus into the wilderness in order that he might be tempted there. This statement is so obscure that we find it difficult to think of it [with any clarity]. Following upon the baptism it gives the impression that Christ had received the Spirit for the first time at his baptism; that, infused with a wholly new life principle, he had been led into the wilderness. The sojourn in the wilderness

149

has been explained as Christ's attempt to secure privacy in order to think through the course his life was to take. This hypothesis is based on an interpretation of the baptism that we have rejected, namely, that the baptism had been a significant event for Christ himself, or even that after his baptism he became aware for the first time of his own mission. All this is quite incompatible with the way we have conceived his human development. The course of his life had already been determined by *the inner self-consciousness peculiar to himself,* and in all that follows there is nothing that gives any evidence of a plan that was the result of a definite, specially instituted reflection, and even less of one so constituted that it would have required a forty-day period of complete retirement from the world about him.

Leaving all that out of consideration, what is the story that Christ had to be tempted by Satan intended to say? If we wish to think of him as we do of all other similar men, we have to assert: He had to meet temptation throughout his entire life. In order to be tempted he had no more need of a special confrontation with Satan as the principle of temptation than any other man. Temptations emerged of themselves in the course of his life. However, if we view him in the light of his peculiar dignity and as equipped with divine power, by means of which he was free of all sin, then such a state of being tempted appears as purposeless. For whom was it actually intended? Was it designed to give him the consciousness that he had a power which made him incapable of sin? He must already have had such a consciousness, for that is what distinguished him from all other men. He could not have obtained this consciousness for the first time by the temptation, for the three elements in it could not have constituted a temptation for him. If we were to imagine that this temptation was as it were a test to which Christ was exposed and that after he had as it were withstood this test in God's sight he had become sure of his mission, we should have to conclude that he had an easier task than any other man. We are not tested so briefly, but the test lasts throughout our entire lifetime, and it appears as an outer form that has to be observed. But we are not in this connection to think of a natural law or to establish a theological point that represents the purpose for anyone of this outer form, for God must also have known that others did not possess this relationship. There is also no evidence that Christ's disciples were led to believe in him because he told this story of his temptation.

Well then, in what relationship are we to think of Jesus as opposed to Satan? Did he recognize him or not? The story says nothing about this except that at the end, when he ordered him to depart from him, he addressed him as *Satan*. If we conclude from the natural place this temptation has in Matthew that this command was obeyed and that this temptation was *the last,* then it is possible to believe that Christ recognized Satan for the first time when Satan demanded that he should worship him. But this understanding of the matter is not clear. If Christ had recognized Satan, it is natural that *he was not able to accept anything of what he offered him,* and then one would have to abandon the idea that the proposition was a temptation. It could only have been a temptation for him *if he had been afraid* that he stood under Satan's power, but that is not the kind of story we have. Satan would have *threatened* him, but there is no indication that that happened. On the other hand, Satan would not have been able to tempt Christ if Christ had recognized him. If Christ had recognized him only in the course of the last temptation, this would necessarily have introduced a difference into the last temptation, of which there is no indication. And so far as the content of *the first two* temptations is concerned, the proposals they contained were not of the sort that could have enticed Christ. If his hunger had endangered Christ's life, the use of his miraculous powers would in no case have been a sin. *The temptation, therefore, cannot be regarded as a fact.*

This conclusion has frequently been reached, and all sorts of attempts have been made to explain the narrative. In the first place, it has been said that the story is not history. Christ only presents in the form of historical account what had happened *within him* at the time when he was about to begin his life's work. In my judgment this hypothesis would make it impossible for us any longer to believe in Christ. If Christ had been able to entertain the thought of witnessing to himself

151

and thereby of arousing belief in himself on the part of the people by such an act as that of hurling himself to earth from the pinnacle of the temple, then his very entertainment of this idea would at once mean the end of my faith. Furthermore, if the thought of founding an earthly kingdom had been able to enter his mind, he would then *eo ipso* not have been the one who was to found the kingdom of God, for the desire for an earthly kingdom presupposes an entirely different disposition. Consequently this hypothesis can be similar (or: acceptable) only to those who put Christ wholly on the same level with all other men — in fact, *below* them. Just as clearly as an understanding of the event as offers and proposals on the part of Satan would make it no temptation for Christ, this other hypothesis, that he could entertain such an idea, does not agree with what we otherwise know of him. It would make him appear as *one inconsistent with himself, who had experiences that cannot be understood on the analogy of the whole and who stands on a level lower than other men — men who can be the object only of ordinary attention.*

The situation is little different when others have said that the narrative is an account of an inner process, but of the nature of a vision. It was a *vision* that Christ experienced, and he told his disciples of this *vision.* Similar to this is the idea that the whole affair was a *dream* that Christ dreamed which he recounted with such vitality that his disciples were misled into regarding it as a historical account. If we think of a *vision* as something effected supernaturally, it must therefore have been the result of *a foreign influence* that entered into his soul. On the other hand, if we think of a vision as a product of a heightened condition of an individual's soul power, in other words, as a product of *an exalted fantasy,* then, if it is *his own work,* it can never be untrue to *the character of the man.* The same thing is true of *a dream,* to the extent that the dreamer can believe it is worth the trouble of recounting the dream. If the dream is something that represents an individual as acting otherwise than is in accord with his nature,* we regard it as a physical rather than as a

* or add: in such a case one tells only the strange content of the dream, and any confusion with fact would be impossible

psychical phenomenon, and it loses all value for him. So far as I am concerned, then, all these hypotheses get us nowhere.

However, there is still another explanation, one that has already often been advanced, which also presents several difficulties, but the fewest difficulties of all, namely, that the whole account was a parable, a parable in which Christ presented himself as the subject, a parable about himself, but *for his disciples.* The various parts of the temptation story contain rules for the disciples which were of the greatest importance with reference to the manner in which they should organize their leadership in the office entrusted to them. (1) In light of all that Christ elsewhere had told them of the way they would fare, an unlimited trust in God with respect to their external needs, such as is set forth in the first temptation, was indispensable to them. The meaning of the saying, Man does not live by bread alone, etc., is clearly that, if ordinary ways do not suffice, God knows how to use extraordinary means to achieve his ultimate purpose. In accordance with this rule the disciples were to have a firm trust in God. As long as their ministry would be necessary, God would know how to support them, whether by ordinary or by extraordinary means. (2) It was equally necessary, to the extent that they shared Christ's wonderworking powers, that they should abstain from making any display of what was entrusted to them and never to use such gifts in order to obtain a vain renown. They were to regard every such inclination as proceeding from a principle opposed to Christianity. (3) What has been said above applies also to the last temptation. The possibility of exercising civil power and lordship was remote so far as the disciples were concerned, but the temptation to exercise a personal authority and a personal, spiritual lordship was ever present, and as Christ warns them elsewhere against it, he did so also in this instance in terms of a symbolic warning. Thus the individual temptations take on a significance, but not if they are related to Christ himself. All that makes it impossible to understand the story if it is regarded as history loses its difficulty if the account is viewed as a parable,* for

* or add: so I do not hesitate to adopt an interpretation that removes all difficulties

in a parable such presuppositions were permitted in order to give expression to the thought.†

There are only two difficulties that remain: the difference in the order of the temptations, and how to explain the transformation of what Christ told as a parable into a historical account (for it is clear that the narrative is represented in both Gospels as history). 1) It is not difficult to discover a certain principle at work in Matthew's arrangement, and also one in Luke's, although a different one. In Matthew the principle of arrangement is *an inward one*. The relationship between both actors develops from one temptation to the other. The first proposal is one that anyone could have made, and therefore the relationship is not definitely apparent. The second temptation presupposes an attitude of hostility. Either Christ could perish if he were to follow the advice and God were not to protect him in some direct way, or he could acquire a morally unhealthy influence in public opinion. In the final temptation the hostility becomes most evident, for Satan demands that Christ subject (or: subordinate) himself to him, and that is the strongest proposal. In all this, however, the outer congruity of the temptations is surprisingly neglected, for the first scene is located in the wilderness, from which Satan conducts Christ to the pinnacle of the temple and then to a high mountain, which cannot be thought of as in the vicinity of Jerusalem. A mountain from which the "kingdoms of the world" can be pointed out is wholly inconceivable, (for) even if we do (or: do not) limit ourselves to Palestine,* no such mountain exists. In any case, such a mountain would be a long way from Jerusalem, and consequently it is difficult to think of such journeyings hither and yon. The narrative in Luke is governed by a *geographical* principle, which on its part neglects the inner development of the parable. We can most easily think of the high mountain as located in the wilderness, for the wilderness bordered on a mountain range. Accordingly, the Lukan account makes Jerusalem and the pinnacle of the temple the location of the last temptation, and then Satan

† or add: and these were a suitable framework for this parabolic form
* or add: even if we include Herodian and Roman territory

disappears. On the other hand, this arrangement has the disadvantage that the temptation in which Christ bids Satan "begone!" is the second rather than the last, so that it represents Satan as not obedient to Christ and as tempting him for a third time. We see again what in the temptation were words of Christ is identical. If Luke had been free to do as he pleased with the tradition, he would have transferred the words to the final temptation, but as it was he left Christ's words in their original setting. To the extent that we understand these differing principles of arrangement it is not difficult to explain the difference in the two accounts. Christ related the various temptations separately.

2) Let us now turn to the second remaining difficulty. The parable was later regarded as history. This transition must account for the two variant arrangements, the one concerned mainly with the inner development, and the other with the outer. So we see that the different arrangement itself is an argument for such a transition and that such a transition took place is the conclusion that can most easily be drawn from the difference in arrangement. But the fact that what was originally a parable should have been understood as history presents a peculiar difficulty. Here we must start by properly assessing the distance that separated the original narrative from our present Gospels. So far as the narrative in *Luke* is concerned, the distance between it and the original is generally acknowledged. If we assume that Luke did not get his account from those to whom Christ directly told it and who must have known that it was a parable (for the disciples could not have erred in this connection) and that it passed through several hands, the transition from parable to history is understandable. Rabbinical writings provide any number of illustrations of how what were obviously parables are related so clearly as histories that one cannot distinguish the one from the other. If we recall in addition that in certain thought circles, namely, in those that inclined to Ebionite and Nazorean ideas, it was easy to think of Christ as in a situation in which he would set the seal on his mission by such a victory over Satan, we can readily see how the parable came to be regarded as a historical narrative.

SECOND PERIOD

The Public Life of Christ to the Time of His Arrest

Lecture 24 (June 22). Since the state of the material does not permit a coherent presentation within the limits of this period, it appears appropriate to deal with the main natural points of view of an account of the life of Christ. We distinguish between *the outer and the inner side.* To the first belong *locality and external relationships,* as well as also *the external arrangement of life.* To the *inner* side belong *teaching* and *the foundation of a community.* The national relationships and the miracles are ambiguous. We reckon the former as belonging to the inner side, for they form the counterpart of the foundation of a community, while we place the latter among those that are related to the outer side, for they are always performed on specific occasions. We do not view the baptism as the beginning of Christ's public ministry. There remain, however, thirty years of general *usus.* If the age relationship between John and Christ that is specified by Luke is historical, then both men were about the same age. If Jesus had submitted to baptism as soon as John appeared, less would be known of the fact and it would have exercised less influence. So we accept the estimate that Christ was thirty years of age when he began his ministry, for he would not have spent more time than was necessary in education. We also must think of him as imparting much as a preliminary exercise, although not under the guise of public teaching. ' We regard his arrest as the end of this period. From that point on everything constitutes one act, and the source material we have has a different form.

Without attempting to define the point at which Christ's public life began — I cannot accept the idea that Christ's baptism by John had any special'significance for him — we can only hold fast to what Luke tells us and what corresponds to the custom of the time. It was the custom that no one should appear as a public teacher before his thirtieth year, and Luke designates Christ's age as thirty years. John's baptism can hardly have been administered only to people who had reached a certain age, and therefore we cannot maintain that Christ did not permit himself to be baptized until he had attained the age of thirty years. Let me note another circumstance. For the relationship between Christ and John we have no other authority than the account in Luke which, in light of its whole composition, is not easy to accept as a historical witness. The same Lukan narrative is also our only authority for the age relationship between John and Christ — information that we also cannot accept as a historical datum. Were we to regard it as historical we should also have to accept the general view, namely, that if John were only six months older than Christ, he could not have appeared and would not have begun to baptize before he had reached his thirtieth year. But we cannot assume that Christ was among the first who accepted John's baptism. Only after this baptism had become something public could it have been worth John's trouble to protest Christ's coming to him for baptism, etc. So then, if we accept the Lukan· narrative as historical, the baptism of Christ and the beginning of his public life must have virtually coincided. However, if we doubt the historicity of that account, such a conclusion also becomes doubtful. Once we think of Christ's public appearance as the result of an inner urge to communicate himself, we think of it as *a gradual process*. To the extent that his outer perception of the state of his people became complete, to that extent the inner urge to communicate himself must have become stronger and have expressed itself in an outer act. Having said this, however, it does not follow that Christ had to restrain himself and repress this urge without expression until he was thirty years of age. On the contrary, it is possible to think of many forms of communication that do not correspond to the actual type of public appearance and that could have preceded that public appearance, in the first instance as practice, and secondly as the satisfaction of his inner urge. Only his *actual public teaching* cannot be thought of as beginning earlier than this point of time. In this connection, however, it is uncertain whether Christ had not already engaged in public teaching before he accepted baptism. I myself regard it as possible that he did, for only then can the act of accepting John's baptism take on significance. I am also driven to this conclusion because of the statement in the Gospel of John that presupposes that Christ had disciples before anything could have been known of his baptism.*

So far as *the conclusion* of this second part of Christ's ministry is concerned, it is inevitable that we should regard the end of his public ministry as coinciding with his *arrest* and the beginning of his sufferings. To be sure, Christ was a public person also during this time of his life, but the ministry that was characteristic of this earlier period no longer is pursued. In addition, the material that is introduced from the moment that the sufferings begin is different from what precedes it. Prior to the passion story the material is disconnected and the individual narratives are beset with contradictions. The passion story, on the other hand, appears in all the Gospels as a connected account and, although even here apparent contradictions are not lacking, such contradictions are of quite a different character. The passion story is concerned with a judicial process and the contradictions are related only to individual elements in the same whole, whereas the individual elements from the actual life of Christ are isolated and the connection of events can be viewed much more variously.† Therefore it is desirable to make the division as we have suggested and to give a separate treatment of that part of the life of Christ that begins with his arrest.

Now the question arises: How are we actually to proceed in this section? If our task were to deal with all the narratives of the four Gospels in general and in the same way, since they form an unconnected collection of material we should have to abandon all attempts at giving a connected presentation, and then we should be necessarily compelled to follow a different procedure. To be sure, all the Gospels are not equally composed of disconnected material. There is a significant difference in this respect between the first three Gospels and the Gospel of John. The first three are so unmistakably an account composed of originally separate narratives that, even

* or add: and only so could disciples of Jesus have been invited to Galilee before anything was known there of his baptism
† or add: On the other hand, contradictions in unconnected narratives are much more difficult.

if the composition were complete and without a gap, the problem would remain the same and no account of the life of Christ as a unity could be discovered in them. That, however, is not the case with the Johannine Gospel, for such a composition from earlier unconnected details cannot be observed there. On the contrary, the Gospel of John reveals one and the same tendency from beginning to end. It evidently comes from one who narrates what he himself had experienced. However, because it has a definite tendency, what it narrates as the content of a period is just as full of gaps as the other Gospel accounts. The periods which John skips he specifies, and he skips them because they contain nothing of interest to his special tendency. The tendency of this Gospel can be described as follows: The author wishes to make understandable the disaster in Christ's destiny together with the authentic nature of his activity, while — regarding the matter from John's own standpoint — the two conflicted with one another. Everyone who had, like John, won through to faith, had to expect that Christ would be recognized by all in the same way, and the catastrophe had therefore to be viewed in general as something that appeared unexpectedly. However, he wishes to make it comprehensible, and consequently everything is set forth in order to give a clear picture, in the first place of the actual nature of Christ's activity, and in the second place of the development of his relationship to the people and to the authorities among the people, and to make both comprehensible side by side with one another. A relationship exists, but only in this particular connection. For those, however, who undertake the task of viewing the life of Jesus in its *continuity,* the Evangelist John is just as unsatisfactory as the others. For our task, then, the difference is not as great as if we were to compare the Gospels in and for themselves with one another. Therefore John does not ease our task as we might actually expect in view of the significant difference between him and the other three.

If we ask what would be the essential points for viewing the life of Christ, (or add: in its continuity) we are reminded here in every respect of the relative contrast in every individual life between its *inner unity* and the limitation placed on its appearance by *the external relationships*. If one is to be able completely to carry out the task of giving an account of a life, both must be kept in view in their connection and interconnection with each other. If one has therefore reached such a point as that on which we now stand, the task is: If one has reached the point in the development of a life where the public, connected influential activity (or: spontaneity) of the man begins in the world, then a certain view of *his internal side* already exists because of what has gone before, and also a knowledge of the totality of his *external* relationships. We have attempted to achieve the former by means of our common presupposition and from what we were able to reconstruct from the few notices that were at our disposal. Assuming that Christ was such a one as he appears to be by reason of the historical connection of his entire ministry, how did he gradually develop in this period of his life, if we regard that life purely as a human one? We have solved this problem.

We have also tried to acquire knowledge of his external relationships, but that knowledge has been very incomplete, and putting it all together we find that there emerges [follows] no sure and certain picture of the way Christ occupied himself during this period of his life. We have only picked out certain points and have said: That must have happened, and that cannot have happened. But we lack all source materials for understanding how Christ behaved in the totality of his external life relationships during this period. For example, if we were to say that Christ acquired, more or less by the employment of available helps, a knowledge of the Old Testament writings and of the history of his people such as was necessary for him as a public teacher, or if we were to say that it is not certain where he stayed throughout this whole period, but it is improbable that he spent the whole time with his family in Nazareth, significant gaps in our knowledge of his life would still remain. These gaps cannot have been filled entirely with studies, but if we do not know his social relationships with his people (or: his interests in his people), we have to leave these gaps blank. If we ask whether Christ followed the custom of the day and engaged in some business in addition to his studies, as Paul, for example, did, it would not be unnatural or improbable that, if Joseph had lived on until late in this period, Christ was a partner with him in his business and was helpful to him in it, as the apocryphal gospels distinctly report. But we have no knowledge of all this. Such activity on Christ's part would have been in accordance with custom, but it is certain that the more the whole time in this period was filled with the activity of instruction and the more he became attached to this profession, the more the other subordinate element disappeared. There is no reason to believe that Christ carried on any business activity during the period of his public ministry, but for the preceding period there is a significant gap in our knowledge. We should have to repeat here a survey of the period during which his inner life developed, as well as of the totality of his relationships, if we were to be able to pursue any further the reciprocal effect of each on the other. But both were so little connected in our source material concerning the public life of Christ that we cannot pursue this reciprocal effect with any assurance. So then, in light of the state of our source material, I know of no other way to proceed than to divide the task and pursue the individual parts for themselves. Then it will become clear of itself how important for the whole task are the unavoidable gaps, or how far we can get a coherent picture to some extent of the whole appearance of Christ.

Obviously everything that belongs to the *outer* side constitutes as it were only the framework, but it puts *a limit to the inner side* of Christ's life, *his spiritual activity.* Our main task would be *to seek to inform ourselves first of the external life of Christ* for this period and to present it as fully and clearly as possible, and *then to take into consideration his actual spiritual influential activity, which forms the inner side of his life.*

However, the fact remains that both aspects of the task cannot be completely separated. On the contrary, there are important points which belong as well to the one as to the other. For example, if we are to have a clear picture of the appearance of Christ as a connected whole, it is necessary for that picture that we know, on the one hand, what was Christ's relationship at various times to those whom he attracted to himself, his relationship to his pupils in the widest sense of the word, increasing and proceeding in an unbroken line, or composed of different movements. Viewed in and for itself, that is an external relationship, but it is connected in the closest possible way with Christ's inner activity, and one cannot easily be separated from the other. The same thing is true of that part of his contemporary world that was opposed to him. This outer relationship had such an important influence on the inner that it is impossible to keep them separate. Consequently their separation presents some difficulty. It is inherent in the state of the source material, but we could wish that it were not necessary, for it interferes with a full understanding. As things are, however, we must submit to this necessity.

Two things in the main belong to the *outer* life of Christ: in the first place, the determination of the locality in the widest sense of the word, *the where* of the life of Christ, viewed in the different points of this period; and secondly, the way and manner in which *he filled in the time* with respect to the more external parts of his life, to which, therefore, belongs his condition with respect to all external relationships of life. Both these things taken together constitute the outer side. To be sure, the *inner* side also consists of two essential parts. The first is *the self-communication of Christ under the form of teaching.* and in this connection we should have to observe how this, if we can describe it, took one form and another at different times and under different circumstances and in what way it developed. The second main part is then *the self-communication of Christ under the form of attraction.* This latter element was an important part of Christ's vocation, the task of *founding a community* (or: fellowship) bound to himself and subordinated to himself. We must seek to understand what he did to accomplish this and its result.

It will probably occur to all that something else must necessarilybe included in our presentation, something which is difficult to classify in one category or the other, namely, those expressions of Christ's life that we are accustomed to call his *miracles.* Do they belong to the inner or to the outer side? If we were to think of them independently of what distinguishes Christ inwardly from all other men, they would have no interest at all for us, except that of external facts that are difficult to explain, for they would have no relation to what makes Christ the object of our faith. If they are therefore to have a place in our account, they must have a connection with the specific dignity of Christ. However, they do not belong to the inner side of his life because they are always individual acts that are related to external matters, and proceed from and depend on Christ's external relationship to men. In this connection we see the difficulty of separating one aspect of Christ's life from the other, but we shall have to reckon the miracles, nevertheless, to the outer life, because, as they are connected, they coincide wholly with the external relationships.*

Lecture 25 (June 25). Locus 1. *The locality.* Lack of agreement in the first instance between Matthew and John, not only with reference to Jerusalem, but also with reference to the view of his homeland. John always makes excuses for a departure from Judea, whereas Matthew presupposes a domicile in Galilee, especially in Capernaum. In addition, a special disagreement with respect to the way Jesus comes for the final Passover festival. According to Matthew, from Galilee through Perea by way of Jericho. According to John, no definite indication of absence from the time of the Feast of the Tabernacles to that of the Feast of the Dedication of the Temple. After the Feast of Dedication Christ goes to Perea to an area in which John had at first baptized, returns for the raising of Lazarus, goes from there to the town of Ephraim near the wilderness, and proceeds from there to Bethany for the Feast of the Passover. These contradictions cannot be explained if all our Gospels are equally close to Jesus. If the other Gospels are more remote, we find the key to the solution of the difficulties in the fact that John also records it as the prevailing opinion in Jerusalem that Jesus was a Galilean. Luke, after passages that betray artistic combination and that have been correlated by reason of the similarity of content, presents everything in the course of a narrative of travel toward Jerusalem. According to this analogy, overlooking the fact that Jesus must often have

---

* or add: because they can only be understood in terms of the external relationships. We must therefore begin with the outer side of Christ's life as the limitation and condition of the inner, "because they [the miracles] always issue from special occasions."

had yearly reasons for going to Jerusalem, what must have happened there was gathered together in one collection. Only Hellenists could have done this.

THE EXTERNAL ASPECT OF CHRIST'S ACTIVITY

The Locality

However, here we run into very serious difficulties. It is impossible to harmonize the reports of the various Evangelists. I do not mean the differences that are to be found within the three Gospels themselves, but the great gulf that separates the first three from the Johannine Gospel. In the first place, all three of our first Gospels know of no stay on Christ's part in Jerusalem during his public life, with the exception of the one that brings his life to an end, the one that followed upon a journey by Jesus to attend the Feast of the Passover and that resulted in his arrest, whereas John has Jesus go to Jerusalem soon after his ministry began, and then often at later times. Secondly, the way in which Jesus comes to Jerusalem to this last Passover festival is quite different in the other Gospels than it is in John. Another circumstance is closely connected with this, namely, that in Matthew, the representative Gospel of the first three, the prevailing point of view is that Christ made his home in Galilee. Whenever he left Galilee a special reason for so doing is given or the absence appears as something temporary or accidental. In John, on the other hand, a different point of view is to be found. It would appear that John assumed that Jesus belonged to Judea and, whenever he leaves that territory, John gives special reasons for his doing so. In Matthew Capernaum is represented as actually Christ's usual place of residence, but of that John appears to know nothing. These differences are so important that we scarcely know how to explain them, at least if all the authors are equally close to Christ. I can explain them only on the assumption that the various apostles stood at various distances from him, a fact that accords with the nature of the Gospels. If I am compelled to adhere to the belief that our Gospel of Matthew comes from the apostle whose name it bears and if I am to assume that Mark was written as a record of the memories of Peter, I am wholly at a loss to explain how such extraordinarily different views could have arisen. We shall be in a better position to view these difficulties after we have gone into them in detail and have examined the references to localities that are made in the various Gospels.

According to Matthew, after the temptation Jesus heard that John had been put into prison, and then he returned to Galilee, that is, from the place where he had been exposed to temptation.* At this point Matthew's connected account of Christ's ministry begins for the first time. Many have claimed to have found in this the key to the whole apparent difference between Matthew and John. Matthew overlooks everything that had preceded John's arrest.† But it is by no means the case that the key is to be found here, for it is impossible that all the occasions on which the accounts of John and Matthew differ could fall into this period. If we only recall that in Matthew we have the first example of Christ's public teaching in the Sermon on the Mount, it is quite impossible that all else could be compressed into this period after John's arrest.** Jesus then settled in Capernaum, and the Matthean narrative implies that it was there that he made the acquaintance for the first time of Andrew and Peter. In John, on the other hand, the relationship with these first disciples begins immediately after Christ's baptism and, if we accept the usual view, we should have to assume that Christ had no companions, no apostles, prior to John's arrest. Then we are told in Matthew 4:23 ff. that Christ went about all Galilee, teaching in the synagogues and healing every disease and infirmity, so that his fame spread throughout all Syria. This presupposes, to be sure, a lengthy ministry on Christ's part, which could be the cause of this fame, but we cannot explain how it happens that Matthew doesn't tell us of it. All that happens in Galilee is presented according to this pattern of travel from

* apparently from the area where the temptation had taken place, and that cannot have been an exact location
† and abandoning Nazareth, Christ took up his residence in Capernaum
** all Johannine material cannot fall into the period between the Baptist's arrest and the Sermon on the Mount

one place to another, although Capernaum is regarded as the actual base of operations. The account in chapter 8 forms an interlude. Christ crosses over the Sea of Galilee by boat to Perea, and then returns by the same means "to his own city", that is, to Capernaum as his place of actual residence. Then, rather unexpectedly, we are told in chapter 10 that Christ empowered and sent out his twelve disciples. We are given the names of the apostles but are not told how these twelve had been assembled. Then Christ gives the disciples his instructions, and at the beginning of chapter 11 we are told that he left them in order to teach "in their cities," etc. This implies that Christ was quite separated from his disciples. That is a very peculiar passage and one that has no parallel elsewhere. And then comes the story of John's embassy from prison. This visit provides the occasion for a curse that Christ lays upon Chorazin and Bethsaida, towns in which he had done great deeds without result. But, we are not told previously of any visit to these towns, and we can only assume that such a visit was included in the course of one of the many journeys Christ took. In chapter 13 we are told that Christ suddenly came to Nazareth. That visit was one part of his journeyings about Galilee, so that the pattern is constant in this section of the Gospel. In chapter 14 we are told that Christ received news of John's beheading and that he withdrew to a lonely place. The feeding of the five thousand follows upon this withdrawal, and then a journey into Phoenicia, which bordered on Galilee. All that follows, the journey to Magdala [textus receptus] on the Sea of Galilee and to Caesarea Philippi, are only separate journeys within Galilee. Then follows the story of the transfiguration, and finally the journey to Jerusalem by way of Perea in chapter 19. In Matthew, then, the actual site of Christ's ministry from the beginning was Galilee, and this Gospel says nothing of Jerusalem until Christ goes there for the Feast of the Passover. If we reflect on the fact that Christ was obligated to attend the national festivals, especially since he had no fixed place of residence, we should have to conclude that all that Matthew recounts falls within the confines of a single year and that the Passover which preceded that on which he was arrested must have occurred before Matthew begins his account.* But there were many other great festivals in addition to the Passover, and Christ must have had the urge to journey to Jerusalem for them, or have been hindered from doing so in some special way. John, on the other hand, tells us that Christ journeyed to Jerusalem for the Feast of Tabernacles and did not return thereafter to Galilee.

Localities as they appear in t'.e Gospel of John. John knows nothing of the temptation story. After the baptism John has Christ go from the place where he had been with John by way of Cana and Capernaum, but in company with his mother and brothers. He remained there only a few days. This appears to have been a sort of family visit, but not the assumption of residence, "he dwelt", as in Matthew. Now the Passover was near, and therefore Christ and his disciples went to Jerusalem. Then comes the story of Nicodemus, and then (John 3:22) we are told that Jesus and his disciples went into the land of Judea. Here Jesus baptized, and John was also baptizing there at the same time. Christ learned that the Pharisees had heard that he had been making more disciples than John, and then he left Judea for these definite reasons. Otherwise he would have remained. Then he takes the road through Samaria, and then comes the story of the Samaritan woman. At the beginning of chapter 5 we are told: "After this there was a feast of the Jews, and Jesus went up to Jerusalem." This is the second time after the baptism that John conducts Jesus to Jerusalem. Whether John the Baptist had already been put in prison at this time does not directly emerge from the Johannine text, but in the course of chapter 5 John is regarded as having withdrawn from the scene (v. 33: "You sent to John . . ."), and that is a visit to Jerusalem that Matthew also ought to have told about, since he began his account with John's arrest. From chapter 6: After this Jesus went to the other side of the Galilean sea, and the Passover feast was at hand. This indicates that the first feast that had been mentioned was another. Now the story of the feeding of the multitude is introduced, Christ goes to Capernaum, and

* and the Passover before the last had already occurred before the beginning of Matthew's narrative of Christ's public ministry

afterward he went about in Galilee (John 7:1) and would not go into Judea, because the Jews had sought to kill him. *He had therefore to absent himself from the Passover Feast that followed upon the feeding of the multitude,* but thereafter he went to Jerusalem for the Feast of Tabernacles, a journey of which Matthew knows nothing. It follows that from the time of the feeding of the multitude John and Matthew each locate Christ's activity in different areas. The fact that Matthew records two feedings of multitudes does not alter the situation, since we can regard the account of the feeding in John as identical with either the first or the second in Matthew. Jesus therefore goes to Jerusalem for the Feast of Tabernacles. To be sure, there are places in John where we learn that Christ was regarded as a Galilean, but by others than the Evangelist. If John had held that view it would be difficult to understand why he gives a special reason every time for Christ's departure to Galilee. Toward the end of chapter 7 we find discourses that Christ delivered on the final day of the Feast of Tabernacles. In chapter 8 other discourses of Christ are introduced with the adverb "again," a fact that indicates that Christ tarried in Jerusalem after the feast was over. Then we have the story of Christ and the adulterous woman — a story that has probably been interpolated into the Gospel. At the beginning of chapter 9 the Johannine account gives the impression that Jesus had left Jerusalem, but the locality of the incident narrated there is obscure, and we cannot be sure that Christ had actually departed from the city. In John 10:22, however, we are told that the Feast of the Dedication of the Temple was celebrated in Jerusalem and that Jesus walked at that time in the temple. It follows, then, that either he had spent the whole time between the Feast of Tabernacles and the Feast of the Dedication of the Temple in Jerusalem, or that he had returned to the city for the Feast of Dedication. Since nothing is said of any absence, the most probable assumption is that he had spent all this time in the neighborhood of Jerusalem. Then, toward the end of chapter 10, we are told that, as a result of antagonism on the part of the Jews, Christ went to Perea, and from there he returned to the vicinity of Jerusalem (the raising of Lazarus). Then he goes to Ephraim, a place that has not hitherto been mentioned, and then on to Bethany.

From the time of the feeding of the multitude there is no agreement between the accounts in John and in Matthew. It is worthy of note that the two other Gospels also represent Christ as not coming to Jerusalem before the occasion of the last Passover. *Mark* is the Gospel that can always be shoved into the background, since it is not comprehensible apart from comparison with Matthew or Luke. In the Gospel of *Luke* we run across a very peculiar phenomenon, namely, the intentionally artistic composition of the various elements that occurs as early as the birth narratives and that is evident to a striking extent in the narratives that follow, which are combined in groups and aggregations (see my essay on Luke).[24] In chapter 9 Christ says that he and his disciples should now go to Jerusalem, and all that follows (an enormous mass of narratives) is represented as having taken place on this journey to Jerusalem, a representation that agrees neither with that in John nor with that in Matthew. This representation can probably be explained if* we reflect that it was an idea that somehow had come to be accepted that Christ had maintained his residence in Galilee during the period of his public life and that he had only gone to Jerusalem as it were for the purpose of his passion, a prevailing opinion that is set forth in Luke. So it appears that individual events that had not been precisely located were connected with one another in the form of a narrative of the journey to Jerusalem. This leaves only the question: How can this idea of a predominantly Galilean ministry have arisen at that time, although the apostles, Christ's immediate companions, must have known that Jesus spent most of his time in Judea? The key to the solution of the problem is to be found in John. It was the prevailing

---

24. This work is found in Schleiermacher's *Sämmtliche Werke* (Berlin: G.Reimer, 1836), I, 2:1-220. There is an English translation by Connop Thirlwall, *A Critical Essay on the Gospel of Luke* (London, 1825). Cf. above, Introduction, pp. xxix-xxxi.

* if one recalls that Luke, unlike Matthew, does not carry the name of an apostle, and that Mark reports indirectly. Therefore these Gospels can be regarded as being second or third hand. We should also recall that it was a generally accepted idea that Christ had lived in Galilee until the time of the final Passover, etc.

opinion that Jesus was a Galilean. If the narrator did not know that Christ had a strong motive to be in Jerusalem, he could easily have compressed everything that happened outside Galilee into the course of this single journey that he knew about. This, however, could not have been the work of an apostle.

Lecture 26 (June 26). Therefore only John can be made basic, since, in the form in which we have it, Matthew's Gospel . . . * ever more clearly is not the work of an apostle. John himself did not regard Galilee as the main seat of Christ's activities, but he puts that notion into the mouth of others as the prevailing idea in Jerusalem.[26] This belief can have arisen very probably as a result of the Galilean idiom or accent that Christ acquired [by] his education in Nazareth and that a large part of his constant companions had from birth. There were two ways by which Christ could fulfill his vocation to spread his message as widely as possible in Palestine: in part by a constant residence in Jerusalem, and in part by repeated journeyings in the different territories that comprised the country. His journeyings would not have taken him to Jews in the Dispersion, in addition legal custom drew him to Jerusalem. Christ made use of both methods and himself laid the foundation for the spread of the gospel in Samaria. Also, by means of his attendance at festivals, he was able to draw himself to the attention of Hellenists.

We know little of Christ's personal acquaintances in Jerusalem (only the host at the Passover meal), but we do know of some in the vicinity of the city, for example, the family with many branches with which he stayed in Bethany in order that he might daily come into Jerusalem. John speaks only of one stay in Samaria and has nothing definite to say of any in Perea. We must always keep in mind the high regard in which members of the teaching profession were held and the respectful hospitality extended to them. Homes were readily opened to them. In Galilee, Capernaum was

* reveals itself, or can be seen to be?[25]
25 Rütenik is evidently unable to decipher Schleiermacher's note. [LEK]
26. Paulus also takes the temporal ordering of the Gospel of John as basic; *Das Leben Jesu als Grundlage einer reinen Geschichte des Urchristentums*. 2 vols. (Heidelberg, 1828), I 154. This is worthy of note because Paulus was known as an extreme version of an Enlightenment rationalism and a thoroughly moral approach to the message of Jesus, a very different theological perspective than that of Schleiermacher. Paulus shared much with the Kantian influenced school of theology, one of whose members, Karl Bretschneider, had seriously challenged the Gospel of John as a historical source in 1820. The fact that Paulus takes John as basic is indicative that there is more than Schleiermacher's theological propensities involved in his adherence to the Fourth Gospel. Such a basic reliance upon John, of course, is virtually no longer extant in New Testament research.

Christ's most important center of activity, in part because of family connections there that we have to assume because his mother and sisters accompanied him thither, and in part because Peter's residence was there, although he had originally come from Bethsaida. It is very probable that Jesus resided with Peter. (That Peter was a householder is evident from the reference to Peter's wife's mother and from the story of finding a stater in the fish's mouth.) Luke 8:1–3 can be regarded as a general pattern of the frequent journeys, although the number of Jesus' companions may not always have been so large. Indeed, even the twelve may not always have been present for many a one could be kept away by his business duties.

If we wish to avoid unrewarding conjectures, we can only conclude from this contradiction that our Gospels have different relationships to the facts. In this connection we should not overlook the excellent character of the Gospel of John, which everywhere gives evidence of having come from an immediate eyewitness, whereas the character of the others as composites of originally separate elements is just as apparent, and all the Gospels except John must be viewed as having come down to us second hand. Although the one bears the name of an apostle, doubt has recently been cast by several persons on the tradition that the Gospel in its present form really is the work of an apostle, and I am convinced that the question of Matthew's apostolic authorship will increasingly be answered in the negative. We must, therefore, make the Gospel of John basic to our studies, and if we view the relationship of Christ to localities in light of this Gospel, this is what we see: According to John it was not the prevailing opinion that Jesus' homeland during his public ministry was Galilee, the way Capernaum is expressly designated Christ's "own city" in Matthew. John actually regards Judea as the site of Christ's public ministry, and Christ goes elsewhere only temporarily and for definite reasons. The question, then, arises: How can the view have arisen that Galilee was the site of Christ's public ministry? Even in John Jesus is referred to in Jerusalem as a Galilean, but only by others, never by the Evangelist himself. What was the reason for that? We can make the following suggestions: (1) Before he began his public ministry Jesus received his education in Galilee. If there were certain differences of idiom in Palestine — Peter, in fact, was recognized by his speech as a Galilean — it can have been that Christ's ordinary speech betrayed Galilean characteristics. (2) The majority of Christ's pupils that were in constant attendance on him was made up of Galileans. This we know was true of the two pairs of brothers, of Nathanael, of Matthew, and, to judge from their nicknames, also of several others. These were reasons enough for the idea to win acceptance among those who did not belong to Christ's immediate entourage and to become the one generally held in Judea, and in this way it found its way into our Gospels.

If we now take a look at all the local relationships and ask how the public life of Jesus was related to the totality of the Jewish country, since he himself considered his vocation as limited to Palestine, this is the way things appear: At that time Judea was a Roman province and the other parts of the country were sometimes under various members of the Herodian family and sometimes united, but the terms that were in common use were Judea, Galilee, Samaria, and Perea. If we now have to say that Christ thought of himself as called to proclaim the kingdom of God and to establish it among his people by that proclamation, this fact explains why he put himself as much as possible into contact with them. That could happen only in two ways. One method would be to stay continually in Jerusalem, for that city was the center of the land, partly because great crowds from all parts of the country came there at the time of the festivals, and partly because many were in the city from all the different districts of Palestine for business reasons. At the same time this was the means by which attention could be called to Christ on the part of those members of the Jewish people who lived in the dispersion, that is, outside of Palestine. The other method would have been a constant journeying in order to visit all parts of the country. We find that Christ combined both methods. In John we see that the occurrence of one of the great festivals was the occasion of a journey to *Jerusalem*. Then Christ spent some time in the vicinity of Jerusalem, or in Perea, or he went for a while to Galilee, but in John such a departure from Judea is always given some motivation. To be sure, it cannot be demonstrated that Christ could not have achieved his purpose by remaining constantly in Jerusalem. However, it must be clear to everyone that he would not have achieved it by avoiding Jerusalem and employing only the other method of journeying hither and yon. If he had not come to Jerusalem he would at least have been unable to attract attention from those sections of the Jewish people who lived outside Palestine, for such people had no concern for Palestinian affairs outside the capital city. Just as there were synagogues of Hellenists in Jerusalem, so foreign Jews also came to the city because of the great festivals. However, even if we left this factor out of consideration, Jesus could not have avoided Jerusalem. He stood under the law, and that compelled him to celebrate the festivals as far as possible in Jerusalem. Jesus had certain family connections in Galilee, and also connections with earlier acquaintances.

Samaria was of least importance for the task he had assumed, for the Samaritans, strictly speaking, were not members in the same way of the Jewish people. The Samaritans were a mixed race of Jews and others, and, so far as the cult was concerned, a separate people. However, there were two roads from Jerusalem to Galilee. The one went to the west of the Jordan river through Samaria, while the other went to the east of the river through Perea. For most people the former route was the more direct, but the latter was preferred because people wished to avoid coming into contact with Samaritans, who were regarded as ritually unclean. Very early in the book of the Acts of the Apostles we hear of a great advance of the gospel in Samaria, which was associated with the preaching of Philip. In John we learn that Christ also traveled through Samaria. We see, then, that Christ did not observe the custom of avoiding the route through Samaria, and by his presence in Samaria he prepared the way for the later spread of Christianity in that land. The synoptic Evangelists represent Christ as crossing the Galilean lake from Galilee to make a brief visit to *Perea* on the other shore and as traveling through Perea on the journey from Galilee to Jerusalem, and John makes him take an intentional route (or, journey) to Samaria. We see, then, that Christ neglected no part of the Jewish land and excluded no part of it from the scene of his personal ministry.

To be sure, he had special points of contact in Galilee. The fact that he had earlier been educated there seems to retreat into the background. Matthew (4:13) begins his story with the statement that Christ, "leaving Nazareth," went and dwelt in Capernaum, and speaks only of a single visit at a later time to Nazareth. We learn from John, however, from the story of the marriage at Cana, that Christ also had family connections in Capernaum. Peter and Andrew had their residence in Capernaum, and Christ found the two sons of Zebedee, James and John, in a business partnership with them at Capernaum. From the statement in John 1 we learn that Bethsaida was regarded as the original home of Andrew and Peter. Since Andrew is mentioned first, we may perhaps conclude that he was the elder of the two brothers. This may also emerge from the fact that he and John had been disciples of the Baptist. Bethsaida, then, is designated as their actual native town, as it was also, according to the same verse, of Philip. But Matthew declares distinctly that Peter had a house establishment in Capernaum, and the other Evangelists agree with him on this point. In this way, then, Christ had a double interest in Capernaum, and it is probable that, when he settled in Capernaum, he was a member of Peter's household. We see, then, how this could easily give rise to the statement that he took up residence in Capernaum and that Capernaum was his "own city," that is, his usual domicile. There is little reference to Christ's special relationships in Jerusalem, with the exception of that implied in the story of the preparation for the final Passover, where Christ refers his disciples to one to whom he has them say that he wishes to celebrate the Passover in his house. Such a request could only have been made of one with whom Christ was already well acquainted. In John special emphasis is laid on Christ's relationship with the family in Bethany, of which Lazarus and his two sisters are named. This relationship was not limited to the time of the last Passover. John tells us that on an earlier occasion Christ left the city at evening time and took the road from Jerusalem to Bethany as far as the Mount of Olives, at whose foot lay the town of Bethany. Definite relationships of this sort in other parts of the country are not mentioned, and we know nothing of how Christ lived in Perea. Only one stay in Samaria is referred to — one during which Christ was welcomed as a guest in the city where the event took place.

In this way we can form a picture, although an imperfect one, of Christ's *outer existence*. This was related to the households of his disciples in various Galilean towns and, in the vicinity of Jerusalem, to the households of those who either recognized the Messiah in him, or at least honored him as a prophet. Relationships in other localities remain in the dark. However, we know in general that the profession of the scribes and of those who were entitled to engage in public teaching was a highly honored one and that everyone made a point of showing courtesy to anyone who belonged to it. Because he had no special means of subsistence, the support of a person of this profession was often dependent on the respect in which his profession was held and on the hospitality extended to him as a member of it. When we are told that Christ journeyed hither and yon and we ask, How did this happen, and on what did his subsistence depend? we find a passage that bears on the question, although we cannot be sure whether it refers only to a specific journey or to the sources of Christ's subsistence in general. At the beginning of chapter 8 of Luke's Gospel we are told that Christ went through cities and villages, preaching the kingdom of God, and that the twelve were with him, as well as some women, etc. These women are named: Mary Magdalene and two others, as well as many others who are unnamed. Then we are told that they provided for Jesus and his disciples out of their means. The picture we get is that of a rather large company of travelers. The disciples had their professions and their income, and there were others who gave practical expression to their thankfulness to Christ, and Christ's *subsistence* was provided for in these ways. It is probable that we can regard this single instance as illustrative of what happened in general.

Lecture 27 (June 27). In this way we can account at the same time for the problem of the nature of Christ's *outer subsistence* during this period. The usual idea of an actual poverty that contributed significantly to his lowly estate is indefensible. The saying that he knew not where to lay his head refers more to the fact that he had no settled home than to the lack of a lodging, which was certainly always at his disposal. The statement that Judas carried what was thrown into the money box (John 12:5–6) would have no connection with what precedes it if it had not been a fact that what was intended for the poor passed through Judas's hands. So the society, which often had occasion to use them, was entrusted with charitable gifts. But also gifts of love to a teacher, and especially hospitality to traveling teachers, were quite in the spirit of the time and the people. Christ retained no close connection with his family, and it is unlikely that he obtained any of his subsistence from its members. On one occasion his brothers wanted him to go to Judea rather than to stay in Galilee (John 7:3), and at another time (Matt. 12:45–50; Mark 3:31–35; Luke 8:19–21) they wished to have him by themselves. In this latter instance Christ's mother was also with his brothers. This does not mean that she shared their unbelieving conviction, but only that she stood with them. His mother does not accompany him on his journeys. She was not even with him on his last journey, but came to the festival in some other way. Although Christ did not have his own dwelling, he certainly shared Peter's house in Capernaum. Our information is insufficient to say that this was the reason for Peter's status in relation to the other apostles, a status that can scarcely be explained by his personal character, especially after the denial, and in light of the preferential relationship John enjoyed, although this last was purely personal. The earnings of the apostles, whatever profession they may have followed, went into the common fund. Then we have to keep in mind the hospitality and the love gifts.

In this connection we have to reflect *on the activities of Christ and the way he occupied his time.* Public instruction in a specific form was restricted to the days on which there were synagogue assemblies. In addition great numbers of people collected only on journeys to the festivals or on the marketplaces. Assemblies at marketplaces were not adapted to teaching but were often used for that purpose. Since people suffering from disease are not easily moved, we cannot think that many people gathered about him with sick friends or relatives. The Gospel of Matthew often gives us the impression that they did, but this is due to the method of narrating events employed by this Evangelist, a method that has not yet been wholly clarified.

The general discussion of the localities involved in Christ's public ministry enables us to conclude that we cannot specify a definite residence to which Christ always would have returned. To be sure, in Matthew's Gospel this is the prevailing idea, but in John we do not find it at all, and this fact is all the more significant since John himself stood very close to what was Christ's point of contact in Capernaum. Apart from Christ's family connections in Capernaum, it was Peter's house that could attach him to that town. John and his brother were in some business partnership with Peter. They are represented as carrying on the business of fishing together with him. Such business had to do with trade in dried fish at the outlet of the Sea of Galilee, and this business could lead to a comfortable living. In the Gospels we see the two pairs of brothers in partnership, engaged together in the business of fishing. Consequently John could have been inclined to lay a certain stress on Christ's connection with Capernaum, but actually there is no trace of it. So the emphasis on Capernaum in the other Gospels is not due to accurate recollection of facts but to the view of the matter that developed later and at a distance from events. This is connected with another point that is of very great importance. The idea runs through all the narratives of the Gospels, and to a still greater extent through those of the book of the Acts of the Apostles, that Peter held a unique position among the disciples. Even while they were still with Christ, Peter appears in individual instances as the spokesman, the foreman as it were of the apostles, and in the book of the Acts he is often the foremost among the company, the one who speaks for all. How can we account for this preeminence? Was it just the result of his personal character? To be sure, Christ emphasizes this character in a special way in the familiar passage, but the story of Peter's so-called denial (I do not value it as highly as is often the case) could detract from this impression of a dominant strength and power of character. Even after the story of the denial we find that Peter occupies the same leading position among the disciples as before, and that could scarcely have been due to the fact that Christ after the resurrection restored him to a place of trust and affection. An explanation of Peter's role is to be found in Matthew's Gospel. Peter had a house in Capernaum, and whenever Jesus was in Capernaum he stayed with Peter. This led to a special relationship of Peter to Christ by which Peter obtained an ascendancy over the others, and in this way we can account for the role he played. However, if we cannot share Matthew's point of view and if Capernaum cannot be regarded as Christ's actual hometown, this idea loses its importance. Nevertheless, the role Peter played is most easily explained in this way. It is apparent that this relationship to the other apostles that Peter enjoyed is not stressed as much in John's narrative as in those of the first three Gospels. For the book of the Acts of the Apostles we have no such counterweight as the Gospel of John for the other three Gospels, and in the book of the Acts the relationship of Peter as the spokesman and foreman of the apostles is very prominent. In the Gospel of John, on the other hand, it is a special relationship of the apostle John to Christ that is emphasized, but this has a purely personal character and was of no influence on the apostle's profession.

Another question concerns *the way and means by which Christ obtained external subsistence.* If a person has a definite residence, this question is not urgent, for such possession pre-supposes a source of help for outer subsistence. However, if we have to deny such a permanent residence to Christ we must ask: How did Christ actually obtain subsistence? It is very doubtful that he spent the whole time until his thirtieth year with his family in Nazareth. That becomes quite improbable if you think in an unprejudiced way of the account of his appearance in Nazareth. That story indicates that Christ's family was well known in Nazareth, that his sisters lived there, but if he himself had lived there, the story would have been told differently. His relationship to the other members of the family, regarded as the basis of his external support, must have ceased at a much earlier date. However, we cannot venture to advance hypotheses with respect to ways in which he may have supported himself prior to the beginning of his public ministry in the absence of any source material on which to base them.

Christ's mother disappears almost completely from our Gospels, and appears again only at the very end. John tells us that Christ was invited together with his mother and brothers to the marriage at Cana and that he went with them from there to Capernaum. However, even there he seems to have separated from them. What really is meant by the term ''his brothers'' is still the subject of dispute. The Gospels do not tell us in what sense they are called his brothers. Were they younger brothers, or older brothers from an earlier marriage of Joseph, or were they called his brothers although they were actually his cousins? These questions are still debated. Whatever the term may mean, his brothers appear in the Gospel of John specifically as not sharing the idea of himself and his vocation that Christ set forth and as lacking belief in his messianic dignity. In John 7 we are told that they asked him, when he on one occasion had spent some time in Galilee, to go to the festival, and they asked him in such a way as to suggest that they would rather have him in Judea than in Galilee. Consequently we cannot think of a close relationship as existing between Christ and his brothers. In the other Gospels there is an account which makes one suspect that for a long time Christ's mother had been with his brothers. That does not mean that she shared their conviction, that she had no faith in him, but only that she took part formally in what they did. Whereas in John 7 we are told that his brothers wanted him to leave Galilee so that they might not be confused with him, in these other passages (Mark 3:21, 31) we are told that they wanted to seize him and remove him from public life, as though he were one who had lost control of his senses, as though he were mad. They had heard this report and regarded it as better to keep him at home. From all this it is apparent that Jesus had no close connection with other members of his family. Similarly we have no reason to believe that his mother stood in any close relationship to him during his stay in Galilee, whether he spent the time in Capernaum or in traveling about. In his detailed enumeration of Christ's traveling companions, Luke does not mention Christ's mother, and even when Christ made his last journey to Jerusalem to attend the Feast of the Passover, she did not accompany him, although she later was in the city. The other Evangelists would have had occasion to mention Christ's mother as a member of his entourage if she had been with him, for they have him go directly from Galilee to Jerusalem. This is not the case in John's Gospel, where Christ at first lived in Jerusalem and its environs, then went to Perea, then to Lazarus, then to the wilderness to Ephraim, and from Ephraim to the festival. His mother could not have been with him on those travels. Only later, after Christ's death, does his mother appear in close relationship to John and the apostles, and not his mother alone, but also his brothers, who therefore must have changed their attitude. This later relationship, however, does not seem to have existed during the period of his public ministry.

How are we to think of Christ as supporting himself? It is generally held that Christ lived in a state of acute poverty, but there is no evidence to support such a belief. When Christ says that the Son of man has nowhere to lay his head, we do not have to explain that saying in the sense that he was poor. It means only that he had no definite home, but that he was always compelled by circumstances to wander to and fro. If Christ was recognized as a public teacher, we cannot think of him as poor. Teachers were the objects of respect and the recipients of hospitality. We have every reason to believe that this was so to a high degree at all times and in all places. The difference between teachers and others cannot be regarded as a contrast between poverty and affluence. In the first place, the satisfaction of a teacher's essential needs was something exceptionally easy, and in this respect we cannot speak of poverty. When we recall that Christ lived at times in Peter's house, that at times he was on journeys to areas where he would receive hospitality when he appeared as a teacher, and that he attracted more and more pupils and adherents, the question of how he obtained his subsistence ceases to require an answer. At the same time we have to give up the idea that he was especially poor, for there is no reason to hold it. To be sure, one passage, that in John 12, seems to support this idea, but the interpretation of that passage is very difficult. This is the passage in which John tells of the anointing in Bethany. He says that Judas Iscariot complains of the waste. The ointment should have been sold and the money given to the poor. At this point John remarks that Judas had not said what he did out of concern for the poor, but because he had always carried the money box and looked after what was put into it as gifts. That gives the impression of a common fund that was used for the direct support of Christ and his company, to which each contributed. This presupposes that each of Christ's disciples had his income, income not earned personally but by members of his family, and that each received what was necessary and shared it with others. The other expression, "he used to take what was put into it," is explained as meaning that those who honored Christ had made contributions to his support. I have no intention of denying that. It was the way the Jews of the day treated traveling teachers. After they had delivered lectures in the synagogues they received their support in this way. But the passage does not have to be interpreted after this fashion, for such an interpretation does not explain how Judas could have said what he did. If there is to be a connection here, we must assume that in this "money box" there was also something for the poor. The passage means that contributions were made to Christ and his company to be distributed by them to the poor. That is the natural explanation of the passage, for the Gospels plainly tell us that there were often beggars who sought support from passersby, and Christ must often have had such requests, for he was regularly engaged in travels. The more we think of Christ as constantly in the company of several people, whether in one place where he had those who honored him, or in travels, the less we can accept the idea of a poverty on his part that required the receipt of alms. He did not lead a lonely existence. We would have to say that Christ's whole company was in a state of poverty, but in that case he would not have been able to hold it together, for its very existence would have depended on external circumstances. Consequently we conclude that he obtained his subsistence in part from the pooling of the resources of those who belonged to his immediate entourage and in part from contributions that others made to this common life. But these latter are only to be considered as support for his undertaking, (or: his affairs) as contributions to assure the continuance of Christ's company, on whose existence the whole ministry of

Christ primarily depended, not as charity that Christ personally received.

Let us turn now to another question. If we now know in what area Christ moved about and in which he stayed here and there for a shorter or longer time, usually teaching and surrounded most of the time by at least the majority of the twelve, how did he occupy the whole time? It could not have been taken up only with teaching. Public instruction was limited to the time that was set apart for rest from work. In other words, it was associated with the day on which the synagogue assembled. This, then, was essentially the time during which Christ exercised his public ministry. To be sure, there are narratives in the Gospels that represent Christ as teaching at times on a mountain, at times by the lake in the presence of a crowd, at times on journeys, with people following him. These pictures are more difficult to verify. They are dependent on two facts. In the first place, crowds of people were engaged at the time of the great festivals in journeying to Jerusalem, and at such times Christ would have masses of people near him and there would be times when he could teach. In the second place, his miracles, his extension of help to people in dire need, would be responsible for gathering crowds about him. This latter fact presents some difficulties, however. We cannot easily think of Christ as constantly surrounded by sick, helpless people and at the same time ·by many others. This could happen only in especially favorable circumstances, and we cannot think of this as occurring very often. This, to be sure, is the impression we get from Matthew's Gospel, but it is due to the special point of view that is characteristic of that Gospel.

Lecture 28 (June 28). Christ's use of his time involves two factors, the daily ordering of his life and a ministry that differed according to place and time. The time set aside for prayer was only a brief period, for it was at the same time the beginning of the day's work. The disciples pursued their ordinary tasks, sometimes with Christ accompanying them without taking part in their activities. This was also the time of his meditation and his study of the Scriptures. Then came their social assembly, which would be occupied with instruction whenever they were by themselves and with inspiring teaching when they were surrounded by others. The disciples had many prejudices that had to be overcome, and the foundations of the Christian church had to be laid in them. This, then, was the simple form of the ordinary order of Christ's life, which was enriched on sabbaths by public teaching, more rest from regular work, and greater companionableness. So far as the other factor is concerned, our source materials are unevenly divided, and in this unevenness Matthew and John differ greatly from each other. The latter passes frequently from one activity to another, although he at least fills in the gaps by commencing each new account with some reference to the passage of time. Matthew only introduces separate accounts and general descriptions and lumps everything into them in such a way that they lack any indication of the passage of time. In this fashion Matthew's Gospel gives the impression of days in Christ's ministry that were filled to the full, but this impression is usually not defensible. I cite the Sermon on the Mount and the various collections of parables as examples.

We have a large number of narratives from this period of the life of Christ, but we are still faced with serious problems. If we ask how much time Christ spent in public teaching, which would ordinarily be teaching in the synagogues, we have to answer that this would be limited to the sabbaths. In addition it is natural to assume that Christ could find great crowds of people together only insofar as they assembled in caravans to journey to Jerusalem, and that was limited to certain times of the year. In addition we can also assume that there was a definite place *(forum)* in centers that had no synagogue where people could assemble at definite times for prayer. In Jerusalem these took place in the temple, at the place where offerings were made, but such assemblies were only brief, and each attendant soon scattered to fulfill his special duties. Accordingly, there was not much time in the course of an ordinary day, except under unusual circumstances, when Christ could count on listeners. To be sure, in Matthew's Gospel we find accounts of large crowds of people which assembled about Christ. At times these Matthean reports give the impression that there were rather remote places to which people brought their sick folk for Christ to heal. This is difficult to imagine. Preparations would have to be made for such occasions, and the place where Christ would be at the time would have to be known, as well as how long he intended to remain there. An assembly of large numbers of people under such circumstances can only be regarded as accidental. It does not fit into the picture of a regular day's activities, and we may well ask whether the references of this sort that Matthew makes are not to be regarded more as summaries by which the Evangelist seeks to fill in gaps in his narrative rather than as indications of separate, specific assemblies. There are two parts to our task. In the first place, if we regard the day as an individual, recurring occasion, we have to ask: How did Christ ordinarily occupy himself during such a day? In the second place, with reference to the whole period, can we form a clear picture of the continuity of Christ's activities?

1) *An ordinary day in the life of Christ during his public ministry.*[27] (a) We can only think of the sabbath as the day when as a rule Christ could make any significant use of his teaching ministry and on which it occupied any considerable amount of time. On all other days we can assume only social activity on Christ's part. This, however, took many forms and was in every respect *unique*. Those who made up his regular entourage had to pursue their professional tasks, and we run across occasional instances of this. The disciples attended to their occupational duties, for example, those of fishing on the Sea of Galilee, and Christ accompanied them to their tasks, simultaneously exercising his unique activity, for that was the time available to him for meditation. (b) Then there was *social activity,* partly in the circle of his disciples and partly in a wider relation to others. We are particularly concerned in this connection with whether we may assume that Christ carried on any kind of regular activity within the narrower assembly of his disciples for the purpose of instructing them, correcting their ideas, and preparing them for their future ministry. We have no definite reports concerning such activity. The discourses of Christ to his disciples have a definite occasion and do not appear to conform to a specific teaching

---

27. The subhead titles for this and the following section have been supplied by the translator.

pattern. On the contrary, they appear to have been occasional. However, we have to assume without question that Christ was regularly in the company of a number of his disciples. The number was limited at times when the disciples pursued their professions and more extended when they gathered for social purposes, but the fact of such gatherings cannot be denied. After Christ had finally departed, we see the disciples appearing, filled with assurance and certainty. They knew what they wanted with respect to their task of founding and ordering the Christian fellowship as the externalization of the kingdom of God, and having abandoned all earlier ideas of a politically oriented theocracy, they were agreed on appealing to God's earlier revelation. This was the fruit of their common life with Christ, not just of Christ's public teaching, which they shared with others. Christ had exercised a special ministry to them. *So then, Christ's daily life was occupied with meditation and study of the Scriptures by himself, with public teaching, and in general with a social life which was especially filled with instructing the narrower circle of his disciples and with whatever else was opportune.*

2) *The whole time of Christ's public life, considered as a continuum.* The task of forming a picture of this in accordance with the available material is very difficult. Comparing the two Gospels, John and Matthew, we find both a great similarity and a great difference. There are large gaps, periods of which nothing is recounted. John notes these gaps largely with references to time, for example, at Christ's baptism. At the beginning he is very specific as to the passage of time. He tells of the day on which John gave his witness to Christ before the deputation from Jerusalem. Then in 1:29 we are told that "on the next day" John saw Jesus, and then follows the account of Christ's baptism. Then again on the following day (v. 35) John was standing with two of his disciples, Andrew and Peter, who left him and went to Jesus. On the following day (v. 43) Jesus found Philip and Nathanael. On the third day (2:1) he went to the marriage feast at Cana, etc. Here the references to time are so exact because they had to do with the beginnings of the relationship between Jesus and John, and in this connection even the slightest detail was

noteworthy. Gaps show up later which, however, John does not indicate. After the account of the marriage at Cana, the Evangelist tells us that Christ found his way to Capernaum, where he spent "not many days", [i.e., a few days], and then went to Jerusalem to celebrate the Passover. Then come the accounts of what he did in Jerusalem. Then we are told in chapter 3:22 that he went into the land of Judea, where his disciples baptized. News of this reached Jerusalem and made quite a stir. Then Christ went to Galilee by way of the road through Samaria to the west of the Jordan. The stay in Samaria lasted only for a few days. In 4:43 we are told that "after two days" he resumed his journey and came to Galilee, and then there is no further specification of the passage of time. Then in 5:1 we are told that a feast of the Jews was at hand and that Jesus went to Jerusalem to attend it. At the beginning of John 6 the Evangelist proceeds: After this Jesus went to the other side of the Sea of Galilee, and then there follows the story of the feeding of the multitude. In this way John summarizes a considerable period of time. At the end of chapter 6 he says that many of Jesus' disciples began to draw back. In chapter 7 we are told that Christ stayed in Galilee until the time of the Feast of Tabernacles and that at the time this feast began he went to Jerusalem. In this way John's account clearly reveals gaps and fails to fill them in with information as to how Jesus used the time.

How does Matthew represent Christ as occupying his time? We start with Christ's assumption of residence at Capernaum. There Jesus began to proclaim (4:17): "Repent, for the kingdom of heaven is at hand." He meets the two pairs of brothers. Then we are given a general description: Christ went about all Galilee, teaching in the synagogues and healing (4:23). Then reference is made to an indefinite period: Christ's fame spread throughout all Syria, and people brought him all their sick and he healed them (4:24--25).* There is here no mention of a passage of time or of a definite locality, and to this general notice chapter 5:1 is attached: "Seeing the crowds, he went up on the mountain," etc. Then follows

* or add: for which he required a lengthy period of travel round about

the Sermon on the Mount. So a specific detail is linked directly with an indefinite account, for which there is no note of the passage of time. At the end of the Sermon on the Mount we read: "And when Jesus finished these sayings, the crowds were astonished at his teaching." There is no account of Christ's activity as a healer among the people. Only an isolated story of the healing of a leper and another of the healing of a servant of a centurion are attached, and then that of the healing of Peter's mother-in-law. Then we read (8:16): "That evening they brought to him many who were possessed," etc. It is assumed, then, that all that had previously happened had been done on one day. Christ then withdraws from the crowd by crossing over the lake in a boat. There follows a storm, the incident of the Gergesenes [*textus receptus*], the return voyage, and then (9:2) the healing of the paralytic. In all this we have on the one hand a general description without reference to the passage of time, and on the other hand a mass of separate events compressed into a brief period. If we are to take this literally and are to regard Matthew's Gospel as our primary source, then we get the picture as it is painted by Dr. Paulus in his commentary and in his *Life of Jesus,* a picture of *separate days, filled to the full with events.* In the course of this, however, the whole rest of the time would remain in the dark. We should know nothing of it except what is given in the indefinite generalizations, and points become evident where we see clearly that it is impossible to take Matthew literally. For example, chapter 12 begins with a general reference: "at that time" Christ went through the grainfields on the sabbath. Then in v. 9 we are told that he went on from there into the synagogue, where he healed a man that had a withered hand. Then we are told very vaguely that the Pharisees took counsel against him, how to destroy him, and then Jesus withdrew from there. In v. 22 we are told that a "demoniac" was brought to him, and the healing of this sick man is the occasion for a long discourse by Christ, and, while he is still speaking, his mother appears outside, and so on till we come to chapter 13. We get the impression that all this took place on the same day, as well as the delivery of a parable to the assembled crowd. Then his disciples came to him and asked him why he spoke to the people in parables, and he answered by explaining one of the parables. Then comes still another parable, and then still another, and so on. By this time it must have grown late. How can we possibly think of all this as a continuum! And yet Dr. Paulus speaks of it as a day that was particularly rich in events. We see that there is still need for a closer examination of the actual character of Matthew's Gospel. In comparison with Matthew, we have no choice but to make John's Gospel basic.

The Gospel of *Luke* presents still other difficulties in connection with the continuum of time, for it includes small collections of narratives of separate events which are assembled because of their similar character. Then follows a similar collection, and toward the end of chapter 9 we are told that the journey to Jerusalem begins, and then everything that is recounted is represented as having happened in the course of this one journey. We cannot use Luke to get an idea of the way Christ occupied his time during this period of his life. John is the only Gospel that can give us that, although even in John the picture is incomplete.

Lecture 29 (June 29). Of the two other Gospels, *Mark* obviously tends to agree with Matthew, and the references to time in *Luke* appear most clearly to be only the introduction to and the conclusion of previously independent (or: separate) narratives, which is the natural way for such general descriptions to appear. There is no other alternative than to make the picture of the arrangement of daily life basic also for the ministry in general. Though we cannot assume that Christ had a fixed residence, there was, nevertheless, a difference between places where he usually and frequently stayed and those that he visited infrequently. In the former the order of the day varied, whereas in the latter hospitality was more to the fore, as well as social discourse. Most time for formal public discourse was available at the festivals in Jerusalem, as well as during the course of journeys thither and when, as usually happened, the festivals were celebrated at Bethany; the companionship was also richest during such periods. In this connection we must also mention the question of *Christ's miracles,* all the more because, according to a few accounts, a significant amount of time must have been necessary for them. The narratives pass over large numbers of miracles in silence, of which only a few are later occasionally mentioned, for example, Matthew 11:21, John 2:23, John 4:45, and John 10:41.

Many miracles are also referred to only in summary fashion, although this occurs only in the three synoptic Gospels. Comparable summaries are not to be found in John's Gospel, which mentions miracles only when they are the preface to noteworthy discourses and specific developments. Of the mass of miracles, however, many serve only as the introduction to or the conclusion of individual narratives and consequently can lay no claim to separate discussion.

We see how little we are in a position to carry out the task of clarifying the continuity of Christ's ministry at various places. Both *Mark* and *Luke* leave us in the lurch, though in different ways. *Luke* begins by describing an indefinite period of Christ's teaching in Galilee, a period that follows immediately upon the temptation story in chapter 4. Luke is wrong in his reference to time. After a few narratives we are told, "And reports of him went out into every place in the surrounding region."* This statement stands between the two accounts in such a way that it cannot be regarded as a special element. So we see quite clearly that the whole has been constructed out of previously separate accounts. It is not possible to form a picture of the place of the various activities that Jesus engaged in, sometimes here, sometimes there. In this connection Mark is closer to Matthew, although, while for a time he agrees with Matthew, he sometimes follows Luke's order. For example, according to Mark 6 Jesus goes to Nazareth but can accomplish nothing there. Then he summons the twelve and sends them out two by two. Then comes the news of the Baptist's death. Then the apostles return and Christ goes with them into the wilderness. Then follows the incident of the feeding of the multitude and then the visit to Capernaum, where Christ permits people to bring their sick to him from the whole surrounding country. It is virtually impossible to form a coherent picture of all this.

Mark tells us much of individual localities, but we learn nothing from him of the way in which Christ occupied his time. While John's account in this connection is somewhat preferable, since, while John also narrates only separate

* or add: and when later events are narrated, we do not know whether they are to be included among those that precede the generalization

events, he at least fills in the gaps between them by beginning each new element with references to time and place, we must say that, had he told us of how much time had passed between one event and another and had he added general summaries as Matthew does, his account would be more instructive and more important for our purpose. But that was no part of his intention, for he wished only to emphasize certain details. There is a twofold tendency in John's Gospel. In the first place, there is a tendency to stress the *teaching* of Christ, and in the second place, there is a tendency to emphasize the development of Christ's relationship to the people in order to make the catastrophe of his fate understandable. Since here also there are very few general references to which we can appeal, we can only make use of what we have said about Christ's way of daily life in order to fill out the whole of the time.*

Wherever Christ went he engaged in public teaching in the synagogues. Sometimes this consisted of discussions between him and those who turned to him. Then there were certain social relationships, based on hospitality and personal contacts, healings, etc.

Another particular point needs to be included here, one especially emphasized in Matthew's narrative, namely, Christ's *miracles*. If we reflect on those general descriptions that Matthew gives, which occur between the separate and detailed accounts of Christ's deeds and discourses, the miracles always appear to occupy a large part of the time. So we should have to say that a large part of Christ's time must have been taken up with the performance of miracles. If we consider the individual facts that are narrated in detail, we see that the miraculous act itself is but a matter of a moment and takes up no time, but it is always related to an account of Christ's dealings with those on whom a miracle had been performed. If we imagine large numbers of people gathering about Christ with sick and suffering folk and think of Christ as treating them all separately, a great part of his time must have been devoted to the performance of miracles.

* we can only make the picture of Christ's ordering of his daily life basic to an understanding of his life in general

How are we to think of this with reference to Christ's use of his time? In this connection we find narratives that give very different impressions. If we look at many passages, we see that they say nothing at all of large numbers of miracles in our Gospels. In Matthew 11: 20-21 we read: "Then he began to upbraid the cities where most of his mighty works had been done . . . for if the mighty works done in you had been done in Tyre and Sidon, they would have repented long ago in sackcloth and ashes. But I tell you," etc. Nowhere in any of our Gospels are we told of a stay by Christ in Chorazin and Bethsaida, and yet the most of Christ's miracles were performed there. Such passages are also to be found in John 2. There we are told that when Christ was in Jerusalem at the Passover, many believed in his name when they saw his signs which he did, but we are told nothing of these miracles. There is just the story of the cleansing of the temple. Then Nicodemus refers to the signs that Christ did, and we are told that the Galileans welcomed him, having seen all that he did in Jerusalem. It is noteworthy that during Christ's stay in Samaria, where people believed in him, no miracles occur, though he stayed there several days.* To be sure, another fact ought to be mentioned. John always narrates miracles of Christ only when they were the occasion for discourses or conversations, or to the extent that they led to a change in his relationships to people. Therefore it is possible that Christ performed miracles also in Samaria and that John passed over them in silence.

In the three synoptic Gospels we find many passages in which large numbers of miracles are mentioned without being enumerated in detail. Such passages occur so early in Matthew that it is scarcely possible to believe that they had been performed so early. Matthew 4:23 gives us the impression of large numbers of people and also of the passage of a considerable amount of time, but almost leads us to believe that something earlier must have been basic to it. *Just as we sus-*

---

* or add: though there certainly were sick people there and though there was faith, and Christ never is reported as having rejected such a request. Yet, during an unsettled stay in Jerusalem all kinds of miracles are said to have been performed.

191

pect that Christ had taught some time before his baptism, we are also led to suspect that he had engaged before that time in the performance of miracles. There is a passage in Luke that makes this assumption very plausible. Immediately after the story of the temptation we are told that Christ taught in the synagogues and said in Nazareth, "Doubtless you will quote to me this proverb, 'Physician, heal yourself; what we have heard you did at Capernaum, do here also in your own country.'" This shows that the report of his miracles had already reached Nazareth before he himself had arrived there. However, the uncertainty that arises out of the location of this incident in Luke's Gospel means that we cannot lay much weight on this passage. Just as these Evangelists present all sorts of accounts of miracles, they also abound in descriptions that differ completely from one another. Take the story of the feeding of the multitude as an example. One Gospel tells us of many miracles in connection with it, whereas Mark in his account in chapter 8 mentions none. *If we reflect on the numerous miracles that are not recounted, on the numerous miracles that are narrated, and on the miracles that are described in detail, we must conclude that the performance of miracles required a large part of Christ's time during his life.*

However, if we take all that is told of this in the Gospels literally, it is difficult to form a total picture of it. In the first place, these great numbers of miracles presuppose quite disproportionate numbers of sick, diseased, and ailing folk, and particularly many that are referred to under the inclusive term "demoniacs," who are mentioned along with the lunatics. If we were to consider these numerous marvelous healings, which presuppose a massive suffering, we should get a picture which would differ greatly from that we have formed of Christ's ordinary day, and it would be impossible to understand how such large numbers of sick people could have gathered about Christ again and again for the same reason and in the same area. *Therefore we must treat these statements with caution and see how far they are due to the structure of the Gospels. Many of them may be the conclusion to or the beginning of individual narratives and merely repeat what has already been said or what is about to be said, rather than refer to different miracles.* In the narratives in John the matter takes a natural form. If Christ spent a period of time in Jerusalem and was not the last who came there and not the first who left, since this time was important for his task and he had more time and a larger audience for his teaching, we can imagine that more such miracles were performed during his stays at festivals, but not so many that they could not be considered separately. But if we are to imagine such numbers in the course of travels about Galilee, numbers that could not have been drawn from among the immediate inhabitants of a single place, we cannot conceive of them in the same way as the stories in John enable us to do.

But this is the only suitable place in our account of the life of Christ to deal with these marvelous acts of Christ in their peculiarity, for they belong essentially to our picture of Christ and his ministry, and it is important to arrive at a clear picture of them. For that purpose, however, it is not enough to use the general term *miracle,* for that includes very different things that cannot be compared with each other. The expressions that the New Testament writers use and that we translate by the word "miracle" do not refer to the same thing. Our word "miracle," because of our use of terms, is definitely opposed to natural events. The term "miracle," because we have a greater and better systematized knowledge of nature, has a greater meaning for us than it had in Christ's time, and we must put ourselves back into that time. I do not wish to say that a contrast between the unnatural and the natural was not already implied in the expressions "signs, wonders, mighty works." It is present to the greatest degree in the word *teras*["wonder"],but that word occurs least frequently and only incidentally. In *sēmeion*["sign"]the *significance* of what we are to infer from the outcome is to the fore. In *dynamis*["mighty work"]the main emphasis is on the fact that the actor has a certain nature (power) in him. In *teras*["wonder"]the comparison of this result with the others constitutes the main content. In Christ's time, however, no such contrast in meaning was possible. Among us it occurs less frequently in popular usage than among those who view nature in its scientific aspects, and, in the sense that it was intended at that time to convey, the contrast between the natural and the supernatural signified not much more than that for us between the ordinary and the unusual or extra-ordinary. But I do not wish to say this in order to put an end to the use of our strict contrast, for what has been said is related only to the idea that is basic to it. We, however, must reach our judgment according to the nature of the events, whether or not the contrast between the natural and the supernatural is employed.

Lecture 30 (July 2). Viewed as a whole, we can understand the miracles only as follows. It is uncertain whether some were not performed even before the baptism. In any case, they gradually became more frequent after their renown became current. We can only explain the fact that few or no miracles were performed during Christ's final stay in Jerusalem by the observation that those who sought help were kept away by those who accompanied Christ, whereas previously they had been brought to him. Apart from Jerusalem Christ spent any length of time only in small towns, where only a few people in need of healing would be found. Those who longed for help would naturally be stationed chiefly in synagogues, at places set apart for prayer, and along the highways that were traversed by folk going to festivals.

If we are to deal properly with the matter we must disregard the scholastic contrast between the natural and the supernatural in these accounts, for there was no knowledge of nature in Christ's time. What was not understood could be a *sēmeion* ["sign"] and what was merely unusual a *teras* ["wonder"]. The narrators cannot be regarded as witnesses or authorities in these matters, but we must ascertain the facts as far as that is possible and base our judgment on them. To the extent that they were also moral acts we must pay attention to the motives and the way the miracles themselves arose. (1). Most of the miracles were performed because of Christ's love of people. Our Lord always refused to perform miracles for the purpose of display or ostentation. Therefore, what looks like ostentation must be carefully examined. The temptation story represents Christ as rejecting miracles as means of obtaining self-preservation, and what applied to himself must also have applied to those who were associated with him. To perform such miracles would not have been a sin, but the idea of doing so never occurred to him. So what appears to have been of that sort (the stilling of the storm, the finding of a coin in the fish's mouth) deserve our closest attention. So we discover gradations of motives, from deliverances on down. (2). Miracles were prompted usually by request, at times without being asked for (as in the feeding of the multitude), even on occasion because they were almost forced upon him (as at Bethesda). In these we can discover the motives more precisely. Many others, on the contrary, were performed involuntarily (the healing of the woman with the hemorrhage). They happened in connection with him but were not done by him. They were done by God through him (the raising of Lazarus from the dead). Related to these are those miracles that were associated with him or that happened to him (the baptism, the voice from heaven, the transfiguration, the resurrection).[28]

John usually includes individual miracles in his account only to the extent that they give rise to other acts or to our Lord's discourses, which are a necessary element of his Gospel. Although occasionally reference is made to a more extended miraculous activity on Christ's part, that always refers to a lengthy period in which miracles were performed but which is not included in his account. In Matthew,* on the

28. Schleiermacher's statement on miracles in *The Christian Faith* holds that a true recognition of Jesus is never properly to be based upon miracles, however such recognition might be confirmed by them. Most pointedly, they are superfluous for later times. In their occurrence they operated as signs to direct attention to Jesus, an impressiveness which they lose in ratio to our distance from them in space and time. The place of miracles in performing this function is now taken by our knowledge of the historical influence which Jesus Christ has had in the world. See *CF*, §103, 4. There is a partial parallel between Schleiermacher's position on this point and that of G. E. Lessing in *On the Proof of the Spirit and of Power*: "But since the truth of these miracles has completely ceased to be demonstrable by miracles still happening now, ... What then does bind me? Nothing but these (Christ's) teachings themselves. Eighteen hundred years ago they were so new, so alien, so foreign to the entire mass of truths recognized in that age, that nothing less than miracles and fulfilled prophecies were required if the multitude were to attend to them at all." *Lessing's Theological Writings,* trans. Henry Chadwick (Stanford University, 1956), p. 55. However, there are far-reaching differences between Schleiermacher and Lessing which are pointed to in Schleiermacher's contention of congruence between miracles and Jesus Christ's historical influence. For Lessing holds that religious truth resides in the inner deliverances of rationality and for that reason this truth is not intrinsically dependent upon accidental historical formation. Christianity can be surpassed. In contrast, Schleiermacher maintains that Jesus Christ has transformed the religious self-consciousness of those living within his sphere of influence, providing truth which would not have been without his appearance and which is unsurpassable. Cf. Introduction, p. xlvi, the historical relation of Schleiermacher to Lessing, Wilhelm Dilthey's statement still is valid: "An influence of Lessing's view of religion, which appears similar to that of Schleiermacher, has up to the present time not been established." *Leben Schleiermachers* (Göttingen: Vandenhoeck & Ruprecht, 1970; 1st ed. 1870), 1:395. Analyses of Lessing's views may be found in Bernhard Punjer, *History of the Christian Philosophy of Religion,* trans. W. Hastie (Edinburgh: T. & T. Clark, 1887), and in Henry E. Allison, *Lessing and the Enlightenment* (Ann Arbor: University of Michigan, 1966).

* the miracles are related in part for their own sake, and so with an entirely different purpose than in John's.

other hand, we find general accounts or, rather, general statements of miracles performed en masse by Christ, which we have to think of as belonging to a limited period. So we have two different representations of what happened. The latter, however, that in Matthew, is explained by the fact that such general statements occur at transition points from one group of accounts to others and in such a way that we cannot be sure what they refer to and cannot say whether they do not contain essentially what has already been narrated. Many of these statements of miracles performed en masse are of such a sort that they cannot be taken (or: understood) literally. For example, when Christ comes to Capernaum the inhabitants summon all the sick from the surrounding district.

If we gather together everything that belongs in this field and ask how we are to think of the miraculous power of Christ as having been apportioned, there are two points to keep in mind. I have already indicated that there are passages which suggest that Christ's wonderworking powers had already been exercised before the beginning of his public appearance. Christ's mother is represented as already believing in his miracles, and that permits us to infer that he had previously performed miraculous acts. When Luke has Christ go to Nazareth, where his public ministry begins, and makes the residents say that he should perform the same miracles there that he had done in Capernaum, that cannot be limited to a few days. On the contrary, it seems to refer to something that had happened earlier. The only question is: Has Luke given the incident its proper chronological setting? In any case, Christ's miraculous ministry must have been gradually expanded, since naturally the class of miraculous healings can have been performed only on people who took advantage of Christ's wonderworking power. This presupposes experience with that power, and that would have been acquired only gradually.

So far as the end of Christ's public ministry is concerned, Matthew reports in chapter 21 only quite incidentally that in Jerusalem, after Christ had entered the temple, the blind and the lame followed him in order that he might heal them, but later the Evangelist has nothing to say of such healings.

It remains doubtful whether we are to think of the statement in this way, or whether it is to be thought of as a description of Christ's daily activity. During this time he usually spent the night in the vicinity of Bethany and only went to the temple in the mornings. We can imagine that it was improbable that people who could be moved only with difficulty, who needed the help of others, would have come to Christ when great crowds of people assembled in Jerusalem at the time of the festivals. And this leads to another point. If we think of Christ as remaining for any length of time at one and the same place, whether during his Galilean stay or, according to John, during his stay in Judea, we must reflect on the fact that there were few large towns apart from Jerusalem, and that actually none (or: few) of the larger towns except Jerusalem is mentioned. On the contrary, most places had a small population, and there would scarcely have been many there at the same time who could lay a claim to Christ's help. Furthermore, the less certain the length of Christ's stay in a given place, the less people could come from different places to claim his help.

We conclude, then, that Christ's performance of healing miracles was incidental and occasional. When we run across narratives that give a different impression, namely, that those in need of help crowded around Christ in great numbers, we surely find other narratives that counteract them, stories that the sick were restrained and pushed back by the people who surrounded Christ in order that they might not bother him at an unsuitable time. From these stories we see that the desire for miracles, the demand that Christ work miracles, did not emerge among the masses except on certain occasions, and always to confirm his messianic office. So the part that the masses played in his wonderworking activity was sometimes to bring people to him and sometimes to restrain them from coming. Consequently a certain limited period was provided in which Christ exercised this activity and in which he performed his healing miracles.

When we look at the matter itself, the contrast between the supernatural and the natural that we include in the term "miracle" on the basis of scholastic terminology does not

197

appear as strongly in the general designation of Christ's influential activity that the Evangelists use. This contrast could not be so strong at that time, for there was nothing known of what we call natural science. There were only confused references to nature and natural power in ordinary life, without a clear distinction and classification of the concepts and of their limitations. As a result the unusual and the astonishing could be designated without examination as *teras*["wonder"],*dynamis*["mighty work"],or *sēmeion*["sign"].So then, if we consider this fact from our point of vantage, we must first overlook everything in the narratives that belongs to the category of judgment and must try to envisage the facts of what happened. The way the Evangelists narrate the events presents great difficulties. To get at the facts so far as possible it will be necessary for us to avoid regarding in advance all acts of Christ as identical that are subsumed in the New Testament accounts under that general expression. On the contrary, we must classify them, for otherwise we should regard many as of the same sort, and the decisions and judgments would have to be of unequal worth if they appear in the same form with reference to very different facts. In this connection two matters must be kept in mind. In the first place, we must remember the variety of facts, regarded as acts of Christ, that must be presupposed with respect to the power that accounts for them. In the second place, we must never forget the motives on which Christ acted, for all these acts of his must be capable of being viewed as moral acts. In this respect the facts as narrated present a great difference.

If we distinguish between the miracles in the first instance according to their *motives,* we see that most of them are acts that arose out of concern for people and their needs. They were acts by which Christ alleviated the sufferings of men by using a power inherent in himself. But not all are to be regarded in this way. There are others that appear to have had different motives. If we approach the matter from a different direction, we find that Christ always refused to perform acts that had a holy (or: divine) character, that were only intended to be valid in their own right, rather than to be a response to moral motives. He always refused to perform miracles to replace unbelief with belief. We must make this distinction: He appealed to miracles as familiar acts that implied an indwelling power in himself such as was not possessed by other men, and yet he never performed such acts in order to appeal to them. If some miracles seem to be capable only of this latter explanation, we must remember that Christ never intended them to be so explained. This must lead us to look carefully for another explanation of every miracle performed by Christ that could have been meant, according to the narrative, only as a display of his office. If we go back to the story of the temptation, the throwing of himself down from the pinnacle of the temple would have been purely a display miracle. Christ's rejection of the suggestion made by Satan is in accordance with the pattern we observe. It expresses the maxim that such behavior was contrary to his nature, and it would be regarded as acting against the divine will if he were to perform such a merely ostentatious miracle. Since he indicates everywhere clearly that faith in him is the will of God and that the purpose of his coming was to realize this and to lead men to faith, and since we find that in this connection Christ rejected all miracles performed merely for display, it follows that he did not regard that as the faith that he was to call forth that was awakened by such display miracles. That is to say, in appealing to his miracles he never wanted to separate their physical content from the motive, but to regard them only in the light of the motive.

Nevertheless, miracles are recounted that could only have had this character of display, for instance, the story of the cursing of the fig tree. Are we to say that Christ wanted to punish the fig tree? Such a statement would be absurd. It would have been only the expression of a disappointed expectation and would have had only a sensuous, passionate motivation. Our only conclusion is that it was performed as a display miracle. The narrators understood and represented it as such. If it was an act of Christ it was either the expression of a sensuous motive, and we cannot believe that, or a piece of ostentation, which we also cannot believe, since those about him did not require such an exhibition to establish or under-gird faith. According to the temptation story the first* would also have had to involve rejection. The miracle is represented there as one related to Christ's need to nourish himself, and yet he thrusts it aside with an answer which asserts that he puts his trust in divine providence for such matters. That must be regarded as the rejection of all miracles that were con-cerned with self-nourishment. We should not expect such miracles, and where they appear we must try to discover whe-ther they do not have another explanation.

In this connection we can draw no distinction between those miracles concerned with his personal nourishment and those concerned with the nourishment of those who were members of the company about him. He could only treat the latter as he treated himself. Nevertheless, such miracles are recorded. If, for example, we look at the miracle of the still-ing of the storm, we see that it took place during a time of danger to life in which the disciples believed him and them-selves to be involved and in which they went to him and laid claim on his power for help — a plea that he did not reject. But that is something we must try to harmonize with the maxim we have articulated. We are in a similar situation when we consider the story of the coin that Peter is said to have found in the fish's mouth. The only purpose of this miracle could have been to give assistance to Peter. In the same category we must also place the story of the miraculous draught of fish, for that was also a miracle that affected the disciples' income. It was either an increase of their income miraculously effected by Christ, or an alleviation of their worry and need. Here, then, we find a gradation of motives, where miracles performed purely out of concern for human needs pass over gradually into those that no longer relieve suffering. Some even appear to have involved the element of display, in contradiction to the general position Christ ex-pounded, but which we must nevertheless regard as in con-formity with his maxims.

We find an equally important distinction in Christ's rela-

* the sensuous motive would also have to be rejected?

tions to those on whom the miracles were performed. Usually we find that Christ was requested to do some mighty work and a claim on his help was advanced. However, there are also instances when Christ as it were forced his help on others. I cite the story of Christ's healing of the sick man at the pool of Bethesda, as it is reported in the Gospel of John. Christ healed the man, though he had made no request and had not asked for help, and his whole way of expressing himself later does not indicate that he felt any great degree of gratitude. Similarly, in the miracle of the feeding of the multitude we find no request for help emanating from the crowd. The disciples made a different sort of request, namely, that Christ should dismiss the crowd early and let the hungry among them shift for themselves. So we find that at times the request was one that issued from Christ's own inner being. Quite opposed to such miracles as we have discussed so far are the descriptions of those that Christ performed involuntarily, for example, the healing of the woman who pressed on him in the crowd and was cured of her trouble by touching his garments. In this instance Christ became aware of the miracle only after it had happened. This was a result that he had not actually willed and intended. According to the content of the story it was the consequence of a physical contact whose issue was not intended, and this is the picture that all three Evangelists give us. Here, too, there is a significant gradation, which means that we must make a distinction. The last example cited leads us to distinguish between miracles that happened through Christ as the medium and miracles that he actually performed. And this leads us to still another example. The miracle of the raising of Lazarus does not look like one that Christ performed, for in no other miracle are we told that he first uttered a prayer and asked God to do something. By first offering a prayer and by representing what follows as the answer to his prayer, Christ leads us to believe that the act was not his but God's. There are also miracles that happened to him and in connection with him, but in which he himself played only a passive role, for example, the miraculous events associated with his baptism. The voice that declared that he was the Son of God, what happened at the transfiguration and when God raised him from the dead — all these are miracles performed on him but not performed by him.

Lecture 31 (July 3). To sum up, we must consider two other matters. In the first place, there are miracles performed on living people whose success depends chiefly on the persons on whom they are performed. So we are told that Christ could not [perform miracles] where there was no faith, even if this faith involved nothing more than the element of eager expectation. Likewise he himself is almost passive when the effect of the miracle, while proceeding physically from him, is due merely to the activity of others (the healing of the woman with the hemorrhage who touched him). In the second place, we must ask whether the effect of the miracles is to be found purely in the human realm, or whether it involves the elementary powers of nature. (The latter is the case also when the miracle is effected on people, but by an *actio in distans.*) Summing up the results we can say: Those miracles are clearest to us where the effect is limited to the human realm (for there are analogies which show that purely organic illnesses can be cured by spiritual powers) and which are performed because of Christ's concern for human need. These enable us to understand, at least as free acts, those miracles that were performed on nature, not actual healings but acts of good will (as at Cana), and also those — for Christ must have been able to use such powers, just as everyone else uses those that he possesses — that were performed in his own and his disciples' interest (the stilling of the storm, the healing of Peter's mother-in-law). But those miracles performed wholly for display, such as the feeding of the multitude, the finding of the coin in the fish's mouth, are the most difficult to understand and therefore must be examined most carefully. And the most difficult of all are those miracles performed outside the human realm.

In order to make a complete survey of this difficult area we must make two further comments. Every success is dependent on more than one person. When someone does something to another, the latter can never be purely passive, and that is the case* if he to whom something happens is a human or free being. This twofold character of any activity is to be presupposed everywhere. That is to say, anyone's ability to achieve success is dependent on the activity of some other person. Christ's activity has not always the same conse-

* and that is true always to the extent that, etc.

quences. Sometimes he is the only one who plays a role, and in such instances we can only assume a lively receptivity on the part of the other person involved. On the other hand, we have already seen that there were miracles in which Christ's part was much less, miracles that Christ had not deliberately intended, and even miracles which happened through him without any volition on his part. Many instances of these occur in general statements in the Gospels. In Matthew we read: "All who touched him were healed." The same thing is true of the story of the woman with the hemorrhage. Christ took no initiative in this instance, and the result of the miracle was a physical result. So we have a gradation. This takes on still another appearance when we recall how often we are told in Gospel narratives that Jesus now and then could do few mighty works because of the unbelief of those about him. We do not need to exaggerate this to the point of saying that Christ's wonderworking powers were always conditioned by faith. There are examples to the contrary. However, even if he could perform only a few miracles because the faith that was necessary for the demand for help was lacking, it follows that Christ's activity in this respect was conditioned by something else* that determined its success.

With reference to the contrast between the natural and the supernatural, as we are accustomed to view it, we must note the difference in the way Christ acted. By far the most of the miracles of Christ that are recorded are concerned with human life and the organic condition of people. They lie wholly within the realm of human nature. On the other hand, there are others, whose results were successful, that were performed on inanimate nature, and this sets them off from the rest. If we assume that all Christ's acts must always be capable of comprehension as purely human acts, because otherwise we should find them inexplicable, and if at the same time we must presuppose what definitely sets him apart from all other men, though it takes human form, or if we assume, on the other hand, that we can never define the area of the supernatural because nature has not been fully explored and we

---

* depended on a request made by someone else, although, as we have seen, this was not always the case

have not reached its outer limits, we find ourselves, despite our knowledge of nature, in a position very like those who were immediate witnesses of Christ's acts. According to the circumstances we cannot definitely distinguish the unusual from the supernatural. With these points in mind we have to say: We cannot think of an act performed by a man on a man as absolutely supernatural, to the extent that we regard the agent as a natural one and the effect also as natural.

If we now wish to bring the different miracles of Christ under a formula, those, namely, that were performed on people, we find that in most of them the effect was an organic one, the removal of states of organic illness, but that the agent was predominantly a spiritual one, the will of Christ. To be sure, however, a physical element was also present, for we never find that Christ left this will unexpressed, and this expression of will was at the same time something physical. If we cannot regard everything that is said here and there of contacts that Christ made and of other definitely external acts of Christ as what was really effective, we must nevertheless say that what we otherwise should have to regard as purely imitative, that is, as an expression of his purely spiritual activity, produces an effect on others. Consequently, if the spiritual effect is conditioned by something organic, the effect (or: the transition) is provided for the organic result. To the extent that we regard these acts as miracles, that is, as acts which depend on the peculiar dignity of Christ and were only possible because of it, they appear to us, and must appear to us, in the form of human acts, and we must therefore look for analogies to them, although such analogies appear similar rather than identical. Natural science in its research has observed many analogous instances at the present time of the sudden effects on the human organism of another, but of one who exercises a certain power over men, a spiritual and physical ascendency. It reports many such effects that* have not yet been explained by natural law. *They are similar rather than identical cases, and it has not been possible to accomplish by physical effect on people what Christ brought to pass through*

* so that an exact boundary line between organic and spiritual effects cannot be drawn

204

organic relationships by means of the dignity peculiar to him, that is, by employing a quite different power of spiritual ascendancy, on which we can place no limits. Because Christ's power remains analogous to human acts, it is not contrary to nature, but it is supernatural to the extent that it rests on his unique dignity and character. But these acts in individual instances take on a quite different character.

The analogy ceases to apply in several miracles that are recorded, miracles in which Christ performs his mighty work as an *actio in distans*. When a man's servant is healed without asking for it (or: by a mere word) and without being in Christ's presence, a medium intervenes that puts an end to the analogy, for if we wish to account for this as something natural, we have to think of nature as the bearer of the will of Christ to the subject who is to be effected by it, and this destroys the connection between one human being and another. So there are some cases in this area that belong to this class by virtue of their results, but by virtue of their genesis belong in the other. Since we have to think of gradations in this connection, we have to recognize a whole series of such differences in Christ's miracles, and then the following will represent a summary of them: *The more the deed can be understood as a moral act on the part of Christ and the more we can establish a comparison between Christ's way of accomplishing a given result and that employed by other people, the more we can comprehend the acts as genuine constituents of the life of Jesus. The less we can understand them as moral acts on Christ's part and the less at the same time we can discover analogies, the less we shall be able to form a definite idea of the account and understand the facts on which it is based.*

In this connection we become aware at the same time of a class of miracles that we can most easily understand as *real events in the life of Christ.* This class consists of those miracles of Christ that according to their tendency were performed out of concern for human need, healings of people in distress, and that were performed in the realm of human life, that is to say, miracles that can be regarded as the consequence of the concern of one man for another. To be sure there was always a significant difference in the manner and sort of the suffering, because we always have to think of the spiritual power that emanated from Christ as conditioned in its organic results by the psychic state of the person on whom the miracle was performed. Our experiences, to which we have to restrict ourselves, are very incomplete, and we cannot say anything that is decisive. However, if the suffering is located in a function of life that is in constant relation to the psychic element, we can think of it as ended by a psychic effect. The less that is the case, the more difficult it is to form an opinion of the matter, but in the life of man there is nothing that is completely unrelated to the psychic side of life. To be sure, if we think of disorders that are connected with the mental state (demonic possession), the dominant influence of an overwhelming (or: superior) spirit must be able to produce a psychic effect, which is analogous to ascendancy. The more (or: even if) the suffering is purely organic, [the more] the connection between the psychic and the organic becomes apparent to us everywhere, although not equally distinctly. It is therefore possible to think of psychic influences on the organism as inherent in nature. They do not occur because such a spiritual ascendancy as Christ possessed is not present, but there are analogies to it, and these analogies can be cited.

We now raise the question: How are we to think of Christ as making use of these powers that were latent in him? In such a way that we can understand the individual acts as moral events. Everyone is called to use his powers for the common good, and if Christ could bring about such effects, he was called to relieve the human misery of men and to free them from what limited their activity. However, since that was not his *actual* mission, he was able to make only occasional use of his powers. No doubt he ignored many suffering people, without extending help to them, because he was involved in another mission. Sometimes he was not able to exercise his healing powers because those in need of them did not put themselves into contact with him. In all this we are made aware of the completely moral character of Christ's actions.

Now let us take a further step. To the extent that we put

our powers to work for the benefit of all, we ourselves and those who are near to us are involved, and we cannot maintain that such a work of Christ would not have been capable of being performed on those who were in closest contact with him, as soon as something existed in circles near him that could be placed again in its natural, free condition by the exercise of his powers. Reflect, for example, on the story of how Christ cured Peter's mother-in-law. We are not told that she asked to be cured, but when she was cured she served Christ and the rest. Consequently we conclude that her "service" was expected, but she was incapable of it because of her state of illness, and it is natural that Christ cured her in order that she could carry out her duties and serve him and his disciples. That could be applied to all similar cases. In this area, then, we can observe a gradation from cases where Christ was urgently petitioned to intervene with his helpful powers, to cases where he exercised his powers wihout being requested to do so, to cases where he was as it were compelled to act. We can explain* them in the same way, only under different external circumstances. In a moment of free leisure, as, for instance, during a walk, as in the case of the sick man at the pool of Bethesda, he would not have performed the act if he had been engaged in a definite activity. However, he would have performed it if he had been petitioned for help. So then, Christ made use of his powers as does everyone who employs his gifts with moral precepts in mind.

However, when we look at another class of such acts, which did not lie within the human realm but were miracles performed on inanimate nature, we see that we can discover no analogy, and we think of them at the same time as more difficult to understand than the moral acts of Christ. Where elements of both are to be found we find ourselves greatly embarrassed, and this may go to the extent that we have to say: If the story is to be taken literally, it is incomprehensible. So the suspicion arises that the narrative is not of the sort that we can distinguish what is factual in it. Take, for example, the story of the stilling of the storm. Here we are told of a

---

* We can think of them as issuing from himself

miracle that Christ performed on the elements, a miracle for which we can find no analogy in our experience if the event is recorded as it actually happened. If all those on the ship faced an imminent threat to their very lives, it was natural that Christ should perform such a miracle, that he should make use of his powers, and, while we should be unable to explain the act on physical grounds, we could understand it completely as a moral act. The story of Christ's miracle at the marriage at Cana is a similar one. Anyone can make use of his powers, provided that no other use is prescribed, when it is not in conflict with duty, to cheer up people in social life. There was no case of need at the marriage at Cana. What arose was a situation of social embarrassment. We can discover no analogy to the miracle as a physical one. We cannot understand its physical results. However, if Christ had been able to perform such a miracle, we can understand and can have no objection to the act as a moral one.

However, if we were to discover acts of this sort that could only be acts of ostentation performed by Christ, we should not be able to understand them as moral acts, and if we were not able to comprehend them physically we should be involved in acute embarrassment. Take, for example, the story of the feeding of the five thousand or the four thousand. Here was an instance which did not involve actual need. The disciples asked Christ only to dismiss the people in order that they might look for physical nourishment in the vicinity, and if such nourishment were available, we cannot speak of a case of need. Furthermore, the disciples would not have been able to say what they did if the people present had been so weary that they would not have been able "to go into the villages and country round about, to lodge and get provisions." What was Christ's purpose in performing this miracle? What is the moral motive of the act? We cannot discover it, for the miracle did not involve a case of need and no request was made of Christ. It looks to us as though Christ performed the miracle for the sake of performing a miracle. That, however, we cannot assume. The motive is as elusive as the physical results of the miracle are incomprehensible. We seek to remove the act from this category and to view it in a different light. In such cases we have a problem, but not necessarily one that must be solved.* The story may have been constructed in such a way that we are no longer able to explain it. We have found that we can most easily understand the miracles that most clearly show themselves to be moral acts by virtue of their motives and that can be viewed as the acts of a man on another man. In order to remove any possible misunderstanding in this matter, I now should like to say: *It is not my intention in any way to say that we have to explain these acts of Christ as they were performed in any specific way. I only wish to maintain that we do not need to assume anything supernatural, anything that is at the same time contrary to nature, but only a potential ascendancy on Christ's part, which was a constituent of his peculiar nature and disposition.*

Lectures 32, 33, 34 (July 4, 5, 6). In this connection we are under heavy pressure to place the blame on the narratives and to try to explain them by means of hypotheses, particularly when Christ is represented as acting in ways that do not seem appropriate to him. For example, the words addressed to the sea and the storm could have contributed nothing to the success of the miracle. Here we have to assume either an alteration or some other context. We reject the explanation that Christ developed a theory of miraculous effects when he saw the withered fig tree. This would imply that he had wanted the fig tree to wither away (despite the fact that it was not the season for figs) and that what he wanted was brought about by miraculous means. Since Jesus himself, according to John, excluded the feeding of the multitude from the category of signs, we have the task of trying to imagine what must have happened, if the whole event is not to be regarded as miraculous. Such tasks as these have nothing to do with ordinary, naturalistic methods of explanation, for everything comprehensible, which includes the bulk of the material, is to be understood as the consequence of Christ's unique nature. For nature miracles we have miracles that happened in response to prayer and miracles of prophetic vision as connecting links. The former lie outside our immediate interest, though it remains difficult to understand how Christ could have had such a firm conviction about them in individual instances, since we know that he always refused to perform miracles in order to prove that he was the Messiah. So far as the miracles of prophetic vision are concerned, we have

* but one whose solution is often impossible

209

analogies. We can place no limits on the ability to anticipate events. When we extend this to include the realm of nature, the ability to anticipate is closely bound up with the effect on the body. (The story of the stilling of the storm can be explained in this way, but not that of the finding of the coin in the fish's mouth.) All this does not solve our problems, and we must accept the fact that many such phenomena are inexplicable. Even a theory that the first three Evangelists exercised a great measure of freedom is not of any help, for we still have to contend with the story of the marriage at Cana in the Gospel of John. The situation is similar when we consider the miracles performed on Christ. The miracle at the time of Christ's baptism was performed for· John's sake and is comprehensible, but what purpose was served by the miracle of the transfiguration? Elijah and Moses could have had no significance for Christ, and the disciples had no need of the voice. Finally, if Christ was able to use his miraculous powers to support himself, why did he not employ them at the time of his catastrophic death? We conclude that his actions were sufficiently motivated by the fact that he was under the law.

(July 4) The question of whether the performance of miracles necessarily belongs to the idea of Christ must be clarified to some extent before the individual miracles can be viewed from the proper point of vantage. We have already noted that Christ absolutely refused to perform miracles when people demanded them in order to provide grounds for faith, that is to say, in order that his messianic dignity, unique nature, and redemptive mission might be made manifest by miracles. Taking our departure from this well-known fact, we conclude that he did not want to obtain recognition in this way. At the same time, nevertheless, and in a certain sense he appealed to his mighty works. He did not perform his miracles to demonstrate his messiahship, but he pointed to them as evidence of his office, as signs that witnessed to his nature, as an expression and measure of the power that was his or that he used in a definite way. In this sense he appealed to his miracles. Faith in Christ could also have been aroused without miracles. If Christ had not been convinced of that he would always have performed miracles for this purpose,*even when the request for them revealed the desire to be able to believe.

* He would never have repudiated this only possible means of arousing faith. We are not to assume the necessity of performing miracles in order to give rise to faith

But the matter takes on a different appearance when we ask whether the specific nature of Christ which distinguishes him from all others, namely, that he was able to be a redeemer who himself required no redemption, at the same time involves the ability to perform miracles. We can scarcely provide a wholly satisfactory answer to this question. I can only say: If reports that are genuine and authentic intimate that Christ performed miracles, I can account for them by reason of his unique dignity and nature, but if we are not certain of the miracles, that uncertainty would not give me cause to doubt that specific dignity and uniqueness. I am all the more sure of this since Christ himself declares that miracles similar to his own can also be performed by others. The request that he should perform miracles did not come as a result of the idea that they would demonstrate his peculiar dignity, but because of his likeness to the prophets* and because of his messianic office. So far as the former is concerned, everyone will agree that, if we presuppose something that distinguishes Christ from all others, the possession of a distinctive power that he can exercise in his relation to other men can also be presupposed. How far that can include a power over inanimate nature for which we have·no analogy is unclear to the extent that we can demonstrate no connection between human and inanimate nature. If we can imagine an original moral purity on Christ's part that was maintained at every stage of development — a moral purity by means of which he always subjected the sensual to the control of the spiritual principle as both developed — in other words, if Christ had a spiritual power over both the psychic and the physical world that was always adequate, this furnishes us with an analogy which, if we follow it through, can explain a great deal. It is helpful to reflect on the fact that the psychic condition affects the bodily condition, that a sudden change in attitude results in a change in one's bodily state. The more the suffering from which Christ freed men was psychic in nature, the easier it is for us to understand it by means of the analogy of our own experience. If we doubt the existence of evil spirits and the idea of

* or add: of whom he is said to be the greatest

demoniacal possession, we consider the condition basically a psychic one, and if we consider the cause to have been a free agent, then a lapse into such a state must have taken place, and this must end whenever the reason for it disappears. The effect of a dominating will on one that is depressed, which leads to the latter's freedom, is something we can envisage in accordance with the analogy. And if we reflect on one of Christ's discourses in which, after having healed someone who was regarded as possessed, he went on to say that if one were not powerful enough to bind the strong man, the spirit that had been driven out would return and the latter state of the individual would be worse than the former, we see that others performed similar exorcisms but, since they were not effected by the same power, they did not have the same durability, and the former state of the individual recurred. However, Christ represents his own healing act as one that would put an end to the old condition. The more that organic states exist in the functions of life where the connection between the psychic and the organic elements are most evident, the easier it is to think of such a healing effect in this area. However, I never believe that such healings can be explained as the result of purely natural causes. We cannot overlook the fact of Christ's unique dignity and nature.

Let us now consider the opposite point. We can take it for granted, and it does not interfere with the pursuit of our task. In other words, assuming the unique nature of Christ, these healings appear to us under the categories that determine human life and are adapted to the general conditions that prevail in human life, although we can only think of them in connection with the unique nature of Christ as such. However, if we wish to understand effects in inanimate nature, without the employment of natural powers that are at man's disposal, and especially the effect on such functions of nature as still lie outside the area of human influence — if we wish to understand these in connection with the unique dignity of Christ, the continuity and unity of human life are threatened. If one were to say, Christ did that because he was all-powerful, one would therefore assume an element of human existence that exercised powers that cannot be explained in human terms, and that would interfere with our basic task, and there would be gaps in our account to the extent that we have to assume such acts of Christ. In other words, they are in opposition to our interest in understanding and presenting Christ in human terms, and to the extent that we make such exceptions we cease to some extent to assume the human existence and work of Christ. So such acts deserve closer consideration from our standpoint than the others, for the others and the way of explaining them do not interfere with the continuity of our task.

It is true of many, if not of all, acts of this sort that they could only be understood as moral acts in a way that would cause us some concern. The story of the finding of the coin in the fish's mouth is one example of what I have in mind. Christ returns with his apostles to Capernaum after a journey through Galilee. He seems to have preceded them with Peter. An official whose task it was to collect taxes meets Peter and asks him: Does not your teacher pay the tax? Christ explains that he was actually free of any obligation to pay but, since the tax was collected and paying it was customary, he says to Peter: In order not to give offense to them, go to the sea and cast a hook, and take the first fish that comes up, etc. If we regard such powers as belonging to the life of Christ, I cannot see why he should not employ them in the same way as we, being morally free, employ our powers in a certain sense in order to assure our self-preservation. I ask, however: Was there at that time a situation that compelled Christ to perform a miracle? I cannot say, under the circumstances, that there was any such situation. In the first place, we have no reason to assume that Christ and his disciples were so poor that he could not have found a coin with which to pay the tax, especially a tax that was regularly collected and for which periodic provision had to be made. Furthermore, there was no great hurry. The tax did not have to be paid at once. The circumstances were not such as to demand a miracle. Accordingly it is hard to understand the moral motives of the act. There must have been other circumstances than those that are referred to. Furthermore, in terms of its effect it goes beyond anything that can be explained in human terms. First

213

of all, it was a miracle of prediction. Christ must have seen a fish that had swallowed a coin. This in itself would be something extraordinary. In the second place, he must have ordained that the fish would bite on no other hook than Peter's. That can only be explained as the exercise of pure magic. The miracle, then, combines two improbabilities.

The story of the fig tree that withered is a miracle of the same sort. If we were to think of it as a result of the will of Christ that the fig tree, assuming that it was in an entirely healthy state, withered away so quickly, we should have to say that this was the consequence of magic, for it was wholly contrary to nature. From the moral point of view, the act takes on the appearance of a punishment and presupposes a frame of mind that, with respect to the subject, is incomprehensible, for who can get angry about a fig tree? Furthermore, in chapter 11: 13 the Evangelist Mark says that it was not the season when figs would be ripe.* Christ cannot have been offended at failing to find figs at a time when no figs could have been on the tree. To assume otherwise would be to ascribe a frame of mind to Christ that would be quite incredible. Here, also, two improbabilities coincide.

A third story belonging to the same class raises still a further difficulty, namely, that what actually happened cannot be ascertained from the narrative. In the two stories we have already considered, what happened is clear. In the case of the cursing of the fig tree we are told that Christ uttered the curse and then went away. On the following day he returned and saw the effect of the curse. The fig tree had withered. The same thing is true of the story of the finding of the coin in the fish's mouth. In the case of *the miraculous feeding of the multitude,* however, no one would be able to say what happened. A certain quantity of bread and of dried fish, easily breakable, was divided among a crowd of several thousand people, and after all had eaten their fill more bread and fish is said to have been left over than there was to begin with. As the apostles distributed the food, what did they see and do? If the loaves multiplied in their hands, it would have

---

* This presupposes that the fig tree, though it had no figs, was not diseased.

been remarkable if they had not seen the miracle, (or add: and told of it), but nothing is said of that in the account. If they had only distributed tiny bits (portions) of food, these must have increased in size and the miracle must have been observed, but none of the Evangelists has anything to say of such a happening. Furthermore, no explanation is given of the abundance of food left over after all had eaten. Consequently it is impossible to form a picture of what happened, although the distribution of the food and the collection of the remainder must have been open to view. The story is involved in such difficulties that no judgment on it is possible, for the facts that would enable us to form such a judgment cannot be recovered. Therefore this is a case in which we are justified in resorting to a hypothesis, but only to the extent of supplying what is necessary for an explanation. This is a procedure quite different from the ordinary attempt to explain a miracle as entirely a natural event. Such attempts are surprisingly superficial and seldom touch on the actual (or: basic) problem.

The story of Christ's voyage across the Sea of Galilee in a ship is of the same sort. Christ is represented as asleep in the ship. A storm comes up and the disciples, facing danger, wake him. He then stills the storm and calms the sea. Here again we have something whose accomplishment we cannot understand, for it involves an effect on natural powers and their activity which lie outside the human realm. We are told that Christ spoke to the sea and the storm and ordered them to quiet down and be still. Were such words necessary to bring about the effect? No one can believe that. The effect must have been due to Christ's will, and loud orders could not possibly have brought about the result, and their utterance was quite superfluous.* However, since the words of Christ in all such narratives are what tradition has preserved most exactly and most harmoniously, it would be quite exceptional if Christ had actually said nothing and if the words were only those of the narrators. Are we then to think that Christ addressed the storm? Christ cannot have believed that he had

* or add: Elements have no ears!

215

to speak in order to calm the storm and the sea. But if his words were addressed to his disciples in order that they might be aware that what was to happen was due to his will, then it would have been natural for him to say to them: You will see that everything soon will be calm. This is a case, I think, where some such hypothesis is necessary. We cannot believe that Christ's words were addressed to the sea. Otherwise Christ himself must have been so excited by the occasion that he threatened the storm and the sea as though they could hear what he said,* and that seems incredible to me. The other alternative is that his words were for the purpose of ostentation, since they had no bearing on the miracle itself, and this also I find it impossible to believe. Even if we assume that what distinguishes Christ from all other men involved the ability to do what other men cannot, we can only think of this analogically in the realm of human life. But if we see that all those cases where the analogy disappears are characterized by other difficulties, we are justified in advancing hypotheses in order to fill in gaps in our knowledge and to put what is factual in the record into a setting in which the analogy applies. We must undertake this but not expect always to be successful, for the narrator often told the story from a point of view other than ours.

(July 5) If we were to be content with what we have said to this point, the result of our present discussion would be unsatisfactory. There is a sphere in this area of the miracles of Christ in which we have reached results that are satisfactory to the extent that all effects on human conditions lie in an area for which we have analogies. To understand them as human effects we need only think of the difference between Christ and all others in terms of the usual difference between men. On the other hand, all miracles for which there are no analogies defy our attempt to understand them. From another point of view, the recorded miracles can also be divided into two groups. To the extent that we can understand them as free acts and grasp their moral content, only their physical

* that he personified the storm and the sea, or that the whole event was a display miracle

216

content remains obscure to us. On the other hand, to the extent that they are incomprehensible as moral acts, we must assert the right to make inquiries about the narrative as we have it that could afford a different result, and this is all the more the case when there is something in the act that is incompatible with a moral way of acting. This does not mean (I am referring to the freedom to make inquiry) that we wish to represent Christ's miracles, as is often done, as ordinary events. We should be quite satisfied if we could regard them as analogous to that part of this area where we could be content with the results that the narratives afford, although we do not account for them on natural grounds, but in terms of Christ's higher nature. So a few of these miracles present difficulties because they presuppose a way of acting that makes it impossible for us to think of Christ as remaining a human being and acting as a man. In others we are perturbed by the lack of moral motive in the act, and to the extent that we find something out of harmony with Christ's characteristic way of acting we are dissatisfied with the story.

Let me cite a few examples to illustrate what I have in mind. Among the miracles whose effects we cannot understand are those whose effects are on purely inanimate nature, on the elements, and those whose effects are on human nature to the extent that they are purely physical. The raising of a person from the dead is a miracle of such a sort. If we assume that death has actually taken place, we cannot say that the psychic element explains the result of Christ's act, for we cannot assume that the psychic factor still exists. How are we to treat such a story? Three cases are recorded: (1) Christ reanimates the young man of Nain as he is being conveyed to his tomb. (2) Christ reawakens Jairus's daughter, whose death had been announced. (3) Christ raises Lazarus from the dead after his body had lain in the tomb for four days (John 11:39). None of these three cases is similar to the other. Christ says explicitly that Jairus's daughter was not dead but only asleep. Unless we are to contradict what Christ himself says, this cannot be considered an actual miracle of raising a person from the dead. Furthermore, for Christ to tell a dead child to rise up would be like addressing the sea and the storm, for a dead person cannot hear a voice. On the other hand, if we assume that the girl was not dead, Christ's voice can bring about the desired result, and we are compelled to believe that people who seem to be dead can still hear, although all other signs of life are missing. The story of the raising of the young man of Nain from the dead, a story reported only by *one* Evangelist, also involves Christ's speaking and touching. The case is similar to that of the raising of Jairus's daughter. When we recall the haste with which Jews buried their dead and the fact that the declaration that a person is dead is only a judgment and that death can only be said to be probable rather than certain until decomposition sets in, we see that the question of whether the young man of Nain was really dead permits of no certain answer. But the resurrection of Lazarus cannot be placed in this category. We must accept what was only a statement based on the senses,* namely, that Lazarus's body was in an advanced state of decomposition. If this were the case the miracle of resurrection was not Christ's act. Viewed as an act of Christ, the miracle lies in quite a different sphere. By asking God to answer his prayer, Christ does not claim that he himself performed the miracle. He ascribes it to a divine act that was performed in answer to his prayer. In this instance we cannot speak of Christ as the doer of the miracle, *except to the extent that he was certain that God would answer his prayer.* So we cannot say that Christ performed something for whose effects there is no human analogy.

We have cited two examples of miracles performed on the elements and entirely outside the sphere of human life. One of these, the story of the feeding of the multitude, is so unclear that we cannot hazard a hypothesis concerning it. The other, the stilling of the storm, contains an element that cannot have belonged to the miracle itself and that suggests that Christ acted in some other way than the story itself implies. To still the storm he did not have to address it. The words that are quoted must have had some different context. Con-

---

* The statement that Lazarus's body was already in a state of decomposition may have been based on a preconceived opinion. If this were not the case, the miracle cannot be regarded as an act of Christ's.

218

sequently there are elements of uncertainty in the story that make it impossible for us to recover the facts that lie back of it. In addition, when Christ later reproaches the disciples for their lack of faith — when he says that they had wakened him because of their lack of faith in him and in his wonder-working power — this shows that the reproach had to do with something that had happened earlier. He blames them for having wakened him.* If the danger had been real and he had fended it off, he cannot have reproached his disciples. So we see that unclarities in the account make it difficult for us to understand it.

If we turn again to the story of the feeding of the multitude, this time as John narrates it, we see that something that Christ said in the discourse that follows throws another light on the narrative. To those who followed him to the other side of the Sea of Galilee and found him there he says: "You seek me, not because you saw signs, but because you ate your fill of the loaves." If we regard this as precisely what Christ said, as we must, we have to say: Christ excludes the miracle of the feeding of the multitude from the category of signs. If Christ's reference here had been to the singular rather than the plural — "sign" rather than "signs" — we should understand his remark differently. It would have meant: "to the extent that the miracle satisfied your needs." In this case the reference would have been to a specific miracle, rather than to miracles in general. If Christ had viewed the feeding of the multitude as a miracle, he would not have stated the contrast as he did. Let me try to clarify the difference. If Christ had used the singular he would have been referring to the incident as a miracle. Since he used the plural the reference is to signs in general. Christ is contrasting the event to miracles in general, and so it is excluded from the category of a *sèmeion* ["sign"]. This conflicts with other facts, for the story represents the incident as a miracle, but in such a way that we cannot see what probably lay back of it. There are other similar cases. In the story of the cursing of the tree the difficulty is great-

---

* or add: Christ wants them to have some other sort of faith. Of what that was to consist we are not told. If Christ had meant the faith that led them to waken him, how could he have blamed them?

er to the extent that a general promise with respect to miracles is attached in the narrative to the disciples' remarks, a promise that implies that Christ himself regarded the incident of the withering of the fig tree as a miracle. However, we cannot understand the act in moral terms. We are quite at a loss regarding it, and our lack of understanding can only be removed by some hypothesis concerning the character of the story.

Taking all this into consideration and recalling that there are other acts whose effects take place outside the realm of human existence, for instance, the miracle at Cana, Peter's miraculous catch of fish, and the meaningless walk on the sea — the last-mentioned reported as having taken place at night and under conditions which would make observation uncertain — we see that the field of explanation is reduced in size. In many cases we can put the blame for this on the story, and we are entitled to do this also in instances where we cannot understand the moral motivation of the incident. This is not the case with respect to the miracle at Cana. Christ could have employed his miracle-working power to increase the sociableness of the occasion. The act had a moral motive and was in conformity with all his social life. Peter's miraculous catch of fish is open to similar explanation. Christ had taught from the ship. The act was one of thankfulness to him, and Christ could have employed his miracle-working powers as narrated. However, the concept of this miracle is open to criticism. It cannot be denied that the possibility of Christ's knowing of the presence of fish in that area by purely human means is open to question.

So it is apparent that we must say that the miracles whose effects are represented as being performed outside the area of human existence and which interfere for this reason with the unity of the human behavior of Christ are those that have the least value for faith. They are not necessary. Faith in Christ could be the same if Christ had performed no miracles. However, assuming a specific difference between Christ and all other men, by reason of the connection between the psychic and the physical and with reference to what Christ was able to do for others because of this connection, we must presuppose a specific difference, and this difference is illustrated by the miracles he performed in the area of human existence. That is what we can *expect* of him as a *verification,* but not as a verification that was *necessary* for faith. On the other hand, the acts that lie outside the realm of human nature do not have this value. The unique dignity of Christ applied only to his human life, and we have no reason to give it wider application. To wish to maintain that, because of his specific dignity, Christ must have known everything that lay entirely outside his vocation and his mission would be to destroy the human understanding of his life. So it is something that simply surprises us and that we can do nothing about. If with the passage of time we were to learn something about the genesis of these accounts that would eliminate the miraculous element, such a development would not disturb our faith but would advance the purely human understanding of Christ. We can only regard that as a problem whose solution awaits the emergence of a perfectly certain theory of the origin of the first three Gospels. But it is not *necessary* to solve the problem. Other miracles within this period that were not performed by Christ but that were related to him or were performed on him, including that of Christ's own resurrection, also present serious difficulties.

We have already seen that the miracles associated with Christ's baptism were miracles that happened for John the Baptist's sake. If we go back here to the original authentic story, everything actually miraculous disappears,* and all that is left is that something happened at the baptism that led John to associate the promise he had been given with Christ. Something similar must have happened at the time of Christ's presentation to Simeon in the temple, but we are not told what it was. The story of Christ's transfiguration exhibits some analogy. It contains miraculous elements, but we are not told that what happened was due to an act or accomplishment of Christ. He only appears for a time as set in a miraculous environment. We are not told that he had summoned Moses and Elijah. They only were where he was. Here the

* we can understand how the other narratives arose

purpose that we have to think of as present in everything miraculous seems to be missing. We cannot believe that the presence of Moses and Elijah was necessary if Christ were to experience something or to reach some decision, any more than he needed John's baptism. Consequently we can assume no purpose that the miracle served, so far as Christ himself was concerned. If we wish to hold that the miracle served a purpose for the disciples, we point out that there are accounts of later discussions that Christ held with them after the event. But there is nothing in these accounts that had any bearing on the purpose of the miracle for the disciples. The questions that are discussed could have been raised without any miracle at all. In accordance with the mythology of the day, Elijah is mentioned among those who would prepare the way for the Messiah, and in all this nothing is said of any effect of the miracle on the disciples. To be sure, one of the narratives says that the disciples were in a state of drowsiness at the time. If this were the case, they would have been unable to give any certain account of what they saw. Since there were no other witnesses of the event except those who were in this drowsy state, we cannot expect to recover from their account a picture of what actually happened or form any judgment of it. So we are compelled to confine ourselves mainly to those miracles that happened in the area that is most important and most significant. All the rest seem more or less problematical. In Luke there is a passage that implies that there were many instances of Christ's raising of people from the dead. However, on examining the setting of the saying we see that it refers to what Christ told John's emissaries to tell their master, and we can lay no weight on it.*

(July 6) If in our examination of Christ's miraculous activity we contrast what we can explain relatively satisfactorily and what remains obscure and whose obscurity in some cases we can show to have been the fault of the narrative and compare this with our sources, we reach a result that to some ex-

---

* or add: No other passage in the Gospels refers to this. Another possibility: The passage in Luke that implies that Christ raised many others from the dead probably rests on a misunderstanding.

tent sets John apart from the other Gospels. To be sure, we find the story of the miraculous feeding of the multitude also in John's Gospel, but there it is followed by a remarkable discourse that Christ delivered.* John is the only Evangelist to tell of the resurrection of Lazarus, but in doing so he makes it clear that Christ was only the suppliant who was confident that his prayer would be heard, not the one who performed the miracle. In the other Gospels we find the account† without any explanatory discourse of Christ's. As a consequence we must expand and restate the narrative if we are to make it comprehensible, and we must look for a moral motive back of the miracle, which is very difficult to discover. All other accounts that compel us to do this are peculiar to the Synoptics and are not to be found in John. It is a fortunate circumstance that in our task of recreating the life of Jesus we are not compelled to regard the narrative in the Gospel of John also as derived from second or third hand sources, as altered in many ways, and as no longer reliable.

On the other hand, I have to admit that there are many who think of it as a sort of prejudice on my part that I always regard John in this way as the basic and authentic authority and represent the other Gospels as needing careful criticism, a task that I believe is the most important task of our day. But I see no other way of dealing with the issue. If we are convinced that the three so-called synoptic Gospels are a later composite of originally separate accounts and narratives, whether they existed in oral or in literary form, we must note their difference from the account in the Gospel of John. Furthermore, if we regard the canonical Gospels as the product of the church and consequently view the Holy Scriptures as the basis of all the tradition of a later age and as due to a special divine providence, we must say that, so far as we can understand Christ in terms of a life that was subject to the general laws that govern all life, the Holy Scriptures can only be understood as a book subject to the law that governs human transmission and one that can only be comprehended when all the resources of the intelligence are brought into play. There must

* Cf. the preceding lecture.
† namely, of the miraculous feeding of the multitude

be a continuous application of all the skills of criticism and exegesis to the canonical books. In this way only can we gradually arrive at an artistic, that is, a complete, understanding and use of Scripture.

From this it follows that we cannot yet say that we are able to deal adequately with all the problems that arise. The task is still unfinished, and must remain so until we have a more complete and objective recognition of the criticism of the Gospels and its results. The desirable consequences of the examination of the Gospels for our task can be enumerated as follows: We wish we could dispense with all the miraculous accounts in the life of Christ that go beyond the sphere of human life and existence. We wish we could explain all the stories of Christ's miracle-working activity in terms either of his specific dignity or of the general laws that govern the use of human power on earth. In other words, we wish we did not run across accounts of effects on inanimate nature which lie entirely outside the visible boundaries of human power, such as the Spirit can only perform by means of the organization.

There is a guideline here that we can draw and for which several points can be noted. Summing up all the differences in this area, two clearly distinguished points stand out: (1) There are miracles that Christ performs in his own person on other people with a perfect certainty as to their effects. (2) On the other hand, there are acts, such as we have been able to reconstruct from the story of the raising of Lazarus from the dead, where Christ appears as one confident that his prayer will be heard, acts that are not the work of Christ himself but of God. We also find discourses of Christ to his disciples in which he declares that they also will perform mighty works and which justify us in associating his disciples' miracles with those that he himself performed. For example, Christ says: If you have faith you will be able to move mountains out of their place. This, then, is what faith is. We cannot believe that Christ wanted to use faith as a pictorial expression for such mighty acts as the disciples would regard as due to their own power, but for those that involved the removal of hindrances and for whose performance they could be assured of divine help. So then, faith is not the knowledge of a power already given, but faith in the necessary divine help. Between these two points we find other accounts where the miraculous appears to be conditioned in its results by a foreknowledge, but we can only regard this as a foreknowledge of results that are possible in light of general human belief and the general laws of nature, even although they are accidental. Take, for example, Peter's finding of the coin in the fish's mouth. Here the actual miracle consists of the foreknowledge, not of a knowledge of something perceived. That a fish should swallow a coin and should also be at a given place is something accidental, but something possible. The miraculous element consists of the fact that Christ, while removed from the scene and not viewing the event, knew of such accidental possibilities. However, we cannot treat the story of the miraculous feeding of the multitude in the same way. If Christ had known in advance that the loaves would multiply, that would have been something that could not be accounted for according to the laws that govern phenomena. This affords us some guidance.

If we are compelled to form a hypothesis of the connection of the elements of an event which lie outside the way they are presented in the account, as in the case of all miracles that were performed outside the realm of human life, the necessity is less if we need only to appeal to such a foreknowledge and have to think of such a reformulation of the narrative that would make this central, for here we find ourselves in a sphere where we again can point to an analogy. There are experiences of such a knowledge of something not perceived, and yet of a knowledge that is subjectively one, that is to say, that has an element of certainty and that can stand examination, for the ability to anticipate is of such a sort that we have to think of it as raised to that potency. However, so far as individual cases are concerned, and granted this restriction and these aids, we have to leave the solution of this problem in abeyance because, if we are to proceed with confidence we must be able to make use of criticism and of a firm and assured understanding of the origin and character of the first three Gospels. Until that is available we have no proper basis of procedure for solving the problem.

Let me make still another comment. If we return to the

temptation story as we understand it, we discover in it a canon of Christ's that we do not find observed in this sphere of his miraculous acts, namely, that he did not wish to use miracles and the prayer that he uttered in the confidence that it would be heard in the interest of his own self-preservation. On the other hand, I have already said: If we regard the miraculous acts of Christ as morally free acts, then Christ had to perform them under the same laws and maxims as govern everyone else in the exercise of the whole complex of his powers. Now, self-preservation is a general human duty, and everyone has to care for his health in this respect. So I have had to conclude that Christ could have used his miracle-working power for his own preservation and that of his disciples. As soon as we understand this, as opposed to what appears to be the moral of the temptation story, we cannot avoid the question, whose answer forms an essential part of our present special task: Why did Christ not make use of his miracle-working power at the moment at the very end when his life was in danger? That is the question which was raised by the mocking comment of his enemies: Christ ought to save himself and come down from the cross. We have to draw certain limits to Christ's wonder-working power which it could not cross. Christ was so far from making use of that power that the idea of doing so did not even enter his mind. From the moral point of view, therefore, that is one of the most interesting points we have to investigate. Why could Christ not have entertained such an idea? If we recall the story of the storm on the lake and accept it as it is told, whether or not it can be regarded as dependent on Christ's foreknowledge or on something else, the fact remains that this was an instance when Christ made use of his miracle-working power for his own preservation and that of his disciples. An important difference emerges when we ask: If Christ made use of his power in one instance, why not also in another? In the former case he was dealing with nature and in the latter with people, but not with an individual person; rather, with human authority which he had to recognize. In the first place he had to act as a subject of the Roman state and in accordance with his own saying: Render to Caesar the things that are Caesar's. In the second place, he stood under the law, and so under the authority of the Sanhedrin. On these matters we have Christ's own saying that, if he wished to ask his Father for power to save himself from his enemies, God would render him supernatural assistence. All this shows that Christ had decided not to make any use of his wonder-working power that might disturb human relationships and never to interfere in them. This serves to bring the different instances into harmony. Those in which Christ made use of his higher power in the sphere of self-preservation and those in which he abstained from doing so are not in contradiction. Both conform to the rules of human morality, as does Christ's entire ministry.

If we go further and say that he would have used all his power for everything that concerned the building of the kingdom of God and the performance of his whole mission, to the extent that it did not collide with the existing human order, we should also have to say: Exercise of his wonder-working power had nothing to do with his essential task, namely, that of arousing faith in himself in men and of summoning them to take possession of the kingdom of God. For that purpose the only means available was the communication of the truth and the natural effect that this must have, but in such a way that it could be communicated by means of his unique dignity. In this respect, however, we must not overlook the difference between the impression made by his discourse and that rising out of the discourse of others. If he had wanted to include his miracles for the accomplishment of this end, the kingdom of God would have been built from the beginning on quite a different foundation from that on which it was actually erected and would have been at the mercy of magic instead of taking form within the framework of the historical process. It was inevitable, then, that Christ should make use of no other powers. However, if we recall that people had a different receptivity for the kingdom of God and were prepared in very different ways to take part in it, and if we consider the sum of what Christ did during his lifetime, someone might say: If Christ had used his power of foreknowledge in this connection he would have been able to make his appeal only to those who were most receptive and thus have had much greater results. This would not seem to involve any conflict with human order, and Christ's refusal to make use of his power in this connection seems to require some special explanation. We must go back a bit and say: Just as Christ was under the law, so also he was governed by morality, and it would have interfered with his work more than it would have helped it if he had wished to free himself from that morality.

This is what I mean. If we wanted to think of Christ as acting as we have suggested above, his life would have been unpredictable, incomprehensible to others. He would have had to leave large areas untouched in order to reach those who were most receptive. In short, his entire mission would have had an arbitrary and fragmentary character, for which ordinary life would afford no analogy. He would have seemed utterly different to others than he actually was and, since his way of acting would have been incomprehensible, the bond between him and others would have been looser and his life would not always have been regarded as a human one. So the morality and order that men took for granted must have been as sacrosanct to him as the actual, literal law. This, then, is a rule that places a limit to Christ's actions. No doubt Christ was able to know that many of those with whom he came into contact had little or no receptivity for his message and that he could count only on its ultimate effect. He could also have had the idea that there were really receptive folk whom he could not reach. He himself actually said that he had been sent only to the lost sheep of the house of Israel. This is the bridge to all that the analogy provides and is intelligible. If we are to understand Christ's way of acting in its purely human form, regardless of the higher power he possessed, I could not leave this subject until I had pointed out its limits.

Lecture 35 (July 10). So far as our task is concerned, we have filled in all the gaps with respect to Christ's miracle-working activity We assume that the miracles were performed only to the extent that their performance can be understood in human terms and that Christ made use of his miracle-working power in a way that was in conformity with his office. We proceed to a consideration of his *activity as a teacher*. The natural divisions here are discourses delivered in synagogues, incidental discourses to groups of people, didactic utterances in social intercourse, and private conversation with the apostles. The last is connected with his community-forming activity in which everything belonged that was preparatory exercise on their behalf. But there is no reason to assume that Christ taught his disciples an esoteric doctrine in the proper sense of that term, for we are told that they later were to proclaim all that he had taught them from the housetops. In terms of form we can distinguish two elements: the gnomic, which in turn can be divided into parables and didactic discourses, and the canonical or exegetical, which was usually the type of his discourses in synagogues. In the few actual specimens of synagogue discourses that we possess the exegetical interest is messianic. This must also have characterized Christ's discourses in the course of his travels. During longer stays in one place other interests could also have been stressed, but only in concentric circles. From this we see how little truth there is in the distinction often made between the teaching of Christ and the teaching about Christ. Whoever wishes to regard the latter as something that belongs to the time after Christ must not only question John's Gospel but also the others, for everything that has to do with the kingdom of God is also teaching about Christ.

Although we are not able to form a final judgment on all instances of Christ's miracle-working activity, it is nevertheless true that for our task, that of viewing the life of Jesus in its unity and totality, there remain no gaps, to the extent that we have been able to point out adequately the moral motivation involved in all these acts of Christ. Where this has not been possible we have said: So far as that which cannot be explained by these maxims is concerned, we believe it must have had some other context. We have also pointed out that such an existence as we assume was that of Christ makes possible effects in the area of human life such as no other man could have achieved. The only difficulty is that we can not determine the limits of Christ's unique power. So we have obtained a clear picture of the way Christ exercised his miracle-working powers, and that is all that is necessary for our task.

A Consideration of the Teaching Activity
of Christ during This Period
(From the time of his public appearance to that of his arrest)

We have already discussed the external conditions that were characteristic of Christ's teaching activity. *The most specific form of his teaching activity was that he appeared as an acknowledged teacher in the synagogues.* There were also many occasions when large crowds of people gathered round him, and his natural task then was obviously that of communicating his own spiritual existence (or: that of his self-communication) in the form of thought. This form of teaching was less definite, however, for it was bound up with the variety of occasion, whereas the teaching in the synagogues had a quite different form, always being linked with a passage from the Old Testament Scriptures. In the former case Christ was free to discuss anything that was suggested by the occasion.

This leads us to refer to the general social relationships that Christ enjoyed with individuals or with small groups. Wherever he found opportunity for discussion we have to assume a teaching activity on his part, for he was always conscious of his vocation and of his superiority. This suggests another question, related to another point. A special social relationship existed between Christ and the twelve. Originally this social relationship differed from others only because it was continuous. The disciples were neither closer to him in point of view than others nor more removed. They were on the same level as others. Now the question arises: Have we reason to presuppose that for both parties, for the disciples as well as for Christ, this steady association meant something else than a social relationship in which Christ could carry out a teaching mission more continuously? When we look ahead and reflect on the fact that the apostles were destined to become Christ's witnesses, we ask: Did the disciples fulfill this destiny, or could they have fulfilled it, simply because of the association with Christ that we have assumed, or did they have to be qualified for their calling in some specific way?

It is easier here to ask this question than to give it an adequate answer, for it is bound up with what Christ did to constitute the Christian church, that is, to create a community of people related to himself. If we are to assume that something more was necessary for the training of the apostles than Christ's continuous association with them, an association that did not differ in kind from that with other people, two possibilities emerge. In the first place, the association of the apostles with Christ may have been intended to prepare them for their later calling, to give them some preliminary practice. In the second place, Christ's teaching to them may have had a different content than that to others. If the former possibility were the one we are to accept, it would not require discussion at this point. If Christ were giving his disciples practice, this would not be teaching, but something else. However, if the latter alternative were the right one, we should have to distinguish in Christ's teaching between an *esoteric* type and an *exoteric* type, between what Christ taught his disciples exclusively and what he taught in other relationships. If we were to think that mere constant association with Christ had ultimately to lead to a different sort of relationship of Christ's disciples to their master's whole personality than was true of others, we can assume that his message to them came to include something not in his message to others. To put it in other words, much that it would have been useless to say to others because they would not yet have been able to understand it could have been comprehensible to Christ's disciples and could have been included in his message to them. If this were the case, the precise difference between Christ's exoteric and esoteric teaching would disappear. All we can say would be that the disciples heard what only later was to be preached to others. So we do not have to look for a specific difference in Christ's teaching. When we encounter a saying of Christ that seems to imply that his disciples were given a special message, this impression is immediately corrected when we recall the other saying: "What you hear whispered, proclaim upon the housetops." Christ's teaching to his disciples was not a body of secret lore. The difference was only a matter of the time at which the message was proclaimed.

The extent to which a preliminary practice for the disciples took place, or the extent to which a significant difference in the capacity to accept Christ himself emerged in the disciples, will depend on another consideration, namely, on the activity of Christ as the founder of a human community. Everything that we can think of as related to preliminary practice must have been oriented toward this. This accounts for the different forms of Christ's teaching. The most definite form was the one he used in his teaching in the synagogues, but unfortunately few specimens of this have been preserved. Then there was his teaching delivered to mixed groups of hearers. Then there was his teaching in the course of limited social contacts. Finally, there was his teaching specifically directed to the twelve.

When we take a look at the form of Christ's didactic message in our Gospels we note a difference there also. To begin with the briefest sayings, there is the *sentence,* the *gnome* or aphorism, where the form is proverbial, that is, where the saying is applicable to different cases which are illuminated by its content. Another related form is the *parable,* which has similarities to the gnome. We always distinguish between a didactic and a pictorial aphorism. The pictorial includes the basic content of the parable, just as the didactic includes that of a longer, more elaborate discourse. The gnome, then, is the common element in these two other forms of teaching, the parabolic address and the consecutive discourse. These two forms, of course, can again be combined. A parable can give rise to a strictly didactic discourse in which the pictorial element disappears and what remains can be treated as purely didactic. In like manner a purely didactic discourse can be concentrated in a parable, if this sums up pictorially what preceded it in a general form.

However, when we look at the specific teaching form that Christ employed when he appeared in synagogues we see that we unfortunately have very few specimens. In fact, all we have is the introduction to one such synagogue address that Christ delivered when he went to Nazareth. There may be another passage that belongs in this category, but it is difficult to recover a specimen from it. I have in mind the passage in which the Evangelist John tells the story of the feeding of the multitude and goes on to say that Christ then went to Capernaum, that many came from the other side of the lake to hear him, and that he entered into conversation with them. Then John concludes the account by saying that Christ spoke his words to them in the synagogue at Capernaum. It is improbable that the day was the sabbath, for if it had been the feeding of the multitude would have taken place late in the evening that formed the first part of the sabbath day. If the day were not the sabbath, the address was not actually a synagogue address. In this case we can only speak of an address that happened to be delivered in the synagogue at the time in the morning which was set apart for prayer. So we have a dearth of examples of addresses that Christ delivered in synagogues, although the Gospels may contain many which are not identified as such. We do not always know the occasion and locality of a discourse. An individual dissertation is often attached to or incorporated into other material. But we do know that addresses in the synagogue were related to passages of Scripture, either to one that was the lection for the day or to one that was arbitrarily chosen or that happened to stand on the page that was opened. The one example afforded by the Gospels does not imply that Christ's address was based on the passage of Scripture that had already been read. It seems that Christ turned to a passage that had a messianic content and to which he could relate his preaching. Can we conclude from this instance that he always employed this practice? That is improbable when we bear in mind the variety of circumstances that attended his appearances. In the first place, the passage in question belongs to an account of Christ's travels to various places. In the second place, we are led to believe that Christ often stayed for some time in one and the same place. It is very probable that on his travels Christ's addresses were related to his basic proclamation and were messianic in character and had to do with the kingdom of God. On the other hand, during lengthy stays in one place he could have developed his theme in detail, and it is possible that his discourses did not conform strictly to the type he delivered during his travels. Perhaps the polemical element in his teaching, of which we have many examples, was also found in his synagogue addresses. Certainly they would have exhibited especially the antipharisaic emphasis.

I should like here to look at the matter in a more general context. All the actual messianic discourses of Christ that relate directly to the type indicated by "the kingdom of heaven is at hand" were such that he could not do otherwise than make reference to himself and to speak of himself. To the extent they were messianic they had to have the tendency to indicate himself as the Messiah. Frequently people have wanted to distinguish between the teaching of Jesus and the teaching about Christ, that is, the teaching that makes Christ the subject, and have tried to show that the latter came later and derived from the apostles. This theory is refuted by what we said above and is contrary to what must naturally have happened. As soon as we return to the general formula that sums up all Christ's teaching, we see that it must have been at the same time a teaching concerning himself and not just concerning general human affairs,* and when we reflect on the verb "to preach," which sums up everything, it would be inconceivable if Christ's views and discourses on general conditions had been summed up in such expressions without any reference to himself. If we were to make a distinction and were to speak first of the actual teaching activity of Christ and then of what he did to lay a basis for a specific human community, we should be attempting the impossible, for all Christ's teaching was simply a part of the latter task. The teaching of the kingdom of God could only have been an invitation to belong to it and an encouragement to do what it demands. Consequently we can only distinguish an occasional development of such teaching. The general rubric sums it all up: Christ did what he did to found the kingdom of God, and we can represent his teaching activity only as a specific form in which he endeavored to carry out his mission. It follows that we cannot make a distinction between the teaching of Christ and the teaching about Christ. Rather, the teaching about Christ was central to all his teaching. To be sure, the Gospel of John contains more discourses in which Christ speaks of himself than do the other Gospels, but we cannot say that the others lack this element. Take the parables, for example. Most of them are concerned with the kingdom of God, and likewise refer to it by way of Christ's founding of a community.

Keeping all this in mind we see how great a place the idea

---

* or add: the teaching of Christ must also have been teaching *de se*

of the kingdom of God occupied in all these public forms of Christ's teaching.[29] It follows that there was no actually *esoteric* teaching, no secret doctrine that Christ communicated only to his disciples. What they received before others did was only an advance installment, given them only because they had already received more than others. Therefore we shall have to regard what in Christ's teaching is related to the community he came to found as what is central to it, and all else as only a development of that central idea. We cannot think of the latter as theoretical over against the practical. Both what is a further development of what is involved, and must be involved, in the idea of the kingdom of God and what is unrelated to the idea are always associated with it.

Lecture 36 (July 11). More important is the distinction between what Christ himself said and what he took over from the tradition. According to the custom of the time, Christ adopted the exegetical method and developed the exegesis of a passage in Scripture metaphorically, as well as in other similar ways. He turned most frequently to later ideas, such as those of the resurrection of the dead and of the last judgment. We have to distinguish between the instances when Christ develops the idea in a scriptural passage and those when he uses the idea only as a point of departure. We also have to make a distinction between the direct discourse and the indirect. The apologetic discourse is more closely related to the direct form than is the polemical discourse. With respect to all these differences, John's Gospel is more helpful than the others, for John specifies the occasion of almost all of Christ's discourses. The other Gospels sometimes give the discourse without mentioning the occasion, and in such instances the interpretation must remain doubtful. In other cases one Gospel (usually Matthew) omits any reference to the occasion, while another gives it. In this instance the latter version is preferable. In some cases the various Gospels give different occa-

29. Recognition of the centrality of the kingdom of God in the Gospels in modern thought has derived from Schleiermacher. The importance of this rubric had been seen by Hermann Samuel Reimarus in his *Fragments,* ed. Charles H. Talbert, Lives of Jesus Series (Philadelphia: Fortress, 1970), but his interpretation of Jesus as wanting to be a ruler of an earthly kingdom was too eccentric for his time. Schleiermacher's influence on the role of the kingdom of God did not come from these lectures but through the central place he gave it in *The Christian Faith.* See above, Introduction, pp. xxxiv and xliii. Cf. Norman Perrin, *The Kingdom of God in the Teaching of Jesus* (Philadelphia: Westminster, 1963), p. 1: "The modern discussion of the Kingdom of God in the teaching of Jesus may be said to begin with Schleiermacher."

sions. In view of all these differences and, where possible, in light of whether one account indicates progress or not, we must now attempt to interpret the material in our sources.

I have already drawn your attention to the differences between what Christ himself teaches and what he takes over from the tradition, but this distinction is not an absolute one. Otherwise there would be no point of contact between one part of his teaching and another. The messianic idea, for instance, was part of the tradition that Christ had received. In this connection we see how what is peculiar to Christ's teaching always appears at the same time as a polemic against the tradition. In another respect we also see this twofold character, namely, when we reflect in general on the relationship of Christ's teaching to the Old Testament. Here we note as primary a peculiar modification of the gnomic, namely, of the exegetical, of the canonical, the introduction and adaptation of Old Testament passages as a means of presenting what he wishes to communicate, or as an occasion for presenting it. This reveals Christ's twofold use of the Old Testament. Sometimes he uses an Old Testament passage as a means of presenting his own thought.* He adopts it, so to speak. At other times he only uses an Old Testament passage as a point of departure, with the result that what he says in connection with it and about it is something different. We have to keep this twofold use of the Old Testament in mind if we are to form a clear picture of the content of Christ's teaching. We could have said the same also regarding the gnomic element. Sometimes it is used as a full expression of Christ's own thought, but at other times Christ uses what is current in the thought of the day as something to which he can attach his own interpretation.

During the period immediately preceding Christ's advent the Jewish people, no longer living in isolation, had adopted many ideas whose essential content is not to be found in its original national memorials, that is to say, in the ancient canonical writings. These foreign ideas had nevertheless become widely accepted, and it is in connection with these that the two relatively opposite methods of approach that Christ

* or add: at the most with slight modifications

236

used are frequently confused. The doctrine of the resurrection of the dead and that of the last judgment are examples of ideas that have no place in the Old Testament. When they are referred to in the discourses of Christ, they appear not as distinctive elements in Christ's teaching, but as parts of generally accepted doctrine. It would be possible to believe that this is due to the nature of our Gospels. The discourse in which Christ originally developed these doctrines has not been preserved, and when he mentions them he has in mind his earlier defense of them. But we know that the doctrine of the resurrection of the dead was a matter of dispute between the Sadducees and the Pharisees. It was therefore an idea that Christ adopted from the tradition, and the same is true also of the doctrine of the last judgment. We must examine Christ's teaching carefully in order to determine whether a given element in it is his own or is a part of the tradition he accepts.

It is difficult to discover general rules that would help us here. We can only return to Christ's way of using the Old Testament. When Christ speaks of a passage we must make a distinction between those instances when he expounds the passage in question and those when he uses it as an introduction to something new. In the former instance Christ makes use of the passage as an expression of his own thought, whereas in the latter he uses it only as an occasion to develop his own unique ideas. We observe the same practice in the use of Scripture in the case of other Jewish teachers. This use was natural under the circumstances, for all that was in Scripture was a condensation of the wisdom of the nation. In this way we can explain the allegorical interpretation, which often departs a long way from what was the thought of the original author, as well as the various connections of an Old Testament passage. The same rule must also be applied to the later ideas which we mentioned, for example, the passage in Matthew where Christ speaks of the last judgment. There he refers to the idea as one common to the tradition, and it is questionable whether by doing so he also wishes it to be regarded as one that he himself accepted. So I shall have to say, in accordance with the rule: If the whole content of the discourse is nothing but a precise explanation of the fact, then Christ represents it as his own knowledge and expands it in detail. However, if what follows cannot be so understood, we shall have to give another answer. The latter is the case with respect to the passage in Matthew concerning the last judgment. The triple repetition of the same form by Christ on the one hand and by the hearers on the other in the form of question and answer and the measure that here is propounded cannot be regarded as a different interpretation of an idea generally familiar. On the contrary, in this passage the idea of the last judgment appears as one to which Christ can attach some definite teaching of his own, for the whole discourse is based on the gnomic saying: What is done to those who belong to Christ is also done to him [and vice versa]. Everything depends on this point, and the idea of the last judgment is just the form it takes. If we had nothing else than this, and similar passages that are concerned with ideas such as these, we should be unable to conclude that Christ represents and adopts such ideas as his own and as truth that is valid generally for the kingdom of God.

If we reflect on our task and compare the state of our Gospels so far as the *content* of Christ's teaching is concerned, we find ourselves in this respect rather unfortunately situated to carry out that task fully. We can completely understand any given discourse only in light of its entire context. We must see it in its entire setting. We must know on what occasion and for what purpose it was delivered, for all this determines the relative value of its various elements. Consequently we can only carry out our task to the extent that we have didactic discourses of Christ that are as full as possible and to the extent that the circumstances under which they were spoken and the occasion on which they were uttered are specified as exactly as possible. The fact is that we have very few discourses of that sort, and once again we note that those in the Gospel of John are very different from those in the three other Gospels.

In the Gospel of John it is almost invariably the case that the occasion of Christ's discourses is specified, and there are only a few examples of Christ's discourses that are presented without any context. Take Christ's conversation with Nicodemus as an instance. The occasion and the main content are given. Only at the very end is there any obscurity, for there we cannot be sure whether the words are Christ's or those of the narrator. The conversation with the Samaritan woman is also given in full. The same thing is true of Christ's defense of himself after healing the sick man at the pool and of the discourse of Christ that develops out of the speech that he delivered in Capernaum after the incident of the feeding of the multitude. We also know the setting and occasion of the discourse delivered at the end of the celebration of the Feast of Tabernacles, when Christ was in Jerusalem. Christ makes his speech as an invitation, and into this speech other elements are introduced. The occasion could have been none other than the end of the festive gathering. To be sure, a new discourse seems to begin at the end of chapter 8. This has no apparent connection with what precedes it. But this is one of the rare examples of discourses whose connection is not apparent. The fact that the Greeks wanted to see Christ provides the occasion in chapter 12 for a discourse on the success of Christ's work after his death. Then follows a discourse to the crowd, and then a short discourse for which no occasion is given, the declaration that belief in him is also belief in God who sent him. The occasion of this last speech is unclear, as it is of the final discourses that Christ delivered before his death. Such speeches for the most part deal with the person of Christ and the immediate reason for his mission, and these are matters about which we are well enough informed. Few instances occur of discourses that are related to ideas that belong to the tradition and also few that are examples of the use of Old Testament passages. Of these latter, there are few where any uncertainty exists about whether Christ appropriates the passages or uses them only as points of departure.

However, the state of affairs is quite different when we turn to the other Gospels. In the first place, many discourses of Christ are introduced there without any indication of what immediately preceded them and without providing us with any account of their occasion. Then it often happens that the same discourse appears in the three Gospels with a wholly different context in each instance. Finally, it is usually the case that the numerous discourses without occasion in Matthew are provided with an occasion in Luke. They cannot be understood in Matthew's version in the same way that they are in Luke's, where the occasion is given. Often the difference is qualitative, and often quantitative. In Matthew, for example, the Lord's prayer is included among general polemical rules about prayer, whereas in Luke it is given in response to the request of the disciples: Lord, teach us to pray, as John taught his disciples! We see, then, that Luke gives the Lord's Prayer an entirely different occasion than does Matthew. Luke says that the Lord's Prayer was given in answer to the disciples' needs, whereas Matthew represents Christ as giving it unasked. We must choose the version that provides an occasion, and by following this rule we see that one Evangelist often takes much of Christ's teaching out of its original context and associates it with other similar material.

Now, however, we must reflect on the most difficult instances, namely, those in which the same discourse is given a different context, an entirely different setting, in one Gospel than in another. In such cases it is very difficult to decide which setting is the right one, and the more different the circumstances, the greater can be our embarrassment with respect to the interpretation of the discourse, with respect to the context within which it is to be understood, and with respect to its value. We find ourselves in such cases in a situation where we cannot arrive at satisfactory results because we have no exact knowledge of the way our Gospels came into being. If we knew the facts about the genesis of the Gospels of Matthew and Luke we should be able to carry out our task in this respect much more adequately. Here again we must mention the fact that the Gospel of John provides us with our most important source material and at the same time with the matter that we can use with the greatest confidence, for most of the material in John's Gospel has to do with what Christ said of himself and of the kingdom of God that is to be founded upon himself, as it were in an inner way. On the other hand, the further development of Christ's teaching in the other Gospels has to do largely with external matters, and most of the time the polemical form is employed to·present what is basic to the doctrine of Christ.

The point I have just made leads me to mention a general point of view that we must adopt with reference to the basic differences we have noted between John and the Synoptics. When we consider the whole teaching activity of Christ in this connection we can distinguish a direct and an indirect method of presentation, and in the latter, moreover, an apologetic and a polemical form. These two last-mentioned forms are variously related to the first or direct method. The apologetic form is more closely related to the direct form of address than is the polemical. However, there are also transitional forms, and also cases where it is difficult to decide whether a discourse is direct or apologetic, although such a decision is important for its understanding. A direct discourse is one in which Christ communicates his view, what for him is the truth, purely from within himself. There is always an occasion for doing so, but as long as this only means that he communicates himself under specific circumstances, the discourse remains direct. When Christ defends himself against a false interpretation of what he has said, or against a false view of his person, or of the messianic age and the kingdom of Heaven, he must have regard in each instance for the definite idea against which he defends himself, and the discourse he delivers has therefore a *polemical character*. It is more difficult to isolate what is peculiarly Christ's own in such a discourse than it is in a direct one. When Christ could express himself and himself alone, he was subject to no limitation except that of his general view of the capacity of his hearers. This could mean either that he left something unsaid, or that he said something in a different way, but the content of his discourse in such instances is to be understood directly, and Christ reveals himself then to the greatest extent. When his discourse was polemical, his purpose was to oppose someone else's view, and he could often achieve this without imparting his own unique message as directly as otherwise. Take, for instance, the discourse in which Christ defends himself for calling himself the Son of God, despite the fact that Scripture gives this name to men. It does not follow from this that he

241

thereby equates himself with such men. The more Christ's discourses are apologetic and polemical, the less sure we are that we can isolate in them directly what was his own conviction. The more Christ's discourse proceeds from within, without reference to the views of others, the more it must be the expression of his own innermost belief and conviction.[30]

If we wish to view Christ's whole activity as a teacher in order to form as unified and as clear a picture of it as possible, we must keep the differences in mind to which we have already referred. However, we must first bring the total content of his teaching as it lies before us in the Gospels under certain main headings and attempt to discover, in light of the differences noted, what he said with respect to them. If we then can recognize either some progress in his communication, in other words, if we can distinguish a later element as more complete than the earlier, or if, on the other hand, we find that the earlier and the later examples of his teaching are the same in their content, the clearer and more complete would be the picture of the whole.

Lecture 37 (July 12). Because of the state of our source materials we cannot discover any progressive development in Christ's teaching activity. There could have been such progressive development only in Christ's intercourse with a more constant circle of disciples in connection with his activity directed at the formation of a community. The Johannine discourses delivered within the

30. Joachim Jeremias offers an instructive comparison with Schleiermacher's view of the distinction between direct and polemical speech. In his book on *The Parables of Jesus* (New York: Scribner, 1963), p. 21, Jeremias holds that Jesus' parables deal primarily with a situation of conflict, and by means of this polemical situation open up what is most distinctive in Jesus' message, a result quite the contrary to the conclusion at which Schleiermacher arrives. Yet there are definite areas of agreement evidenced when Jeremias says of the parables: "their main object is not the presentation of the gospel, but defence and vindication of the gospel..." (p. 100). For Schleiermacher such a direct presentation would come above all through the Fourth Evangelist's report of Jesus' discourses on his own person and his relation to God in the circle of his disciples. The other form is mainly present in the Synoptics — the material analyzed by Jeremias — where Jesus must engage in polemic in his founding of the kingdom of God and thus be indirect in stating his own convictions about his person. Consistent with this distinction is Schleiermacher's view of the Synoptics as an aggregate of separate incidents while John is a continuous whole. Cf. Introduction, p. xxx. Schleiermacher also has a theory of language related to this direct/polemical contrast in *CF*, § 15, 2, and § 16, 1-2.

inner circle of confidants all have in mind Christ's forthcoming separation from his followers, but that is not the case with the discourses in the other Gospels.

When we take a look at Christ's teaching activity in terms of its content, we find it summed up in the general formula employed to describe his preaching. The idea of the kingdom of God is not to be separated from that of the Son of God; therefore Christ's teaching was *teaching about his person and about his mission.* All else is a development of this according to the degree of relationship, including random expressions and uncertain appropriations of ideas taken over from the tradition. We note first of all that Christ represents himself as *the promised one* and that, in doing so, he appeals to the prophecies. We have to ask what governs this appeal. Two extremes: (1) Everything is literal interpretation. In other words, in all the passages Christ cites from them, the prophets had him in mind as he actually was. (2) There was nothing here to interpret. Rather, the passages expressed hopes that were applicable to an entirely different good. John 5:39–40 provides us with the main key. (Extreme literalists would be able to use this passage as a proof that Moses really wrote the whole Pentateuch, but Christ speaks here only of the book and employs the ordinary designation of it, without having examined whether or not it was correct.) The Scriptures bear witness of Christ to the extent that men seek eternal life in them. Everything in the Old Testament is theocratic. If restoration was prophesied as the means by which the people could obtain blessedness and illumination, then Christ was able to make use of all such passages. The reverse, however, was not possible. Since it was also the general practice of the time to use words of Scripture in the most varied ways, Christ adopted this practice, and it would be a misunderstanding to assume that his every exposition of Scripture was regarded by his hearers as exact exegesis.

If we now want to begin to form for ourselves as complete a picture as possible of Christ's teaching activity, we must say in advance that our Gospels make it virtually impossible for us to isolate the progressive element in that teaching, although it must have been there. So far as the public teaching of Christ as a whole was concerned, there was no real need of such a progressive element, for the body of Christ's hearers varied and his teaching activity itself was conditioned by the occasion of its delivery, which meant that it had a fragmentary character. However, if we think of Christ's teaching activity with relation to his pupils and disciples in general, not merely to the twelve, but to a larger circle of people who followed his teaching activity with a certain regularity, it is natural that in this instance there must have been an element of progression in the teaching. The capacity of a stranger to appropriate teaching grows with his exposure to it.The more he understands, the easier becomes the understanding. The more we recall how closely Christ's teaching activity was bound up with his purpose of building a community, the more obvious it becomes that in this connection certain general principles had to provide the beginning. These expressed the actual tendency that had to be understood and that made possible the execution of the details. The difference between Christ's public, fragmentary teaching and the other sort that he delivered within a narrower circle provides us with a common formula. His public life had to express the same principles because it was governed by the intention of establishing a community, but it could not often go beyond these or include individual developments of them, for new hearers were continually coming to him. On the other hand, in the narrower circle the clear presentation of the principles involved a progressive development. However, we are not in a position to say anything more of this.

There are several passages in the synoptic Gospels that appear to belong to Christ's teaching to this inner circle of followers. This is not true in the same sense of the Gospel of John. To be sure, the last section of John's Gospel consists almost exclusively of discourses of Christ to this inner circle. However, since they are all related to Christ's imminent separation from his disciples, they are of a special type and do not acquaint us with any progress in what the disciples regarded as Christ's actual teaching. On the other hand, the material in the first three Gospels lacks any certain indication of time. There is a different reason for this in Matthew than there is in Luke. Luke has gathered together numerous details and fragments under the form of an account of a journey to Jerusalem, which gives them the appearance of having taken place within a very short period of time. This journey at the same time was Christ's last. Matthew also knows only of one journey that Christ made to Jerusalem, but he gathers together everything that he believes had been uttered most probably in Jerusalem. This method of composition makes it impossible for us to demonstrate a progressive development in Christ's teaching or to indicate a time in terms of John's chronology when this or that discourse was delivered by Christ.

So then, how are we to proceed to get a picture, so far as that is attainable, of Christ's teaching activity? We are referred by all our sources to a general formula of all Christ's teaching activity, a formula that we have to accept as one that sums up all he taught, as the living seed from which his teaching developed, namely, "the kingdom of heaven is at hand" [Matthew 4:17]. This formula contains the invitation to join the kingdom. That is to say, it implies the founding of a community. At the same time it also sets forth the idea of a kingdom of God that is related immediately to the person of Christ as its founder and central point. This demonstrates that the main points in Christ's teaching, points to which all else is related, are *Christ's doctrines of his own person and of his mission.* We can develop all other elements in Christ's teaching only in relation to these two points and can regard them only as occasional utterances. Our study of these two central themes will show us how far in fact we can speak of a teaching of Christ that is a unified system, what we are to think of (or are not to think of) as belonging to that system, and, with reference to the important point of difference, what Christ presents in his teaching as his own and what he only uses because it is part of the tradition he had taken over, in order to introduce or illuminate his own thought.

Christ's Teaching Concerning His Person

This brings us at once to another point. All our sources agree that Christ represents himself as the object of earlier divine promises that had been given through the prophets. This faces us with a problem that it is most difficult to solve. *When Christ relates these promises to himself, does that mean that always and in every instance he regards them as referring to himself, or does it mean only that he applies them to himself?* To understand the problem we must have the two opposite solutions of it in mind. At one extreme there are those who say: By representing himself as the promised one, Christ declares that with respect to the nature of his person and the various expressions of his life he was actually the one described by the prophets. In this case Christ's representation of himself as the promised one was pure *exegesis* of the prophetic passages. At the other extreme there are those who say: Christ only took over the idea of a promised one from the prophetic passages. They had spoken of a future good, and Christ represents himself as the one in whom everything they had in mind was realized and through whom everything is to be fulfilled that can truly be thought of as a future good. In this case Christ's use of Old Testament passages was not their actual exegesis, but only their *application*. The possibility of this is due, in a definite but in this case unique way, to the idea of a theocracy as it was prevalent among the Jewish people during the whole period from which the prophetic promises derive. In the idea of a theocracy two elements were combined: the political and the religious. Christ had no intention of renewing this combination. Since the prophets thought of the future as naturally connected with the reality of their own lives, they always included in their thought something that Christ did not want, for they were compelled by the very nature of their experience to think of a combination of these two elements [in one concept]. Moreover, since their promises were not intended for the whole world, but only for their own people, they could expect that they would not be understood in any other way. However, the prophets' main concern was with the religious element, although it was never separated from the political.

But we can also look at the matter from the opposite point of view. Christ can have made no use of those passages in which the religious element appeared only as a means and a form, whereas the political element appeared as the essence. Or is it possible that Christ could have made use of the passages and have said: I am the actual object of the hope; the form it took was only one that belonged to that time? In this case Christ's employment of the promises was not their exegesis but their application. The question for us is: At what point between these two extremes do we take our stand, or which of the two extremes do we accept? To answer this question we must reach a clear understanding of Christ's use of Scripture, in order to see whether we have to assume a significant variation in his usage.*

Before we deal with this question there is a preliminary one that demands our attention. How far are we justified in taking literally, in the strictest sense, all that Christ says about the Old Testament? There is a passage in the Gospel of John, in chapter 5:39 and 45, which is particularly pregnant and decisive in this connection: "You search the scriptures, because you think that in them you have eternal life, and it is they that bear witness to me ... Do not think that I shall accuse you to the Father; it is Moses who accuses you ... If you believed Moses, you would believe me, for he wrote of me." If we take this quite literally it follows that no one could any longer ask whether the Pentateuch is from Moses or not. This would put an abrupt end to all recent investigation, for in that passage Christ states unequivocally that Moses wrote the Pentateuch. In fact, I cannot understand why the defenders of the literal interpretation have not appealed to this passage.† But Christ could have said what he did in that Johannine passage without having examined the question of the authorship of the Pentateuch. He simply makes use of the generally accepted designation of the book, and the truth of his words is related only to their definite sense in this given connection. But how are we to understand the remark that the Pentateuch speaks of Christ? This is part of the passage I have just quoted. If someone wished to maintain that there are passages in the Pentateuch whose real meaning is that the promises they contain refer to a specific individual such as Christ was, so that he could say: "The Pentateuch speaks of me," our answer is that no one could prove that. All the passages in the Pentateuch are of a general sort and of such a kind that

---

* If the usage is always the same, then one or the other of the extreme positions we have noted is probably the correct one, for it represents everything as definite. If we find a difference, then our position must lie at some point between the two extremes.

† Why do the literalists not appeal to this passage? Because the healthy instinct still has a certain power even in those who suppress it. Christ speaks not of a man but of a book (the former lies outside the area of his concern), without having any conviction with respect to critical problems concerning the author of the book.

Christ could say: I am the one spoken of there — without maintaining that* what the Pentateuch said had a definite idea of him in mind, but only that it contained an idea that had been realized in him. In spite of that he can say that the Scripture condemns those who believe in what it says but, when he appeared, did not apply it to him as he himself did. Therefore we cannot assume an absolute literalness here.

When Christ represents himself as the promised one, he does not mean that in his unique, personal being or in his peculiar destiny and life's accomplishments he had been foreseen. On the contrary, that can only be maintained when Christ expressly indicates that such is the case. Here we have an example of a use of Scripture in a wider sense. The way Christ employs it lies outside the bounds of actual interpretation. We are also not to overlook the fact that he looks for the whole motive in that use when he says: You search the Scriptures, because you think that in them you have eternal life, that is to say, because you are looking for the essential constituents of eternal life, and the search initiates the process of discovery. A similar passage is to be found in John 3:14-15. This is part of Christ's conversation with Nicodemus in which reference is made to the use of the serpent which Moses lifted up in the wilderness: So must the Son of man be lifted up, that whoever believes in him may have eternal life. If anyone wishes to use this passage as the basis for the belief that the brazen serpent was a type of Christ, we observe how far this departs from what Christ says, and we get the distinct impression that in other connections Christ would have expressed himself quite differently. The whole passage is a comparison, not of the brazen serpent with himself, but of the lifting up of the brazen serpent with what he believes to be involved in his own coming exaltation. The lifting up of the serpent had a purpose, and the attainment of that purpose was related to (or: conditioned by) a specific process. It was in this that the similarity was to be found. The lifting up of the serpent had the purpose of healing those who had been bitten, but the method was the all-important factor. Those

_____
* that the writer had his person specifically in mind

who had been bitten had to view the serpent after it had been lifted up. In similar fashion the exaltation of the Son of man had the purpose of healing men, of saving them from threatening death, but this purpose could be achieved only by viewing the exaltation, that is to say, by *faith*. The whole passage is concerned with the way in which Christ carries out his mission, but his words give no indication that he had something similar (or: something about Moses?) in mind.

If we reflect on the way that Jewish teachers themselves used the Old Testament, even at the time that Christ lived, we find that (or: that there was a mixture that) it ranged from actual exegesis and application to mere analogy. They tended to make use of every opportunity to weave something from Scripture into the expression of their own thought. If we think of this as the traditional and usual practice, we must assume that it was so understood by those who listened to the teachers. The hearers knew how to adjust themselves to the varied use of Scripture, without requiring that on every occasion a specific formula that defined the kind of use should be specified. Christ appeared as a public teacher and was understood by his hearers to be such. Consequently he would have acted unnaturally if he had used a different method of employing Scripture than was customary, without drawing attention to the fact that he was doing so. Since we find no such announcement in our sources and observe that the differences between Christ's way of teaching and that of the other teachers are not to be noted in this area, but concern only Christ's activity (or: energy) we have to say that, assuming that his hearers would understand his use of the Old Testament passages in the proper way, he made use of Scripture in the same way that the other teachers of the time employed it. In the aspect of his teaching that we are now examining the same is true. We find the same varied use of Scripture. In some passages Christ quotes the actual words of the Old Testament and gives an exact exegesis of them. At other times he only refers to the Old Testament passages remotely. In all this we have to assume that Christ's hearers were familiar with the passages quoted or alluded to and that they produced a definite effect. So, in order to make a point emphatically and to impress it on the memory of his hearers, it was desirable that Christ should make use of Scripture as was the custom of the time. We must pay attention to the character of the passages and the context in which they appear. Only then shall we be able to determine the manner of their use.

Lecture 38 (July 13). The passage in Luke 24:26 affords similar results. There is no other way of solving the problem [of the meaning] of the passage. The verb "to suffer" cannot refer literally to the death on the cross, and the noun "glory" cannot be a reference to the resurrection. The passage can only be a reference to the hope that the disciples were not to abandon. It is therefore a prophetic assurance that the Messiah can only overcome resistance after he has suffered. The use that Christ makes of Isa. 61 in Luke 4 is in agreement with this. The promise of external restoration is only fulfilled by the appearance (or: emergence) of Christ which* was conditioned by it, and this was the innermost meaning of all the divine decrees given to the Jewish people. The messianic element of prophecy in Pauline theology would also have the same relationship. (Isa. 61 is superbly adapted to this purpose because it contains no legalistic element. The restoration is prophesied *simpliciter.*) The statement that glory is conditional on suffering could not have been made in any other sense than this.

In Luke 24, after Christ's conversation with the two disciples who were walking to Emmaus, he says to them harshly: " 'O foolish men, and slow of heart to believe all that the prophets have spoken! Was it not necessary that the Christ should suffer these things and enter into his glory?' And beginning with Moses and all the prophets, he interpreted to them in all the scriptures the things concerning himself." Here we have a summary account of how Christ demonstrated that all the prophets spoke of him. Obviously the summary is directly related to the words that Christ used, namely, that he had to suffer those things to be able to enter into his glory. When Christ asks, "Was it not necessary that the Christ should suffer these things and enter into", etc., to what is he making reference? The subject is the crucifixion and resurrection. However, since the disciples had previously said

* which fulfillment, or, what was conditioned by it

250

that they had hoped that he was the one to redeem Israel, their remark implies that there had been no redemption. Christ cannot have blamed them for what they did not know, namely, that they had seen Christ. Christ could not have blamed them for failing to draw a conclusion from their contact with him. He could only have blamed them because, having set their hope on Christ, they had abandoned it after he had been crucified. This is why Christ appeals to the prophets. The passage gives us no definite information concerning what Christ sought to prove by his appeal to the prophets. It would be assuming too much to say that he must have interpreted some passage as a reference to his crucifixion and resurrection, for the verb "to suffer" may have been used quite generally, and the clause "to enter into his glory" must be related to the definitive attainment of Christ's goal, not just to the resurrection. So then, if we wanted to attempt to specify what Old Testament passages Christ probably appealed to in order to show the disciples that, had they properly understood the Old Testament, they would not have had to abandon their hope, we have to admit that we have undertaken a task that we cannot carry out with any confidence.

However, the way the disciples use the Old Testament throws some light on Christ's use of it. The passage in Luke that we have been discussing stands by itself, but it is unthinkable that Christ had not earlier said similar things in his conversation with the apostles. Consequently, when we examine the apostolic exegesis in the New Testament we have to regard it as based on the exegesis that Christ himself used. In such exegesis we find much that is not exact interpretation, but only application. Take, for instance, that part of Peter's sermon at Pentecost where he quotes the familiar passage from the psalms which declares that God's Holy One will not see corruption and applies it to Christ, going on to say that it could not have had any reference to David. How can anyone draw a definite distinction between what is actually death and what is actually corruption? Corruption is just the consequence of the operation of chemical laws instead of the laws that are responsible for life, and it is impossible to think of any intermediate state. The operation of the chemical process to begin with is minimal, but it is impossible to conceive an intermediate state when there is neither life nor death. So we have to understand the verse in the psalm as saying: Thou wilt not permit thy Holy One to die. Then Peter goes on to say that, since this could not have referred to David, it must have referred to Christ. This involves rules of procedure that we cannot regard as exact exegesis. We must also conclude that when Peter says that the verse could not have referred to David and that therefore it must have referred to Christ, he makes a statement that stands in great need of proof. However, we know that the messianic party among the scribes of the Jewish people held that all prophetic passages that cannot be shown to be references to a specific person are messianic, and Peter therefore only followed scribal practice.

Now we have to ask: Is it possible that Christ could have found among all the writings of the prophets passages which say in essence that the Messiah could only fulfill his destiny by rejection, suffering, and death? No one can find passages that contain this to a greater degree than others that can be used similarly to that passage from Psalm 16. This enables us to see in what area of precision or generality this appeal to Old Testament prophecy lies. Christ distinguishes between what was the outer shell or form which the idea had to assume and its inner meaning. The latter is as follows: *What the men of God of the old covenant wished and expressed as their hopes and as divine promises was fulfilled in Christ. Although the outer form and fashion of their utterances could lead us to believe that they had something quite different in mind, these utterances actually refer to the kingdom of God, which was to be founded and whose founder was to come from among the Jewish people. That is the glorification of what they saw, although what they saw was seen in terms of quite different images.*

This could appear to be a venturesome statement if it were not for the fact that we have an account that says this unequivocally. In chapter 4 Luke says that Christ was handed the Old Testament scroll when he went on the sabbath into the synagogue at Nazareth and that he read from chapter 61 of the Book of Isaiah. He read only one section, the beginning of the chapter. Then he closed the scroll and said concerning the words he had read, "Today this scripture has been fulfilled in your hearing." Luke gives only the opening part of Christ's address on that occasion. If we read further in the chapter in Isaiah we see that it is a prediction of the return of the people to Palestine and of the reconstruction of their country and of a high degree of prosperity, so that the people no longer have to engage in heavy labor — a symbol of general well-being. Christ must have known that the passage he had read had this connection, and he cannot have arbitrarily isolated the beginning of the chapter from what follows. Yet he says, "Today this scripture has been fulfilled in your hearing." So he relates the passage he had read to his own appearance. His appearance was its actual fulfillment. This means: *All divine decrees relating to the Jewish people, including this, that it would return and after the dispersion would be gathered together again — all this must refer to him, must have had him in view, and to that extent he could say that this promise had been fulfilled in him. To the extent that this passage was regarded as a divine ordinance, what it had in view was realized in his appearance.* All this is justified, but it is not what we call exegesis in the strict sense. If from our point of view we had asked Christ: Is it your opinion that the author of Isaiah meant what he wrote as a reference to the appearance of an individual teacher? he would have denied it. But he entered further and deeper into the truth of the idea, and in so doing he acted quite properly. If we were to ask: Does everything that Christ relates to himself as messianic prophecies and regards as passages that represent him as the one foreseen by the prophets mean that he was convinced that the prophets had him in mind as he actually was when he appeared? we should have to answer that we have no right to make such a claim, for the passages in question have a quite different reference.

If we examine Paul's theology with reference to the whole Old Testament field and look at his idea of the law in connection with the promise given to Abraham, we see that his theory amounts to this: When God chose Abraham in order to assure for himself from among the patriarch's descendants a people apart from other peoples and a people that would continue in the unity of God, this had the closest possible connection with the divine intention of redeeming men through Christ, for Christ could not have appeared among a people laboring under pagan illusions and sharing in pagan perversities, but only among a people in whom the consciousness of God could have been aroused. In this connection the Mosaic law was purely an incidental element. It was a *pareisakton* ["something secretly brought in"][31] that in this connection had no direct value.* Paul's theory is that the original divine decree was realized in these two factors, by the choice of Abraham in order that such a people might be created from among his descendants and by Christ's birth among this people. If Paul had worked out a similar theory regarding Old Testament prophecy, what would it have included? What place would he have made for Abraham and the Mosaic law in prophecy? He would naturally have regarded everything as messianic prophecy and would have related it to the divine promise that had been given to Abraham and would have said: Prophecy is a divine institution that was always intended to point to the promise given to Abraham. That is precisely the way and manner in which Christ used the messianic promises. However, the extent to which the prophets proclaim divine blessings or divine punishments to the people in light of their obedience or disobedience to the divine law is another part and section of the law.[†] They could hope for success from their reference to a future disclosure of the original divine destiny of the people only to the extent that they contributed to keeping the people to-

31. This is a reference to Gal. 2:4 which Schleiermacher has misinterpreted as referring to the Mosaic law in the centuries before Christ. Actually, Paul by this Greek word is speaking of certain Christians whose Judaizing tendencies are a threat to Christian freedom from the law and representing in Paul's eyes a surreptitious entry of false brothers into the church. In the discussion of the adding of the law in Gal. 3:17-18 there is nothing secret involved and the Greek word cited in the text here does not appear.
* that therefore could be of no value to the Jews
† of their service to the law; Another possibility: is something quite different, and is related to messianic prophecy as is the law itself

gether under the law, which was the nation's external bond. So the two elements of prophecy are connected.*

So most of the difficulties that would otherwise beset this subject disappear as soon as we examine the use that is made of the Old Testament passages from the prophets and the psalms in light of our rules of exegesis. However, if someone wished to add that the messianic prophecies were thought of as referring literally to the person of Christ and that similarly there was a definite idea in the mind of the writer identical with the application that was made of it, this would be a statement that could not be justified. But that was not the way that messianic prophecy was understood. What mattered was not the detail but the basic idea. But there is still another point to be considered. The prophets were able to think only in terms of a theocracy. They could not think of the divine election, when they reflected seriously on it, apart from a political formulation of it. But Christ from the beginning separated the religious from the political element in his people's destiny. He must have thought of the political element only as something external, as the outer form by which the destiny was expressed, rather than its actual inner content. He retained only the spiritual element in prophecy, namely, that Christ would be a light to enlighten the Gentiles. The prophets had never been able to separate the political element in the messianic hope from the religious, and Christ viewed this as a limitation of what was the actual meaning and spirit of the hope, and he himself retained only the religious element. With this in mind it is impossible to maintain that all use of Old Testament passages was exegesis in the strict sense of the word.

I cannot resist the temptation to say something here that perhaps I should not introduce at this point in our discussion. Among the claims of recent theology is the theory that Christ, to begin with, accepted this theocratic idea and thought of the kingdom of God that he was to found as a political system and devoted himself to its establishment, and that he only

* Therefore prophecies were excluded that would be fulfilled in another way and that had another significance, and the canon of the scribes is in agreement with this.

later abandoned this idea. This question actually belongs to another part of our investigation, namely, to our study of what Christ did to found the Christian church as a community. If he had thought of the church as a political system, his regulations would have had to be quite different than they were. At this point in our discussion let me phrase the question this way: Can we find anything in Christ's teaching in the Gospels that says that the kingdom of God would and must come by means of external power and might? In my opinion no one can find anything of this sort. The theory can only be defended by saying: Christ must have kept that element of his teaching secret. Otherwise the Romans would have interfered directly and would have had him arrested.* However, to say that Christ kept that teaching quiet is not the same thing as proving that he taught any such doctrine. In fact, not only are there no traces of it,† but everything we find, even in the earliest tradition of his teaching that has been handed down to us, contradicts the theory in its entirety.[32]

Lecture 39 (July 16). The content of Christ's teaching concerning his person is identical with the content of Christ's teaching concerning his mission, because Christ invariably speaks of his person in connection with his mission and vice versa. But here again we note a difference in our sources. The Gospel of John speaks chiefly of Christ's person, while the other Gospels are concerned more with his mission and contrast the kingdom of God that Christ preached with the ancient theocracy. A consideration of this difference is all the more necessary because the prevailing opinion is that John everywhere has added his own interpretation to the tradition. But John's relationship with the Baptist cannot be harmonized with a dominantly mystical concern. Furthermore, it is also impossible to demonstrate that Alexandrian speculation was widespread in Palestine, for Jerusalem had no attraction for the Alexandrians. Since John the Baptist's messianic views made no place for Alexandrian thought, there is even less reason to believe that anything of that sort had penetrated into the Johannine circle. Even if we assume that the apostles were the main source

* and would have treated him quite properly as a rebel
† or add: even in discourses delivered to the inner circle of his followers
32. Schleiermacher could well have in mind here Hermann Samuel Reimarus and his *Fragments,* ed. Charles H. Talbert, Lives of Jesus series (Philadelphia: Fortress, 1970), for Reimarus argued that Jesus had a worldly Kingdom in mind in his preaching and that he would be established as ruler. Cf. Introduction, p. xxxv.

of the narratives of Christ and, more specifically, of the discourses of Christ in the synoptic Gospels, the Evangelists employed chiefly oral tradition, which made it necessary for them to restrict themselves to what could be least misrepresented in this way. John, on the other hand, supplemented the evangelical tradition (but not the Gospels themselves) with a view to its publication and consequently so fixed the literal account that, while misunderstandings were not completely ruled out (that would have been a superhuman achievement), it remained possible to obtain the correct understanding from it, since misrepresentations could no longer occur. This is an adequate explanation of the difference that exists between our sources. In addition we must keep in mind that the disciples, some to a greater degree and others to a lesser degree, Judaized Christ's teaching.

Our starting point can only be what Christ taught concerning his person and his mission. These two elements of his teaching are always so intimately connected that one cannot be separated from the other. Although it is true that they are always closely interrelated, we note a significant difference in our sources. The Gospel of John differs in this respect from the three other Gospels, and we cannot treat the subject adequately without taking this difference into account. If we consider the Gospel of John separately from the others and ask first of all: What did Christ say about his person, and how did he represent his mission? we discover that it is virtually only in the Gospel of John that we get information about the first part of the question. In the other Gospels there are only a few isolated references to it. So we must ask: How are we to understand this difference? The problem is all the more insistent because for a long time the idea has been prevalent, even among our German theologians, that the first three Gospels, because of their apparent simplicity, are our more authentic and more reliable sources, while John has included in his account much that is his own.[33] This opinion would raise some doubt about everything in the Gospel of John that is represented as Christ's witness to himself. In the other three Gos-

33. Schleiermacher has in mind here especially, Karl Bretschneider. While there had been some scattered opinions raised prior to Bretschneider regarding the authorship of the Gospel of John by a disciple, he was the first to call this genuineness into question on critical grounds in his *Probabilia de evangelii et epistolarum Ioannis Apostoli indole et origine cruditorum iudiciis modeste subjecit* (Leipzig, 1820). See Introduction above, p.xxxi.

pels the subject of discussion much more frequently is Christ's mission. That is to say, Christ speaks of the kingdom of God which it was his intention to found, and the kingdom of God is most frequently discussed in its relation to Jewish thought and to the idea of a theocracy. The synoptic Gospels do not discuss the person of Christ in its essential difference from that of others in the same way that the subject is discussed in the Gospel of John. Since the kingdom of God that Christ was to found is considered only in light of its relationship to Jewish theocracy, it follows that the account can only adequately stress those points that have analogies in the Jewish idea, and therefore a really complete representation of it cannot be expected. If we wish to contrast this view with another opposed to it, we should have to say that John was in an excellent position to be able to preserve what Christ had to say of himself, and we cannot pay attention only to what can be regarded as the relation of the kingdom to Jewish theocracy and legislation, but must ask: Of what does the kingdom of heaven consist, to the extent that it could be founded only by someone such as Christ represents himself to have been?

How are these two opposite points of view related to one another? What is presupposed by the first assertion? It is not maintained that John wished intentionally to distort the picture or that he deliberately said things about Christ that Christ never said of himself. However, it is said that in John, considered in and for himself, there was a tendency that could have led him to misunderstand Christ's discourses and that his enthusiasm for Christ, combined with that tendency, had the effect that, unknowingly and unconsciously, he made something of what Christ said that was not actually inherent in it. If we were to admit that for the moment and ask what actually led John to do this, we should have to fall back on something that we learn from his own account, namely, that to begin with, he had been a disciple of John the Baptist. However, in all the rather detailed accounts of John the Baptist that we have, there is nothing to suggest that he exhibited such a particularly mystical tendency. On the contrary, one who had been attracted by John the Baptist would later have written an account of Christ that would have resembled the one we find in the first three Gospels. John the Baptist was a man of the old covenant and remained so, even though he proclaimed something new that was at hand. Everything we know is against ascribing to the Baptist the tendency that is said to characterize John's Gospel, for in the Baptist's teaching everything is derived from prophetic sources, and the unique element in it was that the Baptist demanded that members of the Jewish nation itself should repent if they wished to have any claim on the kingdom of heaven. What he had to say of him who was to found the kingdom was not the sort that it could be said to have that character. In the first place, the Baptist subordinated himself to the Messiah who was to come. When he refers to the Messiah as the Lamb of God who was to bear or take away the sins of the world, it is difficult to define the content of the statement, for it has been handed down as an isolated remark. In the second place, the Baptist says that the Messiah would baptize with the Holy Spirit and with fire, whereas his baptism had been with water and was for repentance. This statement presents a contrast between a preparatory mission that had a negative character and a positive mission by which the Messiah would bring about a unity among men and would distribute a new spirit among them. This would exhaust what the Baptist had to say. There is nothing in this that would be especially attractive to an enthusiastic personality such as is presupposed in John. The Baptist had nothing to say of a specifically miraculous, incomprehensible relationship between God and the one whose coming he proclaimed. All we know of the Baptist's teaching about Christ is what I have already stated. What was it, then, that made John ready at once to turn to Jesus when the Baptist identified him as the Messiah? The reason was a practical one: He turned to him who was to realize what John the Baptist had proclaimed. So then, from everything external that we know of John, there are no grounds for the conclusion that the tendency we note in his Gospel was due to the influence on him of the Baptist. If someone were to say that the conclusion is based on the discourses that John ascribes to Christ, we should have to answer that this is a *petitio principii,* for it remains to be proved that he ascribed to Christ anything that Christ did not say. So the whole discussion revolves about this single point.

If we take our departure from the observation that the two chief Gospels of the three, Matthew and Luke, are composed of originally separate constituents and that they are therefore only end results of a process of oral transmission, we must think of the problem in such a way that we raise the question: What are we to regard as the immediate source of the individual accounts? Only to the extent that they contain something that happened between Christ and the intimate circle of his disciples can we regard the disciples as the actual source. Whenever anything is narrated that Christ spoke to a large crowd of people, all those who were present could have spread the account. But those who wanted to gather information about Christ for themselves, or in order to retell it, will have turned first of all to the apostles, and only those stories will have become generally current that went back to the apostles themselves or were in agreement with the stories the apostles told. But this raises the question: Can the apostles and those who most frequently accompanied Christ have narrated everything they had heard from Christ in order that it might become generally known? Obviously it was natural and a primary precautionary measure on their part that they should have most carefully withheld what could most easily have been distorted in retelling. When we take the additional fact into consideration that they were so occupied with their immediate didactic responsibilities that they could only regard either the communication of the individual acts and discourses of Christ themselves or the correction of the accounts of others as a matter of secondary concern, we see that they were unable to give the time that would be necessary to attach their own explanations to these accounts and thus to insure that something else was not made of the story at second or third hand.

To be sure, if the apostles had been interested in providing a written account of Christ's acts and discourses, the situation would have been a different one. Then they themselves could have given the narratives a fixed form for all time to come. But John was the only one of that first circle of Christ's pupils who communicated his account directly in written form, and he was able to report those discourses and sayings which had been left out of the oral tradition because they could easily have been distorted. So the other Gospels restrict themselves to reporting only the discourses in which Christ represents his mission in connection with the Jewish theocracy, legislation, and prophecy. I do not share the opinion that has been popular in recent times that John wrote his Gospel as a supplement to the others. However, it is quite another matter to say that he wrote his Gospel, in part at least, as a supplement to the oral tradition. So phrased, I accept the suggestion at once. From this it follows that John preferred to include in his written account teachings of Christ that had no place in the oral tradition. To this extent the Gospel of John can be characterized as a supplement to the oral tradition that was ultimately incorporated in the other Gospels.

But the differences between John and the Synoptics cannot be said to be due to much that John added of his own ideas. What could possibly have led John to put anything into the discourses of Christ that did not belong there? Usually it is said that John's own ideas can be detected in what Christ says of his own person and of his relationship to God. However, how can John previously have formed such ideas that he is said later to have introduced into Christ's discourses? We are told that the prologue to John's Gospel provides the actual key to an understanding of his point of view. There, we are told, John shares with us his own ideas, ideas that he had previously held and had then introduced into Christ's discourses. If this were the case, how are we to explain that the basic ideas of the prologue do not recur in the discourses of Christ that John later reports? Christ has nothing to say in his discourses that has anything to do with the Logos ["Word"] as that term is used in the prologue. Moreover, where could John have got this idea? It cannot be said to have come from any Jewish-Alexandrian speculation that can be said to have been current at the time. There is even less reason to say that such speculation was current in Palestine, and still less to think of it as having penetrated the circle in which John had previously moved. To be sure, there were many Hellenistic

Jews in Jerusalem, but few of these were Egyptian, for Egyptian Jews, since they had built their own temple and did not regard the temple in Jerusalem as particularly holy, had least reason to move to Jerusalem. Even if we were to admit that among the Jewish scribes there were those who had some literary connection with Egyptian Jews, it would still be impossible to see how John, who had no Jewish education, could have become familiar with the ideas they may have held. There is also not the slightest indication that Egyptian speculation had been publicly discussed by the Jewish scribes. That they engaged in such speculation is only a fiction that is most improbable. John the Baptist was the son of a priest and had been trained in priestly ways of thinking. To claim that he shared Alexandrian speculation is to make a claim that has absolutely no inner probability. If John had previously held such ideas, they would not have inclined him to enter into collaboration with John the Baptist, for that association would have provided no support for them. Consequently I cannot understand how anyone can believe that those ideas were John's. Furthermore, the First Letter of John is characterized by a practical tendency that makes no place for such speculation. So our task is that of understanding the prologue to the Gospel of John in such a way that it can be harmonized with other facts we know about the author. *So then, what John represents as the content of the discourses of Christ must have been what Christ really said, and there is no reason to believe that John introduced any of his own ideas into Christ's discourses.* What shall we say of the account in the first three Gospels? Although many of their narratives may derive from the apostles, the fact that we do not find in them discourses such as those in the Gospel of John is readily explained. The apostles reported the discourses orally, and in doing so they suppressed what was difficult to understand and what could most easily be misrepresented as it passed from one mouth to another.

Lecture 40 (July 17). We have a twofold interest in the content of Christ's teaching, namely, whether it supports our presupposition

262

of a specific dignity on Christ's part, and whether it indicates that it is possible for us to carry out our task of discussing the life of Christ in purely human terms. What is not supportable we abandon. In addition to representing himself as the promised one, he also represents himself as *the one whom God has sent,* but without basing this claim on a single fact or on a specific event. He did not make his claim as the prophets had, but in the same way that we all to a different extent are sure of our own calling, that is to say, as included in the development of his self-consciousness. There is nothing, then, in the way of our task. Rather, the more spiritual the mission and the greater the certainty, the more each one of us assumes that his mission has been given him by God. Assured that he had been called of God, Christ maintained: (1) He could do nothing of himself, but must always look to the Father. In other words, his consciousness of God never failed him, and apart from it he amounted to nothing.[34] (2) Only he had true knowledge of God, so that only he could communicate it. Both these claims can be understood only in light of our presupposition, for Christ does not derive his consciousness of God from the Old Testament, and he asserts that there is no one else in whom it exists as originally and as purely, and therefore as specifically. Christ's statement that he alone has seen God, in the sense we have just indicated, is to be understood as meaning that others have neither seen God's form nor heard His voice. Furthermore, when he says that he "is with God" he has in mind only the constancy of his consciousness of God. This does not imply an *anamnēsis* ["recollection"], any more than the *doxa* ["glory"]of John 17:5. *The glory that he had with the Father* is the place God had given him as the center of all things, as we are told in Colossians 1, and also as the statement in Genesis 1 that "God saw everything that He had made, and behold, it was very good," must mean that Christ also had been foreseen. Also it cannot be said that John 6:38 and 62 imply any recollection on Christ's part. If he had had any memory of a preexistent state it would have been constant, and there would have been no truth in the teaching he delivered to his disciples if he had not frequently referred to it.

First of all we have to determine whether in Christ's sayings there is an expression of what is the presupposition of faith in Christ, and secondly whether, if that is so, we can continue to assert the pure humanity of his life in terms of its whole historical manifestation. Under no circumstances may we make it a canon of interpretation that the discourses of

34. J. Ernest Davey in his book, *The Jesus of St. John* (London: Lutterworth, 1958), has carried through a comprehensive interpretation of various aspects of John's presentation of Jesus by means of the rubric "dependence," which Schleiermacher sees as constitutive of the God-consciousness. Cf. Introduction, p. xl.

Christ must be so understood that both our goals are proportionately attained. On the contrary, the possibility that both may be achieved must be demonstrated by the observation that Christ made these statements of himself. If that is not the case, we are faced with a choice between the two. We have already dealt with one point, namely, that Christ again and again represents himself as the promised one and appeals to Old Testament prophecy, by demonstrating in connection with his own sayings how that claim is to be understood. Now we have to consider the fact that Christ also represents himself as *the one whom God has sent*. The sending is the fulfillment of the promise. Both are inextricably connected. What made Christ believe that he had been sent by God? How did he reach this awareness, this conviction? I assume that certain passages of Scripture, especially in John, are familiar. Christ never appeals to any single fact in connection with his commission. He never speaks of his own calling as the Old Testament speaks of that of the prophets: "The word of the Lord" came to this man or that, telling him to do this or that. Christ never says that he was called to his mission on any particular occasion. This agrees with the fact that he regards the age of the prophets as having ended with John the Baptist. He did not explain his commission from God as that of the prophets had been explained. He did not look back to a particular event that had marked its beginning. Therefore we ask: How are we to think of his commission? If it was not related to a particular event, or to any definite outer or inner fact, we can only think of it as belonging to the natural development of his self-consciousness.

At this point we must first raise the question with reference to our own interest: Is there anything analogous to this anywhere in the area of human affairs? I do not think we shall have any difficulty in finding it. Among individuals we frequently discover the development of such a certainty concerning a particular destiny or calling, wholly unrelated to any specific event or fact. It is the pure development of the self-consciousness concerning the individual's relationship to the world. However, this exhibits an astonishing variation. Some do not have the capacity to make the decision themselves, but let others decide for them, or the decision is brought about by circumstances. Sometimes individuals hesitate to make a decision, and when they finally reach one it appears to have been a pure accident that they did so, and when something later gets in its way they change their vocation and strike out on a new path. With some people this vacillation lasts throughout their entire lifetime. That is the one extreme, assuming many different forms. There are also those who are sure of their way of life in a purely negative fashion. They never question it. They go their way as though they were boxed in. Even when there is a greater or more definite certainty, this is not always the certainty of a vocation in life that God has ordained. However, the more spiritual and, at the same time, the more unique the vocation, the more the conviction that it is ordained of God, and so it offers the analogy we have been seeking. There are many such analogies in the religious field. There are individuals who are so certain in terms of their self-consciousness of what they have to do in the religious field that they regard this as the destiny that God has ordained for them, and consequently their conviction that God has called them is nothing else than their own self-consciousness.

So then, if Christ was one who was distinguished from others by a specifically divine communication that had entered into a purely human life, it follows automatically that he was conscious of this in a very special way. That, however, is only a general view of the matter, and we must now go on to ask more precisely: What did Christ actually understand by the statement that he had been sent by God? Here we find that he often introduced two points concerning himself that we have to regard as essential correlates. (1) He declares that *he had received his teaching from God*. This involves the claim that he alone was able to put men in possession of the truth, to give them the consciousness of God, for he claims that his consciousness of God was exclusive. (2) The correlate of this is that he says that *he could do nothing of himself. He attributes everything to the constancy of his relationship to God, to the constant, uninterrupted vitality of his consciousness of God*. By this claim he certainly does not wish to suggest that he was ever without this relationship to

God and this consciousness of God. When we combine these two correlates, what we said earlier emerges for the first time with real clarity, and we have the indication that this is the most direct expression of the specific divine communication, that at no time in his life had he ever been without the consciousness of God that was associated with every moment. He describes this at the same time in such a way that it belongs within the framework of human development. God not only shows him the works that he has to do, but God would also show him still greater works. That is to say, Christ thinks of his consciousness of God as something involved in the process of human development. That is in accordance with the task we have set ourselves.

When Christ says, "No one knows the Father except the Son," he asserts most definitely that his knowledge is exclusive and that the truth of his consciousness of God is exclusive. From this it follows that he does not derive it in any way from the Old Testament writings. If that were not the case, the authors of those writings would have possessed the same knowledge that he did, and he could not have said that it was exclusive to him. Furthermore, he cannot have regarded his knowledge as something acquired from the total life of his people by education. The comparison between himself and the people who surrounded him, as well as the comparison between himself and the world in which he lived, must have confirmed him in his belief. This consciousness of exclusiveness developed more and more as the result of the comparison between what was in him and what he found in the world outside, and it grew along with his general human consciousness so exactly that he represented it as something exclusive also for the whole of mankind: "and to whom the Son wishes to reveal it." Therefore he regards himself in a general way as the only source of such a consciousness of God, and this implies that he was conscious of this divine communication as something unique to himself and entrusted to him individually and personally, but still within the framework of human existence. When this at times is expressed in such a way that we find in Christ's sayings something that would obliterate the human form of his existence, we must examine such sayings most carefully and see whether they have been understood as he himself meant them to be. Take, for example, the saying, "No one has ever seen God except him who is with God." That seems to deny Christ's humanity, but when we add to it the saying that Christ said to others in analogous fashion, "You have never seen God's form or heard His voice," we find ourselves necessarily obliged to regard the expression as pictorial and to understand the reference to seeing as a way of contrasting full and complete knowledge with mere formulas. Having established this, we must explain the other saying similarly and say: Christ says of himself, not that he *had been* with God, but that he *is* with God, because God is continually present in his innermost consciousness. In other words, no consciousness of God and no knowledge of God can be in accordance with the truth unless it be continuous. Consequently he represents his knowledge of God as exclusive because it was constant, and this is connected with the fact that he does not base his divine mission on any single event. The prophets always base their call on some particular event. This indicates that their consciousness of God was dissimilar to Christ's, for a word of God came to them only on specific occasions, without continuity. So the two facts are related, namely, that Christ had his consciousness of God as a continuous possession, and that he did not find it necessary to base this consciousness of God on a single event. As a child he had neither the one nor the other, neither the comparison with others nor the *continuity* of the consciousness, for the latter develops only gradually in the course of the continuum of his being. And so we see that these two correlates are in agreement. Christ had continuously to look to God, and his consciousness of God was complete and exclusive, so that all the consciousness of God that others possessed had to proceed from him. Both correlates are in complete harmony.

It follows naturally from this that Christ should also claim that his consciousness of God was infallible, that he should represent himself as the truth and as the source of truth for others, and that is the most complete expression of the specific divine communication as something that belonged to the constitution of his personality.

There is still another matter to be considered. If I reflect on the fact that Christ represents himself as the one who is with God and recall other passages where he speaks of the "glory that he had with the Father before the foundation of the world," both assertions seem to rule out the humanity of his being. To be sure, that would be the case if we had to say that these sayings of Christ mean that he had a recollection of a state of being before the foundation of the world. However, as soon as we try to expand this and make it really comprehensible, we see that it is opposed to all his sayings and that, if he had meant it in such a way, we should have to conclude that many of his sayings were intended to say something that they do not. Nowhere does Christ speak of a real consciousness that he had of a preexistent state, and nowhere does he speak of a contrast between his being before his human state and his being as a man. If we wished to think of him as possessing the memory of such a preexistent state, we should find it impossible to think any more of his life as a truly human one. He could not have wholly identified himself with humanity. Even if it were true that all men preexisted, if a few had a recollection of an earlier life that others did not share, we should not be able to regard them any longer as belonging to the same species. In like manner we could not regard the life of Christ as a human one.

However, if Christ had remembered some preexistent state he would necessarily have had to refer to it in his teachings in a different way than he does in such general references as we have noted, which permit of a different explanation. If we reflect on the saying that Christ had a glory with God before the foundation of the world, we have something definite with which to associate it. If we assume the standpoint of the creation story and ask whether God, when he said that all that he had made was good, had foreseen sin and regarded it as good, no one would say that he had foreseen sin, which he could not have regarded as good. But if we say that he had foreseen both sin and Christ, this means that he had regarded the passage of men through sin to redemption as good. That was the glory that Christ had with God at that moment, namely, the knowledge that through him all things would become good. But he also had it before the foundation of the world, because all things were related to it. However, this does not mean that Christ had it as a *recollection*. It was only the consciousness that it was his destiny that men through him would be guided to their own destiny, or that he would be responsible for the blessedness of men, and that the world was founded with that destiny in view. Otherwise the expression "before the foundation of the world" would have had no specific meaning. Christ could as well have said "from all eternity." So it appears that the purpose of God for the world and the glory of Christ in God's design amount to one and the same thing.

Lecture 41 (July 18). Christ's reference to his descent from heaven is only the appropriate expression of his mission, and his reference to his ascent to the place where he had been before is only a way of saying that he had fulfilled within time the eternal divine decree. Christ's *oneness with the Father* is to be explained in light of our oneness with him. It is only a way of saying that he was wholly governed by his consciousness of God. The title *Son of God* is not to be distinguished from the title *Son of man* and is explained by the contrast between Christ as Son and Moses as servant. There is nowhere any suggestion that Christ distinguished between the divine and the human in himself. He always speaks of himself in terms of the unity of his being. However, the title Son of God draws attention to his difference from all others, while the title Son of man emphasizes his identification with all others. It would interfere with all human treatment of the subject and Christ would be a completely ghostly figure if we were to ascribe to him either the recollection of a consciousness of a prehuman state of being along with his consciousness of his state of being as a man, or a parallel awareness of his divinity and his humanity. If he had been such a being but had not been able to inform his disciples of the fact because they were still incapable of understanding it, the Spirit would have had to do it, and there is no trace of that. If the disciples had known anything of that, it would have been much more important for them to have testified to it than to Christ's resurrection. Nevertheless, we can continue without qualification to affirm Christ's consciousness of divine indwelling, or of original and constant divine influence.

In the course of the preceding lecture I said that we must hesitate to accept any interpretation of Christ's sayings, such as that concerning the glory that he had with the Father, that presupposes a recollection on his part of a state of being prior to his life as a man. We must consider whether, if he had spoken of such a memory, his teaching would not have taken on a quite different form in the consciousness of his disciples than what we actually find. We should have to think of the truth in Christ's message as gravely restricted if he had had such a consciousness of which he could have spoken but had not communicated it in any definite and distinct way to his disciples. There is not a trace of it, and we have to say that this fact in itself makes such an explanation very doubtful.

It is equally difficult to assume that Christ must have told his disciples about it, as we should have to presuppose since he says that he told them everything, but that they on their part had kept what he told them in this respect to themselves. If they had done so they would have overlooked the most important means of awakening faith among men. If they had to appeal either to Christ's resurrection or to what Christ had told them of his preexistent state and of his heavenly being, and we should ask which of these two would have been the more effective means of leading men to faith in him, we should have to answer that the latter would have been a more powerful means than the former. Furthermore, the latter would have been of more help to people who desired more assurance than earthly and sensual evidence could afford. If this had been the case, the disciples would have made a very poor choice. However, if anyone wishes to appeal to the fact that, while Christ says that he had revealed everything to his disciples that he had received from his Father and that this would include the form of the eternal witness — that he had borne witness to the Father's revelation to him of the form that had been his — he also said, on the other hand, that he had still much to tell them that they could not yet hear — if anyone wants to get out of the difficulty in this way, my answer would be that Christ refers the disciples to the Spirit, who would lead them into all truth by revealing to them what Christ himself had been unable to reveal during his lifetime.

So I insist that the apostles ought to have received the revelation of Christ's preexistent state from the Spirit. If they had, they give little indication of the fact. Even if we take all the passages into consideration — I do not even exclude the prologue to the Gospel of John — we see that they say nothing of a prehuman state of being on Christ's part of which he had any recollection. So I can only continue to insist that we are not in a position to reach such explanations and that we must be suspicious of all that necessarily lead to such a conclusion.

To be sure, Christ does say that he had come down from heaven, and that statement would seem to afford the strongest possible support for the assumption that Christ had a recollection of some preexistent state. However, let us consider what this utterance can mean when it is associated with the related one, namely, that the Father had sent him. If we compare these two statements in John 6:38, "I have come down from heaven, not to do my own will, but the will of him who sent me," we see that the expression "come down from heaven" is directly related to what follows it about God's having sent him. If we now reflect on the commission of the prophets, we see that Christ never appeals to a belief that a definite task had been committed to him on a certain occasion. A prophet could have said, "This task was committed to me from heaven," but that could only have been a reference to a specific occasion. In Christ's use of it the statement that he had been sent by God can be nothing else than a reference to his personal self-consciousness. So, because he related it entirely to his divine commission, he could say of his own existence what the prophet said only of a definite occasion. Let me now turn to another passage that has frequently been misinterpreted. In John 6:62 Christ says, "What if you were to see the Son of man ascending where he was before?" In this saying interpreters are always inclined to look for the distinction between Christ's divine nature and his human nature that generally forms part of our christological concept. They say that Son of man refers to Christ's human nature and Son of God to his divine nature. If this were the case they would have to abandon their whole interpretation, for this passage contradicts it. Christ's human nature was not in heaven. But I

271

do not accept this distinction between "Son of man" and "Son of God". In either case, whether he uses the title "Son of man" or the title "Son of God", Christ means his whole being. Because. he cannot have had any such separation of natures in mind and because he never refers to it, I cannot take John 6:62 to mean that in any literal sense Christ had a consciousness of an earlier state of being in heaven, for what the phrase "Son of man" designates could never have been a consciousness of his personality. So the passage indicates that Christ had in mind his exaltation and also his having been sent by God, and in both taken together, the fulfillment of his destiny, of his earthly existence. He says the same thing in the verse that follows: "My personal existence counts for nothing; the words that I have spoken to you are spirit and life." That other explanation wholly disregards the context. Clearly we could not think of such a consciousness in Christ as anything else than as a constant one, and we could not do that without utterly destroying the humanity in him.

If we now go further, we see that we have many sayings in Christ's teaching concerning his person where he speaks of his unity with his Father. The question arises: What is the actual central point which will enable us to explain this statement? If we examine Christ's prayer in John 17, where we find several such statements included, we see that he speaks of his unity with the Father and of the unity of his disciples with him in such a way that one statement is directly related to the other. This happens again and again. In v. 18 Christ compares his commission from the Father with his own commission to the disciples and goes on to say in v. 21: "that they may all be one; even as thou, Father, art in me, and I in thee, that they also may be in us." If we compare this double parallelism, that the Father has sent Christ and Christ the disciples, and that God is one with Christ and Christ is one with his disciples (cf. v. 22: "that they may be one even as we are one") we see that both are identical in meaning. As soon as we regard this as the central point of any explanation and go on to ask: What is this unity of the disciples which Christ makes the object of his prayer, their unity in Christ and in God? I am not content to answer: It is a unity of the will. That is something much too limited. Rather, it is a unity of life and being. However, if we have to relate this to what Christ says elsewhere, we have to say that Christ's statement that he was one with the Father must belong with the assertion that he could do nothing of himself, but must always look to the Father. If we do this we see that the only explanation possible is that Christ in all things was governed by his relationship to God (or: in God). However, this relationship always existed. That implies not only the unity of the will, but also the unity of thought. Everything that Christ taught was related to the divine will, and this unity is a genuine unity of life. Similarly he thought of himself as having mediated a unity of the disciples with himself and with God. This contains the most complete expression of his self-consciousness as one specifically different from other men, but it does not indicate a consciousness of an earlier existence.

There may still be those who would ask: If we do not wish to assume that Christ's sayings express a consciousness of an earlier existence, what bearing has this on the divine element in him? It seems to me that the one has nothing to do with the other. It would affect only the wholly transcendental idea that has its origin in other, even non-Christian concepts, the idea that Christ had a purely separate divine being before the creation of the world. There is not a trace in Christ's sayings that he believed that he had possessed such a separate divine being. According to that idea, when Christ said that he was one with the Father, what he actually meant was that he was not one but two.* His sayings that are related to the divine in him assert the very opposite. He had no recollection of a separated being of God in him apart from his person.

We are now in a position to ask: What did Christ mean when he spoke of himself as the Son of God? I do not wish to say, for I should not know how to justify it by anything I know of Christ, that he used this title of himself only because it was customary at the time to apply it to the Messiah. If this designation of himself had not been appropriate, he could not have employed it, for he felt himself called to justify

* If Christ had been a special being before the creation of the world, then he and the Father would not have been one but two.

its use by others with reference to himself. He could not have gone on using this expression as a title for himself simply because it was the custom of the day to apply it to the Messiah, although he himself was aware that he was not entitled to it. We can only apply to ourselves, because it is customary to do so, things that we do not have to investigate. The claim that he was the Son of God was central to Christ's consciousness and life. We cannot separate Christ's use of the title Son of God for himself from his use of the title Son of man. Both must be considered in relation to each other.

If at the same time we reflect on the fact that these expressions are used similarly in other New Testament passages, this brings us back again to the comparison between Christ and the Old Testament organs of the divine will and of divine decrees. I refer to the passage in the Letter to the Hebrews where the author says, in the course of a comparison between Christ and Moses: "Now Moses was faithful in all God's house as a *servant* . . . but Christ was faithful over God's house as a *son*." Similarly in other passages [the letter to the Galatians] we find the comparison of the son with the child and with adoption. There the term "son" contains the idea of a full-grown son, familiar with the whole will of his father and in complete agreement with that will. That is the idea that is found in the passage just quoted from the Letter to the Hebrews, and this is what Christ meant by his saying about the unity that existed between himself and the Father. When we observe how very often Christ applies these two titles to himself, sometimes "Son of God" and sometimes "Son of man", and how he does so without ever differentiating between the two, we see that he uses both to describe himself in the totality of his being, but in different respects. The one title draws attention to the specific difference between himself and all men, while the other emphasizes the identity between himself and all other men. There is another passage, John 5:25 ff., where both titles stand side by side: "The hour is coming, and now is, when the dead will hear the voice of the Son of God, and those who hear will live. For as the Father has life in himself, so he has granted the Son also to have life in himself, and has given him authority to execute judgment, because he is the Son of man." There, in vv. 25 and 27, Christ calls himself first the Son of God and then the Son of man, and in the verses in between he says, "As the Father has life in himself, so he has granted the Son also to have life in himself." If we wish to regard that as something unique, we must go beyond the words "have life". Rather, according to the context (it is said in v. 25 that the dead will come alive) to say "to have life in himself" amounts to saying *"to have life in himself as a life-communicating power"*. Christ ascribes that power to himself as "Son of God", and the title "Son of man" is explained by the words "to execute judgment". In other words, Christ had been given authority to rank men or make decisions about men in accordance with human differences because he was "Son of man", that is to say, because he was identical with other men, or because he shared other men's consciousness of differences.* The whole passage declares that Christ is to be thought of as a single whole. We are not to think of the divine in him in isolation from the human. His nature includes what is specific, what is unique, as well as what is human, for only as men could they hear his voice. So the title "Son of God", in terms of its essential content, is based on what is said of the unity of Christ with the Father.

This brings us to the limit of what Christ teaches concerning his person, to the extent that we wish to separate that teaching from what he has to say concerning his vocation. However, since this brings us back to his specific relationship to God and since, on the other hand, everything he teaches about God, that he advances as his own teaching, is associated with this specific relationship to God that was his, we intend at this point at once to set forth what he imparts as his unique teaching about God. It is evident that he believes that he has a unique teaching to impart, for he says that he alone knows the Father. By such a claim he distinguished his knowledge of God most definitely from that in the Old Testament. If he had obtained his knowledge of God from the Old Testament he would have uttered an untruth. This is not in

* or add: and conditions

any contradiction to what I said at an earlier point. If Christ's familiarity with the Old Testament writings and with the whole religious life of his people contributed to the development of his consciousness of God in human terms, that is quite another matter. To that extent it is true to say that he drew his consciousness of God from the Old Testament books. This is all we are trying to say: Christ recognized the inadequacy of the consciousness of God as it was portrayed in the Old Testament books. Building upon it, he developed what is unique in his consciousness of God in such a way that he could say that he alone knew the Father and that through him alone could others obtain a knowledge of the Father.

Lecture 42 (July 19). Christ's *teaching about God* is connected in the closest possible way with his teaching about himself, but at the same time also with other matters that are not our immediate concern, especially the relationship between the old and the new covenants. So then, the doctrines of Christ's person and vocation, of God, and of the divine plan of salvation are not wholly to be separated. In the first place, Christ calls God his Father. But he also calls God the Father of his disciples, although not as definitely, but in [a more] general way. To be sure, the same is indirectly true of the prophets in reference to the people, and a passage in which the prophet Hosea calls Israel God's son is applied in Matthew [2:15] to Christ. But the prevailing idea in the Old Testament is that of the theocratic nature of *the Lord.* When Christ calls his disciples the children of God, he is actually anti-Jewish, for in so doing he substitutes the idea of the household for that of the state. In the second place, *God is Spirit and seeks spiritual worshipers.* To be sure, in the Old Testament God is not directly thought of in physical terms, and even the prophets protest against the inadequacy of merely ritual worship, but they thought of a dwelling of God from which his revelation proceeded, and this Jewish idea of the *shekina* ["dwelling"] was something quite different from our thought of Christ as the source of God's communication of himself. God *loves Christ* and sends him because of *love,* which, like God's paternal relationship, expands so that he dwells with those whom the Son loves. This is something quite different from the thought of God's love for Abraham and God's dwelling with the nation Israel. Most anti-Jewish of all was Christ's *dissolution of nemesis* by the complete separation of the divine favor (those who love the Son) from the divine ordering of external welfare (the sun shines on both the evil and the good). In these propositions lies the seed of the whole apostolic teaching: Peter, Paul, the Letter to the Hebrews.

The two matters, Christ's presentation of his person and his teaching about God, and his presentation of his consciousness of God, are so directly related that it is impossible to separate them, for the one contains elements of the other. On the other hand, however, Christ's teaching about God is also connected with still another matter, namely, his teaching concerning his mission. These four matters are so connected with each other that it is not really possible to separate one from the other, and any order in which they are discussed must have an element of arbitrariness about it.

If we take up where we left off in the preceding lecture, the first point of Christ's teaching about God will be that concerning the divine decree, to the extent that it involved the sending of Christ. In other words, the first subject to be discussed is Christ's teaching concerning the relationship existing between God and his own person. The first thing we notice is that Christ always calls God his Father. I believe we can say categorically that he was unique in making this designation. To be sure, there are certain passages in the prophets where God, speaking through the mouth of the prophets, represents the Jewish people as his son. One instance is the familiar verse in Hosea, which is applied in our Gospel of Matthew to Christ. However, such prophetic passages are isolated and did not influence the theology of the Jewish people. Because the Jews thought in terms of a theocracy, their prevailing idea of God was by far that of an overlord, a lawgiver, and a regent. Christ, then, was virtually the first to use the name of Father for God. He uses it in the first instance to describe his own relationship to God. Whenever he refers to his disciples as God's children, he does not do so in the same original way that he calls God his Father. Rather, as it is said in John 1: 12, those who believe in him receive power to become children of God. Christ's relationship to God is transferred to those who believe in him. This is the explanation of the fact that Christ addresses God as his Father and then also speaks of the disciples as children of God. That is a polemic against the dominant Jewish idea, for in speaking of God as Father Christ at the same time *substitutes the idea of a household for that of a state, and that had a decisive influence on the pre-*

sentation of the whole relationship between God and men.[35]

We find the same usage recurring in the writings of the apostles, both in the Pauline and in the Petrine letters. There the Christian church everywhere is represented as the household of God in which Christ has first rank as the actual and therefore the only-begotten Son, but in which the others are also thought of as standing in the same relationship to God. Here, then, we find both things united in an original way: The same expression by which Christ describes his consciousness of God has also at the same time a tendency wholly to transform and to modify the idea of the general relationship of God to the people who stand in an association with Christ.

However, if we take our departure from the use of the name Father for God as Christ employs it directly to describe his own relationship to God and ask: What does Christ say of God with reference first to his own person, and then also to his mission? we find that we can sum up the essential points as follows. Christ represents himself as the object of the divine love and of an absolutely original manifestation of God that took place in him. He declares that the Father loves the Son and shows him what He does. In other words, God makes himself known to him in his manner of dealing with the general world order, so that everything, then, that Christ later speaks of as unique to himself is only represented as the consequence of a divine indwelling in him, as a self-manifestation of God in him for others. Directly connected with that, just as Christ is represented as the object of the divine love, so also his mission is described as the work of the same divine love. Since Christ represents himself as the original source for others of the knowledge of God, this involves the further fact that *he actually sums up the whole knowledge of God in an original way by declaring that God so loved the world*

35. In recent New Testament scholarship Joachim Jeremias has emphasized the central role of familial language in the words of Jesus, especially in regard to Jesus' introduction of the intimately familiar word "Abba" in his addressing God as father. Furthermore, Jeremias connects Jesus' eschatological proclamation of the kingdom of God with this familial language in the following manner: "Only the one who belongs under the kingly rule of God may call God 'Abba,' *already* has God as his Father, is *even now* a child of God. For the disciples, being children means sharing Jesus' sonship." *New Testament Theology* (New York: Scribner, 1971), p. 181; cf. pp. 36, 63-64, and 178-79.

that he sent him into the world as the object of his love. These are matters that Christ emphasizes again and again in his teachings, but this divine activity in the sending of Christ enlarges its scope, just as the Father-Son relationship that Christ originally applied to himself was generalized to include others. God is his Father, and the Father of those who have entered into direct association with him. Just as God manifests himself in him and the Father is in him, so also this manifestation extends beyond him, and God takes up his dwelling with those and manifests himself in those whom the Son loves. The direct involvement in the work of Christ means that it can be regarded in the same way either as the work of the Son or as the work of the Father, to the extent that Christ is viewed as the actual central point of this entire manifestation of God. By describing what proceeds from it alone and exclusively as the knowledge of God, Christ asserts that his work is something new, something different, something apart from all that preceded it. (This implies at the same time that Christ did not derive this knowledge of God from the sources of the old covenant. These were only a stimulus to the development of his own unique consciousness of God.) This unique character of Christ's revelation of God is stressed even more clearly in the later apostolic teaching. When it is said that the law had been only something provisory, an interlude, a *pareisakton* ["something secretly brought in"],[36] and this characterization is extended to include the entire Old Testament, this is just another way of saying what was inherent in the teaching of Christ.

What bearing has this on the viewpoint that has recently been set forth in theological circles, the view, namely, that we have to distinguish between the theology of the apostles and the theology of Christ? There are those who say that a teaching about Christ was first advanced by the apostles and that this must be strictly distinguished from the teaching of Christ.[37]

36. See n. 31 on p. 254 for Schleiermacher's use of this Greek word.
37. The contrast between the message of Jesus and the writings of the apostles had been present in the eighteenth century at least as early as certain writings of the English deists such as Thomas Chubb in *The True Gospel of Jesus Christ* (London, 1738). Hermann Samuel Reimarus made such a contrast one of his main points in his *Fragments,* ed. Charles H.

The truth is that the theology of Christ is connected in the closest possible way with his Christology, that is to say, with his teaching concerning himself, and the theology of the apostles is nothing else than the combination of the elements we discover in our incomplete and fragmentary expositions of the teachings of Christ as we find them in his discourses.

This brings us to another point. Christ on one occasion declares that God is Spirit and at the same time asserts that He is engaged in a process of search, that is to say, that He wishes to create or produce purely spiritual worshipers. Is this an idea that is purely Christ's own, or is it contained already in Old Testament theology? We can answer the question either in the affirmative or in the negative, depending on whether we look at one part or another of the Old Testament. If we have in mind the dominance of the theocratic idea among the

Talbert, Lives of Jesus series (Philadelphia: Fortress, 1970) although Reimarus's particular way of understanding it was sharply different from the normal interpretation in this vein and not the differentiation to which Schleiermacher refers here. Reimarus agreed that a teaching about Christ was already present in Jesus' own message but that it had reference to a strictly worldly kingdom; therefore, the catastrophe of his crucifixion caused his disciples to fabricate a new teaching of a spiritual kingdom mediated by the atonement, resurrection, and second coming of Christ. Much more typical was the manner in which Lessing formulated the issue in *The Religion of Christ* (1780) in *Lessing's Theological Writings*, trans. H. Chadwick (Stanford: Stanford University, 1956), saying that the religion Jesus himself practiced was one which every man could have in common with him. On the other hand, the Christian religion is that which takes Christ as the object of its religion, accepting him as more than a man. The usual phraseology for the dissimilarity was "the religion of Jesus" and "the religion about Jesus" such as used by J.G. Herder in his *Briefe, das Studium der Theologie betreffend* (1785). A new point of departure in the discussion was made by Immanuel·Kant in his *Religion Within the Limits of Reason Alone* (1793), trans. T.M. Greene and H. Hudson (New York: Harper, 1960). Despite agreeing with the deists' distinction of rational and statutory religion, and like his precursors regarding Jesus as the teacher of a purely moral religion, Kant proceeded to interpret apostolic teachings such as Incarnation and atonement in strictly moral categories, thereby ostensibly overcoming the separation. The principle Kant manifested in this work is that one finds a profounder level than the terminological expressions themselves by which to bring out the continuity between the message of Jesus and the apostolic testimony. In so doing, however, Kant removed specific reference to Jesus from the apostolic doctrines. Schleiermacher avails himself of the principle of the deeper level by means of his analysis of religious self-consciousness and then includes "the religion about Jesus" in Jesus' own message by interpreting the preaching of the kingdom of God as Jesus' communication of his God-consciousness. See above p. 243 (S) and p. 245. His approach formally parallels the present new quest of the historical Jesus which employs existentialist interpretation to bring out the continuity between Jesus' eschatological proclamation and the early christological kerygma of death and resurrection. Cf. James M. Robinson, *A New Quest of the Historical Jesus* (Naperville, Ill.: Allenson, 1959).

Jewish people, we have to say that on the whole the Old Testament is dominated by still very undeveloped, and if I may be permitted the expression, very corporeal ideas of God. The whole body of Mosaic writings from the very beginning thinks of a definite locality as the actual dwelling of God, as a point from which the manifestation of God proceeds. This involves a subjection to externalities of a sort that appears to be purely arbitrary and, as it were, mechanical, because it is not related to anything living. This is a point to be carefully noted. Otherwise it could be said that, by representing Christ as the one in whom God manifested himself fully and in a unique way, we have also bound God's activity to something corporeal and external, which we represent as the actual dwelling place of God with respect to men. However, it is not the corporeal but the spiritual to which we have reference. It is God's activity through something spiritual, and so it is neither something external nor something arbitrary. By saying that God seeks spiritual worshipers Christ at the same time utters a polemic against the sensual and corporeal element in the Jewish cult. He contrasts the spiritual worship of God to the worship of God that is bound to a particular place.

We have to admit, to be sure, that there is a very vigorous polemic in the writings of the prophets against the ritual worship of God, insofar as it purports to mediate between men and God. The prophets constantly protest in the name of God against ritual worship, to the extent that it is unrelated to obedience to God's commands. However, when we consider these commands we see that the prophet has understood them purely from the point of view of Jewish theocracy. They are laws that God has given to govern the life of the people of his choice. They are, therefore, laws with a limited application, and the welfare of the Jewish people in the land that God has given them is represented as the actual purpose of the Lawgiver. That is something that Christ wanted to deny, although something else than he had in mind was already denied in the thought and spirit of the prophets. If we think only of the value ascribed in Old Testament practice to the ceremonies of religion, we see that the prophets objected to the same things that Christ did. However, if we think of the particularism of the prophets, we see that Christ polemicizes against them.

When we reflect on how Christ polemicizes against another leading idea that runs through the whole Old Testament, we are completely convinced for the first time that Christ's teaching about God was something new, something original. The cardinal idea to which I refer, an idea that pervades the entire Old Testament account, is that of nemesis, namely, the idea that obedience to the divine will is rewarded and disobedience to the divine will is punished, rewarded by earthly prosperity and punished by earthly disaster. That idea is typical of all prophetic asceticism. All prophetic expectations are based on it. It was also expressed in Jewish legislation, and it was a necessary component of theocracy in its public, civic aspect. Christ repudiates this idea by saying that the natural laws that God has ordained, that govern all events and that exert a constant influence on the welfare of men, operate independently of God's moral judgment: ''Your Father who is in heaven . . . makes his sun to rise on the evil and on the good, and sends rain on the just and on the unjust.'' So Christ separates this ordering or nonordering of men's experience of good and evil completely from the matter of God's good pleasure, for he represents God's order in nature, so far as it relates to men, as something quite independent of it. There could be no more definite polemic than this against the leading idea of the Old Testament with respect to the relationship which exists between God and men, and in particular, between God and the Jewish people.

Furthermore, it is also evident that the whole apostolic teaching in this respect is nothing but the further developed reproduction of this saying of Christ's. When Paul says of the Jewish people, ''When we were still children, we were slaves to the ordinances,'' these ordinances are the Mosaic laws that had their sanction in the promises and threats associated with them. Paul declares that that was a divine order designed for a state of immaturity, and thus a lower level of human development that could only have temporary validity. He then sets forth, in contrast to the old order, the idea of Christians as those who have received adoption, that is to say, as those who have been declared to be fully grown children of God and people emancipated from their former state as minors. This is bound up with the fact that the new covenant is represented as a state in which the divine will is written on the hearts of men, in which the divine will has become men's own will, and for which the sanction that had been part of the old world order would no longer make any sense. What proceeds from the inner impulse of men can never be encouraged by the promise of reward, and men who act in this way are not frightened away by the threat of punishment from what they themselves abhor, without any need of external sanction.

Another essential point in Christ's teaching about God, with reference to the whole development of the new order of things that he was to introduce, the new age, is that he says that the Father has given him those who come to him. In other words, God determines those who come to Christ. It is God who ordains that at the same time some people come to Christ and others do not. If we relate this to another saying in which Christ declares that he did nothing on his own authority but spoke only as the Father taught him, we see that this too has a bearing on the subject we are discussing. This utterance of Christ's is clearly the seed of the doctrine of predestination as we find it further developed in the apostolic writings, and especially in Paul's letters. This doctrine, then, is not one that first emerged at a later time. It is grounded on Christ's own sayings. To be sure, predestination is an idea that can be understood in many different ways, and it should cause us no concern that it is possible so to understand and articulate it that it contradicts other sayings of Christ, or even general rules that Christ lays down, which no one can ignore. We can brush such a possibility aside. We need not look for any closer definition of the idea in what Christ says. But the general expression of the idea as it applies to all men is unquestionably there.

When Christ says that the Father gives him those who come to him, he is asserting that the conditions that determine whether individuals may be united with him are laid down; that they are based on the general divine order (the Father draws them to Christ). If we wish to approach the matter from another direction and to say that it follows that whoever does not come to Christ does not come because the Father has not drawn him, or because God has not given him to the Son, we are drawing a conclusion that is much more definite than the saying on which it is based and that can have been drawn incorrectly. Paul develops the theme of predestination extensively, but he applies it generally rather than specifically. It was God's decree that the Jewish people should begin by rejecting Christ in order that Christianity might then be taken to the Gentiles. However, when the fullness of the Gentiles had been brought in, the Jewish people as a whole would participate in this salvation. We see how carefully Paul proceeds in his discussion. The nonacceptance of Christ, the failure to come to Christ, is regarded as something only temporary. The divine ordinance determines an earlier rejection of Christ and a later acceptance of him, but it is not regarded as determining a total inclusion or a total exclusion. This is a guideline of how far we can go, with any certainty in respect to detail, in applying Christ's saying that the Father gives him those who come to him to the other matter of those who do not come to him.

Lecture 43 (July 20). The Father gives the Son, or draws to him, those who come to him. Christ therefore declares that the acceptance or nonacceptance of the call depends on the way the individual is both affected on the natural side and determined by the other social relationships that proceed from the governance of the world. The Father draws whenever the calling of those who were distant in and for themselves is made easier by such combinations. He always gives, however, because those who in themselves are not distant can only too easily be held back by unfavorable connections. All this, then, is quite opposed to those who give the whole governance of nature and of the world to Christ and push the Father into the background.

Teaching concerning Christ's mission. This is connected in the first place with the point that Christ makes in his theology that the Father has granted him *to have life* in himself, that is, as *a self-communicating power.* His picture of the vine and its branches and his disciples' picture of the head and the body are the same, except that the one is drawn from the vegetable world and the other from the animal. When he elsewhere associates having life with faith, we must understand that as meaning the acceptance of the offer of his communication of life. The area of this life he imparts is the kingdom of God, and he never speaks of the communication of life to the individual apart from this community. No one can remain in him apart from remaining in his new and only command. As a consequence there is no promise extended to an individual by himself, but only in association with one or more other persons. Consequently all separatism, all personal withdrawal from society, is contrary to his teaching.

Christ ascribes his sending to the Father, and the expression "to draw" means that God constantly attends his work; the effect of his preaching is determined by the Father. It is quite wrong to ascribe the whole governance of nature and the world to Christ, as some do, and, as it were, to push the Father into the background in the New Testament ordering of the world. This would contradict Jesus' own words, for he says that while he makes the proclamation, the effect of that proclamation is determined by the Father. Everything in human affairs that is independent of the preaching of the gospel but that plays a part in the way it is accepted depends on the divine governance of the world. Here we see, then, how Christ in another direction makes a similar statement. He says that he can do nothing of himself. The actual success of his work does not depend on his share in the undertaking, but on that of his Father. This is evident in the words: No one can come to him unless the Father draws him. It is also present in the other saying: No one comes to the Father except through the Son. In other words, Christ is the only mediator of the living relationship of men to God, but it is the Father who determines who is drawn (or: comes) into this area of mediation.

When we examine this coefficient to the preaching of the gospel somewhat more closely and in its various relationships, we see that the influences of what belongs to the general government of the world are often so overwhelming that the saying that no one comes to the Son except the Father draws him is literally true. There are general world relationships that in part directed the proclamation of the gospel to certain specific regions and in part to those people who by reason of their inner constitution seemed to be furthest removed from the acceptance of the gospel. Therefore the effect, since it was wholly unexpected, gives the impression of compulsion. On the other hand we find, to be sure, entirely different instances. Although everything seems to be in the natural course of the preaching of the gospel — as completely as Paul represents it when he says that faith comes from what is heard, and what is heard comes by the preaching of Christ — yet on the other hand this natural course can easily be disturbed and its result destroyed by influences that lie in the area of the general governance of the world. Consequently, in the natural course of things a giving by the Father must take place, a consent on the Father's part, in order that the natural effect can really be produced. This is the type of reciprocity with respect to the effect that Christ ascribes to himself and that he ascribes to the Father, which pervades all elements that concern the kingdom of God. However, we restrict our attention to this one type.

Taking all this into consideration and going back to the fact that the teaching of Christ concerning God is only to be attributed to his own inner life, to the presentation of his self-consciousness, which made him certain of his own inner relationship to God and of the destiny that God had ordained for him, we have to admit that we can discover nothing in this that has actually been acquired by routine, but only a purely unique development, and that the knowledge of God that the Jewish people possessed could be regarded as a cause of this inner development, but nothing more. The necessity that Christ had to be born among the Jewish people is not to be taken in the positive sense that he had to draw his knowledge of God from that people, but only that otherwise he would have had to be born and to have grown up in a pagan area, and therefore would have had to enter into an absolute opposition to the total life to which he belonged in order to be able to develop his inner consciousness of God.

Let us now go on to the next subject to be discussed, namely, the teaching

Concerning Christ's Vocation

We relate this to a saying that also belongs to Christ's teaching about God: "*As the Father has life in himself, so he has*

granted the Son also to have life in himself" [John 5: 26].
We cannot take the noun "life" in this passage as it were in
an intransitive sense, as in the passive, but transitively, as the
power to communicate life as a life that passes over into
others. This contains the point from which Christ's whole
mission, as he was conscious of it and as he presents it, can
be developed. He had been permitted to have and had been
presented with the life by the Father in order to impart it to
others. He had been sent by God as the source of life. We
find that Christ everywhere represents himself in this way and
that this is the content of his preaching, just as the formula
that the kingdom of God is at hand is at the same time a
formula for saying the same thing in a different way. The
communication of life that had its source in him could only
take place within such an organic complex and could only
so be assured to the whole of human history. However, *its
material content is that Christ invites men to come to him in
order to receive from him all the elements of the spiritual life,*
to the extent that they appear both as the liberation from a
state of death or suffering and directly as positive elements
of blessedness, of peace. At the same time he always presents
this in connection with his saying that *he had been sent by
God.*

Just as this saying is the expression he relates to himself,
so the expression for the same divine act that he relates to
other people is that it is the will of God that they should
believe in him whom He had sent. If we add to this the fact
that in other passages Christ makes the whole effect of his
existence dependent on a fellowship of life between him and
men, it is evident that we must regard the term "to believe"
as identical with it. To be sure, this expression as it occurs in
Christ's use of the words "faith" and "to believe" and as it
passed over later into the terminology of the apostles (for we
must regard it as an idea they took over from him) has a
certain indefiniteness, a relation both to theory and to practice. However, for that very reason we must explain it in
terms of those expressions that obviously have the same content, by which Christ must have meant the same thing, but
expressed it in quite a different way. When he tells the parable

of the vine and its branches and then says that his disciples could only bring forth fruit as they remained in him as the branches remain in the vine, he describes a complete fellowship of life and says the same thing as does the later image of Christ as the head of the body. Christ maintains that this bringing forth of fruit is the actual goal of his activity and is the life that he had come to impart. When he says, on the one hand, that whoever believes in him has eternal life and, on the other hand, that whoever remains in him in such a living way brings forth fruit, *we must think of eternal life and of bringing forth of fruit as identical terms.* It is clear that the conviction, the certainty, that is involved in the word "faith" cannot be regarded as a theoretical matter, for the word has at the same time a practical reference. It is the certainty which dwells directly in the self-consciousness and which expresses itself in that self-consciousness, and this always involves an essential relationship to behavior. *It is always a certainty that is the basis of action, though not in a specific and determined direction, but the basis of all action so far as it is wholly connected with the relationship to God and the divine will in general.*

We are now in a position to develop Christ's whole teaching concerning his mission and his destiny. In so doing we must always keep in mind both points from which alone the whole can be construed. There is a return to him, to the extent that he makes himself known in his teaching concerning himself, and there is a going on through him to the kingdom of God as a totality, a totality of a life that has its source in his. We find this most distinctly and most completely articulated in the words that Christ uttered when he said that *those whom God had given him, and who therefore constitute the kingdom of God, are not only to be one with him, but are also to be one with each other.*[38] In other words, the life

38. Schleiermacher understands by the kingdom of God the dominance and penetration of the God-consciousness — that is, a teleological unqualified dependence — over and throughout the human self. As such, the kingdom takes three forms. First, the kingdom has drawn near in the person of Jesus himself in the absolute power of his God-consciousness. Second, under the decree of God the kingdom will be effective in the future for all men of all times and places. Finally, the kingdom of God resides in the communion of the new corporate life informed by Christ that is in

that he made possible and imparted to them was to be one common to them. This pervades all Christ's discourses and all his actions in such a way that we must say: It is impossible to separate the attainment of Christ's purpose for individuals from the founding of the kingdom of God, that is, a life in which individuals are interrelated.* This is what we find in all Christ's sayings.

To be sure, in recent times an entirely different idea has had currency in different forms. There are many who always prefer to think of redemption and of the attainment of its purpose with respect to individuals exclusively as a relationship between Christ and the individual as such and who always regard the common life as of secondary importance and as a mere aid to individual redemption. We find nothing of that in Christ's teaching. On the contrary, the unity among themselves of those who are his is just as originally the object of his prayer as the unity of the individual with him. One is connected with the other. The commandment that those who belong to him should love one another was Christ's only commandment. He emphasized nothing else as he did this: *"This is my commandment, that you love one another as I have loved you."* Therefore this summons to concretion, this exhortation that the life of men should become one, is Christ's original commandment. So then, we cannot believe that he separated the one from the other, or that the one was to a greater extent purpose and the other to a greater extent means. In fact, it is quite evident that this alone does justice to all proper evaluation of human life in general. The individual in isolation is a minimum, and he only becomes what he actually is (or: is to be) in terms of his essential nature in the life of fellowship. Just as in the natural sense of the word both elements always reproduce each other, the individual life and the common life, so this also is true in the purely spiritual area. To be sure, part of what differentiates Christ from all other men is that he comprehends the spiritual life

the process of becoming as it develops in the course of time. For a discussion of the kingdom in Schleiermacher's theology by way of the doctrine of election, see Richard R. Niebuhr, *Schleiermacher on Christ and Religion* (New York: Scribner, 1964).
* or add: the two are correlates

within himself as individual, and that is what Paul means when he refers to him as the second Adam. The natural man to begin with was an individual, to the extent that his life had not sprung from the common life, but at the same time he was the source of all common life. Christ is presented in the same way. The whole kingdom of God, that is to say, the actual power of God in human nature, was original in him and had developed from him, but could develop only under the form of the common life. The winning of individuals as such, considered as an end in itself, is not the main concern. What really matters is the way and manner in which the kingdom of God exists as a totality and how it can maintain itself with the passage of time. The essential character of every organism is this relation of the individual to the whole and this identity of means and purpose in the whole and in the individual. So Christ's impartation of his unique life to men and his foundation of a kingdom of God as a life together is one and the same thing.

If we now consider this as the form in which Christ himself predominantly presented his destiny, this leads us back again to the question: If we regard this as the actual purpose of Christ's mission, how can he appeal to the Old Testament promises, of which no one can say that this idea is anywhere to be found in them? To be sure, the idea of the kingdom of God can also be expressed by the term theocracy, and this in fact lay at the basis of all messianic utterances and promises of the prophets. However, the meaning which the word has in the one instance and in the other seems to be quite different. The Old Testament theocracy had essentially a political character, whereas the kingdom of God that Christ wished to found was essentially unpolitical. It was to be compatible with all political forms, to include all political orders, and so naturally could not itself be a political entity. This brings us back to what we have already pointed out. It all depends on what we consider to have been the actually dominant emphasis. If the political element had been everywhere the dominant one in the messianic promises and if the prophets had regarded the knowledge of God and obedience to the legislation God had given as the means of maintaining the political existence of the nation, then Christ could not have adopted these ideas. However, if there were passages which regarded it as the destiny of the nation that through it other peoples also would be blessed by the knowledge of God, that regarded the political independence of the nation only as a means to an end, then those were the prophecies that Christ could relate to himself. Such prophecies were naturally included among the Old Testament predictions and at Christ's time were understood by others as he himself understood them. So Christ could also adopt certain aspects of the theocratic idea, though for him the founding of a political union could not form any part of the constitution of the kingdom of God. It was for him only a preliminary phase.

If we now inquire how far Christ himself developed the characteristic features of the kingdom of God in the form of his teaching, we run across a great difference when we distinguish two facts but think of them as necessarily related: (1) the genesis of the kingdom of God, and (2) its actual type, its characteristic features, its constitution.

Lecture 44 (July 23). The former of these elements, the fellowship of life of each with Christ, we intend to call the mystical element; the other, the fellowship of believers among themselves, the element of the church. The latter (or add: not?) in the sense that every life unit higher than a single, personal one is regarded antimystically as a mere abstraction. Both lead back to one another. We intend to begin with the churchly element, and more specifically, with the relationship of the New Testament society to that of the Old Testament. Some think that the invalidation of the law was an addition to the gospel made by the apostles, and therefore the first example of the perfecting of Christ's message. However, although Christ says that he had not come to destroy the law and the prophets and that not a tittle of the law would pass away, he also says that the age of Moses and the prophets lasted until John, that the temple will be destroyed, and that God seeks spiritual worshipers. All these sayings taken together show that he regarded the form of the community he founded, a community limited to Jews, only as the first stage and that he himself made arrangements for the later form; that even in the former he rejected the validity of the oral tradition and therefore established again the exclusive validity of the contrast by denying spiritual value to the prohibitions of the law as mere external matters (what goes into a man does not make him unclean) and, instead of the Pharisaic restriction, by adding attitude to the commands, as a transition to the spirit of his community. Consequently here also the later practice of the apostles (the law was not to be invalidated, but with the destruction of the temple and the end of the common life of the Jewish people its fulfillment became impossible) agreed entirely with his intimations.

We can designate the first element in Christ's teaching, that there is to be a fellowship with himself, as the mystical, and the other element, the foundation of the community, as that of *the churchly*. These two are bound up inextricably with each other. I am loath to use the latter term because it has been badly misused in the field of science. However, in this connection no misinterpretation is possible. If the statement is made, for example in the field of politics, that there is a national life as an actual entity, that would likewise be a mystical statement in the actual sense of the word, because it goes beyond the idea of a single unit of life. The antimystical assertion is that it would be an abstract concept that would arise out of the comparison of the individual units of life with themselves and with others, but there would be no reality to that.

It makes no difference with which of the two elements we begin our discussion, for we must always return from the one to the other. In my judgment it is more practical to begin with the churchly element. Here the chief question at issue is: How did Christ conceive the relationship of the community to be founded by him to that which existed under the old covenant, namely, the theocratic existence of the nation? That is a most debatable matter that is related to many others. We find that, very soon after Christ himself withdrew from the stage, the religious validity of the Mosaic law was denied in the Christian community. In other words, the Christian community exists without any connection at all with the religious side of the Old Testament community. It is frequently said that this was an advance of the apostles beyond the actual thought of Christ. To be sure, that would then be a striking example of the perfectibility of the Christian church. In other words, the Christian community did not have to restrict itself to what Christ had said, but was able to go beyond his teachings to something better. Such a view, however, contradicts the idea of Christ and of faith in Christ that we have to regard as the core of Christianity. To be sure, there are sayings of Christ in this connection that seem to support such a view. However, when we compare them with others there emerges such a contradiction between them that it becomes immediately necessary either to explain one group or the other as not genuine or to interpret one of the two in such a way that it is compatible with the other.

In the familiar passage in the Sermon on the Mount where Christ declares that he had not come to destroy the law or the prophets, but to fulfill them (Matt. 5:17), the antithesis to "destroy" cannot be *"to observe,"* but rather "to complete, to complement." However, when we compare other passages such as Matthew 11:13, where Christ says that all the prophets and the law prophesied until John and that from that time on a new order existed, we see that this means that he assumes an end of the law and the prophets and that he actually designates the preaching of the Baptist, which had the imminence of the kingdom of God as its content, as the end. In other words, Christ said that the kingdom of God marks the end of the era of the law and the prophets. Moreover, in John 4:23, in the course of his conversation with the Samaritan woman, Christ says that the Father seeks worshipers who will worship in spirit and in truth. This puts the matter the other way round. This worship of God in spirit and in truth depends on the disappearance of the Jewish temple. Furthermore, Christ says that he was sent only to the lost sheep of the house of Israel, and yet he commissions his disciples to make disciples of all nations. On another occasion he speaks of other sheep that are not of this fold but that nevertheless belong to the same herd. All this together indicates that Christ regarded the full formation of the community that he wanted to found and the end of the theocratic constitution as conditioned one by the other. As soon as we reflect on this difference that occurs frequently in Christ's sayings, we see what meaning the saying in the Sermon on the Mount must have. The law is not to be invalidated by any human act that had such an invalidation as its goal, and least of all by one that lay in this area of the founding of the kingdom of God. Rather, it was to collapse of its own accord. Its end came with the destruction of the temple, for the whole legislation in all its parts revolved about the temple as its center, for the temple was as much a political as a religious institution.

Now we raise the question: What was the teaching and the practice of the apostles in this respect? We find nothing in this teaching and practice that was in opposition to Christ's teachings. The apostles recognized the validity of the law for **all who were bound to it, but only in the political, national** respect, and so only in the land in which the national rights lay within which the whole legislation moved. In this sense even Paul declares that Christ was born under the law. He acknowledges Christ's practice so far as he himself was concerned, and yet wholly denies the religious authority of the law.

Let us now ask: In connection with the fact that he represents his mission as that of founding a community that would worship God in spirit and in truth, what did Christ mean by the verb ''to fulfill'' in contrast to the verb ''to destroy''? When we observe the practice of his time we see that it was predominantly determined by the Pharisees, that is to say, by those who maintained the validity of the so-called *paradosis* [''oral tradition''], the interpretation of the law given by outstanding scribes which was often made up of additions to the law. The school of the Sadducees, of those who rejected this tradition because they wanted to preserve Mosaism in its purity, was not widespread and not popular. Everywhere Christ denounced these traditions and invalidated them both by his own practice and by his teaching, since most Pharisees regarded them equally as binding as the regulations of the law. All this seems to be in contradiction to the verb ''to fulfill''. Other sayings of Christ in this connection sound even more decisive, particularly those in which he opposes the whole idea that a man can be made unclean by external things, especially by foods. Whatever belongs only to the animal side of man's life cannot make him unclean. In this way Christ abrogates an essential part of the law. However,

Christ wished only to isolate the moral element in this concept, which was not originally inherent in the law. This does not mean that he had come to destroy the law. He does not say: I allow you to eat unclean foods. He only says that unclean foods do not make a man unclean. This led to the whole catastrophe of his earthly fate, but that is another matter that we cannot pursue at this point.

What does Christ mean by saying that he had come to fulfill the law? He added nothing to the statement. He gave no external prescript of any kind. Consequently we are inclined to understand this expression in terms of his own practice. However, that is also a vain undertaking. We cannot separate his practice from his teaching. Every act of Christ's was also teaching and instruction, for every act was symbolical. If we say: Everything was always brought to completion and made whole when it was illustrated by his own practice, we must add: The liberation of the law from the traditional additions to it, on the one hand, and the relation of that tradition to the political aspect of theocracy, on the other hand, could be regarded as the actual fulfillment of the law. To be sure, there are passages in which Christ seems to assume the permanence of the law, its continued and indefinite validity. He says, for instance, that not the smallest part, not a tittle, of the law can fail. But such an interpretation would be in evident contradiction to specific sayings of Christ such as his prediction of the destruction of the temple and the end of the worship of God in the form laid down in the law. When Christ in the same passage says that not a tittle will pass away from the law until all is accomplished, we see that this is only a way of saying that no one could invalidate any single part of the law by an arbitrary act until that event had taken place by which the observance of the law would become impossible and it would collapse of its own accord.

To be sure, several passages appear to indicate that Christ himself attempted to defend the religious validity of the law. Take, for example, the familiar story of the one who asked him, "What shall I do to obtain eternal life?" Christ answers, "Keep the commandments" if you wish to enter into life.

This seems to be a defense of the religious validity of the law. However, we should not tear the saying out of its context. It is only an introduction to the discourse that follows. Christ only wanted to draw out another answer and a wider explanation. Later on he gives another piece of advice. When the questioner expresses himself as still dissatisfied, Christ refers him to the community which he was to found and says that he will find a satisfactory answer in that. Consequently we must say that Christ wholly separated his community from the theocratic form in the same way that that separation was achieved in the Christian church. The form in which he founded his community, by keeping it in terms of his own person within the confines of the Jewish people, was only the first stage of its development. That had to give way to another, and this supersession was conditioned by the collapse of the Jewish theocratic order. Within the community in its first form the law was traced back to its original form and all Pharisaic additions were declared to be corruptions of it, probably (1) because they necessarily laid unbearable burdens on the people as a consequence of the consciousness of the impossibility of their fulfillment, and (2) because they lent support to the idea that it was possible to obtain divine favor by means of such externalities. By saying that much was forbidden so that when it yet happened it did not lead to the spiritual deterioration of men and that the basis of the prohibition was to be found in the way and manner of the external existence of the people, Christ related what in the law was command and prohibition to the civil maintenance of the people in the form of a theocracy. So far as the commands are concerned, we must say that we have to look for the meaning of "to fulfill" in its entire sense in this connection. This is involved in the whole comparison of Christ's teaching with respect to the law with that of the Pharisees. The latter always had the tendency to lay the actual worth of the legislation on the letter, on the literal fulfillment, and to leave attitude as far as possible out of consideration. When we reflect on the comparison as it is made in Matthew's version of the Sermon on the Mount, we find there the actual key to that formula. Christ came to fulfill the law and the prophets by this summary of both. Even the prophets had declared the outer behavior in and for itself as valueless, and consequently had penetrated to the attitude, but Christ himself was the first to present this interpretation of the law in its complete form.

From this point of view let us now consider the passage in which Christ declares that *on two commandments depend all the law and the prophets.* We have to regard this passage as a sublimation of Old Testament passages and as a bringing together of two quite separate commands. In so doing Christ gives a meaning to the statements of the law that differed completely from Pharisaic exegesis. The Pharisees interpreted the command "You shall love your neighbor as yourself" only within the area covered by the law. By neighbor the law understood only the fellow countryman, and the command to love such a person was quite compatible with that to hate one's enemy. The way in which Christ employs the command not only invalidates this restriction, but also goes beyond the content of the law. The law sought to prevent any communication between the Jewish people and other peoples and so was incapable of teaching any such love as Christ had in mind, since it made it impossible to practice it. So then, by saying that he had come to fulfill the law and the prophets, Christ meant that he had come to abstract and isolate what in the law ought to be spiritual, but which by reason of its limitation could only be political. He had come to stress the purely moral and religious element in the law* and to give it its foundation. If we bring together Christ's various sayings in this way and consider them in their proper relation to one another, we see that they actually involve no contradiction, either in what he said or between his teaching and what the apostles and the Christian church later taught. However, his sayings do involve an absolute separation of the messianic kingdom, of the community based on himself, from the whole theocratic system, without interfering (or: invalidating) by an outer act to the slightest degree with the duty of those who belonged to his community, to the extent that they were subject to the law by descent or by personal acceptance of it.

* the latent moral element in the law

Lecture 45 (July 24). Furthermore, Christ's mission was not to found a community of a political sort with an external sanction (for otherwise he would have had to make the attempt by the use of force at the time of his arrest). It follows from this either that this community must be able to be compatible with all political orders, or that it is to put an end to all civil bonds. There are those who maintain the latter alternative, and even apart from Christianity it has been advanced as a philosophical axiom. However, Christ never gave any mandate to that effect, but always [thought] of his followers as part of the civil order and instructed them to pay taxes to Caesar. It was the other alternative that everywhere prevailed. In this conviction Christ teaches a perfect equality of all under him. To be sure, this is related originally only to the equality prescribed by the synagogue constitution. Christ does not mention the contrast between priest and people, but only because this has already ceased to exist, since priest and the temple are correlates and there was no suggestion that there was to be a new temple. This community, since it is based on a love similar to Christ's own, can therefore only exist in the communication of the divine life of Christ to the extent that that is possible, and any individual can belong to it only to the extent that he has this divine life in him, to the extent that he is in Christ. At this point, however, an apparent contradiction arises between Christ's sayings concerning the way of entering this community, for according to what has been said it depends on faith in him, but elsewhere he conditions it on being born again by the work of the Spirit. So here we must insert a discussion of *Christ's teaching concerning the Holy Spirit.* We have two main sources for this: John 3 and John 14–16. In the latter source the Spirit appears as a substitute for Christ's physical presence, whose task it is to continue the communication of life from Christ. However, since Christ at the same time promises his spiritual presence, which must fulfill the same function, it follows that both Christ's spiritual presence and the presence of the Spirit denote the same thing.

The next aspect of Christ's teaching about the community that he was to found that we can deal with is related to a point that has recently been much debated, namely, the fact that this community has no political character. Christ asserts that expressly when he says that his kingdom is not of this world, in the sense that it cannot be maintained by force. It is apparent that no political order can exist without such employment of force, for external power is always the sanction of every political order. If the society were attacked in connection with his person, force would have to be used if it was to be a political society. Members of it would have had to

298

offer resistance. But Christ declares that his community has no such sanction and therefore is not a political order. If we reflect on what is immediately involved in this, we see that there can be only two alternatives: either the community founded by Christ is to make the political order superfluous, or it is to be compatible with any political order with which it is connected. Our premise permits only one or the other of these two possible alternatives. It is well known that the former has frequently been taken as the actual postulate. In fact, it has even passed over into philosophical theories. There are those who say that the state must strive under certain circumstances to make itself superfluous. Historically speaking, however, it is the latter alternative that has prevailed. Since the Christian community has no political character, it is *eo ipso* neutral with respect to all political orders and must be able to be compatible with all. The former demand, wherever it has tried in practice to validate itself, has always returned to a theocratic form, and the political element has always had to find its way back in again whenever the religious community by itself has tried to be responsible for the relation of men to one another. Such an attempt was made, for example, in the Jesuit colony in Paraguay, where the association of commissions* was. at the same time to constitute the political order. However, that experiment gave rise to a priestly and legislative power, and consequently the political character found its way in again and the result was a restoration of the old theocracy. When papal power was at its zenith the same thing soon happened. Moreover, in comparison with the religious conditions that had previously prevailed, Christ sets forth his teaching of the absolute equality of all members of his community, but naturally in such a way that at the same time he puts himself at its head. It is doubtless unnecessary for me to cite the specific passages that demonstrate this.

When we reflect on this more carefully, we see that there is nothing in it about the unequality that is to be avoided, the contrast between priest and people that formed part of the Old Testament idea, but only the contrast between teacher

---

* teaching authorities. Where the authority of the teachers was to give leadership to the state.

and master, on the one hand, and disciples on the other. "None of you is to let himself be called master with respect to the others." This saying makes it clear that the Christian community modeled itself to begin with on the constitution of the Jewish synagogue — an influence that persisted throughout all its subsequent development. The contrast refers back to the synagogue constitution, according to which the scribes were the masters, those from whom in all relevant cases the others had to obtain advice. So far as the other contrast is concerned, that between priest and people, Christ had no occasion to negate it, for it had already been negated in a much more general way. In Jewish thinking priest and temple were correlates. The entire priesthood was related to the conduct of temple worship, and the activity of the priests, who lived in various parts of the country, consisted of maintaining the communication of the people with the temple by conducting temple worship. So, if anyone had a sacrifice to offer or had anything else to do with the temple, he had a priest do it for him. Christ did not want to put an end to the temple worship as long as the temple stood, and he had even less intention of putting a new temple in place of the old. Rather, his society was to be made up of those who worship God in spirit and in truth, those who had no need of temple worship. Consequently, when the temple ceased to exist the priesthood also came to an end, and there is nothing in any of Christ's sayings that is based even remotely on an analogy to temple worship.*

Thinking of this mutual fellowship of those who believe in Christ, apart from and excluding any political tendency and with each member enjoying an absolute equality, so that the difference lay in Christ alone, we proceed to ask: What was the actual life, the actual content of this fellowship, that was the result of it? Here we can only go back to Christ's saying that his followers were to love one another with a love similar to his. In every Christian community that is the principle of action, and that expresses the demand that the relations of members of the community to one another, so far as their

---

* that is intended to have any bearing on temple worship

common life is concerned, are to be analogous to his own relations to men. This, then, leads us back to the other element that I called the *mystical*. When Christ bids his followers to love one another with a love identical with that which he had for them, we have to ask, first, How did Christ act? and then, What was the nature of the fellowship of life between him and those, considered as individuals, who believed in him and who in relation to one another were to form that fellowship? Here we can only return to the idea that Christ himself advances, both in didactically defined formulas and in parables that convey the same meaning. When Christ says, "I in you, and you in me," where the second "in" cannot have the same meaning as the first, and when he tells the parable of the vine and its branches, the latter parable and the former saying must be related and have the same meaning. If we take our departure from the parable, we see that its content is that the vine is a unity that actually includes the branches, and the one can only be distinguished from the other in such a way that the vine is regarded as a unity and the branches as parts of an organic whole which is dominated by this unity. Therefore the unity is the source of all life activity in the individual. Furthermore, when Christ says that, as the Father is in him, so he is in the believers, we find the same truth also expressed in this comparison. When Christ says that the Son can do nothing by himself, that is the same as saying that a branch is of no use by itself. Its activity proceeds from the Father.

This brings us to a difficulty concerning the way that has become common in church circles and in Christian doctrine of keeping the relations separate. When we think in general of the contrast between those who stand in a fellowship of this sort with Christ and others who do not, we conclude that the former are those who constitute among themselves the community of disciples and that the latter are those who stand outside that community. The one group constitutes the kingdom of God and the other the world as something separate from the kingdom of God. The relationship between Christ and the individual exists whenever the individual submits himself to Christ's influence. The effect is always Christ's, but the person who heeds Christ's call must consciously submit to him. He must open himself to Christ's influence. Only in such a way can Christ's influence be effective. By opening himself to Christ's influence the individual enters the kingdom of God. That opening of himself establishes a fellowship of life between the individual and Christ, and thereby the individual becomes a member of the fellowship of believers with one another. But how does Christ say this in another way? A man can only enter the kingdom of God when he has been reborn as a result of the work of the Spirit, and he himself plays no part in the process.

Now we have to ask: How far can the one statement mean the same as the other, or are the two statements necessarily and essentially different? In the latter case we should be faced with an insoluble contradiction, for when Christ speaks of the one or the other way of entering the kingdom of God, he speaks in a definite manner that excludes all else. Since in our doctrine we find stress on both the activity of Christ and the activity of the Spirit, we are accustomed to distinguish between Christ and the Spirit, and this raises the question of how we are to harmonize this distinction with Christ's own sayings. We can scarcely consider this problem by itself, but must pay some attention at the same time to the other main element in Christ's teaching of the Spirit that we find in another discourse in John's Gospel [chaps. 14-16], where Christ speaks of the *pneuma* ["Spirit"] as the *paraklētos* ["Counselor"]. In this passage he clearly represents the *pneuma* as the *paraklētos* under the form of a representative, a substitute for his own immediate presence and influence. If we were to regard this as the full explanation of the Spirit and as exhausting the content of the idea and then were to apply it to Christ's conversation with Nicodemus, we should have to conclude that no one could enter the kingdom of God apart from the work of the Holy Spirit. In that case the disciples could not have constituted the kingdom of God before having received the gift of the Spirit and could not have been constituent parts of it. On the other hand, Christ acknowledges the living bond between himself and his disciples and all that is to be regarded as the natural consequence of that, namely, that like him they have the Father in them and that they have a fellowship of life with God that he had granted them. If we were to regard this as the complete description of the way and manner in which the individual is in the kingdom of God, then all that Christ says in other passages about the Holy Spirit would become superfluous. We seem to be involved here in a conflict, and the only way we can resolve the threatened contradiction is to show that these different sayings of Christ's are only different ways of presenting the same truth in different contexts. This is the only way that the two groups of sayings can be harmonized and such a harmonization is mandatory. If we were to believe that only after the gift of the Counselor were the disciples born of the Spirit and that their previous state was only a preparatory one, then all the sayings in which Christ promises eternal life only as a consequence of a union of life with him and without the slightest reference to the *pneuma* and the *parakletos* would form a contradiction and could not be so explained.

We can discover the key to the solution of this problem only in one of two ways. In the first place, so far as the context of Christ's individual discourses in which he represents the *pneuma* as the *parakletos* is concerned, Christ speaks of the Spirit in connection with the termination of his own personal work. However, in other passages he denies this termination and says that he would be among them, at any gathering of believers, even when he was no longer physically with them. In the conversation with Nicodemus there is a clear relationship between "being born of the Spirit" and "being born of water," and in each case there is a special relationship, but both do not mean the same thing. On the other hand, when we look at the other way of presenting the matter, namely, union with Christ himself as the condition of inheriting the kingdom, we see that this is made without reference to any special relationship. So then, we must regard the latter as the original way of expressing the truth of the matter, and the former as one introduced only in a special context.

However, this gives rise to a new difficulty. If these relationships are not the same, we have no assurance that what

Christ means by the word Spirit is just the same in both instances, and this introduces the possibility of still another difference. Our first task is clearly that of asking: When Christ speaks of his continuing activity, apart from his physical presence but at the same time identical with that which was manifest during his lifetime, is what he represents as the result of that activity something different from what he ascribes to the *pneuma* as *paraklētos?* When he says that whenever any of them gather in his name, there he would be among them, he means that inward presence among them, and when he says that the *paraklētos* would bring to their remembrance all that he had said to them [John 14: 26; 17: 7ff.] he means the same thing. When he relates the former to the gathering of several people and does not speak of it as a relationship which he was to have with the individual as such, and when he promises the disciples the *pneuma* as the *paraklētos* only as they constitute a group and does not represent it as a relationship to an individual, we see again that both statements are identical. Whether Christ says, My continuing activity is dependent on your existence as a fellowship, or whether he says, You will experience this continuing activity by means of the principle that holds you together, the meaning is the same. In terms of its original meaning, Spirit is therefore the actual basic form of the unity of life. For the time when he will no longer be physically present, Christ relates the continuance of his activity to the principle of the believer's union with him and of a common life based on him, and he describes this state by means of an expression that at the same time guarantees his presence as a continuous one. Consequently Christ's continuing presence, related to the union of his followers, and the unity of life of their fellowship that he had founded are only two different ways of saying the same thing.

Lecture 46 (July 25) Faith and rebirth are also two ways of saying the same thing. The phrase "not by water alone" relates to a part of the conversation that has not been recorded and probably refers to John's baptism, which did not involve entrance into the kingdom of God. Just as the divine element in Christ was operative in founding the community, so it becomes operative also in every individual believer. Consequently everyone who opens himself to the influence of Christ (which is the same as having faith) begins a life that founds a fellowship (which is the same as having been born of the Spirit or from above). The same divine element at work in Christ is therefore called the Holy Spirit as the principle of a common life. Christ's mission was to begin the struggle against the world in the kingdom of God. This is not to be understood as the opposition of the world to the external existence of Christianity and as the struggle of Christianity against persecutions, for that would reintroduce the political element. In this sense not even Christ overcame the world, but was overcome by it. Rather, it is the struggle of the Spirit against the flesh. In this sense the kingdom of God and the world are opposed to each other. More often, however, Christ speaks as though the world formed a unity and had a common life principle. All these different expressions have been reduced to *Satan or the devil,* and so at this point we have to insert a discussion of *Christ's teaching concerning the devil.* If we identify the "ruler of this world" with the devil and yet admit that it was the Jewish hierarchy that rejected Christ, along with the new principle of life, we have to conclude that Christ must have thought of that hierarchy as standing under the hegemony of the devil. Our task would then be either to demonstrate when this change took place or, in opposition to all other clear statements, to show that it existed from the beginning, which would then result in a complete dualism.

We closed the preceding lecture with a discussion of Christ's teaching concerning *the Holy Spirit.* At first glance there seems to be a contradiction between this teaching and what Christ says of his relation to the individual believer and of his continued spiritual presence, independent of his earthly appearance. If we regard both as different statements, each of them, considered from the vantage point of the other, seems to be superfluous. If what Christ understands by having faith in him, that is to say, by opening oneself to the communication of Christ's divine life, is something different from being born of the Spirit, then the one or the other is superfluous, for Christ ascribes everything to each. It follows that, if we do not wish to assume a contradiction (that is to say, if I regard both as the same, so that I exclude them), both can only mean the same thing but in different contexts. I have already pointed out that, when Christ speaks of his continuing presence, he also presupposes a community of believers. However, his relationship to his disciples was originally his relationship to them as individuals, and as long as he was physically with them they did not form a fellowship among themselves, but each had only a fellowship with him. Any fellowship that they had among themselves was only accidental. So then, if we consider the individuals as such in the community he wished to found, we designate their fellowship by referring to Christ's continuing presence. However, Christ employs that expression only with reference to individuals in the community. If, on the other hand, we consider the community as a living unity, we designate Christ's relationship with it by using the expressions *pneuma, parakletos*. From this it follows that this unity of the life based on him through this fellowship of believers represents his personal presence, but only because his activity continues in it. So the formulas, *"The Spirit will declare it to you" and "I will be with you,"* *can be regarded as essentially identical.*

But the case is somewhat different with the saying. *"Those who believe in me have eternal life,"* that is to say, have their place and location in the kingdom of God. By faith one has eternal life, and by rebirth one enters into the kingdom of God. To enter into the kingdom of God and to have eternal life are one and the same, and from this it follows that the other two must also be one and the same. The sayings by which Christ relates blessedness, eternal life, a share in the kingdom of God, to faith in him are free sayings that he himself uttered spontaneously, whereas the other saying occurs only in the course of a conversation where what one says is determined by what the other says and, furthermore, in a discourse that we have only in fragmentary form. So we cannot escape ascribing a certain priority to the former saying, but it occurs repeatedly in Christ's ongoing discourse and must be regarded as his own. We do not know how far the other saying was conditioned by some statement Nicodemus made. To be sure, it appears to have come directly from Christ, but it is nevertheless clear as we examine it that Christ related it to something that had preceded it, namely, that one must be born anew if he wishes to enter the kingdom of God, not merely of water, but of the Spirit, and later retained only the reference to the Spirit. So the phrase "of water" must have been related to some other statement that had preceded it. Most probably the phrase refers to baptism, more specifically, to John's baptism, and we shall have to assume that at some earlier point in their conversation Christ and Nicodemus may have been talking about John and of his relationship to Christ and that the phrase "kingdom of God" is conditioned by that preceding discussion. This is analogous to the way John the Baptist himself spoke of the difference between himself and Christ. John also contrasts water baptism with Spirit baptism and reserves the latter for Christ. The phrase "not with water alone" must imply that Christ said that John's baptism in and by itself could not afford entrance into the kingdom of God. There is no evidence that John had founded a community in the same way that Christ had. Whenever disciples of John are mentioned, the expression has only the meaning given to it at that time. The pupils of one and the same scribe had no fellowship among themselves. Their gathering about a teacher was only an accidental meeting and point of temporary contact. So Christ uses the word Spirit in the same way for the form of the existence and of the communication of all that he wanted to accomplish among men under the form of a fellowship. Consequently Spirit is the principle of the unity of life. In other sayings Christ declares himself to be the principle of this fellowship, and in such cases he had the fellowship just as much in mind. So the different sayings are simply different ways of saying exactly the same thing. *The divine communication for the raising of human life to a higher potency was originally in Christ. However, to the extent that it can only continue after his disappearance from the earth in the form of a fellowship, Christ designates what is peculiar to this life in contrast to human life apart from this fellowship, which type of life had issued from himself as the principle that bound believers together, by the word "Spirit."* If you examine Christ's sayings you will discover that this is the only explanation you can reach.

So Christ's teaching in this respect is that his work, his influence, the effect of the divine in him upon men, can persist after his disappearance only in the unity of a truly common life. But this is the same divine element that (was) also in him and which he communicated to men and which influenced them. So then, to the extent that we attribute to this divine element the character of absolute equality, we can understand the actual function of this common life only under the form of a pure mutuality. What takes place, then, is a mutual communication of Christ, the communication by each of what he has from Christ. It is the living circulation of what is awakened in each believer by the special relationship of each to Christ, but in such a way that in each it is regarded as a shared spirit and as common property, and in this fellowship the absolute equality of all consists. To be sure, in later developments this unity seems to have been destroyed by the organization of the church itself, in which those who in general exercise the function of giving leadership to the whole are not on the same level as the others. However, in the connection in which Christ establishes this equality, it is not destroyed. (1) Although, to be sure, Christ himself placed the twelve in a special relationship to himself, through which his relationship to the whole mass of those who were connected with him closely or more remotely was mediated, we cannot say that that involved an unequality with respect to the actual subject. The divine life that issues from Christ is the same in all, and with respect to that they are equal to one another. The differences of perfection and imperfection with respect to insight or moral power are regarded as differences that disappear at the moment they arise, but in such a way that they also can arise in others. It is nothing else than the *division of responsibilities* that is necessary in every corporate life and without which there could be no society. (2) The definite way in which Christ forbids his twelve disciples to assume the role such as was that of a teacher in their relationships to the others affirms the element of equality most distinctly, and so the task of each can only be regarded as a *diakonia,* a rendering of service in the area of the common life. What some in the course of this service could communicate to others was *not their own but Christ's, and for that reason could give them no superiority, for it was the property of all in the fellowship and in no sense anything that belonged to an individual.*

As we proceed we discover that Christ says that this fellowship would be engaged in a constant struggle with the world, but a struggle in which his followers were already assured of victory. This is related directly to the subject we have so far had under discussion, for what is responsible to the greatest extent for the appearance of inequality is not something within the fellowship. Rather, it is that by which the whole relationship of the Christian fellowship to the world is mediated, namely, the actual apostolic office, which was one of the offices that issued from the church,* the office of preaching the gospel, the continuation of the original service of Christ. To be sure, that constituted an unequality, but only between the apostles and those who performed the same function to a lesser degree and those who did not yet belong to the church, but were only brought by them into the Christian fellowship. Once they were in the church this inequality in this sense ceased to exist. They entered into the area of circulation, where all to that extent were equal. To be sure, there is an inequality between those who communicate and those who receive. However, to the extent that the latter only received, the fact is that they previously had had no higher life and that this began only after the reception of the proclamation.

We now go on to ask: What can Christ have had in mind in the various passages in which he describes this relationship in terms of a struggle, and what did he mean by the victory of which his followers had already been assured? It is certainly a remarkable fact that, however clearly we are told that the kingdom of God is not of this world and has no political character, there are still those who frequently understand this struggle and this victory in ways that only make sense in light of the contrary presupposition. If Christ had thought of that struggle in terms of the external opposition of the world to Christianity, the attempt by the world to destroy the Christian community, and of that victory as the survival of the Christian church, then his ideas would have belonged to the political area and the victory of which he spoke would have been

* that was not an office in the church, but was related to the church's work with outsiders

the historical development by which the civil order itself in a great part of the world came to be subjected to Christianity. The struggle of which he spoke is only what Paul pictures as the lusting of the flesh against the Spirit, the opposition to the divine principle in its inner working. It had nothing to do with the outer existence of the society, except to the extent that this was one of the consequences of the inner working of the divine principle. The victory of which he spoke was only the overcoming of that opposition, when the spiritual life was accepted and human nature was no longer opposed to it. Only in this sense could Christ say that he had overcome the world and that the victory has been given him, for in the other sense he was actually overcome by the world.

We now have to insert a discussion of a particular teaching of Christ's. (I use the word "teaching" only provisionally.) It is clear that Christ occasionally in this opposition represents that human state of existence that lies outside the kingdom of God as a power, and therefore as though there were a unity in it such as exists in the kingdom of God itself. Just as the Holy Spirit or the Spirit of truth is represented as the unity of life in the kingdom of God, a comparable unity of life is apparently assumed to exist in the world outside the church. The sayings differ greatly, to be sure, but they are all summed up in the statement that Satan constitutes this unity of life in the world. We now have to ask how far was this a teaching of Christ's, and to what extent can we regard the following as contrasting ideas: The kingdom of God as a unity of life and a totality, and the world likewise as an organic whole, with the divine Spirit the principle of the former and Satan as the principle of the latter? If we assume this opposition in extreme terms, we ascribe a dualism to Christ, and Christ's whole presentation of the matter takes on a character that closely resembles that of later Manichaeanism. That very fact must raise some doubts, and for that reason we must now examine the matter more carefully.

For the time being I shall only remind you of one thing. In this connection Christ uses the phrase "ruler of this world", he who exercises lordship over this world, and this phrase is often regarded as identical with the words "Satan" and

"Devil". If this were the case, the various terms would have the same meaning. "Ruler" presupposes a true community, and "Satan" would constitute just as much its unity of life as does the divine Spirit in the Christian church. From this it would follow that Satan is assigned the actual lordship over the world, and that is a complete dualism. So it appears necessary to ask: If these various expressions are actually identical in meaning, can Christ have assumed that, despite their verbal difference, they would have been understood by those to whom he spoke directly as having the same meaning? Does what he elsewhere has to say of Satan bear the same stamp of didactic certainty, which it would have to have, to be sure, if we understand this as the actual meaning of the word? If we ask: Where at that time did the opposition to Christ come from, the opposition of which he could say that the ruler of this world could attack him but that he could do him no harm? we have to reply that this came from the Jewish authorities of the day. So Christ represents these as subject to the rule of the devil, and then we have to ask: Was this subjection always the case, or when did it take place? No one would maintain the former, for otherwise we should have to assume that the new covenant was wholly opposed to the old. It is also impossible to demonstrate the latter, and yet such a demonstration would have to be given in order to distinguish between the time when the Jewish constitution existed as a divine ordinance and when it came under the hegemony of Satan. So we see that the whole idea that the ruler of this world is synonymous with Satan or the Devil suffers shipwreck on the rock of this one expression that Christ employs.

Lecture 47 (July 26). In most cases these expressions occur only in the speeches of others. When objection is raised to Christ's healing of the demoniac, Christ does not employ the phrase "ruler of the demons" that was current in the vernacular, but reduces it to the Old Testament idea of Satan, although he uses the word in the plural. This refutation does not mean that Christ was convinced of the existence of one or more Satans. In the passage in which the word Satan occurs without reference to what others have said, in the passage about Satan sifting the disciples like wheat, Christ uses the idea in the same way that it is employed in the Book of Job. The other passage about Satan falling from heaven like lightning has also the reference to demons. The term is also used in some of the parables. No teaching is apparent in the explanation of the parable where "devil" is equated with "the evil one" and "Satan" with "the enemy" (further discussion later). When Christ calls the devil the father of the Jews, he does so in contrast to their claim that God is their Father and as a rebuke for doing the desires of the devil. In this instance there is clearly a reference to the story of the fall. So the Jews cannot boast that they are subject to any other *ek patros* [from the Father]) than him who is represented as the devil. An attempt is made to return as far as possible to the beginning.

I can probably assume that you are aware that I do not believe in any so-called teaching of Christ concerning Satan. There is no passage that can be said to contain an idea that had a definite influence on Christ's consciousness and whole way of acting. It has often been objected that, if Christ had no idea of the existence of the devil, he would have protested against it. However, I cannot agree with that. It is impossible for anyone to protest against everything that does not correspond to his belief. What good would that do? All passages which refer to the devil and in which Christ would have had occasion to protest against this idea are not of the sort that lie in his field. To be sure, the expressions of the idea are very different and must be kept apart. There are four terms that actually occur in the New Testament in this connection. The first two are *diabolos* ["devil"] and *satanas* ["Satan"], terms that most commonly assert that there is a powerful spiritual being at the head of a spiritual organization opposed to the kingdom of God. The third is *archōn tōn daimoniōn* ["ruler of the demons"], which is related to the term *daimonion* ["demon"] and which implies a multiplicity, of which an individual is regarded as the *archōn* ["ruler"]. At this point we ask: Is that the same as the terms "devil" and "Satan," or does it mean something else? The fourth is *archōn tou kosmou toutou* ["ruler of this world"], a term that Christ uses to designate the origin of resistance to himself and his mission. This term cannot be understood as meaning the devil without admitting that an absolute dualism is part of the teaching of Christ.[39] It would mean that the ruling power in the Jewish theocracy stood under the influence of that principle.

Our most helpful procedure will be to consider first of all the passage in which the phrase "ruler of demons" first occurs. This expression is used by other persons rather than by Christ himself, and Christ argues against it by beginning with their presupposition. According to one account the Pharisees, and according to another "certain people" of the crowd, accused Christ of driving out the demons with the aid of the ruler of the demons. The reference was to miraculous healings that Christ had performed, and that had actually nothing to do with the kingdom of God. No one can say that the conditions from which Christ freed so many people, however they may be regarded, had been a barrier to the kingdom of God in any other way than other evils, for they were not moral, not a conscious striving against the kingdom of God. Men in such a state can actually exercise no spiritual activity and are not responsible for their condition. So the idea that certain conditions are caused by demons that bring them forth in men is a matter for natural science to judge. The question has to do with our understanding of conditions of human life that are caused by psychical and physical states. Therefore this was not an occasion on which Christ could have had any duty to protest against the prevailing idea, any more than against the various theories concerning other evils from which he freed people.

What does Christ himself have to say about this in the familiar passage? It is found in Matthew in chapter 12, be-

39. In *The Christian Faith* Schleiermacher finds no place in Christian theology for a distinct doctrine of the devil. He also holds that: "There is not a single passage in the New Testament where Christ or his apostles definitely and indisputably refer to the devil with the intention either of teaching anything new or peculiarly their own, or of correcting and supplementing current beliefs. They make use of the conception in its current popular form." CF, §45, 1. The devil represents a common idea of the time of which they avail themselves just as people in other times might speak of ghosts without any real conviction about such entities. Accordingly, Schleiermacher says that the devil is actually a fusion of various elements which include the following: the inexplicable and abrupt occurrence of affections antithetical to the power of the God-consciousness, the interlocking and cooperation of evil forces, and the fact that Christians look for divine aid in face of the source of evil being beyond their own will and intelligence. Such elements as these are united in a poetic personification which is acceptable outside the conceptual task of theology.

ginning with v. 24, in Mark 3:22, and in Luke 11:15. The Pharisees say: It is only by Beelzebul, the prince of demons, that this man casts out demons. Jesus heard their comment and answered them, first of all in general: Every kingdom divided against itself is laid waste, and then he makes the application: If Satan drives out Satan, the result is that he is divided against himself. Here Christ goes beyond the presupposition of the Pharisees, or he makes a combination that is not contained in their remark. They call the ruler of the demons Beelzebul, and Christ ignores this title altogether and argues from the term Satan. He also ignores the plurality "demons" by designating him who drives them out and him from whom they are driven out with the same name. This contains another idea. Christ does not assume demons which differed from Satan. Satan had no physical area. Rather, the dominant idea in "demon" is one that is taken over from foreign sources. On the other hand, the expression "Satan" occurs even in the Jewish national writings. Consequently Christ rejects the foreign idea. Is not the fact that he wants to get rid of the foreign idea rather than approve it an indirect protest? He abandons the foreign practice and returns to the national idea of Satan and makes no reference to the terms "Beelzebul" and "demon." All our accounts agree on this. Christ was able to say what he did without assuming such demons and without having any definite connection with them. In fact, since his whole refutation is based on this hypothesis, he was also able to say what he did without having a definite idea of Satan. We can draw no conclusions from this, except to the extent that Christ expressly relates the idea to that of Satan. In other words, Christ tried to free himself from the foreign idea, to the extent that it was to be related to the kingdom of God. However, since he repudiates the charge entirely, he did not have to share the positions related to it. The situation is the same in the passage in Matthew. The only difference is that there the charge is made by the Pharisees. We can leave the whole matter to one side. The passage had to do only with an idea that was dominant at the time and which was believed to explain certain acts of Christ, and Christ says only that his healings could not be explained by that idea.

In addition to the passages we have considered, the term "Satan" occurs on two other occasions. One of these is a very difficult passage to interpret. The context is not sufficiently developed properly to determine what Christ intended to say. I refer to the incident in Luke 10 which tells of Christ's sending out of the seventy who in dependence on him (or: in his name) were empowered to put an end to such demonic possessions. In v. 18 Christ says to them, "I saw Satan fall like lightning from heaven." There is much doubt concerning which word the phrase "from heaven" refers to. Probably we must relate it to "lightning," for Christ could not possibly have meant that Satan had his seat in heaven, unless he understood it in the sense that it has in the Book of Job, where Satan is seated along with other angels and has access to God. But what could falling in this sense mean? Christ cannot have said it with the prevailing idea of fallen angels in mind. Thus he meant, "like lightning falling from heaven, so ....." In this passage Christ also abandons the idea of demons and returns to the title "Satan." He deliberately avoids using the idea that had no place in the actual development of Jewish ideas, to the extent that they have any content at all, but reduces them to the term "Satan." Now, can we develop any sort of teaching in this matter from what Christ has to say, or is it of such a kind that we can conclude that Christ himself had a definite conviction of the existence of one spiritual being, or of a class of spiritual beings, which was designated by this name? Nothing more is said in this connection. Christ immediately leaves the matter and confers on the seventy still more far-reaching powers, including that over all the power of the enemy. There is nothing supernatural in all this, except the term "enemy," which it is possible to regard as a reference to Satan. We now have to ask: Are we to understand that "enemy," the expression of a quality, has been substituted for "Satan," or that the expression "Satan" is to be carried over into the general term "enemy?" The second explanation, which actually has the same tendency as the

315

elucidation of the idea of "demons" by the term "Satan," speaks against the first. Furthermore, Satan appears only as the cause of the evil, but, it must be granted, with a hostile tendency. However, if we understand "enemy" in its general meaning, we have to conclude that the enemy has been personified by the addition of the article. But this only involves the summation of all hostility in a single unit. It remains doubtful whether this is part of the term "Satan," or whether Satan itself is to be traced back to the idea of hostility.

The other passage is the one in which Christ says to Peter that Satan has demanded to have the disciples, that he might sift them like wheat [Lk 21: 31]. In this saying Christ goes back entirely to the idea of Satan as it is in the Book of Job. According to the later view, a transaction between Satan and God over a single matter could not take place. In this passage Satan is represented as wishing to do to the apostles what Satan had demanded that he be permitted to do to Job. Satan wished to test the disciples' loyalty to Christ. He was the tempter in the sense of the tester, and the whole matter was thought of as a sifting that remained under divine control. This is the only occasion on which Christ uses the term on his own, without having reference to what others had said, and it contains not a trace of dualism.

Now let us take a look at the expression "devil." In several passages in our Gospels the title "devil" is substituted for "enemy." Similarly, in the temptation story Matthew and Luke use the term "devil," while Mark uses "Satan." In the parable of the sower Luke uses the term "devil," while Matthew uses "the evil one," which is related to "devil" as "the enemy" is to "Satan" in the other passages. "Devil" also occurs in the explanation of the parable of the sower and in the parable of the weeds in the field. The term is also used by Christ in the discourse on the last judgment. There he speaks of the eternal fire that is prepared for the devil and his angels. It follows from this that the devil has his angels. The term also occurs in the discourse in John 8, where Christ charges the Jews with being "of (their) father the devil." They had previously maintained, "We have one Father, even God." Christ denies their claim and says that if God were their

Father they would love him. As it was, they were "of (their) father the devil" and they wanted to act according to the "desires" of their father. It is further said that Satan was a murderer and that the lie was his actual sphere of dominion. This is a reference to the serpent in the story of the fall, for the serpent achieves its purpose by a lie. Since in the story of the fall death is introduced as the consequence of sin and the serpent is represented as its actual cause, the devil is said to have been a murderer. That the serpent was the devil is an interpretation that is not part of the passage in Genesis. Did Christ adopt this interpretation? When we reflect on how Christ says that the Jews were "of (their) father the devil" over against their own claim that God was their Father and on how he explains that by the dependence of their will on his desires, it appears that he contrasts one state with another. "If you had the right to call God your Father, you would have to be inclined to do his will, and that will is that you believe in me." This is a reference to the subordinating similarity. On the other hand, Christ traces their desire back to the devil. The direction of their will was a similarly murderous one and one opposed to the truth. Consequently he traces it back to the one from whom it originally issued. That involves going back to the one responsible for man's first sin. It is a return to the narrative in Genesis. But Christ could not say: The snake is your father. The generally accepted interpretation of the narrative was the form in which he could make this accusation. Therefore *Christ had no intention of presenting a doctrine.* He only wanted to rebuke the Jews as severely as possible. So *I should not assume that Christ was actually convinced that the devil existed. No such conviction is presupposed.*

The other passage, Matthew 25:41, where Christ speaks of the eternal fire prepared for the devil and his angels, is the most decisive. However, *Christ's whole discourse is not a didactic treatment of the subject it deals with, the end of human things. Rather, it has didactic content only with respect to the way that opposite fates are determined. Those who have neglected to work for the kingdom of God will share the fate that is prepared for the devil, etc.* Therefore there is

317

no dualism here, except to the extent that Christ makes use in passing of an idea that was generally accepted at the time in order to express the attitude of opposition to the divine will. However, neither with respect to the way evil originates in men nor in any other respect does he make use of this idea. So then, *Christ does not advance any teaching about the devil.* He only sums up ideas in a single unit.*

Lecture 48 (July 27). Furthermore, "devil" and "Satan" are both appellatives, occur as such, and are to be understood as such. While in the explanation of the parable of the sower not all but only some evil is ascribed to the devil, and popular belief only credited the devil with responsibility for some illnesses, it nevertheless became customary to blame him for everything injurious whose cause was unknown. When Christ, in his reference to Satan's intention of sifting the disciples, assumes a transaction between Satan, God, and himself over the apostles, we are not to understand the scene literally. So what we get is not a consistently tenable idea of the devil, but a very unstable picture. The idea arose among the people (whom otherwise, contrary to all analogy, we should have to regard as the original seat of a divine revelation) like our idea of a ghost, and they used the idea of the devil as we still use that of a ghost, without presupposing belief in it or seeking to settle the dispute as to whether it exists or not.

Christ declares that his mission is to command his disciples to spread Christianity beyond the borders of Judaism. In connection with this we have to ask *what he taught about his death* with reference to the kingdom of God. In this connection we take only his own words into consideration. That is not to say that the apostles had added anything contrary to them, but that what they added was only illustrative. This, however, is something we cannot demonstrate here. John 3:14 and chapter 6 are passages whose interpretation is doubtful. In the latter everything must be capable of being reduced to bread from heaven, and "to eat flesh" cannot refer to Christ's death. John 10:11, 17, 18 speak only of Christ's willingness to die. The most important passages are John 12:24 and 16:7, both of which belong together, for the outpouring of the Spirit and the general dissemination of Christianity are conditioned each by the other. In Matthew 20:28 the context leads us to think of Christ's death as issuing from his service and of ransom as a deliverance. However, according to John 8:31–36, setting people free was also the result of Christ's active life, and his death was instrumental only in connection with his life. In Matthew 26:28 we do not know whether "for the forgiveness" goes with "poured

* or add: but even in this assumption Christ does not designate anything organized

out" or with "this". Even if it goes with the latter, there would still be no teaching here of any connection between the two. We should have to go back to Christ's teaching in other passages, and then forgiveness could be understood only *pars pro toto* as a constituent of eternal life, and elsewhere peace. So then, Christ's death is nowhere thought of as something special, but as a consequence of his life's work or as a condition of its anticipated fruitfulness.

Both terms, "Satan" and "devil," are originally appellatives: devil the slanderer and Satan the adversary. There are passages in the New Testament where "devil" occurs with this meaning, and also passages in the Old Testament (e.g., 2 Sam. 19:22) where Satan has its original connotation. Personification is something very common in the development of the language in which those terms and ideas arose. If we wished to assume that the use of those terms involves an actual doctrine, we should have to say: People in general actually discovered it and Christ only confirmed it. So the divine revelation would originally have been imparted to the people — something that runs counter to the ordinary idea of the word. Christ doesn't preach Satan, but assumes him as a being already known. So his sayings about Satan would not have been teaching that issued from him, but would have been teaching already accepted.

Let us look at the way Christ makes use of this idea. In the explanation of the parable of the sower Christ says that the seeds that were sown along the path were those who heard the word of God, and then the devil came and took it away from their hearts. Then the explanation goes on to speak of others among whom the word perishes because of the pleasures of life. Here the devil plays no part. However, what is ascribed to the devil is not defined any more distinctly. If it were a fact that the destruction of the influence of the word of God was ascribed to the devil, then the devil would have had to be held responsible for all that is evil. That cannot have been the case, for Christ says that the evil thought comes from the heart. Here we discover a very distinct analogy. Just as some states of illness are ascribed to the activities of demons, so others are not, although physical evil is a barrier to the freedom and activity of men. In theory all illnesses ought to have been ascribed to Satan, but in practice the devil was blamed only for that for which no definite cause was known, if it was something that disturbed and interfered with man's life. In the same way the explanation of the parable of the sower accounts for only some moral evils as the work of Satan.

What of the passage in which Christ tells Peter that Satan had asked to sift the disciples? That would appear to assume a transaction between God, Christ, and Satan. However, if we keep in mind the prevailing ideas of Satan, we see that they do not permit us to assume a transaction between him and God.

This is our conclusion: Christ made use of those ideas as did all others at the time, for he always made himself understandable and worked within the ideational framework of the day. However, those ideas were not tenable as a unity, and from this it follows that such images were constituted of various points of view that gradually coalesced but did not form a unity. If we think of the state of rebellion against God, of a being with great power and at the same time an evil will, we must then assume a limitation of the divine governance of the world. The only other alternative would be that Satan is a necessary instrument of God in certain areas. In the latter case we should have to assume that a great amount of evil had been willed by God and without him would not exist, and that is something quite incompatible with any tenable idea of God. Consequently, if we want to assume that Christ really had a definite conviction of Satan and wanted to impart a teaching concerning him that belongs to the body of faith, he would have had to do this in a different way. Such teaching would have had to include an idea that could be definitely held and instruction as to how in every case we have to meet Satan. No such teaching is found anywhere, and so we are compelled to say: Christ made use of those terms as he knew they were understood, but in such a way that they do not designate an actual being and that the different ways of using them do not constitute a whole. On the contrary, each use must be explained in its own way by the context. So then, Christ was entitled to use this idea. It always occurs, not as a subject about which he speaks, but only as an interpretation of a definite part of a connected discourse. We should consider the whole analogous area as it stands today in order to convince ourselves that this is a general procedure to which no one objects. It is comparable to our use of the statement: The sun rises. No one objects to that, and there are many people who do not know that the words cannot be taken literally. Similarly we speak of *ghosts*, and it occurs to no one to believe that the word ghost refers to a real object, although there are people who are convinced that there really are ghosts. No one pays any attention to this difference. So it is with many ideas that have come down to us from an earlier time and have remained current.

However, the situation is quite different when Christ uses the phrase "ruler of this world." This title occurs in only a few passages in which the crisis of Christ's own earthly fate is under discussion and only when the public authorities were intending to act against him. "The ruler of this world is coming, but he has no power over me." "The ruler etc. shall be cast out." "The ruler etc. is judged." In each of these instances the reference is to the public authorities in their opposition to Christ's ministry. There is no reason at all to say that this phrase is a synonym for the titles "devil" or "Satan." If that were the case Christ would have to have meant something much more definite by it and would have to have ascribed a power over this world to Satan, for in these passages the phrase is a definite predicate, not just a loose indication of an indefinite idea. We cannot object to the fact that Christ represents the public authorities as an individual, although they actually were a collegium. So we can say: Christ's teaching of the warfare of the kingdom of God against the world is independent of this idea. Essentially that teaching is nothing more than that of the continued warfare of the flesh against the Spirit, to use the words of the apostle Paul, and of the opposition that the Spirit experiences as he attempts to overcome the flesh.

Another element of Christ's teaching concerning his mission is his belief that *it was his destiny to spread this kingdom of God among all peoples.* That is expressed most distinctly in the final commission to his disciples, but it is also found earlier in what Christ says of other sheep that are not of this fold, that is to say, of elements of the Christian church that are not analogous to, or identical with, Christ's disciples of the time, who were all members of the Jewish people. The question arises: *What bearing does Christ represent his death as having on his mission?* This is one of the questions that is still debated, not only in theological circles but also in the Christian world in general. Our task is to consider it only to the extent that light is cast on it by Christ's own sayings. This does not mean that I want to make a distinction between Christ's teachings and those of the apostles. That would presuppose that the apostles had taught many things that they had not received from Christ. On the contrary, I believe that, if we understand the word *teaching* in its proper meaning, the apostles taught nothing that they had not received from Christ, although, to be sure, their way of representing it can be different because of the differing personalities and because of the different circumstances under which they had to teach. The apostles did not add anything of their own to the teaching of Christ.[40] This is the situation: All that occurs in the apostolic writings concerning the death of Christ of a sort for which there is no analogy in Christ's own sayings belongs only, without exception, to their method of presentation. So we have to restrict ourselves only to what we find in Christ's sayings and what we can ascertain to have been his view.

The fact is that Christ, at a certain point that is indicated in our Gospels, began to predict his death to his disciples, and it is essentially the content of these predictions that we have to consider. To be sure, there are also a few passages in his discourses apart from the predictions in which there are general references to his death, but the interpretation of these passages is debatable. For example, in Christ's conversation with Nicodemus in John 3 he says that, just as Moses lifted up a serpent in the wilderness, so the Son of man must be lifted up, that is, raised so that he can be seen from afar. Christ regards his exaltation as parallel to the lifting up of the serpent, "that whoever believes in him (analogous to

40. See above, p. 279, n. 37.

322

viewing the serpent with the confidence that it will help) may have eternal life." It is quite arbitrary to regard this as a reference to Christ's crucifixion. By exaltation is meant only the general becoming seen.* In John 6 there is a difficult passage in which Christ speaks of the eating of his flesh and of the drinking of his blood. Many have wished to interpret this as a reference to Christ's death. However, if we consider it in its total context we see that the entire discourse issues from the recollection of the manna which those who spoke to Christ had related to the question they had addressed to him. Christ represents himself as the true bread that comes down from heaven. This is only another way of saying what is declared by the parable of the vine and its branches, a way of referring to the power that nourishes, imparts instruction, and maintains life. When this is expressed by the terms of eating his flesh and drinking his blood, we do not need to regard the passage as referring to Christ's death. The terms are to be interpreted in light of the image of bread that has come down from heaven, and "flesh" can be used only of the living state. So then, the words "flesh" and "blood" refer only to *the personality of Christ as it was made manifest in his life,* the way they were customarily used. Christ in this passage represents himself as the bread that has come down from heaven, of which he wants believers to participate. The passage in which Christ speaks most explicitly of his death is the one in John 12: "Unless a grain of wheat falls into the earth and dies, it remains alone; but if it dies, it bears much fruit." This saying is uttered in connection with the words, "The hour has come for the Son of man to be glorified," and that saying in turn is connected with the reference to "some Greeks" who had wished to see Christ. The context, then, speaks of the attention Christ had attracted and hints at a generally widespread activity of which, however, Christ's death was at the same time to be a necessary condition. We can regard the saying as Christ's definite declaration that the attainment of the purpose of his mission was conditioned in its entirety by his death. A similar explanation must be given of the passage in

* generally becoming known. The *in conspectum omnium* is used in a spiritual sense.

which Christ tells his disciples that his death was the condition of the gift of the Spirit. "If I do not go away, the *parakletos* ["Counselor"] will not come to you" (John 16: 7). The disappearance of his person is related to the attainment of the purpose of his mission. Only when that takes place will the promised Spirit come, and the distribution of the Spirit will result in the wider distribution of Christ's activity. There is another passage in which Christ speaks of his death, but the reference is not as specific. I refer to the parable in John 10 in which Christ speaks of the good shepherd in contrast to the hireling. The good shepherd lays down his life for the sheep, whereas the hireling flees and the wolf comes and snatches the sheep and scatters them. In this image it is not the necessity of Christ's death that is stressed, but Christ's willingness to lay down his life: "I lay down my life for the sheep." Several other similar passages occur that have the same content (cf. chap. 15).

To be sure, when we examine other passages we seem to be compelled to regard them in a different light. In Matthew 20:28 we read, "Even as the Son of man came not to be served but to serve, and to give his life as a ransom for many." The Greek phrase is *lutron anti pollon* ["ransom for many"]. However, the initial "even as" refers to something earlier with which the statement is to be compared. The connection is that Christ summons the disciples, who had been disputing with each other, and tells them that such quarrels of one with another ought not to take place. Their greatness was to be measured only by the extent to which they rendered service to others, and whoever would be first among them would have to be preeminent in his service to all others.* So then, Christ says of himself: My whole life is geared to the rendering of service. I count my whole life for nothing, so far as I myself am concerned. It is for the rendering of service, and that involves the readiness to lay down my life. To be sure, "ransom" seems to refer to something else. However, if we ask: Is that a passage in which Christ wished to advance a teaching

* or add: Christ here has substituted "slave" for "servant," which the Roman hierarchy has strengthened to read *servus servorum* in order to give weight to the *megas* ["great"].

peculiar to himself about the effect of his death? we have to reply: That could not be achieved with such an isolated phrase. Ransoming refers only to the state of slavery and imprisonment. So here and in other places Christ represents what he has come to bring men under the image of setting men free. The Son alone can set men free. The freeing of men[41] was the *object* of his whole life, and so his death is mentioned in connection with that, and with reference to his whole life, rather than specifically for itself.

In the story of the institution of *the Lord's Supper* there is a passage in Matthew 26:28 that could serve most effectively as an excuse for the apostolic explanation. When Christ gave his disciples the cup he used the phrase "for the forgiveness of sins." To be sure, it is uncertain whether this is dependent on "blood" or on "this."* In addition, however, we must take the fact into consideration that in the account of the distribution of the bread there is no parallel to the phrase. We should have to say that it was an elaboration of Christ's statement, a definition of it that occurred only in connection with the second half of what Christ said at the time. If we ask what Christ elsewhere has to say about the forgiveness of sins, we see that it is clear that it is nowhere related to his death. It is nowhere said that his death was the actual cause of the forgiveness of sins. On the contrary, Christ speaks of the forgiveness of sins without making any reference to his death. If anyone wanted to relate "ransom" to Christ's death (in so doing he would have to regard the punishment as payment for the guilt), we should have to say that, when Christ tells his disciples that they were "clean," they could not have been under the control of sin. "You are already made clean by the word which I have spoken to you" [John 13:1-11]. By "the word which I have spoken to you" Christ means all his teachings. Therefore he says that the disciples' purity is the consequence of his influence on them in its entirety, and the forgiveness of sins is part of this purity. So Christ traces this forgiveness

41. Rütenik refers to Luke 24:21.
* in the story of the institution of the Lord's Supper the phrase "for the forgiveness of sins" occurs, which may have been most influential in suggesting the apostolic rule. The phrase may be dependent either on "blood" or on "this"

back to the whole effect of his work, and his death is only one moment in the course of his entire ministry. Nowhere does Christ say that his death has some special and peculiar efficacy apart from his whole life.

Lecture 49 (July 30). The axiom that the kingdom of God is not dependent on any human effort (see the parable in Mark 4) is as true of the time of Christ's life on earth as it is afterward. This stands in sharp opposition to the idea of a plan that Christ is said to have made. In spite of that many, such as Reinhard, have maintained that the best hypothesis is that Christ had developed a plan.[42] In fact, Christ acted only on a constant inner impulse. In his way of expressing it Christ, as did the apostles later, let himself be led by circumstances. The promise given to prayer in Christ's name, often repeated, seems opposed to this. The question of the efficacy of prayer can be left out of consideration in the course of this discussion. However, if we think of definite petitions made in the confidence that they will be granted, we have concern and plan. We have two examples of Christ's own petitionary prayers. The first is the prayer that the disciples' faith might not fail. This was a petition that Christ made. The second is Christ's prayer in the garden. This was a prayer of submission to God's will. In light of this latter precedent, how could the disciples pray for anything external in Christ's time without similar submission? What Christ has to say in Matthew 19:29 and elsewhere of the compensation that the kingdom of God affords leads back to two things. The first has to do with external possessions and is realized by the community of goods that in a certain sense came into being everywhere in Christianity and by the greater security that this sharing of possessions affords wherever it is practiced. The second is the matter of social bonds, and here the compensation consists in the inwardness of brotherly love. The assurance that *the disciples will judge the twelve tribes of Israel* raises other questions. It is undeniable that Jesus often speaks of a higher development of his kingdom, it is difficult to decide whether a second historical period is meant or an end to human things. Christ's personal presence is often to be understood only in spiritual terms and his physical miraculous power is often not to be understood literally. The description of the judgment distinctly bears the marks of a parable, and in the discourses after Christ's

---

42. The reference is to Franz Volkmar Reinhard's *Versuch über den Plan, welchen der Stifter der christlichen Religion zum Besten der Menschheit entwarf* (1781). Schleiermacher often referred to Reinhard in his theological writings, invariably as an example of the "wrong" position which Schleiermacher was combating. Reinhard represented a mixture of old Protestant orthodoxy and Enlightenment rationalism.

last viewing of the temple it is impossible to distinguish between the end of Jerusalem and Christ's return. Consequently this has given rise to chiliasm. However, the reverse is true. Christ only designated that destruction as his victory and therefore as his entry. Concerning the judgment in and for itself there are contradictory sayings. On one occasion Christ asserts that he has not come to judge, and on another that the Father has committed the judgment to him. The latter saying has been understood as a reference to two different presences, but there is no indication that that is what it means. Much more natural is the explanation that the judgment was not to be his work but was related to his mission as a consequence. Equally difficult are the passages where judgment is related to Christ's resurrection. In the same connection resurrection is to be understood spiritually and then again physically.

There is another element in Christ's teaching, expressly found, to be sure, only in one passage, that is very strongly opposed to the frequently debated view that there is a power system of evil and enmity against the kingdom of God which is under the control of a single spiritual being. Christ declares that the kingdom of God is the work of God alone and, as this implies, does not stand in need of any special human effort. This aspect of Christ's thought is set forth only in one parable that is found only in Mark. "The kingdom of God is as if a man should scatter seeds upon the ground, and should sleep and rise night and day, and the seed should sprout and grow, he knows not how ..." (Mark 4:26 ff.). There is absolutely no reason to doubt the authenticity of this parable, and it is impossible to give it any other explanation than the one I have suggested. When we reflect on the way and manner in which the kingdom of God expands we see that the assertion that it is the work of God alone is confirmed. To be sure, the kingdom could not grow unless those who believe in Christ preach the kingdom to others. The continuous proclamation by men of the kingdom of God must precede its advance. However, this does not imply any plan-making on the part of men or the taking of any precautionary measures against individual obstacles that stand in the kingdom's way. On the contrary, everything is left to the spiritual power of life that dwelt in Christ as he appeared upon earth, and it brings about everything in the organization that is in accordance with the divine governance of the world, which we can only regard and understand as the result of its operation. Consequently I can never agree with the view that Christ had a *plan*, whether it be thought of as a plan for the redemption of men or a plan for the establishment of a kingdom of God. Such ideas cannot be credited to Christ (although that is what Reinhard does). Once we admit the existence of that direction of life that led Christ to preach himself, redemption through him, and the kingdom of God, we have to agree that in all individual cases Christ and the apostles let themselves be governed by the circumstances, without formulating a specific design or determining by human reflection that something should be done here or there that would most effectively spread the gospel. Christ's manner of life, alternating between a steady residence in one place and traveling about in the country, interrupted at times by a stay in the temple on the occasion of a great festival, cannot be called a plan, but was simply the result of conditions of living freed from every external responsibility. Everything issued purely from the inner impulse to offer himself to men. The fact that he went here or there at this or that time cannot be ascribed to a plan, any more than we can say that he had a plan in choosing his disciples. Apparently he selected them at random, by inner direction and inclination. The same thing is true of the later church. How can anyone possibly dream of a plan that the apostles made to spread and establish Christianity? Everything happened at the instigation of circumstances, and these gave the impulse to specific acts. So Christianity was bound up with the entire course of general world affairs in its various aspects.

We now have to consider a counterpart to this that we find expressed by Christ in several passages. On the one hand there is the exhortation to leave everything to the working of the kingdom of God itself, under the guidance of the divine governance of the world, and on the other hand there is Christ's definite assurance to his disciples that God would grant them every petition that they could agree to make in his name. I do not wish to present this as Christ's teaching of the efficacy of prayer. It is easy to point out that such efficacy was provided for in advance in the divine governance of the world. What I am concerned with here is that in his assurance that prayer will be answered Christ assumes human concern, wish, desire, and that he opens the prospect to his disciples that such a common desire on their part, associated with the consciousness of the divine governance of the world, would be realized. To be sure, these sayings can be understood in two very different ways. On the one hand we can regard them as an encouragement, a demand, that the disciples should frequently reach agreement as to their petitions so that they would be realized by the divine assent to them. In this case these sayings would be completely opposed to what Christ says in the parable in Mark. On the other hand we can look at them in an entirely different way. We can regard them only as an appeal to the disciples to reflect on whether they could ask of God in Christ's name whatever might arise in them as wish and as desire. In this case the sayings would only be a warning to moderate or set aside everything that in men so easily opposes such a submission of wishes to the divine governance of the world. If the disciples had asked: What can we agree about to ask in Christ's name so that God can grant it to us? they must themselves have said that they could not point to anything that Christ had asked of God, except what is referred to in his saying to Peter, that Satan had demanded from God the right to sift the disciples, but that he himself had prayed that Peter's faith might not fail. The disciples could regard that as an instance of God's assent to Christ's prayer and could conclude that they had been spared the ordeal. On the other hand, the disciples could have found some help in what is told us of *Christ's prayer in the garden*. According to the account that is given of it, Christ suppressed a definite wish and submitted himself to the will of God, but as though that will were unknown to him. The uncertainty is involved in the words, "If it be possible, let this cup pass from me." The resignation is recorded by the words, "Nevertheless, not as I will, but as thou wilt." As soon as they took the former utterance as a positive and the latter as a negative guide in their use of Christ's promise, the disciples had to rid themselves of all concern and of desire for any single thing, because they had to reconcile themselves to the fact that they did not know whether it was the will of God, and they had to phrase their prayers as Christ had phrased his.

This brings us to another point with respect to the kingdom of God. We are told that the disciples had asked Christ what reward they would be given for having abandoned everything else in order to devote themselves to him and his cause. Here the question concerning recompense for loss occurs in connection with the totality of human affairs and a promise of Christ that has reference to it. According to Matthew 19:28-29 Christ's promise follows upon Peter's statement, "Lo, we have left everything and followed you. What then shall we have?" And the promise runs, "Truly, I say to you, *en tē palingenesia* [in the new world], when the Son of man shall sit on his glorious throne, you who have followed me will also sit on twelve thrones, judging the twelve tribes of Israel. And every one who has left houses or brothers or sisters or father or mother or children or lands, for my name's sake, will receive a hundredfold, and inherit eternal life." In connection with this passage we ask to what extent Christ says here that the kingdom of God will afford a recompense for what man, in a worldly sense, has given up for its sake. Since Christ here promises a hundredfold recompense for everything that has been given up, it follows that the promise refers to external possessions as well as to other matters. Consequently we can distinguish between external goods and the social relationships which rest on natural love and on love by choice, and for both Christ promises a recompense to a numerical extent that is intended to suggest something incomparable and immeasurable.

Are we to conclude from this that he thought of the kingdom of God as a state of earthly affluence? Are we to think that, since he speaks of judging and of the twelve thrones of Israel, he intended that the disciples should be responsible for deciding the fate of other men? The question arises: What point of time did Christ have in mind? What point of time is meant by the reference to the sitting of the Son of man on the throne of his glory? The passage speaks of a continuous state, but it does not make it really clear whether an earthly state is meant, or a state after earthly things come to an end. To be sure, there are sayings of Christ that seem to speak of a state after earthly things have wholly ceased to be, but they are of such a kind that we cannot separate them from what was to happen in the course of history. Consequently this whole subject is a very difficult one and raises one of the most serious problems we have to face. We cannot hope to solve it satisfactorily. We cannot expect to clarify Christ's ideas with any certainty. Involved in the problem is the discourse concerning the reappearance of the Son of man on the clouds and that concerning the last judgment. Furthermore, there is the discourse that Christ delivered after he had viewed the temple for the last time, in which he predicted the destruction of the temple and spoke of what would precede it. It requires most devious exegesis to determine where the consideration of what is soon to happen comes to an end and where what is to form the end of human things begins. Certainly that was the main reason for the rise of the chiliastic interpretation of Christianity, which expects that to take place in the immediate future which Christ seems to associate with the end of human affairs. What I have said is not intended to deny that Christ assumed various periods in the development of his kingdom. However, it is difficult to determine whether these periods are different from the early limitation of the kingdom to the Jewish people and the later spread of the kingdom to all peoples. It is hard to say whether those various periods refer to this contrast, or whether Christ had something else in mind.

This problem is directly related to *Christ's teaching concerning his return,* and Christ's sayings about that are uttered from very different points of view and occur in very different contexts. There are two main points of view. The first views the return of Christ from the point of view of repayment. Each person will be repaid according to his works. What is said of the judging of the twelve tribes of Israel seems to belong here, although it is the nation of Israel rather than the individual which is represented as the object of judgment. The second main point of view is that, by reference to his return, Christ proclaims a reunion, at times, to be sure, in such a way that we need to assume only a spiritual presence of Christ as the object of Christ's promise. Take, for instance, the familiar saying, "Where two or three are gathered together in my name, there am I in the midst of them." Or the saying at the end of Matthew's Gospel, "I am with you always, to the close of the age." In other passages, however, Christ's return appears as a personal second coming. This is the case in Matthew's account of the last judgment and in the saying early in John 14, "I will come again and will take you to myself." This latter promise refers to a personal reunion, and the same thing is true of the passage in John 17 where Christ prays, "Father, I desire that they also, whom thou hast given me, may be with me where I am." However, Christ has less of his own actual person in mind when he goes on to say, "in order that they may behold my glory, which thou hast given me in thy love for me before the foundation of the world." If we examine what Christ has to say in the discourse on the last judgment in Matthew, we see that what he says cannot be taken literally, for the last judgment as it is there represented cannot be regarded as a factual event.* On the face of it the discourse bears the character of a parable or of a didactic dissertation.

If the discourse on the last judgment can only be explained as a parable, is any other explanation possible for the reference at the beginning of it to the coming of the Son of man on the clouds? This has posed a serious and much-debated problem. If we restrict ourselves to the idea of the judgment, we find contradictory sayings of Christ with reference to it which, to be sure, are usually very easily (or: freely) harmonized with each other, but the method, to be sure, is then also easy. Christ says on various occasions that he had not come to judge, and in other passages that the Father had committed the judgment to him. There are those who say that in the former passages Christ speaks of his presence at that time on earth and in the latter passages of his second coming, but it cannot be demonstrated that he spoke with this twofold reference. It is also possible to say that Christ declares that judging was not something he did, but that whoever does

* the asking and answering cannot be understood literally, and the assembly of people that are already divided would mean that the judgment had already taken place!

not believe in him is already judged. Therefore God committed judgment to him as the natural result of his mission.

It is now necessary to reflect on the idea of judging. The verb "to judge" is used in very different senses. There are many passages in the New Testament writings where "to judge" means "to condemn," and this is in accordance with the genius of the Greek language. However, in many passages it is difficult to determine which meaning the word is intended to convey, and consequently the whole idea is unclear. In addition this judging, represented under the form of the last judgment which, according to ideas current among the Jews, was to be over all other peoples,* but not over the twelve tribes of Israel, was thought of as connected with the appearance of the Messiah. With this as a point of departure, we find the idea of the last judgment also connected with that of the resurrection of the dead. This idea, however, occurs with a twofold meaning. It may refer to an actual, physical resurrection, or to a spiritual, metaphorical one, and in any given instance it is difficult to determine in which sense the phrase is used. In fact, there are passages in which the phrase is used in one sense and then in another, so that the idea of a physical resurrection passes over into that of a spiritual one. However, if we hold fast to the idea of the kingdom of God as something that develops historically we are compelled to say: The idea of the kingdom of God confirms the fact that judgment is something that is constantly going on. The kingdom of God at every moment separates the believers from the unbelievers and, consequently, the good (in the sense of that which is in agreement with the divine will) from the evil (in the sense of that which is a rejection of the divine will). Wherever the kingdom of God is proclaimed, such a separation takes place and persists, until a subordinate distinction of a relative separation occurs.† So then, we can say that Christ thought of the kingdom of God and presented it as something that resulted in a continuous process of separation. However, since

---

* to the extent that they were well- or ill-disposed toward the Jews

† If a mass of people consists of believers, the distinction is only a relative one and is determined by the extent to which an individual conforms to the principle.

the idea of an end of human affairs was bound up with it, this separation must be regarded as a decision, for the process finally comes to an end. It cannot be said that what lies beyond this end is discussed in any purely didactic form in Christ's discourses.

Lecture 50 (July 31). If by *world judgment* we understand an event that is bound up with the end of earthly things, that would be a matter that no longer belongs to Christ's calling and about which Christ therefore had to form no definite conviction. Christ made use of the idea, but in such a way that he related it to himself rather then to the people. Christ's whole teaching of the kingdom of God is concentrated in the fact that blessedness is found in the fellowship with God that he founded, which as a communication of his life is at that same time a vision of God and the following of His will. All that together constitutes the content of Christ's teaching.

We now proceed to discuss *what Christ did in order to found a community of believers.* What we are definitely told consists of two things: He preached and he had people baptized. To be sure, it is only John who speaks of this latter activity, but he does so in such a way that we cannot doubt what he has to say. If Christ's baptism had been wholly identical with the Baptist's, then both could be regarded as nothing more than different ways of making disciples. Therefore probably Christ's baptism made a more definite reference to him than did John's. That John did not point to Christ more generally and include this in his baptism presupposes no vacillation on his part, but may be due to the difference in their practice. John may have believed that he would not be able to reach the largest part of his hearers in this way. There is no indication that John wanted to found an actual community by means of his baptism, and such a purpose would have been incompatible with his reference to one who was to come. Christ also did not relate his baptism to the establishment of a community, but he did regard it as a preliminary setting apart of those who would belong to one and as a summons that would be issued to follow him. Otherwise it would be difficult to understand how congregations could have come into being so quickly and without further effort wherever Christ had stayed. It is probable that Christ baptized not only in Judea but also in Galilee, but probably not in Jerusalem. It remains uncertain whether he always baptized, or did so only for a certain period.

We cannot go into detail. The view that Christ speaks in his discourses of an imminent twofold return has often been advanced, but has never satisfied me. It has seemed to me to be a forced attempt at explaining something that takes place but once. Christ found the idea of a judgment of peoples already current, combined on the one hand with the idea of the appearance of the Messiah, and on the other also with the idea of the resurrection of the dead. In several passages Christ himself interprets the latter idea in spiritual terms, and his specific descriptions of the judgment as such have a predominantly parabolic character. Furthermore, Christ represents the idea of the judgment itself as a continuous one. Men separate themselves into two groups by reason of their belief or lack of belief in him. In light of all this I cannot say that any certainty issues from the discourses of Christ that he was convinced of any general judgment associated with the end of human affairs or of a personal return, such as we find mentioned in his parabolic discourses. On the contrary, it is my belief that Christ was convinced only of a continuous judgment that takes place in the course of the development of the kingdom of God itself. Those who are received into the kingdom of God separate themselves on grounds of their belief from those who are unbelievers.* *All I find in Christ's teachings that is definitely expressed, but even so only in a general way and without specific clarity, are the ideas of a reunion of Christ with believers and of a continuous spiritual activity of Christ upon earth.*

I have already said that I can find no grounds for believing that Christ had a definite consciousness of a previous existence in him of the divine in a state of union with or of separation from God and that, if he had such a consciousness, it would have nullified his humanity. Similarly I find no definite statement by Christ of a specific consciousness of a personal return to earth or any definite statement of a later human existence, whether as a new one or as a continuation of the one that already was his. Rather, what I find is only a general consciousness of a continuation, not only in the interests of a constant spiritual activity of his personality, but also for his union with believers in fellowship with God. To be sure, Christ did not think of this fellowship in a different way than

---

* or add: The judgment is the negative side of the gathering of men into the kingdom of God.

others who had a premonition of it, but much more completely and with a certainty that we find in all that Christ teaches that issues from his inner being. If we leave this aside as something about which we cannot speak more definitely, we find in Christ's consciousness as an essential component the idea of the kingdom of God bound up with his activity constantly directed to its establishment. He regards this as the complete development of the divine ordinance for the human race.

Let us return to a consideration of Christ's promise of a recompense for all that man gives up for the sake of the kingdom of God. We are compelled to say that the judgment that Christ promises his disciples is nothing else than an expression of their spontaneous and independent participation in the extension of the kingdom of God as that by which the distinction between believers and unbelievers is repeatedly made. The purpose of his promise was only to increase the disciples' consciousness of this participation in the development of the divine ordinance for the human race by bringing about this contrast between believers and unbelievers.

So far as actual recompense for earthly goods and social bonds is concerned, it appears that Christ's promise in this respect had to do only with the earliest period in the history of Christianity. If we ask how this recompense that Christ promises is to be thought of, the answer is that with respect to external possessions this hundredfold return can only be realized in the community of external possessions that exists everywhere in Christianity and that is to be perfected more and more. To the extent that everything is held in common there is no such thing as individual loss, for it appears as a minimum. All external possessions with respect to the kingdom of God must not only be property held in common, but must also give common occasion (or: interest) for keeping every person in such a condition that he can devote his powers to the development of the kingdom of God. So all sorts of securities are available in Christian congregations that do not exist in the civil order. The second main point that Christ stressed was recompense for the loss of social bonds. For that loss Christ promises a hundredfold recompense by means of the inwardness of general brotherly love. This is continuously realized in the fact that all individual human relationships where the Christian church exists and establishes itself are permeated with a religious character. If we include this in the vital view that Christ held of the kingdom of God we are compelled to say: *Christ's self-consciousness as that of activity in his mission was at the same time the consciousness of the complete development of the human spirit and the human race that took place from this point on. The definitive perfection of the human spirit in its development was included in the fullest possible way in his personality, which on the one hand was conscious of God and on the other hand was conscious of the species. Christ was constantly filled with this consciousness, but always strictly in the form of a human consciousness.*

This community which was founded by Christ and in which the idea of the kingdom of God was to be realized is presented from the very beginning as a communication of what Christ calls eternal life. In his use of this term he makes no distinction or even any definite gradation between a present and a future state. Since both in his self-consciousness were one, he could say that whoever believes in him, that is to say, whoever opens himself to the effect of his life on him, has eternal life here and now in the fellowship of his life. It is a diminution of the content of Christ's words that is difficult to justify when they are taken to refer only to a promise and a future gift. It is quite clear that this interpretation has frequently followed quite diverse maxims in order to reach the same goal of ascribing to Christ something magical, something exceeding human consciousness, and at the same time something much less than the truth. Since this is everywhere the way Christ speaks of the kingdom of God and of the individual life so far as it is comprehended in it (in Christ's sayings these two forms, the fellowship of life with him and with God and the communication of eternal life, are the two that prevail), I must confess that *I lay but the smallest amount of worth on what interpreters have often wanted especially to stress, namely, the actual moral content of Christ's sayings. This is predominantly only the polemic against those who oppose the kingdom, and that is always only the indirect side of the communication,* intended under given circumstances to give an impulse, but *something we can*

*never include in an actual account of Christ's teaching be-
cause, although it issues from it, it looks like a foreign element.* As soon as we presuppose what Christ described only in
such a general way, we conclude that *it is quite unnecessary
to enter into a mass of individual moral detail, for the meaning of that is obvious, and the general formula in the apostolic
writings, ''faith is active through love,'' is the same as we find
in Christ's general description, but the former makes everything specific superfluous as teaching, for the application always takes place as an individual matter, according to the
conditions and circumstances that exist at the time.*[43] And now
we pass on to the other side of the consideration, namely,
what Christ did during his public ministry to create a community in which the idea of the kingdom of God was to be realized.

His Activity in Founding a Community

Let me begin with a general statement. In the nature of
things it was impossible that such a community as we find in
existence so soon after Christ's death could have existed during
the period of his public life and work among those who joined
him and acknowledged him. At that time everything had to be
in a sense preparatory, for then all that existed was the union
of each individual with him. This had to be the dominant fact,
and the union of individuals among themselves could only be
complementary to that. There could only be a pooling of the
memories and recollections of several individuals, and a fully
organized community could not come into being among them.
To be sure, we can imagine an approximation to it, but only
to the extent that there was an analogy to the future situation.
To put the matter another way, there could be no real com-

43. This statement represents a polemic against a very prevalent manner
of reading the message of Jesus both in the Enlightenment and in those
theologians active in the early nineteenth century under the banner of
Kantian thought. Kant's *Religion Within the Limits of Reason Alone*,
trans. T.M. Greene and H. Hudson (New York: Harper, 1960) is a great
example of this approach. One prominent New Testament critic in this
line that was contemporary with Schleiermacher was H.E.G. Paulus.
Schleiermacher does not deny the moral content in Jesus' message, yet it
is always more fundamental for Schleiermacher that Jesus does not
primarily point men toward ideals but brings an actuality — the power
of his God-consciousness.

338

munity among those who lived with one another in the immediate presence of Christ; only among disciples in areas where
Christ himself was not present could there be a fellowship that
held individuals more closely together. We can assume this
without holding that this fellowship was organized. There
could not have been any real community. So then, if we leave
Christ's teaching activity out of account, which, to be sure, is
something important as soon as this whole activity with respect to the creation of a community is regarded only as preparatory, there is little left that Christ could have done in preparation.

This can be summed up under two headings: (1) the formation and preservation of the apostolic circle, a group of men
more closely gathered about Christ, from which later the communication of his being and his life was to be made most effectively to the community that was to be founded; (2) the
fact that even during his lifetime *Christ had people baptized in
his name* and consequently built a bridge from baptism, which
proclaimed him and related men to him, to an obligation, if I
may put it that way, to the community that he was to found.
True, reference to Christ's baptism of people in his name is
made only in one passage in John's Gospel [4:1-2], but mention of it there is so definite and uncontrived that not the slightest doubt about it can be entertained. To be sure, the passage does not say that Christ had people baptized. However, we
cannot doubt that it was a baptism in his name. If it had only
been a repetition of the Baptist's baptism it could not have
been contrasted with the latter, which it is, and no difference
could have arisen between the disciples of the Baptist and
those of Christ such as did arise. It would be easier to believe
that John also baptized in Christ's name than that Christ baptized in general only in light of the approach of the kingdom
of God and for repentance, for after Christ's baptism John acknowledged most definitely that it was he who was to found
the kingdom of God which he had proclaimed. He told that to
at least a few of his disciples, who later became disciples of
Christ, and therefore communicated the fact to several people.
If he had the firm conviction that Jesus was the Messiah, it
would have been natural for him to include that in his bap-

tism. However, there is no indication that he did so, and it is probable that he did not, for he could expect that Christ himself would take the initiative in that respect. To the definite assertion that, when Christ commissioned his disciples to baptize, this baptism was to be in his name, the objection could be raised that thereby the fact that he was Messiah would have been assumed as familiar to all. However, then we should expect that at once he would have been subjected to the same persecution and that the Sanhedrin would have demanded that he express himself distinctly, but of that we find also no indication. We are told, however, that, when it became well-known that Christ had made more disciples by baptism than had John, Christ left the area in which the Sanhedrin exercised direct authority. We are told that he left Judea and went to Galilee. There would have been no occasion for him to do that if he had baptized as did John, for the Sanhedrin ignored John's baptism, and if his baptism had been the same as John's there would have been no reason for Christ to leave the area of the Sanhedrin's direct influence.

Well then, what was the nature of Christ's baptism? Did those who were baptized assume thereby a definite obligation that became effective at once? No reference is made in our sources to such obligation, but it is incredible that it was not involved in baptism (naturally not an outer, judicial obligation, but a moral one). It is incredible that those who accepted baptism did not acknowledge something that provided a bridge to the practical. Two things were involved in John's baptism. In the first place, it involved the acknowledgment that the descendants of Abraham as such did not have an unconditional right to the divine favor and blessing promised in the messianic kingdom, but needed first to repent. In the second place, because it was a baptism for repentance John's baptism required that everyone who accepted it should be mindful of the approach of the kingdom of God and that, when it appeared, should undertake to join it, for otherwise any confession of sins would have been an empty rite. It has often been maintained that there was a community of John's disciples, that they constituted a religious corporation, but that claim cannot be proved. It is only a deduction from later historical phenomena. If the baptism practiced by Christ's disciples during his lifetime had been related to John's baptism but had included a definite reference to the fact that the promised kingdom of God was grounded on Jesus of Nazareth and would issue from him, then no one could have accepted baptism from Christ's disciples without attesting his faith in it by the act itself and so undertaking to wait for the manifestation of the kingdom of God. Baptism involved a demand from Christ for a specific activity. Whether the disciples kept on baptizing after the time when John mentions their activity in this respect cannot be determined. We have no way of ascertaining whether, if Christ's disciples were compelled to leave Judea just as Christ himself was, they carried on this work of baptism in areas more remote from the center and from the actual influence of the Sanhedrin and whether this work of baptizing was continuous. If they did continue to baptize, their purpose in doing so must have been that those who accepted baptism should constitute a group that could be counted on as soon as a community had to be founded.

Lecture 51 (August 1). That Christ later expressly instituted baptism does not contradict the fact that his disciples also baptized during his lifetime. The later commission had to do with authorization to baptize also outside Jewish territory. The second thing that Christ did to found the Christian community was to form the apostolic circle. This did not happen all at once. Furthermore, Christ did not form the circle by comparing all personalities with the purpose of his mission in mind. No doubt there were many in Palestine who could have discharged their duties as well as those that were chosen. If Christ had chosen his disciples in such a way, we could not understand how he came to select Judas. Peter was brought by his brother to Christ. This story shows us clearly how Christ was governed by circumstances. We are not sure of the names of all the disciples. Perhaps the disciples were not always the same. One of them could easily have been removed from the group by death or by circumstances that could not be overcome and another have taken his place. It remains uncertain whether Nathanael was an apostle. There must have been others besides the apostles that accompanied Christ just as regularly in his public ministry. What set the apostles apart, therefore, was chiefly that they lived together with Christ. That Christ taught them things in private that he could not have taught in public can be deduced from the words "what you have whispered in private rooms," but the same passage indicates that these teachings must be found in the teachings of the apostles. It is not easy to think of Christ as giving the apostles instructions in the form of their delivery, for they were told not to make preparation. They would have to learn from his example how to construct parables. There was little to teach about parables. Everything in the construction of parables depends on imagination. As a matter of fact, the apostles do not seem to have used this form very much or with particular success. We must naturally assume that Christ gave them explanations of what he had said in public. The Johannine discourses stood most in need of such explanations, but John at least has not included any of them.

The uncertainty in which we find ourselves concerning the point which I discussed at the end of the preceding lecture is dispelled to some extent by the fact that very early in the book of the Acts of the Apostles we read of congregations in Galilee, without being told how they came into being. Because of his long stay in Galilee Christ had a number of pupils there, although some had deserted him because they had hoped that he would lead a national movement. So we must assume that there were a considerable number of believers in Galilee. The fact that they so quickly constituted themselves as a community makes it likely that something had happened there at an earlier time and that in baptism they had been prepared for such a future community and that thereby Christian congregations were later formed. This could have happened the more readily if even during Christ's lifetime the believers had come together, but that does not seem to have been the case.

The second thing that Christ did to prepare the way for the Christian community was to form *the inner circle of apostles.* Several of his discourses cast light on his purpose in doing so. The apostles were to continue his preaching, and he wanted to hand over all his work to them when he left the earth. However, the question of how this circle came into being and became fixed is a difficult one to answer.* In the Gospel of Matthew the twelve are enumerated at the point where Christ gives them instructions. It is not certain whether these instructions were meant to be general or were intended to govern the

*Cf. Schleiermacher, *Ueber den Lukas [A Critical Essay on the Gospel of Luke]* (Berlin, 1817), pp. 87 ff.

apostles in the carrying out of their immediate mission. The latter interest appears to be predominant, but the instruction has nevertheless a more general content. The apostles are enumerated for the first time at this point, but we do not get the impression that they were first formed as a group at that time. Rather, they had already been known as the twelve and therefore already had a special relationship to Christ.

In Luke the situation is quite different. There we get the impression that Christ constituted the twelve at the time that is mentioned in the Gospel. When Luke reports the Sermon on the Mount he enumerates the twelve and does so in such a way that we are led to believe that they were first set apart by Christ at that time. However, if we recall the fact that this Gospel is clearly made up of elements that earlier were quite independent of each other and if we think of this story in that light, it is possible to believe that the account of the choosing of the twelve is used as an introduction to the Sermon on the Mount without having had any original connection with it. In Luke 6 we are told that Christ went out to a mountain to pray and that he continued all night in prayer to God. Then, when it was day, he called his disciples to him and chose twelve from among them, whom he named apostles. It is clear from this that the period immediately before such a public act as the delivery of the Sermon could hardly have been the time for such a choice.

John is the only Evangelist who tells us of several of Christ's first disciples, of how they came to him, and of several personal contacts. However, those who came to Christ were not all members of the twelve. One of them, Nathanael, is not listed as one of that group. Attempts have been made to identify him with one of the twelve, but there is no authority for that, and nothing confirms it. Another difficulty is that even the twelve are not always enumerated in the same way. There are differences in the listings. There is a name in Luke's list that is not in Matthew's, and if we try to solve the problem by identifying the two, by saying that the same person had a number of names, we find no analogy for that. It was not the practice of the time. To be sure, we find that the Jews of the day used a different method of naming people than did the

Romans, but that is of no help to us. It was Jewish custom to add the name of the father to that of the individual. It was also a Jewish custom to translate or Hellenize a man's name. However, when these factors do not come into play it is impossible to regard two different names as referring to one person. Both lists, Matthew's and Luke's, begin with Simon and Andrew, James and John, two pairs of brothers. Then follow in turn Philip and Bartholomew, and then also Matthew and Thomas. Then in Matthew we find the name James, the son of Alphæus, and then Lebbæus, surnamed Thaddæus. At this point, instead of Lebbæus, surnamed Thaddæus, Luke has the name and nickname Simon, called the Zealot. It is impossible that the same man could have had two different names and two different surnames. Then in Matthew we have Simon the Canaanite and Judas Iscariot, but of a Judas son of James, the penultimate disciple in Luke's list, Matthew knows nothing. If an attempt is made to identify Judas and Lebbæus, all we need to do is to point out that Judas the son of James bears his father's name after his own and would also have to have been known as Thaddæus and Lebbæus. It is impossible to identify the two in this way (keeping the practice of the time in mind).

In Mark's Gospel we find a difference in the way the names are listed, and Mark's apparent listing of the disciples in pairs must have some significance, although it is not easy to discover it. To be sure, there were two pairs of brothers, and they would naturally have been placed together, and this precedent could have been followed in presenting the rest. The difficulty with this theory is that Mark breaks up the pairs of brothers in his listing.

The question then arises: Do our accounts agree that the twelve were always the same, or is it not easy and natural to assume that the members of the twelve were not always the same and that the lists come to us from different times? This latter possibility is attractive in and for itself and does not require us to think of an apostasy of one of the apostles from Christ, for that would have been an event that could not so easily have been covered up. Family duties, special circumstances, these could have compelled an individual member of the group to give up constant attendance on Christ and then someone else would have taken his place. This theory is credible in view of the many differences in the lists of these three analogous Gospels. There is also another difference. Matthew is introduced also as the tax collector, and that title is used in the story of his call in the Gospel of Matthew. However, in another Gospel (Luke 5:27) this tax collector is called Levi rather than Matthew. There it is uncertain whether Matthew is given the name Levi or whether it is not true that *Lebbæus* is the tax collector. And that is far from all.

There is still another difficulty of a sort that we are not in a position to solve, namely, the question of how it came about that Christ included Judas Iscariot among the apostles. It is often said: Yes, Christ knew in advance that Judas would come to his end as he did. Prophecy required that he should be betrayed by one of those who were closest to him. He chose Judas as one of his intimate followers in order that one of those ancient prophecies should be fulfilled. I cannot understand how anyone can accept this hypothesis. It means that Christ because of his foreknowledge became coauthor of the deed, for if he had not included Judas among the apostles, Judas would have had no part in the betrayal. Prophecy does not support the hypothesis. Various passages are interpreted to support it, but Christ himself did not use those passages as a prophecy.* If we were to say that Christ, when he included Judas among the apostles, did not have any foreknowledge that he would take the course he did, we should again be taking a position that is untenable. It could not be maintained in view of the extraordinary degree of knowledge of the inner being of men which, in light of what the Evangelist John says, we must credit to Christ. The difficulty is insoluble if we accept Luke's account of the determination of the apostolic circle, namely, that Christ selected his apostles by deliberate

* The hypothesis makes use of similar passage[s], but we do not know whether Christ regarded it as a *prophecy*. Another possibility: It is usually said that Christ chose Judas in order to fulfill various ancient prophecies, according to which the Messiah was to be betrayed in such a way, but this prophecy seems only to be applied to the relationship between Christ and Judas.

choice.* To be sure, it is not only in that passage in Luke that we are told that Christ chose his apostles. Christ himself said, "You have not chosen me, but I have chosen you." However, this is not as definite a saying as it sounds. The positive statement is made only in the form of a contrast and can only be judged in accordance with what precedes it. We could paraphrase it after this fashion: I am what I am through no work of yours and, secondly, Your relationship to me is not one that is due to your own initiative. The former statement is the more important of the two. If we assume that the choice was not something that was wholly and exclusively Christ's work, we can imagine that one man became an apostle as the result of a greater and more specific concern on Christ's part, while another entered the group much more on his own initiative. Even if we assume that certain circumstances must have existed to bring individuals into Christ's immediate presence, it is possible, nevertheless, to think that these circumstances were such that Christ would have had to reject Judas very specifically in order to prevent him from entering the group of the twelve, and his knowledge of men was not a sufficient reason for doing this, since this reason was not understandable to all. This is the only way I can conceive of the fact. *It is impossible for me to think that Christ deliberately chose his apostles.* Otherwise I am inextricably caught in a dilemma. Either Christ did not know what was in Judas, or he himself involved Judas in destruction — made him an apostle in order to destroy him, knowingly and intentionally — and neither of these alternatives is acceptable. According to the view I have put forward, the choice of the apostles seems to have been one that was made freely, much as human choice is made.

John tells us that Andrew, who with John left John the Baptist and joined Christ, went and brought his brother Peter into relationship with Christ. This relationship became at once a very close and intimate one, for as soon as Andrew brought

* Rütenik: This would mean that Christ himself chose Judas and in this way could have been able to exercise control over his spirit, a difficulty that could be much more easily overcome if it had been unnecessary for Christ to issue a specific call. See Schleiermacher, *Ueber die Schriften des Lukas [A Critical Essay on the Gospel of Luke]* ,,p. 88.

his brother Simon to Christ, the latter gave him the name Peter, by which he was henceforth to be known. The other Gospels give a different account. They say that Christ, as he walked by the sea, called Peter and Andrew and James and John. In so doing it is implied that he called them as apostles and that the apostolic circle came into being as the result of a gradual gathering of its members. However, this is in contradiction to the account in John. It is possible to imagine that Christ at that time established a close relationship with Peter, without assuming that any definite group of followers was yet in being. Such an apostolic circle evolved only gradually.

The number twelve is another fact of importance, a number that the apostles themselves considered so significant that after Judas's death they chose another man to keep the number twelve intact. If we reflect in this connection on the passage in which Christ says, in answer to a question that Peter had asked on behalf of the group, that the apostles would sit on twelve thrones to judge the twelve tribes of Israel, we are led to the thought that the number twelve has some relation to the twelve tribes. In that case, however, Christ would have thought of the kingdom of God as limited to these twelve tribes, as limited to the Jewish community, or at any rate would have regarded the twelve tribes as the nucleus of the Christian society, so that non-Jews would first have to enter the Jewish community in order to become Christians. In addition there is the fact that at that time the twelve tribes no longer really existed. The stories in the Old Testament of the return of Jews from exile no longer have reference to the twelve tribes, but only to that part that formerly constituted the kingdom of Judah. The land was no longer distributed according to tribes. In fact, it is also improbable that all parts of the nation any longer had any awareness of their genealogy, or any documentation of it. No doubt the leading families, including the Davidic, had such an awareness, but that cannot be said of the people in general. So then, this reference to the twelve tribes would have been meaningless,* and the

* or add: So then, only the apostles regarded this reference as important and, in doing so, would have given it a meaning that it did not have for Christ. That is something external and does not lessen the importance of

apostles accordingly must have placed a value on this *number.*

This raises the question: Did Christ also do that, or are we to regard the number twelve as accidental (or: as something of no importance)? In the latter case the apostles must have given the number an importance that Christ did not. That, however, was a purely external matter and of no significance in itself, and we need not assume a diminution of the apostolic view, for they did not allow the number to limit membership in the group. We need only recall the conversion of *Cornelius.* Furthermore, this thought would have had no deleterious effect on their actual practice. They continued to use the number only because it remained in their memory, without constantly being aware of gaps in it, and by means of this external matter to retain their identity with the original group.*

Lecture 52 (August 2). The safest assumption seems to be that Christ read Scripture with his disciples and drew their attention especially to the messianic passages. In the apostolic writings we find that it is more his exegesis than their interpretations that cannot be accounted for by means of the ordinary rules. In this connection we have to think not only of the actual interpretation but of all the kinds of use of Scripture that were customary at the time. We cannot say whether the disciples were given any actual training for their future mission. The occasion on which they were sent out seems to have been an isolated one. If that were so, there is all the more reason to think that their mission at that time had a specific purpose. However, if we are to understand that the apostles were sent out in pairs, one pair at a time, then such

the apostolic view, since the apostles did not really allow it to put a limit on their numbers. They could make use of this number only because of their memory of it. At a later time the number twelve was not necessarily associated with the apostles.
* As they looked forward to the fulfillment of Christ's words, they believed that, if they were to begin immediately thereafter to be his witnesses, they would have to be as complete a group as they were when he had spoken to them. So then, aware that they would then have to fulfill their mission in its greatest extent, Peter made the proposal that someone else should be appointed to the twelve to take Judas's place. If we regard the matter in this light, we can only say that Peter at that time spoke under the inspiration of the Spirit of God. See Schleiermacher, *Predigten üeber die Apostelgeschichte [Sermons on the Book of the Acts of the Apostles]*, 1:21-22: "As at that time, on such an occasion the best of the church was perceived." [To what extent this entire note comes from Rutenik is not clear — LEK.]

a mission could often have been repeated. *The seventy disciples* can scarcely be regarded as a different group, similar to but larger than the twelve. However, if Jesus on one occasion sent out such a number in pairs, he must have intended them to exercise a great simultaneous influence, but what that was cannot be more precisely determined. It is possible to think of all sorts of gradations between those who were Christ's constant companions and those who had merely been baptized, but these gradations remain indistinct. Such groups prepared the way for all the later congregations and assured the spread of the gospel. Christ's stay here and there made and confirmed converts. No one can demonstrate that Christ would not have bound believers together (still?) more closely had he not known in advance of his death, but it is possible that that was the case. Had Christ lived longer he would have continued and enlarged his work in the same way. Without any disturbance of Sabbath worship and the law and without any collusion with the priesthood or the Sanhedrin, he could have become a spirtual chief and could therefore have obtained his kingdom. Then the spread of Christianity also outside Palestine would have taken place automatically.

In addition to our uncertainty regarding this intimate circle which surrounded Christ, there is still another matter that has to be taken into consideration. After the ascension but before Pentecost, when Peter makes the proposal *to choose a new apostle,* he says that he must be chosen from among those who had accompanied Christ from the time of his baptism to that of his ascension. From this it is apparent that there were such people, who, however, were not apostles. What constituted the difference between such people and the apostles? Commission by Christ as apostles could only have rested on the constancy of attendance upon him, for much of what Christ taught was occasional and was never given in fixed and final form. So each element in his teaching required explanation by another. By degrees an inward comprehension of these fragmentary details could form an organized whole. Why, then, were the others not also apostles, and what constitutes the difference? This is the key to the puzzle: The difference rests on the distinction between public and domestic life. What Peter sets up as the criterion for the selection of a new apostle was just continuous attendance on Christ during his public ministry. The apostles, however, dwelt with Christ and, because of that, had advantages over the others. But all who had attended constantly on Christ during his public ministry stood next in rank to the apostles, and when it became necessary to fill out the number of the twelve, the choice of a new member had to be made from among this next most intimate group.

There must have been a great many gradations from those who accompanied Christ constantly to those who had acknowledged him.* Many only heard Christ in the centers in which they themselves resided and, because of all the circumstances under which they lived, did not have the opportunity to accompany him beyond the confines of their own place of residence. It is possible to think of several gradations between such people and those who regularly accompanied Christ. Some could listen to Christ both at home and in Jerusalem and on journeys to one festival or another. There can also have been others who at times were able to accompany Christ beyond the limits of their place of residence on occasions other than journeys to festivals. To be sure, the group that enjoyed domestic fellowship with Christ must have been a closed one. If that were the case, it accounts for the peculiar character of the apostolic relationship in contrast to that of those who accompanied Christ only during his public ministry. A number of external circumstances may have played a part in this.

Now we naturally have to ask: What did the twelve have by reason of their domestic fellowship with Christ that the others did not possess? In this connection we shall have to reflect on still another dissimilarity. Not all those who were admitted to this domestic fellowship could always take advantage of the privilege. There would be those who had to withdraw at times because of civil or family responsibilities. So we have to think of still a smaller group within that of the apostles, and we find indications of such a group in our sources. On many occasions we are told that the two pairs of brothers, sometimes both and sometimes only one, were those who at certain times were with Christ. When we recall the fact that these pairs of brothers, according to our sources, were business partners in their trade, something that presupposes some special family relationships, and that Christ when in

* those who had merely been baptized (see above)

Capernaum resided in Peter's house, we see that the close and intimate relationship of the two pairs of brothers to Christ was associated with wholly external matters. Ignoring this difference between the whole apostolic group and the intimate circle of the two pairs of brothers and regarding the apostolic company of those who shared domestic privileges with Christ as a unity, we have to face the question: What connection did Christ have with his apostles and what sort of influence did he exert on them, from which those who followed him during his public ministry with the greatest possible regularity were excluded? The analogy with experience immediately raises another question: Can we regard this sharing of domestic living as a special institution, through which those who took part in it received from Christ a special training for their mission and in which Christ imparted instructions which were not given to others who were excluded from it? As a matter of fact, this is a difficult question to answer. In the Gospel accounts we find many references that would lead us to give an affirmative answer to it, but if we reflect on the later development we find nothing in what the apostles did that presupposes a special body of instruction and a special training. On the contrary, everything can be explained by what we find also in Christ's public ministry. Consequently our sources give to some extent contradictory answers.

It is necessary at this point to make a distinction. It is possible to think of such special training of the apostles under two forms: (1) the impartation of special teachings and precepts; (2) practical training. Both of these together make up the idea of a school in the technical sense of the word. We have no reason at all to assume special practical exercises. Such exercises could only have been exercises in public speaking, and there is no reason at all to suppose that Christ trained his apostles as public speakers. On the contrary, what he has to say points in quite the other direction. At critical moments the disciples would be enabled to say the right thing by the inspiration of the Spirit. On the other hand, there are indications that Christ imparted special instruction to his intimate followers: "What you hear whispered, proclaim upon the housetops." This saying implies a teaching imparted only to the apostles, but we cannot ascertain what it was, since nothing of the sort emerges from the apostolic writings. To be sure, there is an indication of what it was in the Gospels, which is not confirmed by anything we find in the apostolic writings. When Matthew gives an account of a number of parables Christ told, he says that Christ privately explained to the apostles what they had not understood. This may suggest that Christ imparted a more intimate body of instruction to his apostles — a guide to his way of teaching — but we find no evidence that the apostles made use of that at a later time. There is no trace of it in the apostolic sermons that are incorporated in the book of the Acts of the Apostles, and in the writings of the men of this most intimate group there is also no special tendency manifested to employ parabolic discourse. What we find there is usually purely metaphorical.

This leaves only one matter about which it is probable that Christ gave his apostles special instruction and whose consequences can be demonstrated, and that is the use of the Old Testament Scriptures in a variety of ways, the search for and reminder of messianic prophecies, and later the application of other Old Testament passages to the area of the kingdom of God. When we find in apostolic addresses the use of Old Testament passages that were probably not employed by others at that time as prophecies or analogies in the same way as passages which contained the messianic idea, we have every reason to conclude that such use goes back to instruction given the apostles by Christ. That is most probable in view of the fact that such use of Scripture was a very essential element for public speaking in the practice of the synagogue.

However, the apostles were not only set apart to teach, but also to found and maintain the Christian society, and so we raise the question: Did Christ give his disciples special instruction in this respect? If we examine what the book of the Acts of the Apostles has to tell us, we find no evidence there that the apostles put such instruction into effect. On the contrary, everything there occurs as opportunity arises and because of specific circumstances, and the practice of the apostles appears to have been the result of correct instinct rather than of special instructions with respect to specific cases or relationships that they had received from Christ. Let me give an example. At a later time in all apostolic congregations two different forms of public leadership emerged as types, the office of teaching and the office of caring for the external affairs of the congregation, the office of *presbyter* and that of *deacon*. These offices were not original, and the apostles had no occasion to create such institutions from the beginning, as would have been the case if Christ had prescribed them. We see that they developed at the dictation of circumstances, and particularly because of a situation that existed in Jerusalem, where the congregation was made up of different elements. These seem to have been more definitely characterized there in this respect, for the teaching had to remain in the hands of the apostles, who were all Palestinian Jews, while external business affairs came to be delegated chiefly to Hellenists. Therefore these developments led to a sort of equilibrium, as one might expect, but an equilibrium that naturally did not last. So we see that such a general type of church leadership did not emerge as a result of instructions given by Christ but as a consequence of the pressure of circumstances and of a natural development.

When we examine the instruction given to the apostles in Matthew's account, the same, to be sure, that we find in Luke given to the seventy, we discover that this seems to have been given for the immediate task which Christ had then committed to them. It is possible, of course, to doubt that they were meant just for the mission of the apostles at that time, but when we reflect on how Christianity was later spread, we see that such a method was not employed, such a traveling about of the apostles in the country from one place to another. Such a procedure was made impossible in part by circumstances, and in part by the fact that the apostles were compelled to use quite other methods. It follows that also in this respect we find no definite indication of such actual content in the teaching of Christ as he was engaged in domestic association with the apostles. If we then go on to ask what the apostles got from this living together with Christ, we conclude that it was the consistent and more constant effect of his personality on them and the quiet and unbroken understanding of his whole being on their part, rather than the prescription of institutions or other instructions.

In the course of our studies we run across a second group. We learn from an account in Luke that Christ on one occasion sent out seventy disciples in various directions to preach the kingdom of God. Since we have only this one account, I do not believe that the assumption is warranted that this group constituted a second closed circle of followers. If that had been the case, Peter would have mentioned it in the course of the speech in which he proposed the selection of the twelfth apostle, either to limit the choice to a member of this group or to suggest a comparison of those who belonged to it. However, Peter's speech makes no reference to this circle. To be sure, Christ on one occasion may actually have sent out seventy followers to preach the kingdom of God at the same time in various directions, but everything speaks against the assumption that the seventy were a permanent, closed group.

We cannot give any more precise answer to the question whether Christ in addition to what we have discussed did anything to prepare the way for the community that during his lifetime did not yet exist. This does not mean that Christ would not have done more in this respect if the catastrophe of his earthly fate had not occurred so soon. We could form some judgment about that if we could demonstrate that he encouraged a closer association of those who believed in him and strengthened the bonds that united them, but there is nothing in our sources to suggest that he did. To be sure, we hear that he complained that no progress with reference to the kingdom of God had been made, such as he had the right to expect, in places where he had exercised an extended and a frequent ministry, and such a complaint shows that he must have felt himself restricted in his mission by such a failure. This indicates that he would have done something more and something specific if his work had been marked by greater progress. It shows that the various elements of his mission had not yet prospered to the extent that he would have been able to do something definite without acting too hastily.

The Evangelist John reports that, when Jesus permitted his disciples to baptize at the same time as John the Baptist, it

354

came to the attention of the authorities in Jerusalem that Christ's following increased more rapidly than John's, and Christ therefore withdrew to Galilee. We see from this that he wished to avoid unfriendly actions against him (countermeasures). This is the first reason why less happened in this respect than would have happened under other circumstances. In Galilee Christ had to face less opposition, for the influence of the Sanhedrin and the closed leadership of religious affairs were not organized in the same way in all parts of Palestine. However, even in Galilee there were elements opposed to Christ, and if he had wanted to make progress to a certain point he would have aroused the opposition he sought to avoid. The reason for this avoidance of confrontation with opponents was that Christ did not wish to give occasion for outbreaks of antagonism and of open warfare. He wished to avoid all tumultuous situations, and he took steps to see that they were not caused by those associated with him. Consequently he sought to avoid such opposing elements. This state of affairs may account for the fact that even in Galilee and in other areas where the influence of the Sanhedrin was less, no real congregations were founded.* That seems not to have happened as long as Christ lived, although congregations were formed soon afterward.

Lecture 53 (August 3). The previous discussion shows that in any case the opposing party would have been unfriendly to Christ. Even if that had not been so, the group about Christ would naturally have changed considerably from time to time. Some must have grown weary when their political expectations were not fulfilled. Others took offense at Christ's liberalism.

Concerning the development of Christ's relationships with the nation. In this respect the Gospel of John must against be our main source of information. The other Gospels have so little interest in the conditions of the time that they are of little use in determining an intensification of Christ's relationships with the nation. On the other hand, John has **an unmistakable pragmatic tendency to this.**†

---

* or add: that is to say, the Christians could have formed their own synagogue. That would have been quite permissible, for such synagogues were allowed to be established by a certain number of householders.
† Rutenik: Schleiermacher notes, "In the following lectures (53-56) I have described the development as John reports it, with some resort to material

In our materials as we have them we have been able to distinguish only two things that Christ did to prepare the way for the community he came to found, the formation about him of the circle of the apostles and, in the course of his general teaching and preaching activity, baptism with reference to the community as it was to be developed later. As we have seen, an actual community of the followers of Christ was not organized during his lifetime. This preaching and baptizing, beginning as soon as we can think of the apostolic circle as having been formed, continued throughout Christ's whole public ministry. Christ resided alternately in the various territories of Palestine and carried on his task of preaching there. To be sure, we have to think of the apostles as almost always present during this ministry. According to John they were chiefly occupied with baptizing. I have already drawn attention to two points, but points about which one may ask whether they permit us to reach any definite conclusion. One of these is the discourse concerning the sending out of the twelve, and the other is that in Luke concerning the mission of the seventy. If we take the former by itself, we can suppose that Christ arranged for the mission as preliminary practice for the apostles in view of their later task of teaching and preaching, for when they were with him they could get no practice. At such times Christ alone taught and preached. The apostles were recipients rather than imparters. Their sending out was a challenge to teach and preach on their own initiative. To be sure, I have to admit that the fact of the sending out of the apostles is not fully clear. Not all the accounts definitely tell of the return of the apostles, and from none of them do we get a clear idea of what Christ did at that time. Thus our information about the event is not full and clear. This is also true of the mission of the seventy disciples, although in this instance at least we cannot think of it as preliminary practice, since we have no reason to regard this group as an actual institution. Therefore it seems clear that Christ must have had a different purpose in view when he sent out this group, and

in the other Gospels, making use of my old notebooks devoted to the subject." [Evidently this explains the absence of Schleiermacher's notes for lectures 54-56; his notes resume at lecture 57 — LEK.]

this leads us to believe that the mission of the apostles also was not intended to be just for practice. All that we can say is that there were certain times when Christ was not content with his own personal activity and when he wished that the task of preaching the kingdom of God in several places throughout the entire extent of Jewish territory could be carried on at the same time. There were times when Christ wished for more rapid results. How that was related to Christ's activities in other directions cannot be determined, for there is no way of incorporating the elements of the other three Gospels chronologically into John's account. Otherwise the situation would be different,* for in John we see the development of the points that have a historical significance with respect to the catastrophe. But John has nothing to say of the mission of the twelve and the mission of the seventy.

The most natural thing to assume is clearly this: The more the total impression that Christ had of the circumstances in which he was involved was that of a quiet development, the less occasion there would have been for him to undertake a change in his usual practice of having the apostles about him and accompanying him as he taught. However, when this development seemed to him to be threatened, he can easily have entertained the wish to bring the proclamation itself to a certain point before the catastrophe occurred. So the missions can be explained in harmony with all else, although we cannot say anything more precise concerning them. To be sure, there are also occasions in the other Gospels when such concerns on Christ's part could arise, but in these instances we are not sure of the connection of the events that are narrated one after the other, and therefore we cannot reach any certain conclusions.

At this point it is difficult to avoid asking a few other questions that would occur to anyone. We cannot maintain, in fact, we should probably have to deny, that an organized community of Christ's disciples existed during his lifetime. The question arises: Would Christ never have gone on to form such an organization, but always have postponed it to the time when he no longer would be present, or may we suppose that

* otherwise information would be available

357

he himself would have tightened the bonds that bound his disciples together and have given what he had been engaged in preparing for a more definite form of reality if he had been personally active for a longer time? There is no reason, to be sure, to maintain that the founding of an organized community among Christ's followers would have been in conflict with his personal life and work. Only if that had been true would Christ himself never have established a congregation. If that was not the case, we have to think of some other reason that led Christ to postpone the founding of a community. If there was no conflict between his life and work and the founding of a community, the question arises: Why did Christ not organize a community wherever there was a certain number of his followers? To be sure, he would have had to anticipate that by doing so he would bring on the catastrophe of his earthly fate more quickly, although there would have been nothing illegal in founding such a community.

There is still another point to be considered. Christ's anticipation of his imminent death is expressed early in his public ministry, but the point at which this prediction is expressed with any definiteness in our Gospels is not such as to have been occasioned by any special event. So we are compelled to say: Christ's conviction that his personal activity would in no case last for any great length of time must have been the result of the totality of his general impressions. (I restrict myself here to the form of expression that is in accordance with human consciousness and avoid referring to a definite omniscience.) We also find that Christ referred to the prospect of the destruction of the political order as it then existed and of the temple, and this prediction was made earlier than that of his death. Consequently the former must have been a preconsciousness that he constantly possessed, and we have only to presuppose a great interest in the national situation and an unbiased observation of it to realize that a conflict would soon have to emerge, whose issue it would be difficult to foresee. It was this latter point, much more than the former, that restrained Christ from forming a closer union of his followers, for he wanted in no way to give occasion for the outbreak of that conflict, and such a conflict could easily have followed on one that could have broken out among the Jewish people themselves. Unrest, not necessarily against the Romans, would inevitably have brought about such a conflict, and that is what the Sanhedrin at the end warns against: "If we let him go on thus, every one will believe in him, and the Romans will come and destroy both our holy place and our nation." We are compelled to say that Christ did not want the establishment of a closed community among his followers to provide such an occasion, and consequently he did not tighten the bonds between them. We cannot say how these two points, the assumption of his approaching death and the national catastrophe, were related in Christ's thought, but he believed that the generation of those alive at the time would not have died out before that catastrophe occurred. So it is possible that he had wanted to a greater extent to presuppose the actual organization of the community.

Let us now take a further step and ask: If this presupposition on Christ's part had not been so clear and if he had had no cause further to postpone what he wanted, what would he have done? Did the organization of the Christian church that later came into being become what he himself intended, or would he himself under those circumstances have brought about something else? This question is related to another, namely, that of whether the form of the kingdom of God that Christ had in mind would have become in any way something political, and we cannot be satisfied with a general negative answer until we can form a clear picture of what Christ actually hoped for. If we suppose that he wanted everything postponed until the Jewish people themselves would have brought his life to an end and that he thought of the organization of the church as beginning only then, he would have reflected very little on its nature. Here all that we have to go on are Christ's own sayings. He himself declares that he had no wish to put an end to the law by his own authority. The law, however, was bound up with the national sanctuary. Its original connection with the ark of the covenant had been transferred to the temple. Law and temple were essentially correlates. Consequently Christ would not have been able to effect any revolutionary change in the temple worship.

It is often maintained that that is what Christ would actually have done if he had had a free hand. He would have effected a general reform of the temple worship. I cannot accept this hypothesis. It is based on the story of the cleansing of the temple, but this had nothing whatever to do with an actual reform. To oppose malpractices that have no legal ground is not to attempt a reform. In opposing them a man simply exercises his rights. That is something everyone should do. All essential elements of temple worship were exactly stipulated by the law. Christ did not wish to destroy the law; consequently he also did not wish to destroy the temple worship. He would have permitted his followers to take part in temple worship just as he himself did. In fact, there is a suggestion in our sources that Christ had a considerable number of followers among the priests. If someone were to ask whether he would not have forbidden at least these to take any part in temple worship, despite their obligation as priests to do so, because that was not worship of God in spirit and in truth, I should have to answer that I cannot believe that he would have done that.

The whole matter can be looked at only from two points of view, a religious and a national. Christ would have insisted that participation in temple worship had no religious value. However, it would have amounted to a nullification of the law if he had forbidden the priests to take any part in temple worship. As soon as we clarify our thinking about this, nothing is left to which an organization among the followers of Christ could have been attached. All that was left was the institution of the synagogue. At a later time the Christian congregations attached themselves to this, and therefore, if Christ had wished to make such a change, this would have been the only one open to him. That was the only means by which Christianity could obtain an organization and at the same time spread among the Jewish people. Any special organization that had a different form would have come into conflict with the synagogue, and such a conflict would have been a barrier to the spread of Christianity among the people. If Christianity had spread further (there were already followers of Christ among the priests and also among the scribes, for example, Nicodemus and others), it would have come about automatically that the actual temple school in part would have become Christian in terms of its actual spirit, and then Christianity would have found a footing in it for its further expansion. The actual spirit of this community would have consisted of regarding all ritual, legal precepts, ceremonies, as a purely national matter and of grounding the religious element on the foundation provided by the person of Christ. That is to say, Christianity would have been organized by Christ in the same way that it was later organized, and Christ could never have combined anything else than this with the messianic idea, insofar as it expresses a lordship. This whole new religious life, free from externalities, grounded on direct fellowship with God, and equipped with the power that Christ himself imparts, would have constituted his spiritual lordship. This is the sort of Christian church that Christ himself, by his own activity, might have been able to organize. His own person would have had to remain the focal point and the soul of such a community.

So then, if the catastrophe that was to befall him had not been indicated as it is, the same thing would have come about in this way as the direct result of Christ's work as later happened as a result of the work of the apostles, but it would then have happened without any conflict with the authorities. The Jewish hierarchy would not have perished as a result. There would have been no reason for concern about Christ's work on the part of the Sanhedrin, for it would have rested on the temple worship and the law. To be sure, however, the Jewish hierarchy would have ceased to be a religious group. The priesthood would no longer have been the mediator between the believing section of the people and God, but only an organization authorized by the law to carry out religious practices, and these would have become something quite detached — not ended, but altered in their actual significance. However, it is not easy to maintain that Christ's opponents thought of such possible developments and feared only them. On the contrary, they could not avoid the conclusion that anyone who wanted to present himself as the Messiah would have to be aiming at a lordship in the messianic sense, and that, even if some arrangement could be made with the Romans, which would not be easy, a radical change would be effected in them and in their constitution, since the people were to be free of this burden. Christ wished an end to be put to the law by events that he foresaw, but he did not wish to bring it about himself. So the bad relations arose that gave rise to the enmity against him.

Lecture 54 (August 6) We now return to a consideration of Christ's public ministry in order to see how the catastrophe of his fate came about and how the opposition gradually increased from the very beginning of his activity as a teacher.

Those who take their departure from the dogmatic significance of Christ's death easily reach the conclusion that, because his death was necessary for the achievement of the goal of his mission, he himself must somehow also have aimed at his death. I have never been happy with this idea. It contains a secret docetism, for it sets up a rule that no one can wish to apply to another. For example, we may grant that martyrdom was necessary for the growth of the church, but this does not justify setting up the proposition that therefore Christians ought to aim at martyrdom. In that case the result is a moral docetism, which would put an end to any idea of Christ's life as a pattern to be emulated. I should therefore never maintain the proposition that, if Christ's death would not have come about without some action on his part, he would surely have done something to bring it about.

If we therefore here maintain a historical point of view and ask: How did it happen that Christ's fate developed in this way? We find that our sources are unsatisfactory to the extent that they give us too much and too little. What we discover in the first three Gospels is too little because, if we did not have the fourth, no one could achieve an understanding of the actual state of affairs. On the other hand, they give us too much, because what they tell us cannot be fitted into the texture of John's Gospel, because too little is known of the chronology of the Gospels. In addition, the three Synoptics know only of *one* stay by Christ in Jerusalem, and we have no complete and satisfactory solution of the problem of why they do so. In the second place, since they are not arranged chronologically we are not certain that the later sections refer to events that happened at a later time, for they are arranged according to another principle. Consequently we must follow the account that John gives us.

The first three Gospels, in particular the Gospel of Matthew, often refer to conspiracies and plots against Christ that were directed at his life and that originated in Galilee. In John's Gospel, on the other hand, we are told more as an instance that Christ, in order to avoid enmity in Judea, went to Galilee. This represents a point of view opposed to that in the Synoptics. It is undeniable that there is a tendency in the Gospel of John to show the form taken by Christ's relationship to the nation and to those who exercised authority in the nation and over the nation. It is impossible to overlook this pragmatism.

The account according to the Gospel of John. It is uncertain to what extent there is an indication in John's Gospel of a public teaching activity by Christ before his baptism by John the Baptist. Those who first believed in him also applied the idea of the Messiah to him, and that happens in part in such a way that we have to believe that they also had an idea of a political forerunner of the Messiah at that time. John 1:37 ff. tells us how the first disciples became acquainted with Christ. Andrew says to Simon, "We have found the Messiah." Philip says to Nathanael, "We have found him of whom Moses in the law and also the prophets wrote, Jesus of Nazareth, the son of Joseph!" And Nathanael is represented as confessing, after he had overcome his doubts, "Rabbi, you are the Son of God! You are the King of Israel!" This was only Nathanael's way of agreeing with what Philip said. Consequently we have to believe that among Christ's disciples from the beginning there were those who had political ideas of the Messiah's kingdom, and such folk would only give up those ideas gradually under Christ's own influence. Christ's answer is given in v. 50, "You believe," etc., is not a direct rebuttal. He goes on the say, "You will see heaven opened, and the angels of God ascending and descending upon the Son of man." In other words, Nathanael would get to view the constant relationship between God and Christ; the angels of God can indicate who Jesus is, etc. (v. 51). This is compatible with a political view of the kingdom, but the answer contains a tendency in the direction of a spiritual understanding of it, since the spiritual is always indicated by "heaven", etc.

According to John 2, Christ, having been invited to a family festival, left Judea and performed the miracle at Cana. In this connection John makes no suggestion that faith in Christ was spread by this marvel. He only says that Christ's disciples were strengthened in their faith by it. Then Christ goes to Capernaum, and after that to Jerusalem for the Feast of the Passover. Then follows the driving out of the merchants from the temple, an account similar to the one that the three synoptic Evangelists narrate as having happened during the course of Christ's last stay in Jerusalem. I refer you at this point to my book on Luke. [pp. 244 ff.] This is not to be regarded as a failure of memory. It is highly probable that a purification of the temple took place often. Selling and buying in the temple grounds was a malpractice that anyone had a right to prevent. Trade in objects that were used in temple worship often took place in the temple and, since the temple police did not put a stop to it, anyone had the right to clear that area of the temple in which he wanted to carry on teaching activity.* Christ can often have found it necessary to do this, since the situation recurred. Did Christ wish by this act to inform people that he wanted to be regarded as the Messiah? I do not believe that that was the case, since it was the right of anyone who had business that belonged in the temple to pre-empt the space it needed. To be sure, in John the act seems to be represented as a messianic one. In John 2:18 the Jews ask Christ, "What sign have you to show us for doing this?" However, that question amounts only to this: By virtue of what function are you doing this? The only messianic element connected with the incident is Christ's remark, "You shall not

---

* Teaching was carried on in the temple porticos. Consequently the listeners could join in driving out the merchants. Since this had only temporary results, Christ can often, etc.

make my Father's house a house of trade!" But the Jews made no objection to this, as they did later to Christ's use of the word "Father". Christ can only have cleared the temple of merchants by virtue of his office as a public teacher.

John now tells us that at this Passover season many believed because of the signs that they had seen, but Christ established no closer relationship with those who became believers. The reason for that seems to have been that those believers entertained political hopes (John 2:23 ff.). Then we are told of Christ's relationship to one of the most distinguished men in the Jewish nation, an outstanding scribe and a member of the Sanhedrin. When this man came to Christ he refers to the signs that Christ had done, and he says that these signs had convinced him that Christ was a teacher come from God. There is no indication in this that Nicodemus thought of Christ as the Messiah. The saying implies, rather, that he thought of him as a prophet. Christ's conversation with Nicodemus contains definite traces only of the spiritual nature of his calling and of the kingdom of God as the actual area of his influence. Christ suggests his messianic office only indirectly, for the phrase "God's only Son" in John 3:16 could not have been understood otherwise. In connection with this conversation ideas of the outcome of Christ's mission appear. Christ sees that men have a greater affinity for darkness than for light: "And this is the judgment, that the light has come into the world, and men loved darkness rather than light..."

Christ now stays in Judea, but he leaves Jerusalem for the country. Then we are told that the disciples of John were jealous because Christ allowed his disciples to baptize. John the Baptist did not let the fact disturb him, but says that Christ must increase, while he himself would have to decrease. If we reflect on what John said at the time of Christ's baptism, we are surprised that, when John gives his disciples this answer, he does not point in such a direct way to Christ, although he had told some that Christ himself was the object of his preaching, to the extent that it contained a promise of the Messiah. Many have tried to explain this by saying that John himself vacillated in his faith that Jesus was the Messiah. I know of no evidence to support this hypothesis. On the contrary,

John's conviction was of the sort that he ascribed its origin to divine inspiration. Athough he had asked for a sign, that had later been given him and appeared to him as a heavenly confirmation. Most of John's disciples retained the Pharisaic doctrine, as we can see from other passages where they are expressly set over against Christ's disciples. So John could have known that he would not be able to persuade the greater part of his pupils to accept Christ, because he differed from their notion of whom the Messiah would be.

John 4 now tells us that Christ, when he knew that the Pharisees had heard that he and his disciples were making more converts than John, withdrew to Galilee. To get there he took the road through Samaria, although the usual route was through Perea. That was not unintentional. He did it to show that he paid no attention to specific circumstances, indeed, that nothing compelled him to choose this way rather than that through Perea. Then follows the conversation with the Samaritan woman in which he refers to himself clearly as the Messiah.* Then Christ speaks to his disciples. In this conversation there occurs the remarkable passage concerning the harvest (v.34-38), and many have tried to find evidence in this of another secret school that Christ had. However, Christ does not say that he had sent out those who had produced the harvest his disciples now were to gather in. On the contrary, he refers only to the general historical preparation which would make it easier to respond to the summons to enter the kingdom of God.

After a brief stay in Samaria Christ goes on to Galilee. According to chapter 5:1, Christ then went to Jerusalem to attend a festival of the Jews. At that point John gives the first example of Christ's teaching on the Sabbath and describes how it created a sensation when the man who had been healed took up his bed and went home, since the carrying of a bed was regarded as a breech of the sabbath law. Christ does not avoid the man whom he had healed. This man, we are told in v. 12, had been asked who it was who had healed him, and Christ goes to him early and seeks him out. According to

---

* or add: wherein he emphasizes the spirituality of the messianic idea

v. 16, the Jews followed him and "sought to kill him" [*textus receptus*]. The clause I have quoted is of doubtful authority. Only the words that directly follow refer to it.* So then, that must have been the first actual vigorous disturbance directed against him, but it was not of a sort that it could be translated into deed, for immediately thereafter Christ entered into a discussion with his opponents, continuing to speak to them of himself and God in this way, as well as of similar matters. He clearly speaks his mind on these things without any concern lest those who wanted a worldly kingdom would object to what he was saying and would demand that he act in such a way, or that their enmity would turn directly into action against him. *However, the germ of the persecution, from which later all further opposition developed, is presented by this account.*

Lecture 55 (August 7) We have seen how a violent opposition to Christ first arose because of the way he treated the sabbath law. He did not repudiate the law, but explained his action with respect to it in detail. His discourse exhibits the character of great authority, of which Christ must already have been conscious, for individual sayings incorporated in that discourse clearly reveal the consciousness of his higher dignity. The disturbance was the reason for Christ's decision as John 7:1 reports it. To be sure, between chapter 5 and chapter 7 there is the whole story of the miraculous feeding of the multitude. However, if we examine the discourse in chapter 5, we must conclude from it that John the Baptist even as early as that time was no longer teaching publicly and was already in prison. So this traveling about in Galilee is that of which Matthew 4:12 speaks when the passage declares that Christ, once he had heard of John's imprisonment, went to Galilee.

* or add: These closing words ("and they sought to kill him") have an uncertain authority. Nevertheless, reference is made to them. Because Christ referred to God as his Father, we are told in v. 18 that the Jews sought all the more to kill him. This is the first report of such a disturbance, caused by the fact that Christ calls God his Father in a special way and neglects the tradition, that is to say, was not the Messiah in the sense that the tradition spoke of him.

What the other Gospels have to tell us about Galilee must be understood as having taken place at this time and must be placed in part before and in part after John's story of the miraculous feeding of the multitude. We need not look for anything distinct and specific in the other Gospels, for they are not chronologically arranged. We can only recover from them a general description of Christ's acts, which can be regarded as a general result without attaching it to individual events, and then such individual events themselves. This general description makes it clear that a great number of people from this area followed Christ, (or: demanded to see Christ) constrained to do so by Christ's miraculous works, in part because of a desire for help, and in part by reason of natural curiosity. There are individual events, for example, Christ's journey to Perea, in connection with which we do not know whether Christ intended to make a lengthy stay, but, because he was rejected by the Gadarenes, returned to the other side, or whether the journey was undertaken without any definite purpose in mind. After this return from Perea we are told that a gathering of several Pharisees and teachers of the law took place on Christ's account in the house where he was. This group represented an opposition, although a very mild one. Whether we are to suppose that these had been sent to observe him, especially those who were from Jerusalem, is obscure. These were originally isolated narratives, and the connection in which they now stand is so imprecise that we cannot form a clear picture of it. Then there is a comparison of Christ's disciples with those of John the Baptist, where we have to entertain the possibility* of presupposing an intention of directing the favor of the people more to the pupils of John, because they were stricter in the observation of the tradition. Related to this are several sayings of Christ, for example, the parable of the new patches for old garments and that of the new wine in old wineskins, which show that this outer being is wholly incompatible with the inner and outer condition that Christ wanted to bring about. The embassy that John sent to Christ

* or add: refrain from entertaining. Another possibility: probably with the intention of directing the favor of the people to them, because they observed the tradition strictly

from prison seems also to fall into this period of residence in Galilee, as well as Christ's statements concerning John. At this time Christ says that both forms, John's the stricter and his own the freer, had to exist side by side in order that, existing together, they might proclaim the kingdom of heaven. However, he describes the people as following neither one nor the other and as behaving in this way as the result of an uncertain state of mind. This is implied in the parable of the children playing in the market place. This parable shows us that Christ was aware that he could expect no great result from his relationship to the people.

There are other examples in the three synoptic Gospels of people spying on Christ with reference to sabbath laws, ritual washings, and similar matters of external regulations of the law. A particularly notable passage is that in Matthew 12:14, which indicates that even in Galilee plots were made against Christ. Probably Mark 3:6 is a similar passage. There a plot of Pharisees and Herodians against Christ is mentioned. This indicates an element of opposition to Christ of which there is no trace in John. We cannot conceive of any occasion in that Gospel which would have caused Herod and his party to oppose Christ. Clearly the Herodians always hoped to obtain greater power and freedom from the Romans, and it was the politics of Herod's party to throw its support to one or the other side in every dispute between the Jewish people and the Roman authorities in order to further its own ends. However, it is not clear what could have caused the Herodians to take part in a plot against Christ. The only conceivable reason would be that John the Baptist had been imprisoned by Herod because he had condemned his illegal marriage with the seduced wife of his brother. Christ expresses himself strongly regarding marriage, divorce, and marriage with divorced women, and could have included Herod in his condemnation. We also find that Herod identifies Jesus with the Baptist after the latter's execution by saying that Christ may be John the Baptist risen from the dead. The reader must be struck by the fact that this is a peculiar idea of the migration of souls that is found nowhere else, and by the further fact that John the Baptist had performed no miracle. However that may be, the connection that Herod makes between John and Jesus may account for the opposition of the Herodians to Christ. We can hardly think of this alliance of the Herodians with the Pharisees against Christ as anything but an *ad hoc* one, which proved something temporary. As soon as the excitement that John had aroused abated and Christ went to another district the alliance came to an end.

The Evangelist John stresses the incident of the feeding of the multitude as the main event of Christ's stay in Galilee. From John's Gospel we learn that after this miracle the people made the attempt to declare Christ king, to put him at the head of the state, and to engage in a political venture with him. What could possibly have caused the people to do that on that occasion? It was hardly the miracle itself that gave an impetus to it. If we keep in mind what happened, the crowd of people, Christ teaching and healing, and the actual miracle taking place during the gathering dusk ["when it was evening"], we realize that only very few could have known of any miracle involved. Certainly most of the crowd would have been unaware of where the disciples' supplies came from or of how much they distributed. The connection between the miracle and the abundance of food would have been known only to Christ and his disciples.* So the action of the people must have had some other motive. The feeding of the multitude was a kind of fellowship. The people could have regarded it as Christ's attempt to mold them into a special community. They could have thought of the event as a table-fellowship with him. They may have believed that he wanted to establish a closer connection with them and that the meal was to be a *captatio benevolentiae.* According to Josephus the Galileans were eager to rebel. That there were many in Galilee whose messianic expectations were political is well known, and such messianic hopes could easily have been aroused on that occasion.

Now Christ leaves the shore of the Lake of Galilee and goes into the mountains, where he would be difficult to locate.

---

* If we do not think of a miraculous act as involved, that cannot have furnished the motive, and the connection, etc.

However, during the night he meets his disciples on the lake, near the shore, where he had sent them on ahead of him. Later, on the next day, Christ is again with the greater part of the crowd, who ask him, "Rabbi, when did you come here?" They were puzzled by the fact that he had come to that side of the lake. After that Christ speaks in the synagogue at Capernaum. This day could not have been a sabbath, and on such a day no assemblies took place in the synagogue and there was no actual sabbath discourse. If the day had been a sabbath, the people would not have gathered the evening before and would not have made a voyage across the lake. Consequently the synagogue was just the ordinary place of meeting, and the time no doubt was that of the morning prayer, when a larger part of the people who had been together on the previous day gathered once more.

Then we are told that many who had been his disciples "drew back and no longer went about with him." In this discourse Christ makes the mysterious references to the eating of his flesh and the drinking of his blood — references that many did not understand, but they are related to the demand that he should perform a sign, such as Moses had done with the manna. This demand suggests that the people had not come back because of the impetus that had governed their actions on the preceding evening. They had [not yet] the assurance that he would care, by means of miracles, for their physical existence.* Christ says only that he is the actual manna, but not Moses, and this is a spiritual interpretation of his function. It is a deprecation of all political ambitions. Although they did not understand what he actually meant by this saying, they did understand the actual deprecation, and that was the real reason why many left him. Christ did not wish to win them in this way. He was not the Messiah for whom they had hoped. I cannot avoid the conclusion that this whole event is the fullest demonstration of the fact that there was no time when Christ had any political intention or ambition. The whole way

---

* In their impetus to take a political step they still wanted an assurance from him before venturing on it with him. By describing himself as the true manna, but not as a Moses, Christ turns their thoughts in another direction. [From Rütenik?]

he conceives and rejects this idea shows that he did not just want to postpone the attempt to establish political hegemony until a more favorable time   that he regarded the conditions then as unfavorable —or that he had wanted to achieve political power to begin with but had given up the idea.[44] This was the first point at which he could have made his thought on the matter clear, although only indirectly, but there is not the slightest trace that he did so.

There is a great deal more material in the Galilean narratives of the other Gospels that belongs to this period, but we cannot tell with any certainty whether it should be placed before or after the incident that John stresses. Particularly noteworthy is the story of the driving out of an evil spirit, which is described as deaf and dumb. On one side there are the crowds of people, and on the other side Pharisees (according to Mark 3, from Jerusalem) who accuse Christ of driving out the devil with the help of Beelzebub. The people, on the other hand, demand a sign. According to Luke 11:16, the sign they sought was to be from heaven, in other words, a heavenly voice and witness. Christ rejects the demand out of hand and defends himself against the accusation of the Pharisees. In this connection we are told that members of his family tried to remove him from public life and action, and this brings us back to the passage in John where we are told that Christ's brothers demanded that he should go to Jerusalem to the festival and thus tried to get him away from the vicinity of their residence. This demand does not seem to have been due to any special concern for his person, but to the feeling that they did not want to suffer with him in the disturbances that gathered about him and wanted to send him back to a district in which he could have rest and quiet, or in any case get rid of him. This means that they must have believed that an explosion could easily take place against him and that they wished to avoid it in order not to become involved in it.

Then we are also told that scribes and Pharisees from Jerusalem asked him why he transgressed the tradition of the elders, and he replied that it was because they disregarded the

44. This is probably another allusion to the theory of Hermann Reimarus. See above, n. 32, p. 256.

essential elements of the law in the Scriptures in order to obey its externalities. This shows that Christ not only opposed them, but also warned the people against them, and that he described their whole method of interpreting Scripture as something his Father had not planted and that must be rooted out. Consequently Christ appears here in a very positive manner. In the same section of Matthew we are told that the Pharisees and Sadducees joined in a conspiracy against Christ and that he warned his disciples against the leaven of the Pharisees (Matt. 16; in Mark 8 the warning is against the leaven of the Pharisees and the leaven of Herod). What Matthew tells us is improbable, since there was no reason why the Pharisees and Sadducees should have joined forces against Christ, for Pharisaism accepted the authority of the tradition, while the Sadducees rejected it. Furthermore, since Galilee was a long way from Jerusalem, there could have been few Sadducees in that area. Nothing can be deduced from Matthew's remarks. Events are represented so generally in this section of his Gospel that we cannot conclude that this particular reference has to do with any historical incident.

In chapter 7 John tells us that Christ intentionally remained longer at this time in Galilee because the Jews in Judea wished to kill him. At the same time opposition to him had arisen in Galilee also, and this appears to have been instigated from Jerusalem. This could not have prevented Christ from going to Jerusalem, for such a visit to the capital city was a statutory obligation. No circumstances of life could excuse neglecting it. He had to attend the festivals in Jerusalem, but this obligation did not extend to all festivals. So he did not go to the Feast of the Passover, as did the crowd that he had fed, but later, to the Feast of the Tabernacles. His brothers had demanded that he do so.

Lecture 56 (August 8). From the point at which, according to John, Christ goes to Jerusalem to the Feast of Tabernacles, there is such a discrepancy between the Gospel of John and the other three that we cannot insert anything from the latter into the former with any certainty. According to John, Christ later did not return to Galilee, and according to the other three Gospels it appears that he came to Jerusalem for the Feast of the Passover. The two accounts cannot be harmonized, and there is great uncertainty whether everything that the Synoptics tell us of the Passover period belongs to this time or to a previous visit of Christ to Jerusalem, for they make no mention of any previous visit. John tells us that the Jews were expecting Christ at the Feast of Tabernacles and commented on the fact that he was not there. As a result a dispute concerning him arose among various parts of the crowd. Some praised him and others blamed him. In John 7:12 the Evangelist speaks of a tumultuous disturbance. The incident indicates a division of opinion that must have arisen because of something that had happened previously. The judgment of one group was due to the influence of Christ and his disciples on the people, while the other presupposes that the Pharisees, the party that was opposed to Christ, had stirred up sections of the people. Now we are told that Christ came to Jerusalem "about the middle of the feast" and appeared and taught in the temple. It is strange that we are told that the Jews marveled that he understood Scripture so well, since he was not the product of a school. It is difficult to determine whom John meant by the word "Jews". Is there a connection between the "people" of v. 12 and the "Jews" of v. 15 who marveled? Are these Jews identical with the people, or are they others? If they are others, then the people are strangers who visited the festival and the Jews are residents of Jerusalem. In this case the latter included many who became aware of Christ then for the first time. To be sure, however, it is true that, if the passage refers to the larger part of the Jews in Jerusalem, it seems as if John intends "Jews" to mean mostly those who belong to the leading class. So this passage indicates an attention to Christ's teaching that had not previously been awakened but that was connected with the opposition to him that had developed.

After this reference to the amazement of the Jews we are told of sayings of Christ in which he mentions an intention to kill him, and the people reply that the idea that anyone was seeking to kill him was a nonsensical one. This shows that the intention of some to take his life was known to Christ but was still kept secret, for in v. 25 we read that "some of the people of Jerusalem therefore said, 'Is not this the man whom they seek to kill?'" In this passage the people who did not know of the plot were mostly strangers, but not those who had declared themselves for Christ. All this shows that there was a state of disturbance that took many different forms and which indicated that an explosion might be in the offing. John tells us in this chapter that at an earlier point in the course of the feast the chief priests and the Pharisees, that is to say, the Sanhedrin, had sent agents to seize Christ but that these had not done so, but on their return had said that they had never heard anyone speak as this man had spoken. This response shows that their mission had not been an official one, for otherwise what they said would not have been an excuse for not performing it and they would not have been told, "Are you led astray, you also?" Rather, their mission was only one that a few members of the Sanhedrin had given their underlings. It was not actually an official mission, but only a private one, something to some extent hypothetical. At this time Nicodemus is mentioned again, who protests against such a procedure as had been intended. This incident is contradicted by the passage itself and by the fact that in v. 48 the Pharisees had said that no members of the council had believed in him, and none of the Pharisaic party. This shows that Christ's opponents were designated as authorities and Pharisees.

In chapter 8:1 ff. John describes at great length the way Christ behaved as long as he was at the feast. We are told that during the evenings he went to the Mount of Olives and that during the mornings he was again in the temple and that people thronged to him there and that he sat down and taught them [textus receptus]. That indicates a circle of acquaintance that Christ had in the city and its environs. During the time of festivals Jerusalem was overcrowded, and not all who streamed to it from all the districts of Palestine could find lodging there. Many actually had to live outside the city.*

* The "earlier notebook" (see reference above) treats the story of the adulterous woman (John 8:3-11) at this point, but the discussion was omitted in the lecture delivered in 1832.

John now reports a saying in which Christ calls himself the light of the world, which makes a great claim and which the Pharisees oppose by saying that he had no testimony except his own to demonstrate it. After that John also reports sayings from the period in which Christ speaks of the fact that he will soon not be with them, but does so only obscurely: "I go away, and you will seek me and die in your sin; where I am going, you cannot come." If we examine this in its context, we see that the chapter includes specific sayings, such as "I am from above; you are of this world," which point out the contrast between Christ's purpose and goal and the hopes and expectations that were widespread among the people.[45]Questions such as that in v. 25 follow: "Who are you?" Christ evades them by declaring that he had been sent by another, and John expressly says that the people did not understand that he spoke to them of the Father. Christ had often referred to God as his Father and had aroused opposition by the claim, but on this occasion he speaks similarly, and yet his listeners do not understand what he means.* Then Christ continues after the same fashion, but now calls himself "the Son of man" and goes on again to use the expressions "the Father taught me — He who sent me — the Father has not left me alone, for I, etc." Thereupon John says that after this discourse many believed in him. Now another discussion develops, which takes a violent turn (vv. 31-58). In this discussion Christ had to do only with people from the crowd. He appeals to Abraham and speaks of his interlocutors as being "of your father the devil." This indicates a movement against Christ among the people which was quite independent of all provocation on the part of others. In this instance Christ himself provided the provocation by attacking the prejudices on which the people based their privileges.† The discussion ends with an attempt to stone Christ.

45. This is an illustration of the manner in which Schleiermacher draws upon his own theological position to interpret the Johannine text. The words of Jesus quoted here indicate a preexistence in heaven, but Schleiermacher deploys them according to the dominance of Jesus' God-consciousness over the sentient self-consciousness and, thereby, in terms of his goal of a spiritual kingdom rather than a particularistic national theocracy.
* took no notice of it (the "did not understand" of v. 27)
† or add: and against the saying that the sons of Abraham had no need of repentance.

Immediately after this John speaks in chapter 9 of *the incident of the man born blind,* an account that belongs to Christ's same stay in Jerusalem. Here again the leaders of the people take part in the affair, inform themselves of the person Christ had healed, and ask him what he thought of Christ. In the course of the narrative the Evangelist John says that there had already been an agreement that anyone who should confess Jesus to be Christ was to be put out of the synagogue. *This, then, is the first official decision against Christ.* Measures with respect to it must already have been taken and it must have been previously known. So the man who is questioned and his parents give an evasive answer in order not to become "people put out of the synagogue." Later, however, the man who had been healed is not able to contain himself and says that he was greatly surprised that they did not want to recognize Jesus as something [higher]. John 9:34 recalls the threat to excommunicate anyone who confessed that Jesus was the Christ referred to in v. 22, and then we are told that the Sanhedrin excluded the man who had been healed from the synagogue fellowship (they cast him out). That was the first public step taken against Christ. However, there is no indication that Christ was intimidated by that action, or that he did anything because of it, such as change his place of residence, nor do we find that any change in general attitude toward Christ took place at that time. It is difficult to determine whether we should conclude from this that decisions of that sort were relatively powerless and unenforced, or that the story indicates that many could express themselves in support of Christ without claiming that he was the Messiah. In Jerusalem, due to the influence of the Sanhedrin, to which probably all rulers of the synagogues belonged, there was such a close connection with the synagogues that the Sanhedrin could ordain that anyone in general could become "a person put out of the synagogue," but only to the extent that the individual ruler of the synagogue saw fit to enforce the rule. The synagogues were completely free associations, over which the Sanhedrin could exercise no actual authority.

John goes on to tell us in chapter 10:40 that Christ, after the disturbance increased and attempts were made to seize his person, went to Perea, to the area in which John had at first baptized, and that there again many believed in him. Then, beginning with John 11:1, there follows the story of the raising of Lazarus, which seems of great significance for the development of Christ's fate. John tells us that several of those who had come from Jerusalem to Bethany to see what would happen and who had become witnesses of Lazarus's resurrection now went to Jerusalem to the Pharisees and told them what Jesus had done. The chief priests and the Pharisees then assembled the council, and a certain Caiaphas, who was high priest that year, said that it was expedient for them that one man should die for the people, and that the whole nation should not perish. The concern of the council had been previously expressed in the words, "If we let him go on thus, every one will believe in him, and the Romans will come and destroy both our holy place and our nation." The question arises: What was the basis of this concern that led to such a decision, which could hardly have had any outcome other than the one that later took place, unless Christ had decided to withdraw completely? The way it is described here in brief but pregnant form shows that the Sanhedrin had no fear that Christ himself wanted to be a political Messiah, but the council's declaration that all will believe in him, and the Romans will come, lacks the middle term, for if all believed as Christ wanted them to, the Romans could not have intervened. We must assume that they meant: All will demand that Christ reveal himself as the Messiah in terms of the political ideas they had held. In that case there would be an uproar and the Romans would take advantage of the opportunity to suspend the constitution and put an end to the very existence of the nation. So the decision was reached to try to get rid of Christ.

From then on Christ no longer showed himself openly, but went into a district near the desert. We must assume that Christ had learned of the council's decision. He must have been told of it, for *Nicodemus* and *Joseph of Arimathea* were his friends, and he must have been informed of what had happened in the council. Once more he avoids death and leaves Jerusalem, but this step was taken so long after the Feast of

Tabernacles that it can have had no connection with it. The passage does not say that Christ had come to Jerusalem itself. On the contrary, he seems to have remained in Bethany and have learned in Bethany of the council's decision and then have left that village. We cannot clearly determine how much time intervened, but obviously the resurrection of Lazarus occurred after the Feast of the Dedication of the Temple and therefore at some time between the end of our year and Easter. In the meantime Christ went to the district that is called Ephraim, but the location of that village remains unknown.

In John 11:55-57 we are told that the Feast of the Passover was near and that people were looking for Jesus and wondering whether he would come to Jerusalem for it. We are told that before the time Christ could be expected orders had been issued by the Pharisees that if anyone knew where Christ was, he should let them know. This indicates that Christ was expected some time before the beginning of the feast in order that he might perform sacred customs and rites of purification, and that the intention was to arrest him *before* the feast. The purpose of this was to prevent him from appearing any more at the festival. This shows us how this decision was reached, and we must conclude from this that the idea that Christ's opponents held of his following was that it was very large and that there were some, particularly among those who came to Jerusalem to the feast, who could be expected to betray him. Christ does not seem to have had much of a following among the residents of Jerusalem itself. Such folk were more exposed to the counterinfluence of the Pharisaic party, and the greater consciousness of all that belongs to sacred worship in the capital city and the greater interest that people must have had there in maintaining the old order of worship were responsible for an attitude that was unfavorable to Christ. Without this presupposition the measures taken against Christ would have been in vain, for Christ's followers would have kept him hidden and would have disobeyed the orders to reveal his whereabouts. The authority of the Sanhedrin was very limited. There were only certain punishments that they could impose for disobedience to the regulations that governed the temple services. A Roman sanction was applicable to any special disturbance. So then, a threat on the part of the Sanhedrin was not effective for all who had accepted Christ with a firm conviction of his higher destiny.

Under circumstances such as these, then, Christ comes to the Feast of the Passover. However, he does not immediately enter the city. According to John, six days before the Passover he came to Bethany where Lazarus lived with his family, but with a distinct foreboding that he was approaching his death. The other Gospels also tell us the same thing when they speak of Christ's preparation for his last journey to Jerusalem, although they ignore the whole incident involving Lazarus and make no mention of how far the movement against Christ had developed and had been given expression. I believe I have already discussed the way I understand this complete silence on the part of the other Gospels about the incident of the raising of Lazarus. In the accounts of the other Gospels the story of Christ's last journey to Jerusalem is introduced in quite a different way. The synoptic Evangelists speak with a certain solemnity of Christ's departure from Galilee and show that they had no knowledge of this earlier stay of Christ's in Jerusalem. Nevertheless they mention Christ's presentiments of death, and this shows that this foreboding on Christ's part that he was approaching his death must have become known in a very overt way. In John's Gospel it is manifested clearly in the incident of the anointing at Bethany, where Christ speaks of his forthcoming burial. So the natural question arises: Since Jesus on other occasions avoided violent disturbances directed against him, why did he now go to the festival and not avoid the turmoil on this occasion?

Lecture 57 (August 9). The chief reason why Jesus, in order to preserve his life, did not this time evade traps set for him and avoid the festival lies in the fact that even in Galilee agitation against him had arisen and that Herod at that time had become aware of him. Consequently there was no reason for him to prefer being at one place rather than at another, and he went to Jerusalem despite the fact that he had learned of the general decision against him reached after the resurrection of Lazarus and of the public order against keeping him hidden. If the intimation is correct that the authorities did not wish to take action against him during the feast, the purpose of the order can only have been either to keep Jesus away from the festival or to arrest him before the festival began. The entrance to Jerusalem, which was not something planned, must be an incident that occurred twice, for otherwise the various accounts cannot be harmonized. Perhaps an entrance in a less public fashion took place daily, although in order to avoid public acclaim Jesus went intentionally very early to the city. He seems to have tried to avoid a decidedly favorable declaration on the part of the people. The feast seems already to have been underway, and something special must have happened to make Christ's opponents revive the old decision. So I believe that the questions they asked to ensnare him were not intended to give them cause to take immediate action, but were for the purpose of assembling evidence against him. Furthermore, I do not believe that Christ at this time delivered all the anti-Pharisaic discourses, in part purely offensive, that are credited to him, for he could not have wished to annoy his opponents. These discourses have their present context because of Matthew's incorporation of them at this point.

We have reached the point in our description of the relations of Christ to the national authorities when a decision in general had been made to get Christ out of the way and when a public order had been promulgated before the festival that anyone who knew where Christ was staying should reveal his knowledge. The purpose of this order was either to keep Christ away from the feast or, if he should come, to arrest him before festivities began. Christ comes despite this, and the order in and for itself had no results. We are told that Christ comes to Bethany, where he is joyously and festively welcomed by the family that had many contacts with Jerusalem and with persons who were associated with some who were members of the Sanhedrin. At this point we may ask: How did these relationships actually originate? What the Sanhedrin had ordered appears wholly to have been ignored, and this shows us that the Sanhedrin possessed no sure and firm authority. In external matters this was limited to a rather slight extent by the Roman procurator, who demanded that his permission he obtained before any great punishment could be inflicted. However, this limitation would have been suspended whenever the spiritual power of the Sanhedrin would have been really effective, whenever its orders would have been really obeyed. The Sanhedrin must not have been sure of its influence over the people. This accounts to some extent for the leniency with respect to the decisions made concerning Christ. If the Sanhedrin had been sure of its influence over the people, it would not have needed to issue such an order against an individual such as Christ. It could have let him continue with his work in the confidence that it could have suppressed any disturbance among the people by its authority. Since it did not possess this authority, it is easier to understand why it reached this decision. To be sure, this decision cannot be justified on moral grounds, but the lax politics of the day permitted exceptions to moral rules. We must consider the times, and we must excuse the measures taken, since the Sanhedrin had worries that it had no prospect of ending by the exercise of its authority.

Christ came to Bethany six days before the feast. No action was taken against him during this period, despite the fact that he went daily to the temple. This is apparent from the other accounts as well as from John's. This raises another question: Was there no one who could hope to profit from informing the Sanhedrin of Christ's whereabouts, or could the Sanhedrin have been ignorant of the fact that Christ was staying in Bethany? The Sanhedrin must have learned about that, for its members saw him every morning in the temple. There must have been some circumstance that protected Christ against the measure already taken against him. At this point we find the story of his entry into Jerusalem, reported by all the Gospels, although not quite in the same way. In each instance, however, we are told that his entry attracted considerable attention and that Christ himself was asked by the opposing party why he himself did not keep the demonstration within bounds. It appears that Christ's opponents were intimidated by what seemed to be a widespread support of Christ among the people. When we recall that they actually wanted to avoid anything that looked like a rebellion and that the order against Christ had been issued with this in mind, we conclude that they saw that a revolt could arise if they set hands on Christ and that they therefore had to be careful what they did. On the other hand, it is also possible that Christ and his friends had taken measures to protect themselves. In the evenings

Christ went to the Mount of Olives. To be sure, Bethany lay at the foot of the Mount of Olives, but reference to the Mount of Olives does not mean reference to Bethany.[46] It appears that Christ did not go to Bethany because he did not want to involve the family there in trouble or expose them to any unpleasantness. There were a number of small buildings on the Mount of Olives, erected for business purposes by persons in Bethany who had olive orchards on the Mount, and it is natural to assume that Christ spent the night in one or another of these buildings.* This made it difficult for anyone who wanted to denounce him to find out exactly where he was staying. Furthermore, the Sanhedrin was not inclined to take steps in an official way against Christ, for it knew that, because of the attitude of the people, such steps could have led to the revolt that it wished to avoid.

What was the nature of Christ's entry into Jerusalem? This raises still another question: Why on this occasion did Christ not avoid the trap laid for him, as he had at other times, by staying away from the feast? His entry was nothing else than the beginning of his attendance at the feast and the announcement of his presence. At this point we must refer to a few statements which, though they are not entirely clear, stand in our Gospels in such a way that we cannot overlook them. In the first place we are told that various attempts had already been made in Galilee by the Pharisees on Christ's life or freedom. In the second place mention is made of Herod's antipathy to Christ. (The cause and context of this is obscure.) I have tried to connect this antipathy with what Christ had said about divorce, which may have been directed against Herod. When we compare Josephus's reports of John the Baptist with those in our Gospels, we see that they do not agree. Josephus knows nothing of any denunciation of Herod's marriage by John the Baptist. According to Josephus, Herod

46. Schleiermacher's location of Bethany is inexact. Actually, Bethany lies on the east slope of the Mount of Olives with Jerusalem located to the west; cf. *The Interpreter's Dictionary of the Bible* (Nashville: Abingdon, 1962), 1:387-88; also, Gustaf Dalman, *Sacred Sites and Ways: Studies in the Topography of the Gospels,* trans. Paul Levertoff (London: SCM, 1935).

* or add: No doubt Gethsemane was one of these.

had John put to death because he was jealous of the spiritual authority John had over the people. If the stories in our Gospels are correct, they explain Herod's antipathy to Christ. If Josephus is correct, then Herod had just as much reason to be jealous of Christ's influence, especially after such a large assembly as that which took part in the feeding of the multitude. The fact of Herod's antipathy in either case is probable. If we put these two facts together, namely, that Christ was exposed to opposition in Galilee, and that Herod, whose influence would extend also to Perea, was also opposed to him, we see that Christ would not easily have been able to avoid opposition, and therefore extend the period of his mission, as he had been able to do when opposition to him existed only in Judea.

In this connection we do not have to assume that, if Christ's death had not been sought by the opposing party, he himself would have had to seek it. Furthermore, we cannot presuppose any reflection on his part about whether it was right to avoid the traps of his enemies any longer. He was now exposed to them, whether he was in Galilee, in Perea, or in Jerusalem. He could only have avoided such traps as he had done in the interval between the resurrection of Lazarus and the Feast of the Passover, when he went to the wilderness, but such an avoidance could only be temporary, for otherwise he would have had to discontinue his mission. If he had to assume that it made no difference to his safety whether he were in one place or another, it was natural that he should pay no attention to where he was. During the time of a festival the natural place for his work was in Jerusalem, and he had a duty to attend the festival. He therefore went to the city, but with the full consciousness that he would die there, and all our accounts make that clear.

Nowhere is this conviction so apparent and so clearly expressed as in John 12. After John's short narrative of Christ's entry, we are told that among the visitors to the festival were certain Greeks. These could only have been in the outer court of the temple, the Court of the Gentiles. They turned to Philip the apostle and asked to see Jesus. This leads to a discourse of Christ that is thoroughly permeated with the consciousness of his impending death. This is combined with a consciousness of a greater success of his work, but not with any idea that his death was necessary as an essential part of redemption in and for itself. This would have been as good an occasion as any other to include this element in his consciousness and to express it. The request of the Greeks suggested a wider circle of work, and the presence together of Jews and Greeks must have caused Christ to stress the generality of sin and the necessary universality of redemption, and also the necessity of his atoning death, if he had been aware of that.

Let us consider for a moment the demand that some Pharisees made that Christ should rebuke his disciples (either for the disturbance they were making or for calling him Messiah). In order to get a clear picture of the matter we have to consider another fact, namely, that it is impossible to harmonize the various accounts of the entry. We are driven to the conclusion that there were several entries, or rather, several occasions when Christ was accompanied on his way from Bethany to the city. When we look at the matter in this light the problem disappears. Christ's acclamation was not something he had specially to arrange, or anything he could prevent. Whenever he left Bethany or the Mount of Olives and came to the highway, where every morning large numbers of people were making their way to Jerusalem, it could not fail that many always joined him and that those who were his followers acclaimed him. That was something he could not possibly prevent. We see a tendency to avoid it when we are told that Christ went to the city very early in the morning, but this early departure did not achieve the end he had in mind. This is what Christ means when he says, according to Luke 19:40, that it was not in his power to prevent the acclaim. The incident shows that Christ had a large following among the masses, especially when we conclude that the purification of the temple was also an incident that took place more than once.[47] On

47. While Schleiermacher's *A Critical Essay on the Gospel of Luke,* trans. Connop Thirlwall (London, 1825), recognizes the principle of a plurality of sources from the very beginning and that these existed for a time as oral tradition, his opting for a multiple number of entries and cleansings of the temple indicate his lack of recognition for the independent development of the various traditions at this point in the lectures.

the one hand, this must have annoyed Christ's opponents. On the other hand, however, to the extent that they were not motivated by personal hatred, but only by the thought of the probable result of the development of the affair — there is no evidence that they were driven by motives of personal hatred — they must have acted all the more carefully, lest they bring about what they wanted to avoid. So Christ, without defying his opponents, could appear daily in the temple and could return quietly at night to one place or the other, without giving occasion for a denunciation or publicly embarrassing his friends with respect to the order, to which they were obligated to pay some attention.

The incident shows us that Christ did not wish to repel those who regarded him as Messiah or keep his messiahship a secret. However, it also shows that he admits that he wants to be regarded as Messiah but knows at the same time that he will find no recognition. At this point let us return again to what is often told us in the other three Gospels with reference to the miracles of Christ, namely, that he ordered his disciples to keep silent about them, and also not to say that he was the Messiah. The fact that Christ forbade his disciples to say that he was the Messiah cannot be regarded as an actual rule. He must have meant it to apply only to certain situations. He naturally knew that they would only come in contact with people who had only political ideas of the Messiah, and therefore this warning could have been a natural one. However, in the course of his teaching, especially his teaching in Jerusalem, we find that he always designates himself both directly and indirectly as Messiah.

When we reflect on what is told us in all the Gospels about Christ in Jerusalem during this period, we realize that we have no assurance that everything was said at that time. Since the first three Gospels make no mention of previous visits of Christ to Jerusalem, it is natural that they should put together everything that seemed in general to have the character and color of something said in Jerusalem or that it was claimed had been spoken there. If that were not the case, we should have to say that Christ himself in various ways annoyed his opponents, but that is not something that corresponds to his whole way of acting. We cannot think of him as delivering the mass of anti-Pharisaic discourses that is compressed into this period without intentionally wishing to anger his opponents. We have no data that would enable us to distribute these discourses in various other periods of residence in Jerusalem. When we reflect on the fact that in Matthew 19 we are told that Christ was asked by the Pharisees about divorce, we realize that this question was not put to him in Jerusalem but on the way to it actually while he was in Perea. We can scarcely avoid concluding that this was not a theoretical question, but one that was related to Herod, and that it was an insidious one. If he were to answer it one way, it might lead to a united front between the Pharisees and the Herodians against him. If he were to answer it in another way, the Pharisees could accuse him to the people of suiting his answer to the circumstances. The question had been prompted by the insidious desire of the Pharisees to incriminate him. However, in light of Christ's actions on other occasions we have no right to assume that he would have let this intention irritate him. A large part of the discourses that Matthew has preserved and that are said to have been delivered at this time is made up partly of anti-Pharisaic material and partly of references to the approach of the kingdom of God. When I reflect on such an anti-Pharisaic discourse as that in Matthew 23, where Christ says without occasion that the scribes and the Pharisees sit on Moses' seat, I cannot believe that this speech was delivered at this time without any occasion for it. On the other hand, everything that refers to a definite decision, the discourses on the kingdom of heaven, seem to me to be properly placed at this time. These discourses were clearly intended to draw attention to something that lay close at hand and to prepare those who followed him for the fact that the point of decision had arrived. The anti-Pharisaic discourses, however, would have been a polemic that would have angered his opponents and which would have been quite out of character. There was no reason for him to appear as one who betrayed an attitude of annoyance.*

* Editor [Rütenik]: I have been unable to clear up the obscurity of this passage.

Lecture 58 (August 10). The last discourses in John and the farewell rites of the Lord's Supper and foot-washing show that, despite this hesitation, Christ clung to the conviction that this festival would mark his end. A parenthetical discussion of how John presents the matter. It is always difficult to combine John's silence about the Lord's Supper and its general introduction into the church at an early date. We cannot maintain that Christ's confident expectation depended only on Judas's project. We also cannot know how it came about that the fact about Judas's individual steps became known. It is improbable that he had always been a thief with the knowledge of the others. Their opinion seems to have been that Judas's decision was determined definitively by Christ's saying at the supper in Bethany. Christ could still have prevented the betrayal by going elsewhere. However, he would still have been found on the road to the Mount of Olives or somewhere else in the neighborhood. The quiet and the inner strength that John describes are in sharp contrast to the prayer that has often been used to show Christ in a state of weakness that is not far from sin. No doubt he could have been concerned about the incompleteness of his disciples and could have wished for their sake to live longer, but not according to the discourses of John 16 or the prayer of John 17.

We can scarcely believe anything else than that the Sanhedrin was in a vacillating state with reference to Christ. To be sure, the decision had been made, but its actual purpose seemed likely to be hindered rather than furthered by its execution. So it seems that something special had to happen to put an end to this hesitation, and that is the actual historical significance of Judas's betrayal. If the Sanhedrin had simply gone its way without vacillation, it undoubtedly would have been able to arrest Christ in a normal way. The members of the Sanhedrin must have known that he was in the vicinity of Bethany, and they could have overpowered him as easily as they did with Judas's help. However, in the state of indecision in which they found themselves Judas's assistance seems to have given them the final impetus they required. If they had rejected Judas's offer when he made it, they would have compromised seriously, for Judas was only obeying the order to reveal where Christ was. This is not the place to make a judgment on Judas's act. As a matter of fact, it is very difficult to make such a judgment. Here we have to restrict ourselves to the fact that Judas only obeyed the order of the Sanhedrin.

It is obvious that for someone to do that who was a member of Christ's intimate circle was something quite different than it would have been for someone else. If we ask what led Judas to do what he did, what gave him the impulse to it, we conclude that it was what Christ said at the supper in Bethany. At that meal it was Judas, according to the Gospel of John, who protested against the anointment of Christ as an act of waste. The ointment could have been sold and the money given to the poor. John adds an explanation at this point. Judas had not said this because he cared for the poor but because he had been embezzling the funds of the group. He had wanted to do the same with the proceeds of the sale of the ointment. In his reply Christ spoke quite distinctly of his impending burial, and it looks as if it was this saying that decided Judas to make his offer to the Sanhedrin to betray Christ's whereabouts. It is uncertain whether the comment that John makes about Judas rests on earlier observations of the disciples or is a conclusion that the Evangelist draws. *It is certainly strange that they should have tolerated Judas as a member of the group* if he had actually been embezzling their funds. If we go on to ask whether Christ also knew what Judas had been doing and whether the disciples, aware of this, had done nothing against him, but had left the matter to Jesus, we find the question unanswerable. There is nothing we can say further on the matter.

We have now come to the end of Christ's influential activity and are at the point where the catastrophe is actually complete. Judas makes his offer to the chief priests; they accept it; in the evening they provide him with a guard and he leads it to the place where Christ was spending the night with his followers; Christ is arrested. There is only one further question. What do we learn from the narrative of the Last Supper, the meal which Judas left in order to bring the servants of the chief priests to the place that Christ was now about to leave? Jesus seems to have been aware of Judas's intentions and to have said something to him about it. "Truly, truly, I say to you, one of you will betray me." Peter beckoned to John and asked him to inquire who it was of whom Christ spoke, and in the course of the discussion Christ says to Judas, "What you are going to do, do quickly." The Evangelist now says that when Jesus gave Judas the morsel, Satan entered into him. Since John has already said that the devil had already put it into the heart of Judas to betray Christ, he must mean by this second reference that Judas was confirmed by Christ's sayings in his intention of carrying out what he had begun.

If I had assumed that Christ had not sought his death and that there was no reason to seek it, we should have to ask whether that does not amount to saying that Christ had looked for his death, or to admitting that he could still have avoided it without doing anything contrary to duty or unworthy of himself, and yet did not avoid it. He could have avoided it if he had remained in the city, or had gone to spend the night somewhere else than he originally had in mind. However, what purpose would that have served? The situation would have remained as it was, and the opposing party would have been made more determined than ever by its initial failure, and Christ would have had to abandon his own decision and have left Jerusalem, or the same thing would have happened on the following day. I do not mean to say that Christ reflected on the matter in this way. There is not the slightest indication that he did so. I only want to show that the idea never occurred to him. The certainty that he had expressed that his death would be brought about during the festival could not be imperilled by any possibility. He continued in his ordinary way of life, and this meant that he was determined to accept what could not be prevented.

The fact that Christ speaks of swords that were to be kept ready and the further fact that they were brought present difficulties. However, when Peter later made use of his sword at the time of Christ's arrest, Christ rebuked him for so doing. That seems to involve a contradiction. It seems to indicate that Christ to begin with had the idea of offering resistance but later reprimanded Peter for doing what he did. This is the only way I can explain the matter: There were two ways that the chief priests could have gone about the arrest, an official and an unofficial. If they had sent people who had no official office, that would have been an act of violence, a wholly illegal procedure. They could have used this method because of the uncertainty whether it would succeed or not. If the arrest were attempted illegally, they need not have been officially involved. If it failed and they were not officially concerned in the attempt, the failure would not have made them the object of derision. On the other hand, they could undertake the matter officially and send a squad of the temple police. In that case any resistance would have been resistance to legal authority. If the arrest had been planned unofficially, I see no reason whatever why Christ should have thought of himself as obliged to submit to illegal violence. In such a case he could have planned a resistance which he could not have used in the case of legal authority. It is unquestionably true that it was legal authority that was employed to overpower Christ's person. To be sure, the arresting group was a mixed one. In addition to the servants of the chief priests there may have been many ordinary folk in the arresting party. But the group contained some who were legally commissioned, and that meant that Christ gave up any thought of resistance. Furthermore, Christ could not have believed that his disciples would have resisted legal authority. This is the only way I can get a clear picture of what happened. We now proceed to a consideration of the passion story, which brings the public ministry of Christ to an end.

THIRD PERIOD

From the Arrest to the Ascension

THE PASSION STORY

There is still a further point about which I should like to say a few words. Earlier I limited myself to the two central points, the institution of *baptism* and *the apostolic circle,* and all else was related to those institutions. We are now accustomed to link *baptism* and *the Lord's Supper* as belonging together, as it were homogeneous acts, but the idea that justifies joining them, the idea of sacrament, is wholly arbitrary and never appears in the New Testament. Quite apart from that, there was no place to speak of this institution of Christ, for it does not belong to what Christ did to *found* the community. However, now that we find this institution at the close of Christ's public ministry and actually as its final act, I believe we have to ask the question: How much can we show of what Christ intended by this act, and what did he include in it?

First of all, it is clear that we cannot immediately conclude from Christ's own words as they are reported in the three Gospels that Christ instituted this as a permanent rite of the Christian church. The Last Supper was an affair only of a small number of his disciples, of the apostolic circle, and even if he commanded these to repeat the act, it does not follow that he intended the whole Christian church to observe it. It is just as possible that he thought of it as only for the apostles, as a commemorative festival to perpetuate the special relationship between him and them. However, when we reflect on how early this rite was transplanted into the Christian church, and when we cannot avoid finding the same rite related to the Last Supper, as Paul's first letter to the Corinthians shows, we have to admit that the disciples who took part in it at least understood it in that light. The actual words of Christ are unknown to us. We cannot maintain that we have them, for they appear differently in the different accounts. Therefore we have to agree that the disciples understood the rite correctly.

But now we run up against the fact that John, despite the great detail with which he treats Christ's last days, remains wholly silent about this institution. This is usually explained by saying that John only wanted to complement the other Gospels. Because the institution of the Lord's Supper was recounted in those, he could omit any reference to it. However, this hypothesis cannot be maintained. John narrates what the other Gospels do concerning the reference that Christ made at the supper to Judas's betrayal, and then he goes on in the same connection to tell how Christ washed his disciples' feet. Because of the former reference the meal that John describes seems to be the same as the one during which the other Gospels report the institution of the Lord's Supper. We are compelled to conclude that John, if he had had the other Gospels in front of him, would necessarily have had to make mention of the institution and could not have omitted all reference to it, as he does. Otherwise we should be confused by the fact that the other Gospels say nothing of Christ's washing of the feet of his apostles, something that John represents absolutely as a symbolic act of Christ's. This fuller account, together with the silence about the Lord's Supper, makes it difficult to believe that John had the synoptic Gospels before him. John would have had to mention the institution of the Lord's Supper as the common bond between the two. Let us look at the matter in this way: John's Gospel was the first. At the time John wrote his Gospel the constituent parts of the other Gospels were in existence only as separate narratives and were only assembled at a later time.

It seems that, since John makes no mention of the institution of the Lord's Supper, it must follow that he did not regard it as an institution of Christ's for the church. He regarded the foot-washing as more important than the Lord's Supper. He seems to have regarded the foot-washing as a rite that Christ's disciples were to repeat, but says nothing of the Lord's Supper because he did not think of it as a rite that was to be repeated. This means that the account in John's Gospel is in sharp contrast to the fact that the Lord's Supper was introduced as an institution into the early Christian church. If we were to protest that the meal reported by John was not the same as that referred to in the Synoptics, we should have to assume that Christ on two occasions, at two different meals, said that one of his disciples would betray him and indicated that Judas was the one in question. This would present us with a difficult problem to solve. In such circumstances the safest procedure is to hold fast to the facts and to admit that other matters are insoluble. If we assume that when John wrote his Gospel the Lord's Supper was already generally observed as a rite in the Christian church, John could have made no reference to it because it was a generally known fact, but he could hardly have done so without saying that the rite of the Lord's Supper had originated at the time of the Last Supper. We cannot account for this gap in his narrative.

We cannot discuss here the content that Christ wanted to include in the act, for that would involve us too deeply in exegetical matters. Leaving that difficulty aside, the agreement of our three other Gospels in their accounts of the institution of the Lord's Supper with what we later actually know from Paul's letter, that the Lord's Supper had been adopted as a rite by the Christian church, is evidence that the disciples had understood Christ's words as a command that the meal should be repeated. The act, then, was a symbolic institution that was in a special way to bind the participants together and all the participants with him and his unique life. This shows that at the time when he was certain of his impending death he had no doubt at all of the continuance of the community that had scarcely been founded by him but whose first foundations he had laid. This continuance for him was assured and firm.

Shortly before Christ's arrest, when he and his followers had already reached the place where he intended to spend the night, the other Evangelists tell us of a sudden depression and deep concern that came over Christ and that he admitted to his disciples. We are told that he sought guidance for meeting it in prayer and later regained his clarity and resolution. John says nothing about this, and his accounts of what immediately preceded it are in contradiction to it. John describes Christ as speaking with greatest clarity about his impending death. In a prayer that his disciples could overhear, he declared that he had fulfilled his mission and now went with peace and presence of mind to the place where the betrayer could find him. If we are to follow the synoptic account and think in terms of it, we must admit that Christ was under the power of dark ideas and confused feelings, which are difficult to ascribe to him, since they follow upon a clear-headed and firm state that was in accordance with the divine will. The historicity of the synoptic account has been especially stressed by those who do not want to admit any specific difference between Christ and other men, and relate the fact that Christ shared in human "weakness" to the moral field, since the difference between weakness and a sinful state of being cannot be maintained.

Lecture 59 (August 13). The accounts of this prayer are clearly not in their original form, as is apparent from the threefold repetition of the prayer. The reference to the angel is a special accretion. The accounts have an ascetic turn and their historical basis possibly is to be found in some earlier incident. Furthermore, the command to keep swords ready is in contrast to Christ's firm conviction. The command must have been issued with the thought in mind of a possible case of a tumultuous, extralegal attack. But even if Christ had endured such an attack, the situation would not have changed in any essential respect. *After the account of Christ's arrest* the narratives differ from each other. Only John refers to the role that Annas played before Caiaphas appears, but he does so with such circumstantiality that we cannot doubt the reference. The other Gospels mention the assembly before the high priest in such a way that it is easy to see that they have misunderstood the fact that Christ had stood twice before the high priest. This is why they also identify the scene of Peter's denial with that of the actual trial. How Annas came to be involved in this trial is not clear. Probably it was due to local conditions. Perhaps also to the fact that he did not want to go to the assembly at that hour of the day and yet wanted to examine Christ and give his opinion. John has nothing to say of the trial before Caiaphas, probably because he had not been an eyewitness. Nothing can be said about accusations whose content is not reported. The charge that he had wanted to destroy the temple was not a very effective one. Christ remains silent and wishes to indicate by his silence that he submits in advance to all consequences that could rightly follow,

395

and he had a perfect right to maintain such a silence. In any case, the question whether he was the Christ had to bring the trial to the point of decision.*

We cannot assume that Christ's attitude and his view of his situation that John describes must have changed when his death approached, or that a temporary weakness came over him as a sort of death fear. If we examine the story of Christ in the garden of Gethsemane, we see that it is clearly of such a character that we cannot regard it as original. We need only reflect on the threefold repetition of the prayer to convince ourselves that the story is not a literal account, for such a solemn number must awaken the suspicion that the narrative is directed at a specific purpose. So we cannot say what we have to regard as the true fact. It is clear that this example of Christ's prayer in his own personal interest as it is described, beginning with the expression of an urgent wish and closing with submission to the divine will, was a model for other people, and therefore is presented in such a way that it is clearly indicated that it is to be a model. This is shown by the threefold repetition of the prayer. To be sure, Christ could have desired to remain active in his work for a longer period. He could have wished to do more for his disciples: "I have yet many things to say to you, but you cannot bear them now." Consequently the expression of the wish was natural. It was also possible that the crisis could be resolved in some other way, for something could have happened to interfere with the plans of Christ's opponents. However, the reference to Christ's depression belongs to the form that the story was given in order to make it more useful as an example to others who could experience a similar state of mind.

When we go on to examine the account of how Judas appeared with those who accompanied him, we see that the event has the character of an official step. We ask: Who were they? There are two ways in which we can think of them. In the first place, the Sanhedrin could have requested a guard of Roman soldiers from Pilate. In the second place, Judas's companions could have been members of the temple police,

* At this point Schleiermacher's own manuscripts come to an end.

Levites, whom the Sanhedrin had sent against Christ. The word "band" suggests a group of Roman soldiers, who in most instances would be familiar with the Greek language. We do not know that the Levitical temple police were divided into bands. However, the meaning of the other word that is used, "servants," is obscure. It can refer either to the personal servants of the chief priests or to the temple police. It is improbable that a mixed group of Roman soldiers and Levitical temple police would have been used. The chief priests could only use the temple police for purposes directly related to their duties. If they had jurisdiction over Christ,* Pilate would not have spoken the sentence of death over him. So then, a Roman squad must have been necessary, even though the Sanhedrin later subjected Christ to a preliminary examination. In this case "servants" must refer to the personal servants of members of the Sanhedrin.† After they had shown that they had official authority, Christ would no longer think of offering any resistance that he might have been able to offer under other circumstances. He let himself be arrested.

Our Gospels differ very greatly in their accounts. According to John, Christ was brought first before Annas, who had formerly been high priest but who had been removed from office by the Romans. The actual high priest at the time was Caiaphas, Annas's son-in-law. Annas's demotion was an arbitrary interference by the Romans in Jewish affairs, but they had often removed high priests and installed others, though they always chose the new incumbent from among the class of priests, in order that he might be of priestly descent. The other Gospels know nothing of Christ's prior appearance before Annas. They tell only of two appearances before Caiaphas (Matt. 26:57 and 27:1 ff.), and in doing so omit

---

* if they were authorized to deal with Christ

† If they had wanted to bring Christ under their jurisdiction, they were probably able to do so. However, if they wanted to obtain a sentence of death from Pilate, they would have had to demonstrate a revolutionary tendency on Christ's part and would have taken a Roman guard, even though they themselves understood the preliminary investigation. In such a case the "servants" were their own personal servants. The matter cannot be decided either way. If they sent a squad of temple police, they had in mind sentencing Christ to death and only requesting confirmation of the sentence from Pilate. If they then represented governmental authority, Christ allowed himself to be arrested without resistance.

any reference to what John has to say of Jesus before Annas in 18:13-23. Matthew 27:1 ff. seems to refer to a second appearance, or at least to a second session of the trial. In the meantime Matthew asserts that the chief priests had examined witnesses against Christ, but without obtaining any results until Christ declared himself to be the Messiah, a claim that they regarded as worthy of death. When all members of the Sanhedrin called out, "He deserves death," they thereby passed sentence, and the reference in Matthew 27:1 to the fact that they took counsel must refer to something else, no doubt a consultation about bringing the matter before Pilate. However, an assembly was not necessary for that purpose. The account in Mark 14:53 is similar to that in Matthew. They led Jesus to the high priest and the Sanhedrin was assembled. Then witnesses were examined and judgment was pronounced as in Matthew. According to Mark 15, as soon as it was morning the whole council held a consultation and bound Jesus and led him away. Here a second session of the trial is not necessarily indicated.* In Luke's Gospel the proceedings approximate more closely to the account in John. In Luke 22:54 we are told that Christ was brought into the high priest's house, but we are not told that any official trial was held. The only purpose of bringing Christ into the house was to keep him under guard. So we see that the various accounts cannot be traced back to one original. By mentioning Annas, John gives us the only correct account of what transpired.

At this point John mentions Annas's relationship to Caiaphas. Annas examines Christ, but no one else was present, and John does not represent it as a trial before the Sanhedrin. Annas questions Christ concerning his disciples and his teaching, but Jesus appeals to the publicity surrounding his entire life and refers Annas to those who had heard him. After giving a full account of Peter's denial, John goes on in chapter 18:24 to say, "Annas then sent him bound to Caiaphas the high priest." What happened there John does not say. He could therefore not have been there. He was present at Annas's house and was therefore able to relate what

---

* or add: In Mark the morning meeting of the Sanhedrin is not represented so explicitly as a second session of the trial.

had happened there. The appearance before Annas and the one before Caiaphas are confused in the other Gospels because the synoptic Evangelists did not distinguish between the two high priests, but identified the two men.

The actual trial was held before Caiaphas, but nothing incriminating could be produced. It is hard to believe that the Sanhedrin, or individual members of it, should have brought witnesses forward who had nothing else to testify than what is recorded, namely, only a contempt for the temple. The hearing of witnesses can therefore have been only a form. Either it was a veneer to give the hearing an appearance of an actual trial, or evidence that the Sanhedrin would gladly have avoided the main issue if other charges had been advanced. Several days earlier Christ had been asked many tricky questions in order to gather information against him and to get him into the Sanhedrin's power. To be sure, the decisive point in the trial came when the high priest asked Christ whether he were the Messiah. If he had denied it they could have let him go, but would then have had his own witness against him. If he had affirmed it, they could have condemned him by an authoritative decision on the grounds that he was an imposter. It has frequently been said that the Sanhedrin had asserted the right to decide who was the Messiah or a prophet when anyone advanced the claim. However, this hypothesis does not rest on assured facts. On the contrary, it was generally assumed that the prophetic voice had been stilled, that is to say, that no prophet was any longer expected. The messianic hopes were widespread at the time, but the Sanhedrin could not officially claim the right to decide whether one who asserted that he was the Messiah actually was he, especially since it was composed in large part of Sadducees, who rejected the whole idea of a Messiah. To be sure, however, this was a claim that Christ had made of himself, and this could be countered by the opposite assertion, and since the Sanhedrin was an authority in these matters its members could pass the sentence, "He is worthy of death." To be sure, this might have led to an investigation, but that was something the Sanhedrin would not or could not undertake. Since Christ had affirmed the claim, only two courses of action were open. They could either condemn him as a false messianic claimant and as a blasphemer, or they could support him. It was hardly necessary for them to hold a later meeting to bring the matter before Pilate, but they had to observe the wider rules.

One question remains to be answered: To what extent was Pilate already informed of the matter? If he had provided a squad of soldiers to effect Christ's arrest, Christ's opponents must have given him information about the person they wished to seize. Otherwise we could not understand how he could make it convenient to sit in judgment so early — when morning came — before the actual hour of business had begun. They could have told him that the affair had to be settled as much as possible without stirring up the people. This must have been the reason why Pilate acted as he did.

Now we encounter a difficult point, but one of significance for our purpose. In chapter 18:28 ff. John tells us that Christ's opponents led him early in the morning from Caiaphas's house to the praetorium. They themselves did not enter the praetorium in order that they might not be defiled, but might eat the passover. Then Pilate went out to them and asked them what accusation they were bringing against this man. Then they answered, "If this man were not an evildoer, we would not have handed him over." John must again have been present at the scene, for he is able to tell us all that happened. The other Gospels tell us that Christ had eaten the passover with his disciples, and that that coincided with the institution of the Lord's Supper. In John, however, we are told that the Jews did not enter the praetorium in order that they might not be defiled. This is a well-known difficulty. To be sure, it is possible that the expression "to eat the passover" *(Stud. und Krit.)*[48] can have been used in a wider sense. It may refer to the observance of the festival as a whole. However, that does not

48. A reference to *Theologische Studien and Kritiken,* a periodical of the time; however, it is not clear precisely what Schleiermacher had in mind. In 1832, the same year as the lectures, he published two articles in this journal: "Ueber Kolosser 1:15-20," and "Ueber die Zeugnisse des Papias von unsern beiden ersten Evangelien." In the latter article Schleiermacher cites Matthew 26:17-35 which contains the phrase, "to eat the passover" but there is not any discussion of the point he is exploring here. Cf. *Sämmtliche Werke* (Berlin: G. Reimer, 1836), I, 2:363-92, esp. 378.

seem to me to be probable. If that had been the case we should have been told that they did not enter the praetorium in order that they might eat unleavened bread, the only kind of bread allowed for the eight day period. But the words "that they might eat the passover" are too precise a reference to eating the paschal lamb to be used in the other sense. Let me advance a second explanation. It was impossible for all people in Jerusalem to eat the passover on one day. The inspection of the paschal lambs, which was limited to the locality of the temple, must have limited the loss of time (of slaughtering?), and the time necessary for it must have been overlooked in another reckoning.* So it is probable that strangers ate the passover at an earlier time in order to return home earlier, and that the actual residents ate on another day.[49]

Lecture 60 (August 14). For information about the trials before the Sanhedrin we are limited to the accounts in the first three Gospels, for John says nothing about them, and it is not necessary that the charges made at these trials were repeated at the later one before Pilate, and therefore we cannot draw any conclusions about the former from the latter. The three Gospels introduce nothing except the complaint about the rebuilding of the temple, and nothing could be made of that accusation. The fact that Christ said that he would rebuild the temple meant neither that he intended to destroy it nor that he treated it with contempt. How are we to account for Christ's complete silence until the high priest asked him whether he was the Messiah? We may ask whether the report of his silence is correct, since everyone was obligated to speak to and answer the legitimate authorities and comment on the charges brought against him. Christ's silence did not mean a denial of the authority of the Sanhedrin, although it is impossible to demonstrate what constituted its sanction and how it

---

* never allowed for ... and there must have been a certain *latitudo*
49. Schleiermacher's manuscript outline ceased with the material covered in lecture 59. This means that we do not have this very important check from Schleiermacher's own hand for the material covered in the concluding twelve lectures beginning at this point. Consequently, the opinions expressed in the student notebooks cannot claim the same reliability in these final lectures as heretofore.

obtained it. It was recognized by long continued assent.* This
is the explanation of the matter. One who was on trial had
only to act and answer in his own best interests. By keeping
silent Christ left the Sanhedrin the freedom to interpret his
silence as agreement and to act accordingly. This silence of
Christ's was therefore at the same time his definite assertion
of the correctness of all that was charged against him. This
is the only explanation possible.† Between this first trial,
which ended with the declaration that Christ's definite assertion that he was the Messiah was a blasphemy, and the trial
of Christ before Pilate there must have been some period of
time.

During this period we hear of mistreatments that Christ
suffered. In one account we are led to believe that the members of the Sanhedrin were responsible for these. In Matthew
26:66 ff. we read, " 'What is your judgment?' They answered, 'He deserves death.' Then they spat in his face, and struck
him; and some slapped him, saying, 'Prophesy to us, you
Christ! Who is it that struck you?' " It is highly improbable
that members of the Sanhedrin acted this way. Such action
presupposes a personal passion on their part which there is no
reason to assume that they had. The Sanhedrin was governed
only by concern for what Christ's activity might do to the
general situation. Mark says the same thing, but with a significant difference. In Mark 14:65 we read, "and the servants
received him with blows." Since it is impossible that the members of the Sanhedrin and their servants would have been in
the same place, we see here some evidence of confusion in the
account. In Luke 22:63-64 we read, immediately after the
story about Peter, "Now the men who were holding Jesus

† or add: How the authority of the Sanhedrin later developed we do not
know. It did not rest on the law, but long duration confers legality. The
Sanhedrin's authority was not sanctioned by the constitution, but had
accumulated over the years.

* or add: His silence gave the option of regarding everything as admitted
that demonstrates the justice of the charge: "If you act as though I had
admitted the charge, you can properly punish me for it, for you will not
find anything punishable." Rütenik: Schleiermacher speaks of this more
clearly and in greater detail in his sermon *Oculi* (1833), on 1 Tim. 6:13.
In the first part of that sermon he speaks of the silence of the Redeemer
as a victorious confession. (*Sämmtliche Werke* [Berlin: G. Reimer, 1835-
64], 3:496.)

mocked him and beat him and asked him, 'Prophesy,' etc.," almost word for word what we find in Matthew and Mark, and then Luke goes on to say that when day came, the assembly of the elders of the people gathered together, both chief priests and scribes, and they led him away to their council. Luke looks at the affair from an entirely different point of view. His account is the most probable of the three, and must be a record of the same events. It absolves the chief priests of any mistreatment of Jesus. Mark's account gives indications of internal confusion. The mistreatment of Christ was the work of the servants.

Christ is now brought before Pilate. With respect to the proceedings at this point our accounts vary considerably. So far as the beginning is concerned, we see that the narratives differ and are very abbreviated. Matthew begins by saying that, when Christ appeared before Pilate, the latter asked him, "Are you the King of the Jews?" and Christ answered, "You say so." This can have been a way either of affirming or of denying the question, but the usage of language favors the former conclusion. How can Pilate have happened to begin the trial with this question? That would presuppose a familiarity on Pilate's part with the affair, which would mean that he paid close attention to what went on in Jerusalem. If he had learned of the case from the chief priests, he could not have gone ahead with the trial in such a formless way. It must have begun with the Jews presenting accusations. Mark gives the same account, which must be regarded as an abbreviation. Luke 23:2 is the more correct account. Members of the Sanhedrin began to accuse Christ, saying, "We found this man perverting our nation, and forbidding us to give tribute to Caesar, and saying that he himself is Christ a king." This was the charge, specific and substantiated in a very insidious way. John's account agrees with Luke's, which appears in contrast with John's to be abbreviated. John makes Pilate ask, "What accusation do you bring against this man?" The members of the Sanhedrin apparently found it difficult to be specific and only reply, "If this man were not an evildoer, we would not have handed him over." That was no answer, and so Pilate goes on to say: "If you have no charge to lay before me, take him yourselves and judge him by your own law." In other words, Pilate tells them to exercise the right of punishment that was legally theirs. Pilate wants to leave the affair with them to settle. They were to do with Christ as the law permitted. Then they were compelled to say what they actually wanted him to do. They were not allowed to condemn anyone to death, and that is what they wanted Pilate to do with Jesus.

Now John tells us that Pilate entered the praetorium and called Christ to him and asked him in private, "Are you the King of the Jews?" He does this, although there is nothing in the account that gave him occasion to do so. It is possible that at this point we have to supplement John's account with Luke's, for the Jews must have advanced a reason why Christ should be condemned to death. But they could not prove what Luke says was one part of the charge, namely, that he had forbidden the payment of tribute to Cæsar. They make the charge indirectly. If someone maintains that he is the Messiah, this means that he wants to be recognized as king. They take their departure from the political idea of the Messiah. If they had raised the matter of the tribute as a fact by itself, Pilate would have needed no other reason for condemning Christ as a rebel in accordance with Roman law. The main charge made by Christ's opponents was that he claimed to be the Messiah, and that claim involves an instigation to rebellion. To be sure, there was some truth to this. What was incorrect was the statement that Christ had ever represented himself as *such a Messiah. So it was natural that Pilate should ask him about the claim.* The whole charge of the chief priests involved a contradiction, for no actual revolution had taken place, and there was no *corpus delicta.* Rather, they appealed to a presumed tendency. Christ had often been in the temple and no revolution had broken out, so the charge was baseless. Therefore it was natural that Pilate should wish to question Christ privately. Only John gives us this detail.

The others abbreviate the account in such a way that it becomes quite incomprehensible in and for itself. According to Matthew (27:11-14), when Pilate asked Christ whether he was the King of the Jews, Christ replied that he was, but later he made no answer to the accusations of the chief priests and elders, so that the procurator wondered greatly. Since Christ had said that he was the King of the Jews and since Pilate would only think of that claim from the political point of view, that was reason enough to pursue the investigation. When, after they demanded that Barabbas be released rather than Christ, Pilate goes on to say, "Why, what evil has he done?" the whole account becomes hopelessly confused. The account in Mark is similarly mixed up, with even less connection between one part and the other. All this shows that Pilate did not regard the accusation that Christ had claimed to be the King of the Jews as relevant.* In Luke there is still another account of how Pilate passed from the charge against Christ to his support, but everything in this account is wholly improbable. John 18:33-38 is the only account that gives a reasonable version of the conversation of Pilate with Christ in which Christ agrees that he is the Messiah. The Greek word *basileus* ["king"] designated a person worthy of worship, but the Latin word *rex* ["king"] had no such connotation. So for Pilate there was nothing out of the ordinary in the use of the word "king."† This is the key to the whole matter.

The next item in which all accounts agree is Pilate's attempt to put an end to the whole affair by proposing to release Barabbas to Christ's opponents. Such a release is represented as a rite that was observed at each feast. The people were allowed to request the delivery to them of one who had been condemned. This rite was actually not applicable to Christ, for it would have been contrary to Roman law to free a man before his trial had been ended. That would have been an injustice to the defendant. Such an observance can only be explained by the general state of the country. Contrary to all law, Palestine had been made a Roman province, and that had given rise to tumultuous rebellions. The Galileans in particular were given to such insurrections. So there were many who were called "robbers," but given that name because of the illegal situa-

---

* or add: and washed his hands of the whole matter. Another possibility: In Mark's account the matter is also unclear, and is relieved only by the fact that to Pilate Christ's guilt is not evident.
† There was nothing new for Pilate in the use of the word "king" for ecclesiastical authorities, and he had nothing against the use of such a title.

tion.†The rite of releasing such a person was thought of as a sop to the people, and the people were inclined to ask that the person be set free. It cannot have been usual, however, for Pilate to want to free a man whose trial had not yet ended, for there is a difference between declaring a man innocent who is in the process of being judged and setting a condemned man free as an act of grace. To free a man before the end of his trial is to commit a great injustice, for his innocence is still undecided. That was a procedure, then, that could take place only under exceptional circumstances. However, since all the Gospels agree on it, it is no doubt what happened.

Pilate's intention was not just to free himself of the whole matter, but to use this opportunity to cause a division among the people itself. This favor was not extended to the Sanhedrin, for the high court of Judaism could not demean itself to appear before Pilate and ask for a favor, but it was always granted to the people. It was therefore a formless procedure. The people appeared before the praetorium en masse and asked the procurator to free someone. The favor was granted to the *people*. Christ had been accused by the Sanhedrin, and if Pilate had granted the request of the people he would have put the Sanhedrin into a compromising situation, and that was something that would have pleased him greatly. Perhaps that is what moved him to act in such an exceptional way. He must certainly have known something about Christ, and he probably knew that Christ had many followers among the people. That was evident from the accusation of the chief priests. He could easily have supposed that freeing Christ would cause a division between the Sanhedrin and the people.

We have no data to enable us to ascertain why that did not happen. When Pilate asked the people who had assembled and were listening to him whom he should release, he may have believed that these folk were supporters of Christ. He could not have expected anything else.* It is probable that during this time a great crowd of people had gathered and that it expressed itself as the reports indicate, although we cannot reach

† because they found the whole situation illegal
* He obviously did not give the accusers of Christ the choice.

any definite conclusion on the matter. In any case it is certain that Pilate could not have believed that the people had remained assembled from the beginning because of Christ's trial. Otherwise they would have been only servants of the Sanhedrin. In that case he would not have been able to put the question. Furthermore, Pilate's intention of calling forth a vote of the people against the Sanhedrin is quite clear, and he must therefore have thought of the crowd as composed of people free of the Sanhedrin's control. We do not know whether the crowd of people who generally received this favor were made up as a rule of residents of Jerusalem or of strangers. Among the residents of Jerusalem there were not many who were followers of Christ. So it is possible that a mixed group attended. It is clear that the response to Pilate's offer they gave was one contrary to his expectation.

Lecture 61 (August 15) There are two other incidents during the trial before Pilate that are mentioned in individual accounts. Both present difficulties. The first is that Pilate's wife interceded for Christ during the trial itself because of a dream she had had that had been concerned with him. It is difficult to get a clear picture of what happened. It is not easy to believe that such a mission of Pilate's wife to him during the trial could have taken place. It shows that she had already been concerned about Christ and that she and Pilate had talked about him. So it is a kind of confirmation of the probability that there had been some earlier discussion about Christ between Pilate and the Sanhedrin. The members of the Sanhedrin must have obtained a concession from Pilate to hold the trial before him at an unusual hour. So the project to arrest Christ must have been previously known to Pilate, and the information he had of it must have included something favorable to Christ, which aroused such an interest in him.

The second incident is reported only by Luke. When Pilate learned that Christ was a Galilean, he decided to relieve himself of responsibility and send him to Herod, who had come to Jerusalem for the festival. That Pilate could have had the idea of ridding himself of Christ in this way and that there were legal grounds for doing so is quite conceivable, but it is very difficult to understand why there is no reference to all this in the other Gospels. This is especially true when we recall how John treats the trials before Annas, Caiaphas, and Pilate. There can be no doubt that he was an eyewitness of the first and the last, but overlooks the trial before Caiaphas because he was not present. If he had been a member of the crowd before Pilate, it is hard to believe that all that Luke reports could have happened without his knowledge. There is a key to this problem, but it does not solve it fully. John tells us that Pilate called Christ into the praetorium, and so John was not present. It is possible to suppose that Pilate sent Christ to Herod at that time, perhaps by way of another exit* without John being aware of it. However, according to Luke the incident must have taken up quite a space of time.

Herod's behavior in the matter seems quite unworthy of his status as a king. He was involved in the affair because Pilate sent Christ to him as belonging under his jurisdiction (comitium), either to accept or to reject him. If he rejected him, it would be unworthy of him to use the occasion for his own personal satisfaction by engaging, together with members of his court, in all kinds of mockery of Christ. The fact that he sent Christ back to Pilate indicates that he did not want to accept jurisdiction over him. To be sure, Pilate says that Herod had found nothing wrong with him. However, if Herod had sent him a special message to that effect, then that was an inconsistency.† He ought to have set Christ free if he had found nothing wrong with him. If he rejected jurisdiction over him, he did not have to relay any judgment concerning him to Pilate. The situation is clarified somewhat by the fact that Herod and Pilate, as Luke says, had been at enmity with each other. There was jealousy between the two. Herod tried to get support from the people for all future cases that would arise, even where his own authority did not extend, and the Roman procurator must have been suspicious of him. However, Herod may well have been embarrassed about how he should deal

---

* if Christ went in with Pilate alone, he could have been taken to Herod by another exit and have been brought back to same way
† or add: He could not have sent Christ back, but would have set him free.

408

with the case. On the one hand, he wanted to accept it as a response to Pilate's indication of respect, but on the other hand he did not want to oppose the authority of the Sanhedrin. When Herod rejected jurisdiction over the case, it took a turn contrary to Pilate's expectation. However, Pilate must have found it pleasant that Herod was so amiable as to send Christ back to him.

Pilate found no reason to pass the sort of sentence that Christ's accusers demanded. They had condemned Christ of blasphemy, and they now wanted a confirmation of their judgment. If they now attempted to represent Christ as one who stirred up the people, so that Pilate would have to accept jurisdiction over him, their first judgment would have been superfluous. However, this accusation against Christ, for which no evidence could be supplied, was to let Pilate know that they had acted out of concern for public order and in order to avoid all breeches of public peace. That could help to make Pilate favorable to a comfirmation of their judgment. With complete legality he could confirm the judgment without actually running counter to his duty. He could not pass judgment himself, for there was no reason for him to do so. However, if members of the Sanhedrin maintained, "He has done something for which according to our law he deserved death, but you must carry out the sentence," Pilate could confirm the judgment without doing any harm to his duty by saying, "I am not myself concerned with the case, since it is a matter of your law, and that is nothing that concerns me. If your conscience does not trouble you about it, I shall confirm the judgment, but not make myself responsible for it, although as a citizen before my forum he is innocent." That is the meaning of the act in which Pilate washes his hands. He makes use of his right to comply with their wish, but places the actual legal responsibility for the condemnation of Christ on their shoulders. He could avoid confirming their judgment and at the same time consent to it.

There are now two things that put Pilate in a disadvantageous light, and of one of them I do not wish to absolve him. He is often reproached for what he said when Christ declared that he had come to found a kingdom of truth. If we consider his position, we should have to regard it as good and praise-worthy if he had entered into a further discussion of what Christ understood by truth, but that would have been a purely personal discussion and would have had no place in a trial. It seems quite appropriate that Pilate should say: If you do not want a kingdom that is external, that is something that has nothing to do with the trial. What you want is a matter of complete indifference to me and I am not concerned with it. In the second place, however, Pilate seeks to surrender by of-fering a lesser measure of punishment and then suggesting that he let Christ go free, and the case is delayed until the crowd of people say: If he hesitates to pass judgment, we must regard that as a neglect of his duty to care for the respect of Cæsar and Cæsar's authority. There were no grounds for that in the case before him, for Christ's enemies could not prove that he had led an insurrection against imperial power in Palestine. So he could have said: I shall settle that with the emperor. But he may have given occasion for many complaints that could be brought against him in Rome, and if, in addition to those, members of the Sanhedrin were to say that they could cite ex-amples of when he had let dangerous men go free, that could have made his situation worse. So then, Pilate acted as a cow-ard. He actually acted against his own conviction. His hesita-tion, his unmistakable wish to find another solution to the case, indicates that he had a personal share in the affair. He could close the case quickly in favor of the Sanhedrin, without neglecting his duty, but now he had to consider his own con-viction, which he now surrendered, and that was a mark against him.* As things were then, with the inclination of the people to all kinds of excess, with the many executions he had to carry out legally, one judgment more or less was for him in his situation a matter of little consequence, and he could easily appease his conscience and say: You can easily look after this matter *simpliciter,* and then go on to confirm the judgment of the Sanhedrin.†

* or add: That mark would disappear if there were no evidence that he had wanted to save Jesus.
† or add: and could deceive himself thereby. Another possibility: and a Pilate in his situation could reassure himself about it.

If we recall Christ's definite conviction that the end of his life was imminent, despite the various possibilities that could arise — some scruples could have caused Judas to change his mind, Christ could have avoided going where Judas expected him, Pilate could have released him — we find that, despite all this, his conviction that he was about to die remained throughout quite firm. The question arises: Are we to regard that as a human conviction, accounted for by the state of affairs in which he found himself, or was it a miraculous foreknowledge on his part, or did it arise out of his thought of the necessity of his death for the completion of his task? It is the first of these possibilities that I wish to maintain. The last has to do with the question *how*, but not with the question *when*. The second runs counter to the way we have treated our subject from the beginning. If we had to assume a foreknowledge as a way of explaining what differentiated Christ from all other men, that would do more to invalidate the truth of his human nature than all the miracles taken together. If we were to think of him as possessing a constant foreknowledge of what was going on in his circle, he would no longer be a real man, unless we were to regard it as an especially powerful premonition, as a virtuosity of seeing things, and that leads us to the first possibility indicated.

We are now faced with a number of individual considerations. What could Christ surmise, and what could he, or did he have to, desire? Both these questions are related to a third: What could Christ have done if he had been able to extend his life for a longer time? We are compelled to say: The fullest truth of his conviction must have been that the actual fruitfulness of his work could begin only after his death, that the organization of the kingdom of God and his actual presence in the church could only begin when he was no longer present physically. The power by which all individuals were drawn to him, or the relationship of each one to him, made a fusion of individuals with each other impossible. So then, what he would have been able to do can only be understood in light of what he had done. The organization of a community of believers while he himself was still with them would have been a vain endeavor. They could not have felt free or have moved freely

411

in the relationship individuals had with him. On the contrary, the relationship of the individuals to him had always to be the dominant one. Therefore Christ had no direct reason to desire a prolongation of his life in the interests of the actual object of his mission. He thought always of his mission as one given him by God. Convinced that the living nucleus of the church in his disciples, in spite of all the imperfection of their insight, would nevertheless prove adequate to grow in the form of a common spirit, a fusion of the life of all individuals, he could not wish that his life should be prolonged. He says that quite unambiguously. The paraclete as the divine principle of the common spirit of believers would remind them of and elucidate his teachings. Convinced of this, and in view of what he would be able to do in any practical way, he could not have entertained the wish to live longer.

Let me sum up what I have said. The party opposed to Christ had obtained an apparent predominance, at least in external matters, on all points, in Judea by the direct influence of the Sanhedrin, and in Galilee and Perea, on the one hand, by the great ascendancy of the traditional party in their protest against his treatment of the law, in which he disregarded all tradition, and on the other hand by the concern of Herod lest Christ be John the Baptist risen again from the dead. In light of all this we have to say that Christ could clearly anticipate his impending death. To be sure, if we reflect on the definite character of the circumstances, there is still another factor. The treachery of Judas seems to have been only an incidental element in the affair, but it had a definite effect on the time of Christ's death, for, if the Sanhedrin had not received this impulse from Judas, they would have done nothing about Christ's arrest during the course of the festival and would have carried out their decision to put an end to him at a later time.

This brings us to the question of the mysterious relationship of Judas to Christ. We do not know how he became a member of Christ's intimate circle or what caused him to think of betraying Christ. In any case we have to regard him as representing the opposition within the inner circle of Christ's followers. However, the truth of the human life of Christ would wholly disappear if we had to think of Christ as being compelled by his fate to accept among his disciples one who he knew was destined by divine decree to betray him. What amounted to a complete sacrifice of freedom could not be regarded as an act of free self-determination. If Christ had known beforehand that Judas would act as he did, he could not have chosen him as a disciple if we are to think of him as acting as a human being. So we cannot think that Christ chose Judas, knowing beforehand that he would betray him. However, we lack sufficient information to say why he made the choice. When I say that in any case we must regard Judas as representing the opposition to Christ within the inner circle of his followers, I do not have in mind such a Judas as Daub assumes, who was wholly unsuitable to be a disciple.[50] I think of him as one who was opposed to the way Christ realized the messianic idea. Since we cannot deny that the disciples of Christ from the beginning were not wholly agreed on their messianic ideas, although some had accepted a spiritual interpretation of the work of the Messiah, we have to think of Judas in this respect as representing those who held fast to the political idea of the Messiah's function and as one who never freed himself from that idea. However, Christ had no satisfactory reason to exclude Judas from the circle of the twelve, although he had not

50. The reference is to Karl Daub of Heidelberg (1765-1836 and his book, *Judas Ischariot: oder das Böse im Verhältnis zum Guten* (Heidelberg, 1816-18). Next to Schleiermacher, Daub was probably the most original systematic theologian of early nineteenth century Germany. Decisively influenced by the philosopher Schelling, Daub in *Theologoumena* (1806) and *Einleitung in das Studium der christlichen Dogmatik* (1810) set the task of theology as overcoming the conflict between traditional supernaturalism's external relation of God and the world as based upon a special temporal history and rationalism's alternative of either rejecting Christian dogma or limiting it to self-evident finite bounds. The resolution of this conflict Daub considered to lie in a speculative approach to the idea of God. The revelation of God in the human spirit through religion reaches its most complete expression in Christianity whose symbolical designations about the person and work of Christ are to be seen as universal metaphysical principles. These are the same general ideas which David Friedrich Strauss later employed in exegetical interpretation in his *Life of Jesus Critically Examined*, ed. Peter C. Hodgson, Lives of Jesus series (Philadelphia: Fortress, 1972). Daub, however, was both speculatively much more robust than Strauss and religiously more interested in traditional Christian doctrines as manifested in concrete history. *Judas Ischariot* is an extension of these same ideas with greater attention to evil. The disciple Judas, therefore, represents the embodiment of the metaphysical opposition to the good that is, in turn, overcome by God. Daub subsequently came under the influence of Hegel and is often recorded now as a member of the Hegelian school in theology.

freed himself from the idea that others had given up. In human terms Christ had to believe that in the future Judas also would overcome the limitations of the human idea of the Messiah as a political figure. Judas's behavior can be understood and to some extent excused only on the presupposition that he held this wholly false conception of the messianic idea and was never able to overcome it, and his end makes his frame of mind to some extent comprehensible. Nevertheless, the whole matter remains obscure.

Lecture 62 *(August 16)*. If we consider the sentence passed by Pilate, the consequence of his approval of the Sanhedrin's request made Christ's crucifixion inevitable, for that was the way people were executed at that time who had no claim to Roman citizenship. Sometimes individual sayings of Christ are interpreted as referring to crucifixion as the manner of his death, but that is due to too narrow an interpretation of them. All that they indicate is that Christ thought that he would be condemned by the Roman authorities. When Christ thought of such an unhappy outcome of his life, he could think of himself either as being killed in a tumultuous fashion by stoning or as executed according to legal means, and this latter would be by way of crucifixion. All Christ's sayings about his death declare only that he would die, not as the result of mob action, but as the consequence of a legal decision. From the beginning we have seen that Christ avoided all situations that would lead to mob action against him. That was intentional on his part, for he did not want to die that way. His command to his disciples to keep their swords ready could have meant only that he intended them to be used only against mob action. The way Christ was received in Jerusalem gave him great assurance against mob action, and the Sanhedrin would not have dared to instigate such a tumultuous act. It would have led to open warfare between two parties, for Christ had many followers, and such warfare was not desired by the Sanhedrin. Consequently Christ's sayings about his death indicated a correct understanding of the situation. Roman practice involved a whipping of the prisoner before his execution. It seems to us horrible that a condemned man should be subject to such physical punishment before execution, but our moral attitude differs from that prevalent at that time, and scourging before crucifixion was a legal Roman procedure.

Before going into further detail there is a general consideration to be made. Recently the manner of Christ's death has frequently been the subject of debate. How far was it natural and in accordance with the fact that Christ should have died so soon after his crucifixion? Can his death at such an early time be regarded as an actual death? The consideration of the details has had a significant influence on the treatment of these questions. If someone wants to represent Christ's death on the cross as a wholly natural event, in view of the fact that most other people who were crucified had to suffer much longer than he, the accounts of the crucifixion are carefully examined and the conclusion is reached that Christ was in a weakened bodily state. The less that can be demonstrated, the more striking must be the fact of Christ's early death and the easier the assumption that it is not to be regarded as a genuine death. Let me give my view of this latter hypothesis. It seems to me to be a matter of complete indifference whether one maintains one view or another. In connection with this I maintain at the same time that there is no way to prove one hypothesis or another. We have no grounds for reaching any conclusion. To be sure, scientific and physiological questions are involved, which I can treat only as a layman.*

I believe we can assume that the only certain indication of death is *the decomposition of the body*. This rule is accepted practically universally in medical law.† If someone says that dogmatic reasons make it necessary to believe that Christ's death was genuine and complete, I will not even bother to draw attention to the fact that it is not necessary for the satisfaction of the divine righteousness that one must believe that Christ's death was simply a physical event, without any moral or spiritual content. When we say that what satisfies the divine righteousness must be something spiritual, rather than something physical, we conclude that it can make no difference to

* or add: and leave the determination of the value of the different points of view to the doctors
† or add: This leads in certain states to regulations by the police against burial before there are signs of decomposition in the corpse.

the divine righteousness whether Christ's death was a real death or a state similar to death. Once the act of dying had taken place in its spiritual significance,* whether the physical part of death had been completed or not seems to me to be of no importance whatever. However, I only want to ask, if someone wants to maintain that Christ actually died, how do you explain the fact that, when people spoke of his revivification, they expressly applied to Christ's state the passage from the psalm, "Thou wilt not . . . let thy Holy One see corruption"? † So it must be admitted that in Christ's state there was not yet the slightest beginning of decomposition, and consequently no genuine death had taken place. Decomposition is only the resurgence of the chemical process that was inhibited during life by the action of life. Between life and death no intervening state is imaginable. It is impossible for the action of life to cease completely without the beginning of the chemical process of decomposition.** *So then, in this connection we can compel a man to maintain one point of view to the extent that he does not want to maintain the other. The debate cannot be resolved one way or the other.* We lack information to determine whether Christ's body had begun to decompose or not. It is sometimes said that, if Christ's death was not a complete death, his revivification was not a complete miracle. Here again we are in a situation in which it is not possible to draw a sharp distinction between one point of view and the other. *As soon as one assumes (declares that there is) an absolute miracle, how can he maintain that a given event is such a miracle?*†† *This requires an infinite amount of investigation that can never be brought to completion. We can therefore regard this whole matter as one of no import-*

* As soon as Christ's consciousness reached zero and he had completed the act of dying in a spiritual sense
† or add: Acts 2:27-32 (Ps. 16:10). Such dogmatic theologians ought not to neglect that messianic prediction.
** or add: Decomposition marks the reintroduction of the chemical process that is inhibited during life by the power of life. When life ceases to be, the chemical process begins. Both cannot exist side by side. With the end of life, the chemical process begins. So to say that there is death without decomposition of the body is to utter a contradiction in terms.
††As soon as one assumes an absolute miracle, one can never maintain that a given event is such a miracle, for that requires an infinite amount of investigation.

ance † *and consider the details without prejudice and without any definite interest in proving one hypothesis or the other.*[51] *However, we are concerned that the picture of Christ that we have formed should be continuous and remain the same to the last moment.*

I do not regard the question of whether Christ's physical constitution bordered on a state of weakness as one of equal importance. However, there is no reason to maintain that, in light of all that we have found to this point in our study of Christ's work. There is no case when Christ would have been hindered in a spiritual activity by anything lacking in his physical constitution. If, in order to explain the death of Christ as an actual fact, one were to assume that it took place so quickly because of weakness, since it generally happened that a man lingered longer than Christ did between life and death after having been crucified, that would be the very first indication that we could discover that had any bearing on his constitution. Every man withstood such attacks on his life that were not in themselves lethal according to the extent of his physical life force. If anyone wishes to avoid concluding that Christ's early death indicates a weak physical condition on his part, he becomes interested in discussing indications that at the time he was crucified he was no longer in possession of his normal physical powers. I confess that I can find no such indications. Christ was scourged before he was crucified, but so were all who were condemned to crucifixion, and so one can draw no especial conclusions about Christ from that fact. If one were to go back to the states of mind that Christ had and maintain that they could have caused a weakening of his physical life powers, it would be better to get rid of this idea than have to deal with all those that would result from it.

We cannot interpret the account of Christ's state of mind in the garden after this fashion. I have to regard Luke's reference, found only in his Gospel, to the angel who had come to strengthen Christ as a later embellishment of the story. It indicates a tendency to interpret the incident ascetically, and John's account in its continuity makes it impossible to con-

† we regard both points of view with complete indifference
51. For the question of an apparent death, see p. 456 below, n. 60.

clude that Christ suffered such a state of mental weakness. Christ could have desired to live longer for his disciples' sake, but I cannot believe that he did so in light of the discourses in John 16 and the prayer in John 17. These passages represent Christ as so calm and assured in view of the certainty of his impending death that I cannot think of any opposition in Christ's soul to the divine decree without distorting and falsifying the whole picture of him. At that time, then, I cannot imagine any condition that could have weakened Christ's physical life force. I could think of such a condition with respect to all others more than with reference to Christ.

To be sure, there is one circumstance related that to some extent seems to support the hypothesis of Christ's weakness at the time of his crucifixion. We are told that a man coming in from the country was impressed into carrying Christ's cross. To be sure, it must have been usual for a man to carry his own cross, but we must not completely overlook the difference between Christ and those who usually suffered the same fate. It must have been very seldom, perhaps it had never happened before, that a person was crucified who belonged to the same class as Christ. Those who were guilty of crimes that could be legally punished by crucifixion were only people of the lower class, and it must have been seldom that others were brought in such an insidious way to crucifixion in view of the close unity of all Jews against the Romans. For that to happen required some special circumstance such as in this instance. The authorities among the people would have to be convinced that one man's crucifixion was a necessary offering on behalf of the whole nation. So a case similar to Christ's had probably never arisen before. Christ was probably the first man who had ever been condemned by the Romans to be crucified at the wish of the Jews. So we may ask: Was someone else compelled to carry Christ's cross because Christ was physically incapable of doing it,* or did some other circumstance bring that about, a circumstance that distinguished Christ from others (or: from ordinary criminals) who had to endure the same fate? We cannot be sure. One conclusion seems as pro-

* or add: as the situation is usually portrayed in pictures

bable as the other. To be sure, once Christ had been crucified he spoke very little, but that cannot be regarded as the result of a weakened life force. On the contrary, Christ's relative silence was due to the fact that he was awaiting death and to the fact that he was exposed to public view. Silence under such circumstances was natural, and it required a special development to break it in individual instances. I cannot say that I find any indication that Christ's physical condition was any different from that of others.

However, it is clear that, since crucifixion was a crude operation, much that was accidental could happen. The wounds that crucifixion necessarily inflicted, whether they were two or four (it is well known that Mr. Hug in Freiburg, the overseer of the cathedral there, has recently come out in defense of four wounds of Christ),[52] were not in themselves lethal, but they could be different in different cases. The loss of blood in one case could be greater than in another, although a complete loss of blood could not be caused by crucifixion. The extension of the extremities of the body must have interfered with the normal circulation of the blood, and a coagulation of the blood must have taken place that would prevent total loss of blood. However, apart from that, the wounds must have been very different in different cases, since crucifixion was carried out by people who had no skill in execution. Similarly, the extension of the extremities would differ, and this difference could affect the speed of death. So it could come about that men who had been crucified could die at different times. It must have been rare for a man to remain on the cross for several days, and just as rare for a man to die as quickly as Christ did, but either case was possible. However, unless you assume a bodily weakness in general, for which there is no evidence, you cannot ascribe Christ's quick death to a weakened bodily condition.

52. Schleiermacher refers to J.L. Hug, a leading Roman Catholic New Testament critic of the day and author of *Einleitung in die Schriften des neuen Testaments*, (Stuttgart, 1808; 3rd ed. 1826). In 1831 Hug wrote an article in the *Zeitschrift für die Geistlichkeit des Erzbisthums* (Freiburg,) vol. 5, on the history of the narrative of Christ's passion which Schleiermacher notes at this point.

Circumstances Accompanying Christ's Death

What is important in these last moments of Christ's life is what is a sign and manifestation of his life, his spiritual life activity, and that is what has been preserved of his last sayings and the accompanying circumstances that are related in the Gospels.

Since I regard the latter as the less important, I shall begin with them. There are two accounts, the darkness that occurred during Christ's crucifixion and the rending of the veil in the temple. Perhaps a third ought to be added to this list, the opening of the graves and the emergence of the dead. So far as the first is concerned, it is impossible to think of an eclipse of the sun. There is nothing in the account that suggests that. The word that represents our "eclipse" is not used. The darkness was caused by other atmospheric conditions. It resembled what we experience, for brief periods, and we do not have to think of it as continuous during those three hours. Rather, it probably came and went. In that case there is no need to speak of a miracle.

Let us now turn to the other two circumstances. So far as the former is concerned we must ask: Where could the information have come from that at Christ's death the veil of the temple was rent in two? Who could have seen in? There were two curtains, the one which separated the Holy Place, the outer part of the temple, from the Court of the Israelites, and the one that separated the Holy of Holies from the Holy Place. No could see the latter except the priests, for they were the only ones who entered the Holy Place. If that curtain had been torn in two the priests would have had the greatest interest in suppressing any knowledge of it, for it would have been impossible to avoid a symbolical interpretation of the fact. However, if this were a fact that became known, it is difficult to avoid the conclusion that the apostles in their sermons would have made reference to it, for it would have symbolized the end of the Jewish cult. The occurrence would certainly have been decisive. So then, the fact cannot have become known during the period of the apostolic preaching, so far as this was concerned with Jesus. If the story must have had a later source, this cannot be regarded as authoritative.

The necessarily symbolic meaning of the occurrence points rather clearly to the origin of the story. It was a way of speaking of the relationship of the new covenant to the old. Christian sermons and, even more, Christian hymns, could speak of the new covenant as superseding the old, much as the author of the Letter to the Hebrews does, in terms of the rending of the veil of the temple at the time of Christ's death. Such an event could not have been known to the author of the Letter to the Hebrews, for he would have referred to it if he had known of it. The teaching of the supersession of the old covenant by the new was presented symbolically in terms of the rending of the temple's veil, and this symbolism was later interpreted as a fact.[53]

Lecture 63 *(August 17)*.* The details of the opening of the graves and of the emergence of many saints are narrated in such a way that they cannot be thought of in physical terms, as they would have to be if accounts of physical occurrences were to be given. When we are told that at Christ's death the rocks were split and the tombs were opened, and then that many bodies of saints who had fallen asleep were raised, and that coming out of the tombs after the resurrection they went into the holy city and appeared to many, we are not told what

53. Schleiermacher's statement here on symbolism becoming transformed into a fact anticipates David Friedrich Strauss's thoroughgoing application of this type of interpretation three years later in his *The Life of Jesus Critically Examined.* Schleiermacher had similarly drawn on symbol to elucidate Matthew's journey of the wise men as representing Jesus' recognition by the non-Jewish world in *A Critical Essay on the Gospel of Luke* in 1817 (*Sämmtliche Werke* [Berlin: G. Reimer, 1836], I,2:35). The difference between Schleiermacher and Strauss apart from the latter's insight into the the more extensive applicability of this rubric lies in the fact that Schleiermacher interprets such symbols as finally referring to the proper union of individuality and universality in Jesus Christ; Strauss, on the other hand, understands the symbol's reference to Jesus' individuality as itself being part of the myth and consequently in need of purging for the true reference of universality. Cf. *The Life of Jesus Critically Examined,* ed. Peter C. Hodgson, Lives of Jesus series (Philadelphia: Fortress, 1972), pp. 895-96.

* Rütenik: This circumstance is presented nakedly, not as something that would have brought forth violent emotion. At the beginning of this lecture Schleiermacher seems to have recapitulated and enlarged his presentation. For the way in which Schleiermacher presented these two points from the pulpit, the darkness at the time of Christ's death and the rending of the temple veil, see his Good Friday sermon on Luke 23:44-49: "A Consideration of the Circumstances that Accompanied the Redeemer's Last Moments," *Sämmtliche Werke* (Berlin: G. Reimer, 1835-64), 2:249.

happened to these saints between the time of Christ's death and his resurrection. We are not told whether at Christ's death the tombs were opened without the dead men stirring and whether it was only at the time of the resurrection that they went into the city. We cannot form a conception of the occurrence. There is such a gap in the narrative that we cannot think of it as a real fact, and we must think of it as having some symbolic origin. There are many indications in the New Testament itself that at a very early time in the life of the church there were both rhetorical and hymnodic productions for which such symbolical interpretation was something quite natural. Since we cannot determine from what time our synoptic Gospels come, it is quite possible that the synoptic Evangelists excerpted statements from such productions as facts, which were not originally described as such. To explain such facts we must take the possibility into consideration. The accounts cannot be in their original form. They must have appeared differently to begin with. So they must have had an origin other than factual. This is the easiest and most natural conclusion we can reach.

The *last words of Christ* from the moment of his crucifixion to the time of his death are distributed among our various Gospels. If we are to think of them as a group, are we to assume that one Gospel includes the sayings that the other has omitted? That is not quite the case. We have three different accounts of the last utterance. Matthew and Mark represent it as an unarticulated cry, as a sound without definite content. In Luke we are told that Christ said, ''Father, into thy hands I commit my spirit!'' In John Christ's last word is ''It is finished,'' and thereupon he bowed his head and gave up his spirit. These three accounts of the last utterance Christ made cannot be harmonized. We can imagine that an involuntary cry such as Matthew and Mark report could have followed upon Christ's last words, and it is possible that it did so, but we cannot think of the last words as reported by Luke and John as following upon one another. Both could have been Christ's last words, and one has as good a claim to that as the other. The other sayings could have been appropriately uttered, and their order can be surmised if necessary from one or the other narrative, since the synoptic Gospels may have been composed of originally separate elements.

I have recently pointed out that I can think of Christ's whole state of mind only as it is described in the discourses in the Gospel of John and that I believe it is improbable that Christ fell back into a state of mental distress. Christ's word on the cross, "My God, my God, why hast thou forsaken me?" has a bearing on this. I cannot think of this saying as an expression of Christ's self-consciousness. I can think of no moment when the relationship between God and Christ could have changed. It must always have been the same. Christ's oneness with the Father can never have been ended, but that seems to be what such a saying indicates. Some claim that such a state of abandonment by God was a necessary part of the plan of redemption. I admit gladly that I do not believe that. It contains an untruth, for if such a one had been abandoned by God he would have to be an untruth. He was an object of divine favor and must always have been that. Therefore his cry of dereliction must have been a self-deception or an untruth. A theologian in Zurich, the saintly Hess, has also said that, and he is not one whom anyone can accuse of rationalism.[54] When we recall that the saying is the first part of a psalm in which a number of circumstances are referred to as descriptions of a state of suffering which literally was reproduced in Christ's experience, it is natural that he cited this state (or: cry) as a beginning of this description. He did not isolate it as a description of his situation, but as a referring of those who could hear him to *the entire psalm*.[55] This is

54. The reference is to Johann Jakob Hess, author of *Geschichte der drei letzten Lebensjahre Jesu* (Leipzig-Zurich, 1768-72; 7th ed. 1823).
55. Opinion is still varied among New Testament critics on the proper way to interpret this word from the cross, and the manner in which Schleiermacher does so has continued until the present. For instance: "We get the point of these words, which were spoken in Aramaic (so Mark) or Hebrew (Matthew), only if we know they are the opening verse of Psalm 22, and then only if we read the entire psalm. It begins in despair (22:1) but ends as a song of trust in God, that he will care for the righteous man in his extremity (see 22:19-31). Pious Jews recited these words when catastrophes threatened, and it is likely that Jesus had in mind the entire psalm or even spoke it in a low, inaudible voice." John Reumann, *Jesus in the Church's Gospels* (Philadelphia: Fortress, 1968), pp. 84-85; also, Sherman Johnson, *A Commentary on the Gospel According to Mark* (New York: Harper, 1960), p. 256.

something quite usual in citations. Passages are often cited whose actual meaning emerges only from what follows. It is even more common to cite a passage, not as a description in itself, but as a pointer to what is said in what follows. This is the only way I know how to explain the saying in question.

One of Christ's last words is notable in another respect. It is found only in Luke: Christ's conversation with those who were crucified with him, and the way in which one of the two turns to Christ and Christ responds to him. This criminal says, ''Jesus, remember me when you come in your kingdom,'' that is to say, when you come in your kingly power. These words imply a basic idea of a two fold appearance of the Messiah, or at least of two periods in his appearance. Here the speaker thinks of a return of Christ in his kingdom, and Jesus answers, ''Today you will be with me in Paradise.'' Clearly ''today'' is used in contrast to the words ''when you come'' that the repentant criminal had used. If we were to ask whether we are to regard this as a definite teaching of Christ about the future state, we should have to conclude that this teaching consisted of two different elements. The ''today'' declares that the future state follows immediately upon the present (for ''today'' expresses the unity of the day and therefore an unbroken unit of time). The other element of the teaching is found in the term ''Paradise.'' Christ uses that word and thus confirms the idea that is contained in it. However, we cannot understand this word literally. An idea of a physical state was bound up with it, an idea of the future life that was current among and accepted by the people of the time and that Christ also adopted in another passage when he speaks of Lazarus lying on Abraham's bosom. This last belongs only to the parabolic framework of the teaching Christ wished to communicate. This is also the case here. If we wanted to assume that Christ wished to confirm an exclusive prosperity of the descendants of Abraham for (in?) union with him, this would form a sharp contrast to the way Christianity later developed. If we cannot accept the one as an actual teaching, we also cannot accept the other. What is the actual content of it? We have to say: Christ only wanted to reject the notion that lay in the request made by the repentant thief, not the request itself — only the way the repentant thief thought of the request as being fulfilled. Whatever his wish actually was, it was independent of his thought of Christ coming "in [his] kingdom". In opposition to that Christ used the word "today", and "in Paradise" to refer to his idea of the future state. It would be quite impracticable to demand that Christ should have repudiated the idea. That was not the time or place for that. He could use the idea as the outer vestment and retain what was essential, namely, the "today". The future life was not something distant, but followed immediately upon death.

I should like to say a few words about another of Christ's sayings, for recently I have noticed a misunderstanding of it. It has been said that Christ's prayer, "Father, forgive them, for they know not what they do," can only refer to the men who personally took part in Christ's crucifixion, to the soldiers, but not to the actual authors of the act. This seems to me to be a very strange limitation of the meaning of Christ's words. Nothing had to be forgiven the soldiers, for no judgment of the morality or the legality of the execution could be passed by them. They could have their own personal feelings on the matter, but these could not influence their actions. They acted only in accordance with their profession. They only carried out a mission that they were commanded by their superiors to perform. They had no right to avoid the duty thrust upon them. So it could not have been the soldiers whom Christ asked to be forgiven. On the contrary, they would have been open to blame if they had not done what they were bidden to do. No one could say that, in terms of the morality of their act, they did not know what they did. If they had had a feeling that Christ was treated unjustly, they could have done nothing more than fulfill the duty of their station against their will. So Christ could not have been referring to them as those who stood in need of forgiveness. It is impossible to deny this on the grounds that Christ's opponents did know what they were doing. They really did not know it, for they did not proceed on the presupposition that Christ was the Messiah. If they had had a conviction of what they were doing, their way of acting would not have appeared as it did. On the contrary, if they had regarded him as the Messiah, they would not have acted as they did. They would have let the matter take its natural course if they had not had the concern that actually determined their action.

Let us retrace our steps for a little. In these different, very straightforward accounts of the last moments of Christ we have found a few elements that do not seem to be literal descriptions of actual facts, such as the rending of the temple veil and the opening of the graves. We may well ask: Can the same be said of many other details? We also have the remark that the sun lost its light and that there was a darkness over the face of the land, which also resembles the two other items we referred to. It looks like a poetical comment that has found its way into the bare account. If we compare John's narrative with the others here also, we find here too that it seems to be partly the account of an eyewitness and partly one of matters of which John could not have been an eyewitness, but it nevertheless bears the character of a direct report. Let me give an example. When John tells us that the chief priests lodged complaints with Pilate about the superscription on the cross, ''Jesus of Nazareth, the king of the Jews,'' and asked him to change it to, ''This man said, I am King of the Jews,'' that is a pregnant moment that makes the event very vivid. The superscription indicated a wish on Pilate's part to mock the Sanhedrin, since its members had used a kind of compulsion to make him pass sentence on Christ. Pilate wished to suggest that what had happened to Christ would happen to any future king of the Jews whom they might set up as a result of their hopes. The same thing could be said of the protest by members of the Sanhedrin that they had done what they did only on the assumption that Christ was not the Messiah, but one who falsely represented himself as the Messiah. John could have learned of this pregnant fact from a member of the Sanhedrin, from Nicodemus, or Joseph. Everything John narrates of the place has the character of an eyewitness report. When he speaks of Christ being led to the place of execution he does not mention the man who was impressed to carry Christ's cross. This does not mean that the detail was incorrect. It is possible that John was not close enough to see what was going on. He gives a detailed account of the course of the crucifixion, accentuates individual details, which he relates to Old Testament passages, and tells us which of Christ's relatives and disciples were near. These are precise statements, but they contain no reference to the darkness. So we have to reckon with the possibility that the detail of the darkness found a place in later narratives of the event, in which many other elements were included, from other poetical and rhetorical descriptions.

John refers to two other circumstances, the piercing of Christ's side with a spear, and the consequence of this, that not a bone of Christ was broken. When we consider how John mentions these circumstances, we see that he does so in connection with Old Testament passages that he cites. That, then, is his point of view. The piercing of Christ's side with a spear has been variously regarded. Some have thought of it as the cause of Christ's death. The story is as follows. Christ seemed to the soldier to be dead. He wanted on his part to be certain of that. The thrust with the spear was therefore not intended to kill Christ if he were still alive. If that had been the custom, why were the others not treated in a similar fashion, rather than having their bones broken? So then, since Christ seemed to be dead while the others still lived, the purpose of the spear thrust was to try to discover whether Christ still showed signs of life. The thrust was made in a sensitive part of the body, but not where an injury would be lethal, if the wound were not very deep. The fact that blood and water came out of the wound was a sign to the soldier that Christ had actually died. If he had still been alive, the lymph and the blood could not have been distinguished. So a chemical decomposition of the body had taken place.* The spear thrust, then, cannot be thought of as a contributing cause of Christ's death. It can only be regarded as a test of whether death had taken place. John cites the Old Testament passage about the paschal lamb as a prediction of the fact that Christ's bones were not broken. That is not to be interpreted as meaning that he thought of the paschal lamb as representing a type of Christ. He also cites an-

---

* or add: The lymph (*serum*) had already separated, although not fully, for otherwise no blood could have flowed out of the wound.

other passage of Scripture immediately following which has just as remote a connection with its subject. So then, we can only say here that even those who had the task of bringing about the death of those who had been crucified as quickly as possible, so that their corpses could be taken away, thought of Christ as really dead, and did so contrary to their expectation, for they marveled at the fact. We cannot discuss the matter in any further detail, for there is nothing more we know about it.

Lecture 64 (August 20). After this fashion Christ was officially declared dead. This whole final act, whose purpose was to hasten the death of those who had been crucified, which was brought about in the case of the other two crucified persons by breaking the bones of their extremities and breasts, an act of violence that was found unnecessary in the case of Christ, was due to the necessity of taking down the corpses before the arrival of the Sabbath. Now the problem arose of what to do with Christ's body. Then we are told that a man, apparently a member of the Sanhedrin, asked permission to take the body and bury it, and his request was granted by Pilate. That is the basis of the accounts of Christ's *burial.*

Here also, however, our accounts do not exactly agree. Matthew (27:57 ff.), after telling us that Joseph, a rich man from Arimathea who was also a disciple of Jesus, had asked Pilate for the body and had been granted it, goes on to say that he took it, wrapped it in a clean linen shroud, and laid it in his own new tomb, which he had hewn in a rock. Compare the account that John gives in chapter 19. In v. 38 John says, "After this Joseph of Arimathea, who was a disciple of Jesus, but secretly, for fear of the Jews, asked Pilate that he might take away the body of Jesus, and Pilate gave him leave." Then he goes on to say that Nicodemus also came, bringing a mixture of myrrh and aloes, and the two bound the body of Jesus in linen cloths with the spices, after the fashion of Jewish burial. Then in vv. 41-42 we are told: "Now in the place where he was crucified there was a garden, and in the garden a new tomb where no one had ever been laid. So because of the Jewish day of Preparation, as the tomb was close at hand, they laid Jesus there." This report seems to indicate quite clearly that the grave in which Christ was laid did not belong to Joseph. Otherwise we should not have been told why the grave was chosen. Here,then,there is a contradiction of the account in Matthew. It is my conviction that in a case such as this we cannot avoid preferring John's account. Since it was a natural assumption that Joseph had buried Jesus in his own new grave, it was natural that Matthew reported this, but John is better informed about the matter. He mentions Nicodemus and the spices, and he must be right on this point also, for it was not something that could have been invented. John must be right.

Joseph got his surname from a place whose exact locality has not been determined. We do not know whether he lived in Arimathea or was only born there. The references seem to suggest that Arimathea was where he had his residence. If this were so, it is hardly likely that he had his family tomb near Jerusalem. Probably he had only come to the city for the festival. The burial of Christ took place hastily and therefore without the consent of the owner of the tomb. If he later refused permission for the grave to be so used, the body would then have to be taken out again. We are faced with a dilemma. Either Joseph deposited the body temporarily, in order later to remove it to his family tomb, or he was concerned only with its burial. We hear no more of Joseph, and therefore there is no evidence that he wanted to do anything further. The reason for this is that Joseph, if it were not his intention to bury Christ in his own tomb, could leave the final disposal of the body to Nicodemus. Perhaps the body could be and ought to have been left where it was. This is a matter we cannot determine.

There is another story to be considered, this one in Matthew: the story of the guard. Matthew tells it in connection with the tale that the Pharisaic party had spread.* The story follows on the declaration made to the chief priests by the guards who had fled from the tomb. However, it is strange that the Sanhedrin should have told Pilate that it occurred to them that Jesus had told them while he was still alive that he

---

* or add: had spread abroad, but only after the report of the guard. Another possibility: but this occurs only after the resurrection.

would rise after three days and that Pilate should see to it that the sepulchre was properly guarded, so that there might be no indication that Christ's prophecy had been fulfilled, and that thereupon he gave them a guard, in whose presence they had sealed the tomb. So the chief priests must have known of such a prediction, which the disciples did not recall, for otherwise they would not have been so unbelieving when the first news of the resurrection was brought to them. The chief priests must have recalled it. How could they have know about it? There was only Christ's saying about the destruction of the temple. To be sure, Christ's disciples had interpreted that as referring to his resurrection. However, nothing was said of that in the testimony against Jesus at the trial. It was not a complaint made against him, and how could the chief priests have become acquainted with the disciples' interpretation of the passage? That the chief priests claimed that Christ had predicted his resurrection is therefore quite impossible. Just as improbable is the readiness of Pilate to comply with the request. He had been compelled to confirm the sentence of death imposed by the Sanhedrin on Christ. He had jeered at the Sanhedrin by means of the super-scription placed on the cross. In light of all this it is highly improbable that he should have supplied the Sanhedrin with a guard to prevent a possible theft of the corpse that had been buried with his permission — the corpse of a man who had been condemned to death and executed.

The Sanhedrin is said to have set the guard as a precautionary measure. After the resurrection some of the guard are said to have told the chief priests what had happened. The chief priests and the elders then met and told the soldiers to keep quiet about the matter. "Tell people, 'His disciples came by night and stole him away while we were asleep.'" All this is something very improbable. The Sanhedrin could better have told the soldiers to say nothing at all. It would have been easier for them to say that everything was in order and that they had left at the proper time.* When the apostles appeared

* or add: In this way they set a story in circulation that they actually ought to have had to prove. Since the disciples later said quite openly that Christ had shown himself only to them, they clearly made no use of the guard's story. It would have been easier to tell them: Why did he

as witnesses to the resurrection, they said quite openly that Christ had not appeared to others. So they made no use of the guard's story. The whole affair has no inner probability. In Matthew 28:15 the Evangelist says that the report that the body of Christ had been stolen ''has spread among the Jews to this day.'' The fact that lies back of the story is that, when the apostles preached Christ's resurrection, the opposing party said: Your claim is false. The body of Christ was stolen. To be sure, this presupposes that the finding of the empty tomb had become a generally known fact and that the Sanhedrin had to explain it. They did so by saying that the body of Christ had been stolen. This statement had to be supported, and in my judgment the story of the guard was invented to support the Sanhedrin's claim. The Sanhedrin said the body of Christ had been stolen, but the story of the guard was a concoction. There is no reason to believe that it has any historical content.

We now proceed to a consideration of the last part of the life of Jesus, namely,

THE STORY OF CHRIST'S RESURRECTION UNTIL HIS ASCENSION [56]

appear only to you? If he had actually risen he would have appeared to others also, that all might believe in him.

56. An oft-quoted proposition of *The Christian Faith* states that: "The facts of the Resurrection and the Ascension of Christ, and the prediction of his return to Judgment, cannot be laid down as properly constituent parts of the doctrine of his person." *CF*, §99. Consistent with his Johannine approach, Schleiermacher there insists that the disciples recognized Jesus Christ as the Son of God without possessing any foresight of such events and the same conviction is possible for Christians of later times quite apart from these events. Nevertheless, the long discussion of the resurrection that follows here in the *Life of Jesus* makes clear that Schleiermacher accepts the so-called historicity of the resurrection even though it has little function in his theology. The resulting situation is a quite striking and unusual one in modern Christian thought. Faith does not need the resurrection as a specific event because Jesus can otherwise communicate what is significant, his archetypal God-consciousness into which he continually assumes believers, and because matters pertaining to eternal salvation rest upon God's eternal predestination which Schleiermacher does not connect with Christ's resurrection. (Cf. *CF*, §119-20, and "Ueber die Lehre von der Erwählung," *Sämmtliche Werke* [Berlin: G. Reimer, 1836], I,2:393-94. One might then expect such a theological position to assume a quite different stance to the resurrection of Jesus Christ than Schleiermacher actually has. In sum, with a modicum of license, I would say that for Schleiermacher what is theologically inconsequential happens historically to be true! He will not impugn the reliability of the Gospel of John; therefore, he says Christ's resurrection belongs to the doctrine of Scripture rather than to Christology. Cf. *CF*, §99, 2.

Schleiermacher's particular view of the resurrection was also held by

We begin this second part of the third period of the life of Jesus with a general observation. It is well known that these stories of the resurrection and ascension of Christ were violently attacked and that the opponents of Christianity took great pains especially to point out contradictions in the accounts of Christ's resurrection. We cannot deny that these contradictions exist. However, comparable contradictions are also to be found in the earlier parts of the life of Jesus. When the opponents of the evangelical story insist that the early part of the life of Jesus is true and that untruth begins with the resurrection account, they are guilty of an illogical prejudice and intention. Contradictions, as we have said, appear in other sections of the life of Christ. Let me cite an example. The Gospel of John speaks of many visits that Christ made to Jerusalem, whereas the first three Gospels tell only of one visit. There are similar contradictions in all the longer accounts. We cannot differentiate between the contradictions in the resurrection stories and those that appear earlier. To be sure, there is an idea that lies back of all this. In other narratives, apart from the biblical narratives, one can imagine contradictions and explain them by saying that when a certain author tells a story, he does not do it so fully that there is no more to tell. If two narrate the story, there can be still more that can be added. In the case of biblical stories, however, that cannot be the case, for these accounts were actually all inspired narratives. On this presupposition it would even be possible to say: One cannot treat the evangelical stories as one does secular accounts. This, however, would require a consistency, and we come to the conclusion that evangelical narratives are not inspired narratives, but accounts such as we find elsewhere. A literal application of the doctrine of inspiration to the Gospel accounts cannot be made. It would be absurd to try to do so. In the story of the resurrection we have to make the same presupposition and to treat it in the same way. We find the same difference there that exists elsewhere between John's Gospel

others of his day and stresses the continuity of the natural body of Jesus after Easter with its state prior to death. The naturalness of the condition to which Jesus returns calls for its inclusion in a discussion of the life of Jesus. Cf. Karl Hase, *Das Leben Jesu*, (3rd ed. Leipzig, 1840), pp. 210-17.

and the other three Gospels. I know no rule to set up except this: The Gospel of John is an account by an eyewitness, and the whole Gospel was written by one man. The first three Gospels are compilations of many accounts that earlier stood by themselves. If the individual sections of the different Gospels are examined, we find differences which are genuine contradictions, and they can only be hypothetically reconciled, not wholly. These always occur when details are related by eyewitnesses which then are repeated by others and when gaps in the narrative are filled out with facts drawn from other sources or by conjecture. It is always possible to recover the fact itself from the narrative, and the contradictions contained in them can often be explained in terms of their sources by conjecture and critical research. Again and again this is the case.

In connection with the resurrection story, however ,the problem is not restricted to the individual data, but is due to general ideas that are basic, and it seems proper procedure to treat these first and clarify them. *Matthew* compresses this part of his account into a single chapter, and half of this is occupied by the story of one event. His account runs as follows. Christ appears to the women and tells them to order his disciples to go to Galilee, where they would see him. Then there is the intervening story of the guard, and then only the comment that the eleven disciples went to Galilee. This Evangelist knows nothing of several appearances of Christ to his disciples in Jerusalem. So he omits so much of what Luke and John narrate that we have to say again: It is impossible that Matthew's Gospel was written by one of the twelve apostles, unless we are to accuse the others of telling deliberate lies. This Gospel must necessarily be ascribed to some other apostolic source. Apart from the first part of the last chapter, in which the resurrection is announced and we are told that Christ appeared to the women, there is a twofold tendency to be noted. On the one hand the Evangelist wants the reader to understand the unbelief of the Jews and the lie that the chief priests spread abroad. On the other hand, he wants us to know that the activity of the apostles in preaching was the result of the command that Christ gave them. The story is not treated historically, for we are not told where Christ went.

Lecture 65 (August 21). Let us glance at the way the whole event of the resurrection is presented in the different Gospels. We have seen that Matthew does not actually treat it historically. All he tells us is how the resurrection became known and of a meeting between Christ and his disciples in Galilee. No details are given of this meeting except that Christ commanded the disciples to preach in his name. The purpose of Matthew's account is to explain after the resurrection this preaching of Christ after his death, and therefore all that happened is located in Galilee.

When we examine the account in *Mark,* we have to note a special circumstance. The greater part of Mark's last chapter, which contains the details of the story, is subject to suspicion. According to ancient reports in several manuscripts, the last section of Mark 16, from v. 9 on, is missing in many excellent Greek manuscripts or is replaced by a shorter account. I do not want to lay much weight on this. In my judgment the passage in question is quite genuine. I only wish to point out that it contains a greater number of details than does Matthew's account. The narrative has a tendency to show the unbelief of the disciples. Christ appears on the one hand to rebuke them for their unbelief and on the other hand to commission them to preach the gospel. In connection with the commission Christ expressly promises support by the gift of miracle-working powers. No actual historical tendency can be observed here.* Rather, the description is one of a disposition, bound up with a description of its result. As in Matthew, the unbelief of the disciples is stressed when Christ appears to them in Galilee.

Luke presents a strikingly different account of what happened. In this Gospel we see a purely historical tendency at work. Various appearances of Christ as a living being are narrated with a measure of detail and exactitude, without betraying any other interest on the part of the Evangelist than that which emerges from the account. However, at different times Luke has apparently gotten different accounts of the matter. In the Gospel everything happens on the same day,

* There is no tendency to present the individual events in any connection with each other.

434

and one cannot deny that the latest events, when Christ leads
his disciples to the Mount of Olives and from there is taken
up to heaven, are directly related to the preceding meeting of
Christ with his disciples on the evening of Easter Sunday. On
the other hand, at the beginning of the book of the Acts of
the Apostles, Luke has an entirely different account. There he
mentions a space of forty days during which Christ appeared
to his disciples and spoke to them of the kingdom of God, and
he tells of Christ's ascension as an event that took place long
after the resurrection. That is clearly a correction of what had
been said in the Gospel, where the resurrection and the ascension are represented as having taken place on the same day.
However, in both the Gospel and the book of the Acts of the
Apostles Luke presents a contrast to the other two synoptic
accounts. His interest in narrating facts is dominant.

This is also what we find throughout John's Gospel. The
way he narrates events during this period does not differ at all
from the way he narrates events from Christ's life before his
death. His narrative shows the same pragmatic tendency and
the same character of immediacy. Everything he includes in
his account is taken directly from the reports of eyewitnesses.
How are we to explain this difference? On the one hand there
is the compression of the whole affair into a single act with
which Christ's resurrection life begins and ends. Then there is
the variety apparent in John's account, with the statement at
the end that much more of the sort could have been told, and
then in Luke there is the definite reference to a period. Two
contrasting explanations are possible. We can suppose that
gradually details were added to the simple account, details
that were not factual but were spun out of the miraculous
character of the event. The other explanation is that the consciousness of such a period during which Christ continued to
appear to his disciples and of which much is told that is not
included in our Gospels was original, but much of that has
been lost in our synoptic Gospels, and consequently the matter
came to be understood as Matthew and Mark present it.*
In Luke's writings we see that he later obtained new informa-

* or add: and therefore everything is briefly summarized by the synoptic
Evangelists

435

tion. In addition, we know from Paul's First Letter to the Corinthians of other appearances of Christ to his disciples that are not recorded in all our Gospels. Since Luke appears to have been a diligent researcher and Paul certainly was not one who would include unattested statements in his letter, we are compelled to prefer the latter of the two explanations we have put forward.

The facts were handed down from the beginning in varied form, and the way by which our Gospels originated at certain times and places that we cannot determine prevented their inclusion. Matthew and Mark each hand on a significant detail. In Matthew we observe the tendency to locate all events of Christ's life in Galilee — a tendency not shared by all the other Gospels. Matthew assumes that Christ came to Jerusalem only in order to die there, and therefore the first thing he does after his resurrection is to tell his disciples to go to Galilee. In Mark we see quite clearly that the detailed story that Luke records of the two disciples who walked to Emmaus was so largely forgotten that only a general reference to it was made. Mark could have given greater place to it without running counter to his principle of brevity. If Mark had had the story in greater detail, he would have had a greater interest in putting into Christ's mouth what he made the angel in the grave say. So we can set up the following principle: When we undertake to recover the facts from all our narratives, we cannot ascribe the same authority to all our Gospels, since all Evangelists were not all in the same position to be familiar with them. If the first reporters obtained different details from different sources, the differences they reflect can be satisfactorily explained.

Let us turn now more to matters of detail and see what is told us of all that spread the report of Christ's resurrection, before he himself was seen by his disciples. Clearly there are contradictions in connection with this in individual narratives which cannot be immediately harmonized, but they can be explained when we assume that each Evangelist felt compelled to make up for the incompleteness and inadequacy of the stories he got from others by expanding them.

Matthew tells of two women, Mary Magdalene and the

"other" Mary (sister of Jesus' mother and wife of Cleopas), who went early in the morning of the day following the Sabbath to see the sepulcher. If they had any other intention in mind, Matthew knows nothing of it. Now follows an account that if taken literally seems to me to be inexplicable: "And behold, there was a great earthquake;for an angel of the Lord descended from heaven and came and rolled back the stone, and sat upon it. His appearance was like lightning, and his raiment white as snow. And for fear of him the guards trembled and became like dead men. But the angel said to the women," etc. Matthew goes on to tell the story of the guard and then comes back to the women. Where did this account of the earthquake and of the descent of the angel come from? Because it is interrupted, the story of the earthquake and all that follows does not seem to be an account of what the women themselves saw. If it were, they would have had to have seen Christ coming out of the grave when the angel opened it before their eyes. What happened was this: the women came to the sepulcher; the angel was there; the guards were like dead men. The rest must have happened before their arrival. Where did the story come from? It cannot have originated in the account that the guards gave to the chief priests, for they suppressed the truth by spreading the lie that the disciples had stolen Christ's body. We cannot assume that the chief priests themselves would have betrayed the truth of the resurrection. It is apparent that the story of the actual resurrection is nothing but an account of what no one saw, linked with the story of the guard, which likewise is apocryphal.

The angel tells the women to see the place where the Lord had lain and then to hurry and tell the disciples that he had risen. Then we have the words: "Behold, he is going before you to Galilee; there you will see him. Lo, I have told you." This story apparently excludes everything else that happened in Jerusalem. The women are told to go quickly to the disciples and tell them, etc. This presupposes that the disciples spent no further time in Jerusalem but went at once to Galilee. So the person who told this story knew nothing of an appearance of Christ in Jerusalem.

Mark knows nothing of the earthquake and the rolling

away of the stone, and he had more women, three in fact, go to the grave with the intention of anointing the body of Jesus with spices. To their astonishment they find the stone rolled away. They now enter the sepulcher and see a young man sitting on the right side, who tells them much the same thing that Matthew's angel had told the women in that Gospel. So we find an agreement in what was said, but a disagreement as to the person who said it. In Matthew it was clearly the angel who had descended from heaven and had rolled away the stone who uttered the words, while in Mark it was a "young man sitting on the right side, dressed in a white robe." There are different ideas of the person who informed the disciples of Christ's resurrection in the Gospels, and Mark's "young man" appears to be the original.

Luke gives the following account. In the time that elapsed the women prepared spices and went to the sepulcher, along with a few others [*textus receptus*]. They found the stone rolled away and, while they were perplexed about this, two men in dazzling apparel stood by them. Whether they were at this time in or out of the sepulcher is not clear from the story. The use of the phrase "returning from the tomb" in v. 9, without any mention of their previously coming out, seems to indicate that the event took place in the sepulcher. In Luke we have two men, and Luke says nothing of an angel, but supports Mark in this respect. Now he goes on to mention three who were present: *Mary Magdalene, Joanna,* and *Mary the mother of James,* as well as other women who were with them. In Luke, then, two men and several women are enumerated, a plethora of persons. There is also a further difference in Luke. We do not find the command to the disciples to go to Galilee. There is a reference to what Christ had said to them while he was in Galilee, but no mention of a command to go there. Since the following facts in Luke and John would conflict with the command as Matthew and Mark report it, we must conjecture that the command to the disciples to go to Galilee must have been constructed out of this mention of Galilean sayings of Christ. It forms a bridge between the two variants.

This is the account as it stands in *John. Mary Magdalene*

came to the tomb and found the stone rolled away. Then she ran and went to Simon Peter and the other disciple, the one whom Jesus loved, and told them that Christ's body had been taken away from the tomb to some other place. That takes us back to the story of the burial, where we are told that this tomb was only an interim burial place and that the body of Christ was to have been brought to Joseph's own tomb. Mary Magdalene knew that this was so, but she did not know where he was to have been brought in order to carry out the original intention. The fact that we are told that Mary returned immediately indicates a great similarity to the account in Luke. The "certain women who were with them," who according to Luke had gone with the women, had certainly remained behind at the tomb. Since they did not know where the personal tomb of Joseph of Arimathea was located, they would have had to go back the whole way to Jerusalem. So a considerable group went out, but Mary Magdalene was perhaps the first who went to the tomb (cf. v. 11), and the "'other" Mary stood at the grave while Mary Magdalene went on ahead. So, if we treat the accounts in light of the way we have seen that they could have come into being, we see that the contradictions can be largely resolved and that we can recover the facts, at least to a large extent.

Lecture 66 (August 22). The first accounts of Christ's resurrection consist of two elements: the tomb was found open and empty, and, quoting the command to the disciples, the information that Christ had risen was imparted. The latter element is not found in John's Gospel. In that Gospel everything takes place without such an apparent introduction of another supernatural factor. In other words, John contains the account of the resurrection. Christ appears, and what occurs between the finding of the empty tomb and his appearance is superfluous, although, to be sure, it is narrated. Mary Magdalene finds the tomb empty. She returns to Peter and John, who go out and inspect the sepulcher. Then Mary stands before the tomb, looks inside, and sees two angels. Then, without anything else happening, Christ meets her and speaks to her. In John's Gospel there is one point hard to understand. In v. 11 we are told that *Mary* stood weeping outside the tomb. As she wept she stooped to look into the tomb, and she saw two angels in white. If that happened after Peter and John had inspected the tomb, we cannot understand how the angels could later have entered it. They must have gone in in an invisible way and have assumed form only after their entrance. However, this assumption is not necessary. The *second Mary* must have been another person than the first. Before Peter and John came out of the sepulcher the one must have returned and the other remained behind. So the conversation of the risen Christ with Mary must have taken place before Mary Magdalene had come back and entered the tomb, and the angels must have then disappeared at once. However, this explanation proves inadequate and cannot be employed. The Mary who saw Christ is later identified as *Mary Magdalene,* and the encounter with the angels must have taken place after Peter and John had investigated the sepulcher. There is no way of knowing how the angels got into the tomb. If Mary had only seen the angels we might conclude that it was a hallucination, but they also spoke to her.* Here we have an insoluble difficulty and, since the other accounts give a more general report, we cannot use them to supplement that in John.

Let us consider the question of the persons involved in this interlude. Matthew and John expressly call them *angels.* Matthew says that the angel descended from heaven and that Mary saw him sitting on the rock. In John there are two angels in the tomb, one sitting at the head of where the body of Christ had lain and the other at the feet (v. 12). In Mark it is *a young man* who sits in the tomb, and in Luke there are *two men,* but in neither case are we told where they were sitting. So this is a variable element. Which variable is more probable, *man* or *angel, one* or *two?* There is one angel in Matthew and two in John; one man in Mark and two in Luke. If from the very beginning several persons went to the tomb and so several accounts were possible, but not of such

* or add: without anything happening as the result of that

440

a sort that they could be fully harmonized, it is easy to imagine how one could have become two, if a later redactor had
assumed that the persons mentioned by the reporters were not
the same. If we now ask: What is more probable, a man or
an angel? We are compelled to answer: In a historical time
such as that, probably the appearance of angels was no longer
imaginable. So I ask: What is more probable, that a reporter
should say that an angel was a man, or that a man or a young
man was an angel? We have to answer: If something miraculous was underway, it is more natural that something natural
was interpreted as something miraculous than the reverse.
The angels appear in this instance completely in human form.
They wear clothes and speak, so the confusion is something
quite natural. These transformations of individual elements
in the individual narratives can therefore probably be explained, and it is only in John that anything inexplicable
remains — something that does not correspond to his way
of narrating events.

It is clear that he was an eyewitness when the tomb was
searched. He himself was with Peter in the sepulcher. What
follows, the address of the angels, etc., he could probably
have gotten from Mary Magdalene herself. No doubt Mary
told of seeing these persons in the tomb and of Christ's appearance to her immediately thereafter. Naturally, if she told
John what she had seen, we must wonder that he did not ask
more precisely how what she had seen in the tomb was related
to his own experience in it. We must conclude from this that
she told it in such a way that it was not possible for him later
to separate the two elements that belonged together. This
appearance in the tomb serves different functions in the different Gospels. We see no particular tendency in John. There
were two in the sepulcher, and Mary was the first who looked
into the tomb, and she enters into a conversation. When Peter
and John went into the tomb there was no longer anyone
there. This I regard as the actual historical element in the
story. As for the other Gospels, in Luke we find that the two
angels have become two men. These men tell the Galilean
women — we do not know how many of them there were —
that Christ had risen and they remind them of Christ's earlier

Galilean predictions. In Matthew and Mark the one angel has the function of giving the women the command to tell Christ's disciples to go to Galilee. In fact, the command could not have been given at the time. Otherwise other developments would have had to take place. The command is therefore a later addition to the story. We must assume that it was suggested by Christ's Galilean discourse and the report that Christ later was with his disciples in Galilee. It is clear that such a command would have been quite unsuitable to the end in view. However that may be, we must say that, whether they were one or two, they contributed nothing by their appearance. Christ appeared immediately to Mary herself and could say what there was to say. So, since I cannot imagine an angel appearing during a historical era, I regard them as superfluous persons. Therefore they are to be regarded as men. It is useless to speculate about who it was. There is also not the slightest reason to introduce the legend of other groups about Jesus that were unknown to his disciples.

Let me recapitulate the story as it has been narrated to this point. Joseph of Arimathea laid the body provisionally in the tomb in the garden, but was not able to attend to the rest of the burial customs until after the Sabbath had passed. So people commissioned by Joseph could have come to the tomb earlier than Mary, who found the grave empty. However, all our accounts necessarily presuppose Christ's resurrection, and it is to be assumed as a fact that cannot be doubted. If it is said that all these accounts of Christ's presence with his disciples after his death on the cross are delusions, then all the narratives of Christ are delusions. The narratives of the resurrection seem to be reports of something actually seen. We are compelled either to dismiss all accounts of Jesus' life or to accept them. There is no other alternative. It is very natural that there are no accounts of Christ's resurrection itself. In the first place, Christ's disciples show a praiseworthy hesitance to ask Christ questions arising out of mere curiosity. If we find in the story itself an indication of how the fact is to be explained that someone was in the tomb, there is no reason to conclude from the two facts, that such persons appear and that positive accounts of the resurrection

442

itself are lacking, that the presence of an individual in the tomb points to the existence of groups of secret followers of Christ. Such an assumption is groundless.

We now come to the first announcement that was made by the risen Christ. In the accounts either Mary alone was given it, or indefinite reference is made to several women. The latter is the case in Matthew's Gospel. There we are told that on the instructions of the angel the women went to the disciples and told them that Jesus had risen, etc. Then Christ meets them and speaks to them and repeats the commission. The other major account, that in John's Gospel, cannot be harmonized with Matthew's. In John Christ speaks to Mary, but she does not recognize him. He says the same thing to her that the angels had said to her, "Why are you weeping?" but adds, "Whom do you seek?" Then we are told that she thought he was the gardener, etc. Now Christ calls her by name and she recognizes him. Then he tells her of his impending ascent to the Father and commissions her to tell that to the disciples. There are no instructions that the disciples should go to Galilee where they would see him. She was only told to tell them that he would shortly ascend to the Father, although he had not yet done so. This contradicts all the other accounts we have. John's narrative implies that Christ did not want, or was unable, to say anything more definite about the future; that he had no definite idea of the extent of this renewed life* and was unable, or did not want, to say anything about it. So there is a certain solemnity to what he says, and that is quite natural and appropriate to the circumstances, but without giving the occasion any definite color. Now we must make a further division, distinguishing between what happened *on the same day* and what took place *during all the rest of the time,* not only in the narratives of the Evangelists, but also in the notices that Paul gives.

Our sources tell us that two things happened on the resurrection day: (1) Christ appeared to the two disciples on the way to Emmaus, and (2) he went late in the evening to the assembly of the disciples. Before the latter visit he appeared

---

* newly-awakened life. Another possibility: of this new life.

to Peter. We cannot precisely locate this appearance, but certainly it took place before the encounter with the two disciples. Immediately after telling us that Peter went into the tomb and found it empty, Luke goes on to narrate the story of the appearance to the two disciples on the walk to Emmaus that took place on the same day. We learn from what follows that it happened in the evening, for the disciples could invite Christ to share their supper. Then, after Christ had left them they returned to Jerusalem and the disciples told them that Christ had appeared to Peter.

We now have to discuss an important question: How are we to think of the state Christ was in after the resurrection? There are contradictory indications in our sources, and the evidence seems to support one conclusion rather than the other. (1) There is an indication that we are to think of Christ's resurrection state as a reconstitution of his life just as it had been before. (2) There is another indication that leads us to believe that Christ's resurrection state was quite different from his state before his crucifixion. He only appeared to be the same. The first evidence I cite in favor of the former conclusion is that Christ showed himself in the form that had previously been his. Otherwise Mary would not immediately have recognized him, and how would he have shown his disciples his wounds? In fact, Christ expressly says that he is not a being unrelated to the natural course of life, but one with a wholly human body. The picture we get of him in this light is that he was one who moved as men moved and even ate and drank as men did. On the other hand, however, there are also indications that he disappeared, that he passed through closed doors, and that individual appearances were noted without any indication of where he had been in the meantime. These references confuse the picture. However, I believe that Christ's declaration, his specific declaration, by which he tried to convince his disciples that he was the same as he had been before, must clearly carry the greater weight.

That Christ was not continually with his disciples can be explained by the fact that he did not want to come into contact with others, that he wanted to be with them alone. We do not know where he stayed because the disciples hesitated to put the question to him. If someone were to say that that quite clearly presupposes other groups whom Christ reckoned among his followers, I should have to say: There were no such groups outside the disciples who are regularly the subject of discussion. Christ's disappearance and his passing through closed doors have more the appearance of the supernatural than they necessarily need to have. When the apostles were together at evening, no doubt the house* was closed, but there would have been someone there whose duty it was to open it. It would have been quite unusual for the *room* to be closed, and it would have served no purpose to close it.† In view of the definite statement Christ made there is no need to assume anything so ghostly as passing through closed doors. So, too, the two Emmaus disciples were astonished when they suddenly recognized Christ. That they did not recognize him sooner can be explained by their lack of faith in the news that had already been received. Christ can have left them without disappearing in a supernatural way. They only later noticed that he was gone. If we hold fast to what Christ himself said, admitting that not all historical statements are clear because they do not consist of properly arranged elements, we see that nothing incomprehensible remains, except Christ's resurrection itself. However, the same thing is true of Christ's whole appearance upon earth. His coming was a miraculous act, but all that followed it was wholly natural.

Lecture 67 (August 23). There is still another difficult question that I believe neither the author of the Wolfenbüttel fragments nor anyone else has noticed.[57] I want to point it out to all, for it has much to contribute to the proper understand-

---

* the *pylē* ["gate"] was naturally closed
† or add: There was no reason for the room to be closed, and no analogy for so doing, for the disciples could have been isolated by closing the gates. Their astonishment was such that they did not observe how Christ came and went.
57. Hermann Samuel Reimarus's *Fragments* are included in the Lives of Jesus series (Philadelphia: Fortress, 1970). Reimarus in his section on the resurrection of Jesus Christ presents a long cataloguing of the discrepancies and contradictions found in the New Testament on this subject.

ing of the actual state of our accounts. We have two references to Christ's appearance to Peter. Luke tells us that when the two Emmaus disciples came to the assembly of the eleven they were greeted with the words, ''The Lord has risen indeed, and has appeared to Simon'' [Peter]. Peter must have been alone on that occasion, or at least without any other of the apostles. In 1 Corinthians 15 *Paul* mentions the appearance to Cephas [Peter] and lists it as *the first,* for he says in v. 5 that Christ was seen by Cephas and then by the twelve. It is impossible to ascertain whether Paul knew nothing of the earlier appearance to the women, or only omitted reference to it. If we isolate the final narrative in John, when Christ addressed himself especially to Peter and spoke to him about his relationship to him, we see that the narrative seems to presuppose that there had been no previous communication between the risen Christ and Peter. This occasion seems to have been the first when the two had been together. To be sure, the reference to Peter's denial is not quite clear, but if we leave that out of consideration, what we have is a renewed instruction (or: institution) of Peter, although it does not contain anything that did not apply also to the other eleven. So this must have been the occasion of Christ's first appearance to Peter. Although we get this impression, according to both Luke and even John himself Christ had seen Peter earlier, on the evening before, together with the other apostles. So then, if this institution had to take place in the presence of the other apostles, since Christ's fellowship with Peter was the same as his fellowship with them, the natural place for that would have been on the occasion of the first time they saw each other again. However, these accounts are so interrupted that we cannot fill in the gaps. On the other hand, there was no occasion on which Christ had been able to ask Peter whether he loved him. (It is improbable that it refers to the denial, which did not include this.) So this conversation can naturally have its basis in something that happened in between, but what that was we cannot determine, for our sources lack the necessary connection.

If we take Christ's conversation with the two Emmaus disciples as the central point, we see that in Luke Christ had appeared previously to Peter, and that later he appeared also to

446

the eleven. In Luke's account it is noteworthy and an important proof of the truth of the narrative that everything that we know from the story of the two disciples has the character of describing Christ's appearance as something miraculous. This can be observed in the nonrecognition and the later sudden recognition, as well as in Christ's disappearance. On the other hand, the whole account of what happened at the meeting with the eleven tends to represent Christ's appearance as a perfectly natural one and as identical with that of his earlier life. Two appearances are referred to in the same connection, the one reported by the disciples and the other Christ's appearance to the eleven. Everything Christ says and does tends to discredit any thought of an unnatural state of his resurrection body. He does not want anyone to think of his resurrection state as differing from his state as he was before. He lets himself be touched to show that he has a genuinely human body as others have. He shows the wounds he had received on the cross. He eats in the presence of the disciples. This last is something decisive as a proof of the wholly natural corporeity of his state. If Christ had only eaten to show that he could eat, without having any need of nourishment, the whole thing would have been a deception, something docetic. This ought to give us an indication of all else that we want to know of the way Christ represented himself. Everything that appeared miraculous to the disciples was due to their apprehension of him.*

However, there is still another remarkable difference in the account. John also tells us that Christ came in the evening to the eleven as they were assembled, although, since he expressly says that Thomas was not present, the number of the disciples was actually ten. He says nothing of the two Emmaus disciples. That is due to his practice of emphasizing only what he himself had heard and of which he himself had been an eyewitness. Of the rest he adds only what is absolutely necessary to fill out his account. In Luke Christ in his conversation with the two Emmaus disciples appeals to the Old Testament. They ought to have known from the Scrip-

* or add: They were responsible for it.

tures all that had to happen to him. Similarly in v. 44 ff. he says to the disciples, "These are my words which I spoke to you, while I was still with you, that everything written about me in the law of Moses and the prophets and the psalms must be fulfilled." Then he goes on to say, "Thus it is written, that the Christ should suffer and on the third day rise from the dead." Then he adds, "Repentance and forgiveness of sins [are to be] preached in [my] name to all nations, beginning from Jerusalem." In John we find no reference to the Old Testament and also no such definite commission, which actually would have been only a renewal of their original mission. To be sure, there is a mention of the fact that he was sending them out even as he himself had been sent, but with the definite addition that he communicated the Holy Spirit to them and uttered the familiar words about the forgiveness of sins.

Two things are remarkable about this. In the first place, there is the negative element. Are we to conclude from John's silence that Christ made no reference to Old Testament predictions of his death and no reference to the fact that he himself had predicted it? Although John seldom refers to such predictions we can hardly avoid concluding that he intentionally omitted reference to them here. We cannot regard his silence on the matter as accidental. His omission of such references could only have been intentional if he had been aware of them but had not used them, and the only reason for that could have been that he wrote his Gospel for a non-Jewish public. Christians drawn from among the heathen were to be referred only to the story and its fulfillment in Christ. If John had not heard Christ say anything such as Luke reports, it must have been accidental. He could not have omitted it intentionally. Of course, it is possible that Christ did not say it. John was always a member of the intimate circle about Christ, and we have no reason to believe that he was often absent, or long absent, from it. But this hypothesis is not probable. The book of the Acts of the Apostles in chapter 1 tells us that Christ let himself be seen for a considerable period by his disciples and spoke to them of the kingdom of God. In the course of their preaching the apostles appealed to Old Testament passages that they held were predictions of the death and resurrection of Christ, even passages that were not regarded as having messianic content by ordinary (rabbinic) exegesis. So it is probable that among Christ's discourses with his disciples about the kingdom of God there were such references to Old Testament passages and that the interpretation of them by the apostles was based on Christ's own exegesis. However, that does not mean that what Luke reports was part of Christ's discourse at that time. It is so general that in and for itself it could have had no result. In reporting the conversation of Christ with the two Emmaus disciples Luke says that he had interpreted to them in the Scriptures the things concerning himself. It is not necessary to assume that this explanation was given only during the period after the resurrection, but it is improbable that Christ before his death made use of Old Testament passages to demonstrate that he must rise from the dead. It is much more likely that passages of this sort were ascribed to Christ before his death* from what he actually said after the resurrection. If Christ had given such detailed instructions it is improbable that his disciples would have so completely forgotten them that they were not able to presuppose his resurrection. The statement that they were amazed when they saw the tomb empty and that it never occurred to them that Christ could have risen is so natural that it demonstrates that Christ had not predicted his resurrection while he was still in the course of his earthly mission.

All this is clearly proof that many of Christ's discourses are introduced in the Gospels in contexts that are not original, set in a context in which they were not originally delivered. So elements from discourses of Christ after the resurrection have found a place in his earlier discourses. Christ expresses himself at his first meeting with the disciples as Luke records his words. In John's account Christ says to Mary: "I have not yet ascended to the Father," etc. and expressly refers to the Spirit who is to take his place and assures his disciples of what they should do with respect to the forgiveness of sin. According to Luke Christ repeated the general commission.

* at the time of his crucifixion

All this shows that Christ at that time had no certainty that he would see his disciples often again. He was conscious of a genuinely human life, but had no assurance of how long it would last. His words give the impression of a farewell. There is no definite difference between what he says in the evening to his disciples and what he says in the morning to Mary. So a command by Christ to his disciples to go to Galilee is not in harmony with the rest we know. However, John's account has such a character of inner truth that we must say: The command must have had some other origin. John's account is the true one by which we can explain Christ's whole state of being. In light of this we must regard it as a new and unexpected development that still other appearances of Christ are mentioned. The first Evangelist also represents Christ's first meeting with his disciples as though it were also his last. The ascension follows this first and last meeting. In the book of the Acts of the Apostles and in the Gospel of John, however, the resurrection story extends over a period beyond the first day. This period in Luke's account is specified as lasting forty days, but it is indefinite in John's narrative. The period ends in Luke with the ascension, but this is not the case in John. This is another indication of the remarkable variation we have to note in our historical records.

Our first task is to discuss what we are told happened after the day of the resurrection, and our second task is to examine the state of our historical records of the ascension.

For this further study we have three different sources: the narrative at the beginning of the book of the Acts of the Apostles; the conclusion of the Gospel of John; and the account given by the apostle Paul in his First Letter to the Corinthians.

In Luke's account the length of the resurrection period is given, but the story of it is presented in a very general and condensed form. Let me paraphrase his narrative. During the forty-day period after his sufferings Christ presented himself alive by many proofs and spoke to his disciples of matters related to the kingdom of God. Then follows the story of his last farewell. The phrase "appearing to them" does not describe a regular life of fellowship with his disciples but a series of separate appearances. However, the clause "he presented himself to them alive" shows that his disciples recognized that Christ's life was genuine. In John we find an aggregation of separate elements. However, there are two sides to the question of how we are to fill in this interim period. In the first place, why did Christ not live together with his disciples as he had done before, since it would have been possible to do that? Christ found them together. They remained together, for he found them assembled eight days later. In the second place, since he was not with his disciples, where was he? What was the constant factor that was only interrupted by his occasional appearances to his disciples?

There seem to be two ways to solve this problem. In the first place, we can say that there was no constant factor. Christ led a consistent life, but only appeared on occasion, though each time as a full man. However, this view lacks clarity. Despite that, however, there is a strong probability that Paul held this idea. In 1 Corinthians 15 he speaks of Christ's resurrection as he tells us he had taught it from the beginning. Christ died for our sins according to the Scriptures, was raised on the third day according to the Scriptures, and appeared to Peter and then to the twelve. Later he appeared to more than five hundred brethren at one time, then to James, and then to all the apostles at one time. "Finally he appeared also to me." It is worthy of note that Paul refers to the appearance to himself as though it were identical with those to the others. There are only two possibilities open. Either we assume with the notorious Mr. Brennecke that Christ was still alive as Paul took the road to Damascus,[58] or

58. Schleiermacher refers to Jakob Andreas Brennecke who thirteen years previously had published a book with the revealing title, *Biblical Demonstration: That Jesus Has Lived Bodily upon Earth Twenty-seven Years after His Resurrection and Quietly Was Continuously Active for the Benefit of Humanity* (*Biblisher Beweis: dass Jesus nach seiner Auferstehung noch siebenundzwanzig jahr leibhaftig auf erden gelebt und zum Wohl der Menschheit in der Stille fortgewirkt habe*) (n. p., 1819). The little book stirred up considerable response and a barrage of works came forth from several German pastors debating Brennecke's position. One of the book's central theses concerns the ascension of Jesus Christ which Brennecke denies by carefully showing the lack of evidence for the occurrence in the New Testament. The ascension is an abomination for it turns the one who is the image of the deity into a vehicle of absurd astronomical mechanics. In order to overcome the blight of the ascension Brennecke thinks that

we must assume that Paul thought the other appearances were of the same order as that to himself.

However, if we wish to reach a basic judgment on the matter, we have to view Paul's account in the connection he makes between Christ's resurrection and ours, the general resurrection. This is a comparison between one order of existence and an entirely different one. Paul had two things in mind when he put these two orders of existence in the same account. He wished to show that Christ's resurrection was documented by his appearances to the disciples and that his exalted state after the ascension was the type of ours. By putting them together he lost sight of the difference between the two, between the risen and the exalted Christ. He makes no definite distinction between the two. He actually thinks of Christ as risen in such a way that he does not have to undergo any change in order to enter into the state of exaltation. Consequently the ascension does not have to represent a special time of change. However, it does not follow from this that he thought of the matter other than he later describes it in general. The seed of his new life (or: glorified body) is found in the present, and therefore Christ after his resurrection appeared to him differently than he had before his death. We cannot conclude from this that Paul thought of Christ's state as a truly human one and that he made no distinction between the appearance of Christ before the ascension and that which he personally encountered.* The didactic element makes it im-

---

New Testament history must be radically reconstructed, which he does in the following manner: Jesus would have died at the crucifixion but God helped him by means of a hundred pounds of refreshing ointment, applied by Nicodemus, which roused him. For the next twenty-seven years Jesus lives and, like a general of an expanding army, directs matters from behind the scenes, including the recruitment of Paul. The earlier eschatological passages of the New Testament letters concerning "the coming of the Lord" refer to Jesus' traveling around from congregation to congregation. Brennecke brings out the emphasis in many passages on "the living Christ" and uses the speeches of Peter in Acts and Paul's earlier letters to trace Jesus' activity. The letter of James was written in the year 60 and he can still speak of Jesus' coming in 5:7-8, but the next year Peter in his first letter reports that Jesus is now with God and the angels. By this means Brennecke dates Jesus' death in late 60 or early 61 when he was sixty years old. Strange as all this may now seem, Brennecke was in earnest and he prayerfully closes his book by addressing Jesus Christ, "Praise and gratitude be yours eternally."
* in which Christ appeared to him

possible for us to view this passage purely historically. On the other hand, the individual statements are to be taken as fully historical.

In the second place, this Pauline passage shows that there were a number of appearances to which no reference is made in our Gospels, and two that we cannot locate at a definite place, namely, the appearance to James and that to more than five hundred brethren. If we also reflect on the fact that Paul omits reference to many facts that are documented in the Gospels, we conclude that he can have omitted still others. There must have been still other appearances of which we have no knowledge. So the appearances of Christ were not so fragmentary and so interrupted as they appear in our accounts, and not so limited to the few moments of his activity with his disciples.*

Lecture 68 (August 24). At the beginning of the book of the Acts of the Apostles Luke rectifies his account in the Gospel. How far does this rectification extend? There is an analogy here with Christ's other periods of stay in Jerusalem. During the festivals he usually stayed in Bethany, and so it is probable that he also stayed there during the period of his resurrection life.

It is certain that what Luke tells us in Acts represents a later version of the facts than he had at his disposal when he wrote the Gospel. Whether he had learned at the same time of still more details or not cannot be determined. He could attach the Acts of the Apostles to the last commission of Christ and then make corrections, but it would have led to misunderstandings if he had wanted to weave in still further details, even if they had been known to him.

Now let us make a general comparison of John with 1 Corinthians 15. In John we still have to discuss the story of the second appearance of Christ to the eleven in Jerusalem, which took place eight days later in the presence of Thomas and which forms the last part of chapter 20, the preliminary

* So there can have been many such appearances, and we can legitimately place the one at the end of John's Gospel in this period. So the life of Christ loses its apparently fragmentary character.

conclusion to the Gospel. I have no doubt about the authenticity of chapter 21. The manner of the account there is quite in harmony with the rest of the Gospel, and for this reason I can ascribe the chapter to no one but the Evangelist himself.[59] Whether he attached the chapter himself to the Gospel as an appendix is uncertain because of the conclusion. It could be said that only the last two verses have another author because of their witness to John, but the whole chapter could also have another author, but he must have got his information from John himself. The chapter includes the only story that John locates in Galilee and is therefore the second that we possess.

In 1 Corinthians 15:5 we are told of the appearance to Peter, then of one to the twelve, apparently on the first evening, then of one to more than five hundred brethren at one time, then later of one to James, and then later still of one to all the apostles, and finally of one to Paul himself. The question arises: Was this appearance to all the apostles the same as the one John reports eight days later, and does Paul follow the same chronology in his account? If that be the case the appearance to the five hundred brethren at one time must have taken place sometime between the first evening and the second appearance to the apostles eight days later. In this case we should have to place it in the vicinity of Jerusalem. The meeting with James alone would also have occurred at some time during this eight day period. In that case Paul would have had nothing to say of anything that happened after the second evening in Jerusalem.*However, it is difficult to believe that Christ could have appeared to more than five hundred at one time anywhere in the vicinity of Jerusalem.

59. This judgment about the authenticity of chapter 21 of the Gospel of John is directly counter to the opinions found in Schleiermacher's lectures on **Introduction** to the New Testament, presented only a few months prior to these lectures on the life of Jesus. Since the discussion in the former lectures is more extended and directed specifically to this point whereas here in the student notebooks the acceptance of chapter 21 comes as something of an aside, I have concluded that the New Testament Introduction is the more reliable indication of Schleiermacher's position, particularly in view of the fact that we have no manuscript outlines for this part of the text. See above, Introduction, p. **liii, n. 111.**
* or add: and he would have no account of what is narrated in John 21

This would have attracted so much attention in the neighborhood of Jerusalem that the event could not have been kept quiet. There is no evidence in all that follows that that appearance was known in Jerusalem. On the other hand, if we think of it as a Galilean event, we can more easily understand why it did not become known in Jerusalem and why the apostles in the sermons they preached in Jerusalem made no mention of it. The presupposition that Christ had a few hundred followers in Galilee is quite compatible with the complaint Christ had made about unbelief in Galilee. We know from Acts that there were already congregations there. So the hypothesis that Christ's meeting with the five hundred brethren took place in Galilee is quite attractive. As long as it was not an accidental meeting, but arranged and intended by Christ, the Galilean locale is quite probable. The final story in John leads us again to Galilee, this time to the Sea of Tiberias, and that would also agree with the hypothesis I have just discussed. However, all this is difficult to harmonize with the fact that the second story of Luke's, that at the beginning of Acts, once more is located in the vicinity of Jerusalem. So we have to assume that Christ spent a part of this period in Galilee but then returned with his disciples to Jerusalem, because they were to remain in Jerusalem and await the outpouring of the Spirit there.

There is nothing improbable about all this. Christ could be more separate and unobserved with his disciples in Galilee than it was possible for him to be in Jerusalem, or between Jerusalem and Bethany. The (commission? cf. Luke 24:47) of Christ had demanded that the disciples should return to Jerusalem and there await the promise, and such a return must appear quite in order. If we think of Christ as bearing the external marks of his crucifixion and of his body as it had been before, that is to say, as a sick man with weakened life force, the journeying hither and yon seems quite improbable, but this improbable action took place as early as the first day. Then he appears as one quite healthy, who walks without difficulty to Emmaus and back again. All this clearly belongs to the picture of his state. We cannot represent him as those do who maintain the hypothesis of an apparent death. We cannot think of him as spending this time with his life force at a low ebb.[60]

60. Unfortunately, Albert Schweitzer in *The Quest of the Historical Jesus* trans. W. Montgomery (New York: Macmillan, 1961) has given currency to the idea that "Schleiermacher's own opinion is what really happened was reanimation after apparent death." This is false as the text here indicates. Schleiermacher's point, as pp. **415-16** above state, is that what is important is the spiritual significance of Christ's death, whatever may be the situation with regard to the chemical process of physical decomposition, information about which is not given in the New Testament. Furthermore, Schleiermacher makes quite clear in *The Christian Faith* that Jesus Christ died on the cross, especially throughout the long discussion under §104 which includes such texts as the following: "He must therefore have accepted it as a duty involved in his vocation to appear in the holy city for this feast, in spite of the foreknowledge he possessed; and beyond question it was an element in the development of this great crisis that Christ met his death in his zeal for his vocation relatively to his Father's Law, just as truly as his opponents — at least the best among them — condemned him to death in their professional zeal for the law. If, nevertheless, we wish to regard even this from the standpoint of the divine decree, then we must concede that it behooved the perfecter of faith to die a death which should be not simply an occurrence, but at the same time a deed in the highest sense of the word, in order that in this too he might proclaim the full dominion of the spirit over the flesh. By a natural death, whether due to accidental illness or the result of the weakness of old age, this could have become evident only accidentally and in a lesser degree." *CF*, §104, 4. David Friedrich Strauss also ignores *The Christian Faith* in his discussion of these matters in *Der Christus des Glaubens und der Jesus der Geschichte* (Berlin, 1865). Furthermore, Strauss in his *A New Life of Jesus in 1864* (London, 1865), p. 24, written before the publication of these lectures, combines Schleiermacher with H.E.G. Paulus's idea of an apparent death; an idea currently found also in Emanuel Hirsch, *Geschichte der neueren evangelischen Theologie* (Gütersloh, 1960), 5:38. But combining the type of rationalism represented by Paulus with Schleiermacher on this particular issue seriously obscures a significant point for early nineteenth-century thought. Paulus has Jesus revived from a state of nondeath by such natural events as the cold temperature of the tomb; other interpreters used the earthquake and machinations of Joseph of Arimathea and Nicodemus. In such cases Jesus still had death to face. But Schleiermacher understands Jesus as having died on the cross, therefore death is behind him in his post-Easter life.

An instructive discussion of this point is made by Karl Hase, Schleiermacher's younger contemporary who had a similar view of the resurrection, in a book written subsequent to the criticisms of Strauss (*Die Geschichte Jesu* [Leipzig, 1876], pp. 602-3). Hase rightfully objects to the lack of distinctions between his own position and the rationalism of Paulus's type, since Strauss handles the topic according to a neat supernaturalism/rationalism scheme. He insists that for Schleiermacher and himself Jesus' death is actual and the phrase "apparent death" only arises because they hold that the body of Jesus is still a usable one. In referring to his interpretation Hase says: "One can name the preceding condition death or apparent death, the revivification out of this condition natural or supernatural. Jesus was not rescued from death through common human knowledge and human will, and his miraculous power was not the commonly natural but something historical (*Geschichtliches*). Believers take offence at the term 'apparent death' insofar as thereby only a suspension of the functions of life is understood, so that life has only withdrawn into that which is most inward and therefore is able to spring forth again

If we also reflect on the story in the Acts of the Apostles, we have to presuppose that much more must have happened during this period. We have to assume that the time was filled to a greater extent by meetings of Christ with his disciples. We cannot determine whether Luke knew more than he reports. I should like to maintain the same of the account in 1 Corinthians 15. We see from the way Paul mentions the five hundred that he refers to those who were still living. He refers to witnesses who could then still be interviewed. That can have been true of Peter and of James. By taking all these bits of evidence into consideration we get a natural picture. The inclination to think of Christ's whole state in such a way that he could no longer make earth his home, but could only spend brief periods there, rests on the isolation of elements in the narratives. However, if we fill out those brief periods, the isolation disappears to a great extent.

Let me now discuss individual narratives. Christ appeared to the eleven the first time with Thomas absent [John 20: 19-29]; and Thomas did not believe the report of the others.* Christ condescends to this unbelief and appears to the disciples again, this time with Thomas present. I do not think that Christ appeared to the disciples this second time simply on account of Thomas or that he did nothing else than bring about faith in his doubting disciple. On the contrary, he must have given his disciples instruction, much as he did according to the general description in Acts. However, John emphasizes this detail, for he does not report any didactic discourses during this period, which could have consisted of supplementation and explanation of what Christ had already said. The narrative shows that even eight days later Christ could con-

from itself or through an accidental aid. But there is also a serious apparent death which is a really being dead that is only named apparent death, a transition to a full — an eternal, if you will — death, from which through some extraordinary intervention the dead life has again been recalled. In this sense some isolated free Christian thinkers such as Schleiermacher and Bunsen, along with myself, have regarded the death and resurrection of Jesus." The contrast here between life that has only receded and can again emerge by means of a cold temperature, etc., and a condition which is a really being dead but which concerns a body that can again receive life was crucial in their own eyes.
* or add: The story of Thomas resembles stories related by the Evangelist Mark, who likes to draw attention to the unbelief of the disciples.

vince Thomas by means of his bodily state. There were still traces of the wounds of nails in his hands, and also of the wound in his side. However, we cannot draw conclusions from this with respect to other aspects of his bodily state All that mattered was that Thomas could still see or feel scars.

What does Christ actually mean when he blames Thomas to some extent for his unbelief and adds that he must declare those much more blessed, give them praise, who can believe without such direct viewing? That is to be taken strictly. A well-grounded witness must supplement direct viewing, and those who wanted only to trust their own sight were limited to their own disadvantage. These words do not seem to me necessarily to presuppose the absolutely miraculous. It can often be the case that it is not possible to believe without seeing, at any rate to the extent that it is not possible to form one's own idea of an event. In this case, however, there were many witnesses to whom no objection could be taken. Thomas must have heard Mary's story and that of the two Emmaus disciples. Furthermore, on the first evening when he believed his fellow disciples had been deceived, it was arrogant of him to assume that, if he had been present, he would not have been deceived, while assuming that the others had been deluded. He could not have meant that he would not believe unless he saw Christ's wounds. That was only a way of speaking of an immediate conviction that would come as the result of the evidence of his own senses. What Christ blamed him for was therefore the lack of a genuinely historical sense which was not allowed to arise from confidence in sufficiently attested and, in themselves, not improbable facts.

John presupposes that many things happened that he did not report. The saying in John 20: 30, "Now [Jesus] did many other signs in the presence of his disciples" cannot be understood to exclude the resurrection story. Rather, it must refer especially to this, for Christ had not performed the other signs during his lifetime in the presence of his disciples, but for others and in the presence of others. This saying was especially fitting for the disciples when Christ had isolated himself from the world and wanted to have nothing more to do with it.

Did Christ have the right to separate himself after his death entirely from the world and to devote the time of his resurrection exclusively to his disciples? Was it in the nature of things and in accordance with the circumstances that he should do so? It is possible to say, of course, that, if Christ had shown himself as the risen One, he would have produced a greater effect; that he did himself harm by this withdrawal. But what kind of effect he would have achieved is quite another matter. A tendency to an external messianic kingdom could have manifested itself, and one needs only to think of this to be able to explain satisfactorily why Christ set himself apart from the world. It is also very noteworthy that in the first sermon in Acts the apostles call themselves in a unique way witnesses of Christ's resurrection and that Peter expressly says that Christ had not shown himself to others. It is remarkable that the Sanhedrin in opposing the apostles paid no attention to the resurrection. They only commanded the apostles not to preach in Christ's name. How easy it would have been to use another method and order the disciples to prove that Christ had risen! Since it was notorious that Christ had not shown himself publicly, the Sanhedrin could have ordered the apostles to prove that he was alive and they would not have been able to do it. They could only have produced witnesses from within their own ranks. However, we find no such demand made. I can only ascribe this to the fact that they all thought that this was not natural.* Even if the disciples had been incapable of producing any proof outside their own circle, they could still make it clear that Christ would not take part in public life.

We do not know how the disciples came to Galilee so that we find them there in Christ's company. The way Matthew speaks of a command that Christ had given cannot give us a lead. He could not have given such a command, and the story only reflects the tradition that Christ had been with his disciples in Galilee. At the end of Matthew's Gospel he tells us that Christ took leave of his disciples on a mountain. All is

* or add: We find no such demand made because it seemed natural to all, for the disciples, although they did not produce this proof, could yet make it clear that Christ could not have wanted to return to public life.

obscure. It is difficult to determine what Matthew knew and did not know and of what sort his traditions were. In the Galilean account in John the eleven are not together. John mentions those who were present: Peter, Thomas, himself and his brother, Nathanael, and two other disciples. This does not add up to the eleven. This seems to indicate that the disciples were not there as the result of an express command by Christ that they should forgather there with him. It is clear that the occasion on which Peter said to his companions that he wanted to go fishing and they replied that they wanted to go with him was not a gathering of the eleven. The eleven were scattered, and this shows that they were not in a fellowship with Christ as a group. Otherwise they would have kept together, whereas they were scattered. However that may be, we cannot regard this as a proof that the disciples had gone to Galilee without any direction from Christ in the matter and that Jesus had only met them there once and accidentally. Even in Galilee Jesus could have found it necessary to take precautionary measures if he did not wish to be seen by others, and that may explain why the disciples were not together.

Lecture 69 (August 27). The Pauline account of the resurrection data in 1 Corinthians 15 gives a strong impression of chronological arrangement. The individual events are introduced by *epeita* ["then"]. In no sense, however, does the account claim to be complete. Its only purpose is to list witnesses. Therefore there can be no doubt that the last appearance of Christ to all the apostles is not the one that John says took place eight days after the resurrection. Rather, it was that with which several of the Gospels associate the ascension. The appearance to the five hundred probably took place in Galilee, and so there are two accounts which document a stay by Christ in Galilee after the resurrection. One is John's definite statement that Christ appeared to his disciples at the Sea of Tiberias. Paul does not say expressly that the appearance to the five hundred brethren took place in Galilee, but it is improbable that such a gathering to which Christ appeared is to be looked for in the vicinity of Jerusalem.

460

Now let us face the question: How are we to think of the journey to Galilee and then of the return to the neighborhood of Jerusalem? The key to much of what we cannot explain in and for itself is Christ's firm decision to have nothing more to do with the world that had been completely satisfied and compensated by his death on the cross. In addition to this, it could not have been easy from this point of view for Christ to stay long in any place, especially near Jerusalem where those who shared the secret of his resurrection were and wished to remain until Pentecost and whom his presence might put into a too precarious position. That was what motivated a change of place. Christ certainly had a large number of followers in Galilee. This is evident from the fact that early in the book of Acts we are told of congregations in Galilee that had come into being without special apostolic activity. We have already seen that Christ, if the catastrophe had not happened, would have organized the Christian community in the places where he had not been for any length of time. When Paul says that Christ appeared to five hundred brethren at one time, he must have had some purpose in mind. That was not just to let them see his person. He could assume and expect that only a few would push their unbelief in his resurrection as far as Thomas did. So his purpose must have been something other than that, and that suggests the supposition that Christ came to Galilee for the purpose of laying the first foundations of the Christian church so to speak with his disciples, and for this reason assembled with them. We must regard it as a fact that Paul believed the appearance to the five hundred to be sufficiently attested, and Paul certainly had his information from eyewitnesses of the appearance and of the assembly itself. So we cannot doubt the fact, unless we wish to cast doubt on all the others.

The case is quite different with respect to the special Galilean incident that John tells about in the last chapter of his Gospel. The purpose that John had in mind in that story was clearly only to correct something that had come to be believed rather generally, namely, that he himself would remain alive until Christ's return. John says that expressly in v. 23. John draws attention to the hypothetical element in the saying and

461

tries to point out that it should not be confused with the positive element. This attempt to correct a mistaken belief is actually the purpose of the whole narrative. This is connected directly with Christ's demand to Peter, "Follow me" This is not an exhortation to discipleship in the moral sense, but a demand that Peter should accompany him for the purpose of a special conversation. After the Lord had so to speak rejected Peter's demand that John should remain behind, John also took part in the conversation, but what its content was remains uncertain. John only wishes to deny the rumor, and so a report of the conversation does not interest him. After his talk with the other disciples, Christ takes Peter aside especially for this conversation, but we cannot determine whether or not Christ appeared to his disciples at that time for the purpose of having such a special conversation. However, there is something unique about the way John describes this. Not all the disciples were present, which was natural if they had been in Galilee for a considerable time. There each had his own special message and story to relate. If they had been expressly ordered by Christ to go to Galilee only for a short time, that would be difficult to conceive. We find it necessary to make room for both elements in our hypothesis. We have already pointed out that Christ, as soon as he rose from the dead, did not command his disciples to go to Galilee. However, it is just as difficult to believe that after they had seen Christ, in some cases individually and in others collectively, they went to Galilee without instructions from him. These instructions must have come later and must have been given because Christ no longer wanted to stay in Jerusalem and yet wanted to be together with his followers.

However, if we now think of the period of forty days and recall that the second appearance of Christ to the eleven took place eight days after the resurrection, we can imagine that Christ appeared in Galilee until he went to Jerusalem for the ascension. There was time enough for the disciples to get involved in the management of their business, which meant that the eleven were separated. In the story that John tells the eleven (?) were together, and clearly Christ had not made an agreement to meet them, for they undertook a fishing expedition and did not recognize Christ at once when he joined them. There is another circumstance to be mentioned. Christ asks his disciples whether they have anything to eat. In particular, he asks whether they have any fish and tells them where they are to cast their net. The event is similar to the incident when Peter at the time he was called to his apostolic office was engaged in fishing. Christ asks about fish for the purpose of a meal. He did not wish to demonstrate that he was actually a living human being.* So then, Christ had not only the capacity for, but also the need of, all bodily sustenance. Christ's meeting with his disciples on this occasion was therefore an accidental one, but it can well be that Christ sought and found the occasion. Since Christ had already often appeared to Peter, we cannot regard this appearance as having any relation to Peter's denial or as a renewal of his apostolic office. Therefore Christ's question that he addressed to Peter and the general commission that he gave him, which was the same as the commission to all the apostles, must have been related to the special conversation as its beginning, and having begun it he took Peter aside.

If we consider the two Galilean events together, two things become apparent: Christ's presence with a large number of his disciples, and his appearance to a number of apostles and to one especially. His resurrection appearances seem to have been an orderly continuation of his life and work, for he continued to teach and commission as he had done during his lifetime. So these may not have been Christ's only appearances in Galilee. Paul emphasizes just one of many. It is improbable that the five hundred to whom Christ appeared was the only large assembly to which he made himself known.

We cannot think of Christ's return to Jerusalem as unintentional. The most certain key to the puzzle is provided by the opening chapter of Acts, where we are told that Christ gave his disciples the charge not to leave Jerusalem but to await the fulfillment of the promise, with the intention that the preaching of the gospel must begin in Jerusalem. If we consider this together with the formula with which the last

---

* or add: The disciples must already have believed that.

appearance of Christ is described in the Gospel of Matthew, the charge to go into all the world, we see that there is a certain analogy between the two. Of his own personal existence Christ had always said that he had been sent to the lost sheep of the house of Israel. He had said that his mission was limited to his own people, and he was content to preach the kingdom of God to that folk and not to begin impatiently with other peoples. His charge to his disciples was similar. They should begin their public preaching not just among the Jewish people in general, but in Jerusalem in particular. What was the actual purpose of that? It was that the public preaching of the gospel should begin in the capital city of Jewry under the eyes of the public authorities. A further opportunity was to be given the Jews after the crucifixion to accept the gospel. However, Christ added to that the charge that is reported. They were not ultimately to be limited to the Jewish people. Since the Jews had rejected him as Messiah, it was very probable that they would also reject the preaching of the gospel by his disciples. So Christ gave the apostles the right to go beyond the Jewish land and even beyond the Jewish people. So the apostles had to return to Jerusalem before the outpouring of the Spirit, and it is natural that Christ accompanied them to that city.

In light of these few bits of evidence, what appears to have been Christ's consciousness with reference to the continuance of his state of revivification and concerning the way that would end? We find a definite development to a certain point. Christ's first saying after his resurrection seemed to assert that he thought of it as a very temporary state. Speaking to Mary he said, ''I am ascending to my Father.'' If we reflect on the weight of the words that he spoke to the eleven on the first evening, we see that they have the character of a final charge, as though the apostles' activity should begin at once. We find no evidence there that Christ thought of a long period during which he would remain with them and no intimation that they were to await his coming again. Then it seems as if Christ came a second time for Thomas's sake, since he was absent on the first occasion. The question arises: Did Christ come to know of Thomas's unbelief in a supernatural way? There is no reason to assume that, for the Gospel of John was not written in order to relate everything that happened. There is no reason to believe that Christ let the eight days pass without appearing to one or another of the disciples. Since he sent the disciples to Galilee and yet wanted them to begin their work in Jerusalem, there is reason to believe that he was conscious that his state of revivification would last longer than at first we get the impression. However, there is no suggestion of how this state would end, except in the words to Mary Magdalene, "I am ascending to my Father," etc. This saying in itself contains no clear idea of Christ's departure. It only verges on giving one. And now (in Jerusalem) comes the definite account at the beginning of Acts, and the possibility that in the first account in Luke's Gospel two events have been combined in one and that much that the second has in common with the first may have been related only to the second. I am referring to what Christ says of a consciousness of his imminent complete separation from them. Related to this is the story of the ascension.

The Ascension

What do these accounts contain, and what assurance have we that they are reliable? John tells us nothing of the ascension. In 1 Corinthians 15 Paul would have given a more effective, more vigorous, and briefer account of what had happened to him and what he describes as a personal apprehension (or: appearance) of Christ in distinction from the event involved in Christ's resurrection if he had inserted a few words about the ascension, but he does not do that. Matthew also has nothing to say of Christ's ascension. Mark, to be sure, does include a reference to the ascension, but it is in the last section of his Gospel, which is missing from many ancient manuscripts, which conclude without any account of the ascension. We have therefore two nonapostolic reports of the ascension, whereas the two apostles, who, especially John, would have had reason to speak of what happened to the risen Christ as the complete conclusion to their accounts, leave it strictly alone.

What can we say about the reports that we do have? That

465

in Mark is of such a sort that we cannot say whether it pre-supposes an exact knowledge of the course of the event, or whether it is a description that an eyewitness could have given. No one could have seen Christ sitting at the right hand of God. The ascent is bound up with what follows and there-fore is not to be regarded as something visible, but as that which makes the sitting at the right hand of God possible. So Mark has no contribution to make to a clear idea of what happened. The situation is quite different in the case of the ending of Luke's Gospel. There we are told that when Christ had blessed his disciples he left them. According to this ac-count, what happened was something visible. However, then Luke adds, "and was carried up into heaven" [textus recep-tus], though he does not give an actual description of the as-cent. So there is some doubt whether it is to be regarded as a description, or only as a communication of a result.* The account at the beginning of Acts is quite different.

Lecture 70 (August 28). If we regard the days Christ spent on earth after the resurrection as wholly normal in human terms, we find it more difficult later to relate the ascension to them, while those who consider these days as already part of Christ's supernatural state have an easier task. In this latter case every departure of Christ from his disciples was to some extent already an ascension. It seems as if we have to under-take a revision of our procedure to this point when we ask: What idea of the event did those people have who originally participated in it? If it could be proved that the disciples had an idea of a phantasmal element in the appearance of Christ, that would support the position of those who hold that the risen Christ belonged to the spiritual world from the time of his resurrection, although we should not yet be compelled to accept their belief. Actually we can say nothing definite about the problem, as some have done who have distorted it, for we have no other apostolic witness than that of John, and John emphasizes the measures Christ took to represent his life after the resurrection to his disciples as fully human. Luke indi-

* or add: The verb "he parted from" takes us only a step further.

cates the same concern on Christ's part, and his account, next to John's, is the most circumstantial. Matthew and Mark compress the story so much that * we can only use their accounts by testing them in this respect. This similarity (or: relationship) between John and Luke later gives way to a complete dissimilarity. Luke attaches the story of the ascension to these accounts of Christ's resurrection activity, which represent Christ as seeking to convince his disciples of the genuineness of his life, whereas John, with the same interest in mind, reports nothing of the ascension.

We now have to say† that something runs throughout these narratives of what Mark emphasizes, namely, the lack of faith on the part of the disciples and the uncertainty of their idea of Christ. Nevertheless, can we not point to evidence that something similar happened during Christ's actual life? What I refer to is something that is very evident in the days after the resurrection, a hesitancy on the part of the disciples to ask Christ about his risen state. If they had done so it is hard to understand why Christ ought not to have told them in what way he came out of the tomb. If he had told them, it is very strange that we have no report of what he said. If they did not ask him, there was no purpose in telling them. This hesitancy to ask him about what was not essential to faith is something that we find even during his lifetime, and there are traces of an inclination to assume something miraculous in his state of existence. This is apparent, for example, after the story of the miraculous feeding of the multitude, when Christ had sent his disciples ahead of him to the Sea of Galilee and when he rejoins them from Capernaum. However, we have to admit that there is nothing there that is fully clear. One gets only a feeling of it by the tone of the narrative, and the feeling can be explained by these circumstances without generalizing it. The case is different with the story of Christ's transfiguration. When we examine that story, we find

* quite apart from the fact that we do not know who their authorities were, we cannot use them
† that the most that can be said of this opposed point of view is that throughout this narrative, as happens so often in Mark, there runs an emphasis on the lack of faith on the part of Jesus' disciples in Christ's natural state of being

reference to the miraculous element associated with both persons who appear in the story, who are said to have been Moses and Elijah. Then we are given a peculiar impression of the figure of Christ which seems to indicate a state that is not to be harmonized with any idea of a completely human body. When we examine all this together we easily come to the conclusion that even during Christ's earlier lifetime his disciples had regarded his existence as not fully human.

However, it would be very rash to attempt to maintain that that was actually the case. On the contrary, docetic aberrations with respect to the person of Christ appeared very early, and these ideas on the part of the disciples are the first indications of them. However, we cannot be sure whether the disciples held them or got them second or third hand, and it is again remarkable that we find no mention of all that in the story in John's Gospel. I do not believe this silence on John's part can be satisfactorily explained by the hypothesis that John only wished to supplement the other Gospels and that therefore he omitted reference to what they had already said. What really matters is the way something is said. There can be fuller accounts of what is said as well as of what is not said. In John we find no ideas that are related to the docetic debate itself, although there are accounts where the docetic idea seems to have influenced the disciples momentarily, but only when they were impressed in an external way. If John had known the story that was current (he probably did not know the written version of the three Gospels) of the time Christ spent with his disciples on the mountain we have to ask: How do we explain the fact that he does not mention it? If he himself had had the miraculous idea, he could have omitted reference to it on the grounds that it was current. However, if such a story was current and he held another idea, he could intentionally have avoided referring to it, since he could believe that that was the quickest way to have it forgotten. The story actually does not compel us to assume anything miraculous in the incident. We have plenty of evidence that the disciples were not always in a waking state, but in a state halfway between sleeping and waking, from which they were roused briefly. If Christ told them that they should say nothing of the matter, the reason for that may have been that they did not fully understand it.

If we take our departure from the fact that even in the accounts of Christ's preresurrection life there were already approximations to the docetic point of view, we must naturally find it much less strange that the same docetic views occurred during the days after the resurrection and that there is a certain color tone to the stories that indicate moments in Christ's resurrection life that do not belong to a real life. However, that does not constitute real evidence, but only judgments, only indications that point in the direction of such an idea. When we contrast to that what Christ intentionally does, we must regard the idea as baseless.*

So then, after the resurrection Christ returned to a truly human life. The contrary appearance is to be explained by the easily explicable decision not to have anything more to do with the world, but to restrict himself to the company of his followers. Furthermore, Christ's first sayings after his resurrection permit us to conclude that Christ had formed no definite idea of, was uncertain of, a specific period during which he would continue to live. However, after he had instructed his disciples to go to Galilee and after he himself had gone there and had been with them collectively and individually, he must have returned as one possessed of a full life, because he acted in quite the same way and under the same conditions. To be sure, the reason why he returned from Galilee with his disciples may have been the same as that which took him from Jerusalem to Galilee in the first place. Dangers could arise there. His presence could become known in places where it ought not to be known. Furthermore, he had already predicted that the disciples were to begin to preach in Jerusalem. Consequently it was the foreboding of the imminent end of this second life that moved him to return from Galilee to Jerusalem.

How are we to think of this end? At this point we must try to form as complete a judgment as possible about the state of

---

* What Christ does destroys such a notion. Another possibility: Nevertheless, that gives us no right to share such ideas.

our sources of information. Matthew has no account of the ascension. John has nothing to say about it. In 1 Corinthians Paul mentions nothing of the ascension between what he tells us of the resurrection life of Christ and his own experience of Christ's presence. In the final section of Mark's Gospel (not fully assured as authentic, although I am compelled to regard it as genuine), the Evangelist mentions the ascension, although not in the form of an actual narrative. So our accounts of the ascension are virtually limited to those that Luke gives. Luke's second account looks like a rectification of the first. His first seems to assert that this ascension of Christ took place after Christ's appearance to the disciples on the evening after the resurrection, whereas the second declares that a period of forty days intervened between the resurrection and the ascension. However, Luke gives no details of Christ's activities during this period. His only extensive narrative is that of the ascension. That Luke says that the period between the resurrection and the ascension lasted for forty days is a fact that we should not ignore. That is such a solemn number that it always gives rise to the easy suspicion that it can be an unhistorical item. It causes us to suspect that it does not rest on actual information, but is only a guess. To some extent that throws an unfavorable light on the state of the narrative itself.

If we begin with the assumption that Christ himself actually required that he be returned in the days of his resurrection to a really human life, how was this state to come to an end? If Christ returned to the same human life he had had, if it was the same body that was revivified, this could have happened only if he had died, for otherwise he would not have been the same, and this requires the necessity (or: possibility) of assuming a second death of Christ. If we had never had Luke's second narrative, we should say that that was a wholly inadmissible idea for the Christian faith,* for *with the spiritual exaltation of Christ* (he sits at the right hand of God) *the way that his human body found its end is wholly incompat-*

---

* no one could regard this faith as inadmissible for the Christian idea, for with the spiritual exaltation, etc.

*ible. We cannot get rid of the idea of Christ's spiritual exalta-
tion in that way, and it also undergoes not the slightest diminution.* So then, no one could advance the hypothesis that
Christ had to die twice. On the contrary, from this point of
view the doctrine of the spiritual exaltation of Christ would be
the most natural idea. However, it would always remain difficult to explain the lack of a report of it. All that we could
say would be that Christ withdrew intentionally into a complete retirement. There could have been motives for that. He
did not want to resume contacts with the world that he had
ended by his death. If he had continued such a life with his
disciples for any length of time, he would thereby have restricted their activities. Their public appearance would not
have been possible, for they would have been bound to him
as closely as they had been during his first life. They could
never say that they had learned enough from him. As long as
he was there and available to them, because they wished to be
receptive they would have to seek him out as often as they
could come to him to get teaching from him, and this would
have made their public appearance impossible. This hypothesis would make no place for any notion of secret groups
(or add: to which he returned) other than the circle of the
apostles. Such ideas are historical nonsense.[61]

There is a report, however, that we should examine to see
whether it is actually a report. What are we to make of the
words that Christ was "carried up" or "taken up" into heaven, in connection with the commission and the statement
that he was seated at the right hand of God? It does not have
to be regarded as an external phenomenon. If we had nothing
more than what Mark tells us at the end of his Gospel, we
should not have to think of the ascension as a visible phenomenon. Mark could have said what he did even if Christ had
actually died a second time, or even if nothing was known of
the end of his second life, for it is the repetition of what
Christ himself had said earlier of his farewell to the world as
a returning to the Father.

61. Karl Friedrich Bahrdt and Karl Venturini in their so-called fictitious
lives of Jesus (see above, **p. 106,** n. 19) record Jesus as retiring after the
crucifixion, in which he had not actually died, to the group of Essenes to
which he had been secretly related throughout his life.

However, as soon as this is formulated as an external phenomenon, we cannot construe it in connection with the idea of Christ after the resurrection without inserting an element into it. But I raise the question of whether we are in any position to do this. At the beginning of Acts we read that Christ was with his disciples, spoke with them, gave them a charge, "and when he had said this, as they were looking on, he was lifted up and a cloud took him out of their sight." Then we are further told, "while they were gazing into heaven as he went, behold . . .". What, then, was the nature of the phenomenon? While the apostles watched, Christ was taken up into heaven. That, we could say, is what was *seen* (leaving the miraculous out of consideration). Now a cloud takes him out of their sight. The cloud, then, veiled him, and his disciples saw him no more. What they could still have seen was the cloud in which they knew Christ was. Now they look toward heaven. So the cloud must have moved upward. With their eyes they followed the movement of the cloud which had veiled Christ. Is that a phenomenon that we can think of as an actual end? Can we do so even if we insert into the thought of it the element that is missing, namely, that such a change took place in Christ's body that it ceased to be a human body (or: that it became weightless)? So we are inclined to believe that Christ was taken up to heaven before his disciples eyes in the state in which he was and was veiled from their sight by the cloud.* The cloud cannot have come from the atmosphere of the earth, and we must then assume that it was originally there without ceasing to be a cloud. So then, something happened in this instance, but what the disciples saw could not have been all there was to know, and the rest is only a supplement.†

Lecture 71 (August 29). Looking at what is told us in the account and then turning from this to the general idea, with-

---

* or add: All this contains an element of the miraculous. Have we in this instance the account of an event that has a beginning and an end? Not at all, for the cloud cannot have come from the atmosphere of the earth.
† and what was seen takes us no farther than we should have been if we knew nothing of what had been seen. Another possibility: They saw only that Christ was taken up into a cloud, not that he was taken up into heaven.

472

out attempting to give it the necessary clarity, the attempt was made to understand the ascension as an event. However, an event must have a beginning and an ending, and in the instance we have been discussing the end by its very nature is not conceivable and is also incapable of being grasped as a definite concept. In Christian confessions the end is the seating of Christ at the right hand of God, but that cannot be regarded as the consequence of a corporeal, special movement. It is a spiritual concept. The ascent to heaven has a twofold significance. According to the one, we cannot think of anything corporeal. However, there are two sides to this. In the first place, with reference to that to which it is applied, heaven is used as an expression of a direct connection with the Highest Being, and to go to heaven is the condition of sitting at the right hand of God. However, it has also a relation to having been on earth and to removal from it, and to that extent has a corporeal aspect, although it cannot be formulated as a definite idea, since heaven is not an actual place and taken by itself is something negative. The movement from earth to heaven begins, then, as a corporeal movement, but it can have no corporeal end. The only thing corporeal about it is the fact that the person is no longer on earth.* The only thing that could be perceived was the removal of Christ from the earth.

However, if we ask whether that was a necessary beginning to the end, we have to answer no! We cannot demonstrate a connection between the two. So we have a report that cannot be understood as complete. If we ask why then was there this beginning, if it is not to be regarded as a necessary condition of the end, we have to admit that there is nothing definite to say. The report is an actual report to the extent that it is satisfactorily authenticated. The testimony we possess confirms the fact that this second earthly life of Christ ended in such a way that the last that was perceptible was that Christ was lifted up and was veiled by a cloud. The question arises: Is

---

* So it begins as a corporeal affair and means that the individual is no longer on earth. If the movement from earth to heaven ends in a certain way, that can be perceived. So then, the exaltation can be seen, but that has no connection with the end.

473

this report really certain and satisfactorily authenticated? In light of all that has been said to this point, I wish only to add that the accounts of what happened between Christ and his disciples after his death in my judgment are so substantiated that I cannot entertain the idea that they were either an invention of a later time or were due to a self-deception on the part of the disciples. So then, the story of the ascension must be accepted as a fact.

However, we must resort to hypotheses to understand the connection between the first and second lives of Christ. If we did not possess the account that Luke gives in Acts, we should say we have as little information about the end of this second life as we do of the resurrection which marked its beginning. The only information that in any way is related to Christ's coming forth from the tomb is in Matthew, but that speaks only of the way the stone was removed from the mouth of the tomb by the angel, not of Christ's actual emergence from the tomb. What Mark says at the end of his Gospel of the ascension cannot be regarded as an actual report because of the close connection between "he was taken up into heaven" and "he sat down at the right hand of God." The report in Luke 24: 51 is not properly connected with what precedes it and is therefore doubtful, for from the other reports we know that the ascension and the arrival at Bethany were not simultaneous. So we are thrown back on the account in Acts, which we must now examine in greater detail.

The history of the apostles, particularly at the beginning, is very explicit. Basic to it seems to have been to some extent documentary-like accounts of what happened in the congregation in Jerusalem, and the same thing is evident in all individual passages. We are therefore dealing with an authentic book. However, that does not prevent us from concluding that there are passages analogous to the one we are considering where it is doubtful whether something that is narrated as a fact is also to be understood as a fact. Let me give two examples. The one is the report of Peter's vision which came to him when he was about to go and see Cornelius [Acts 10: 9-16]. We are told that this vision was granted him while Cornelius's emissaries were on the way to him. Later the same vision was recounted by Peter as part of his defense at Jerusalem. We ask: Which account is probably the original? When we examine the narrative we see that the vision was said to have been repeated three times, and what is represented as seen cannot actually be construed as something seen.* The great sheet, with all that it implies, cannot be construed as something seen. Peter narrates the experience as a vision, and a vision lies in an area that by its nature is very vague. If I ask why the threefold repetition of the vision took place, since in the story of Peter no gradation in effect occurs, but the whole only decides Peter to undertake his mission, I am led by the solemn number three to the supposition that the original content of the story was Peter's account of it, and that the vision which he reports was the way of expressing the hesitation he had experienced and how this was overcome by what he conceived was a divine impulse. All this is in the manner of rabbinical and Jewish teaching. Other example is the account of the course of events at pentecost. There we find elements that are narrated as something seen but which we cannot so construe. One such instance is the distribution of tongues as of fire and the account of how in this way the Spirit was poured out on the apostles. If we were to ask what sort of necessary connection such a phenomenon had with the inner fact of the outpouring of the Holy Spirit, we should have to admit that no such connection is apparent. We are not to assume that the tongues as of fire were actually external phenomena, for we are told that they were distributed to the apostles before other men were there. Probably poetical elements have been transformed into facts, a process that can be observed to some extent in other books. We are compelled to conclude that parts of Acts reflect such a process.

In connection with the ascension story we note the reference to forty days. This solemn number suggests traces of poetic influence and gives the impression that the account is not precise. We note the way that what was perceived was transformed into something no longer perceptible. Furthermore, we note the instruction that the apostles received as they

* the story represents what was invisible as something seen

were gazing into heaven as Christ went, the instruction imparted by the two men in white robes referred to in Acts 1:10-11, who stood by the disciples and said: "Men of Galilee, why do you stand looking into heaven? This Jesus, who was taken up from you into heaven, will come in the same way," etc. How are we to think of this instruction that the apostles received? Is that new information they were given, or is it a reminder of what had earlier been told them? In Christ's own discourses themselves there are references to Christ's return. So the apostles already had the information and did not need a repetition of it. How are we to think of these two persons? The passage speaks of two men, but the ordinary interpretation of it makes them angels.* Whoever the persons were who instructed the apostles, we still have to ask: Is the instruction they received correct? We cannot think of the apostles as understanding it as a reference to an event that would take place after many centuries. The passage seems to say that they were instructed not to look to heaven the way they were doing, but to think of the return of Christ as something that would take place while they still lived. No doubt that was the way they understood it. The idea was also current at a later time and in due course gave rise to the chiliasm that orthodox faith repudiated. No one will admit that the apostles received such a supernatural communication designed to set their minds at rest, but which was not realized in the form in which it was given. Much can be said against the historical character of this element.

Taken together, these facts make it doubtful that many of these accounts rest on actual specific reports and raise the possibility that much that is narrated as fact rests on explanations and ideas that were not meant to be taken as factual. So it is natural that immediately after Christ's ascension his discourses suggested to the apostles the idea of his return. It was also natural that that hope could be represented and described in a different way in poetic form, as well as in hymns and other liturgical matter, and that later, due to misunderstanding, it was understood as fact and transformed into

* or add: If they were angels, why were they not called so?

the historical account. There are many examples of such a process.

Immediately following, however, there is a truly historical element, the reference to the return of the disciples to Jerusalem. When we reflect in addition on the fact that this is the only report of the ascension we have, we are compelled to conclude that at the time Mark and Matthew were written such accounts as this of an ascension that had been definitely seen were not current. Despite the brevity of their accounts, the Evangelists would have made some mention of it had they known of it. How easy it would have been for Matthew and Mark to have mentioned this ascension in a few words at the end of their Gospels! So we are compelled to say that the narrative in Acts contains so many foreign elements that it cannot be regarded as purely historical. It may have been a compilation, perhaps a unique compilation, of really historical and of unhistorical ways of describing things, that was transformed into what purports to be a historical account.

If we generalize from the account (I regard the truth of this second life of Christ as a documented fact in light of all the references to it), the question arises: How did this second life come to an end and, leaving the account in Acts out of consideration, what kind of an idea of the end can we conceive? We begin with the fact that Christ did not wish to come into contact with the world in the course of his renewed life and therefore did not himself continue his fellowship.* We go on to the observation that, as long as he was in this state and appeared only for brief periods to his disciples, these latter were prevented from beginning their mission. In light of this we can assume that this second life of Christ in the form of an occasional meeting with his disciples could not have lasted long. Since the outpouring of the Spirit and the institution of a Christian church followed upon the end of Christ's second life, we can conceive of no reason why that second life should have lasted long, and it stands to reason that when these events took place it had come to an end. There is no doubt that the outpouring of the Spirit took place

* did not want to continue his activity as a public teacher

at Pentecost, and this means that the period within which Christ could have consorted with his disciples was fixed, and this we find associated with the solemn number forty.

There is still a second question. Could Christ's disciples have been witnesses of the way this state of Christ came to an end? If we were to think it possible that Christ died a second time, that, to be sure, would have been conceivable. However, if that were the case, it would be quite inconceivable that there should be no report of it in existence. So, the belief that Christ died again with the knowledge of his disciples is a hypothesis we have to exclude. There is not the slightest mention of it, either in our Gospels or in the missionary sermons of the apostles. The apostles always appeal to the resurrection of Christ and to the fact that he let himself be seen by the disciples, but they say nothing of witnessing another end of this life. If we were to suppose that this second life came to a natural end, we could only think of it as an end that could not be perceived, or rather, that only the negative side of it, the fact that Christ was no longer on earth, could be perceived. But what would have been attained or achieved if the end had been seen by the disciples in a positive way as an exaltation of Christ toward heaven which they could not follow (or: could not use) any further? We have to admit that it would have been a purposeless, supernatural act.

There is still another question. Was there at least a final meeting of Christ with his disciples which he and they knew was the last, or had they no definite awareness of the imminent end of their fellowship with each other? When I reflect on what directly follows, the latter alternative seems to me to be improbable to the highest degree. When the apostles came forth at Pentecost, it was clear from the start that they no longer expected Christ to appear. In fact, if we recall that mention is made of prayers they offered in which reference was made to Christ, no one can imagine that such reference was made if the disciples had been still uncertain whether Christ was not still on earth. The question arises: Were they convinced that they could no longer expect Christ to return in his former state because he had taken formal leave of them, or by the fact that the outpouring of the Spirit had taken place? There can be no certain answer to this, since passages from the days of Christ's resurrection occur which could take the place of the final farewell if nothing were later said of a meeting. The first such passage is the one in John where Christ communicates the Spirit to his disciples. This bears the character of a farewell and of a final commission and assurance. The same is true of what Christ earlier tells Mary as a message she is to give to the disciples. We cannot say that these passages demand a later occasion on which Christ took final farewell of his followers. However, when we examine the closing section of Matthew's Gospel and the discourse of Christ to his apostles in Acts, we have to admit that these passages seem more clearly to be a farewell. This implies that Christ told his disciples that the meeting in question was the last he would have with them. However, our extant sources make it impossible for us to form any definite idea of what more the disciples apprehended with their senses of the end of Christ's life.

The reports we possess are not sufficient to enable us to maintain anything definite, but the same thing must also be said of the first beginning of Christ's second life. I can believe that to be true without doubting in the slightest* that the fact itself is a historical event (or, has a historical nature). If we have to regard him always as an appearance unique of its kind in the human race (or, in the life of men) — if there is to be a true and unique faith in him — I do not see why, that (if) everything marvelous in his life is connected with this character of the uniqueness of his appearance on earth and gets its character only by the fact that it represents (itself?) as something bound up with his peculiar dignity, that should not also be the case with this appearance.† So I gladly waive any claim to understand Christ's second life as a historical event with a beginning and an end. On the contrary, I regard this whole second life appearance of Christ just as I do every individual miracle. There is something in it** that is wholly

* without raising suspicions about intervening events
† or add: that his beginning and end should not be so represented
** in all the marvelous accounts of Christ

factual, but the genesis of it is incomprehensible to us (or: is incapable of comparison) because it is connected with something that in its way is unique and for which there is no analogy. That is true also of the facts that occurred during Christ's second life. The facts are genuine facts, but how that second life began and how it ended are matters which we cannot conceive factually, and we also should not be able to have any factual idea of the end. To be sure, if we had the analogy it would be possible to form an idea of it, and it is only accidental that we lack the accounts.

The man who does not admit this uniqueness in the appearance of Christ has one and the same task. He must account for all the miracles in light of the laws of nature and by this means explain Christ's last life. However, the result is the same. The whole thing is a sham. In the way the hypothesis is put forward a complete confusion reigns, and that is a guarantee of the higher appearances of Christ, which represent him as a higher being, as *ens sui generis,* which is why all attempts to understand him in an inferior way fail and the truth of the fact itself is lost. *However, that is a task that has not been solved and one for which we can find only an approximate solution. This we have to admit, but at the same time we have to treat every detail in a way that is suitable to something that rests on a supernatural foundation but has become something completely natural. So we have to regard this task as a purely theological one.* We must continually treat it as such and repeatedly test all individual efforts in order where possible to come nearer to a complete solution, *even though this may not be the property of all Christians.* The theologian has the task of bringing everything to the highest possible level of conceptual clarity and certainty.* That is the point of view that governed my treatment of the life of Jesus. I make no claim to have succeeded. *However, I was able to carry out my work only on the presupposition that our Gospels belong to the series of historical phenomena* and are to be regarded as products of a definite time. Therefore much that I have presented in our description of the life of Christ

---

* or add: Getting rid of this difficulty is a matter of indifference to our faith itself.

will be quite uncongenial to those who want to assume in the Gospels an inspiration of the letter and a completely settled unity.